Restitution
in
Australia and New Zealand

Cavendish
Publishing
(Australia)
Pty Limited

Sydney • London

Restitution
in
Australia and New Zealand

Charles Cato, LLB (Hons), BCL (Oxon)
Barrister, the High Court of Australia,
the States of Queensland, Victoria, New South Wales,
the Northern Territory and New Zealand

Cavendish
Publishing
(Australia)
Pty Limited

Sydney • London

First published in 1997 by Cavendish Publishing (Australia) Pty Limited,
Governor Phillip Tower, Level 53, 1 Farrer Place, Sydney,
New South Wales 2000

Australia Cataloguing in Publication Data

Cato, CB (Charles Bentley)
1. Restitution – Australia
I Title
344.9403288

ISBN 1 876213 23 X

£34·95

Printed and bound in Great Britain

Coventry University

To my parents, people of equity and good conscience.

FOREWORD

It is a great pleasure to write the foreword for Charles Cato's work on restitution.

More years ago than I now care to remember, Charles Cato was a Judges' Clerk at the High Court in Auckland – there his keen intellect came to notice and I venture to say that more than one judge was grateful for his efforts in researching areas of law in which the arguments of counsel had been deficient.

From Auckland he went to Worcester College, Oxford and read for his BCL. Since then he has lectured and practised in diverse areas of law. But he has never lost the interest, kindled at Oxford, in the developing subject of restitution.

That subject has continued to develop as a body of law since Lord Wright gave it impetus in his discussion of *Sinclair v Brougham* [1938] 6 Camb LJ 305. But there are still some who regard restitution as no more than an amorphous and ill-defined body of material which runs contrary to accepted principles of contract. Mr Cato does much to dispel this notion.

I believe that his carefully researched work will be appreciated by Judges, lawyers and lecturers and students alike and that it will become a leading text, particularly in Australia and New Zealand. It is written in an attractive style, the cases are embodied in the text and the whole work reflects the author's industry and erudition.

Rt Hon Sir Duncan McMullin
Auckland
4 December 1996

PREFACE

In his illuminating discussion of *Sinclair v Brougham*[1] in the 1938 edition of the *Cambridge Law Journal*,[2] Lord Wright observed that he could not understand why it was not more clearly recognised that quasi-contract or restitution involved a definite system of rules, just like the rules of contract or tort.[3] Further, in his Lordship's view, restitution was a distinct branch of law capable of, and worthy of, careful study.[4] Despite these observations, nearly 60 years have passed and many lawyers today still have little appreciation of restitution. One reason for this is that it was not until 1966 that the first influential edition of *The Law of Restitution* by Lord Goff and Professor Gareth Jones was published which marked an important development for this subject in English law. For the first time, the approach was taken, as it had been in the United States 30 years before in the *Restatement on Restitution*,[5] to incorporate common law and equitable doctrines into a systematic work with a unifying theme of unjust enrichment. It was not, however, until the decision of the High Court of Australia in *Pavey & Matthews Pty Ltd v Paul*[6] in 1986, that restitution started to gain recognition as an important subject in Australia and one that has continued to attract attention since. Many practitioners, who have not had the advantage of studying restitution, may similarly not have appreciated its value or scope until recent times. As Lord Wright acknowledged, however, there is a definite body of law which is reasonably well settled and provides a firm foundation for a law of unjust enrichment. Like other areas of the common law, it is not immutable from growth or change and there will continue to be debate as to how far developments in restitution should be taken.

Restitution is an important subject for several reasons. First, as Lord Wright observed, restitution is the third important area of obligation besides tort and contract. Causes of action based on unjust enrichment are fundamental to the concept of civil obligation and integral to the demands of society in a world which it would seem is increasingly

---

1 [1914] AC 398; [1914–15] All ER 622.
2 [1938] 6 Camb LJ 305.
3 *Ibid*, at 321.
4 *Ibid*, at 322.
5 American Law Institute, 1937.
6 (1986) 162 CLR 221. It had received academic consideration. See Stoljar, SJ, *The Law of Quasi-Contract*, 1st edn, 1964, The Law Book Company Ltd.

exposed to unconscientious behaviour, dishonourable dealing and commercial immorality. Secondly, restitution is, both for students and practitioners, a valuable subject. In so far as students are concerned, it is valuable because it affords a sound basis for studying the the opinions of creative judges of the past, who have in their various ways contributed to the development of this subject, as well as more recent developments and judicial opinions on the subject. This assists to provide the student with a better appreciation of the continuity of common law and equity, their strength and resilience, and their infinite genius for change or adaptation to societal demands. Further, restitution is a challenging subject in that it covers a number of discrete topics in various areas of the law with an underlying unity or common theme of unjust enrichment. In that sense, it encourages a measure of lateral thought. Restitution also provides a basis for the student to consider a blend of remedies, at common law and in equity, with both streams aimed at preventing unjust enrichment. Since the fusion of law and equity, it is advantageous for the student to think in this way. Finally, restitution is a pleasurable subject to teach, the cases are interesting and the subject lends itself well either to socratic method or more formal instruction, or both. The study of law should be enjoyable and this is accordingly a worthy end in itself. A strong case can be made out for restitution, like contract or tort, to be a core undergraduate course. Indeed, it is difficult to understand areas of contract, for example, without an appreciation of the part played by restitution. Restitution is also important for the practitioner. The considerable growth in case law in recent years demonstrates that this is so, and how correct Lord Wright was in describing it as a subject worthy of careful study.

In this book, I have attempted to set out the principles of restitution succinctly with appropriate reference to relevant English, Australian, and New Zealand case law and any theoretical argument or debate that may better illuminate these principles. I have also included a consideration of the relevant statutory reforms. This is particularly important in relation to contractual transactions in New Zealand. I wish to thank my wife Caron for her encouragement and patience, Malcolm Holmes QC of the New South Wales Bar and a friend from Oxford days who first encouraged me to write, he appreciating the developing importance and awareness of this subject in Australia, and Sharon Erbacker of Deakin University who read the original manuscript and made various valuable suggestions. I would also like to acknowledge the lively contributions made to my lectures at Auckland University by my friend, Mr Jim Stephens of University College, London, and Mr Richard Calnan a former colleague, now a commercial lawyer in London. Some of the issues we enjoyed debating with students such as the imposition of a remedial constructive trust have featured prominently in restitution in recent years. I would like to take the opportunity of acknowledging the kindly support given to me over the years by Sir Duncan McMullin formerly a Judge of the Court of Appeal of New Zealand, some of whose judgments are referred to in this book, and Dr Francis Reynolds of Worcester College, Oxford where I spent two happy years reading for the BCL. At Oxford, I was privileged to read this subject for the first time under the stimulating guidance of Dr Treital, Professor Peter Birks and Mr JD Davies. They were most enlightening and enjoyable days. I wish also to acknowledge the support of my publisher, Cavendish Publishing Limited and its staff.

Charles Cato, LLB (Hons) BCL (Oxon)
Chambers,
Brisbane

SOURCES COMMONLY REFERRED TO IN THIS TEXT

Birks, P, *An Introduction to the Law of Restitution*, 1985, reprint 1993, Clarendon Press, Oxford.

Burrows, A, *The Law of Restitution*, 1993, Butterworths, London.

Burrows, A (ed), *Essays on the Law of Restitution*, 1991, Clarendon Press, Oxford.

Finn, PD (ed), *Essays on Restitution*, 1990, Law Book Co Ltd, Sydney.

Lord Goff and Jones, G, *The Law of Restitution*, 4th edn, 1993, Sweet & Maxwell, London.

Stoljar, SJ, *The Law of Quasi-Contract*, 1st edn, 1964, 2nd edn, 1989, The Law Book Company Ltd, Sydney.

CONTENTS

TABLE OF CASES

TABLE OF STATUTES

CHAPTER 1

Restitution – An Introduction

The development of a modern law of restitution

Restitution has enjoyed a lengthy gestation. Its origins can be traced to the 16th century to the common counts of moneys had and received, and *quantum valebat* and *quantum meruit*, the latter being claims for payment for the reasonable value of goods and services respectively. The action for moneys had and received enabled a person, to whom moneys were owed, to obtain restitution in a wide variety of situations. Thus, in addition to claims involving debt, it lay where the plaintiff had paid money to the defendant under mistake or compulsion, or where there had been no consideration provided for a payment. It further lay where the defendant was under an obligation to account to the plaintiff, or had been in possession of moneys that he or she had obtained as a result of the abuse of an office of the plaintiff. The common counts grew out of the rivalry between the King's Bench and the Court of Common Pleas. In the 16th century, King's Bench invoked the procedure known as *indebtatus assumpsit* (ie an action on a promise to repay a debt) in order to compete with the Court of Common Pleas which had traditionally enjoyed exclusive jurisdiction over claims in debt and account, the latter being a remedy invoked when it was necessary to ascertain how much a person owed another. *Indebtatus assumpsit* involved the imposition of the fiction of a promise to pay thereby enabling the plaintiff to sue on the case in the King's Bench rather than in Common Pleas. The pleading would allege that the defendant was indebted to the plaintiff in a certain sum and had, accordingly, promised, at the time of the contract or afterwards, to pay that sum to the plaintiff. The promise did not have to be express but could be implied. *Indebtatus assumpsit* was more popular with litigants than debt because the procedure was cheaper, pleading less rigorous and wager of law could be avoided.[1] Common Pleas strenuously resisted this development and apparent usurpation of its jurisdiction but in *Slade's*[2] case, in 1602, the Court of Exchequer Chamber, influenced by the advocacy of Coke and the presence of King's Bench

---

1   For the development of *indebtatus assumpsit*, see Lucke, HK, 'The Origin of the Common Money Counts' (1965) 81 LQR 422; (1966) 82 LQR 81.

2   (1602) 4 Co Rep 92 a. Discussed by Simpson, AWB, 'The Place of Slade's Case in the History of Contract' (1958) 74 LQR 381, and see further Lord Atkin in *United Australia Ltd v Barclays Bank Ltd* [1941] AC 1, at 26–27; [1940] 4 All ER 20, at 35–36.

judges, upheld the existence of *indebtatus assumpsit* as an alternative to debt and from this time on the common counts prospered.[3]

The 18th century case of *Moses v Macferlan* is an important case in the development of the law of restitution.[4] There, Macferlan, who was the indorsee of promissory notes, represented to the indorser Moses that he would not sue him upon the notes because the indorsement was made simply to accommodate Macferlan and enable him to sue a third party who had originally made out the notes to Moses. However, fraudulently and in breach of this agreement, Macferlan called upon Moses to honour the bills which he did by paying their value into court in separate proceedings. Moses was, subsequently, successful in obtaining a verdict for the money against Macferlan on the ground that the money had been fraudulently obtained. The issue that called for resolution was whether Moses could succeed in the action for moneys had and received, or whether he was prevented from doing so because his claim should have been brought upon the agreement that he had with Macferlan. Lord Mansfield rejected the argument that the action for moneys had and received was confined to actions where debt would lie, or that a claim in *assumpsit* depended upon the existence of an express or implied agreement. Having observed that the indorsement was fraudulently procured by Macferlan, Lord Mansfield said of the action for moneys had and received:[5]

> This kind of equitable action, to recover back money, which ought not in justice to be kept, is very beneficial, and therefore much to be encouraged. It lies only for money which, *ex aeqo et bono*, the defendant ought to refund: it does not lie for money paid by the plaintiff, which is claimed of him as payable in point of honesty, although it could not have been recovered from him by any course of law; as in payment of a debt barred by the Statute of Limitations, or contracted during his infancy, or to the extent of principal and interest upon a usurious contract, or for money fairly lost at play: because in all these cases, the defendant may retain it with a safe conscience, though by positive law he was barred from recovering. But it lies for money paid by mistake; or upon a consideration which happens to fail: or an undue advantage taken of the plaintiff's situation, contrary to laws made for the protection of persons under those circumstances.
>
> In one word, the gist of this kind of action is that, the defendant, upon the circumstances of the case, is obliged by the ties of natural justice and equity to refund the money.

---

3   Birks, P, *An Introduction to the Law of Restitution*, reprint 1993, p 79, Clarendon Press, Oxford. And further for a succinct account of the development of quasi-contract remedies subsequent to *Slade's* case, see Lord Atkin in *United Australia Ltd v Barclays Bank Ltd, ibid*, at 26–27; at 35–36.

4   2 Burr 1005; (1760) 97 ER 676. See further the discussion of this case by Stoljar, SJ, *The Law of Quasi-Contract*, 2nd edn, 1989, p 15, The Law Book Company Ltd.

5   *Ibid*, at 1011–13; 680–81.

Many years later, Professor Holdsworth was to argue that Lord Mansfield had attempted in *Moses v Macferlan* to achieve some form of fusion between law and equity. Holdsworth considered that courts subsequently were correct to resist this view.[6] It is doubtful, however, whether Lord Mansfield was attempting to seize the court of equitable jurisdiction; rather it may be argued that he was merely asserting that there was, underlying the action for moneys had and received, a common principle or foundation of unjust enrichment. It is clear, however, that 19th century judges were sceptical about a liberal approach to moneys had and received. Holdsworth asserts that this was motivated by closer attention to the requirements of *indebtatus assumpsit* and the new pleading rules introduced in 1883 which encouraged judges to look for evidence of an actual implied agreement as a basis for such a claim.[7] In this regard, Goff and Jones also consider that this tendency was attributable to the abolition of the forms of action in the 19th century by the Common Law Procedure Act 1852 which induced lawyers to subsequently classify claims into categories of contract and tort.[8] Because quasi-contractual claims had their origin in *assumpsit*, albeit arising from a fiction, they came to be treated as an appendage of contract and a conservative approach was taken subsequently to the scope of their application. Thus, although there was some support for a liberal view of the action for moneys had and received in the later part of the 19th century, a liberal approach was generally discouraged until well into the 20th century.[9] In *Baylis v Bishop of London*,[10] Hamilton LJ[11] was critical of the approach taken by Lord Mansfield to the action for moneys had and received and observed that, whatever the case may have been some 146 years ago, the courts were not now free in the 20th century to administer that vague jurisprudence which is sometimes attractively styled 'justice as between man and man'. The implied contract theory was approved by the House of Lords in *Sinclair v Brougham*.[12] There, a claim by depositors of moneys in a building society, that they should have their deposits restored to them in priority to the shareholders of the society on the liquidation of the society, failed on the ground that the society had no express power to borrow. Since the

---

6 'Unjustifiable Enrichment' (1939) 55 LQR 37, at 40–41.

7 *Idem.*

8 Lord Goff and Jones, G, *The Law of Restitution*, 4th edn, 1993, Sweet & Maxwell, p 9. Further, Mason CJ in *Baltic Shipping v Dillon* (1992–93) 176 CLR 344, at 356–57.

9 *Cf* Lord Lindley LJ in *Re Rhodes* (1890) 44 Ch D 94, at 107.

10 [1913] 1 Ch 127.

11 *Ibid*, at 140.

12 [1914] AC 398; [1914–15] All ER 622.

ultra vires doctrine prohibited the society entering into a contract of loan with the depositors, the House of Lords unanimously held that it would be wrong to allow a quasi-contractual claim founded on implied contract to succeed.[13] It was also the approach adopted by the Court of Appeal in *Re Cleadon Trust*.[14] There, a majority of the Court of Appeal, when declining the claim of a director, Creighton, to recoupment of his advances to Cleadon subsidiaries, were influenced by the limitation of implied agreement. Since a resolution purporting to confirm the advances was invalid, the company could not be said to have ratified them, thus preventing any quasi-contractual claim succeeding that was based on an implied contract approach.[15]

Whilst the implied contract approach enjoyed influential support well into the 20th century, support developed for a more liberal approach to quasi-contractual claims. Professor Winfield asserted that quasi-contract should rest on a basis of unjust enrichment and not on implied contract.[16] The most influential criticism, however, came from Lord Atkin in *United Australia Ltd v Barclays Bank Ltd*[17] and from Lord Wright in *Fibrosa*.[18] Lord Atkin and Lord Wright both observed that a quasi-contractual claim for moneys had and received should not be narrowly based on implied agreement but on wider considerations of justice. After such influential criticism, the implied contract theory was destined for extinction and the underlying foundation for quasi-contractual claims came to be seen as based on the concept of unjust enrichment.[19] The importance of the rejection of the implied contract theory is that the law of restitution was freed from the fetters of contract and given new life to develop as an important area of obligation in its own right. In this regard, Lord Wright in *Fibrosa* observed:[20]

---

13 *Ibid*, at 414–18; 630 *per* Viscount Haldane LC; at 433–34; 638 *per* Lord Dunedin; at 440; 642 *per* Lord Parker; at 452; 648 *per* Lord Sumner.

14 [1939] Ch 286.

15 *Ibid*, Sir Wilfred Greene MR at 299–300, Scott LJ at 315 (who, however, indicated some sympathy for a more liberal development of the law in this area), and Clauson LJ at 319.

16 'Province of the Law of Torts', pp 131–41. Further, Jackson, RM, 'The History of Quasi-Contract in English Law'(1936) *Cambridge Studies in English Legal History*.

17 [1941] AC 1, at 27–28; [1940] 4 All ER 20, at 35–37.

18 *Fibrosa Splka Akeynja v Fairbairne Lawson Coombe Barbour* [1943] AC 32, at 63–64; [1942] 2 All ER 122, at 135–37. Further, see Lord Wright's criticism in *Sinclair v Brougham* (1938) 6 CLJ 305, at 305–26.

19 Indeed, Lord Wright credited Lord Mansfield with having stated the basis of the modern law of quasi-contract in *Moses v Macferlan*. *Ibid*, at 64; 136.

20 *Ibid*, at 61; 135.

It is clear that any civilised system of law is bound to provide remedies for cases of what has been called unjust enrichment or unjust
benefit, that is, to prevent a man from retaining the money of, or
some benefit derived from another which it is against conscience
that he should keep. Such remedies in English law are generically
different from remedies in contract or in tort, and are now recognised to fall within a third category of the common law which has
been called quasi-contract or restitution.

Unjust enrichment, as a source of legal obligation in restitution, has
more recently been recognised by the High Court in Australia in a
number of cases commencing with *Pavey & Matthews Pty Ltd v Paul*.[21]
There, a majority of the court held that, although a building contract
was unenforceable because it was not in writing contrary to the provisions of legislation governing builders, the builder was able to recover
reasonable compensation for his work on a *quantum meruit* because otherwise the owner would be unjustly enriched.[22] It was held that the legislation was not intended to preclude a builder bringing an action in
restitution for the reasonable value of the services that he had performed, and the implied contract approach was rejected.

Modern restitution is not, however, confined to common law claims.
Although critical of an overly liberal approach to restitution based on
a broad notion of justice, Professor Holdsworth acknowledged that
'unjustifiable enrichment' could depend partly upon the rules of the
common law and partly upon the rules of equity.[23] The 'Restatement of
the Law of Restitution on Quasi-Contracts and Constructive Trusts in
the United States', adopted such an approach, and included within the
scope of that work is a systematic consideration of equitable remedies
for mistake, fraud, duress, undue influence and breach of fiduciary
duty as well as the more traditional quasi-contractual remedies.[24] Lord
Goff and Professor Jones also incorporated into their seminal text on
restitution[25] equitable remedies as well as quasi-contractual remedies,
thus giving fresh life in English law to restitution and removing it further from the shackles of implied contract. In this book, consideration
will be given to some of the more important equitable doctrines which
allow an aggrieved person to obtain restitution in order to prevent the

---

21 (1986) 162 CLR 221. Earlier, Griffiths CJ referred to the action for moneys had and
   received as founded in justice and equity, see *R v Brown* (1912) 14 CLR 17, at 25.
   Further, *David Securities Pty Ltd v Commonwealth Bank of Australia* (1992) 175 CLR
   353, at 385 and *Commissioner of State Revenue (Vic) v Royal Insurance Australia Ltd*
   (1994) 182 CLR 51, at 69 *per* Mason CJ.

22 *Ibid*, at 227–28, *per* Mason and Wilson JJ, at 258–60 *per* Deane J.

23 *Loc cit*, at 37. This was a view also expressed of restitution by Lord Wright in
   Fibrosa [1943] AC 32, at 64; [1942] 2 All ER 122, at 137.

24 American Law Institute, 1937, discussed by Lord Wright in (1938) CLJ 305, at 322–23.

25 1st edn, 1966.

unjust enrichment of another. In recent years, there have been very important developments in the law of estoppel, undue influence, unconscionable bargains and fiduciary relationships which have involved difficult issues relating to unconscionable conduct and claims of unjust enrichment. In *Attorney General of Hong Kong v Reid*,[26] for example, a constructive trust was imposed in favour of the Crown over investment properties acquired by a fraudulent officer of the Office of the Director of Prosecutions from the proceeds of bribes that he had received when carrying out the duties of his office contrary to earlier English authority.[27]

In *Hussey v Palmer*,[28] a case involving a property dispute in the context of a family arrangement, Lord Denning MR rationalised the imposition of a constructive trust as being founded in justice and akin to the way in which Lord Mansfield in *Moses v Macferlan* had approached the action for moneys had and received. In *Chase Manhatten Bank NA v Israel-British Bank (London) Ltd*,[29] a constructive trust was imposed where the personal remedy of moneys had and received would not have prevented the unjust enrichment of the general creditors of an insolvent bank to which a very large sum of money had been paid by the plaintiff through a clerical error. The merits of this development, however, have been cast into doubt by the recent observations of Lord Browne-Wilkinson who expressly declined to approve an approach based on the notion of a remedial constructive trust in *Westdeutsche Landesbank Girozentrale v Islington LBC*.[30] It was held there that whilst an interest swap arrangement between the bank and a local authority that was *ultra vires* of the latter entitled the bank to a personal claim to restitution, it did not permit the bank to claim a resulting trust over the advances that it had made to the authority because the payments that had been made did not operate to adversely affect the conscience of the bank. Lord Browne-Wilkinson, similarly, doubted whether the bank in *Chase* should have been liable to the imposition of a constructive trust unless it had knowledge of the mistake.

Lord Goff, however, expressly declined to review the correctness of the *Chase* approach and the other members of the House of Lords made no mention of it. Accordingly, it remains to be seen, whether the approach favoured in the United States to the imposition of a remedial constructive trust to prevent unjust enrichment will be sanctioned in England. The submission is made in this book that the approach of

---

26 [1994] 1 AC 325.
27 *Cf Lister v Stubbs* (1890) 45 Ch D 1. Discussed p 311.
28 [1972] 1 WLR 1286, at 1289; [1963] 3 All ER 744, at 747.
29 [1981] Ch 105; [1979] 3 All ER 1025. Discussed pp 313, 323–28.
30 [1996] 2 WLR 802; [1996] 2 All ER 961. Discussed pp 324–28.

Goulding J in *Chase* is defensible and the remedial constructive trust was rightly imposed in that case to prevent unjust enrichment of the general creditors of the payee bank.[31] Aside from these developments, however, equity has played an important role in denying unjust enrichment in cases involving property disputes and the breakdown of family relationships, oppressive contractual transactions, and in cases involving undue influence and duress. Consideration will be given in this text to these and other important developments in equity which form an essential aspect of modern restitution. With the fusion of law and equity, it is appropriate that the waters of two confluent streams of law are intermixed to form a coherent body of remedies that are commonly dependant upon a foundation of unjust enrichment.[32] That is not to say that the law is or should be, as Professor Holdsworth feared, a mere matter of judicial discretion.[33] As Lord Diplock, in *Orakpo v Manson Investments Ltd* in England[34] and Deane J, in *Pavey & Matthews Pty Ltd v Paul*[35] in Australia have observed, restitution is a principled subject and unjust enrichment constitutes a unifying legal concept which assists to explain why the law recognises that, in a variety of distinct categories of case, there is an obligation upon a defendant to make fair and just compensation.

Theories of unjust enrichment in modern restitution

Having established unjust enrichment as an underlying basis or foundation for a law of restitution, it is necessary to consider when the retention of a benefit can be considered unjust. There are three general questions to be resolved before the retention of a benefit is deserving of restitutionary relief. First, is there a benefit? If so, has the benefit in some way been derived at the expense of the plaintiff, and if the answer is that it has been obtained in this way, is its retention unjust?[36] These issues will be considered throughout this text in the context of the general law as it applies in England, Australia and New Zealand. Where appropriate, statutory reforms will also be considered. This is particularly important in New Zealand where there has been significant legislative reform in relation to contractual transactions and where a

---

31 See discussion pp 323–28.

32 *United Scientific Holdings Ltd v Burnley Borough Council* [1978] AC 904, at 945; [1977] 2 All ER 63, at 84 *per* Lord Simon.

33 *Loc cit*, at 53. For judicial exposition against too liberal an application of notions of unjust enrichment, see Connolly J in *Kratzman Holdings Ltd v University of Queensland* [1982] Qd R 682, at 685; and Mahon J in *Carly v Farrelly* [1975] 1 NZLR 356 and *Avondale Printers v Haggie* [1979] 2 NZLR 124.

34 [1978] AC 95; [1977] 3 WLR 229.

35 (1986) 162 CLR 221, at 256–57.

36 Birks, *op cit*, p 21.

statutory discretionary regime has been preferred to a rules based approach that exists under the general law in England and Australia.

(a) Is there a benefit?

It is important first to determine whether a benefit has in fact been derived by a person from whom the alleged benefit is claimed on the ground of unjust enrichment. In the case of the receipt of money, there is an obvious benefit to the recipient. However, in the case of services this may be less obviously so. The service may not have been requested and so it may be contended that there should be no obligation to pay. An unsolicited benefit is open to the complaint that it may be subjectively devalued.[37] Where a car, for example, has been painted without the owner's request, the owner may decline to pay for the work on the ground that he or she did not want the car repainted and preferred another colour even though the fresh paint may have enhanced its value. In response to this difficulty, Goff and Jones invoked a concept of free acceptance in the first edition of their work. This was explained in these terms: 'the defendant will not usually be regarded as having been benefited by the receipt of services or goods unless he has accepted them or (in the case of goods retained them) with an opportunity of rejection and with actual and presumed knowledge that they were to be paid for.'[38] Professor Birks, also an influential theorist on restitution, later described free acceptance as occurring when a recipient knows that a benefit is being offered to him non-gratuitously and where, he, having the opportunity to reject it, elects to accept the benefit. Birks would argue persuasively that a defendant who has freely accepted a benefit should not be able to advance the subjective devaluation argument. 'The reason is that, if he has freely accepted, he has *ex hypothesi* chosen to receive it, and subjective devaluation is an argument whose premise is that where something has *not* been chosen by its recipient, it cannot normally be said to have been of value to him.'[39]

The concept of free acceptance as a basis for establishing enrichment has been disputed.[40] Professor Burrows contends that free acceptance is a much more limited factor than either Goff or Jones, or Birks would acknowledge. Burrows argues that a person may accept a service out of indifference and the mere fact that he does so does not establish bene-

---

37 Birks, *ibid*, pp 109–10.

38 Lord Goff and Jones, G, *The Law of Restitution*, 1st edn, 1966, pp 30–31 , Sweet & Maxwell.

39 Birks, *op cit*, pp 114–16, 266. Further, see the discussion in *Brenner v First Artists' Management Pty Ltd* [1993] 2 VLR 221, at 257–58.

40 Burrows, A, 'Free Acceptance and The Law of Restitution' (1988) 104 LQR 576. For a further critique of the concept of subjective devaluation, see Scott, SR, 'Restitution and Subjective Devaluation' (1992–93) NZULR 246.

fit. Burrows supports this argument by resort to the window cleaner who cleans another's windows in the belief he will be paid whilst the owner stands by. In Burrow's view, the owner may be completely indifferent to the performance of the service, and so the fact that the service was freely accepted and the owner took no steps to stop the cleaner is insufficient evidence from which to infer a benefit.[41] It may be argued, however, that the fact that the owner has stood by and allowed the cleaner to proceed suggests not indifference but rather that the service was viewed as a benefit, or else steps should have been taken to dissuade the cleaner from proceeding with the work.[42] A more difficult question in the window cleaning example is not whether a benefit was conferred but whether it should be one for which payment should be made. As Professor Jones has commented, the real issue is whether the service was performed officiously in the sense that the window cleaner undertook the risk that he might not be paid?[43]

A benefit may, however, be the subject of restitution, in some circumstances, where free acceptance cannot operate. Services or payments associated with the preservation of health or property, in necessitous circumstances or in emergency, may constitute a benefit and give rise to a claim for restitution. The provision of benefits through mistake may also give rise to successful claims in restitution. Money that has been paid by mistake clearly constitutes a benefit, however, a mistakenly conferred service may be subject to a complaint by the owner that it was a service that he or she did not want and hence should not be the subject of restitution. Where a service has been rendered by mistake it will be argued in Chapter 2 that restitution should generally be permitted if, in the words of Goff and Jones, the service is one that has conferred an incontrovertible benefit on the owner notwithstanding that the

---

41 *Ibid*, at 580.

42 See the discussion by Birks of this example in 'Defense of Free Acceptance', in Burrows, A (ed), *Essays on the Law of Restitution*, 1991, pp 123–24, and Burrow's response to the concept of free acceptance, in his *Law of Restitution*, 1993, pp 14–15, Butterworths. Burrows considers that free acceptance does not have a place in the law of restitution. Burrows instead advocates a narrower test based on whether the defendant has bargained for the benefit. Burrows asserts that if there is evidence of this there will be a rebuttable presumption that receipt of the service was not merely objectively beneficial but was subjectively beneficial to the defendant as well. The rather narrow Burrow's approach would seem to be open to the criticism that it constitutes a return to the forbidden implied contract theory of restitution. The view is taken here that free acceptance is a legitimate determinant of both benefit and unjust enrichment, and that a surreptitious or sly receipt of a benefit can also constitute free acceptance of a benefit. See *Van Den Berg v Giles* [1979] 2 NZLR 111 considered by Birks *op cit*, p 275.

43 Jones, G, 'A Topography of the Law of Restitution', in Finn, PD (ed), *Essays on Restitution*, 1990, p 7, Law Book Company. See also Birks, 'In Defence of Free Acceptance', in *Essays on the Law of Restitution*, ibid, p 144. This issue is further considered below, p 16.

owner may subjectively attempt to devalue the service.[44] An 'incontrovertible benefit' is one that objectively enhances the market value of property or saves the owner an inevitable expense.

Another objection that has been raised in relation to the concept of benefit has been the criticism that where work is carried out preparatory to the completion of a contract which has been wrongfully terminated, the preparatory work should not be treated as a benefit for the defendant and restitution allowed.[45] A claim of this kind was allowed in *Planche v Colburn*,[46] where a publisher had wrongfully terminated a contract for the preparation of a manuscript. Although costs incurred preparatory to a benefit being conferred on another may be claimable as reliance expenditure in damages for the wrongful termination of a contract,[47] the law has recognised the availability of a quasi-contractual remedy aside from any contractual claim where a party has wrongfully repudiated a contract thereby denying the innocent party the opportunity to complete. Whilst it may be open to persuasively argue that damages should be the exclusive remedy in cases of this kind, the availability of a quasi-contractual claim in this context has long been recognised. In *Brenner v First Artists' Management Pty Ltd*,[48] Byrne J, in the Supreme Court of Victoria, recently referred to *Planche v Colburn* without disapproval and further considered that what was important in cases of this kind was the request for the performance of the service rather than the end-product which the service might or might not produce.[49]

(b) Has the benefit been obtained at the expense of the plaintiff?

Having established that the defendant has received a benefit, the second question that must be answered in order to support a claim in restitution is whether the plaintiff can establish that this has been acquired

---

44 Goff and Jones, *The Law of Restitution*, 3rd edn, 1986, p 26; Jones, G, 'Restitutionary Remedies for Services Rendered' (1973) 93 LQR 273, at 275. The concept has received judicial consideration in *Monks v Poynice Pty Ltd* (1987) 8 NSWLR 662, at 664; *J Gasden v Strider 1 Ltd (The AES Express)* (1990) 20 NSWLR 57, at 70, and in New Zealand in *Van den Berg v Giles* [1979] 2 NZLR 111, at 122.

45 Beatson, J, 'Benefit, Reliance and the Structure of Unjust Enrichment' [1987] CLP 71; also *Essays*, 1991, p 35, Clarendon, where Beatson contends that a claim of this kind is based on injurious reliance. The courts have, however, in Australia and New Zealand allowed claims to restitution for services that objectively do not benefit the defendant, see *Brenner v First Artist's Management* [1993] 2 VR 221, at 256; *Dickson Elliot Lonergan Ltd v Plumbing World Ltd* [1988] 2 NZLR 609. It is submitted that services that have been performed non-gratuitously at the request of the defendant should be deemed to be of value to the defendant even though the end product has not been received.

46 (1831) 8 Bing 14; [1831] 131 ER 305.

47 *Commonwealth v Amann Aviation Pty Ltd* (1991) 174 CLR 64.

48 [1993] 2 VR 221.

49 *Ibid*, at 258.

at the plaintiff's expense. As Mason CJ observed in *Commissioner of State Revenue (Vic) v Royal Insurance Australia Ltd*:[50]

> Restitutionary relief, as it has developed to this point in our law, does not seek to provide compensation for loss. Instead it operates to restore to the plaintiff what has been transferred from the plaintiff to the defendant whereby the defendant has been unjustly enriched.

There, Royal was able to recover stamp duty that it had erroneously paid to the Commissioner even though it had collected the duty from its customers. It was held that the Commissioner had no title to the money which had been paid to it by mistake, and was not entitled to retain the money which would otherwise constitute a windfall gain even though Royal had passed on the liability to its customers and was not out of pocket.[51] In order to found a successful claim in restitution, expense to the plaintiff need not, however, always be associated with a monetary loss or the provision of goods or services by the plaintiff that is in some subtraction of the plaintiff's wealth, although often this will be the case.[52] For example, a breach of a fiduciary obligation may entitle the plaintiff to recover the gains made by an agent even though his or her principal would not have been able to acquire the benefit personally. In *Keech v Sandford*,[53] a trustee was held liable to hold a lease in trust for a beneficiary personally even though the lessor had declined previously to renew the lease for the beneficiary. More obvious examples of this kind involve employees who have accepted bribes. In the leading cases of *Reading v Attorney General*[54] and *Attorney General for Hong Kong v Reid*,[55] the Crown was entitled to restitution of the bribes and their product although there was no direct subtraction of wealth from the principal. Restitution was, nevertheless, available because the benefits were derived at the employer's expense in the sense that the duty of good faith that the employer was owed had been abrogated.

A related problem is seen in contract where a contract-breaker acquires an undeserved profit as a result of his or her wrongful termination. Should the contract-breaker, in these circumstances, have to disgorge the gain? This issue has been considered by Professor Jones[56] and

---

50 (1994–95) 182 CLR 51, at 75.

51 In an appropriate case, however, the payer might have to hold the proceeds on trust for its customers. *Ibid*, at 78.

52 See Birks *op cit*, p 134. Further, Mason CJ in *Commissioner of State Revenue (Vict) v Royal Insurance Ltd* (1994–95) 182 CLR 51, at 75.

53 (1726) Sel Cas, Ch 61; [1558–1774] All ER 230; applied *Chan v Zacharia* (1983–84) 154 CLR 179. Further, *Regal Hastings v Gulliver* [1967] 2 AC 135; [1942] 1 All ER 378.

54 [1951] AC 507; [1951] 1 All ER 617.

55 [1994] 1 AC 325.

56 Jones, G, 'A Topography of the Law of Restitution', in Finn, PD (ed), *Essays on Restitution*, 1990, p 7, Law Book Company.

more recently by the English Court of Appeal in *Surrey County Council v Brodero Homes Ltd*.[57] Professor Jones has argued that, in some circumstances, recovery should be permitted even though the gain or profit has not been derived from any transfer of money or services from the plaintiff to the defendant that is in any material loss. In *Bredero Homes*, local authorities sought damages from a developer for part of the developer's profit that was, they argued, reflected in a reasonable premium for contractual permission to relax covenants relating to the number of buildings that could be constructed on land acquired pursuant to contracts between the authorities and the developer. The plaintiffs could not, however, claim that the additional construction was injurious to their adjoining land. The Court of Appeal awarded only nominal damages for the breach of the covenants. Although conceding that, in some circumstances, a claim in restitution could be advanced in the form of a claim in damages in lieu of equitable relief for breach of a covenant,[58] Steyn LJ observed that where common law damages were claimed, there could be no recovery for any part of the gain that was not reflected in a material loss to the plaintiff. It is arguable, however, that a contract-breaker, or a tortfeasor should not be able to profit from his or her wrong and should be accountable to the innocent party for the profit wrongfully derived even though damage is not established. The issue of a restitutionary allowance in contractual and tortious actions is considered later in this book.[59]

On the issue of whether a benefit is acquired at the plaintiff's expense, it is appropriate to briefly consider the judgment of Gaudron J in *Trident General Insurance Co Ltd v McNiece Bros Pty Ltd*.[60] The plaintiff, McNiece, was the insured under a contract of insurance that had been arranged by a third party building contractor with Trident. McNiece was a subcontractor who sought an indemnity for personal injuries suffered by a worker who was at the time of his accident under the control of McNiece. The accident was one for which McNiece was insured within the terms of the policy that had been effected with Trident. Trident, however, declined to honour its liability on the indemnity. In the High Court of Australia, McNiece's claim was upheld principally on the majority view that the privity rule should be abrogated,[61] or that the benefit was one that was held on trust for McNiece.[62] Gaudron J, however, considered, additionally, that McNiece could

---

57 [1993] 1 WLR 1361. Further, see *Jaggard v Sawyer* [1995] 1 WLR 269, at 281.

58 As in *Wrotham Park Estate Co Ltd v Parkside Homes Ltd* [1974] 1 WLR 798.

59 See discussion, pp 189–90; 337–42.

60 (1988) 165 CLR 107.

61 *Ibid*, at 122–23 *per* Mason CJ, Wilson, Brennan J at, 140–41; 167–72 *per* Toohey, at 173 *per* Gaudron JJ, and at 160–62 Dawson J dissenting.

62 *Ibid*, at 147–54 *per* Deane J.

claim in restitution for the insurance proceeds because Trident had withheld a benefit that was due to McNiece.[63] There are, however, certain criticisms that may be directed at the application of restitution in these circumstances. The first concerns the issue of whether a dishonoured obligation in relation to the building contractor, as opposed to Trident, was a benefit of the kind that justified a claim to restitution. It has been argued in this regard that the real benefit to Trident was the proportional part of the premium that applied to the dishonoured obligation.[64] However, assuming that the saving could be considered a benefit, could it be said that this had been derived at the expense of McNiece rather than at the expense of the building contractor whose contractual expectation had not been met?

A further rather curious case in point is the New Zealand case of *Carly v Farrelly*.[65] The plaintiff had agreed to buy a house and land from the defendant. It was a term of the sale and purchase agreement that property vested in the plaintiff prior to settlement. The plaintiff failed to insure and the house burnt down prior to settlement. The case proceeded on the basis that the defendant obtained the proceeds of insurance from his insurer. The plaintiff claimed that there should be a corresponding adjustment in the purchase price because the defendant would be unjustly enriched should he receive the full sale price as well as the proceeds of insurance. Mahon J dismissed this argument on the ground that he knew of no equity which could lend itself to such a claim, and a mere assertion by the plaintiff that it was unfair not to allow a diminution in the price was insufficient reason to allow the claim. Although the receipt of the insurance constituted an unmeritorious windfall for the defendant, this did not entitle the plaintiff to take the benefit of the payment. The windfall was not derived at the expense of the plaintiff but rather, his omission to gain the proceeds of insurance was caused by his negligent omission to effect insurance prior to settlement or to obtain the sanction of the existing insurer under the agreement for sale and purchase.[66]

(c) Has there been unjust enrichment?

The third question that must be determined is whether, assuming the defendant has been enriched at the expense of the plaintiff, it would be

---

63 *Ibid*, at 174–77. Deane J also postulated a possible solution in restitution, at 145–46.

64 Mason, QC, 'Restitution In Australian Law', in Finn, PD (ed), *Essays on Restitution*, 1990, pp 34–35, Law Book Company.

65 [1975] 1 NZLR 356.

66 Certain protection exists for purchasers in this position in Australia, eg s 47 of the Property Law Act 1958 (Vict); s 63 of the Property Law Act 1974 (Qld); s 66M(1) of the Conveyancing Act 1919 (NSW). *Stephenson v State Bank of NSW* (1996) 39 NSWLR 101.

unjust not to order restitution. There are various indicia which may assist to resolve whether the receipt of such a benefit is unjust and provide the basis or foundation for a successful argument for a claim to restitution. In certain circumstances, more than one indicia may be present in support of a claim to restitution. The approach taken in this book is that there is not one all encompassing determinant of a restitutionary claim, such as free acceptance, but there exist a number of indicia that may point to a worthy claim.

(i) Inofficiousness

It is a fundamental principle of restitution that liabilities are not generally imposed upon people without their consent so that the mere fact that a person has been enriched at the expense of the plaintiff will not inevitably lead to relief.[67] Where a person, for example, has assumed the risk of non-payment for services that he or she has provided, a claim to restitution will generally be unsuccessful if the recipient declines to pay. Restitution of unsolicited benefits may, however, be ordered where the benefit has been conferred in necessitous circumstances, or under mistake or compulsion and, in these circumstances, the recipient of a benefit may be ordered to effect restitution even though he or she had not requested the benefit, on the basis that the benefit has not been conferred officiously.[68]

(ii) Free acceptance

The concept of free acceptance, considered above, has an important role in determining whether it is unjust not to order a recipient of a benefit to effect restitution.[69] If the recipient has freely accepted the benefit, then as well as not being able to appeal to subjective devaluation of it, the recipient cannot complain that the provider of the service has acted officiously. Normally, the provision of a service at the request of another will create a contractual relationship and give rise to a claim on the agreement. However, this will not always be so. In *Brewer Street Investments Ltd v Barclays Woollen Co Ltd*,[70] for example, the defendant, who was a prospective tenant, was ordered to reimburse a landlord for the cost of certain work that he had wanted done to premises in anticipation that a lease would be entered into between the parties. When the lease did not materialise, he was obliged to reimburse the landlord, for the work that had been performed on his behalf, on the basis that he had assumed the risk that a contract might not eventuate. Free acceptance may also lead to

---

67 See discussion, pp 23–26.
68 This topic is considered in Chapter 2.
69 See pp 8–9.
70 [1954] 1 QB 428; [1953] 2 All ER 1330.

restitution where the parties to an agreement mistakenly believe that a contract has been concluded but the purported agreement is unenforceable for want of certainty or form.[71] In *Pavey & Matthews Pty Ltd v Paul*,[72] a majority of the High Court of Australia held that a builder was able to recover reasonable compensation for his work on a *quantum meruit* although the building contract was unenforceable because it was not in writing. Deane J observed that, although the contract was unenforceable, it constituted evidence that the builder did not intend to perform the work gratuitously and evidenced a request.[73] In these circumstances, it was unjust for the owner not to pay for the service, and take advantage of the fact that the agreement was not in writing and thus unenforceable.[74] Similar considerations apply where a lender seeks to recoup the proceeds of an unauthorised loan where the proceeds have been applied to discharge the debts of the borrower.[75] Unless there is a very good public policy reason why the loan should not be repaid, restitution will be ordered because it is unjust for the borrower to take advantage of the proceeds of the loan without reimbursing the lender, and thereby attempt to have the best of both worlds.[76] In like manner, a debtor cannot complain that a person, whom he or she has requested to act as a surety, seeks to enforce a security formerly held by the creditor over the debtor's property once the debt has been discharged on the debtor's default. The debtor is not entitled to be in a better position than he or she would have been in had the surety not discharged the debt, and the surety is subrogated to the creditor's rights, including any securities that he or she may hold.[77]

Free acceptance may also involve sharp practice or unconscionable conduct. This may occur, for example, where the recipient of a benefit has stood by and allowed a person to confer a benefit knowing full well that the other mistakenly expects payment or some advantage from the service. Thus, in the New Zealand case of *Van den Berg v Giles*,[78] the plaintiff, who was a tenant of the defendant's holiday home, laid out a substantial sum of money on improving the property in the belief, as the defendant appreciated, that she would be able to purchase it for a certain price. The effect was that the market value of the property was increased considerably. Although the defendant had never requested

---

71 *Way v Latilla* [1937] 3 All ER 759.

72 (1986) 162 CLR 221.

73 *Ibid*, at 257.

74 See further, Chapter 14, pp 351–52.

75 *Bannatyne v D & C MacIver* [1906] 1 KB 103.

76 See equitable recoupment and the discussion of this issue in Chapter 4, pp 74–75.

77 *Craythorne v Swinburne* (1807) 14 Ves 160; 34 ER 1133. The topics of subrogation and contribution are considered in Chapter 3.

78 [1979] 2 NZLR 111.

the work, she had done nothing to disabuse the plaintiff about his prospects of purchasing the house but had chosen to accept the benefit of the work without honouring the understanding that she had reached with him. As a result, the court awarded the plaintiff the market increase in the value of the property. Similarly, in relation to Burrow's window cleaner example,[79] it is arguable that restitution should be allowed if the owner of the property stands by and allows the cleaner to wash his windows when he or she could have easily instructed the cleaner to leave had the service not been considered to be of value. Claims of this kind based on unconscientious dealing effectively estop the recipient from denying a claim in restitution. Misconduct as a determinant is further considered below.[80]

(iii) Shared mistake or misapprehension

Where the parties to a transaction have mistakenly regulated their affairs on a certain common basis of understanding, equity will not permit one to resile from the transaction and obtain an unjust benefit as is illustrated in *Amalgamated Investment & Property Ltd v Texas Commerce International Bank Ltd*.[81] The plaintiff, Texas, lent money through a subsidiary in the Bahamas to a subsidiary of Amalgamated, also in the Bahamas. Both parties acted in the mistaken belief that a guarantee entered into between Texas and Amalgamated was binding and Amalgamated, in its dealings with the bank, had also encouraged it to believe that this was so. The liquidator of Amalgamated, however, subsequently took the point that the guarantee did not cover the loans to the subsidiary. It was held that it would be unconscionable for Amalgamated to disavow its obligation in these circumstances and not pay. Lord Denning MR[82] adopted the reasoning of Dixon J in *Grundt v Great Boulder Mines Ltd*[83] that the parties had entered upon a conventional basis for the regulation of their business from which neither party could subsequently withdraw.[84] Family relationships and *de facto* marriages can also provide illustrations of disappointed expectations leading to claims to restitution in a very different context. People who enter domestic relationships and acquire property together, in the mistaken belief that they will remain together indefinitely, often do not contemplate the possibility that the relationship may terminate and, if so, how their respective interests in property acquired during the rela-

---

79 See discussion, pp 8–9.
80 See discussion, pp 19–21.
81 [1981] 3 WLR 565; [1981] 3 All ER 577.
82 *Ibid*, at 574; 584.
83 (1937) 59 CLR 641.
84 See Chapter 4, pp 86–87.

tionship should be resolved. In these circumstances, the law will be left to attempt to resolve their disputes and endeavour to provide an answer which prevents one party or the other from retaining property and being unjustly enriched. In the absence of a statutory scheme for the resolution of disputes of this kind, the remedies of resulting and constructive trusts have an important role to play in cases of this kind.[85]

Restitution may similarly be available in contractual cases where the parties have shared a common mistake as to an essential matter, or a fundamental basis of the contract has been frustrated by a supervening cause. Where a mistake related to the existence of the subject-matter, the contract at common law was void or unenforceable and moneys pre-paid to obtain performance could be recovered because of a total failure of consideration.[86] Equity developed a more far reaching remedy of rescission, however, to prevent unjust enrichment so that relief could be given in cases where the subject-matter was in existence but there existed a common misapprehension by the parties as to some essential aspect of the contract which led to an unequal exchange of values.[87] In cases of frustration, a party to a contract could stand to gain or lose substantially by a frustrating event which radically altered the foundation of the contract and frustrated the shared intentions of the parties. The common law was generally deficient in this area. Unless there had been a total failure of consideration, in which case the payer would be entitled to restitution, the loss at common law lay where it fell.[88] The inability of the common law to resolve issues of this kind, and its inability to apportion to avoid unjust enrichment in cases of frustration, was the subject of critical comment by Lord Wright in the leading case of *Fibrosa*[89] on frustration and led to statutory reform so that hardship in cases of this kind could be avoided.[90]

(iv) Total failure of consideration

A further indicia of a possible claim in restitution mentioned above is total failure of consideration. This can arise in contracts where the subject-matter of an agreement unbeknown to the parties has ceased to

---

85 See Chapter 4, pp 95–99; 102–06.

86 *Couturier v Hastie* [1843–60] All ER 281; *Strictland v Turner* (1852) 7 Ex D 208; *Norwich Union Fire Insurance Society v William H Price Ltd* [1934] AC 455; [1934] All ER 352; *McRae v Commonwealth Disposals* (1951) 84 CLR 377.

87 *Cooper v Phibbs* (1867) LR 2 HL 149; *Solle v Butcher* [1950] 1 KB 671; [1949] 2 All ER 1106; *Grist v Bailey* [1969] 2 QB 507; [1969] 2 All ER 891.

88 *Fibrosa Spolka Ackcyjna v Fairbairn Lawson Combe Barbour Ltd* [1943] AC 32; [1942] 2 All ER 122.

89 *Ibid*, at 72; 141.

90 Chapter 6, pp 144–53.

exist and the contract cannot be enforced,[91] where there has been no consideration provided and a contract has been frustrated,[92] or where a contract has been wrongfully repudiated and a party has totally failed to honour his or her obligations.[93] In such cases, a person who has already paid in expectation of receiving a benefit under the contract will be entitled to restitution if it is not forthcoming. If there is only a partial failure of consideration,[94] however, the disappointed party will not usually be able to claim in restitution under the general law because the common law cannot apportion. Modern statutes governing frustration of contract remedy this situation. It is arguable, however, that, at least where a partial benefit can be easily quantified, restitution should be permitted even though there has been only a partial failure of consideration.[95] Aside from contract, however, failure of consideration may be an indicia of a claim to restitution in other circumstances. Where *ultra vires* transactions are entered into, one rationale for restitution of advance payments is failure of consideration.[96] Similarly, where a public body claims wrongfully to be entitled to payment of taxes or other dues, a rationale for allowing moneys paid to be recovered is that no consideration has been given for the payment.[97] Where moneys have been paid to another by mistake[98] or stolen[99] and handed to a third party, the recipient will generally be ordered to effect restitution if no consideration has been provided for the payment, unless some countervailing defence is available to the payee such as estoppel or change of circumstance.[100]

---

91 *McRae v Commonwealth Disposals Commission* (1951) 84 CLR 377, at 406, and see discussion in Chapter 5, p 110.

92 As in *Chandler v Webster* [1904] 1 KB 493.

93 See *Rover International Ltd v Cannon Sales Ltd* (No 3) [1989] 1 WLR 912; [1989] 3 All ER 423; *Baltic Shipping Company v Dillon* (1992–93) 176 CLR 345, and discussion in Chapter 8, pp 184–87.

94 For further discussion of this issue, see Chapter 8, p 186. Birks appears to support the view that there should be a claim to restitution where there has been a partial failure, but acknowledges that there can be difficulty in quantifying the value of partial performance. See reprint, 1993, *op cit*, pp 242–45. Also *Goss v Chilcott* [1996] 3 NZLR 389 where Lord Goff approved such an approach.

95 Restitution was allowed on accounting of balances in an *ultra vires* share swap arrangement, see *Westdeutsche Landesbank Girozentrale v Islington LBC* [1996] 2 WLR 802; [1996] 2 All ER 961, and the discussion in *David Securities Pty Ltd v Commonwealth Bank of Australia* (1992) 17 CLR 353, at 383.

96 Lord Goff in *Westdeutske Landesbank v Islington LBC* [1996] 2 WLR 802, at 808; [1996] 2 All ER 961, at 968; *South Tynside MBC v Svenska International* [1995] 1 All ER 545.

97 See Lord Browne-Wilkinson in *Woolwich Building Society v Inland Revenue Commissioners* (No 2) [1993] AC 70, at 197; [1992] 3 All ER 737, at 781.

98 See *David Securities Pty Ltd v Commonwealth Bank of Australia* (1992) 175 CLR 353.

99 See *Lipkin Gorman v Karpnale Ltd* [1991] 2 AC 548; [1992] 4 All ER 20.

100 See Chapter 14, pp 355–59.

(v) Misconduct

Restitution will commonly be ordered in circumstances where there has been actual misconduct so that it is unconscionable for that party to retain a benefit. If the recipient of a benefit has encouraged or surreptitiously misled another, or has unconscionably attempted to resile from a transaction by disavowing an expectation that he or she has sedulously fostered in the mind of the party who has provided the benefit, the recipient may be estopped from disavowing the transaction. If A encourages B to improve his land knowing that B mistakenly believes that he will gain some kind of interest in the land, or knowingly stands by and acquiesces in B's expenditure, A will be estopped from denying B's claim to restitution. The extent of relief necessary to achieve restitution for benefits conferred in this way will be the minimum necessary to perfect the equity and do justice.[101] The origins of this equity known as 'proprietary estoppel' involved, traditionally, cases where improvements had been effected to property,[102] but the concept has been extended in more recent times to other kinds of transactions as the important case of *Walton Stores (Interstate) Ltd v Maher*[103] in the High Court of Australia illustrates. Walton Stores were found to have unconscionably misled Maher into believing he had an agreement with the result that he performed certain work for Walton Stores at considerable cost. After Walton Stores declined to proceed with the agreement, on the basis that no contract had been concluded, Maher successfully sought and gained restitution for the work performed on the ground that Walton Store's misconduct estopped it from denying that there was a contract.

Restitution may also be ordered to prevent unjust enrichment in contractual transactions where there has been misconduct. Where mistake has been induced by sharp practice or other unconscionable behaviour, relief may be ordered so that the guilty party is not enriched. The extent of restitution in cases of misrepresentation will vary according to whether the representation has been fraudulently made or not.[104] Restitution may be ordered where a transaction is illegal. Cases of illegality do not always, however, involve misconduct or reprehensible behaviour, and often difficult issues arise as to whether a transaction is illegal and, if so, whether a party who has provided services or made

---

101 *Crabb v Arun District Council* [1976] Ch 179, at 198; [1975] 3 All ER 865, at 880 *per* Scarman LJ; *Commonwealth v Verwayen* (1990) 170 CLR 394, at 411 *per* Mason CJ; at 429 *per* Brennan J, at 505 *per* McHugh J.

102 As in *Dillwyn v Llewellyn* (1862) 4 De GF & J 517; 45 ER 1285; *Ramsden v Dyson* (1866) LR 1 HL 129; *Willmott v Barber* (1880) 15 Ch D 103.

103 (1987–88) 164 CLR 387.

104 See Chapter 9, pp 208–11.

payments pursuant to such a transaction should be permitted restitution. In this context, Australia seems likely to eschew the strict rules based disciplinary approach to the issue of restitution of gratuitous benefits conferred for a dishonest purpose, that has been adopted by English courts for many years, in favour of a case by case evaluation in which the objects and policy of the statute, including the presence of alternative sanctions, are considered and balanced against the seriousness of the wrongdoing of the claimant. In *Nelson v Nelson*,[105] a case where the High Court allowed restitution of a home to a woman who had placed it in the names of her children in order to fraudulently acquire a concession to a second home under the Defence Service Homes Act 1918, Toohey J observed:[106]

> Although the public policy in discouraging unlawful acts and refusing them judicial approval is important, it is not the only relevant policy consideration. There is also the consideration of preventing injustice and enrichment of one party at the expense of the other party.

In cases of wrongful repudiation of a contract, the innocent party will be entitled to restitution of pre-paid money if the contract-breaker has totally failed to provide consideration. A contract-breaker may also be sued in restitution for the reasonable cost of services provided, although there is a strong body of academic opinion that would suggest either that the innocent party should be confined to a claim for damages or at the very least the contract should provide a ceiling for the claim.[107] Even more uncertain is the extent to which an innocent party may be able to secure any gains or profits derived by a contract-breaker as a result of his or her breach.[108]

Other important instances of misconduct that commonly give rise to claims of unjust enrichment and play a vital role in restitution today, include benefits derived by means of transactions involving duress, undue influence or other unconscionable conduct on the part of the recipient or a third party who has attempted to profit from an oppressive transaction.[109] Another important aspect of unjust enrichment includes claims involving benefits or profits derived from a breach of fiduciary duty. In recent years, there has been extensive appeal to equity in order to gain restitution of profits gained by fiduciaries or third parties who have received or dealt with property that has been

---

105 (1995) 184 CLR 538; (1995) 70 ALJR 47, *cf Tinsley v Milligan* [1994] 1 AC 340; [1993] 3 All ER 65.

106 *Ibid*, at 538; 80.

107 See Chapter 8, pp 190–92.

108 See Chapter 8, pp 189–90.

109 See Chapter 10.

misappropriated. As well as personal remedies, proprietary remedies involving the tracing of trust property, and the imposition of a constructive trust as a remedy to prevent the unjust enrichment of errant fiduciaries and their miscreant associates are important aspects of restitution, today.[110] Other instances of wrongdoing that may give rise to claims to restitution involve gains derived from criminal or tortious activity.[111]

(vi) Discretion

In England and Australia, considerations involving unjust enrichment are principally governed by case law and principles that can be gleaned from them, sometimes described as a rules based system. However, in New Zealand, in the area of contract law, there has been significant reform intended to abrogate the general law and determine issues relating to mistake, frustration, illegality, breach and misrepresentation by resort to a measure of judicial discretion. The discretion is not one, however, that is entirely unfettered but is, in the respective areas, governed by certain statutory indicia. The relevant statutory provisions and case law are discussed in this book. In general, it would seem that the existence of a statutory regime has not greatly troubled New Zealand courts, with the exception being mutual mistake where a difference of judicial opinion and approach is evidenced in decisions of the Court of Appeal. The decisions have, however, for the most part, been predictable. In defence of a case orientated system, it may be argued that it gives greater certainty and is a better foundation for commercial transactions. On the other hand, an examination of the cases would suggest that the general law is not entirely predictable and is arguably deficient in certain areas. Indeed, it was acknowledged to be deficient in the area of frustration which was the subject of legislative reform first in England and later in New Zealand and other jurisdictions.[112] Whilst it may be argued that the New Zealand discretion based system is less certain, there does not appear to have been any call to abandon this approach or indeed restrict the exercise of discretion. The apparent absence of any great volume of cases concerning the legislation would suggest that disputes have lent themselves to settlement which, if this is indeed the case, is a desirable consequence. In Australia, it would also appear that there has been a preference for a more flexible approach to issues of restitution in the area of illegality than is provided by a rules based approach. Whereas English courts have steadfastly adopted a conservative approach which has meant

---

110 See Chapter 11.
111 See Chapters 12 and 13.
112 See discussion, Chapter 6, pp 144–53.

that restitution will be denied where a claimant is obliged to reveal the illegal nature of a transaction in support of his or her claim, Australian courts have chosen to approach claims of this kind more flexibly by examining the objects of the governing legislation, the seriousness of the transgression and any available penalties in order to ascertain whether a claim to restitution should be permitted or rejected.[113] This is not dissimilar to the approach taken in New Zealand to illegality and restitution under the Illegal Contracts Act 1970.

(vii) Countervailing considerations

Although, *prima facie*, a party has been enriched, there may exist countervailing considerations which enable the recipient of a benefit to resist restitution on the basis that it is not unjust to retain the benefit. In the final chapter of this book, consideration is given to defences that may restrict or deny a claim for restitution. The most important recent development, in this regard, is the defence of change of position which featured prominently in the various editions of Goff and Jones and has now been judicially accepted as a defence to money claims in England in *Lipkin Gorman v Karpnale Ltd*[114] and in Australia in *David Securities Pty Ltd v Commonwealth Bank of Australia*.[115] In Western Australia and New Zealand, there has been, for some time, legislation in existence to allow such a defence.[116] As Mason CJ observed in *David Securities*,[117] the defence of change of position is necessary for the development of a balanced law of restitution because it permits a court to consider more fully the competing equities of a claimant payer and a defendant payee in order to evaluate whether it is truly just to order relief.

---

113 See *Tinsley v Milligan* [1994] 1 AC 340; [1993] 3 All ER 65; *cf Nelson v Nelson* (1995) 184 CLR 538.

114 [1991] 2 AC 548.

115 (1991–92) 175 CLR 353.

116 Section 125(1) of the Property Law Act 1969 (WA); s 94B of the Judicature Act 1908 (NZ).

117 (1991–92) 175 CLR 353, at 385.

CHAPTER 2

Unsolicited Benefits

An unsolicited benefit arises when the recipient has not requested the benefit, or had the opportunity to reject the benefit. Where the recipient has had the opportunity of rejecting the benefit, but has chosen to accept it, issues of free acceptance and restitution arise which are considered in Chapter 4. In general, a person who voluntarily or officiously confers a benefit on another will not be entitled to restitution[1] but, where it can be established that benefits have been conferred as a result of a mistake or through necessity or under compulsion so that officiousness is negatived, restitution of an unsolicited benefit may be ordered to prevent unjust enrichment of the recipient.

The volunteer

The cases considered below illustrate how courts are reluctant to assist a person to gain restitution of benefits that have been officiously conferred upon another without request, or in the absence of some unconscionable conduct on the part of the recipient. As Bowen LJ observed in *Falcke v Scottish Imperial Insurance Company*:[2]

> The general principle is, beyond all question, that work and labour done or money expended by one man to preserve or benefit the property of another do not, according to English law, create any lien upon the property saved or benefited, nor, even if standing alone, create any obligation to repay the expenditure. Liabilities are not to be forced upon people behind their backs any more than you can confer a benefit upon a man's back against his will.

In this case, the owner of the equity of redemption in a mortgaged insurance policy, Emmanuel, claimed a lien in priority to the interests of a mortgagee, Falcke, because he had paid a substantial premium to preserve the policy which he was under no obligation to do since he had been discharged from bankruptcy. The policy by agreement with Emmanuel's creditors had not formed part of his bankrupt estate. On his discharge, he thought he had purchased Falcke's interest through a solicitor whom he believed erroneously had been authorised by Falcke

---

1 When a person cleans my shoes, what else can I do but put them on, *Taylor v Laird* (1856) 25 LJ Ex 329. Cited by Lord Denning MR in *Greenwood v Bennett* [1973] QB 195, at 202.

2 (1887) 34 Ch D 234, at 248.

to negotiate the sale. Falcke died and his wife sought to enforce the security. There being insufficient on sale to satisfy the mortgage, the issue for determination was whether Emmanuel was entitled to a lien since he contended that by paying the premium he had kept alive the policy for the benefit of the mortgagee. He also argued that the solicitor acting on behalf of Falcke had requested him to do so. The Court of Appeal held, however, that Emmanuel was not entitled to any lien or priority. The evidence did not establish that any request had been made of Emmanuel. Nor did it establish that Emmanuel had paid under a mistake induced or contributed to by Falcke that would estop his wife from denying Emmanuel's claim.[3] It would seem that the court accepted that Emmanuel believed that he had acquired Falcke's interest but his motive in paying was not altruistic. He had paid to keep the policy on foot so as to preserve his own interest in the property as the ultimate holder of the equity of redemption.

Falcke was a case concerning a claim to a lien and not a claim to a lesser right of reimbursement for expenditure. In that sense, the *dictum* of Bowen LJ, that the law does not accommodate volunteers who seek reimbursement for voluntary services even though they may benefit another, was *obiter*. However, the wider principle is also illustrated in the decision of the High Court of Australia in *Hill v Ziymack*.[4] A farmer, Mrs Ziymack, had paid the debts of her late son that related to his acquisition of a flock of sheep which were agisted on her property at the time of his death. The flock had been purchased with promissory notes and a stock mortgage back to the vendor. Mrs Ziymack contended that the sheep belonged to her and sold them after the death of her son. In an earlier separate action brought against her by the son's wife, she was found to have converted the sheep. In the present action, she sought to set off the amounts she had paid in settling her son's debts against the damages she had to pay in the earlier litigation. She argued that she had discharged her son's debts in the mistaken belief that she was authorised to do so, and in order to preserve the stock. Accordingly, she claimed that she was entitled to reimbursement for this expenditure. The High Court held, however, that the evidence established that, at the time the payment was made, Mrs Ziymack acted at her own risk and there was no evidence of request, ratification or a contribution by the wife to any misapprehension she might have held as to ownership of the flock. Accordingly, she was held to have voluntarily discharged the

---

3   In other words, Falcke had not acquiesced or in any way seduced the payment. See the discussion of estoppel in Chapter 4, pp 78–79.

4   (1908) 7 CLR 352.

debts and was not entitled to any reimbursement.[5] It would appear, however, that, although the court considered that Mrs Ziymack was not entitled to reimbursement on a claim initiated by her, at least Griffiths CJ would have been prepared to allow her compensation had she claimed this in defence in the earlier case of conversion.[6]

Owen v Tate[7] is another case where the officious intervenor has been denied restitution. There, the Court of Appeal held that a surety who officiously assumed the role of a guarantor in the face of opposition from the debtor was not entitled to claim recoupment from the debtor after paying the creditor. The plaintiff, in order to accommodate the wishes of a former employee, had deposited sufficient money with a bank to cover the defendant's overdraft. As a consequence, the bank released the employee's title deeds to her property which had been deposited as security for the overdraft. The substitution was unacceptable to the defendants who protested the release and variation. The defendants eventually told the bank to look to the plaintiff for payment and declined to repay the loan with the result that the bank applied the proceeds of the deposited funds in discharge of its debt. The plaintiff sought restitution from the defendants but his claim was dismissed by the Court of Appeal. The court considered that the plaintiff had voluntarily assumed a legal obligation to guarantee the loan in exchange for the release of his employee's deeds which had been opposed by the defendants. Their invitation to the bank to have recourse to the plaintiff had to be considered in the light of their objection to the new arrangement. Scarman LJ observed that it was not reasonable or just to allow the plaintiff's claim:[8]

---

5   The assertion by Issacs J that Mrs Ziymack erroneously believed that she was discharging debts on her own property would seem to negate officiousness on her part (*ibid*, at 370). The case would seem to turn on the fact that payment of the debt was neither requested or ratified by the debtor, or his estate subsequently, and so in law the payment was deemed voluntary and one that could not be the subject of restitution. It is argued, however, below, pp 37–38 that where debts are discharged by mistake, there should be a right to restitution where in reality the debtor has been incontrovertibly benefited by the creditor accepting payment.

6   *Ibid*, at 358 citing *Peruvian Guano Co v Drefus Bros & Co* [1892] AC 166, at 170, and see discussion of *Greenwood v Bennett* [1973] QB 195, pp 38–39.

7   [1976] 1 QB 403; [1975] 2 All ER 129.

8   *Ibid*, at 411–12; at 135. See the criticism of this case by Birks, P and Beatson, J, 'Unrequested Payment of Another's Debt' (1976) 92 LQR 88, and Lord Goff and Jones, G, *The Law of Restitution*, 4th edn, 1993, pp 597–98, Sweet & Maxwell. It is argued that the case is a consequence of the rule that, unless the debtor either requests a debt be paid or subsequently ratifies payment, there is no effective discharge of the debt and the creditor could still proceed to claim payment of the debt from the debtor. See *Belshaw v Bush* (1851) 11 CB 191; 138 ER 444; *City Bank of Sydney v McLaughlin* (1909) 9 CLR 615; *Hill v Ziymack* (1908) 7 CLR 352. These writers suggest that the plaintiff should have been subrogated to the creditor's rights in order to prevent any possible unjust enrichment of the creditor in this way. Burrows, A, *The Law of Restitution*, 1993, pp 222–30, Butterworths, is critical of the rule that, in the absence of a request or ratification, there is no discharge of the debt, and suggests that debts should be treated as automatically discharged. See further, discussion in Chapter 4, p 76, fn 52. For a case of a denial of subrogation where there was a voluntary discharge of the liability of another in the context of an insurance claim, see *The Esso Bernica* [1989] AC 643. Considered further in Chapter 3, p 57.

In the present case, the evidence is that the plaintiff acted not only behind the backs of the defendants initially, but in the interests of another, and despite their protest. When the moment came for him to honour the obligation thus assumed, the defendants are not to be criticised, in my judgment, for having accepted the benefit of a transaction which they neither wanted nor sought.

These cases illustrate well, in their different contexts, how courts will, in general, deny restitution where it is considered that benefits have been voluntarily or officiously[9] conferred on others. It may seem harsh that this attitude is adopted where a person has undoubtedly received a benefit which could be described as a windfall; however, this approach reflects the *laissez-faire* philosophy that people should, in general, be free to choose whether they want to incur expenditure and, if so, with whom they desire to transact. Where, however, benefits are conferred in circumstances of mistake, through necessity, or under compulsion, officiousness is negated with the result that restitution of unsolicited benefits may be ordered to prevent the unjust enrichment of the recipient.

Mistake

Unsolicited benefits conferred by mistake will be considered under three heads; mistakenly conferred monetary benefits, mistakenly conferred improvements to chattels and mistakenly conferred improvements to land. It will be seen that where money has been paid by mistake, the payer will *prima facie* be able to claim restitution in an action for moneys had and received. In these circumstances, the payee is clearly or incontrovertibly enriched and is not able to 'subjectively devalue'[10] the worth of the benefit he or she has received. Whether restitution will be ordered, however, will depend on the payee being able to show that it would be unjust for a court to require all or part of the money to be repaid. In order to resist a claim to restitution, the payee will have to establish one of the following defences: that the payment was made regardless of whether the money was owing and in order to settle an honest claim, that consideration was given in good faith for the payment, or that an estoppel arises to prevent the payer from asserting a claim to restitution. Finally, it may constitute a defence that the payee has so changed his or her position by virtue of the payment that it would be unjust to order restitution.

---

9   A term used in *Owen v Tate* [1976] 1 QB 403, at 412, and in Australia, see *J Gasdsen v Strider 1 Ltd (The ASP Express)* (1990) 20 NSWLR 57, at 70. In this case, the owner of a ship was unable to charge freight where the goods had been delivered at Melbourne rather than Auckland since this was effected for the owner's advantage. The owner was held to have acted officiously and voluntarily conferred a benefit on the shipper.

10 An expression advanced by Birks, P, *An Introduction to the Law of Restitution*, reprint 1993, p 114, Clarendon Press, Oxford.

In so far as mistakenly conferred improvements to chattels or land are concerned, the owner may well seek to subjectively devalue the value of improvements by asserting that he or she did not want them and they are of no value. Where the improvements are not ephemeral or of value simply to the improver and do objectively increase the value of the property, thereby conferring what Goff and Jones would describe as an 'incontrovertible benefit' on the owner,[11] a persuasive case can be made out for restitution. Restitution should be allowed where there has been an increase in the market value of property or the expenditure has inevitably saved the owner expense. If claims to restitution of money are *prima facie* recoverable, then consistently, it may be argued, improvements to chattels or real estate that incontrovertibly benefit the owner should also be the subject of restitution. Mistake negatives officiousness or any suggestion that improvements effected in this way are benefits that have been voluntarily conferred. However, others contend that restitution should not be as freely available as in money claims, particularly if it involves the hardship of the property having to be sold in order to pay for the improvements.[12] These issues are considered below.

(a) Restitution of money paid to another by mistake

(i) The nature of liability

A person who pays money to another under a material mistake will *prima facie* be entitled to have the moneys repaid. It does not matter that the mistake arose out of forgetfulness or carelessness.[13] Earlier English authority had suggested that, in order to obtain recovery, the mistake had to involve a belief that there was an antecedent obligation or liability to another. Thus, in *Aiken v Short*,[14] Bramwell B observed:[15]

---

11 Lord Goff and Jones, G, *The Law of Restitution*, 4th edn, 1993, pp 20–22, Sweet & Maxwell; Jones, G, 'Restitutionary Claims for Services Rendered' (1973) LQR 273, at 295. An expression adopted by Carruthers J in *J Gasdsen v Pty Ltd v Strider 1 Ltd (The AES Express)* (1990) 20 NSWLR 57, at 70–71. Further, see *Monks Poynice Pty Ltd* (1987) 8 NSWLR 662, at 664 *per* Young J, and considered also by Jeffries J in *Van den Berg v Giles* [1979] 2 NZLR 111, at 122.

12 See Goff and Jones, *op cit*, pp 166–67, and, 3rd edn, 1986, p 138; Birks, *op cit*, p 110.

13 *Kelly v Solari* (1841) 11 LJ Ex 10, careless payment of insurance moneys after the insurer had been informed the policy had lapsed; *Lady Hood of Avalon v Mackinnon* [1909] 1 Ch 476, mistaken settlement of property under a trust where there had been a double appointment; *Barclays Bank v W J Sims Son & Cooke (Southern) Ltd* [1980] QB 677, [1979] 3 All ER 522, careless payment of a cheque overlooking the countermand of a customer.

14 (1856) 1 H & N 210.

15 *Ibid*, at 215. See further *Kelly v Solari* (1841) 11 LJ Ex 10, at 11, *per* Parke B; *Morgan v Ashcroft* [1938] 1 KB 49, at 63, *per* Sir Wilfrid Greene MR.

> In order to entitle a person to recover back money paid under a mis-
> take of fact, the mistake must be as to a fact, which, if true, would
> make the person paying liable to pay the money: not, where if true,
> it would merely make it desirable that he should pay the money.

Although a liability mistake is clearly a mistake of a kind that negatives any suggestion that a payment is voluntary, to limit recovery to a
mistake of this kind would seriously inhibit the scope of recovery in
cases of mistake, and would enlarge the scope for a payee to be unjustly
enriched. In any event, the width of the *dictum* of Bramwell B was
unnecessary because there was a more fundamental reason why the
moneys paid in that case were not recoverable. A bank, at the request of
a customer named Carter, had paid a debt Carter owed to the defendant. It did this because Carter had assigned to the bank an expectation
of an inheritance. This inheritance, which the bank wished to sell, had
been mortgaged to the defendant. After paying off the mortgage, however, the bank discovered that Carter's expectation that he would gain
an inheritance had not materialised because a subsequent will had
revoked his interest. The bank then sued the defendant claiming that it
had paid the debt under a misapprehension that it enjoyed a valid
expectation of securing Carter's inheritance. The defendant successfully
argued that it had, with the consent of the debtor, *bona fide* discharged
the debt and had provided consideration for the payment. Accordingly,
it was not unconscionable for the bank to retain the money.

In *Barclays Bank v W J Sims Son & Cooke (Southern) Ltd*,[16] Robert Goff J
(now Lord Goff) reviewed English authority on mistaken money payments and concluded that recovery was not limited to mistakes concerning antecedent liability. In *Kerrison v Glynn Mills Currie and Co*,[17] for
example, the House of Lords allowed recovery of a payment made in
anticipation that a liability would be incurred. In this case, a payment
was made to the respondent for the credit of a bank in anticipation that
the bank would advance moneys to a mining company in which the
payer was interested. The bank became insolvent and the respondent
claimed a right to retain the money since the bank was indebted to it. It
was held that the payer was entitled to recover the moneys because the
money had been paid in anticipation of a liability being incurred, and
the payer was not indebted to the bank. The money was paid under a
material mistake that the bank could perform its obligations when it
could not. Since the money was paid under a mistake and could not be
said to belong to the bank, the respondent could not claim a right to
retain the payment in satisfaction of the bank's liability to it. In *Barclays
Bank v W J Sims Son & Cooke (Southern) Ltd*, Robert Goff J held that

---

16 [1980] QB 677; [1979] 3 All ER 522.
17 (1912) 81 LJ KB 465; [1911–13] All ER 417.

Barclays, which had honoured a cheque in contravention of a counter-mand by its customer that had been made payable to a company that had gone into receivership, was able to recover the payment from the receiver. The court rejected an argument that recovery was limited to mistakes between a payer and payee with whom there was privity of relationship, and also rejected the contention that English law limited recovery to cases where the payer believed that he or she was under an antecedent liability. In that case, the bank had carelessly overlooked the customer's countermand. Unlike *Aiken v Short*, the payment could not operate to discharge its customer's debt because the customer had not authorised payment. Hence, the payee could not resist the claim on the ground that value had been given.

In *Porter v Latec Finance (Qld) Pty Ltd*,[18] the High Court of Australia considered that, in order for moneys paid under mistake to be recoverable, the mistake had to be one that was 'fundamental'. The expression had also been invoked by Lord Wright in the Privy Council in *Norwich Union Fire Insurance Society v W H Price Ltd*.[19] More recently, in *ANZ Banking Group Ltd v Westpac Banking Corporation*,[20] the High Court of Australia rejected any limitation relating either to privity in relationship between payer and payee, or any necessity for the mistake to relate to a belief that antecedent liability existed. Further, in *David Securities Pty Ltd v Commonwealth Bank of Australia*,[21] the High Court of Australia rejected the notion that a mistake must be 'fundamental' on the ground that this was a vague expression. So long as there was a causative link between a mistake and a payment, restitution was *prima facie* available.

(ii) Payments made under mistake of law and compromise of an honest claim

Another restriction on restitution of money paid under a mistake was the distinction between a mistake of fact and one of law. This distinction was first made in the 19th century, in *Bilbie v Lumley*.[22] There, Lord Ellenborough CJ alluded to the distinction when declining to allow the recovery of moneys paid by an insurer under a settlement. The insurer had possession of all the facts that would have justified its rejection of

---

18 (1964) 111 CLR 177.

19 [1934] AC 455, at 463; [1934] All ER 352, at 356.

20 (1987–88) 164 CLR 662, at 671–72. *Cf Commercial Bank of Australia Ltd v Younis* (1979) 1 NSWLR 444, at 447–48.

21 (1992) 175 CLR 353, at 377–78.

22 (1802) 2 East 469; 102 ER 448. Further, see *Kelly v Solari* (1841) 11 LJ Ex 10, at 12. Lord Abinger CB observed: 'There are indeed some payments that cannot be recovered back; those, for instance, which a man chooses to make without instituting any inquiry, where his determination evidently is to pay, whatever the facts may be; for when a man resolves to pay, without making any further investigation, it is reasonable that he should be bound by his own conduct.'

the claim but, in ignorance of the right to reject, proceeded to settle the claim. It was held that it could not recover the moneys merely because it later appreciated that the claim could have been declined. This case would appear to represent no more than a compromise of a claim, and it being the policy of the law to preserve rather than set aside settlements of this kind, it was unnecessary for the court to advert to mistake of law. However, after *Bilbie v Lumley*, the distinction between mistakes of law and fact hardened into a rule that denied recovery of payments made where the mistake was one of law rather than fact.[23] The distinction was widely criticised as illogical.[24] In New Zealand[25] and Western Australia,[26] the distinction was abrogated by statute. The Supreme Court of Canada also indicated its dissatisfaction with the distinction in *Air Canada v British Columbia*[27] and in *David Securities Pty Ltd v Commonwealth Bank of Australia*,[28] the High Court of Australia considered that the distinction should not be preserved. The High Court[29] emphasised, however, the importance of upholding compromises or settlements of claims and observed that an earlier decision of the court in *South Australian Gold Stores v Electricity Trust of South Australia*,[30] where a distinction of this kind had been upheld, could be supported on the alternative ground that the payments made constituted a settlement of a disputed claim and for that reason were irrecoverable. More recently, in *Commissioner of State Revenue (Vic) v Royal Insurance Australia Ltd*,[31] the High Court of Australia held that where an insurer had, as a result of an error of law, overpaid stamp duty, the payment was *prima facie* recoverable from the Victorian Revenue. The receipt of the excess duty by the Commissioner constituted an unjust enrichment and, in order to justify exercising a discretionary statutory power to retain the excess, the Commissioner had to show an adverse change of position.[32] The mere fact that the insurer had passed the cost on to its clients was insufficient to

---

23 *William Whitely Ltd v The King* (1909) 26 TLR 19; [1908–10] All ER 639; *Sawyer & Vincent v Window Brace Ltd* [1943] KB 32. In Australia, *York Air Conditioning & Refrigeration (A/asia) Pty Ltd v Commonwealth* (1949) 80 CLR 11; *South Australia Cold Stores Ltd v Electricity Trust of South Australia* (1957) 98 CLR 65; *J & S Holdings Pty Ltd v NRMA Insurance Ltd* (1982) 61 FLR 108.

24 The criticisms are set out in *David Securities Pty Ltd v Commonwealth Bank of Australia* (1992) 175 CLR 353, at 375–76.

25 Sections 94A and 94B of the Judicature Act 1908. See *Thomas v Houston Corbett & Co* [1969] NZLR 151; *KJDavies Ltd v Bank of NSW* [1981] 1 NZLR 262.

26 Sections 124 and 125 of the Property Law Act 1969 (WA). See *Inn Leisure v D F McCloy* (1991) 28 FCR 151.

27 (1989) 59 DLR (4th) 161, at 191.

28 (1992) 175 CLR 353, at 374–76.

29 *Ibid*, at 376.

30 (1957) 98 CLR 65.

31 (1994) 182 CLR 51, considered also in *Kleinwort v Birmingham Council* [1996] 4 All ER 733.

32 *Ibid*, at 65–66 *per* Mason CJ.

justify retention because, as between the insurer and the Commissioner, the receipt by the Commissioner of the excess constituted a windfall to which *prima facie* he was not entitled.[33]

Where a payment has been mistakenly made, the payer may be entitled, in the event of the insolvency of the payee, to the imposition of a constructive trust over the assets of the payee in order to secure the proceeds in preference to the general creditors of the payee. A constructive trust was imposed in these circumstances by Goulding J in *Chase Manhattan Bank v Israel-British Bank (London) Ltd*[34] in order to prevent the general creditors deriving a windfall benefit or an unjust enrichment. The imposition of a remedial constructive trust is further considered in Chapter 11.[35]

(iii) Defences to mistaken payments

Recovery of payments made mistakenly may be resisted where certain defences available to a payee are established. If the payment was made to settle or compromise an honest claim, we have seen that restitution will be denied.[36] Other available defences are considered below.

(iv) Consideration

If consideration is provided by the payee, then the presumption in favour of recovery will be rebutted. In *Aikin v Short*,[37] the discharge of a debt with the approval of the debtor was one reason for denying any right in the payer to recover for an alleged mistake. However, in *Barclays Bank v W J Sims Son & Cooke (Southern) Ltd*[38] recovery was permitted where the bank paid a debt of a customer without a mandate to do so after a countermand of a cheque had been overlooked. In *Porter v Latec Finance (Qld) Pty Ltd*,[39] it was the opinion of a majority of the High Court of Australia that a debt existed, had been validly discharged and consideration provided, even though the debtor had fraudulently misrepresented his identity to both the payer and the payee. Accordingly, a claim to recovery of a payment on the ground of mistaken identity failed.

---

33 *Ibid*, at 69–79 *per* Mason CJ, Brennan J, at 90. The court did entertain the argument that in appropriate circumstances moneys reimbursed might have to be held in trust for the customers to whom the tax had been passed on as a separate item, but that was not the case in *Royal*. See Beatson, J, 'Restitution of Overpaid Tax, Discretion and Passing off' (1995) 111 LQR 375.

34 [1981] 1 Ch 105; [1979] 3 All ER 1025.

35 See pp 313, 323–28.

36 See discussion, pp 30; 228–29.

37 (1856) 1 H & N 210; [1843–60] All ER 425.

38 [1980] QB 677; [1979] 3 All ER 522.

39 (1964) 111 CLR 177, at 185 *per* Barwick CJ, at 198–99 *per* Taylor J, at 208–09 *per* Owen J. See more recently, discharge of a debt as consideration for a mistaken payment, *Keith Murphy Ltd v Customs Credit Corp Ltd* [1992] 6 WAR 332; *Griffiths v Commonwealth Bank of Australia* (1994) 123 ALR 111.

A claim that consideration had been provided by a bank for the payment of withholding tax made by a customer of the bank in the mistaken belief that it was lawfully owing, when it was the bank's responsibility to pay, was rejected by the High Court of Australia in *David Securities Pty Ltd v Commonwealth Bank of Australia*.[40] In that case, the bank had insisted that the customer was liable to pay withholding tax and this formed part of the contractual obligation undertaken by the customer in exchange for which the bank claimed that it had agreed to a reduced interest rate for a loan. It was argued successfully for the customer that the obligation it had accepted was unlawful and that the payments had been made under a mistake. It was held that the bank had not provided valid consideration for the payment since the obligation of the bank to pay the withholding tax was not one that could be lawfully imposed on its customer, and the responsibility for ensuring that the legislation was complied with lay with the bank. It could not rely upon its own ignorance of the law in order to claim that it had provided a reduced interest rate in consideration of the customer agreeing to pay withholding tax. In *Prudential Assurance Co Ltd v C M Breedon & Son Ltd*,[41] it was held that an insurance company could not recover an overpayment of the surrender value of a policy, because the insured had entered into a fresh agreement or compromise with the insurer concerning the surrender of the policy and this constituted consideration for the payment.

(v) Estoppel

Estoppel may preclude the payer from claiming restitution of money paid under a mistake if, as a result of the payment, the payee acts to his or her detriment. Estoppel may arise from a misrepresentation that the recipient is entitled to treat moneys as his or her own, or may arise from the conduct of a payer that gives rise to a wrongful assumption by the payee that he or she is entitled to certain money. Where a person is under an obligation to inform a payee of the correct amount that is due or owing, a failure to do so may mean that an estoppel will preclude recovery of any payment mistakenly made.[42] Where the payee is at fault, estoppel will not be available to resist a claim for restitution.[43]

The defence of estoppel was considered by the House of Lords in *R E Jones Ltd v Waring and Gillow Ltd*.[44] There, a rogue enticed the plaintiff to make cheques out in the name of the defendant by misrepresenting himself to be an agent of the defendant. The plaintiff believed that they were

---

40 (1992) 175 CLR 353, at 382–84.

41 [1994] 2 VLR 452.

42 The principles relating to estoppel in cases of this kind were considered by Mackenna J in *United Overseas Bank v Jiwani* [1977] 1 All ER 733, at 736–37.

43 *Larner v London County Council* [1949] 2 KB 683; [1949] 1 All ER 964.

44 [1926] AC 670; [1926] All ER 36.

obtaining an agency to sell motor vehicles and paid the cheques as deposits on motor vehicles. The rogue presented the cheques to the defendant representing that he had earned the money and had arranged for the cheques to be made out in the defendant's name so as to obtain the release of goods that he had previously purchased from the defendant. These goods had been repossessed after the rogue had failed to pay. On discovering the fraud, the plaintiff sued for the return of the moneys on the ground of mistake, and a majority of the House of Lords held that the plaintiff was entitled to recover. There was no representation in any of the dealings that the plaintiff had with the defendant that the defendant was entitled to the money. Nor was this a case where the plaintiff was under any obligation or duty to the defendant to provide an accurate statement of account.[45] It was further considered by Lord Sumner that the release of the goods by the defendant was attributable not to anything said or written by the plaintiff but, rather, was in response to the rogue's fraudulent tale as to how he had come by the cheques.[46] In *Holt v Markham*,[47] however, restitution was denied where a retired air force officer was paid a gratuity at a higher rate than he was entitled, because the payee had been given incorrect information in circumstances where he was entitled to an accurate account. Further, there had been an unacceptable delay in correcting the error with the result that the payee had invested the money in shares in a company which had subsequently become insolvent.

In order to found an estoppel, the payee must have acted to his or her detriment. It will be insufficient to argue that the money has been expended on ordinary household living because, in these circumstances, there has been no change of position.[48] Similarly, if the expenditure would have been incurred irrespective of the payment, a plea of estoppel will be unsuccessful. In *United Overseas Bank v Jiwani*,[49] it was held that the defendant could not rely on estoppel to defeat the bank's claim for the repayment of a substantial sum paid under a mistake, because the evidence established that the moneys were applied to the purchase of a hotel which the defendant intended to acquire in any event. It was also observed that, if the acquisition of an asset as a result of a mistaken payment had proved to be a profitable investment, the payee could not rely on estoppel because the payee had not been

---

45 *Ibid*, at 693; 46 *per* Lord Sumner, at 701; 50 *per* Lord Carson.

46 *Idem*.

47 [1923] 1 KB 504; see further for a case of this kind, *Skyring v Greenwood* (1825) 4 B & C 281; 107 ER 1064 where, over a period of time, an army paymaster erroneously credited Skyring's account with money to which he was not entitled. It was held that the payments constituted an implied misrepresentation that the money was his.

48 *R E Jones Ltd v Waring and Gillow Ltd* [1926] AC 670, at 644; [1926] All ER 36, at 41 *per* Viscount Cave LC.

49 [1977] 1 All ER 733.

50 *Ibid*, at 737.

adversely   affected.[50]
If, however, the defendant can establish detriment and successfully rely
on estoppel, the Court of Appeal in *Avon County Council v Howlett*,[51] considered that the defendant was entitled to retain the whole of the sum
mistakenly paid, even though it was not established that the detriment
suffered exhausted the payment. It would seem unjust, however, to
allow the payee to retain the whole of the payment in these circumstances. This approach would appear to be at odds with modern
English[52] and Australian[53] authority that regard a plea of estoppel as
being satisfied by the minimum response necessary to achieve justice. In
this regard, in *R E Jones Ltd v Waring and Gillow Ltd*,[54] Viscount Cave LC
observed that in circumstances where there was an excess in the amount
of payment over detriment it was proper, as a condition of successfully
asserting estoppel, that the payee should undertake to repay any excess.

(vi) Change of position

A limited form of defence of change of position has long been recognised where an agent pays over moneys that have been mistakenly paid
to him or her to a principal.[55] A recent Australian application of this
defence is seen in *ANZ Banking Group Ltd v Westpac Banking
Corporation*.[56] As a result of a clerical error in a telegraphic transfer, ANZ
overpaid Westpac $100,000 for the credit of a customer. By the time that
the error was discovered, Westpac had applied the moneys in discharge
of the customer's indebtedness and had honoured various substantial
cheques leaving a greatly reduced balance. The customer ratified what
had been done and agreed to pay back the money to ANZ on an instalment basis. However, after only a short period, the customer went into
liquidation. The High Court held that ANZ could only recover the balance because the bank had effectively applied the moneys to the account
of its principal in discharging the existing debt and in honouring

---

51   [1983] 1 All ER 1072.

52   *Crabb v Arun District Council* [1976] Ch 179, at 198; [1975] 3 All ER 865, at 880 *per*
      Scarman LJ.

53   *Commonwealth of Australia v Verwayen* (1990) 170 CLR 394, at 411 *per* Mason CJ; at
      429 *per* Brennan J; at 505 *per* McHugh J.

54   [1926] AC 670, at 684; [1926] All ER 36, at 42.

55   *Continental Caoutchouc & Gutta Percha Co v Kleinwort Sons & Co* (1904) 9 Com Cas
      240; *Baylis v Bishop of London* [1913] 1 Ch 127; *Gowers v Lloyd's and National Provincial
      Foreign Bank Ltd* [1938] 1 All ER 766.

56   (1987–88) 164 CLR 662. For a comprehensive consideration of mistaken payments
      with particular emphasis on New Zealand law, see Rickett, C, 'Banks and the
      Recovery of Mistaken Payments' (1994) 16 NZULR 105.

57   Note that a mere book entry which had not been communicated to the third party
      or which can be reversed without affecting the substance of transactions or rela-
      tionships will ordinarily not suffice. *Ibid*, at 674 citing *Colonial Bank v Exchange Bank
      of Yarmouth, Nova Scotia* (1886) 11 App Cas 84.

cheques.[57]

A more liberal concept of change of position was rejected by the Court of Appeal in *Baylis v Bishop of London*.[58] There, payments by way of rent-charge were made to the Bishop who spent the money prior to being informed that it had been incorrectly paid to him. It was held that the Bishop had to repay the money and could not rely on the fact that the money had been spent on the Church's business and the balance applied to the trustee-in-bankruptcy of an incumbent rector as he was obliged to do under legislation governing the rector's bankruptcy. The Bishop argued that he was in the position of an agent who had simply paid over moneys to a principal and should not be held liable to repay the moneys, but the court declined to treat the Bishop as a principal. Nor was it prepared to accept any extension of this defence in order to accommodate a wider notion of change of position. Hamilton LJ was robust in his condemnation of any concept of a change of position observing:[59]

> The question is whether it is unconscientious for the defendant to keep the money, not whether it is fair for the plaintiff to ask to have it back. To ask what course would be *ex aequo et bono* to both sides never was a very precise guide and, as a working rule, it has long since been buried in *Standish v Ross*[60] and *Kelly v Solari*.[61] Whatever may have been the case some 146 years ago, we are not now free in the 20th century to administer that vague jurisprudence which is sometimes attractively styled 'justice as between man and man'.

However, more recently, courts have entertained a defence of change of position. Contrary to the approach of Hamilton LJ in *Baylis v Bishop of London*, it has been recognised that a change of position defence is necessary to give symmetry to a rational development of a law of restitution. It is necessary not only to consider the position of the person who parts with money, but any proper consideration of whether the money should be repaid or can be conscientiously withheld should involve an examination of any adverse effect that the payment has had on the payee. A defence of change of position has been recognised in the United States[62] and in Canada.[63] In England, Kerr LJ was supportive of the defence in *Rover International Ltd v Cannon Film Ltd*,[64] and in *Lipkin Gorman v Karpnale*

---

58 [1913] 1 Ch 127.

59 *Ibid*, at 140.

60 (1849) 3 Ex D 527.

61 (1841) 11 LJ Ex 10.

62 *Grand Lodge, AOUW of Minnesota v Towne* (1917) 161 NW 403, at 407.

63 *Rural Municipality of Storthoaks v Mobil Oil Canada Ltd* (1975) 55 DLR (3rd) 1, at 13.

64 [1989] 1 WLR 912, at 925; [1989] 3 All ER 423, at 433.

65 [1991] 2 AC 548, at 558, 568, 578–80.

Ltd,[65] a case involving the innocent receipt of stolen money, Lord Bridge, Lord Ackner and Lord Goff considered that this defence should be available in English law. In *David Securities Pty Ltd v Commonwealth Bank of Australia*,[66] the High Court of Australia also observed that the defence should be available where the payee has acted to his or her detriment on the faith of the receipt. Change of position was said, however, not to occur where the payee had simply spent the money on ordinary living expenses.[67] In *Commissioner of State Revenue (Vic) v Royal Insurance Australia Ltd*,[68] Mason CJ further asserted that change of position was available as a defence to a restitutionary claim based on mistake and, where there was a statutory discretion given to the Commissioner to retain excess payments, retention of any excess should be dependent on the Commissioner being able to show an adverse change of position.[69] However, in order to successfully advance such a defence, there must be shown to exist a causative relationship between the receipt of the money and paying it away. In *State Bank of NSW v Swiss Bank Corporation*,[70] the Court of Appeal held that the State bank could not rely on this defence where it had paid over moneys to a customer on the basis of information that was fraudulently given extraneous to the receipt.

In Western Australia[71] and New Zealand,[72] there has been statutory reform to accommodate a change of position defence in cases involving mistaken payments. The provisions enable a court to consider the justice of the case. The Court of Appeal in New Zealand had to consider the application of the statutory provisions in *Thomas v Houston Corbett & Co.*[73] In that case, a clerk in a law firm fraudulently procured a cheque from a friend and client of the firm and facilitated this by also fraudulently obtaining a more substantial cheque from his employer, which was paid into the client's account to enable him to meet the cheque that was made out to the clerk. The firm sued to recover the whole of the payment made to the client, but the Court of Appeal held that of two innocent parties who were defrauded, the firm should be responsible for a greater share of the loss because they had control over the activities of their employee and the means to ensure that cheques were not fraudulently misappropriated. It is less certain whether an approach that takes into consideration the conduct of the payer rather than the payee alone is

---

66 (1991–92) 175 CLR 353.

67 *Ibid*, at 386.

68 (1994) 182 CLR 51.

69 *Ibid*, at 63–66.

70 (1995) 39 NSWLR 350.

71 Section 125(1) of the Property Law Act 1969 (WA).

72 Section 94B of the Judicature Act 1908.

73 [1969] NZLR 151. Further, see *KJ Davies Ltd v Bank of New South Wales* [1981] 1 NZLR 262.

available under the general law of change of circumstance which has traditionally focused on the position of the payee. In *Goss v Chilcott*,[74] Lord Goff recently declined to apply the statutory defence where a borrower had paid over moneys to a third party aware that if the third party defaulted in repaying the advance he would be called upon to do so.

(b) Mistakenly discharged debts or liabilities

Should the principle that allows a payer to *prima facie* recover moneys paid under mistake be extended to a person who has mistakenly discharged the debt of another? In *Hill v Ziymack*, considered above,[75] for example, it may be argued that, if Mrs Ziymack, as Issacs J[76] appeared to find, genuinely believed that the stock in question belonged to her and that the debts relating to their acquisition were hers, she should have been entitled to restitution from her son's estate to the extent that his debts were validly discharged by mistake. Plainly, payments made under such a misapprehension were not officious and, equally plainly, assuming that the creditor's demands were satisfied, the son's estate received an incontrovertible benefit. An objection to allowing a claim such as Mrs Ziymack's, however, is that her son's debt was not in law discharged in the absence of a request for payment or subsequent ratification by the debtor of the payment, albeit that the creditor would in practice treat the payment as a discharge. Accordingly, it is arguable that no benefit had been conferred in law. That is why Issacs J would appear to have treated Mrs Ziymack's payment as voluntary, albeit that it had been made under an erroneous belief that the stock was hers.[77] However, where the creditor accepts the payment in apparent discharge of the debt, it may be argued that since it would be both unconscionable and unlikely that a creditor would sue the debtor for further payment, in reality the debt has been discharged and the mistaken payer should be entitled to restitution of the payment from the debtor who has been unjustly enriched.[78] If, of course, the debt has not been discharged, a mistaken payer like Mrs Ziymack could conceivably seek restitution from the creditor on the ground that no consideration has been given for her payment, but any claim of this kind could be met by defences of estoppel or change of circumstance which might arise if the

---

74 [1996] 3 NZLR 385.

75 (1908) 7 CLR 352. See discussion, p 25, fn 5.

76 *Ibid*, at 370.

77 *Idem*. Griffiths CJ at 364.

78 Goff and Jones would probably argue in favour of subrogation to the creditor's rights, see discussion to fn 8.

79 See discussion Goff and Jones, *idem*, also in text, Chapter 4, text to fn 52. The case of *B Liggett (Liverpool) Ltd v Barclays Bank* [1928] 1 KB 48 would appear to support such a claim in equity. There, a bank, by mistake, honoured a cheque signed by one of only two directors and the proceeds were paid to creditors of the company. Although at law the bank was treated as a mere volunteer, in equity it was permitted to recoup its payment from the debtor.

creditor had altered his or her position on receipt of the payment.[79] On this topic, it may also be argued that in *Falcke v Scottish Imperial Insurance Company*,[80] if Emmanuel was genuinely under a misapprehension that he had purchased Falcke's interest in the policy, he should have been entitled to sue Falcke for the proceeds of the insurance premium which kept the policy alive, albeit that he was not entitled to a lien over the proceeds. Again, his mistake in paying the premium, thereby keeping the policy alive for Falcke's benefit, negated officiousness and arguably *prima facie* should have entitled him to restitution of the cost of the premium.

(c) Mistaken improvements to chattels

If a person who is in possession of a chattel belonging to another wrongfully sells the chattel, having spent money and time and labour in improving it, the measure of damages that the owner is entitled to for the wrongful conversion or detinue of the chattel will be either the actual loss to the plaintiff of the chattel, or the value of the chattel at the date of judgment less a sum representing the cost of the improvements. In *Munro v Willmott*,[81] Lynksey J rejected an argument that the owner was entitled to ignore the fact that the defendant had spent money on improvements for a car, which had been wrongfully sold at auction, and allowed the defendant the cost of the improvements. In a subsequent case, *Greenwood v Bennett*,[82] the Court of Appeal had to consider the position of an improver, Harper, who had spent a considerable sum in effecting improvements to a car in the mistaken belief that he owned it. The car had been wrecked and stolen by a bailee to whom it was entrusted for repairs. The bailee subsequently sold it to Harper who proceeded to effect improvements and then sold the car to a finance company. The finance company let the car out on hire to a third party from whom it was seized by the police. In interpleader proceedings, the true owners were given specific restitution of the vehicle but no order was made to Harper for compensation for his work. It was held, however, by the Court of Appeal that, as a condition of restitution, Harper should be entitled to his expenditure on the car. Lord Denning MR considered that to deny Harper his expenditure would be to allow the owners to be unjustly enriched.[83] In Australia, *Greenwood v Bennett*[84] has been followed in *McKeown v Cavalier Yachts Pty Ltd*.[85] In that case, the issue was whether a builder, who had effected improvements to the hull of a yacht, was entitled to the cost of those improvements as com-

---

80 (1887) 34 Ch D 234.
81 [1949] 1 KB 295.
82 [1973] QB 195.
83 *Ibid*, at 200.
84 [1973] QB 195.
85 (1983) 13 NSWLR 303.

pensation where the owner sought specific restitution. It was held that, as a condition of specific restitution, the improver was entitled to a sum which represented the incontrovertible benefit or the increased value of the yacht rather than the cost of the work.[86]

Should an improver, who has not acted officiously but in the mistaken belief that he or she owns a chattel, be entitled to the cost of improvements if the chattel is subsequently returned to the true owner or recovered by the true owner without the assistance of a court? Lord Denning MR,[87] in *Greenwood v Bennett*, considered that the mistaken improver should be entitled to restitution for the value of improvements whether the owner reclaims the goods with the assistance of a court or not, but Cairns LJ[88] had some doubt about this. It is submitted that where a person mistakenly improves a chattel in the belief that he or she owns it, the improver should be entitled to restitution for the value of the improvements or an amount which represents the actual market increase in the value of the chattel, whichever is less. The owner should not have to pay for improvements which do not enhance the market value of the chattel, unless the expenditure is inevitable in the sense that he or she has been saved an expense that would necessarily have had to have been incurred.[89] If the cost of improvements that do not qualify as inevitable expenditure exceeds the market increase in the value of the goods, the owner should only have to pay the improver the market increase in the value of the chattel.[90] Professor Jones has suggested, however, that a defence of hardship should be available to an owner if the chattel is unique and the owner has no free funds to pay for the improvements.[91]

(d) Accretion

In some cases, an alternative to compensation for improvements to chattels effected by mistake will involve the removal of chattels that have formed an accretion to another chattel. A simple example relates to improvements mistakenly effected to a motor vehicle, such as the provision of a new engine by a person who believes mistakenly that he or she

---

86 *Ibid*, at 313. The incontrovertible benefit approach was also adopted in *J Gasdsen v Strider Ltd (AES Express)* (1990) 20 NSWLR 57, at 70; *Monks v Poynice Pty Ltd* (1987) 8 NSWLR 662, at 664.

87 [1973] QB 195, at 202.

88 *Idem.*

89 See Birks, P, *An Introduction to the Law of Restitution*, reprint, 1993, pp 117–19, Clarendon Press, Oxford and *Craven Ellis v Canons Ltd* [1936] 2 KB 403. In this case, the Court of Appeal considered that the company would have had to have acquired the services in any event, and Birks asserts that the company could not, as a consequence, subjectively devalue the service and assert that it should not be the subject of payment.

90 See Jones, G, 'Restitutionary Claims for Services Rendered' (1977) LQR 273, at 292–93.

91 *Idem.*

is the true owner. If the accretion can be removed without irreparable damage,[92] or there has not been an inextricable mixture,[93] then the improver can withdraw the chattel from the whole. If this cannot be achieved because the chattel including the accretion has been sold, the improver will be entitled to damages for the parts which have been converted and could have been withdrawn from the product.[94] Where accretion does occur and a chattel is the subject of a claim in detinue or conversion, a court may, in its discretion, consider matters such as added value, and compensation may be ordered.[95]

(e) Mistaken improvements to land

Restitution will be permitted under a proprietary estoppel for mistaken improvements to land if the owner has either encouraged the expenditure or acquiesced in it knowing that the improver mistakenly believed that he or she owned the land or had an interest in it.[96] In these circumstances, the owner is unable to subjectively devalue the value of the improvement and a court has power in equity to satisfy the estoppel in an appropriate way.[97] Equity may also be of assistance in other circumstances where improvements have been made by a person in the belief that he or she is the owner of land, and the agreement, under which he or she has assumed ownership, is rescinded or set aside by a court. Thus, in *Cooper v Phibbs*,[98] a condition of restoring the lease of a fisheries to the true owner was that compensation be paid for improvements effected by a party in possession who mistakenly believed that he was the owner. In the New Zealand case of *O'Connor v Hart*,[99] a contract for the sale of land was set aside by the Court of Appeal because it was considered to constitute an unconscionable bargain. The Court of Appeal, however, as a condition of granting rescission allowed the improver compensation for improvements that had been effected during his possession of the farm. In *Brown v Smitt*,[100] the High Court of Australia considered that where an agreement for sale and purchase was rescinded, compensation should be made by the vendor only for the value of permanent improvements or necessary repairs

---

92 *Lewis v Andrews and Rowley Pty Ltd* (1956) 56 SR (NSW) 439; *Rendell v Associated Finance Pty Ltd* [1957] VR 604; *Thomas v Robinson* [1977] 1 NZLR 385.

93 As in *McKeown v Cavalier Yachts* (1983) 13 NSWLR 303.

94 *Thomas v Robinson* [1977] 1 NZLR 385, at 392.

95 *Idem*.

96 *Dillwyn v Llewelyn* (1862) 4 De GF & J 517; 45 ER 1285; *Ramsden v Dyson* (1866) LR 1 HL 140; *Plimmer v Wellington Corporation* (1884) 9 App Cas 699.

97 See discussion, Chapter 4, pp 80–81.

98 (1867) LR 2 HL 149.

99 [1983] NZLR 280; [1984] 1 NZLR 755. Reversed on other grounds in the Privy Council [1985] 1 AC 100; [1985] 1 NZLR 159.

100 (1924) 34 CLR 160, further see *Evans v Benson & Co* (1961) WAR 12.

effected by the purchaser in possession, and not for mere matters of taste. In these cases, the improvements were not effected officiously but in the genuine belief that the person in possession was the owner of the property. As a condition of rescinding or setting aside the various transactions, equity insisted on compensation being paid to the improver so that the restored owner of the property was not unjustly enriched. In cases of this kind, compensation should be assessed on the actual objectively assessed value of the benefit to the true owner, rather than the cost of any improvement. This will mean that it will be necessary to assess the market value of the increase of the property due to the improvement. If repairs or improvements are inevitable, then the reasonable cost of these should be permitted even though they do not necessarily enhance the market value of the property.

Should there, however, be a general right to restitution for the improvements to land that have been rendered under mistake, where the value of the owner's property has been enhanced? Cases of this kind are unlikely to occur often under Torrens land systems of title where it is easily ascertainable who owns the title to land, but it is not beyond the bounds of possibility that a person may confuse a boundary and effect improvements to a property that belongs to another. There exist statutory provisions allowing claims for betterment in New Zealand,[101] Western Australia[102] and Queensland[103] to remedy this difficulty. Courts are given wide powers to make orders including granting compensation for improvements where they are made as a result of mistakes as to the boundaries or identity of land,[104] as a result of a mistaken belief that the land belongs to the improver, or where the land is the property of a person on whose behalf the improvement is made or intended to be made.[105] Where a mistake of the kind to which the respective Acts apply is established, a court, in addition to granting compensation to the improver, may order that improvements be removed or that possession may be given to the improver on such terms and conditions as the court may specify. In New Zealand and Western Australia, a court also has the power to vest the piece of land wrongly built upon in the improver. Courts in each jurisdiction have the power to make such incidental orders as are necessary to free the land from mortgages and other encumbrances or interests. The issue of whether there should exist a right to restitution under the general law for improvements to land has, however, been doubted. Although admitting that, in the case of

---

101 Section 129A of the Property Law Act 1952 (NZ) as inserted by s 3 of the Property Law Amendment Act 1963.

102 Section 123 of the Property Law Act 1969.

103 Sections 195–98 of the Property Law Act 1974.

104 New Zealand, Western Australia.

105 Queensland.

improvements to chattels, there should ordinarily exist a right to recover compensation if an incontrovertible benefit can be shown to exist (even if this means the chattel has to be realised and sold), Goff and Jones consider that such a right of recovery cannot so confidently be asserted in relation to mistaken improvements to land.[106] Birks argues that there cannot be any free acceptance, and nor would it seem is there any incontrovertible benefit where the owner does not desire the improvements. Subjective devaluation in this sense, Birks would contend, eliminates the obligation to pay for the improvements.[107] It is submitted, however, that, in principle, there should be a right to restitution where the improver can establish that an actual benefit has been received by the owner, in the sense that the market value of the property has been improved or inevitable expenditure has been saved. Thus, if an improver builds a dam mistakenly on land belonging to another and this enhances the market value of the property because it has better irrigation, it is arguable that the improver should be reimbursed at least to the extent of the increase in the market value. Should the owner be able to show that the expenditure does not enhance the market value or does not represent an inevitable saving but is one that is merely suited to the individual needs of the improver, then the claim should fail.

In this regard, concern has been expressed by Birks[108] and Goff and Jones that it may be inequitable for an owner to have to pay a substantial sum for improvements that he or she did not request.[109] It could be considered undue hardship for the owner to charge or sell the property depending on the value of the improvements and his or her capacity to pay. However, given that the law has recognised a *prima facie* right to restitution of mistaken money payments, it is inconsistent for the law not to allow restitution where a mistakenly conferred improvement constitutes an inevitable saving, or enhances the market value of the owner's land. If the improvement is of this kind, then the owner will not be out of pocket or prejudiced by having to pay for the benefit. The creation of a mortgage either to enable the owner to pay for the improvements directly or a charge in favour of the improver (should the later agree to a postponed realisation of his or her expenditure) may be inconvenient for the owner, but it is submitted that this is a better and more equitable solution than allowing the owner to retain the benefit without any compensation being paid to the improver at all. Even in the worst case, where the owner is forced to sell the property, he or she will have the benefit of the higher market price and should not be out of

---

106 Lord Goff and Jones, G, *The Law of Restitution*, 4th edn, 1993, pp 166–67, Sweet & Maxwell, and further, 3rd edn, 1986, p 138.

107 Birks, P, *An Introduction to the Law of Restitution*, 1993, pp 109–10, Clarendon Press, Oxford.

108 *Idem.*

109 Goff and Jones, *op cit*, 3rd edn, p 138.

pocket. Indeed, Professor Sutton, in his discussion of this issue, appears to advocate the cause of the mistaken improver, though he admits to some difficulty in formulating a basis under the existing general law for this to occur.[110] Sutton, in this regard, cautioned against accepting too readily the assertion that relief for the mistaken improver ought generally to be denied in order to preserve the owner's special and unique relationship with the improved land.[111] In any event, even if a conservative approach in relation to mistaken improvements to land is adopted, this should still, *prima facie*, allow a claim in restitution upon a *quantum meruit* unless the owner can establish special circumstances which would render it an undue hardship to pay the full value of the improvements or increase in market price. Such an approach, it is submitted, more closely approximates the modern approach to the recovery of mistaken payments of money and is preferable to one which inexorably denies restitution.

Necessity

There is no universal or overriding principle that allows restitution of an unsolicited benefit whenever necessity can be established, but restitution has been permitted in a variety of circumstances where necessity has been shown to be the motive for conferring a benefit. Out of these cases, it is possible to argue that the courts should recognise a general principle of restitution based on necessitous circumstances.[112]

(a) Agency of necessity

Agency of necessity arises when a person, in a pre-existing legal relationship with another, sells goods or incurs expense in preserving goods that are in his or her custody or control, in circumstances where he or she is unable to communicate with the owner and action is necessary to protect the goods.[113] Although there will exist an antecedent relationship between the parties, agency of necessity arises from circumstances of need and not from any real or presumed agreement between the parties, and the claim is in restitution rather than contract.[114] Agency of

---

110 Sutton, RJ, 'What Should be Done for Mistaken Improvers?', in Finn, PD (ed), *Essays on Restitution*, 1990, p 241, Law Book Co Ltd, Sydney. A view also taken by Stoljar, SJ, *The Law of Quasi-Contract*, 2nd edn, 1989, p 58, The Law Book Company.

111 *Ibid*, p 295.

112 See Muir, G, 'Unjust Enrichment and the Officious Intervenor', in Finn, PD (ed), *Essays on Restitution, op cit*, pp 297; 309–29.

113 *China Pacific SA v Food Corp of India* [1982] AC 939, at 961; [1981] 3 All ER 698, at 695 *per* Lord Diplock.

114 *Burns Philp & Co Ltd v Gillespie Bros Pty Ltd* (1947) 74 CLR 148, at 175 *per* Latham CJ.

necessity was historically associated with acceptors for honour of bills of exchange, and carriers of goods by sea and land,[115] but, although there has been some uncertainty judicially expressed about its scope, in *Prager v Blatspiel Stamp and Heacock Ltd*[116] it was considered that the principle would apply where a vendor of goods was unable to deliver the goods because of war and they were sold *bona fide* out of commercial necessity. In *Sachs v Miklos*,[117] the Court of Appeal observed further that the principle applied to a gratuitous bailee who has to sell goods out of necessity or in an emergency. However, on the facts of that case, the bailees failed to make out a case of necessity. The furniture had been sold after no contact was made with the owners, in order for them to make better use of their premises for profit. Lord Goddard CJ in rejecting the defence of necessity to a claim in conversion observed:[118]

> In this particular case, whatever else there may have been, there was certainly no emergency. It was not a case where the house had been destroyed and the furniture left exposed to thieves and the weather. There was nothing perishable here in the sense in which that term is used when applied to goods.

In an earlier case, *Great Northern Railway Company v Swaffield*,[119] a carrier was entitled to claim restitution of livery charges he had paid for a horse on behalf of an owner who had unreasonably declined to accept delivery. It was held by the Court of Exchequer that the carrier was entitled to recoup the charges because they had been properly incurred and were necessary in order to protect the animal and ensure that it did not become a danger to others. The court reasoned that the situation was analogous to a shipowner who is entitled to reimbursement from the owner for expenses incurred in order to protect cargo from damage.[120] A more recent example of a bailee succeeding in gaining reimbursement for an action taken to preserve property is seen in *China Pacific SA v Food Corpn of India*.[121] In that case, the House of Lords allowed a salvor, who had completed the salvage of cargo, to claim storage charges after the cargo owners had failed to give instructions to the salvors as to what should be done with the goods. It was held that the salvors were entitled to be reimbursed for expenses reasonably incurred in preserving the cargo against loss.

---

115 *Prager v Blatspiel Stamp and Heacock Ltd* [1924] 1 KB 566, at 570.

116 *Idem*.

117 [1948] 2 KB 23; [1948] 1 All ER 67.

118 *Ibid*, at 36; 68.

119 (1874) LR 9 Ex D 132; [1874–80] All ER 1065.

120 *Ibid*, at, 138; 1068 *per* Pollock CB. See further in relation to shippers of cargo and reimbursement for action taken to preserve cargo in necessitous circumstances. *Cargo ex 'Argos'* (1873) LR 5 PC 134 .

121 [1982] AC 939, at 961; [1981] 3 All ER 689.

As a general rule, the person claiming reimbursement as an agent of necessity should attempt to secure instructions concerning the property before incurring expense or disposing of the property.[122] Where this would be impractical, it may be acceptable to dispense with this obligation.[123] If the service is not performed in order to preserve property, agency of necessity cannot be claimed simply because incidentally a benefit is conferred on another. Thus, in *Burns Philp & Co Ltd v Gillespie Brothers Pty Ltd*,[124] the High Court of Australia held that a shipowner was not entitled to claim freight charges associated with a return trip to Australia after the ship had been forced to return without discharging its cargo at the port of destination, because of war. The shipowner was not entitled to claim return freight as an agent of necessity because the voyage back to Australia where the cargo had been loaded was not taken for the purpose of saving the cargo exclusively, but was for the security of both the ship and its cargo.

In cases of bailment, courts have appeared cautious about whether a bailee, who has been put to expense in preserving property, should be additionally able to claim a lien for services rendered out of necessity. In *Great Northern Railway Company v Swaffield*,[125] there was a division of opinion as to whether the carrier should be entitled to a lien for warehousing expenses.[126] The issue did not have to be resolved in that case, however, because the horse was eventually delivered to the owners and the carrier sued successfully to recover the livery costs that were incurred. In *China Pacific SA v Food Corpn of India*,[127] Lord Diplock observed that a salvor which had cargo in its possession should be entitled to a lien for additional costs incurred in warehousing goods to prevent their further deterioration, at least until the time when the owner demanded delivery. Reimbursement for action taken, however, by a lienor to preserve the value of a lien after the owner had made demand could not be claimed.[128]

(b) Salvage

Salvage is a doctrine that can apply in equity in circumstances where there has been expenditure incurred by a person in preserving the property of another. It has arisen, for example, where a court has been asked to

---

122 *China Pacific SA v Food Corp of India, ibid*, at 695.

123 *Burns Philp & Co Ltd v Gillespie Bros Pty Ltd* (1947) 74 CLR 148, at 172 *per* Latham CJ.

124 *Ibid*.

125 (1874) LR 9 Ex D 132; [1874–80] All ER 1065.

126 *Ibid*, at 137; 1067, Pollock B doubted whether a lien arose for warehousing whereas Amphlett B, at 139; 1068 suggested that it should.

127 [1982] AC 939, at 962; [1981] 3 All ER 689, at 696.

128 *Somes v British Empire Shipping Co* (1860) 8 HL Cas 338; [1843–60] All ER 844 referred to with apparent approval by Lord Diplock in *China Pacific SA v Food Corporation of India, ibid*, at 962; 696.

sanction a mortgage to raise sufficient finance to enable a vineyard held in trust for infant beneficiaries to be preserved against further deterioration.[129] However, the most important application of salvage is in relation to maritime law and the protection of shipping from the hazards or perils on the high seas, or in areas recognised as appropriate for salvage according to statutory limits.[130] A salvor is, in general, entitled to a reward for services performed in saving a ship and its cargo from destruction. The reward may be fixed by agreement or, in the absence of agreement, by a court. An agreement may be set aside in equity if its terms are unconscionable, oppressive or fraudulent. Salvage will not be payable unless the service was necessary to protect the ship or cargo or both from danger or exposure to destruction, even if the danger cannot be described as imminent.[131] Further, it must be of a kind that a reasonably prudent owner would have accepted.[132] Nor will salvage be payable if the salvor is under a legal obligation to render salvage whether arising from agreement, or in some other way that constitutes a binding obligation to render services to a ship in distress unless unusual services are performed or unusual danger is encountered.[133] If the salvage is voluntary and not subject to any legal obligation, the salvor is entitled to a reward which is greater than the cost actually incurred in the salvage operation, as an incentive or encouragement for persons to undertake salvage missions in order to better ensure the protection of shipping from the perils of the sea.[134] A salvor, in the absence of agreement with the owner, will not, however, be entitled to a reward unless the salvage operation has met with some success.[135] Once a service has been performed, a salvor will have a lien over the ship and its cargo to secure the payment of the reward, if in possession of the ship and its contents.[136] When not in possession, the lien remains inchoate and crystallises when the ship is arrested and bought before a court exercising

---

129 In *Re Montagu* [1897] 2 Ch 8; *Cousins v Cousins* (1906) 3 CLR 1198.

130 In England, the issue of whether salvage could apply in certain areas was considered in *The Goring* [1988] AC 831; [1988] 1 All ER 641, non-tidal inland waters did not fall within the provisions of the Merchant Shipping Act 1982; and further, *The Powstaniec Wielkopolski* [1989] 1 All ER 199 as to what constitutes a tidal water. Further, see Commonwealth and state and Territory legislation on Salvage, Navigation Act, Cth, Commercial Vessels Act, 1979, NSW, Marine Acts, 1958 Qld, 1936 S Aust, 1976 Tas, 1988 Victoria, 1982 W Aust, 1981 NT, and in New Zealand, Maritime Transport Act 1994.

131 *The Charlotte* (1839) 3 Wm Rob 68; 166 ER 888; *The Troilus* [1950] P 93; *Southern Cross Fisheries Ltd v New Zealand Fisheries Ltd* [1970] NZLR 873; *Fisher v The Ocean Grandeur* (1972) 127 CLR 312; *The Texaco Southampton v Burley* [1982] 2 NSWLR 336; *The Ship MV Santo Roco* (1991) 101 ALR 491.

132 *The Emilie Galline* [1903] P 106.

133 *Ackerblom v Price* (1881) 7 QBD 129, at 135; *Fisher v The Ocean Grandeur* (1972) 127 CLR 312. Cf *The Ship MV Santo Roco* (1991) 101 ALR 491. Note, that, although in that case the owner was under an obligation to render service under the terms of the ships' insurance policy and could not be regarded as a salvor, this did not extend to the master or crew who were entitled to claim a reward for towage.

134 *The Queen Elizabeth* [1949] 82 Lloyd's Rep 803; *The Sandejford* [1953] 2 Lloyd's Rep 557; *The Tantalus* [1957] P 47, at 49 *per* Willmer LJ; *The Majorie Maude* [1959] NZLR 969.

135 *The City of Chester* (1884) 9 D 182, at 202.

136 *The Zephyrus* (1842) 1 W Rob 329; (1842) ER 596.

admiralty jurisdiction.[137] The lien attaches to the ship, freight and cargo severally but not jointly, and each person interested in the property salvaged is liable to contribute to the salvage in proportion to its value.[138]

English courts have not recognised a lien for the preservation of property in inland waters. In *Nicholson v Chapman*,[139] Eyre LCJ was not prepared to grant a lien over logs that had been found drifting in a river and made secure in defence of a claim for delivery up of the goods by the true owner. Public policy did not require the recognition of a lien in cases of this kind since the imposition of a lien could easily lead to abuse if the owner were to be held to ransom over the return of the property. However, the court considered that a person who had performed a meritorious service in preserving the logs should be entitled to reasonable compensation for expense and exertion.

In *Falcke v Scottish Imperial Insurance Company*,[140] it was argued by analogy with salvage, that Emmanuel was entitled to a lien over the policy for paying the premiums because, by doing so, he had preserved the insurance policy for Falcke's benefit. Bowen LJ, however, declined to apply principles applicable to maritime law, to cases that did not involve ships at peril on the high seas.[141] In any event, it is plain that Falcke paid the premiums not altruistically but to preserve his own interest in the policy. Any benefit that the mortgagee enjoyed as a result of Emmanuel's payment of the premium was incidental to Emmanuel's motive for the payment.

(c) Liens and life insurance premiums

A number of rather difficult cases involving claims for liens, of which *Falcke*[142] was one, have arisen in relation to the payment of premiums to preserve life insurance policies. In *Falcke*, it was argued that Emmanuel should have a lien for the payment of the premium because he had preserved the policy. However, it was held that he was under no obligation to preserve the policy and did so merely to advance his own interests. In the absence of any request by the mortgagee to pay or other unconscionable conduct by the mortgagee, of which there was no evidence, Emmanuel

---

137 See *China Pacific SA v Food Corporation of India* [1982] AC 939; [1981] 3 All ER 688, at 695 *per* Lord Diplock. Further, see s 4(3)(g) of the Admiralty Act 1988 (Cth); ss 113–24 of the NZ Marine Transport Act 1994.

138 Lord Goff and Jones, G, *The Law Of Restitution*, 4th edn, pp 398–99, Sweet & Maxwell.

139 (1793) 2 H Bl 254; 126 ER 536. In *Aitchison v Lohre* (1879) 4 App Cas 760, Lord Blackburn seems rather to have overstated the case when he asserted that the effect of this decision was that no claim for remuneration from the owner was given at common law to those who preserve goods on shore, unless they interfered at the request of the owner. Eyre LCJ left this point open.

140 (1887) 34 Ch D 234.

141 *Ibid*, at 248–49. Fry J in *Re Leslie* (1883) 23 Ch D 552; [1881–85] All ER 274 also declined to accept this analogy with regard to insurance premiums.

142 (1887) 34 Ch D 234.

was not entitled to a lien. In an earlier case of *Re Leslie*,[143] Fry J defined the circumstances in which a person would be entitled to a lien for preserving an insurance policy by paying a premium. Fry J, who was also a member of the Court of Appeal in *Falcke*, identified four situations where a lien would be recognised. First, where the beneficial owner had requested payment. The second arose where a trustee had paid to preserve the policy. In those circumstances, the trustee was entitled to an indemnity out of the proceeds of the policy.[144] The third arose where a third party at the request of a trustee had advanced moneys for the preservation of the policy. In that case, the third party would be entitled to be subrogated to the rights of the trustee.[145] The fourth related to mortgagees or other parties who were entitled to add the cost of expenditure required to preserve the policy to the value of their security. This is an illustration of a wider equitable rule allowing encumbrancers to add to their security for payments made to preserve it.[146] A fifth situation was considered in *Re Forster*.[147] It was held that a person was entitled to claim a lien where insurance premiums were paid in the belief shared by all other interested parties that the policy belonged to the payer when in fact it did not. In *Re Leslie*,[148] Fry J rejected an argument that part ownership could be sufficient to justify a lien being imposed for the payment of an insurance premium.[149] A mortgagor, who in equity was a part owner of a policy with the mortgagee, could not claim a lien in priority to the mortgagee; a principle which the Court of Appeal later endorsed in *Falcke*.[150]

(d) Reimbursement for services rendered out of common humanity or in the public interest

In *Great Northern Railway Company v Swaffield*,[151] Piggott B held that a carrier, who had possession of a horse as a bailee, was bound from ordinary feelings of humanity to keep the horse safely and feed it.[152] A husband has been held liable to repay the expenses of a decent funeral that had been incurred by a third person.[153] The law has imposed an obligation to

---

143 (1883) 23 Ch D 552; [1881–85] All ER 274.

144 *Re Smith* [1937] 3 All ER 472.

145 Subrogation is considered further, see Chapter 3, p 58.

146 *Re Leslie* [1883] 23 Ch D 552, at 560; [1881–85] All ER 274, at 276.

147 [1938] 3 All ER 610; and see further on this point, *Falcke v Scottish Imperial Insurance* (1887) 34 Ch D 234, at 242 *per* Cotton LJ, at 251 *per* Bowen LJ, at 253 *per* Fry LJ.

148 (1883) 23 Ch D 552; [1881–85] All ER 274.

149 *Ibid*, at 563; 278–79.

150 (1887) 34 Ch D 234, at 243 *per* Cotton LJ, at 251 *per* Bowen LJ.

151 (1874) LR 9 Exch 132; [1874–80] All ER 1065.

152 *Ibid*, at 137; 1067.

153 *Jenkins v Tucker* (1788) 1 H Bl 90; 126 ER 55; *Ambrose v Kerrison* (1851) 10 CB 776; 138 ER 307.

repay expenses incurred in providing the necessities of life for a child or a mentally disabled person. However, in *Re Rhodes*,[154] the Court of Appeal held that there was no obligation for the estate of a mentally handicapped woman to repay nursing home fees that had in her lifetime been paid by relatives gratuitously, and with no intention that the expenditure should constitute a debt.

Does a person who incurs expense preserving the life or health of another have a claim to restitution? Where there is evidence that the services were not intended as a charity and a court finds that they were reasonably necessary to preserve the health of the person receiving the assistance; a person, who either provides the service or pays for it, should be entitled to restitution from the person for whom the service or expenditure has been incurred. Whether the evidence suggests charity will depend on the kind of service and the amount of expense incurred. In *Matheson v Smiley*,[155] it was held that a surgeon, who had been summoned by a doctor to perform an operation on a person whom friends found severely injured, was able to claim reasonable professional expenses from the estate of the patient who died shortly after. Plainly, in these circumstances, the operation could not be considered a gratuitous service and, although unsuccessful, it was necessary in order to attempt to preserve life. Similarly, in *Greenspan v Slate*,[156] a physician was able to claim the reasonable cost of professional services incurred when a child was referred to him for treatment to avoid permanent injury after the parents had declined to assist. It was held that the parents of the child were, in equity, under a legal obligation to supply a child with the necessities of life and were liable for the cost of the surgeons' services although they had not requested his intervention and indeed had rejected it.

(e) Necessitous intervention and the discharge of another's debt or liability

In *Owen v Tate*,[157] Lord Scarman considered that a person who had assumed a liability and discharged the debt of another might be permitted reimbursement if the payment was made through necessity. In that case, however, the payment was made after the officious assumption of liability by the plaintiff, in order to guarantee a debt so as to accommodate an employee who desired the bank to release her security for the overdraft of the debtors. Where a person incurs liability and discharges a debt out of a necessity so as to preserve property for the owner, as in

---

154 (1890) 44 Ch D 94.
155 [1932] 2 DLR 787.
156 (1953) 97 Atlanta Rep (2nd) 390.
157 [1976] 1 QB 403; [1975] 2 All ER 129.

Great Northern Railway v Swaffield[158] and *China Pacific SA v Food Corpn of India*,[159] a court has ordered restitution of the fees paid on the owner's behalf. Similarly, in cases like *Matheson v Smiley*[160] or *Greenspan v Slate*,[161] if the third party, who requested the intervention of the surgeon, was to have paid the surgeon for his services, he or she should be entitled to reimbursement.

(f) Restitution for necessitous intervention

The above cases would suggest that a general claim for restitution for unsolicited benefits conferred in necessitous circumstances should be recognised where the plaintiff is able to show that the service was not performed officiously and was necessary in order to preserve property, the health of another or provide the necessities of life. It was recognised, in *Re Rhodes*,[162] that claims of this kind are not based on implied contact or agreement, but arise in law because the benefit conferred is meritorious. Courts, however, appear reluctant to recognise liens other than in situations where maritime salvage, warehousing of goods is involved or where payments have been made in the limited circumstances referred to in *Re Leslie*[163] in regard to insurance premiums. The difficulty with increasing the ambit of the possessory lien in cases of necessitous intervention is that the owner of property may be held to ransom by an unscrupulous intervener. Thus, in *Nicholson v Chapman*,[164] Eyre LCJ declined to allow a salvor, who had taken possession of logs floating down a river, a lien, which would have allowed him to resist an action for delivery up of the logs and left him instead to pursue a possible claim for compensation for his services.

Compulsion

Restitution may be available to a person who has paid money to another or rendered a service under compulsion in order to prevent unjust enrichment. Compulsion may operate in a variety of circumstances. Thus, a person may make payments or render services to another under duress emanating from the recipient of the benefit. This important subject is considered in Chapter 10.[165] In this chapter, compulsion is concerned solely

---

158 (1874) LR 9 Exch 132; [1874–80] All ER 1065.

159 [1982] AC 939; [1981] 3 All ER 689.

160 [1932] 2 DLR 787.

161 Restatement of Restitution, para 113(2d); 97A 2d 390 (1953) described, perhaps uncharitably, as a doubtful case, see Goff and Jones, *op cit*, 4th edn, p 382.

162 (1890) 44 Ch D 94.

163 (1883) 23 Ch D 552; [1881–85] All ER 274.

164 (1793) 2 H Bl 254; [1793] 126 ER 536.

165 See pp 223–36.

with the more limited issue of restitution of an unsolicited benefit, where a person has discharged the debt or liability of another because of a legal obligation to do so. The fact that a debt or liability has been discharged in this way, negatives officiousness and renders the person primarily liable subject to a claim in restitution. Legal obligations giving rise to compulsion in this sense do not, however, include obligations that have been undertaken by agreement as, for example, occurs when a person agrees to stand surety for another's debt. Restitution where a relationship of this kind exists is considered in the next chapter.[166]

The compulsory discharge of another's debt or liability

If a person is compelled by law to discharge the debts or liability of another, he or she will be able to claim restitution from the person who is primarily liable for the debt. In *Exall v Partridge*,[167] the plaintiff had left his carriage on the defendant's premises for repair. In order to obtain its release after the landlord had distrained for the failure of the defendant to pay rent, he was able to successfully sue the defendant for restitution in an action for moneys had and received. In *Johnson v Royal Steam Packet Co*,[168] the plaintiffs were mortgagees of a ship over which the crew had a maritime lien for unpaid wages. In order to clear their security, the mortgagees paid the crew and successfully claimed reimbursement from the defendant owner whose primary responsibility it was to pay. Similarly, in *Brookes Wharf and Bull Wharf Limited v Goodman Bros*,[169] the plaintiffs, who were bonded warehousemen, were obliged, under legislation relating to importing, to pay import duties on goods even though the primary liability for the payment of the duty fell on the importers. Having paid the duty on the goods which had been stolen, the plaintiff was successfully able to sue the importer in restitution for the duty. Where the payment, however, is not made under some form of legal compulsion, the payment will be regarded as officious and is irrecoverable. Thus, in *Macclesfield Corporation v Great Central Railway*,[170] the defendants were under a statutory liability to maintain a bridge in good repair. They declined to comply with a notice served upon them by the corporation, which subsequently proceeded to complete the work and sought restitution from the defendants for the price of the work. It was held that the defendants were not liable to pay because, although they

---

166 See pp 53–56.

167 (1799) 8 TR 308; ER 1405.

168 (1867) LR 3 CP 38.

169 [1937] 1 KB 534. See further, *Moule v Garrett* (1872) LR 7 Ex 101 where an assignor of a lease, who was obliged to pay damages for breach of a covenant to repair, was able to successfully claim restitution against a subsequent assignee.

170 [1911] 2 KB 528.

were saved what could be described as an inevitable expense, the plaintiff was officious and a volunteer.[171] In Australia, it was held in *Re Gasbourne Pty Ltd*,[172] that compulsion does not mean practical, as distinct from legal compulsion. As a result, shareholders, who had discharged a taxation liability of the company with a view to obtaining a tax advantage, were unable to seek restitution from the company of payments made on its behalf.

---

171 *Ibid*, at 541.
172 [1984] VR 801.

CHAPTER 3

Discharge of the Debts or Liabilities of Another

In the previous chapter, we have seen that restitution may be ordered where a person is compelled, by statute or other legal process, to discharge the debt or liability of another. In this chapter, the important remedies of subrogation and a related topic, 'contribution', will be considered as they apply to prevent unjust enrichment in other situations where debts or liabilities have been discharged and the payer seeks recoupment from the person primarily liable.

Subrogation

In *Orakpo v Manson Investments Ltd*,[1] Lord Diplock described subrogation as a remedy that embraced more than one concept in English law. In the opinion of Lord Diplock, subrogation was a convenient way of describing a transfer of rights from one person to another without assignment or assent from the person from whom the rights are transferred, which takes place by operation of law in a whole variety of widely different circumstances.[2] Some rights of subrogation are contractual in origin as with contracts of insurance. However, others do not depend upon contract. Thus, in *Craythorne v Swinburne*,[3] the concept of suretyship was said to stand not upon contract but upon natural justice. Lord Diplock observed that some rights of subrogation appear to defeat classification except as an empirical remedy to prevent a particular kind of unjust enrichment. His Lordship warned, however, against relying upon analogy to justify applying to one set of circumstances a remedy of subrogation that might be appropriate in another so as to prevent unjust enrichment.

(a) Suretyship and subrogation

A surety who discharges the debt of a creditor on behalf of a debtor, for whom he or she has agreed to stand guarantor, has a right to be indemnified by the debtor.[4] Having acceded to the request of the debtor, the surety will be legally liable to discharge the debt should the debtor default and, in so doing, the surety cannot be regarded as

---

1   [1978] AC 95; [1977] 3 WLR 229. See further, *Boscawen v Bajwa* [1996] 1WLR 329.
2   *Ibid*, at 104; 234.
3   (1807) 14 Ves 160; [1807] 34 ER 1133.
4   *Exall v Partridge* (1799) 8 TR 308; [1799] 101 ER 1405; *Israel v Foreshore Properties Ltd* (1980) 30 ALR 631; *Meates v Westpac Banking Corporation Ltd* [1991] 3 NZLR 385.

officious.[5] It may be a matter of complete indifference to the debtor if the surety discharges the debt or not at the stage of default. However, having requested a person to stand guarantor, the debtor is not able, subsequently, to contend that the discharge of the debt was officious. Although the origins of subrogation in relation to suretyship are obscure, equity allowed a surety to recoup a payment made to discharge a debt from the debtor. A surety also has the right to stand in the place of the creditor, to enforce all the securities held by the creditor and to have them transferred to him, even though he may not know of their existence or have stipulated for this in the contract of guarantee once the debt has been paid in full.[6] Equity considered that it was unconscionable for a debtor to regain the securities from a creditor on the discharge of the debt by a surety. A surety, who pays off a mortgage given by the principal debtor, is accordingly presumed to keep the mortgage alive for his or her own benefit.[7] The terms of a guarantee may, however, expressly regulate or deprive the surety of the benefit of any security, or may expressly or impliedly give the creditor the right to release securities without prejudicing the creditor's rights against the surety.[8]

If the surety's obligations under the contract of guarantee are ambiguous, the contract will be construed *contra proferentem* against the creditor.[9] Should the terms of the obligation of the debtor be materially altered to the detriment of the surety, the surety will be discharged unless there is a provision authorising the change in the contract of suretyship, or the surety approves it. In *Burnes v Trade Credits Ltd*,[10] the Privy Council held that a variation in providing for a higher interest rate was material and, as a consequence, a surety was discharged from liability under a guarantee.[11]

---

5   *Cf Owen v Tate* [1976] 1 QB 403; [1975] 2 All ER 129. Considered in Chapter 2, pp 25–26.

6   See *Craythorne v Swinburne* (1807) 14 Ves 160; [1807] 34 ER 1133; *Wuff v Jay* (1872) LR 7 QB 756, at 764. *Spicer and Son Proprietary Ltd v Spicer & Howe* [1932] 47 CLR 151; *Australasian Conference Association Ltd v Mainline Constructions Pty Ltd* (1978) 22 ALR 1; *National Bank of NZ v Chapman* [1975] 1 NZLR 481. This principle is embodied in s 58A of the Usury Bills of Lading and Written Memoranda Act 1902–34 (NSW); s 72 of the Supreme Court Act 1958 (Vict); s 4 of the Mercantile Acts 1867 (Qld);s 17 1935 (S Aust), s 13 1935 (Tas); Act 31 Vict No 8 (WA).

7   *Re Davison' Estate* (1893) 31 LR Ir 249; affirmed [1894] 1 IR 56.

8   *National Bank of NZ v Chapman* [1975] 1 NZLR 481.

9   *Eastern Counties Building Society v Russell* [1947] 1 All ER 500.

10 [1981] 1 WLR 805; [1981] 2 All ER 124. *Cf Moschi v Lep Services* [1972] 2 All ER 393 where the House of Lords held that an election to accept repudiation of a contract by a debtor to pay a certain sum by instalments did not constitute a variation because the creditor's debt was transformed into a claim for damages.

11 See further, *Ankar Proprietary Ltd v National Westminster Finance Ltd* (1987) 162 CLR 549 where a breach by the creditor of various clauses in a contract of guarantee justified the discharge of the surety. Further, *Dan v Barclays Australia Ltd* (1983) 46 ALR 437; but *cf Williams v Frayne* (1937) 58 CLR 710 where a failure to obtain a landlord's consent to an assignment of lease, said to constitute security, was not a departure from the contract between the parties that was material for the discharge of the surety. Also, *Dunlop New Zealand Ltd v Dumbleton* [1968] NZLR 1092; *Nelson Fisheries Ltd v Boese* [1975] 2 NZLR 233; *Farrow Mortgage Services Ltd v Slade* (1996) 38 NSWLR 636.

Should a creditor act in such a way that the value of a security is diminished or lost, the surety will be discharged at least *pro tanto* to the extent of the loss.[12] In *Watts v Shuttleworth*,[13] a creditor, having covenanted with the surety to insure mortgaged goods, failed to insure them against loss. As a result, he was unable to convey the security to the surety with the consequence that the surety was discharged to the extent of the loss. The Privy Council, however, held in *China and South Sea Bank Ltd v Tan*[14] that there was no obligation on a creditor to elect to realise a security in order to satisfy a debt on the default of the debtor rather than proceed directly against the surety for satisfaction. Although at the time of default the security, if realised, would have been sufficient to discharge the debt, the creditor elected to proceed against the surety. The security in the meantime became worthless and, as a result, the surety argued that he had been prejudiced by the creditor's failure to realise the security and extinguish the debt in that way. The Privy Council held that the creditor was free to elect which option to pursue and the surety could not claim prejudice merely because in the intervening period the security had become worthless.

Should a creditor give further time to a creditor to pay a debt without the surety's assent, the surety will be discharged.[15] The validity of this principle would seem open to doubt because it may not be prejudicial and, indeed, may be advantageous for the surety that the debtor is given further time to pay. However, the rationale would seem to be that further time may mean that the debtor's position worsens and should he or she become insolvent, the surety will be deprived of an indemnity.[16] A compromise, however, with a debtor in which the creditor accepts a lesser sum by way of discharge of the debt will generally operate to discharge the surety, unless the surety is a party to the composition or there is an express reservation at the time of the making of the composition of the creditor's rights against the surety.[17] A surety may expressly covenant to

---

12 *Pearl v Deacon* (1857) 24 Beav 186; 44 ER 802; *cf Taylor v Bank of New South Wales* (1886) 11 App Cas 596.

13 (1860) 5 H & N 235; 157 ER 1171. Further, see *Wuff v Jay* (1872) LR 7 QB 756 where a failure to register a mortgage prejudiced the surety and he was discharged. Note that in *O'Day v Commercial Bank of Australia* (1933) 50 CLR 201, the High Court of Australia held that a debenture and floating charge over a company did not give the creditor a security interest of the kind that would justify a surety's discharge, on the ground that, having improperly dealt with a security and being unable to restore it to the debtor, the surety was entitled to be discharged. In any event, the guarantee expressly provided that the surety did not have any interest in any security given by the debtor.

14 [1990] 1 AC 536; [1989] 3 All ER 839. Further, see *Buckeridge v Mercantile Credits Ltd* (1981) 147 CLR 654, at 670; *Omlaw Pty Ltd v Delahunty* [1995] 2 Qd R 389.

15 *Deane v The City Bank of Sydney* (1905) 2 CLR 198.

16 The rule was the subject of some criticism by Blackburn J in *Pollak v Everett* (1876) 1 QB 669, at 673; *Swire v Redman* (1876) 1 QBD 536, at 542 and by Goff and Jones, *op cit*, 4th edn, p 314.

17 *Bank of Adelaide v Lorden* (1972) 127 CLR 185, at 191.

remain liable although the debt is compromised. Where the debt is extinguished, the surety will be discharged. Thus, in *McDonald v Denny Lascelles Ltd*,[18] a contract for the sale and purchase of land was rescinded by the vendor with the result that certain instalments were treated as prepayments, and the purchaser in equity was entitled to their return. As a result, the obligation of the surety to guarantee the payment of the instalments was also terminated. Once a debt has accrued, a surety has the right to call upon the debtor to pay the debt, and can seek an order from a court that he be discharged on the debtor paying the amount due. The surety is not under an obligation to live under the threat or cloud of proceedings indefinitely.[19]

(b) Indorsers of bills of exchange and subrogation

A drawer or indorser of a bill of exchange who is secondarily liable, may be called upon to pay by the holder of the bill, whereupon an entitlement to subrogation arises against the acceptor of the bill. Upon paying the bill to the holder in full, the payer is entitled to require the holder to deliver up the bill and once he or she has gained possession of it, the acceptor can be sued in restitution. An indorser of a bill has been said to be analogous to a surety, so that where a holder proceeded against the indorser first, the indorser was entitled to be recouped from a security deposited by one of the acceptors with the holder to cover the bill.[20]

(c) An insurer's right to subrogation

An insurer will, usually, after paying an indemnity to an insured have the right to be subrogated to the insured's rights against third parties arising out of the indemnified event. An insurer has the right to be subrogated in full to the extent of the indemnity for loss that has been provided.[21] Although the insurers right of subrogation may be contractual, it has also been held to constitute an equity.[22] The rule does not apply to contracts of insurance that are not indemnity contracts and hence, life insurance policies are not within the principle. Once the insured has been indemnified, the insurer is entitled to whatever advantages the insured may have in relation to the means of lessening its loss.[23] These

---

18 (1933) 48 CLR 457. This case was distinguished in *Hyundai Heavy Industries Co Ltd v Papadopoulos* [1980] 2 All ER 29, where the guarantor remained liable to pay accrued debts, and the mere fact that the creditor and ship builder had rescinded the contract did not discharge the surety.

19 *Thomas v Notts Incorporated Football Club* [1972] 1 All ER 1176.

20 *Duncan Fox & Co v North & South Wales Bank* (1880) 6 App Cas 1.

21 See Goff and Jones, *op cit*, 4th edn, p 547; *Parr's Bank Ltd v Albert Mines Syndicate Ltd* (1900) 5 Com Cas 116.

22 *Morris v Ford Motor Co* [1973] QB 792 at 800 *per* Denning MR; *Rankin v Potter* (1873) LR 6 HL 83, at 118 *per* Lord Blackburn.

23 See Goff and Jones, *op cit*, 4th edn, p 606 *et seq*.

also include rights that have accrued to an insured. Thus, where, as in *Castellain v Preston*,[24] the insured vendor had received from the purchaser the full purchase price of a building which had burned down after the assured had contracted to sell it, it was held that, although ignorant of the sale, the insurer who had satisfied the loss was entitled to the price received by the vendor in diminution of its loss. An insurer is not, however, entitled to recover more than the payment that has been made to indemnify the insured against loss. In *Yorkshire Insurance Co v Nisbet Shipping Co Ltd*,[25] it was held that insurers were not entitled to a gain arising on the loss of a ship from a favourable currency advantage earned by the insured subsequently as a result of litigation by the insurer against a foreign third party for damages. The insurer was entitled to recoup from the insured only the amount that had been paid in satisfaction of the indemnity. A person who voluntarily assumes responsibility will not, however, be entitled to subrogation. Thus in *The Esso Bernica*,[26] Esso had voluntarily paid crofters for losses incurred as a result of oil spillage caused by the *Esso Bernica*. It paid pursuant to an arrangement that it had with tanker operators that it should be liable for such loss but not as a result of any contract of insurance it had with the crofters. It was not able to sue the party responsible for causing damage to the *Esso Bernica*; the designer of a faulty tug boat which had caused the tug to burst into flames breaking a tow line which led to the *Esso Bernica* colliding with a jetty. The House of Lords held that the rights of action were the crofters and theirs alone. Since Esso had not paid under an indemnity with the crofters, it could not be subrogated to their claims.

An insured has power to enter into agreements for the settlement of claims against third parties but he or she must consider the interests of the insurer. If prejudicial to the insurer, it may operate to release the insurer from a duty to make payment in respect of that loss.[27] An insured may be liable to compensate his or her insurer for damages for breach of an implied term of the contract of insurance should a settlement be prejudicial and binding on the insurer.[28] Exceptionally, a court has declined subrogation where it was considered that to allow such a right would be unacceptable and unrealistic in an industrial setting.[29]

---

24 (1883) 11 QBD 380.

25 [1962] 2 QB 330.

26 [1989] AC 643. Described by Goff and Jones, *op cit*, 4th edn, pp 597–98 as a surprising but inevitable result of the stringency of the volunteer rule.

27 *Andrews v Patriotic Insurance Co* (1886) 18 LR Ir 355.

28 *Commercial Union Assurance Co v Lister* (1874) LR 9 Ch App 483; *Boag v Standard Marine Insurance Co* [1937] 2 KB 113, at 128, *per* Scott LJ.

29 *Morris v Ford Motor Co*, [1973] QB 792, at 800–01 *per* Lord Denning MR, at 815 *per* James LJ.

(d) Creditors, trading trusts and subrogation

Where debts are incurred by a trustee or a personal representative in properly carrying on trust business, the trustee has a right to be indemnified by the trust for any expenses that are properly incurred and enjoys a beneficial interest[30] or an equitable lien to that extent.[31] The creditors will not only have a claim against the trustee for payment, but also a claim in equity to subrogation to the lien that the trustee enjoys.[32] The right of subrogation will be lost where the trustee is in default to the trust estate and has no right to be indemnified.[33] Where the original creditors of the testator or settlor of the trust had not assented to the continuance of the business, the trade creditors were not entitled to a priority over the original creditors, and their interests were postponed in favour of the interests of the original creditors. Merely standing by has been held to be insufficient to constitute assent.[34]

Contribution

Where parties are subject to a common legal obligation, and one accedes to the demand by discharging a debt or liability more than his or her proportionate share, he or she will be able to seek recoupment of the other co-obligor's proportional share of the debt. The equity arises because of the inequality of the burden resulting from the enforcement or satisfaction of the creditor's rights against a sole co-obligor.[35] However, where, as in *Smith v Cook*,[36] there was no common obligation but merely a discretion under separate wills for trustees to prefer a certain person, no question of contribution between the two estates could arise. The principle is of wide application in cases where there is a community of interest,[37] and

---

30 *Chief Commissioner of Stamp Duties v Buckle* (1995) 38 NSWLR 574.

31 *Re Pumfey* (1882) 22 Ch D 225; *Re Staff Benefits Pty Ltd* [1979] 1 NSWLR 207; *Octavo Investments Pty Ltd v Knight* (1979) 144 CLR 360; *Marginson v Potter* (1976) 11 ALR 64.

32 *Re Evans* (1887) 34 Ch D 597; *Custom Credit v Ravi Nominees* [1992] 8 WAR 42, at 53.

33 *Re Johnson* (1880) 15 Ch D 549; *RWG Management Ltd v Commissioner for Corporate Affairs* [1985] VR 385; *Corozo Pty Ltd v Total Australia Ltd* [1987] 2 Qd R 11.

34 *Re Oxley* [1914] 1 Ch 604; *Vaccuum Oil Pty Ltd v Wiltshire* (1945) 72 CLR 319.

35 *McLean v Discount & Finance Ltd* (1939) 64 CLR 312, at 347; *Mahoney v McManus* (1981) 180 CLR 370, at 388. *Scholefield Goodman and Sons Ltd v Zyngier* (1985) 63 ALR 43; query *DJ Fowler (Australia) Ltd v Bank of New South Wales* (1982) 2 NSWLR 879 and *Maxal Nominees Pty Ltd v Dalgety Ltd* [1985] 1 Qd R 51 which would appear to have been incorrectly decided because there was no coordinate liability.

36 (1911) 12 CLR 30.

37 *Bonner v Tottenham & Edmonton Permanent Investment Building Society* [1879] 1 QB 161, at 176 *per* Vaughan Williams LJ. Further, see *Muschinski v Dodds* (1986) 160 CLR 583. It may apply to sureties, insurers, co-contractors, co-adventurers, mortgagors, co-owners, directors, partners and trustees and by statutory intervention in the case of joint tortfeasors. See Muir, G, 'Unjust Sacrifice and the Officious Intervenor', in Finn, PD (ed), *Essays on Restitution*, 1991, pp 342–48, Law Book Company. For a comprehensive discussion of contribution, common maritime adventures and general average, see Goff and Jones, *op cit*, 4th edn, pp 333–42.

has been the subject of further legislative intervention in England[38] and elsewhere.

(a) Contribution and suretyship

Although the common law recognised the right of a surety to contribution as an action for money paid to the use of another surety or co-obligor,[39] equity appeared to supersede the common law in so far as contribution between or amongst sureties was concerned.[40] The doctrine of contribution has been described as founded on doctrines of equity not in reference to chancery doctrine but to doctrines of equity in the sense of reason, justice and the law.[41] In *Deering v The Earl of Winchelsea*,[42] it was held by Eyre CB that a right of contribution in equity existed irrespective of whether the sureties were bound jointly and severally in the one instrument or had guaranteed a debt in separate instruments, provided that they were co-obligors in relation to the same and not different debts. Further, it did not matter that the sureties were unaware of the existence of one another or that one surety agreed to become a surety before another was approached. The basis of a claim for contribution, like subrogation, is that it would constitute an unfair or unjust enrichment for a person to avoid payment of a debt that he or she had agreed to honour in common with others by virtue of what might be mere chance that another co-obligor had been called on first to pay and had discharged more than his or her proportion of the debt.

A surety may claim contribution if he or she has paid more than his or her proportion of the principal debt.[43] Payment of an excessive amount of an instalment of a debt, however, does not entitle the payer to claim contribution since there can be no obligation on a co-surety to pay a contribution until the total proportionate share of the debt is paid by the payer.[44] A surety does not have to actually make payment and will be entitled to a

---

38 The Civil Liability (Contribution) Act 1978, considered by Goff and Jones, *op cit*, 4th edn, pp 272, 289–99. Also, see the Wrongs (Contribution) Act 1985 (Vic). Contribution under these statutes is based on the justice of the case having regard to the extent of the responsibility for the damage caused by the party against whom contribution is claimed.

39 *Godin v London Assurance Co* (1758) 1 Burr 489; [1758] 97 ER 419; *Newby v Reed* (1763) 1 Wm Bl 416; [1763] 97 ER 419.

40 For judicial discussion on the basis in law and equity for the existence of contribution, see *Albion Insurance Company Ltd v Government Insurance Office of New South Wales* (1969) 121 CLR 342, at 350–52; also *Mahoney v McManus* (1981) 180 CLR 370, at 376.

41 *Ibid*, at 351.

42 (1787) 2 Bos & Pul 270, [1787] 126 ER 1276.

43 Contribution will be permitted if a payment is made by a surety to a debtor for the express purpose of paying debts which have been guaranteed by the surety. *Mahoney v McManus* (1981) 180 CLR 370.

44 *Stirling v Burdett* [1911] 2 Ch 418.

declaration prospectively of his or her right to contribution on payment of more than a proportionate share of the debt, if he or she is the subject of judgment or the threat of it.[45] The extent of liability of a surety to contribution will depend upon the proportion of the common debt or obligation that he or she has agreed to undertake.[46] In the absence of fraud, the right to contribution may be modified by contract.[47] Unless the sureties have made an agreement varying their liability *inter se*, each solvent surety must contribute equally to the common debt. If one of the sureties is insolvent, his or her share of the common debt will be assumed by the sureties according to the share in which the remaining sureties agreed to be bound.[48] Thus, where four sureties are jointly and severally bound in a surety bond, and one of them pays the amount of the bond but one of the remaining sureties is insolvent,[49] the right to contribution amongst the other two is for third not fourths of the sums paid. Should a surety obtain the benefit of a security as a result of discharging a debt, any realisation of that security will be for the benefit of all the sureties in the proportion to which they have agreed to guarantee the common debt.[50] Contribution may also not be enforced if it would be inequitable to do so. Thus, in *Official Trustee v Citibank*,[51] it was held to be unconscionable for co-sureties who had requested others to become sureties in order that money would be advanced to a company which the former owned and controlled to subsequently seek contribution from them.

If a creditor releases the principal debtor from his or her liability, the debt is discharged and sureties are released.[52] It would seem, however, that a covenant not to sue the debtor does not exonerate a surety because

---

45   *Wolmershausen v Gullick* [1893] 2 Ch 514; *McLean v Discount & Finance Ltd* (1939) 64 CLR 312, at 341 *per* Starke J; or where a debt has been repaid in circumstances in which the surety and claimant is liable to reimburse the person making that payment more than a proportionate share. *Woolmington v Bronze Lamp Restaurant Pty Ltd* (1984) 2 NSWLR 242, as explained in *Trotter v Franklin* [1991] 2 NZLR 93.

46   *Ellesmere Brewery Company v Cooper* [1896] 1 QB 75, at 79–80. More recently in New Zealand, it has been said that equal sharing was a *prima facie* rule but, as the right to contribution was founded in equity, the ultimate question was to do what was just. Equity might well require unequal sharing if the court can discern either that this was what the parties must have intended or that such unequal sharing is necessary to do justice in the particular case. *Trotter v Franklin* [1991] 2 NZLR 93.

47   *Scholefield Goodman & Sons Ltd v Zyngier* [1986] AC 562, at 574–75; *Trotter v Franklin* [1991] 2 NZLR 93.

48   *Idem.*

49   It would seem that, although a creditor's rights against a surety will lapse on the death of the surety, a right to contribution survives but the legal position is uncertain. Goff and Jones, *op cit*, 4th edn, p 317 consider that contribution should be available in these circumstances.

50   *Idem.* Further, see *Re Ackerdekne* (1883) 24 Ch D 709.

51   (1995) 38 NSWLR 116, at 124; *Trotter v Franklin* [1991] 2 NZLR 93.

52   *Commercial Bank of Tasmania v Jones* [1893] AC 313; *cf Kenworthy v Avoth Holdings Pty Ltd* [1974] WAR 135 where there was no discharge because there was tacit agreement by the sureties to one of the co-debtors being discharged.

the debt is not discharged. If further time is given to the debtor to pay a debt, this is also said to discharge the surety on the ground that, if the time had been adhered to, the surety might have been repaid by the debtor whereas, should time have been extended, the debtor might become insolvent.[53] A creditor's release of a surety from a guarantee will discharge the remaining sureties if their liability is joint, or joint and several, since this will constitute a breach of contract.[54] In *Walker v Bowry*,[55] a surety was released from a judgment debt on payment of a lesser sum. It was held by the High Court of Australia that this discharged the other sureties to the extent of any sum in excess of the sum that was paid pursuant to the release. The discharge of a several surety will not be a breach of any contractual obligation but will deprive the remaining surety of his or her right to contribution in equity.[56] In these circumstances, the remaining surety should also be discharged from liability *pro tanto* for the amount which represents any prejudice suffered by the discharge of a co-obligor.[57]

(b) The joint liability of insurers and contribution

An insured is not able to recover more than the loss that he or she has suffered even though two or more insurers have covered the insured for the same risk. The insurer who discharges more than its proportionate share of the common liability will have a right to seek contribution against the other insurers.[58] In order for a claim of contribution to succeed, the claimant must show not only that there was a common peril insured against but also that the policies covered the same interest in the policy.[59] Where there are two insurers and it is a condition of one of the policies that the insured take certain action consequent upon loss, such as informing the insurer of a claim within a certain time, the fact that this was not done will not prevent the first insurer successfully claiming contribution. In these circumstances, the equity, upon which contribution is based, is

---

53 *Philpot v Briant* (1828) 4 Bing 717; [1828] 130 ER 945. This principle has been doubted by Blackburn J in *Swire v Redman* (1876) 1 QBD 536, at 542, and by Goff and Jones, *op cit*, 4th edn, p 314.

54 *Ellesmere Brewery Co v Cooper* [1893] 1 QB 75.

55 (1924) 35 CLR 48.

56 *Ward v National Bank of New Zealand* (1883) 8 LR 8 App Cas 755, at 766.

57 *Idem*.

58 *Newby v Reed* (1763) 1 Wm Bl 416; [1763] 96 ER 237; *Albion Insurance Company Ltd v Government Insurance Office of New South Wales* (1969) 121 CLR 342; *Commercial and General Insurance Ltd v Government Insurance Office of New South Wales* (1973) 129 CLR 374.

59 *North British and Mercantile Insurance Co v London, Liverpool and Globe Insurance Co* (1876) 5 Ch D 569; and *Borg Warner (Aust) Ltd v Switzerland General Insurance Co Ltd* (1989) 16 NSWLR 421 where different injuries led to an overall total incapacity, and contribution was permitted.

unimpaired by the existence of some limiting provision relating to the insured in the contract of insurance.[60] Where liability insurance is concerned, the Court of Appeal, in *Commercial Union Assurance Co Ltd v Hayden*,[61] rejected an argument that the approach to the assessment of contribution should be based on the maximum liability which each could incur by analogy with the approach to sureties. This was considered to be an artificial manner of assessment, and an approach based on an independent liability concept was adopted. This means that where there are two insurers with differing upper limits for claims, they should both be considered to have accepted the same level of risk up to the lower limit of the claim. Thus, there will be an equal division of liability up to the lower limit but, should a claim exceed this, the burden of meeting that part of the claim should fall on the insurer who has accepted liability on the basis of the upper limit.[62]

(c) Other situations in which contribution may arise

(i) Co-obligors

Under the general law, contribution may be available in other relationships where there exists a common liability.[63] Thus, in *Muschinski v Dodds*,[64] a right of contribution was permitted where one of two purchasers under an agreement for sale and purchase of land had paid considerably more than the purchase price.[65] Joint tenants and tenants in common may have rights of contribution between themselves if the obligation to effect improvements is required by law.[66] A joint contractor who pays more than his or her due share of a common obligation is entitled to contribution unless there is a contrary agreement.[67] However, the importance of there being a common venture and a joint obligation to share losses was emphasised in *Cummings v Lewis*.[68] In that case, Cummings contended that there was an obligation upon two firms of

---

60 *Legal and General Assurance Society Ltd v Drake Insurance Co Ltd* [1992] 1 All ER 283.

61 [1977] 1 All ER 441.

62 *Ibid*, at 453. Note that it is uncertain whether the same principle should apply to property insurance. In *Government Insurance Office of New South Wales v Crowley* (1975) 2 NSWLR 78, Helsham J favoured the independent liability approach. See further Goff and Jones, *op cit*, p 321 where the independent liability approach is also suggested as the appropriate approach to adopt in relation to marine insurance. However, s 80(1) of the Marine Insurance Act 1909 (Imp) appears to provide for the maximum liability basis.

63 *Ruabon Steamship Co v London Assurance* [1900] AC 6.

64 (1986) 160 CLR 583.

65 *Ibid*, at 596–98.

66 *Bonner v Tottenham & Edmonton Permanent Investment Building Society* [1899] 1 QB 161; *Didmore v Leventhal* (1936) 36 SR (NSW) 378.

67 *Bartels v Behm* (1990) 19 NSWLR 275.

68 (1993) 113 ALR 285.

accountants to contribute to losses that he had incurred in relation to the purchase of horses. He had entered into an arrangement to acquire horses and it was envisaged that the firms would prepare tax effective packages through which the horses would be marketed. Each party sought to gain in different ways from the arrangement both in terms of how they would participate and in what they expected to get out of the venture. Cummings hoped to sell the horses and obtain fees from training them for owners, whereas the firms intended to derive professional fees for their participation. It was held that the arrangement did not constitute a relationship whereby it was intended that each would share profits and losses from a common enterprise and, accordingly, there could be no responsibility on the firms to share in Cumming's losses. Contribution is also available in the following cases.

(ii) Trustees

Trustees who are subject to a common liability in equity are jointly and severally liable to the estate for any loss resulting from a breach of trust.[69] A trustee, who has been called to account, will have a right of contribution from a trustee who is under a common obligation.[70] The death of a trustee does not exonerate his or her estate from liability.[71] In equity, there are some exceptions to the general rule. The first arises where a contract of indemnity exists between trustees.[72] The second arises where there has been a misappropriation of a trust fund solely for the use of a trustee,[73] and a third arises where a breach of trust occurs as a result of the advice given by a solicitor-trustee.[74] Finally, a trustee-beneficiary is liable to indemnify a trustee for a breach of trust for which they were both liable to the extent of his or her beneficial interest.[75] Care should also be taken to consider the application of legislation governing trustees in a given jurisdiction because statutory provisions may exist that limit the liability of a trustee for the default of a co-trustee.[76]

---

69   *Jackson v Dickinson* [1903] 1 Ch 947.

70   *Robinson v Harkin* [1896] 2 Ch 415; *Wilkie v McCalla* [1905] VLR 278.

71   *Jackson v Dickinson* [1903] 1 Ch 947.

72   *Warwick v Richardson* (1842) 10 M & W 284; [1842] 152 ER 477.

73   *Wynne v Tempest* [1897] 1 Ch 110. *Chillingworth v Chambers* [1896] 1 Ch 685; *Palmer v Permanent Trustee Co* (1915) 16 SR (NSW) 162.

74   *Re Linsley* [1904] 2 Ch 785; *Bahin v Hughes* (1886) 31 Ch D 390.

75   *Chillingworth v Chambers* [1896] 1 Ch 685.

76   In the United Kingdom, s 2(1) of the Civil Liability (Contribution) Act 1978, which provides that the amount of contribution which is recoverable is that which the court considers to be just and equitable having regard to the extent of the trustee's responsibility for the damage. In other jurisdictions, a trustee, in certain circumstances, may not be liable for the default of a co-trustee unless he or she has been wilfully in breach. For example, s 38 of the Trustee Act 1956 (NZ).

(iii) Directors

A director is entitled to contribution from his or her co-directors if they have concurred in a transaction that is *ultra vires* the company in respect of which money has been recovered from him or her.[77] This is a right available against the estate of a deceased director.[78] A director, however, who has the sole benefit of a breach of trust is not entitled to claim contribution against his or her co-directors.[79] Contribution will depend upon a director being able to show that a co-director has been at fault. This is necessary because, whereas trustees act jointly and severally, directors act by majority.[80] Should a director not have attended a meeting at which an *ultra vires* transaction has been authorised or dissented from, he or she will not be liable to contribute.[81]

(iv) Partners

A partner, who pays more than his or her share of a partnership debt whether voluntarily or not, is entitled to contribution from his or her partners.[82] Where one of two partners, who are jointly liable, has paid a judgment debt, he or she will be entitled, in order to enforce contribution, to an assignment of all securities for the debt subject to equities that subsist between the debtors as partners.[83] Unless it has been otherwise agreed, the right of contribution and the duty to contribute survive the deaths of partners.[84]

---

77 *Ashurst v Mason* (1875) LR 20 Eq 225; *Ramskill v Edwards* (1885) 31 Ch D 100. Further, note also the statutory obligations under the Corporations law in Australia may attract contribution in relation to a breach *Spika Trading Pty Ltd v Harrison* (1990) 19 NSWLR 211.

78 *Jackson v Dickinson* [1903] 1 Ch 947.

79 *Walsh v Bardsley* (1931) 47 TLR 564.

80 Sealey, L, 'The Director as a Trustee' [1967] CLJ 83.

81 *Marquis of Bute's Case* [1892] 2 Ch 100.

82 *Boulter v Peplow* (1850) 9 CB 493; [1850] 137 ER 984; *Batard v Hawkes* (1853) 2 E & B 287; [1853] 118 ER 775; *Bartels v Behm* (1990) 19 NSWLR 275; *Cummings v Bruce* (1993) 113 ALR 285, at 319–23.

83 *Dale v Powell* (1911) 105 LT 29.

84 *Mathews v Ruggles Brise* [1911] 1 Ch 194.

CHAPTER 4

Benefits Derived from Ineffective Transactions or Relationships

This chapter will focus upon the remedies available to obtain restitution of benefits conferred on another pursuant to an ineffective transaction or an ineffectual relationship. A contractual transaction may be ineffective, for example, because it lacks formal validity, a party lacks contractual capacity or it is void for uncertainty. Benefits may also have been conferred where the underlying assumption or expectation upon which a transaction or relationship is based either does not materialise or has ceased to exist. The parties may have given little consideration to what should occur, should this happen. The quasi-contractual claims of *quantum meruit* or *quantum valebat*, the equitable remedy of recoupment, the doctrine of estoppel, and resulting and constructive trusts can play an important role in preventing unjust enrichment in cases of this kind.

Quasi-contractual claims for services rendered pursuant to an ineffective transaction

If a person enters into a contract to perform work or to supply goods, the issue of remuneration will ordinarily be governed by the contract.[1] Thus, in *Luxor (Eastbourne) Ltd v Cooper*,[2] the House of Lords had to consider whether Cooper, who was a real estate agent, was entitled to a commission for introducing a prospective purchaser to Luxor. Luxor had entered into an agreement with Cooper which entitled the later to commission on the completion of an agreement for sale of the company's real estate. Cooper had introduced a willing and able purchaser but Luxor determined to effect the transaction it had in mind by the sale of shares in the group rather than the sale of its real estate. Cooper argued that a term should be implied in the agreement that Luxor would not without just cause prevent him earning his commission. It was held that no such term could be implied and that Luxor was not liable to pay Cooper commission. Where the price is not included in the contract, a court may be able to imply a term that a reasonable price should be paid for goods or services.[3] This represented an early form of *quantum meruit*. However, if price is an essential term of a contract and

---

1   *Update Constructions Pty Ltd v Rozell Child Care Centre* (1990) 20 NSWLR 251, at 275.

2   [1941] 1 AC 108; [1941] 1 All ER 33.

3   *Foley v Classique Coaches Ltd* [1934] 2 KB 1; [1934] All ER 88; *Hillas & Co Ltd v Arcos Ltd* (1932) 147 LT 503; [1932] All ER 495; *cf May and Butcher Ltd v Regem* [1934] 2 KB 17; [1929] All ER 679; *Brenner v First Artist's Management Pty Ltd* [1993] 2 VR 221, at 256.

has not been the subject of agreement, the contract will fail for want of certainty. Whether price is an essential term is a matter of construction.[4] Where an agreement is void for uncertainty, a plaintiff may be able to invoke a quasi-contractual claim for reimbursement for services that he or she has rendered. This topic is considered below.[5]

(a) Services rendered pursuant to a contract that is ineffective

A claim for a *quantum meruit* or *quantum valebat* may succeed where the plaintiff renders services or delivers goods to the defendant under a mutually mistaken belief that there exists a binding agreement when there is not. Should the contract be void, the defendant will be liable to pay the reasonable value of the services or goods. In *Craven-Ellis v Cannons Ltd*,[6] the plaintiff, Craven-Ellis, was employed as a real estate agent for a company without a written agreement. Subsequently, he became a managing director of the company and a resolution was passed which provided for the terms of his appointment and remuneration. After he had performed work for the company and had not been paid, he sued the company on the agreement and in the alternative in *quantum meruit* for the reasonable value of his services. The resolution was found to be invalid since neither Craven-Ellis nor the directors were qualified to act under the Articles. However, the Court of Appeal held that Craven-Ellis was entitled to reasonable compensation for the services that he had provided upon a *quantum meruit*. The obligation to pay did not depend upon a finding that there was an implied contract but was imposed by law. Greer LJ observed:[7]

> In my judgment, the obligation to pay reasonable remuneration for the work done when there is no binding contract between the parties is imposed by rule of law, and not by an inference of fact arising from the acceptance of service of goods. It is one of the cases referred to in books on contracts as obligations arising *quasi ex contractu*, of which a well known instance is claims based on money had and received.

The obligation arises by operation of law in order to prevent the defendant being unjustly enriched. Craven-Ellis did not intend the services to be given gratuitously and the company freely accepted the benefit of those services which saved the company the expense of employing another

---

4   See *Courtney & Fairbairn Ltd v Tolaini Bros (Hotels) Ltd* [1975] 1 WLR 297; [1975] 1 All ER 716, as explained by Robert Goff J in *British Steel Corp v Cleveland Bridge and Engineering Co Ltd* [1984] 1 All ER 504, at 511.

5   See further, Stoljar, SJ, *The Law of Quasi-Contract*, 2nd edn, 1989, p 222, Law Book Company, *et seq.*

6   [1936] 2 KB 403; [1936] 2 All ER 1066; further, *Lawford v Billericay Rural District Council* [1903] 1 KB 722; *Hansen v Mayfair Trading Co Pty Ltd* [1962] WAR 148; *Regalian Properties v London Dock Development Corp* [1995] 1 WLR 212.

7   *Ibid*, at 412; 1073.

person to carry out the work.[8] In *Way v Latilla*,[9] the House of Lords held similarly that Way was entitled to a *quantum meruit* for work carried out in assisting to locate gold mines and concessions in West Africa. Way sued for damages for breach of an alleged agreement under which he claimed that he had been promised participation in the profits of the concessions which were extremely valuable. The House of Lords held that there was no concluded contract since the parties had not agreed on the amount of commission that Way was to receive. However, because he had performed work for Latilla in circumstances which the parties knew were not intended to be gratuitous, he was entitled to reasonable remuneration. The approach in *Craven-Ellis* was also adopted in *Societe Franco Tunisienne D'Armement v Sidemar SPA*.[10] In that case, a shipowner, who had carried goods to Genoa via the Cape of Good Hope rather than through the Suez canal, was entitled to payment on a *quantum meruit* because the original contract of carriage via the Suez canal was held to have been frustrated by war. The goods had been carried after that to their destination via the Cape for the charterer's benefit and at its request.[11] More recently, in *Rover International Ltd v Cannon Film Sales Ltd (No 3)*,[12] *quantum meruit* was available to reimburse Rover for the performance of services for Cannons associated with the distribution of films after it was found that the agreement between the parties was void because, at the time of formation of the contract, Rover had not been incorporated.

A case which caused difficulty in this area is *Re Cleadon Trust Ltd*.[13] There, the Court of Appeal took a more conservative approach to the

---

8   Burrows, A, 'Free Acceptance and the Law of Restitution' (1988) 104 LQR 576, at 594 notes the observations of Birks, P 'Negotiorum Gestio and the Common Law' (1971) 24 *Current Legal Problems* 110, at 120–23 that this could not truly be a free acceptance case because the company had no mind due to the failure of the directors to take up their qualification shares. Gareth Jones appears to admit the validity of this criticism in his comments in 'A Topography of the Law of Restitution', in Finn, PD (ed), *Essays on Restitution*, 1991, p 7, Law Book Company. However, it would seem that Greer LJ in *Craven-Ellis v Canons Ltd* [1936] 2 KB 403, at 412; 2 All ER 1066, at 1073–74 did not consider that the failure of the directors to take up their qualification shares was an impediment to the quasi-contractual claim, a factor being that, in his view, the company had accepted the services which if they had not been performed by the plaintiff would have had to have been carried out by an agent. Birks preferred the explanation that restitution was available because the defendant had been incontrovertibly benefited. And further Birks, P, *An Introduction to the Law of Restitution*, reprint 1993, pp 118–19, Clarendon Press, Oxford. In *Monks v Poynice Pty Ltd* (1987) 8 NSWLR 662, Young J adopted the incontrovertible benefit approach when ruling that a receiver of a company, who was invalidly appointed, was entitled to recover reasonable remuneration for acting as a manager from the liquidator to the extent to which there was such a benefit to the company.

9   [1937] 3 All ER 759.

10   [1960] 3 WLR 701; [1960] 2 All ER 529.

11   *Ibid*, at 725; 548.

12   [1989] 1 WLR 912; [1989] 3 All ER 423.

13   [1939] Ch 286.

failure of directors to comply with the Articles of Association than in *Craven-Ellis*. An invalid resolution that purported to approve an advance made by one of the directors, Creighton, to pay off debts of Cleadon subsidiaries had been passed. Creighton had been asked to do this by the Secretary of the company. Although the payment benefited the company because it was discharged from its obligation to guarantee the debts of the two subsidiary companies on the voluntary winding-up of the company, the liquidator declined to recognise the advances as binding on the company because the resolution was invalid. Creighton challenged the liquidator's opinion. A majority of the Court of Appeal considered that he could not recover even though his actions had benefited the company. The court unanimously ruled that a claim for money lent failed since there had been no valid request or even acquiescence by the company in the payment. Although declining the common law claim, Sir Wilfred Greene MR considered that in equity Creighton could recover because his actions in discharging the debts had undoubtedly benefited the company.[14] The majority, however, considered that recoupment was not available merely because the company had received a benefit. In relation to the common law claim, the court adopted the now outmoded implied contract approach, rather than the approach favoured in *Craven-Ellis* which had treated reimbursement as an obligation imposed by law in order to prevent unjust enrichment. It would appear, however, that even if the court had adopted the modern approach, this would still not have assisted Creighton because the court considered that he had flagrantly abused his position as a director under the Articles of Association. Scott LJ observed of the argument that the common law claim did not depend upon implied agreement:[15]

> If that principle or anything like it could be established at law today, the conduct of the appellant would be germane to the inquiry, in that it might well be regarded as neither 'fair or just' for the court to reward such misconduct by excluding its help.

Considered in this light, *Cleadon* illustrates how a claim to restitution may also be defeated by considerations involving the application of an adverse principle or rule of public policy.[16]

Where a contract is unenforceable because it does not accord with the form required of it by statute, a quasi-contractual remedy will be available where the defendant has requested and freely accepted the

---

14 *Ibid*, at 304.

15 *Ibid*, at 311. Noted by Young J in *Cadorange v Tanga Holdings* (1990) 20 NSWLR 26, at 39. Young J observed that, although he had sympathy, these remarks were made some 52 years ago, at a time when perhaps judges had a greater expectation of company directors than is the experience of judges in this Division in the 1990s.

16 See Chapter 14, pp 351–52.

benefit of the plaintiff's work. Thus, in *Scarisbrick v Parkinson*,[17] an action in *quantum meruit* for services rendered by an employee for his employer was upheld by the Court of Exchequer, where there was no written agreement satisfying the Statute of Frauds. In Australia, it was held in *Stincombe v Thomas*[18] that a housekeeper, who relied on a promise by the deceased to reward her if she stayed with him until she died, was entitled to a *quantum meruit* for her services. The court considered that, although the deceased's promise did not constitute a legally binding contract because it was not in writing, she was entitled to reasonable remuneration for her services because both parties had proceeded on the basis that payment would be made for services rendered and it would be unconscionable for the estate to subsequently disavow payment. In *Pavey & Matthews Pty Ltd v Paul*,[19] the High Court of Australia held that a builder who had failed to comply with the requirements of certain legislation that rendered a building contract unenforceable unless it was in writing, was able to claim on a *quantum meruit* for the value of the work that had been performed at the request of the owner and freely accepted. It was the view of Mason, Wilson and Deane JJ that the right to recover on a *quantum meruit* in this kind of case did not depend upon an implied contract but arose in law as an obligation imposed to prevent the unjust enrichment of the defendant who had requested and freely accepted the builder's services in circumstances where it would be unconscionable for her to deny an obligation to pay a reasonable sum.[20] Although unenforceable by the plaintiff, the contract was of relevance and evidence at least that the plaintiff had not performed the work gratuitously.[21] Deane J also considered that the legislation would not preclude the owner relying on the agreement should the reasonable cost of the work exceed the contract price.[22]

---

17 (1869) 20 LT 175. Approved by Lord Atkin in *Way v Latilla* [1937] 3 All ER 759, at 764. Followed in Australia, in *Ward v Griffiths Bros Ltd* (1928) 28 SR (NSW) 425 and considered by Brennan J in *Pavey & Matthews Pty Ltd v Paul* (1986–87) 162 CLR 221, at 233. See also the approach of Jordan CJ in *Horton v Jones* (1934) 34 SR (NSW) 359 at 367–68, approved in *Pavey & Matthews Pty Ltd v Paul*, *ibid*, at 250 *per* Deane J. In Canada, a similar approach was taken in *Deglman v Guaranty Trust Co of Canada* [1954] 3 DLR 785.

18 [1957] VR 509.

19 (1986) 162 CLR 221. Applied in *Brenner v First Artist's Management Pty Ltd* [1993] 2 VR 221, at 256. Further, in *Pohlmann v Harrison* (1995) 2 Qd R 59, a builder succeeded in claiming restitution for the construction of a house where he proceeded mistakenly thinking that there was a contract and the owner freely accepted the work but argued there was no obligation to pay in the absence of a contract. Distinguished in *F J Richards Pty Ltd v Mills Pty Ltd* (1995) Qd R 1 on the ground that the legislation in question prohibited proceedings in question being taken by an unlicensed agent.

20 *Ibid*, at 227–28 *per* Mason and Wilson JJ, at 258–60 *per* Deane J.

21 *Ibid*, at 257 *per* Deane J.

22 *Idem*.

(b) Services rendered in anticipation of a contract that does not materialise

A more difficult situation arises when one party agrees to perform services at the request of another and both parties are confident that a contract will be entered into which will incorporate payment for the work performed in anticipation of contract. If the preliminary work performed is no more than is customary such as a tender for a contract, a *quantum meruit* will not be available for the cost of the tender should a contract not eventuate. Expenditure of this kind is a cost that a person tendering for a contract customarily bears.[23] However, where the circumstances suggest that the parties are mutually confident that a contract will eventuate, work requested of one party by another may be compensated for on a *quantum meruit* should a contract not be concluded. Whether compensation will be permitted will depend upon the circumstances of the case. In *Jennings and Chapman Ltd v Woodman Mathews and Co*,[24] the English Court of Appeal held that a lessee was not entitled to recover the cost of effecting alterations to premises in order to sub-lease to a solicitor, where the landlord subsequently declined to give his consent to the premises being divided into offices. Although the alterations had been effected at the request of the sub-lessee in anticipation of the sub-lease, the court considered that since the lessee and not the solicitor was aware of covenants in the lease relating to the use of the premises and alterations, the lessee was held to have assumed the risk of non-payment if there was a failure to procure the sub-lease.[25] In *Brewer Street Investments Ltd v Barclays Woollen Co Ltd*,[26] however, compensation was ordered where the defendants, who were prospective tenants, requested the plaintiffs to make certain alterations to premises and accepted responsibility for their cost prior to an agreement being finalised. After the alterations had been commenced, the defendants insisted on a provision being included in the lease which the plaintiffs had refused from the outset of negotiations. After it had become apparent that no lease would be concluded, the plaintiffs ceased the alterations, paid the contractor and sought restitution from the defendants as moneys paid to their use. The Court of Appeal upheld the claim and ordered restitution because the defendants had assumed the risk of an agreement not being reached and also because they had insisted on a provision which they knew from the outset the plaintiffs opposed. In both of these cases, it was emphasised that whether restitution for the services provided should be allowed depended upon the circumstances

---

23 See *William Lacey Ltd v Davis* [1957] 1 WLR 932 at 939; [1957] 2 All ER 712, at 719.

24 [1952] 2 TLR 409.

25 *Ibid*, at 413 *per* Somervell LJ, at 414 *per* Denning LJ, at 415 *per* Romer LJ.

26 [1954] 1 QB 428; [1953] 2 All ER 1330.

of the case. Thus, in *Jennings*,[27] Denning LJ considered that the result might have been different if the landlord had been prepared to give his consent but the tenant had refused to enter into the lease. Conversely, in *Brewer Street Investments*,[28] Denning LJ agreed with Morris LJ in the court below, that if the landlord had refused to go on with the lease capriciously or had demanded a higher rent than that agreed upon earlier, he could not have recovered. In this regard, Somervell LJ further considered that if the improvements had been of benefit to the landlord that might have provided some defence to a claim for restitution.[29]

Another case in point is *William Lacey Ltd v Davis*.[30] Following a tender for the reconstruction of premises damaged in the war, the plaintiff was led to believe that it would win the contract. At the request of the owner, the plaintiff prepared various additional estimates to enable the owner to make submissions to the War Damage Commission for an increase in compensation. The owner subsequently requested further estimates and additional work was carried out which enabled the owner to successfully negotiate a higher award. The owner, however, subsequently decided to sell the premises having first intimated to the plaintiff that he intended to contract with another builder. It was held that the plaintiff was entitled to a *quantum meruit* for the additional work that had been carried out at the plaintiff's request. The court considered that the work had been performed under a mutual belief and misunderstanding that the building would be reconstructed and the plaintiff would succeed in winning the contract. Having considered *Craven-Ellis v Canons Ltd*, Barry J observed:[31]

> I am unable to see any valid distinction between work done which was to be paid for under the terms of a contract erroneously believed to be in existence, and work done which was to be paid for out of the proceeds of a contract which both parties erroneously believed was about to be made. In neither case was the work to be done gratuitously, and in both cases, the party from whom payment was sought requested the work and obtained the benefit of it. In neither case did the parties actually intend to pay for the work otherwise than under the supposed contract, or as part of the total price that would become payable when the expected contract was made. In both cases, when the beliefs of the parties were falsified, the law implied an obligation and in this case, I think the law should imply an obligation – to pay a reasonable price for the services which had been obtained.

---

27 [1952] 2 TLR 409, at 415.
28 [1954] 1 QB 428, at 436; [1953] 2 All ER 1330, at 1335.
29 *Ibid*, at 434; 1333.
30 [1957] 1 WLR 932; [1957] 2 All ER 712.
31 *Ibid*, at 939; 719.

William Lacey was subsequently followed by Robert Goff J in *British Steel Corp v Cleveland Bridge and Engineering Co Ltd*.[32] The plaintiff, who was an iron and steel manufacturer, successfully claimed a *quantum meruit* for the manufacture of steel nodes requested by the defendant, Cleveland Bridge. The parties had confidently expected a contract to be concluded and the defendant had requested work to commence immediately. The parties were, however, unable to come to terms and conclude an agreement. The court held that the plaintiff was entitled to a reasonable sum for the work that had been carried out at the defendant's request. The approach in *William Lacey* was also followed in New South Wales in *Sabemo Pty Ltd v North Sydney Municipal Council*.[33] It was held that a developer was entitled to a *quantum meruit* for extensive proposals it had prepared for the council at the council's request in connection with the redevelopment of certain land. Eventually, the council resolved not to proceed with its plan but declined to fully compensate the plaintiff for the work that it had performed. It was held that the plaintiff was entitled to reimbursement for the work. The court considered that there should be reimbursement where the plaintiff and the defendant had proceeded on the joint assumption that a contract would be entered into, but the defendant had unilaterally abandoned the project for reasons pertaining only to his own interests and not arising out of any disagreement on terms of the proposed contract. However, self-interest was not considered a definitive factor in either *Brewer Street Investments Ltd v Barclays Woollen Co Ltd* or *British Steel Corp v Cleveland Bridge and Engineering Co Ltd*. In neither of these cases was it considered that either party was at fault in not concluding an agreement. Rather, relief was granted because the plaintiff had been requested to carry out the work by the recipient in the mutual belief that a contract would be concluded. In cases of this kind, the risk that a contract will not be concluded should be *prima facie* born by the party who requests preliminary work and encourages the other to believe that a contract will result. It is only if the failure to come to terms is due to some capricious or unreasonable expectation of the person who has performed the service that restitution should be denied. In *Regalian Properties v London Dock Development Corp*,[34] restitution was declined where the services performed in anticipation of contract were found to be for the benefit of the plaintiff rather than the defendant.

In New Zealand, quasi-contractual claims have also been entertained to permit a plaintiff to claim reimbursement for services that were rendered on the basis of an understanding that a contractual relationship would be

---

32 [1984] 1 All ER 504.

33 (1977) 2 NSWLR 880. Considered further in *Brenner v First Artists Management Pty Ltd* [1993] 2 VR 221, at 258–59.

34 [1995] 1 WLR 212.

formalised later. In *Watson v Watson*,[35] the plaintiff successfully claimed a *quantum meruit* for work he had performed for a joint venture he had with his brother, in the expectation that a formal partnership agreement would be concluded. The defendant prevaricated with formalising an agreement and the plaintiff withdrew from the arrangement and successfully claimed a *quantum meruit* for the service that had been performed. In *Van den Berg v Giles*,[36] the court held that the defendant had freely accepted services that she knew had been performed in the belief, which she had encouraged, that the plaintiff would be able to purchase her holiday home which he had improved at considerable expense. The plaintiff was allowed reimbursement on a *quantum meruit* based on the increase in value of the property that was attributable to the improvements. In *Dickson Elliot Lonergan Ltd v Plumbing World Ltd*,[37] the court held that, where a developer had commenced work at the defendant's request in anticipation of contract, the developer was entitled to recover the reasonable value of his services which normally would include a profit element. The fact that the defendant derived no actual benefit from the services was considered irrelevant.[38]

(c) The assessment of reasonable remuneration

As the case of *Way v Latilla* illustrates, the assessment of what constitutes reasonable remuneration is not always easy to determine. The House of Lords considered that the court was entitled to have regard to the declarations of the parties in their negotiations as evidence of the value which the parties placed on services in cases particularly where a trade usage rate was inappropriate or non-existent.[39] The negotiations contradicted any suggestion that the plaintiff should be paid on a fee basis. Rather, the court accepted that Way was to be remunerated on the basis of his participation and results. Lord Wright acknowledged that the assessment of what was a 'reasonable participation' award could only be an approximate estimate and that this was a consequence of the parties leaving such a matter in an uncertain state.[40] The court took into account that Latilla had spent large sums of money in developing the concessions which had also prospered with the passing of time so that the award of compensation that Way received was not very significant

---

35 [1953] NZLR 266.

36 [1979] 2 NZLR 111. The court considered that the same reasoning would have permitted the plaintiff to claim on a proprietary estoppel.

37 [1988] 2 NZLR 608.

38 *Cf* Beatson, J, *Benefit, Reliance the Structure of Unjust Enrichment*, 1991, p 35, Clarendon Press, Oxford, where the writer asserts that a claim of this kind is for injurious reliance rather than benefit.

39 [1937] 3 All ER 759, at 763–64 *per* Lord Atkin; at 766 *per* Lord Wright.

40 *Idem.*

in terms of the overall profit of the venture. In *Stinchcombe v Thomas*,[41] the court considered that it was entitled to take into account all the surrounding circumstances in assessing an appropriate sum. In *Pavey & Matthews Pty Ltd v Paul*,[42] Deane J considered the manner in which compensation should be assessed on a *quantum meruit* and held that, ordinarily, it would be the fair market value for the work or goods supplied. His Honour also considered that the owner should be able to rely on the contract price if it was less than that which would be regarded as fair compensation under a *quantum meruit*.[43] This point, however, did not directly fall for consideration in *Pavey* since the owner had agreed under the unenforceable contract to pay a reasonable sum for the work calculated by reference to prevailing rates of payment in the building industry. Difficulties in assessing the appropriate rate for a manager involved in promoting an artist in the popular music business influenced the court to award an appropriate hourly rate in *Brenner v First Artist's Management Pty Ltd*.[44]

Equitable recoupment of invalid or unauthorised loans which have been used to discharge the debts of the borrower

Ineffective loan transactions have given rise to claims in restitution where, although unauthorised, the proceeds have been used to discharge the debts of a person on whose behalf the advances were made. Where the advances have been applied in this way, the fact that the loans were invalid or unauthorised and hence unenforceable will not prevent the lender gaining recoupment in equity. Restitution based on equitable recoupment was sanctioned in *Re Cork and Youghal Railway Co*[45] which involved unauthorised borrowings by a company. Advances to the company had been secured by means of bonds which were invalid and unenforceable. The proceeds, however, of the loans were used to discharge the company's debts. It was held that the bondholders were entitled to recoup the loans in equity in so far as the proceeds had been used to discharge the company's debts even though the bonds were unenforceable. Lord Hatherley LC observed:[46]

---

41 [1957] VR 509, at 513–14. See *Hansen v Mayfair Trading Co Pty Ltd* [1962] WAR 148 for the assessment of casual professional charges.

42 (1986) 162 CLR 221, at 262–64.

43 *Ibid*, at 257. In *Pohlman v Harrison* (1995) 2 Qd R 59, the quotation would seem to have been regarded as an appropriate guide to restitution for the construction of a home completed under the erroneous belief by the builder that there was a contract in existence between him and the owner.

44 [1993] 2 VR 221, at 262–66.

45 (1869) LR Ch App 748.

46 *Ibid*, at 761.

The proper course to be taken seems to me to be this: that, so far as the Company have adopted the proceedings of their directors by allowing these moneys to be raised on the issue of these debentures, and in so far as the money raised by the issue of the debentures has been applied in paying off debts which would not otherwise have been paid off, those who have advanced the moneys ought to stand in the place of those whose debts have been so paid off.

The issue of an unauthorised loan was further considered in *Blackburn Building Society v Cunliffe.*[47] There, *Cork and Youghal Railway* was explained as a case in which the indebtedness of the company had not been increased by the unauthorised borrowing; rather all that had occurred was that there had been a change in creditor. Accordingly, it was considered inequitable to allow the borrower the benefit of having debts discharged at the expense of the lender.[48] *Re Cork and Youghal Railway Co* was followed in *Banantyne v D & C MacIver.*[49] In that case, an agent who was unauthorised to do so borrowed money from the plaintiff, part of which was used to discharge debts of the defendant firm. The lender claimed recoupment from the principal because the moneys had been used to discharge the principal's debts. The Court of Appeal agreed and ordered an inquiry to determine what debts had been discharged in that way.

A debt may be validly discharged either by the debtor requesting a third party to make payment to a creditor or subsequently adopting a payment that is made on the debtor's behalf.[50] In *Re Cleadon Trust,*[51] the Court of Appeal was concerned with unauthorised loans from a director, Creighton, which had been applied by the secretary of the company in reduction of the debts of subsidiaries, thus purporting to relieve the company from a liability under a guarantee. Since the resolution purporting to confirm the loans and ratify the payments was invalid under the Articles, it was held by a majority of the Court of Appeal that Creighton was subsequently unable to enforce the loans against the company which went into liquidation. Creighton was held to have assumed the risk that the unauthorised loans would be ratified by the

---

47 (1882) 22 Ch D 61.

48 *Ibid,* at 71.

49 [1906] 1 KB 103. See further, *B Liggett Liverpool Ltd v Barclays Bank* [1928] 1 KB 48. There the Bank was able to recoup in equity a payment it had erroneously made on a cheque drawn by one of only two of the required directors of the company where the proceeds had been paid to creditors.

50 *Belshaw v Bush* (1851) 11 CB 191; [1851] 138 ER 444; *City Bank of Sydney v McLaughlin* (1909) 9 CLR 615; *Hill v Ziymack* (1908) 7 CLR 352.

51 [1939] Ch 286.

company and consequently failed in his application after the court declared the resolution purporting to ratify the transactions invalid.[52]

In the cases considered above, there was no suggestion that the lender should enjoy a priority as a secured creditor. In *Re Wrexham*,[53] an argument was advanced and rejected that a lender, who had paid off debts owing to debenture stockholders of a company, should be entitled to succeed to the creditor's security. The advances had been made pursuant to an unauthorised borrowing. Lord Lindley MR considered that it would be incorrect to give an *ultra vires* lender priority over an *intra vires* lender. Rigby LJ further considered that the equity with which the court was concerned in cases of this kind had little to do with subrogation.[54] Exceptionally, however, courts have permitted a lender, who is a party to an invalid loan, to accede to a security held by a creditor. This occurred in *Thurston v Nottingham Permanent Building Society*.[55] In that case, a building society lent money to an infant unaware that the borrower was under age. The legislation governing such a loan provided that the transaction was void.[56] The society paid part of the loan to a vendor with whom the borrower had contracted to acquire land. Subsequently, the borrower mortgaged the land to the society to secure the loan. In proceedings brought by the borrower after she had come of age to have the title deeds she had deposited with the society delivered

---

52 Lord Goff and Jones, G, *Law of Restitution*, 4th edn, 1993, Sweet & Maxwell, p 624 comment that the plaintiff was defeated more by the rules of company law than any defect in the principles of restitution. Sir Wilfrid Greene MR in dissent considered that the company had received a benefit and would have been prepared to grant restitution. Goff and Jones, however, reject this reasoning on the basis that it failed to reconcile the equitable right with the rule that paying another's creditor without request or ratification by the debtor will not alone entitle a stranger to repayment by a debtor. *Ibid*, at 624–25. Burrows, *The Law of Restitution*, 1993, pp 222–30 is critical of the rule requiring debts to be discharged by request or ratification arguing for an automatic discharge principle which would permit the payer to obtain restitution from the debtor.

53 [1899] 1 Ch 440. See further, *Wylie v Carlyon* [1922] 1 Ch 51 and *Paul v Speirway Ltd* [1976] 1 Ch 220.

54 *Ibid*, at 455. Goff and Jones, *op cit*, p 631 consider that the reasoning of Rigby LJ was unfortunate and suggest that the remedy is one of subrogation but, in their view, subrogation is a flexible concept which does not inevitably mean that accession to a creditor's securities is an inevitable consequence of subrogation. For a case where subrogation were allowed where a fiduciary had wrongfully applied a building society's advance to discharge a mortgage owner property, see *Boscawen v Bajwa* [1996] 1 WLR 329.

55 [1902] 1 Ch 1.

56 See ss 6–7 of the Minor's Contracts (Miscellaneous Provisions) Act 1979 (Sth Aust). Restitution may be ordered where property had passed prior to the avoidance of a contract on minority. Further, see s 37 of the Minors (Property and Contracts) Act 1970 (NSW), where a court may make validating orders in whole or in part with adjustments. The minor may be ordered to make just compensation. In New Zealand, see s 7 of the Minors' Contracts Act 1969, where courts are given wide discretionary powers to validate or set aside contracts with minors and have wide powers also to effect appropriate restitution.

up to her, the Court of Appeal held that the lender was entitled, in so far as part of the money had been paid to the vendor in discharge of the purchase price, to succeed to the unpaid vendor's lien even though the loan and mortgage were invalid. *Thurston's Case*, however, was unusual and restitution can be justified there because the borrower could not conscionably take advantage of the society by obtaining the title deeds and the freehold without repaying the moneys that had been advanced to her. In any event, in the absence of the court finding that restitution was precluded by adverse public policy considerations embodied in the legislation governing the transaction, it may be argued that the society should have been entitled to a personal equity of recoupment on the *Cork and Youghal Railway* principle. By advancing the money it had not increased the borrower's liability but it had merely substituted itself as a creditor in place of the vendor.[57] More recent authority also suggests that, where a lender pursuant to a valid loan discharges a liability directly on behalf of another, it will be assumed that the lender intends to stand in the shoes of the creditor and accede to any security that the creditor enjoys.[58] On this basis, it may be argued that, once the payment to the vendor in *Thurston* was adopted after the borrower had come of age, the debt was validly discharged and it was not unreasonable for the court to rule that the society stepped into the shoes of the creditor and enjoyed the benefit of the unpaid vendor's lien.

Where, however, it is clear that the policy of the legislation will be defeated should an equity of recoupment be recognised so as to permit either a personal or proprietary claim to a lender, then the equity must give way to any prohibition contained in the legislation. This principle is illustrated in *Orakpo v Manson Investments Ltd*.[59] The House of Lords held, in relation to an application to set aside a money-lending transaction, that to permit the money-lender subrogation to an unpaid vendor's lien would defeat the policy of the legislation. The House overruled earlier English authority to the contrary.[60] *Thurston* was considered and not overruled, although Lord Diplock observed that, in view of the difference in the respective statutory provisions, a court should not proceed by analogy.[61] *Orakpo* is authority for the proposition that transactions entered into by lenders that seriously contravene the objects of legislation governing them cannot be indirectly enforced by an appeal to

---

57 [1902] 1 Ch 1, at 11 *per* Romer LJ.

58 *Ghana Commercial Bank v Chandiram* [1960] AC 732, at 745 *per* Lord Jenkins. If all that can be inferred is that the parties intended an unsecured loan, it was considered that there was no room for the lender to assert that it should be subrogated to any security interest that the creditor might have. *Paul v Speirway Ltd* [1976] 1 Ch 220.

59 [1978] AC 95; [1977] 3 WLR 229.

60 *Congresbury Motors Ltd v Anglo-Belge Finance Co Ltd* [1971] Ch 81.

61 [1978] AC 95, at 106; [1977] 3 WLR 229, at 236.

equitable doctrine.[62] This is another illustration of the manner in which a claim to restitution may be defeated because of conflicting public policy considerations embodied in a governing statute.

The doctrine of estoppel and ineffective transactions

Estoppel may operate to enable restitution of benefits that have been acquired by a party to a transaction that is ineffective if the conduct of that party is such that it would be unconscionable for the party to deny restitution and the other party has acted to his or her detriment. Recent developments in the law has meant that estoppel is important in ensuring that otherwise ineffective transactions are rendered sufficiently effective to enable an innocent party to obtain restitution from a party who has behaved unconscionably.

(a) The nature of estoppel

In recent years, there has been a rationalisation of the concept of estoppel and a tendency to assimilate the various categories of estoppel into a single doctrine. In *Commonwealth v Verwayen*,[63] Mason CJ observed that:[64]

> In conformity with the fundamental purpose of all estoppels; to afford protection against the detriment which would flow from a party's change of position if the assumption that led to it were deserted, these developments have brought a greater underlying unity to the various categories of estoppel. Indeed, the consistent trend in the modern decisions points inexorably towards the emergence of one overarching doctrine of estoppel rather than a series of independent rules.

The acceptance amongst some Australian justices that common law estoppel should not be limited to a representation of existing fact, thus abrogating the rule in *Jordan v Money*,[65] and the extension of the equitable concept of promissory estoppel in Australia and New Zealand to include not only a forbearance to enforce an existing legal obligation but a promise to enter a future legal relationship means that there has been a significant trend towards assimilating estoppel into a universal

---

62 Further, see *Burston Finance v Speirway Ltd* [1974] 1 WLR 1649, and Chapter 14, pp 351–52. Evans, M, *Outline of Equity and Trusts*, 1996, 2nd edn, p 187, Butterworths, Australia criticises the distinction between *Thurston* and *Orakpo*, but for reasons given above it is submitted the cases are reconcilable.

63 [1990] 170 CLR 394.

64 *Ibid*, at 410–11.

65 (1854) 5 HLC 185; 10 ER 868. See Mason CJ in *Foran v Wright* (1989) 168 CLR 385, at 411; at 435 *per* Deane J; also *Moorgate Mercantile Co Ltd v Twitchings* [1976] QB 225, at 242. In New Zealand, the principle in *Jorden v Money* was affirmed by the Court of Appeal in *NB Hunt & Sons Ltd v Maori Trustee* [1986] 2 NZLR 641, at 655.

doctrine.[66] Where estoppel is pleaded, inquiry should be directed at determining whether it would be unconscionable for a party to be allowed to resile from a representation or action that has led another to suffer detriment. This approach is to be preferred to one that proceeds by attempting to accommodate the case within the confines of some pre-conceived formula.[67] The substance of an equitable estoppel consists of a representation by words or conduct (be it overt encouragement or pas-sive acquiescence) by a person, A, that encourages or allows another, B, to act to his or her detriment in circumstances which render it uncon-scionable to permit A to disavow or resile from the expectation that he or she has created. Estoppel plays an important role in restitution where it can be shown that, as a result of A's representation or conduct, B has conferred a benefit on A or has expended money in preparation for con-ferring a benefit on A in circumstances that preclude A from disavow-ing the expectation in an attempt to gain enrichment at B's expense. In this context, estoppel may assist an innocent party to perfect an other-wise ineffective transaction and thus prevent the unjust enrichment of the other.[68] A representation must be precise and unambiguous and, if so, will be sufficient to found an estoppel even though innocently made.[69] If a clear and precise representation is established, there is an onus on the party alleging estoppel to establish proof of his or her belief in the representation and consequent detriment. If there is evidence that he or she had been aware of the error or was in possession of certain information that reasonably necessitated inquiry, knowledge of the true

---

66   *Legione v Hateley* (1982) 152 CLR 406; *Walton Stores Ltd v Maher* (1988) 164 CLR 387, at 405–06 *per* Mason CJ and Wilson J; 425–26 *per* Brennan J; 448–52 *per* Deane J. *Cf* in England, *Crabb v Arun District Council* [1976] Ch 179; [1975] 3 All ER 865. In *S & E Promotions v Tobin Brothers* (1994) 122 ALR 637, at 653, the Federal Court observed whilst they share much in common, common law and equitable estoppel are sepa-rate doctrines. Equity may require terms be imposed as a condition of relief whereas this will not be the case at common law. In *Burbery Mortgage Finance & Savings Ltd v Hindsbank Holdings Ltd* [1989] 1 NZLR 356, at 359 *per* Cooke P, at 361 *per* Richardson J, at 364 *per* McMullin J, the Court of Appeal considered that promissory estoppel was not limited to dealings between the parties who have a prior legal relationship.

67   *Taylors Fashions Ltd v Liverpool Victoria Trustees Co Ltd* [1981] 2 WLR 576, at 593; [1981] 1 All ER 897, at 915–16 *per* Oliver J, and further, *Habib Bank Ltd v Habib Bank AG Zurich* [1981] 1 WLR 1265, at 1285; [1981] 2 All ER 650, at 666 *per* Oliver LJ.

68   *Crabb v Arun District Council* [1976] Ch 179, at 188; [1975] 3 All ER 865, at 872 *per* Lord Denning MR and further, Brennan J in *Walton Stores Ltd v Maher* (1987–88) 164 CLR 387, at 423.

69   *Low v Bouverie* [1891] 3 Ch 82, at 106; *Woodhouse AC Israel Cocoa Ltd SA v Nigerian Produce Marketing Co Ltd* [1971] 2 QB 23; [1972] 2 All ER 271; *Spiro v Lintern* [1973] 1 WLR 1002; [1973] 3 All ER 319; *NB Hunt & Sons Ltd v Maori Trustee* [1986] 2 NZLR 641, at 655; *General Bills v 'Betty Ott'* [1992] 1 NZLR 655.

position may be presumed and the plea will fail.[70] In order to constitute an equitable estoppel, it is essential that the party who induces an expectation intends or knows that the other party will act in reliance on what has been said or done.[71] If knowledge or intention is not established by the party asserting estoppel, it will not be unconscionable for the other party to a transaction to disavow an expectation that his or her conduct may have unwittingly created. In some circumstances, considered below, an obligation to speak out may found an estoppel if a party is misled by the other's silence and breach of duty.[72]

(b) Proprietary estoppel

In *Dillwyn v Llewelyn*,[73] a father made an incomplete gift to his son of a parcel of land and subsequently approved his son erecting a building on the land in the belief, of which his father was well aware, that he would obtain title. It was held that it was unconscionable for the father not to fulfil the expectation of title in reliance on which the son had expended money. The equity was satisfied by the father fulfilling his son's expectation and securing title for him. In *Ramsden v Dyson*,[74] the issue was whether a court would assist a tenant at will to secure a lease where he had built on the defendant's land in the belief, allegedly encouraged by his landlord, that he would be entitled to a long lease. The House of Lords held that the landowner had not encouraged such an expectation and hence the claim to a lease failed. Lord Kingsdown, however, in his dissenting judgment, expressed the principle of law applicable to the case as:[75]

> If a man, under a verbal agreement with a landlord for a certain interest in land, or, what amounts to the same thing, under an expectation, created or encouraged by the landlord, that he shall

---

70 *Cooke v Eshelby* (1877) 12 App Cas 271; *Colonial Bank v Cady and Williams* (1890) 15 App Cas 267; *London Joint Stock Bank v Simmons* [1892] AC 201; *Bloomentahal v Ford* [1897] AC 156; *NB Hunt & Sons Ltd v Maori Trustee* [1986] 2 NZLR 641, at 656–57. Richardson J observed, citing Spenser Bower, GS, and Sir AH, Turner, *Estoppel by Representation*, 3rd edn, 1977, p 133, Butterworths, London, that the cases have exhibited a marked and growing reluctance to extend the principle in question in commercial cases. *Cf Standard Chartered Bank of Australia Ltd v Bank of China* (1991) 23 NSWLR 144 and text to fn 100.

71 *Walton Stores Ltd v Maher* (1987–88) 164 CLR 387, at 406–07 *per* Mason CJ and Wilson J, at 428–29 *per* Brennan J, at 442–43 *per* Deane J, at 463 *per* Gaudron J; *Milchas Investments Ltd v Larkin* (1989) 96 FLR 464, at 474; *S & E Promotions v Tobin Brothers* (1994) 122 ALR 637.

72 See discussion in text to fn 83.

73 (1862) 4 De GF & J 517; [1862] 45 ER 1285; considered by Kitto J in *Olsson v Dyson* (1969) 120 CLR 365 to be a case founded on unconscionable behaviour, an interpretation which was adopted by Brennan J in *Waltons Stores Ltd v Maher* (1987–88) 164 CLR 387, at 419. Applied *Raffaele v Raffaele* [1962] WAR 29.

74 (1866) LR 1 HL 129. Applied *Wood v Browne* (1984) 2 Qd R 593; *Riches v Hogben* (1985) 2 Qd R 292.

75 *Ibid*, at 170.

have a certain interest takes possession of the land, with the consent of the landlord, and upon the faith of such a promise or expectation, with the knowledge of the landlord and without objection by him, lays out money upon the land, a court of equity will compel the landlord to give effect to such promise or expectation.

This principle, which came to be known as proprietary estoppel, was adopted by the Privy Council in *Plimmer v Wellington Corporation.*[76] In that case, a landowner requested Plimmer to effect improvements to a jetty but subsequently attempted to revoke his licence and prevent him from using it. The Privy Council held that the actions of the landowner were unjust and he was estopped from denying Plimmer's interest. As a consequence, Plimmer had a sufficient interest to claim compensation under the relevant confiscation statute for the loss of its use. In *Inwards v Baker,*[77] proprietary estoppel was invoked by the court of Appeal to protect the interest of a son who had built a bungalow on his father's property after he had been encouraged by his father to believe that he would be entitled to live there for his lifetime or however long he wished. His father, however, made no provision for him under his will and the trustees commenced proceedings for possession of the bungalow. The court held that he was entitled to remain in the house as long as he liked. Following *Dillwyn v Llewelyn, Ramsden v Dyson* and *Plimmer v Wellington Corporation,* Lord Denning MR observed that the equity the father had created would bind any purchaser with notice as well as successors in title. In the opinion of Lord Denning MR:[78]

It is an equity well recognised in law. It arises from the expenditure of money by a person in actual occupation of land when he is led to believe that as the result of the expenditure, he will be allowed to remain there. It is for the court to say in what way the equity can be satisfied. I am quite clear in this case it can be satisfied by holding that the defendant can remain there as long as he desires to as his home.

In *Pascoe v Turner,*[79] the Court of Appeal held that a woman, who had remained in the house of her former lover on the assurance that the house would be hers and with his knowledge and encouragement spent

---

76 (1884) 9 App Cas 699.

77 [1965] 2 QB 29. Further, see *Chalmers v Pardoe* [1963] 1 WLR 677; [1963] 3 All ER 552 (PC); *Silovi Pty Ltd v Barbaro* (1988) 13 NSWLR 466; *Kintominas v Department of Social Security* (1993) 103 ALR 82.

78 *Ibid,* at 37. In an earlier New Zealand case of *Re Whitehead* [1948] NZLR 1066, a son who had laboured and expended money on a cottage in the expectation, encouraged by his father, that he would be entitled to the cottage was held to be entitled to a lien for the amount of his expenditure and labour. To similar effect, see *Hamilton v Geraghty* (1901) 1 NSWSR (Eq) 81. In *Stratulatos v Stratulatos* [1988] 2 NZLR 424, the plaintiff was allowed reimbursement for expenditure and effort and an amount for the increase in capital growth of the property in question. Also, *Van den Berg v Giles* [1979] 2 NZLR 111.

79 [1979] 2 All ER 944.

part of her savings on improvements, was entitled to the property and could not be evicted. The court considered that the plaintiff had manifested a ruthless determination to evict her and her quiet enjoyment could only be assured if title was vested in her rather than her being awarded a mere licence to occupy for the rest of her life.

(c) Silence and estoppel

Where a person spends money on the property of another in the mistaken belief that it was his or her own or under a mistaken expectation of gaining an interest in the land, no estoppel will arise by virtue of the fact that the landlord permitted improvements to be carried out on his or her land, unless the mistake was known to the landowner.[80] Thus, in *Willmot v Barber*,[81] a landowner was not estopped from refusing his consent to the assignment when it was accepted by the court that, at the time the improvements were effected by the plaintiff, he was unaware of his right to object to an assignment of a lease. The court also considered that there was no evidence that the landowner was aware that the plaintiff had entered into possession under a sub-lease and had spent money in the allegedly mistaken belief that he would be able to purchase the lessee's interest without the consent of the landowner. In *Taylors Fashions v Liverpool Victoria Trustees Co*,[82] Oliver J considered that, in the absence of a duty to speak, protest or interfere, which could not arise in the absence of knowledge or at least a suspicion of the true

---

80 See *Ramsden v Dyson* (1866) LR 1 HL 129, at 140–41 *per* Lord Cranworth LC. *Willmott v Barber* (1880) 15 Ch D 96, at 105 *per* Fry J.

81 *Idem.* Further, see *Armstrong v Sheppard & Short Ltd* [1959] 2 QB 384; [1959] 2 All ER 651 where a landowner did not object to drains being placed on his land because he did not know they were over his property. Also, *Svenson v Payne* (1945) 71 CLR 531, where a remainderman did not protest at a lease by a tenant for life because he believed that he had no right to challenge.

82 [1982] QB 133; [1981] 1 All ER 897. For a New Zealand illustration of a proprietary estoppel arising from the breach of a lessor's obligation to speak out when it ought to have appreciated that the lessee was expending money on refurbishing the premises in the belief that it could expect a new lease, see *Andrews v Colonial Mutual Life Assurance Society Ltd* [1982] 2 NZLR 556, at 569–70; further, *S & E Promotions Pty Ltd v Tobin Brothers* (1994) 122 ALR 637, where the silence of a sub-lessor concerning the renewal of a lease led the sub-lessee not to comply with the formalities required for the exercise of the option, and an estoppel disentitled the sub-lessor from denying the sub-lessee a further term. Cf *W & R Jack Ltd v Fifield* [1996] 2 NZLR 105, where a claim of estoppel was rejected on the basis that the lessor had no duty to inform the lessee that a notice relating to a rent renewal assessment was out of time.

position, no estoppel could arise.[83] Cases of this kind require close scrutiny of the evidence to ensure that there has been no sharp practice or unconscionable dealing. An Australian case in point is *Grundt v Great Boulder Pty Gold Mines Ltd*.[84] There, a gold mining company had contracted with miners permitting them a tribute in a certain area of a mine owned by the company in exchange for which, on delivery of the ore, they would be remunerated according to terms set out in their agreement. The miners obtained ore from an area of the mine outside the agreed limits. The company was aware of the situation but elected to allow them to continue working the mine and furnished assistance in the form of plant and machinery. The company later unsuccessfully claimed to recover moneys it had paid over to the miners for their work in mining ore from this area. The High Court held that, even though the miners were trespassers, the company was estopped from claiming restitution because it had failed to take steps to stop the mining and had given active encouragement to the miners to work.[85]

(d) Estoppel and an ineffective contractual transaction

The principle that a person cannot knowingly stand by and allow another to act to his or her detriment in the mistaken belief that he or she will gain some advantage from doing so has been applied in a wider context than the traditional proprietary estoppel or land owning cases. Thus, where a party is aware that another has performed work for his or her benefit under a mistaken assumption that the parties have reached agreement and fails to take steps to disabuse that party of his or her error before the work is carried out, an estoppel may render an otherwise ineffective transaction effective. In Australia, this issue was consid-

---

83   In *Walton Stores (Interstate) Ltd v Maher* (1987–88) 164 CLR 387, at 423, Brennan J appeared to require actual knowledge as a pre-condition of a duty to speak. Further, Mason CJ and Wilson J at 406–07 and Deane J at 453 to similar effect. See also, *Milchas v Investment Pty Ltd v Larkin* (1989) 96 FLR 464, at 474 *per* Young J. However, Gaudron J in *Walton Stores, ibid*, at 462 spoke of knowledge in terms that Walton Stores ought to have been aware that there was a real possibility or likelihood that the respondents had commenced work in the reasonable expectation that exchange would take place. Imprudence was suggested by Gaudron J as a sufficient basis to sustain an estoppel if it were a proximate cause of the other party acting to his or her detriment. This issue was further considered in *S & E Promotions Pty Ltd v Tobin Brothers* (1992) 122 ALR 637, at 652–54, where an estoppel was found because the sub-lessor ought, in the circumstances, to have been aware that the sub-lessee was labouring under a misapprehension that the sub-lessor would not rely on the strict formalities being adhered to in relation to the exercise of an option to renew. In *Panchaud Feres SA v General Grain Co* [1970] 1 Lloyd's Rep 53, at 54, Winn LJ expressed the court's reluctance to introduce constructive notice into commercial transactions.

84   (1937) 59 CLR 641. Further, see *Thompson Palmer* (1933) 49 CLR 507.

85   *Ibid*, at 678–81 *per* Dixon J.

ered by the High Court in *Walton Stores (Interstate) Ltd v Maher*.[86] Walton Stores and Maher had entered into negotiations for a contract in which Maher was to carry out demolition works and construct new premises which the latter was to lease. Maher indicated to Walton Stores that there was urgency in the finalisation of the terms of the lease since, in order for construction to be completed within the period desired by Walton Stores, supplies had to be ordered. Further, Maher indicated that he wanted the transaction finalised by an exchange of contracts before demolishing the building and proceeding to construct the new premises. It would appear from the communications between the parties' solicitors that there had been verbal agreement on the terms of the lease. Maher sent an executed lease by way of exchange to the company's solicitor and then commenced to demolish the building in accordance with their agreement. About a week later, Walton Stores had second thoughts about the transaction and, having been told by its solicitor that it was not bound to proceed unless it completed the exchange of an executed lease, told its solicitor to 'go slow'. Shortly after this, Walton Stores became aware that demolition was proceeding. Some weeks passed before Walton Stores informed Maher that it did not want to proceed with the work. By this time, Maher had constructed about 40% of the new building. Walton Stores contended that it was not bound to proceed with the agreement because no agreement had been concluded. The High Court thought otherwise. It was held that, although no binding agreement had been concluded, the actions of Walton Stores in not proceeding to inform Maher that it might not proceed to completion after it became aware that Maher had started to demolish the existing building had led Maher to believe incorrectly that a contract had been concluded. Thus, Walton Stores were estopped from denying the existence of an agreement. Deane J observed:[87]

> Waltons, knowing the mistake which Maher laboured under, refrained from correcting [them] when it was [its] duty to do so. Its silence was deliberate and intended to produce the effect which it in fact produced – namely, the leaving of the respondents in

---

86 (1987–88) 164 CLR 387. See further, *West v Commercial Bank of Australia Ltd* (1936) 55 CLR 315, where the failure to inform his bank as to the circumstances surrounding the irregular indorsement of cheques and the improper use of them by his son constituted an estoppel and precluded the owner from claiming the proceeds of the cheque from his bank which had honoured the cheques. Also, *Austotel Pty Ltd v Franklins Self-serve Pty Ltd* (1989) 16 NSWLR 582; *S & E Promotions Pty Ltd v Tobin Brothers* (1994) 122 ALR 639. In *Silovi Pty Ltd v Barbaro* (1988) 13 NSWLR 466, an estoppel was held to protect the rights of an unregistered leaseholder where the landlord vendor and the purchaser had unconscionably conspired to defeat the leaseholder's interest.

87 *Ibid*, at 444, adopting the terminology of Dixon J in *Thompson v Palmer* (1933) 49 CLR 507, at 547, which was subsequently repeated in *Grundt v Great Boulder Pty Gold Mines Ltd* (1937) 59 CLR 641, at 676.

ignorance of the true facts so that no action might be taken by them
to withdraw from the negotiated arrangement ...

It is useful to compare *Walton Stores* with an earlier decision of the
Privy Council in *AG of Hong Kong v Humphreys Estates Ltd*.[88] The Hong
Kong government and Humphreys agreed in principle but subject to
contract, that the government would grant the latter a Crown lease of
government property with the right to develop it in exchange for 83 flats
forming part of Humphrey's property. It was agreed that terms could be
varied and there was to be no binding agreement until the documents
necessary to give legal effect to the transaction were executed and registered. Both parties proceeded upon the expectation that an agreement
would be finalised. The government proceeded to occupy the flats and
refurbish them for senior civil servants whose existing residences were
sold. Humphreys paid the government the difference between the
Crown land and the value of the flats. The government granted
Humphreys a licence to enter and demolish existing buildings on the
Crown land with a view to redevelopment, but this licence was
expressed to be revocable at any time. Subsequently, after all the necessary documentation had been drawn up and terms agreed upon,
Humphreys declined to proceed. When the government contested
Humphreys withdrawal, the latter successfully sought a declaration
that it was entitled to possession of the flats. The government counter-
claimed alleging that Humphreys was estopped from denying the
agreement. The trial judge held that Humphreys was entitled to possession and dismissed the counterclaim. The government's appeal was dismissed in the Court of Appeal of Hong Kong and in the Privy Council.
In giving the advice of the Board, Lord Templeman considered that
Humphreys had not created or encouraged a belief or expectation on
the part of the government that it would not withdraw from the agreement. The government proceeded in the confident expectation that
Humphreys would not withdraw; but at no time had Humphreys
encouraged or allowed the government to think that it would not withdraw. Humphreys had continued to negotiate the provisions of the
agreement which had yet to be executed. In these circumstances, the
government had chosen to commence work and elected to continue on
terms that either party might suffer a change of heart and withdraw.
Unlike *Walton Stores*, there was no underhand or surreptitious dealing
on the part of Humphreys from which an estoppel could be inferred,
and it was not suggested that it had concealed its true intentions so as to
mislead the government as Walton Stores were found to have done. It
was simply a case where the government took a risk that Humphreys

---

88 [1987] 1 AC 114; [1987] 2 All ER 387. Considered in *Walton Stores (Interstate) Ltd v
Maher* (1987–88) 164 CLR 387, at 405–06 *per* Mason CJ and Wilson J; at 421–23 *per*
Brennan J.

would not resile from their arrangement and it could not complain when Humphreys took advantage of the understanding it had reached with the government in its pre-contractual negotiations and did so.[89]

(e) Estoppel and mutual mistake as to an underlying assumption of a contractual relationship

In *Taylors Fashions Ltd v Liverpool Victoria Trustees Co Ltd*,[90] Oliver J was asked to determine whether, in order to found an estoppel, the party alleged to be estopped had to be aware that the other was labouring under a misapprehension as to the true state of affairs. Oliver J considered that, although knowledge was a factor in cases of passive acquiescence where a duty to speak out might arise on proof of knowledge that an improver was labouring under a mistake, this was not so where the estoppel was based on an actual representation. Knowledge was merely one of the relevant matters for a court to consider.[91] This meant that the defendant landlord, Liverpool, was estopped from denying an option to lease to a company, Old & Campbell Ltd where, at the time of entering into the lease, the landlord had represented to Old & Campbell that the option was valid although, unknown to the landlord, it was invalid because it had not been registered. Both parties were labouring under the same misapprehension that a valid option existed. In addition, Liverpool had encouraged Old & Campbell to incur expenditure and alter its position irrevocably by taking additional premises on the faith of the supposition that the lease was valid. In relation to the first plaintiff, Taylor Fashions, however, it was held that, although it had also spent money on improvements, Liverpool had done nothing to encourage it to alter its position in the mistaken belief that the option of renewal in its lease was valid. Accordingly, its claim to restitution failed.

Shortly after Taylors Fashions was decided, Robert Goff J, in *Amalgamated Investment & Property Co Ltd v Texas Commerce International Bank Ltd*,[92] considered a similar issue in relation to a claim commenced by the Texas bank to enforce a liability under a guarantee which Amalgamated had entered into purportedly guaranteeing loans made by the bank through a Nassau subsidiary to a subsidiary of Amalgamated in the Bahamas. Although both parties had acted in the mistaken belief that the guarantee was binding and in its dealings Amalgamated had encouraged the bank to believe that this was so, on the liquidation of Amalgamated, the liquidator claimed that the bank could not enforce

---

89 See the discussion of this case by Brennan J in *Walton Stores (Interstate) Ltd v Maher*, *ibid*, at 422–23, and further, see *Sustar Print Pty Ltd v Cosmo* (1995) 2 Qd R 214.

90 [1982] QB 133; [1981] 1 All ER 897.

91 *Ibid*, at 152; 916.

92 [1982] QB 84; [1981] 1 All ER 923.

the guarantee since it did not include an advance through the Nassau subsidiary. Robert Goff J considered both parties had regulated their relationship on a mistaken assumption and that it would be unconscionable for Amalgamated to disavow its obligation in these circumstances. Robert Goff J observed that cases like *Old & Campbell v Liverpool Victoria Trustees Co Ltd* provided an illustration of the way in which estoppel could render effective an otherwise ineffective transaction.[93] The Court of Appeal[94] upheld the judgment of Robert Goff J, with Lord Denning MR[95] adopting the *dictum* of Dixon J in *Grundt v Great Boulder Gold Mines Ltd*[96] that the parties had adopted a 'conventional' basis for the regulation of their business. In *Cadorange v Tanga Holdings,*[97] Young J in the Supreme Court of New South Wales adopted a similar approach when allowing Tanga an equitable lien over land owned by Cadorange, a related company which was in liquidation. Tanga had purchased land from Cadorange and had improved it in the mutual belief that it would be leased back to Cadorange which instead went into liquidation. The sale to Tanga was held to be a transaction that was ineffective against the liquidator. Young J considered, nevertheless, that it would be unconscionable to deny Tanga an equitable lien over the property for the improvements because the expenditure had been made pursuant to an inter-company transaction which, as a result of the companies being under common control, had engendered a common expectation that a contract would in due course be concluded.

(f) The necessity for a causal connection between the plaintiff's detriment and the defendant's actions

In order to substantiate a plea of estoppel so as to render an otherwise ineffective transaction effective, the party claiming estoppel must estab-

---

93 *Ibid,* 107; 938.

94 [1981] 3 WLR 565; [1981] 3 All ER 577. This approach was approved by the High Court of Australia in *Con-Stan Industries of Australia Pty Ltd v Norwich Winterthur Insurance Australia Ltd* (1986) 160 CLR 226, at 244–46. In *Queensland Independent Wholesalers Ltd v Coutts Townsville Pty Ltd* (1989) 2 Qd R 40, McPherson J doubted whether estoppel by convention could apply, to add to or vary a written agreement.

95 *Ibid,* at 574; 584. Estoppel by convention was applied by the Court of Appeal in *Hiscox v Outhwaite (No 1)* [1991] 3 All ER 124. *Cf Keen v Holland* [1984] 1 WLR 251; 1 All ER 75, where its application in the context of contracting out of protective legislation relating to a lease was rejected. Further, see *Hexagon Pty Ltd v Australia Broadcasting Commission* (1975) 7 ALR 233, at 253–56; *Coghlan v SH Lock (Aust) Ltd* (1985) 4 NSWLR 158; *Eslea Holdings Ltd v Butts* (1986) 6 NSWLR 175; *Newcrest Mining (WA) Ltd v Commonwealth* (1993–94) 119 ALR 423, at 499, where the Commonwealth was estopped by convention from denying the validity of certain transfers of leases, the subject of litigation. Further, see *National Westminster Finance NZ v National Bank of NZ* [1996] 1 NZLR 548; *Denning v Tri-Star Customs and Forwarding Ltd* [1996] 3 NZLR 630.

96 (1937) 59 CLR 641.

97 (1990) 20 NSWLR 26, at 40.

lish that he or she was misled and acted to his or her detriment as a result of the other party's representation or conduct. In *Taylors Fashions Ltd v Liverpool Victoria Trustees Co Ltd*,[98] a further reason for Taylors Fashions failing in its claim was that the court did not think that Taylors had effected improvements as a result of representations made by the landlord as to the validity of the option to renew but had done so to better serve its own interests on the basis that the existing lease had several years to run. In *Winterton Constructions Pty Ltd v Hambros Australia*,[99] estoppel failed where Hambros, a merchant bank, had a financing arrangement with a property developer but had declined to advance further funds to enable the plaintiff, a builder, to be paid final progress payments after the development was completed. The plaintiff claimed that Hambros encouraged the developer to continue to proceed to completion despite its knowledge that the developer was insolvent with the result that the bank's security over the development was enhanced. As a consequence, it was claimed that Hambros was estopped from denying the developer access to funds for the final progress payments. Hill J considered, however, that there was no evidence that Hambros' conduct had encouraged Winterton to complete the contract and therefore a plea of estoppel was unsuccessful. Where a false representation has been made, Giles J in *Standard Chartered Bank Aust Ltd v Bank of China*,[100] observed that in determining whether a plea of estoppel should be defeated, account should be taken of a representee's actual knowledge of the falsity of a representation and that estoppel should not be defeated by constructive knowledge or awareness of facts which ought to place a reasonable person on inquiry.

(g) Detriment

In order to found an estoppel, detriment must be established. In *Greasley v Cooke*,[101] the Court of Appeal held that where a representation was intended to influence the plaintiff to adopt a certain course of action, there was a presumption that she did so act. In circumstances of this kind, the court held that the onus of rebutting the presumption that a person did rely and act upon the representation to his or her detriment was imposed on the

---

98 [1982] QB 133; [1981] 1 All ER 897.

99 (1992) 111 ALR 649. In New Zealand, in *Avondale Printers & Stationers Ltd v Haggie* [1979] 2 NZLR 124, a claim to proprietary estoppel failed on the ground that the plaintiff did not act on the basis of any representation made by the defendant. In *Dinyarrak Investments Pty Ltd v Amoco Australia Ltd* (1982–83) 45 ALR 214, estoppel failed in relation to the renewal of a franchise arrangement where there was an absence of evidence of significant expenditure being attributable to misleading conduct of the franchisor. Also see, *Furness v Adrium Industries Ltd* (1996) 1 VR 668.

100 (1991) 23 NSWLR 164. See further fn 70.

101 [1980] 3 All ER 710. Further, see *Brikom Investments Ltd v Carr* [1979] QB 467, at 482–83; [1979] 2 All ER 753, at 759.

party attempting to avoid estoppel. In *Newbon v City Mutual Life Assurance Society Ltd*,[102] the High Court of Australia considered that any general presumptive connection between inaction and a belief in a state of facts must depend upon probabilities which arise from the common course of affairs.[103] Detriment is not confined to financial loss. In *Commonwealth of Australia v Verwayen*,[104] several of the justices of the High Court of Australia[105] agreed that detriment could not be measured in financial terms alone. The strain or distress of embarking on litigation was a factor which could be taken into consideration as detriment and was an additional feature to be considered on the issue of whether the Commonwealth in that case was estopped from pleading a limitation period which it assured the plaintiff it would not rely upon prior to the commencement of the action.

(h) The measure of relief

Where estoppel is relied upon, the appropriate measure of relief is the minimum necessary to do justice to the person successfully claiming the estoppel.[106] The extent of what constitutes minimum justice will vary. In *Pascoe v Turner*,[107] an order perfecting a gift of a house from the plaintiff to the defendant was considered necessary in order to give the defendant quiet possession from the plaintiff's determined attempts to evict her. In *Inwards v Baker*,[108] an order was made giving the plaintiff a right to occupy the house he had lived in on his father's property for the rest of his life. In *Re Whitehead*,[109] the court imposed a lien for the cost of materials and labour associated with the plaintiff's construction of a cottage on

---

102 (1935) 52 CLR 723.

103 *Ibid*, at 735, *per* Rich, Dixon Evatt JJ.

104 (1990) 170 CLR 394. Further, see *Commonwealth v Clark* [1994] 2 VR 333.

105 *Ibid*, at 448–49 *per* Deane J; at 461 *per* Dawson J; at 487 *per* Gaudron J; at 417 *per* Mason CJ and at 504 *per* McHugh J appeared to suggest that detriment could involve matters other than financial considerations but required proof of additional detriment to be demonstrated.

106 *Crabb v Arun District Council* [1976] Ch 179, at 198; [1975] 3 All ER 865, at 880 *per* Scarman LJ; *Pascoe v Turner* [1979] 2 All ER 945, at 950 *per* Cumming Bruce LJ; *Commonwealth of Australia v Verwayen* (1990) 170 CLR 394, at 411 *per* Mason CJ, at 429 *per* Brennan J, at 501 *per* McHugh J.

107 [1979] 2 All ER 944.

108 [1965] 2 QB 29.

109 [1948] NZLR 1066. See *Chalmers v Pardoe* [1963] 1 WLR 677; [1963] 3 All ER 552, where a lien for the reimbursement of expenditure incurred at the request of another was denied because the imposition of a lien would have infringed an applicable statutory proscription. The Privy Council queried whether a *quantum meruit* claim for reimbursement for the improvements would have been more successful if pleaded. Compensation was considered an available remedy to prevent unconscionable dealing in New Zealand in *Gillies v Keogh* [1989] 2 NZLR 327, at 332, and *Cossey v Bach* [1992] 3 NZLR 612, at 632.

his father's land. In *Stratulatos v Stratulatos*,[110] in addition to reimbursement of expenditure and effort, the plaintiff was permitted a proportional share in the capital gain of the property on which she and her deceased husband had been encouraged to spend a considerable sum of money and effort by her mother-in-law prior to her husband's death. In other cases, relief has involved the perfecting of an incomplete gift,[111] the granting of a right of access,[112] the recognition of a right of way or mutual licence over neighbouring property or by the performance of a promise or assurance so that an otherwise ineffective transaction can be perfected.[113]

The restitutionary importance of a resulting or constructive trust in the context of ineffective transactions or relationships

A resulting or constructive trust may arise when a person confers a benefit on another for a purpose that fails to materialise. Underlying both the resulting and constructive trust is the sentiment that it is unconscionable to allow a person to retain a benefit which has been conferred conditionally upon a shared expectation or for a shared purpose which has failed. In relation to the resulting trust, a court will attempt to ascertain the intention of the relevant parties as to the nature and extent of any beneficial interests in property from the evidence that is available. In the absence of intention, certain presumptions will operate to identify the beneficial interests in property. A court may impose a constructive trust where it would be unconscionable for a person to deny another's interest in property. In this context, the doctrine of estoppel may provide a foundation for the imposition of a constructive trust where a party denying another an interest in property is guilty of unconscientious behaviour. In recent years, the resulting trust has been closely involved with the constructive trust in property disputes arising out of marriage or, more commonly, *de facto* marriages. Before proceeding to consider this important topic, however, it is necessary to consider the application of the resulting trust and the constructive trust and their individual operation more generally.

---

110 [1988] 2 NZLR 424.

111 *Dillwyn and Llewelyn* (1862) 4 De GF & J 517; [1862] 45 ER 1285.

112 *Crabb v Arun District Council* [1976] Ch 179; [1975] 3 All ER 865.

113 *Dillwyn and Llewelyn* (1862) 4 De GF & J 517; [1862] 45 ER 1285; *Old & Campbell Ltd v Liverpool Victoria Trustees Co Ltd* [1982] QB 133; [1981] 1 All ER 897; *Amalgamated Investment & Property Co Ltd v Texas Commerce International Bank Ltd* [1982] QB 84; [1981] 1 All ER 923; [1981] 3 WLR 565; [1981] 3 All ER 577 (CA); *Walton Stores (Interstate) Ltd v Maher* (1987–88) 164 CLR 387.

The resulting trust as a remedy for preventing unjust enrichment

(a) Money paid for a particular purpose which fails

Where money has been paid for a particular purpose which fails, a resulting trust may arise so that the money that remains is held on trust for the donor. For example, the imposition of a resulting trust in relation to the disposal of moneys consequent upon the winding up of a non-charitable fund was considered by Goff J in *Re West Sussex Constabulary Fund Trusts*.[114] In that case, an issue for consideration was whether, on the winding up of the fund, moneys raised by entertainments, raffles and sweepstakes and proceeds were *bona vacantia*. It was held that, there being an intention on the part of each donor to part with his or her money irrevocably, the proceeds were to be applied in this way. However, moneys representing donations and legacies were held on resulting trust for those who had made the donations or granted the legacies because it was considered that those had been given for a particular purpose which had failed on the winding up of the fund.[115] The same principle will apply in the case of a charitable donation or legacy which is given by a named donor rather than one who is anonymous. A donation or legacy which fails in these circumstances will not be regarded as a general charitable gift and be able to be applied *cy-pres*.[116] In *Westdeutsche Landesbank Girozentrale v Islington LBC*,[117] the House of Lords held that a payment made pursuant to an interest swap contract that was *ultra vires* the payee was not held on resulting trust for the payer because the payer had intended to part with the money pursuant to the transaction and this rebutted any presumption of resulting trust. The plaintiff was limited to a personal remedy of restitution for moneys had and received.

(b) The *Quistclose* principle

When money has been paid for a purpose which fails to eventuate, a resulting trust may arise in favour of the lender, as occurred in *Barclays Bank Ltd v Quistclose Investments Ltd*.[118] Quistclose agreed to lend Rolls Razor a large sum of money to enable it to pay a dividend. Rolls Razor was in financial difficulties and its bank, Barclays, had declined to advance it further credit whilst its overdraft exceeded its limit. The bank was informed by Rolls Razor that the advance had been made for a

---

114 [1970] 1 All ER 544.

115 Following *Re Abbott Fund Trusts* [1900] 2 Ch 326.

116 *Ulverston & District New Hospital Building Fund* [1956] Ch 622; [1956] 3 All ER 164.

117 [1996] 2 WLR 802; [1996] 2 All ER 961. Discussed further, pp 32–28.

118 [1970] AC 567; [1968] 3 All ER 651.

particular purpose and a cheque was credited and paid to a particular account. Rolls Razor subsequently went into voluntary liquidation and the bank applied the loan in reduction of its debt. It was held by the House of Lords that the loan moneys were held on trust for Quistclose because it was clear that the moneys were never intended by the lender to become part of the assets of Rolls Razor. It could be clearly inferred that the lender intended to create a secondary trust in its favour if the primary trust could not be effected.[119] Subsequently, *Quistclose* was applied in *Carreras Rothmans Ltd v Freeman Mathews Treasure Ltd*.[120] There a cigarette manufacturer was concerned that the advertising agency it employed would not be able to pay the debts incurred on its behalf with its production and media advertisers. As a result, prior to the agency going into liquidation, it paid into a special account at the agency's bank, a sufficient sum to meet the debts as they fell due. Subsequently, the plaintiff commenced proceedings against the liquidator seeking an order that the moneys were held for a special purpose, and a further order that they be applied in reduction of the debts incurred on behalf of the plaintiff. It was held that the plaintiff had a right to compel the performance of the primary trust in favour of those creditors.

In Australia, *Quistclose Investments* has been approached cautiously. In *Re Associated Securities Ltd*,[121] it was held that a payment made pursuant to an offer to allot shares became part of the assets of the company available for the general creditors on liquidation, and there was, unlike *Quistclose*, nothing in the circumstances surrounding the payment that could be said to impress it with a trust. In *Re Miles*,[122] it was considered that *Quistclose* should be limited to resulting trusts arising from loans entered into for the purpose of the discharge of debts and did not apply in relation to other transactions. In *Re Australian Elizabethan Theatre*

---

119 *Ibid*, at 582; 656 *per* Lord Wilberforce.

120 [1985] 1 Ch 207; [1985] 1 All ER 155.

121 (1981) 1 NSWLR 742. The *Quistclose* approach was also rejected in *Austinel Investments Australia Ltd v Lam* (1990) 19 NSWLR 637 on the ground of an absence of intention to create a trust. In *Re Groom* (1977) 16 ALR 278, *Quistclose* was applied to moneys paid by a husband to the official receiver on the grounds that it was given as a composition for creditors. It was held that payment, in these circumstances, did not give the Commissioner of Taxation statutory priority since the payment was impressed with a trust. *Quistclose* was also applied in *Theiss Watkins White Ltd v Equiticorp Australia Ltd* (1991) 1 Qd R 82. In New Zealand, *Quistclose* was distinguished in *Security Bank Ltd* [1978] 1 NZLR 97 on the ground that the subject-matter, promissory notes and securities of the claim did not constitute a loan to the transferee. It was applied in rather doubtful circumstances in *Dines Construction Ltd v Perry Dines Corp Ltd* (1989) 4 NZCLC 298. For critical comment, see Maxton, J, 'Equity' [1990] *NZ Recent Law Rev* 89, at 95–96. In *Dines*, it is difficult to see how the letter accompanying the payment could be construed as creating a trust, since it purported to allow the transferee to use the funds interest free until conversion into shares at the appropriate time. See Rickett, C, 'Different Views on the Scope of the Quistclose Analysis' (1991) 107 LQR 608.

122 (1988–89) 85 ALR 216, at 221.

Trust,[123] it was considered that an unconditional donation to the Trust, expressed to be a preference for a nominated arts organisation, formed part of the Trust's assets and was insufficient to create a primary trust for the nominated organisations within the *Quistclose* principle.

In *Carreras*, it was held that if the primary trust is irrevocable, intended beneficiaries had enforceable rights.[124] This issue was considered further in New Zealand, in *General Communications v DFC*.[125] DFC, at the request of a customer, Video Workshop, had agreed to lend money to Video Workshop so that it could pay for supplies of video equipment by General Communications. It assured General Communications that payment would be made through Video Workshop's solicitors causing General Communications to depart from its original insistence that payment should be secured by letters of credit. Video Workshop was placed into receivership before General Communications were paid, and DFC sought and received from the solicitors repayment of the loan moneys which had not been distributed to General Communications. The Court of Appeal held that the assurance given by DFC concerning payment meant that the arrangement could not be conscionably revoked.[126] DFC became a constructive trustee of the funds held for the benefit of General Communications.

(c) Joint bank accounts

A resulting trust will arise where a person deposits money in a joint account with another and subsequently one of the parties dies. Although the intention of the depositor may be that the parties will be able to operate for their several enjoyment on the account for their lives, in the event of the death of the depositor any credit in the fund will be held on resulting trust for his or her estate.[127] If, however, the other party

---

123 (1991) 102 ALR 681.

124 Following the opinion of Megarry VC in *Re Northern Developments (Holdings) Ltd* (Unreported, 6 October, 1978). The issue of whether third parties have enforceable rights under the primary trust needs to be treated with caution, see Millet, P, 'The *Quistclose* trust; who can enforce it?' (1985) 101 LQR 269 considered by the Court of Appeal in *General Communications v DFC* [1990] 3 NZLR 406, at 432–33 *per* Hardie Boys J, and by Gummow J in *Re Australian Elizabethan Theatre Trust* (1991) 102 ALR 681, at 694–95.

125 [1990] 3 NZLR 406.

126 Compare *Trident General Insurance Co Ltd v McNiece Bros Pty Ltd* (1988) 165 CLR 107, at 124 *per* Mason CJ Wilson J, at 140 *per* Brennan J, at 145 *per* Deane J and at 172 *per* Toohey J, where it was suggested that estoppel might be invoked as a basis to enable a third party insured to sue under a contract of insurance and so circumvent the privity doctrine.

127 *Standing v Bowring* (1886) 31 Ch D 282, at 287; [1881–85] All ER 702, at 704 *per* Cotton LJ; *Tinsley v Milligan* [1994] 1 AC 340, at 371; [1993] 3 All ER 65, at 87 *per* Lord Browne-Wilkinson; *Russell v Scott* (1936) 55 CLR 440, at 451 *per* Dixon and Evatt JJ; *Golding v Hands* [1969] WAR 121.

establishes an intention that he or she should beneficially enjoy any credit in the account on the depositor's death, then the presumption that the depositor's estate enjoys the balance will be rebutted.[128] In some circumstances, a presumption of advancement may arise. Thus, where a father nominates his wife or children as joint account holders, a presumption of advancement arises so that the spouse or children will take the balance.[129] This is a rule of evidence and may be rebutted by circumstances that show a contrary intention.[130] A presumption of advancement does not operate to assist *de facto* wives[131] nor close family other than siblings.[132] Nor does it operate to assist a husband where his wife has contributed the funds to the joint account.[133]

(d) The resulting trust and its application to real and personal property

Where the parties have formally and in accordance with legal requirement expressly declared their respective interests, a court will have no jurisdiction to intervene and vary those interests.[134] However, in the absence of a valid declaration as to interest, the principles that apply in relation to money in joint accounts also apply to other property, namely personalty or realty.[135] Where a person purchases property in the name of another or in the name of himself and another jointly, the question whether the other person who provided none of the purchase money acquires a beneficial interest in the property will depend upon the intention of the parties. If a common intention can be inferred that both parties are to enjoy a beneficial interest in the property, then a court can give effect to this intention. However, where a common intention is not proven and there does not exist a relationship which gives rise to any

---

128 *Young v Sealey* [1949] 1 All ER 93; *Russell v Scott* (1936) 55 CLR 441; *Palmer v Bank of New South Wales* (1974–75) 133 CLR 150.

129 *Re Harrison* (1920) 90 LJ Ch 186; see *Golding v Hands* [1969] WAR 121.

130 *Marshal v Crutwell* (1875) LR 20 Eq 328.

131 *Napier v Public Trustee* (1980) 32 ALR 153; *Calverley v Green* (1984) 155 CLR 242.

132 *Russell v Scott* (1936) 55 CLR 440, at 451 *per* Dixon and Evatt JJ. It would seem also to apply to step children, see *Oliveri v Oliveri* (1996) 38 NSWLR 665, *cf Re Bulankoff* (1986) 1 Qd R 360. Further, see fn 136.

133 *Brophy v Brophy* (1974) 3 ACTR 57.

134 *Goodman v Gallant* [1986] 2 WLR 236; [1986] 1 All ER 311; *Turton v Turton* [1988] Ch 542; [1987] 2 All ER 641.

135 *Tinsley v Milligan* [1994] 1 AC 540, at 571; [1993] 3 All ER 65, at 87 *per* Lord Browne-Wilkinson.

presumption of advancement,[136] it will be presumed that the purchaser did not intend the other to have a share. If a common purpose can be inferred, this does not necessarily mean that beneficial interest ownership will be shared jointly,[137] although in some cases it may.[138] It will be for a court to decide, taking into account the respective contributions made by the parties, what interest each will have. Where no common intent can be inferred and no presumption of advancement arises, the property will be held beneficially for the purchaser under a resulting trust even though legal title is in the name of another.[139] If the property is purchased in unequal shares but placed in the names of the parties jointly, in the absence of a special relationship giving rise to a presumption of advancement or evidence of common intention to share equally, it will be presumed that the property is held by the purchasers in trust for themselves as tenants in common in the proportions in which they contributed to the purchase price.[140]

(e) Resulting trusts and domestic relationships

The principles stated above have particular relevance to matrimonial property cases and cases arising out of *de facto* marriages or relationships. Where a relationship ends, litigation commonly arises to resolve the division of assets acquired during the relationship. In the absence of legislation governing the division of matrimonial property on divorce, the resulting trust was seen as the appropriate means of resolving matrimonial property disputes by the House of Lords in *Pettitt v Pettitt*[141] and *Gissing v Gissing*.[142] Mindful of the fact that in many cases involving

---

136 For an application of the presumption in relation to father and daughters, *Charles Marshall Proprietary Limited v Grimsley* (1956) 95 CLR 353; *Wirth v Wirth* (1956) 98 CLR 228, where the presumption was extended to an intended wife. *Cf Scott v Pauly* (1917) 24 CLR 274, at 281–82, where Issacs J doubted whether there was a presumption of advancement between mother and daughter. In *Calverley v Green* (1984) 155 CLR 242, at 266–69, Deane J recognised that the presumption might need to be widened to meet modern conditions but agreed with Mason and Brennan J (with Gibbs CJ dissenting) that it should not apply to a *de facto* relationship. Note in *Gissing v Gissing* [1971] AC 886, at 907; [1970] 2 All ER 780, at 791. Lord Diplock was critical of the application of the presumption of advancement in matrimonial cases.

137 See May LJ in *Burns v Burns* [1984] Ch 317, at 345; [1984] 1 All ER 244, at 264.

138 As in *Bernard v Josephs* [1982] Ch 391; 3 All ER 162; *Hayward v Giordani* [1983] NZLR 140.

139 *Re Kerrigan, ex parte Jones* (1947) 47 SRNSW 76, at 83, and the discussion by Scheller JA in *Brysan v Bryant* (1992) 29 NSWLR 188, at 214–16.

140 *Block v Block* (1981) 180 CLR 390, at 397 *per* Gibbs CJ, Murphy, Aicken and Wilson JJ; *Calverley v Green* (1984) 56 ALR 483, at 485 *per* Gibbs CJ; *Robinson v Preston* (1858) 4 K & J 505, at 510; 70 ER 211, at 213; *Ingram v Ingram* [1941] VLR 95; *Pettitt v Pettitt* [1970] AC 777; [1969] 2 All ER 385; *Gissing v Gissing* [1971] AC 886; [1970] 2 All ER 780; *Tinsley v Milligan* [1994] 1 AC 540; [1993] 3 All ER 65.

141 [1970] AC 777; [1969] 2 All ER 385.

142 [1971] AC 886; [1970] 2 All ER 780.

matrimonial property it is difficult to infer any true intent, in *Pettitt*, Lord Reid and Lord Diplock observed that a court should be able to resolve the division of matrimonial property by imputing a fair and just solution.[143] A similar approach had been adopted earlier by Lord Denning MR,[144] however, a majority of the House of Lords in *Pettitt* would not support such a liberal approach preferring the more traditional approach of inferred intent and the resulting trust. In so far as matrimonial disputes were concerned, statutory reform was subsequently enacted in England allowing a court a wider jurisdiction to the recognition of spousal interests in property on the dissolution of marriage.[145] In the absence of legislation, *de facto* relationships continue to be governed by the general law.[146]

Two Australian cases illustrate the approach of courts to issues of this kind. In *Calverley v Green*,[147] the High Court divided a home on the basis of the parties' financial contributions to its acquisition despite the fact that the house was in the parties' joint names. The parties had been involved in a lengthy *de facto* marriage. The appellant had provided an amount of $9,000 and the balance was provided by a joint mortgage in the sum of $18,000. The property was ordered to be held in proportion to their contributions and not jointly. Thus, the partner who had provided the cash and half the balance derived from the mortgage commitment was entitled to a greater proportional share than the partner who had simply contributed to a half share of the mortgage. The court held that, in the absence of any subsequent common intention being inferred to share equally, the interests were to be determined at the time of the acquisition of the property and that later contributions by way of mortgage were not to be taken into account in assessing the extent of the beneficial interests, although they might give rise to a claim of contribution by one partner who had paid more than the other. No principle of advancement operated in this case because parties were unmarried. It

---

143 [1970] AC 777, at 795 *per* Lord Reid, 824–25, *per* Lord Diplock; [1969] 2 All ER 385, at 390 *per* Lord Reid, at 415–16 *per* Lord Diplock.

144 *Appleton v Appleton* [1965] 1 All ER 44, at 46. In *Pettitt v Pettitt, ibid*, at 824–25; 415 Lord Diplock was careful to distinguish his approach from that of Lord Denning MR but the distinction between an imputed intention and a division that was fair and just may be no more than a matter of expression.

145 Section 37 of the Matrimonial Proceedings and Property Act 1970, which related to substantial contributions by a spouse to the improvement of property entitling the court to recognise a beneficial interest in that spouse, and s 25(1)(f) of the Matrimonial Causes Act 1973, whereby contributions to the welfare of the family could be taken into consideration in making property orders in divorce proceedings.

146 In New South Wales, *de facto* marriages are governed by the De facto Relationships Act 1984. A court has power to make orders under s 20 which are just and equitable. See *Dwyer v Kaljo* (1992) 27 NSWLR 728; *Wallace v Stanford* (1994) 37 NSWLR 1; *Green v Robinson* (1995) 36 NSWLR 96; *Theodoropoullos v Theodosiou* (1995) 38 NSWLR 424.

147 (1984) 155 CLR 242, discussed by Gummow J in *Re Stevenson Nominees* (1987–88) 76 ALR 485, at 501; applied *National Australia Bank v Maher* [1995] 1 VR 318.

was also found that the property had been placed in the parties' joint names merely to satisfy the demands of the mortgagor.

Conversely, a common intention may displace the presumption that beneficial interests in property are held in accordance with the parties' direct financial contribution to the purchase price. In *Muschinski v Dodds*,[148] the High Court of Australia declined to find a resulting trust in favour of Muschinski who had paid for land out of the sale of her house. It was intended that her partner, Dodds, would pay the construction costs of a prefabricated house and restore a cottage for use by Muschinski as an arts and crafts centre with the balance being financed by bank loans for which both would be liable. After legal advice, the property was conveyed to them as tenants in common. Although some improvements were effected by Dodds, the erection of a house could not proceed before the parties separated. Muschinski had contributed $25,259.45 and Dodds $2,549.77 to the purchase and improvement of the property. Muschinski sought a declaration that Dodds held his half share in trust for her on a resulting trust. The High Court held that the transaction evidenced a common intention that each was to share equally in the property. Dodds was liable under the agreement of purchase to provide the purchase moneys, although, in fact, Muschinski paid the price and both intended to raise finance and pursue the arrangement. Further, legal effect had been given to their intentions. Muschinski was, however, permitted to recoup out of Dodd's share, a contribution towards satisfying her disproportionate share of the purchase price[149] or under a general principle which allowed the proportionate repayment of capital contribution to joint venturers on the failure of a joint venture.[150]

The principal difficulty for the courts in cases of this kind has been to identify the nature of contributions that are able to be taken into account as contributing to an inferred common intention that a party is to enjoy a beneficial interest in property even though there has been no direct contribution to the purchase price and thereby displace the presumption that property will be held in accordance with direct financial contributions to the purchase price. What weight should a court place on indirect financial contributions such as contributions made to the cost of running the household rather than contributions made directly for the acquisition of property? Should substantial improvements to property be considered a contribution to an asset? Should a court take into

---

148 (1986) 160 CLR 583. Considered by Gummow J in *Re Stevenson Nominees* (1987–88) 76 ALR 485, at 506. In *Cossey v Bach* [1992] 3 NZLR 612, at 627–28 Fisher J referred to *Muschinski v Dodds* when emphasising the importance of intention in overriding any division based on contribution.

149 *Ibid*, at 597–98 *per* Gibbs CJ.

150 *Ibid*, at 618–24 *per* Deane J, Mason J concurring.

account non-financial contributions such as the labour involved in running or organising the household freeing the other partner to earn an income and acquire assets? In answer to questions of this kind, the courts have cautiously recognised that substantial contributions made indirectly to the purchase price of a home and substantial outlay and labour associated with effecting improvements may be taken into account in determining whether a party should have a beneficial interest in a home that is held in the name of another.

In *Pettitt v Pettitt*,[151] the House of Lords held that a husband who had carried out certain decorative work and built a wardrobe in a cottage paid for by his wife and held in her name only was not entitled to any beneficial interest in the property. The improvements carried out were ephemeral only and there was no justification in inferring a common intention that the parties intended that the husband should acquire a beneficial interest by carrying out such work in his leisure time. In *Gissing v Gissing*,[152] the House of Lords held that a wife who had not expended money in the purchase or in discharging a mortgage over the family home was not entitled to any interest in the matrimonial home. Although she had spent some money on furniture and in improving the grounds, it was not established that either her efforts or earnings had influenced the husband's ability to discharge his financial liabilities in relation to the home. However, it was considered that there was no distinction between direct contributions towards the purchase of the matrimonial home and indirect contributions that assisted the reduction in any financial liability that was associated with the purchase, although the latter might be more difficult to assess in terms of an appropriate beneficial interest. Where, however, a spouse had made no contributions to the acquisition or discharge of liabilities on the house, the mere fact that she contributed to some of the expenses of the household was insufficient to justify an inference that the parties intended her to have a beneficial interest. Expenditure of this kind was regarded as no less consistent with an intention to share the daily costs of running the household.

In *Burns v Burns*,[153] the Court of Appeal emphasised that, in the case of unmarried couples, a partner who had not contributed to the purchase could not enjoy a beneficial interest unless the court could infer from the conduct of the couple down to the date of their separation that a common intention existed that the non-contributing partner was to have a beneficial interest. This depended on whether the partner claiming an interest had made a substantial financial contribution towards the

---

151 [1970] AC 777; [1969] 2 All ER 385.
152 [1971] AC 886; [1970] 2 All ER 780.
153 [1984] Ch 317; [1984] 1 All ER 244.

expenses of the household which could be related to the acquisition of the property. The court considered that this would occur where the financial contribution to the household expenses enabled the other to pay the mortgage instalments. The court did not, however, regard factors such as the parties' residence together for a lengthy period, the undertaking of domestic duties, or redecoration of the house and bringing up the children as sufficient to rebut the *prima facie* inference that the woman's partner had an exclusive beneficial interest in the house.[154] Conversely, in *Bernard v Josephs*,[155] the court had little difficulty in inferring a common intention to share equally where the parties had purchased a house in their joint names, had both contributed to the purchase price, were liable on the mortgage jointly and had pooled their incomes. Accordingly, the defendant's claim for a greater share on the ground that he had spent a further sum on improvements was disallowed. It was, however, recognised that, subject to the recognition of joint beneficial sharing, credits should be permitted for initial contributions and the cost of improvements.

In New Zealand, in *Hayward v Giordani*,[156] a common intention was found that a *de facto* husband should enjoy a half share in a house purchased by the other prior to the relationship where a substantial amount of work in improving a property had been performed by the husband prior to their living together. After some years of living together in the house, the woman died leaving the property under her will to her partner, Hayward. The document, however, had not been attested and could not operate as a will. Hayward claimed a half share in the property based on the substantial work he had done in renovating and upgrading the house and its grounds, his provision of his earnings to his *de facto* wife, and her expressed desire to have the property placed in their joint names. Cooke J considered that, since substantial capital contributions had been made to the acquisition of a property and a common intention of shared beneficial ownership could be inferred, the court could hold that a trust of a half share in favour of the plaintiff existed.[157] The fact that

---

154 For a precise formulation of the principles, see the judgment of May LJ, *ibid*, at 345; 264–65.

155 [1982] Ch 391; [1982] 3 All ER 162.

156 [1983] NZLR 140. *Cf Jansen v Jansen* [1965] 3 WLR 875; [1965] 3 All ER 363 and *Smith v Baker* [1970] 2 All ER 826, where significant labour content contributed in all the circumstances to an inference of common ownership. In *Pasi v Kamana* [1986] 1 NZLR 603, the Court of Appeal declined to infer a common intention to beneficially enjoy a home equally where the evidence did not establish that a woman in a *de facto* relationship for nearly 10 years had made a financial contribution to the home or that her contributions to the household expenditure had been any more than was necessary for her own support. Also see *Butler v Craine* (1986) VR 274, where an intention to share jointly was formed subsequent to the acquisition of the asset by one of the partners in a *de facto* relationship.

157 *Ibid*, at 143.

the plaintiff had not, during her lifetime, accepted her offer to place the property in their joint names was explained by the fact that this would involve cost and Hayward expected to pre-decease her.

(f) The nature of relief

In the absence of an expression of common intention as to the share or division of property,[158] the extent of a beneficial interest will be judged by the nature of the contributions, whether direct or indirect, that have been made to the acquisition of the property by the parties once a court is able to infer on the evidence that the parties intended that both should enjoy a beneficial interest. In some cases, the evidence may point to an equal division of the property. In other cases, involving indirect contributions, it may be more difficult to assess the appropriate beneficial interest, but, in such cases, it has been said that the courts should not lightly assume that justice is achieved by the principle that equity is equality but should attempt to arrive at a solution which approximates a true reflection of the parties' contributions.[159] Where it is possible to infer a common intention that a property will be shared jointly, or in some proportion other than that reflected in the contributions made to the property, as we have seen in *Muschinski v Dodds*[160] and *Bernard v Josephs*,[161] there may be a need to grant allowances or credits in order to ensure that a person is not unjustly enriched by a finding in his or her favour of joint ownership. It may also be appropriate for a court to make allowances for additional payments made by a party that benefit both or make deductions for benefits derived from his or her sole use of a property.[162]

The constructive trust as a remedy for preventing unjust enrichment in property disputes

(a) Generally

The constructive trust has become popular in recent years as a remedy to prevent a party unconscionably claiming an interest in property in domestic or family relationships, especially in cases involving *de facto* marriages. Resulting and constructive trusts have tended to be assimi-

---

158 See the discussion of Fisher J in *Cossey v Bach* [1992] 3 NZLR 612, at 628 on the importance of an expressed intention in overriding any division based on contribution.

159 *Gissing v Gissing* [1971] AC 886, at 905; [1970] 2 All ER 780, at 793 *per* Lord Diplock; *Burns v Burns* [1984] Ch 317, at 345; [1984] 1 All ER 254, at 265 *per* May LJ; *Hammond v Mitchell* [1992] 2 All ER 109, at 119.

160 (1986) 160 CLR 583.

161 [1982] 3 All ER 162.

162 See *Calverley v Green* (1984) 155 CLR 242, at 253 *per* Gibbs CJ, where a credit was allowed for additional mortgage payments made by a partner remaining in occupation of the home, and a deduction made for occupation rental for his sole use and enjoyment of the home after the parties had separated.

lated in cases relating to marriage or *de facto* relationships. In *Gissing v Gissing*,[163] for example, Lord Diplock remarked:[164]

> A resulting, implied or constructive trust – and it is unnecessary for present purposes to distinguish between these three classes of trust – is created by a transaction between trustee and the *cestui que trust* in connection with the acquisition by the trustee of a legal estate in land, whenever the trustees has so conducted himself that it would be inequitable to allow him to deny to the *cestui que trust* a beneficial interest in the land acquired. And he will be held to have conducted himself, if by his words or conduct, he has induced the *cestui que trust* to act to his own detriment in the reasonable belief that by so acting he was acquiring a beneficial interest in the land.

The constructive trust as a remedial device to prevent unconscionable gains will arise where there has been an agreement or understanding reached between parties which one party attempts to disavow in order to dishonestly acquire a benefit. An example is seen in *Bannister v Bannister*,[165] where the plaintiff attempted to evict a woman who had agreed to sell to him adjacent cottages on the condition that she be permitted to remain in one for life. The plaintiff, who was her brother-in-law, agreed but he subsequently argued that she was a mere tenant at will and issued her with a notice to quit. The Court of Appeal held that the oral undertaking given by the plaintiff created a life interest in the cottage in the defendant's favour determinable only on the defendant ceasing to live in the house. It was a fraud in equity for the plaintiff to attempt to take advantage of the fact that the understanding was not recorded in any written agreement or conveyance. Similarly, it is fraudulent for a party to seek to rely on the fact that a transaction is unenforceable because of an omission to record the transaction in a manner which satisfied the requirements of the Statute of Frauds.[166] The High Court of Australia, in *Bermingham v Renfrew*,[167] imposed a constructive trust where a husband and wife entered into an arrangement whereby the wife would leave property to her husband under her will if he agreed that, were he to survive her, he would leave his property to certain individuals whom the wife had nominated. The husband agreed to do so but on his wife's death dishonoured the agreement and left his property to those whom he chose. It was held that the property was held on a constructive trust for the persons whom his wife had nominated and that the agreement was not void for any failure to record the transaction in

---

163 [1971] AC 886; [1970] 2 All ER 780.

164 *Ibid*, at 905; 789–90.

165 [1948] 2 All ER 133; *Rassmussen v Rassmussen* [1995] 1 VR 613.

166 *Rochefoucauld v Bousted* [1897] 1 Ch 196; *Gissing v Gissing* [1971] AC 886, at 904–05; [1970] 2 All ER 780, at 789 *per* Lord Diplock.

167 (1936) 57 CLR 667.

writing. In *Block v Block*,[168] a son attempted to dishonour an agreement with his parents in which they had contributed to the purchase of land which was placed in his name. The son resold the property but declined to credit his parents with any part of the proceeds. The trial judge accepted the father's evidence that whatever they put in they would receive back from the proceeds of resale. The High Court of Australia held that the arrangement was sufficient to create a trust arising either by implication of law or by way of a constructive trust and was not invalid for failure to comply with the appropriate provisions of the Statute of Frauds.[169] In *Kais v Turvey*,[170] it was held that gifts made in contemplation of marriage were not necessarily given absolutely and that equitable relief was available where the marriage did not proceed.

(b) The application of the constructive trust on the breakdown of a domestic relationship

The constructive trust, as a device to prevent unjust enrichment, was received enthusiastically by Lord Denning MR in *Hussey v Palmer* in the context of the breakdown of a domestic relationship.[171] The plaintiff, Mrs Hussey sold her home and was invited by her daughter and son-in-law to build an extension to their home which was too small for them all to live in. It was the common expectation that she would live with them for the rest of her life. The extension was completed and paid for by the plaintiff who resided in the house for about six months before family differences led to her moving out. She subsequently asked her son-in-law to assist her financially but he declined. She claimed a beneficial interest in the house on a resulting trust but this claim was rejected by the trial judge because she had expressed the expenditure as a loan to her family. Her appeal succeeded. Lord Denning MR considered that the moneys were not advanced as a loan but as part of a family arrangement. In the opinion of Lord Denning MR, there was a shared expectation that the plaintiff would reside in the house for the rest of her life and this gave rise to a constructive trust because it would be inequitable for the son-in-law to deny her claim after the arrangement could not be effected because of family discord. In approaching the case in this way, Lord Denning MR relied on

---

168 (1981) 180 CLR 390; *Re Bulankoff* (1986) 1 Qd R 366.

169 This was described as a classic resulting trust, in which the presumption of resulting trust had been rebutted, *ibid*, at 396–97 *per* Gibbs CJ, Murphy, Aicken and Wilson JJ; Brennan J did not define the trust, holding that it would constitute fraud in the son to repudiate the confidence placed in him by his parents. Further, see in New Zealand, *Hayward v Giordani* [1983] NZLR 140, at 144 *per* Cooke J and in a commercial context, see *Avondale Printers & Stationers Ltd v Haggie* [1979] 2 NZLR 124, at 155–65 *per* Mahon J; *South Yarra Project Pty Ltd v Gensis* [1985] VR 29; and more recently *Carson v Wood* (1994) 34 NSWLR 9.

170 [1993–94] 11 WAR 357.

171 [1965] 2 QB 29. In Australia, to similar effect, see *Morris v Morris* (1982) 1 NSWLR 61.

proprietary estoppel cases such as *Chalmers v Pardoe*[172] and *Inwards v Baker*.[173] Reference was also made to *Cooke v Head*,[174] where Lord Denning MR had earlier held that a woman who had laboured hard on her partner's property and had shared her savings in the common expectation that the parties would marry and the property would be their home was entitled to a one-third share in the property after they had separated before marriage. Lord Denning MR described the claim as one in restitution, likening the equitable remedy of the constructive trust to the common law action for moneys had and received and Lord Denning MR referred to the opinion of Lord Mansfield in *Moses v MacFerlan*[175] in which it was said that such an action was very beneficial and therefore much to be encouraged. These remarks exposed Lord Denning MR to the criticism that he was advocating an approach to the constructive trust which justified its imposition whenever a court considered it necessary to do so in order to prevent unjust enrichment.[176] However, just as Lord Mansfield's remarks were circumscribed by reference to the kinds of claim that the courts had favourably entertained by way of the action for moneys had and received, so Lord Denning MR predicated his remarks by reference to cases where courts had granted equitable relief in accordance with well established principles. In this case, the claim satisfied the essentials of estoppel. In the shared assumption that she would have a home for the rest of her life, Mrs Hussey had expended a substantial sum of money which was never intended as a gift to her family. When the family relationship broke down and the mutual expectation of the parties was frustrated, it was unconscionable for her son-in-law to deny her an interest in the property or the return of her money.

In subsequent cases, the imposition of a constructive trust based on conditions giving rise to estoppel became more common in cases involving domestic property disputes. In *Eves v Eves*,[177] the Court of Appeal allowed a young woman a quarter share in a house in regard to which she had laboured hard as well as looking after the defendant and

---

172 [1963] 1 WLR 518; [1963] 3 All ER 552.

173 [1972] Ch 359; [1972] 2 All ER 70. Further, see *Binions v Evans* [1972] Ch 359; [1972] 2 All ER 70.

174 [1972] 1 WLR 1286; [1972] 2 All ER 38.

175 (1760) 2 Burr 1005, at 1012.

176 See Gibbs CJ in *Muschinski v Dodds* (1984–85) 160 CLR 583, at 594; Toohey J in *Baumgartner v Baumgartner* (1987) 164 CLR 137, at 152. There is reference to unjust enrichment in Canadian authority, *Pettkus v Becker* (1980) 117 DLR (3rd) 257, 273–74 *per* Dickson. Considered also by Cooke J in *Hayward v Giordani* [1983] NZLR 140, at 147–48. A consideration of *Pettkus v Becker* suggests that it was a case of estoppel arising from the fact that Mr Pettkus had accepted services for many years from Miss Becker in circumstances that imposed on him an obligation to disabuse her of her mistaken expectation that she would benefit from her work by having an interest in the property.

177 [1975] 1 WLR 1338; [1975] 3 All ER 768.

their children. The defendant, a married man, had falsely represented to her that he would put the house in their joint names but would not do so because of her age. In *Grant v Edwards*,[178] a false representation that were it not for the plaintiff's pending matrimonial proceedings her name would have been placed on title deeds was found to have induced the plaintiff to act to her detriment in such circumstances that it was considered unconscionable for the defendant to subsequently deny her a proprietary interest in the property. Sir Robin Cooke, when delivering the judgment of the Privy Council in *Maharaj v Chand*,[179] considered that a *de facto* wife should be protected from eviction after she had acted to her detriment in moving into the home of the plaintiff who represented that he would provide a permanent home for her and her children. Subsequently, in *Lloyd's Bank v Rosset*,[180] the House of Lords considered that estoppel could justify a trust being imposed where a party had induced another to act to his or her detriment as a result of a representation that the other would enjoy an interest in a property. There was no evidence, however, of any definite assurance that the wife would enjoy a beneficial interest; nor was her contribution other than *de minimis*. Hence, a constructive trust was not imposed.

In Australia, in *Baumgartner v Baumgartner*,[181] the High Court imposed a constructive trust over property acquired during the course of a *de facto* union where the parties had pooled their resources for the purpose of their joint relationship and had purchased a home in order to secure accommodation for themselves and their children. After the parties separated, it was considered unconscionable for the male partner to deny the woman's interest in the home.[182] She was awarded a half share in the property subject to allowances for her partner representing his initial financial contribution regarding the sale of a unit that he had owned and mortgage payments he had incurred after separation. This case represents an illustration not of estoppel arising out of representation or encouragement as in *Eves v Eves*,[183] but one arising out of a common assumption or

---

178 [1986] Ch 638; [1986] 2 All ER 426.

179 [1986] AC 898; [1986] 3 All ER 107. A constructive trust was not imposed but an action for possession of the premises failed.

180 [1991] 1 AC 107; [1990] 1 All ER 1111. This approach is further illustrated in relation to the division of assets in a complex case involving an unmarried couple in *Hammond v Mitchell* [1992] 2 All ER 109. The necessity for detriment was emphasised in Victoria in *Cooke v Cooke* [1987] VR 625; further, see *Higgins v Wingsfield* [1987] VR 689.

181 (1987) 164 CLR 137. Considered in *Miller v Sutherland* (1990) 14 Fam LR 416, where it was held that work of the kind the woman and her family had performed in renovating the man's house justified the imposition of a constructive trust on the basis that resources had been pooled for their mutual benefit. Further, see *Ryan v Hopkinson* (1990) 14 Fam LR 151; *Conn v Martusevicius* (1991) 14 Fam LR 751; followed in *Woodward v Johnston* (1992) 2 Qd R 215.

182 *Ibid*, at 149 *per* Mason CJ, Wilson and Deane JJ.

183 [1975] 1 WLR 1338; [1975] 3 All ER 768.

convention of mutual co-operation and benefit. In New Zealand, in *Gillies v Keogh*,[184] the Court of Appeal considered that estoppel could provide a basis for the imposition of a constructive trust in cases involving property disputes in the context of *de facto* relationships. Cooke P observed that underlying such concepts as constructive trust, unjust enrichment, imputed common intention or estoppel, there was a general principle asserting the unfairness or injustice of resiling from underlying assumptions that have been acted upon.[185] Richardson J observed that the doctrine of estoppel provided an appropriately principled approach, in the absence of legislation, to the resolution of property disputes arising on the breakdown of *de facto* relationships in cases where the parties have not expressly made provision and a common intention could not be inferred. In this regard, Richardson J observed:[186]

> The three elements, encouragement (of a belief or expectation), reliance and detriment have to be considered in the light of the actual relationship of the parties, the way they lived their lives. The existence of a sexual relationship standing alone is obviously not enough; nor is mixed flatting even though it may involve a degree of pooling of resources to meet current living needs; and those living together may have investments or other assets which they clearly wish to exclude from the pool. But where there is a *de facto* relationship of substantial duration in which, as in marriage, the parties contribute to their lives together in their different, and agreed ways, through financial contributions and through other services, and family assets are acquired or improved for the purposes of that relationship, but with title to an item of property being taken or retained in the name of one alone for reasons not inconsistent with a sharing of property, those circumstances without more, may lead to the ready inference that contributions made in those circumstances were made in reliance on an expectation of sharing and constitute a detriment to the other party.

Where there is evidence that one party, as in *Gillies v Keogh*, informed the other that he or she is not entitled to any interest in property acquired by the other, the fact that he or she proceeds to voluntarily effect improvements on the property does not justify the imposition of a constructive trust. Further, the imposition of a constructive trust may be rebutted by the circumstances of the case. Thus, in *Bryson v Bryant*,[187] a married couple had lived together for many years and died within a few

---

184 [1989] 2 NZLR 327. The principles relating to the division of property in *de facto* relationships were summarised in *Cossey v Bach* [1992] 3 NZLR 612, at 631–32 *per* Fisher J.

185 *Ibid*, at 330–31.

186 *Ibid*, at 347. The reasonable expectation of sharing approach was further adopted in *Phillips v Phillips* [1993] 3 NZLR 159, and in *Lankow v Rose* [1995] 1 NZLR 277.

187 (1992) 29 NSWLR 188.

months of each other childless. The wife's brother who was her sole beneficiary argued that her estate was entitled to half of the husband's
estate under a constructive trust because she had contributed in various
ways to the property during the marriage. The husband had devised all
his property to charity. Although the New South Wales Court of Appeal
was divided on the issue of whether a constructive trust should be
imposed,[188] a majority held that there was nothing unconscionable in the
husband retaining the sole beneficial interest in the property on her
death even assuming that the wife could have established an equitable
interest during her life.[189] As Mason and Brennan JJ had earlier observed
in *Calverley v Greene*,[190] many spouses contribute to the assets on the
basis that the other spouse will enjoy those assets after the other's death.

Where there is an absence of legislation governing the division of
assets acquired during the course of a domestic relationship,[191] the equitable remedies of resulting trust based on common intention and contribution and the constructive trust based on estoppel and unconscionable
conduct should enable courts to adequately resolve most property disputes upon the breakdown of a relationship. Equitable interests that a
partner enjoying the legal estate unconscionably refuses to recognise
may be affected by the imposition of a resulting or constructive trust.
Where the evidence suggests that relief should be given under a constructive trust, a court can make such orders as will practically advance
a just resolution of the dispute. In *Gillies v Keogh*,[192] Cooke P observed
that, in an appropriate case, equity could be satisfied by compensation
rather than division of an asset. These remedies, however, do not permit
a court simply to impose a trust or grant relief according to a broad
assessment of what is fair and just. Nor does the law recognise a regime
of community of assets from which a fair and just allocation may be
made.[193] Any change in the law to permit a court to make such orders on
this basis must depend upon legislative intervention as the House of
Lords emphasised in *Pettitt v Pettitt*.[194]

---

188 See Kirby P in favour of a constructive trust, *ibid*, at 200–05; Samuels J rejected
a constructive trust on the basis that there was insufficient evidence of direct
contribution, *ibid*, at 229–31.

189 *Ibid*, at 222 *per* Scheller JA.

190 (1984) 155 CLR 242, at 259–60.

191 In New South Wales, *de facto* marriages are governed by the De facto Relationships
Act 1984. The court has power to make orders under s 20 which are just and
equitable. See *Dwyer v Kaljo* (1992) 27 NSWLR 728; *Wallace v Stanford* (1994) 37
NSWLR 1; *Green v Robinson* (1995) 36 NSWLR 96; *Theodoropoullos v Theodosiou* (1995)
38 NSWLR 424.

192 [1989] 2 NZLR 327, at 332 following Canadian authority; *Everson v Rich* (1988) 53
DLR (4th) 470 and *Cossey v Bach* [1992] 3 NZLR 612, at 632 *per* Fisher J.

193 See *Hepworth v Hepworth* (1963) 110 CLR 309, at 317–19 *per* Windeyer J; *Greene v
Greene* (1989) 17 NSWLR 343, at 353 *per* Gleeson CJ; *Lankow v Rose* [1995] 1 NZLR
277 *per* Hardie Boys J.

194 [1970] AC 777; [1969] 2 All ER 385.

CHAPTER 5

Mistake in Contract

Mistake as a ground for restitution in a contractual transaction has had a troubled and rather uncertain history. As with mistake in non-contractual situations, mistake in the context of contractual transactions raises important issues of restitution since a mistake of a material kind may lead to a substantial loss or gain for one of the parties that was never contemplated. The law, however, has for commercial reasons adopted a generally conservative approach to mistake in this context and has preferred an objective approach to the issue of formation of contract. In order to preserve the security of bargains, the parties to a contract will generally be held to a contract where it outwardly appears that the parties have reached agreement. A party, who is unilaterally mistaken about some feature or quality of the subject-matter of the contract, will not usually be able to resile from the contract. It may constitute hardship for a party acting under mistake to be held to a contract as this may result in a substantial disparity in the exchange of values, but this has been justified as Lord Atkin said in *Bell v Lever Brothers Ltd*,[1] because it is of paramount importance to commerce that contracts are observed.[2] Lord Atkin further observed that:[3]

> ... if parties honestly comply with the essentials of the formation of contracts, ie agree in the same terms on the same subject-matter they are bound; and must rely on the stipulations of the contract for protection from the effects of facts unknown to them.

A further factor restricting relief for mistake is the *caveat emptor* principle. In *Smith v Hughes*,[4] the importance of this principle in commercial transactions was emphasised when a party claimed a mistake as to the quality of the oats, new rather than old, that he had purchased and argued that he should not be bound by the contract. In this regard, Sir Alexander Cockburn CJ observed:[5]

> I take the true rule to be that where a specific article is offered for sale without express warranty, as where, for instance, an article is ordered for a specific purpose and the buyer has full opportunity of inspecting and forming his own judgment, the rule *caveat emptor*

---

1   [1932] AC 161; [1931] All ER 1.
2   *Ibid*, at 224; 31.
3   *Idem*.
4   (1871) LR 6 QB 597; [1861–73] All ER 632.
5   *Ibid*, at 603; 635.

applies. If he gets the article he contracted to buy, and that article corresponds with what it was sold as, he gets all he is entitled to, and is bound by the contract.

However, in certain circumstances, considered below, a party may be relieved from the consequences of his or her mistake with the result that the other is not unjustly enriched.

Absence of consensus *ad idem*

Although it might outwardly appear that an agreement had been reached, if the evidence established that in fact the parties were not *ad idem* on an essential aspect of a contract, the apparent agreement was not enforceable. In *Raffles v Wichelhaus*,[6] for example, the plaintiff agreed to sell cotton to arrive *'ex Peerless* from Bombay', and made available cotton which had been carried by a ship, *Peerless*, from Bombay in December. The defendant refused to accept delivery claiming that he had agreed to purchase cotton from another ship called *Peerless* which had sailed from Bombay in October. Judgment was given for the defendant. Although no reasons were given for the decision, the case would appear to support the proposition that there was outwardly no consensus as to the subject-matter of the contract and, accordingly, there was no contract.[7] Consensus was also lacking in *Falck v Williams*.[8] In that case, the plaintiff and the defendant were negotiating about charter parties and a telegram intending to confirm a copra charter from Fiji to Barcelona was understood by the defendant to refer to another charter. The Privy Council held that the terms of the purported acceptance were ambiguous and it was impossible to contend that there was a contract. The argument that consensus was absent failed, however, in *Smith v Hughes*.[9] The plaintiff, a farmer, intended to sell new oats and the buyer, a racehorse trainer, thought mistakenly that he was acquiring old oats more suitable for racehorses. It was argued that there was no obligation to pay for the plaintiff's oats, however, it was held that the mistake was not one that could be said to relate to the subject-matter of the contract but merely to its quality. Sir Alexander Cockburn CJ observed:[10]

> All that can be said is that the two minds were not *ad idem* as to the age of the oats; they certainly were *ad idem* as to the sale and purchase of them.

6   (1864) 2 H & C 906; [1864] 159 ER 375.

7   A view taken of the case in *Smith v Hughes* (1871) LR 6 QB 597, at 609; [1861–73] All ER 632, at 638 *per* Hannen J.

8   [1900] AC 176.

9   (1871) LR 6 QB 597; [1861–73] All ER 632.

10 *Ibid*, at 606; 637.

Mistake of the kind that would mean that an apparent contract could not be enforced, could have adverse repercussions for a party who incurred expense or suffered detriment in the belief that a binding agreement existed. In these circumstances, the injuriously affected party was able to claim that the other was estopped from denying that there was an agreement if, objectively, the evidence established that the parties had outwardly reached agreement.[11] In practice, execution of a written agreement would suffice to raise an estoppel of this kind. A party who was estopped might complain that his or her expectations were defeated. However, of the two essentially innocent parties, the interests of the party who had acted injuriously on the objective manifestation of an agreement were preferred. An attempt to argue estoppel, however, could not succeed if the mistake had been induced by the party seeking to enforce the agreement. Thus, in *Scriven Brothers v Hindley*,[12] it was held that a contract entered into by auction, in which the vendor intended to sell tow and the buyer believed that he was purchasing hemp, did not give rise to a contract as the parties were not *ad idem*. The defendant was not estopped from disavowing the apparent agreement because the court considered that the auctioneer had unwittingly caused the purchaser's mistake by the careless manner in which the tow had been presented for sale, thus incorrectly inducing the buyer to bid for what he believed was hemp when the vendor intended to sell tow. It would have been unconscionable for the vendor in these circumstances to be allowed to enforce the apparent agreement.

Relief for common mistake

(a) At common law

At common law, restitution could be had for common mistake where it related to the existence of the subject-matter of the contract. Thus, in *Couturier v Hastie*,[13] the plaintiff was unable to recover the price of corn from an agent who had entered into a contract of sale with a purchaser. Unknown to the agent and prior to the sale, the corn had been sold abroad as a result of deterioration during shipping. The sale had occurred before the defendant had entered into the transaction. The court considered, as a matter of construction of the agreement, that the parties contemplated that the subject-matter of the contract would be in existence at the time the contract was made and, because it was not, the

---

11 See *Smith v Hughes, idem, per* Blackburn J citing *Freemen v Cooke* (1848) 2 Exch 654 which was discussed by Richardson J in *NB Hunt and Sons Ltd v Maori Trustee* [1986] 2 NZLR 641, at 657.

12 [1913] 3 KB 564.

13 [1843–60] All ER 280.

plaintiff's claim was dismissed.[14] A similar approach was taken in an earlier case, *Strickland v Turner*.[15] There, a purchaser of an annuity was allowed to recover the purchase price where the annuitant had died prior to the making of the contract. In cases of this kind, one theory is that the contract is void or a nullity at law.[16] In *McRae v Commonwealth Disposals Commission*,[17] Dixon and Fullager JJ, in the High Court of Australia considered, however, that agreements of this kind were not void but merely unenforceable because of a total failure of consideration.[18] In that case, the plaintiff had tendered for the salvage of a freighter which the defendant had represented was at a certain location. After succeeding in its tender, the plaintiff, at considerable expense, attempted to locate the sunken vessel. Subsequently, it was discovered that there was no tanker at the location. The plaintiff sued for damages for breach of contract. The defendant argued that there was no contract in existence because the contract was entered into upon a common misapprehension that a tanker was in existence at that location. The court held that the plaintiff had relied on the assertion by the defendant that a tanker existed. Accordingly, as a matter of construction, the defendant had warranted the tanker's existence and the agreement was not void for mistake. In any event, the court considered that the defendant ought not to be able to rely on mistake where the belief was entertained without any reasonable ground and had thereby induced a false belief in the mind of the plaintiff.[19]

Common mistake at law was also considered by the House of Lords in the difficult case of *Bell v Lever Bros*.[20] The company sought to set aside severance agreements into which it had entered with certain directors on the ground that the contracts of service had already been effectively terminated as a result of misconduct and, as a consequence, the directors would be unjustly enriched if they received compensation. Since the company was unaware of the misconduct until after the agreements had been entered into, the company argued that they had been entered into under a common fundamental misapprehension that they were not liable to immediate termination when they could have been had the true

---

14 *Ibid*, at 284.

15 (1852) 7 Ex 208. Further, in equity, see *Scott v Coulson* [1903] 2 Ch 249.

16 See the discussion in *Associated Japanese Bank Ltd v Credit Du Nord SA* [1988] 3 All ER 902, at 911.

17 (1951) 84 CLR 377.

18 *Ibid*, at 406. Further see, *Svanosio v McNamara* (1956) 96 CLR 186, at 209. This view also appears to have been adopted earlier by Lord Atkin in *Bell v Lever Brothers Ltd* [1932] AC 161, at 222; [1931] All ER 1, at 30 and further, in equity, by Vaughan-Williams LJ in *Scott v Coulson* [1903] 2 Ch 249, at 252, and Denning LJ in the later case of *Solle v Butcher* [1950] 1 KB 671, at 691–92 [1949] 2 All ER 1106, at 1119.

19 *Ibid*, at 408.

20 [1932] AC 161; [1931] All ER 1.

facts been known. It was successfully argued for the company, at first instance and in the Court of Appeal, that the compensation agreements were void. Lord Aitkin (one of the Law Lords in the majority) observed, however, that in order to avoid a contract for mistake of this kind, an assumption had to be fundamental or essential to the existence of the contract. In the opinion of Lord Atkin, the misapprehension of Lever Brothers did not affect the subject-matter of the contract. Although Lord Atkin recognised that there was a distinction between a contract immediately determinable and one for an expired term which could not be terminated unless a substantial fee was paid, this was a distinction of quality rather than substance. Lever Brothers, in paying for the release, got exactly what it bargained for and it was immaterial that it could have got the same result in another way or, if it had known the true facts, it would not have entered into the agreement.[21] Lord Thankerton considered that there was insufficient evidence to find that the company regarded the indefeasibility of the service agreements as an essential and integral aspect of the contract.[22] In the opinion of Lord Thankerton:[23]

> The phrase 'underlying assumption by the parties' as applied to the subject-matter of the contract, may be too widely interpreted so as to include something which one of the parties had not necessarily in his mind at the time of the contract; in my opinion, it can only properly relate to something which both must necessarily have accepted in their minds as an essential and integral aspect of the subject-matter.

A case which may be usefully compared with *Bell v Lever Brothers* is *Norwich Union Fire Insurance Society v William H Price Ltd*.[24] In that case, an insurance settlement was set aside and the insurer obtained restitution of moneys paid to an insured for the purported loss of a cargo of lemons, where the settlement had been effected under a mutual misapprehension that a cargo of lemons had perished. The parties had proceeded on a fundamental mutual assumption that the cargo had been lost which was a fact that was essential and integral to the foundation of the insurers' liability under the policy. To have declined relief would have meant that the owner of the cargo was unjustly enriched.

---

21 *Ibid*, at 224; 30.

22 *Ibid*, at 235; 36.

23 *Idem*.

24 [1934] AC 455; All ER 352. Further, for setting aside a consent order based on common mistake of fact, see *Huddersfield Banking Co Ltd v Henry Lister* [1895] 2 Ch 273.

(b) In equity

In order to found relief at common law, we have seen that the mistake had to be so essential or fundamental that the contract was devoid of subject-matter in the sense that a condition essential to the contract was absent or it could be said there was a total failure of consideration. However, equity adopted a less rigorous approach in cases of common mistake. In *Solle v Butcher*,[25] the Court of Appeal considered that a contract would be set aside in equity on terms that could achieve an equitable result for both parties when they shared a common mistake which, whilst important, did not totally deprive the agreement of substance. In that case, a landlord let property in the mistaken belief, shared by his tenant, that the property was not subject to rent restriction legislation. The tenant was a surveyor who had been employed to oversee improvements to the building. He had, in misrepresenting that the building was not subject to the legislation, contributed to his landlord's error. As a result, the landlord did not serve a notice of increase, as he was obliged to do under the legislation, if he desired lawfully to effect an increase in rent. The tenant, however, after entering into possession, sought a declaration that the lease was not subject to increased rental and that he was entitled to recover the excess he had paid. The landlord sought to have the lease rescinded on the ground that it had been entered into under a mutual mistake. By a majority, the Court of Appeal upheld the argument that the lease could be rescinded but gave the tenant an opportunity to have a fresh lease executed on terms which were acceptable to the landlord. In approaching the matter in this way, Denning LJ relied on *Cooper v Phibbs*.[26] There, the House of Lords set aside a lease for common mistake where, unknown to either of the parties, the fisheries which constituted the subject-matter of the lease, already belonged to the tenant. The lease was set aside on terms that the landlord be paid compensation for the cost of improvements that had been effected when he was mistakenly thought to be the owner. The reasoning of the majority in *Solle v Butcher* is open to the criticism that *Cooper v Phibbs* was a case of total failure of consideration, whereas the mistake in *Solle v Butcher* was not so vital as to rob the contract of all substance. However, *Cooper v Phibbs* sanctioned the setting aside of an agreement on terms, and in adopting this approach, the Court of Appeal recognised that relief should be granted to the landlord so that the tenant was not unjustly enriched. This approach is defensible on a restitutionary analysis. To have permitted the tenant to have retained the lease at the lower rental

---

25 [1950] 1 KB 671; [1949] 2 All ER 1106. See Cartwright, J, 'Solle v Butcher and the Doctrine of Mistake in Contract' (1987) 103 LQR 594.

26 (1867) LR 2 HL 149. *Beauchamp (Earl) v Winn* (1873) LR 6 H L 223, and *Paget v Marshall* (1885) 28 Ch D 255; [1881–85] All ER 290.

and recover the excess payments would have provided an unjust benefit for the tenant who had significantly contributed to his landlord's error. *Solle v Butcher* was followed by Goff J in *Grist v Bailey*.[27] There, a vendor contracted to sell a freehold property at a considerable undervalue in the mistaken belief shared by the purchaser that the property was subject to a protected statutory tenancy in favour of a third party when it was not. Goff J considered that the sale should be rescinded since the mistake was fundamental and one which greatly affected the purchase price. The agreement was rescinded on terms that the purchaser had the opportunity of entering into a new agreement, at a proper price.

In *Solle v Butcher*, Denning LJ observed that a party seeking to rely on mistake could not do so if he or she were at fault.[28] In *Grist v Bailey*, Goff J observed, however, that there must be some degree of blameworthiness beyond the mere fact of error.[29] In *McRae v Commonwealth Disposals*,[30] Fullager and Dixon JJ considered that a party could not take advantage of a unreasonable mistake that had induced a false belief in the mind of the other party. If, however, a contract contemplates the possibility of error and expressly allows a certain time for a party to investigate that possibility, the failure to investigate should not entitle that party to claim relief for mistake.[31]

Equity has allowed relief where the mistake involved an error of law affecting a private right as in *Cooper v Phibbs*.[32] In *Davidson v Atlas Assurance*,[33] a New Zealand Court set aside a worker's compensation settlement upon the ground that the parties had taken an incorrect view of the status of the term 'worker' under the relevant legislation. The distinction between errors of law and fact has been substantially discredited in both England and Australia in *Woolwich Building Society v Inland Revenue Commissioners (No 2)*,[34] and *David Securities v Commercial Bank of Australia*.[35] Error of law should have no greater place in contract. Providing the mistaken assumption is shared by both parties and is fundamental to their contractual relationship, relief should be

---

27 [1967] Ch 532; [1966] 2 All ER 875, and in New Zealand, although observing that there had been some academic and judicial criticism of *Solle v Butcher*, Chilwell J adopted the approach in *Waring v SJ Brentnall* [1975] 2 NZLR 403, at 406–10 prior to the introduction of the Contractual Mistakes Act 1977.

28 [1950] 1 KB 671, at 695; [1949] 2 All ER 1106, at 1120.

29 [1967] Ch 532, at 542; [1966] 2 All ER 875, at 880–81.

30 [1951] 84 CLR 377, at 408, and further, see *Associated Japanese Bank Ltd v Credit Du Nord SA* [1988] 3 All ER 902, at 913.

31 *Svanosio v McNamara* [1956] 96 CLR 186, at 205.

32 (1867) LR 2 HL 149. Further, see *Earl of Beauchamp v Winn* (1873) LR 6 H L 223.

33 [1932] NZLR 1163.

34 [1993] AC 70; [1991] 4 All ER 577, at 602. See discussion, pp 231–38 below.

35 (1992) 175 CLR 353.

available. Relief may, however, be denied if a party has affirmed the contract with knowledge of the true position[36] or has unreasonably delayed in seeking relief.[37]

Relief for unilateral mistake

(a) At common law

The objective approach to the formation of a binding agreement will generally preclude a party seeking relief from an agreement on the ground of unilateral mistake as to the value or quality of the subject-matter of the contract. Unless the mistake was attributable to fraud or a party complaining of a unilateral mistake could not gain relief at law. In *Smith v Hughes*,[38] Blackburn J considered that a vendor was under no obligation to disabuse a buyer of a mistaken belief as to the quality of an article for sale even if he was aware that the purchaser thought that the article possessed a certain quality. Although in *Smith v Hughes*, Sir Alexander Cockburn CJ appeared to suggest that deliberate silence might constitute fraud, the approach of Blackburn J was subsequently approved by Lord Atkin in *Bell v Lever Bros*.[39]

(b) In equity

Equity was not, however, so tolerant of unconscionable dealing. If one party had sought to 'snap' at a bargain in the knowledge that the other party was labouring under a mistake, the agreement could be set aside in equity so that the wrongdoer was not unjustly enriched. In *Tamplin v James*,[40] James LJ considered that specific performance could be declined for such conduct, and Brett LJ considered that it would amount to equitable fraud. In *Hartog v Collins & Shields*,[41] a claim for damages was successfully resisted on the ground that the buyer must have known that the vendor of certain goods had offered them for sale on an incorrect basis at a certain rate per pound rather than per piece as had been intended. The High Court of Australia considered the issue of equitable relief for unilateral mistake in *Taylor v Johnson*.[42] There, the owner of 10

---

36 See *Frederick E Rose (London) Ltd v William A Pym* [1953] 2 QB 450.

37 *Leaf v International Galleries* [1950] 1 All ER 693, at 695.

38 (1871) LR 6 QB 597, at 607.

39 [1932] AC 161, at 223–24; [1931] All ER 1, at 30–31.

40 (1880) 15 Ch D 215; [1874–80] All ER 560. Further, see Denning MR in *Solle v Butcher* [1950] 1 KB 671; [1949] 2 All ER 1106.

41 [1939] 3 All ER 566.

42 (1983) 151 CLR 422. Further, for the setting aside of a consent judgment for a mistake of this kind, see *DCT v Chamberlain* (1990) 93 ALR 729. *Cf General Credits Ltd v Ebsworth* [1986] 2 QR 162.

acres of land had mistakenly granted an option in writing to the plaintiff to purchase the land for $15,000 when she intended the price to be $15,000 per acre. The High Court considered that there was sufficient evidence to conclude that the purchaser had appreciated the owner was mistaken and had surreptitiously taken advantage of her error, and so the agreement should not be enforced.

A similar approach is taken in equity where a mistake has been induced by misrepresentation. In *Torrance v Bolton*,[43] a purchaser was relieved of an obligation to purchase an hotel where the vendor had failed to clearly describe the nature of the interest that was for sale, and it was unconscionable for the vendor to avail himself of the legal advantage which he had unjustly obtained. Later, in *Solle v Butcher*,[44] Denning LJ relied on this case as authority for the proposition that a contract would be set aside in equity if the mistake of one party had been induced by a material misrepresentation of the other, even though it was not fraudulent or fundamental. More recently, in *Laurence v Lexcourt Holdings Ltd*,[45] a contract for the rental of premises was set aside for misrepresentation and common mistake after the premises had been described as available for use as offices for a term of 15 years when in fact the only available planning permission was limited to two years. The fact that the true position could have been ascertained had the lessee made inquiry was considered an insufficient reason to reject the claim.

Where a party is under an obligation to disclose information adverse to his or her interests and fails to do so thereby inducing a mistaken belief in another, any benefit deriving from the mistake may be the subject of restitution. In *Bell v Lever Bros*[46] such a claim failed because it was held by Lord Atkin and Lord Thankerton that an employee at common law was not obliged to reveal his or her misconduct. Where a duty of disclosure exists, however, an omission to disclose will lead to the restitution of benefits that have been induced as a consequence. Thus, in *Sybron Corporation v Rochem Ltd*,[47] a director omitted to reveal the misconduct of subordinate employees which he had a duty to do because this would have implicated him in fraudulent conduct. The Court of Appeal held that as a result he was not entitled to retirement benefits that had been mistakenly conferred on him by his employer. Where a relationship is *uberrimae fide* as in a contract of insurance, an innocent misrepresentation may result in a settlement being set aside as was

---

43 (1872) LR 8 Ch App 118.
44 [1950] 1 KB 671, at 692; [1949] 2 All ER 1107, at 1120.
45 [1978] 1 WLR 1128.
46 [1932] AC 161, at 227, 235; [1931] All ER 1, at 32, 36.
47 [1983] 3 WLR 713; [1983] 2 All ER 707.

illustrated in *Magee v Penine Insurance*.[48] There, a majority of the Court of Appeal set aside a settlement of an insurance claim involving damage to a motor vehicle, where it had been innocently misrepresented in the policy application that the insured had a driver's licence.

In a case of unilateral mistake, specific performance of a contract may be refused even though the party seeking performance is ignorant of the mistake, if the mistaken party can demonstrate that enforcement of the contract would cause hardship in the sense of injustice or the plaintiff has in some way albeit unintentionally contributed to the defendant's mistake.[49] Damages may be a sufficient remedy.[50] However, it is clear that a plea of hardship will not be entertained lightly.[51] In *Goldsborough Mort & Co Ltd v Quinn*,[52] Issacs J emphasised that it was no hardship to be compelled to carry out a fair bargain because a more advantageous one might possibly have been exacted.[53] In his dissenting judgment in *Taylor v Johnson*,[54] Dawson J suggested that hardship might be established if the land which was the subject of the contract had special value for the defendant, but this was not established in that case.

Mistake as to identity of the offeree

Difficult issues of unjust enrichment and restitution arise where third parties have in good faith purchased goods from a vendor who has obtained them fraudulently by assuming the identity of another. In *Cundy v Lindsay*,[55] for example, goods were ordered in writing from a vendor by a rogue giving his address as 'Blenkarn & Co, 37 Wood Street, and 5 Little Love Lane, Cheapside' and signed in such a way that his name appeared as 'Blenkiron & Co' which was a respectable firm well-known to the vendor

---

48 [1969] 2 QB 507; 2 All ER 891. Mason, K and Carter, PW, *Restitution Law in Australia*, p 546, Butterworths, Sydney, are critical of this decision on the ground that the insured had not acted unconscionably. However, it is submitted that cases of this kind turn on a pre-existing obligation of disclosure. In the event that the insurer disowns the contract for a failure to disclose, the premium should be refunded.

49 *Tamplin v James* (1880) 15 Ch D 215; [1874–80] All ER 560; *Preston v Luck* (1884) 27 Ch D 497; *Goldsborough Mort & Co Ltd v Quinn* (1910) 10 CLR 674; *Dell v Beasley* [1959] NZLR 89.

50 Either at common law or in lieu of specific performance when damages may be calculated as at the date of a court declining to enforce the agreement. Further, see *Bosaid v Andry* [1963] VR 465; *Wroth v Tyler* [1974] Ch 30; *Souster v Epsom Plumbing Contractors Ltd* [1974] 2 NZLR 515; *Grocott v Ayson* [1975] 2 NZLR 586.

51 *Axelsen v O'Brien* (1959) 80 CLR 219, at 226 *per* Dixon J.

52 (1910) 10 CLR 674; *Gall v Mitchell* (1924) 35 CLR 222; *Slee v Warke* (1949) 86 CLR 271; *Fragomeni v Flogliani* (1968) 42 ALJR 263.

53 *Ibid*, at 700.

54 (1983) 57 ALJR 197, at 207.

55 (1878) 3 App Cas 459; [1874–80] All ER 1149. See also *Hardman v Booth* (1863) 1 H & C 803; 158 ER 1107; *Kings Norton Metal Co Ltd v Eldridge, Merritt & Co Ltd* (1897) 14 TLR 98; *Roache v Australian Mercantile Land & Finance Ltd* [1964–65] NSWR 307; *Fawcett v Star Car Sales Limited* [1960] NZLR 406.

that traded from an address in Wood Street, Cheapside. It was established that the vendor had no knowledge of Blenkarn & Co and had intended to deal only with Blenkiron & Sons. Subsequently, the owner successfully sued Cundy who had purchased the goods in good faith from the rogue for the value of the goods. It was held that the vendor did not intend to deal with the rogue but with Blenkiron and hence there was no agreement between the owner and the rogue under which property could pass to the latter. Lord Cairns LC observed:[56]

> ... is it possible to imagine that in that state of things any contract could have arisen between the respondents and Blenkarn? Of him, they knew nothing, and of him they never thought, with him they never intended to deal. Their minds never, even for an instant of time, rested upon him, and as between him and them there was merely the one side to a contract where, in order to produce a contract, two sides would be required. With the firm of Blenkiron & Sons, of course, there was no contract, for as to them the matter was entirely unknown, and therefore, the pretence of a contract was a failure.

To similar effect are the dissenting judgments of Windeyer J and Kitto J in the High Court of Australia in *Porter v Latec Finance (Qld) Pty Ltd*.[57] One of the issues in that case was whether a loan by Latec Finance to a rogue, Lionel Herbert Gill, was void when the latter had obtained an advance by fraudulently representing that he was another, Herbert Henry Gill, whose land he mortgaged for the loan. Windeyer J observed that:[58]

> This is a case where A offered to lend money to be secured by mortgage on B's land. C, by representing himself to be B, had procured A to make the offer, but it was meant for B not for him, as he well knew ... . Only with him could, the contract proposed, a loan mortgage of his loan, have been made. A man cannot bind another in contract by accepting an offer which he knows is not meant for him but for someone else ...

Kitto J observed:[59]

> ... it seems to me the proper inference is that the respondent's officers dealt with Lionel Herbert Gill solely on the footing that he was in truth the Herbert Henry Gill whose land was offered as their principal security. The grant of the loan, as I see it, was implicitly if not expressly on the condition precedent that the recipient was identical with the registered proprietor of the land.

---

56 *Ibid*, at 466; 1151.

57 [1964] 111 CLR 177. Barwick CJ also appeared to agree that an agreement for a loan was void, in these circumstances, but His Honour differed from the minority when he took the view that after the money had been passed over as a loan, Lionel Herbert Gill could not deny the existence of a loan, and hence the payment in issue was authorised by the rogue (at 183).

58 *Ibid*, at 200.

59 *Ibid*, at 194–95.

Where the parties contract *inter praesentes* and a rogue obtains goods fraudulently by assuming the identity of another, more difficult questions relating to identity and third party rights arise. In *Phillips v Brookes*,[60] a rogue visited the shop of a jeweller and chose some pearls and a diamond ring. Whilst writing the cheque, he represented that he was Sir George Bullough with an address in London. He also signed the cheque in the same name. The vendor had heard of Sir George Bullough and knew him as a man of some means. He also ascertained from a directory that he lived at that address and allowed the rogue to take the property. The ring was subsequently pawned for value and, on finding that the cheque was worthless, the vendor sued the pawnbrokers for the return of the ring or its value. It was held that the vendor had intended to transact with the person present. There was no error as to the person with whom the vendor had contracted although he would not have consented had there not been a fraudulent misrepresentation. Accordingly, property in the ring had passed and the pawnbroker had good title. However, in *Ingram v Little*,[61] the Court of Appeal considered that where apparent agreement is reached after negotiations *inter praesentes* but there is a deception as to the identity of the offeree and there is evidence to displace the presumption that the offeror is intending to contract with the person physically present, the contract will be void and consequently property in the goods will not pass to the rogue. There, a majority of the Court of Appeal held that the plaintiffs could recover a motor car from a third party, who had acquired it from a rogue, after he had fraudulently represented to the plaintiffs that he was a reputable person named Hutchinson who resided at a certain address. On being satisfied that a person by the name of Hutchinson lived at that address, the cheque was accepted and the rogue permitted to depart with the car. A majority of the Court of Appeal felt unable to disagree with the finding of the trial judge that the plaintiffs had intended to transact with the person by the name of Hutchinson. This result, however, moved Pearce LJ to say that he was reluctant to accept the argument that there has been a mistake in such a case as this because it created hardship on subsequent *bona fide* purchasers.[62]

A differently constituted Court of Appeal, however, in *Lewis v Averay*[63] exhibited a reluctance in similar circumstances to prefer the vendor. A rogue personally entered into negotiations to buy a car. He deceived the vendor into believing that he was Richard Green, a film

---

60   [1919] 2 KB 243; [1918–19] All ER 246. For a similar conclusion on an issue of identity, see *Sowler v Potter* [1940] 1 KB 271; [1939] 4 All ER 478, and *Lake v Simmons* [1927] AC 487; All ER 49.

61   [1961] 1 QB 31; [1960] 3 All ER 332.

62   *Ibid*, at 62; 344.

63   [1972] 1 QB 198; [1971] 3 All ER 907.

actor, and showed the vendor documents which, although forged, plainly supported his identity. As a result, the vendor accepted a worthless cheque, parted with the motor vehicle and, having learned of the fraud, subsequently sued a firm of auctioneers to whom the rogue had sold the car in conversion. The court considered that the plaintiff had not displaced the presumption that he had intended to deal with the person to whom he had sold the vehicle. Megaw LJ considered that the plaintiff had failed to show that at the time of offering to sell his car to the rogue he regarded his identity as of vital importance. It was merely a mistake as to his attributes, or as to his creditworthiness.[64] Lord Denning MR, however, doubted the merits of this approach and preferred simply to treat transactions of this kind as voidable rather than void thereby protecting the interests of *bona fide* purchasers for value.[65]

It is submitted that Lord Denning's approach is preferable to the approach taken in *Ingram v Little*, at least in cases where both parties negotiate *inter praesentes*. Where the vendor, in cases of this kind, has offered the goods for sale to the public and personally dealt with the buyer, the mistake relates only to the creditworthiness of the buyer. By releasing the goods to a rogue without insisting on immediate payment, the vendor not only places himself at risk of non-payment but purchasers as well, who without notice, transact with the rogue in good faith. In these circumstances, the vendor should not be able to take advantage of his or her generosity or obtuseness and gain precedence over the interests of third parties who have transacted with the rogue in good faith and for value. Retention of the property by a *bona fide* purchaser should not give rise to restitution in these circumstances because the purchaser, in dealing with the rogue honestly and for value, cannot be said to have been enriched unjustly.

Non est factum

A plea of *non est factum* (it is not my deed) may be available in exceptional circumstances to allow a person to resile from a transaction where he or she has executed a document in the belief that it constituted an entirely different transaction from the one that he or she had intended to enter, and so avoid unjust enrichment. Apart from blindness and illiteracy, *non est factum* is approached very critically by the courts. Where the circumstances suggest that the other party has acted unconscionably in obtaining the execution of a document, there should be no need for the plea to be invoked since the transaction can in any event be set aside for fraud or sharp practice. However, in cases where a party is innocent of any wrongdoing, in order for *non est factum* to be successfully entertained, the

---

64 *Ibid*, at 209; 913.
65 *Ibid*, 207; 910–12.

mistake must be one that was not only radical but was also not attribut-able to carelessness on the signatory's part unless the mistake was known to the other party. This approach is evidenced in *Petelin v Cullen*,[66] a deci-sion of the High Court of Australia. In that case an agreement was set aside because the plaintiff's agent was aware that the defendant had little understanding of English, no capacity to understand the agreement in question and had executed a letter of extension in the mistaken belief that he was signing a receipt for a sum of money, a document which was radi-cally different. The court observed that fault of the signatory was not a limiting factor:[67]

> ... when the defence is asserted against the other party to the trans-action, who is aware of the circumstances in which it came to be exe-cuted and who knows (because the document was signed on his representation) or has reason to suspect that it was executed under some misapprehension as to its character. In such a case, the law must give effect to the policy which requires that a person should not be held to a bargain to which he has not brought a consenting mind, for there is no conflicting or countervailing consideration to be accommodated – no innocent person has placed reliance on the signature without reason to doubt its validity.

New Zealand authority is also instructive in this area. In *Conlon v Ozolins*,[68] the Court of Appeal adopted the observations of the High Court in *Petelin v Cullen* and held that the plea could not succeed where the carelessness of the plaintiff or her solicitor in executing an agreement for the sale of land under the mistaken belief that she was selling a small-er portion was unknown to the purchaser.[69] The plea, in any event, could not have succeeded because the transaction was not radically or funda-mentally different from that intended. In *Chiswick Investments v Pevats*,[70] however, *non est factum* succeeded where a company secretary had signed a document believing that he was doing no more than attesting to the affixing of a company seal. He had unwittingly signed the document as a guarantor. The court held that he had not been negligent in signing the document intending only to attest to the affixing of the seal and the transaction was one that was radically different from that intended. A general warning, however, was sounded for those who sign documents

---

66   (1975) 132 CLR 355. See also *Saunders v Anglia Building Society* [1971] AC 1004; [1970] 3 All ER 961.

67   *Idem.*

68   [1984] 1 NZLR 489.

69   *Ibid*, at 503; 508. Further, on the issue of carelessness precluding a plea of *non est factum*, see *IFC Securities v Sewell* [1990] 1 NZLR 177, and *Bradley West Solicitors Nominee Co Ltd v Keeman* [1994] NZLR 111.

70   [1990] 1 NZLR 169. The plea also succeeded in *Landzeal Group Ltd v Kyne* [1990] 3 NZLR 574.

without reading them in reliance on a solicitor explaining their contents in *Bradley West Solicitors Nominee Co Ltd v Keenan*.[71] It was held that parties seeking to avoid a guarantee could not rely on *non est factum* where they had relied on the explanation given by their solicitor and had not bothered to read the document. Only in exceptional circumstances should this plea succeed where the other party to the transaction is unaware of the signatory's error because in circumstances of this kind, it will be more difficult to assert that there has been unjust enrichment.

Rectification

Rectification of a written agreement may also be sought where it does not represent the true accord of the parties in order to prevent unjust enrichment. A contract[72] may be rectified if there is clear or convincing proof[73] that a written agreement does not reflect the common intention of the parties. Rectification may be necessary because the agreement as recorded is more onerous or burdensome for the party seeking rectification. The view that the common intention had to have reached the level of a concluded contract had been expressed in earlier English[74] and Australian[75] authority but was rejected by the High Court of Australia in *Slee v Warke*,[76] by the English Court of Appeal in *Joscelyne v Nissen*[77] and by the New Zealand Court of Appeal in *Dundee Farm Ltd v Bambury Holdings Ltd*.[78] The omitted matter must be capable of proof in clear and precise terms.[79] A court must not assume the task of making the contracts for the parties.[80]

---

71 [1994] 2 NZLR 111.

72 Rectification may also remedy voluntary settlements where mistake can be shown to materially affect the settlor's intention. *Re Butlin's Settlement Trust, Butlin v Butlin* [1976] Ch 251; 2 All ER 483, *cf* the remedy of rescission *Lady Hood of Avalon v Mackinnon* [1909] 1 Ch 476.

73 *Joscelyne v Nissen* [1970] 2 QB 86, at 98; *Pukallus v Cameron* (1982) 43 ALR 243, at 247.

74 *Mackenzie v Coulson* (1869) LR 8 Eq 368, at 375; *Frederick Rose (London) Ltd v William Pym & Co Ltd* [1953] 2 QB 450, at 461. *Cf* Clauson J in *Shipley Urban District Council v Bradford Corporation* (1936) Ch 375, and Simmonds J in *Crane v Hegeman-Harris Co* [1939] 1 All ER 662, where a more liberal approach was advocated.

75 *Australian Gypsum Ltd v Hume Steel Ltd* (1930) 45 CLR 54.

76 (1952) 86 CLR 271, at 280–81; *Australian Performing Rights Assoc Ltd v Austarama Television Pty Ltd* (1972) 2 NSWLR 467, at 473; *Hooker Town Developments v Director of War Service Homes* (1973) 47 ALJR 320, at 323–24; *Bishopsgate Insurance Australia Ltd v Commonwealth Engineering (NSW) Pty Ltd* (1981) 1 NSWLR 429.

77 [1970] 2 QB 86; 1 All ER 1213.

78 [1978] 1 NZLR 647.

79 *Australian Gypsm Ltd v Hume Steel Ltd* (1930) 45 CLR 54, at 64.

80 *Pukallus v Cameron* (1982) 43 ALR 243, at 247 *per* Wilson J; *Bishopsgate Insurance Australia Ltd v Commonwealth Engineering (NSW) Pty Ltd* [1981] 1 NSWLR 429, at 430–31; *Elders Trustee and Executor Co Ltd v EG Reeves Pty Ltd* (1987) 78 ALR 193, at 254.

Although the mistake must be apparent from the actions or words of the parties, the preferred approach adopted in Australia[81] and New Zealand[82] is that there need not be formal communication of the common intention by one party to the other or outward expression of accord. What must be established by clear evidence is that the parties had a common intention which continued up until the time when the contract was executed and the written agreement did not reflect that understanding. In this regard, the decisions of the High Court of Australia in *Maralinga Pty Ltd v Major Enterprises Pty Ltd*[83] and *Pukallus v Cameron*[84] are instructive. In *Maralinga*, a property had been purchased at auction. Prior to the auction, the auctioneer had represented that the purchaser could insist on a certain building on the property being demolished at the vendor's expense and sold on terms rather than entirely for cash. After the auction, the vendor declined to execute an agreement embodying this representation. The purchaser's representative executed the written agreement under a misapprehension that there was an enforceable collateral warranty as to demolition and means of payment. The High Court, however, found that he did not execute the written agreement under any continuing belief that the written document manifested the common understanding the parties had reached after the auction and so there could be no rectification. In *Pukallus v Cameron*, rectification was denied where the purchasers failed to prove that the written contract did not embody the true intention of the parties as to the area of land that was sold. The purchasers claimed that there was a common mistake in the agreement as to the position of a bore and that this was relevant to the appropriate parcel of land that the vendor had agreed to sell. The High Court, however, held that the evidence did not disclose that the parties had agreed to buy and sell any block other than that expressed in the contract. Further, there was no misapprehension as to the boundaries of the land but merely a misapprehension as to its features. In the opinion of Brennan J:[85]

> Rectification of the contract to include a parcel of land lying outside and to the south of subdivision 1 could not be decreed merely on proof that the parties mistakenly believed that the bore and cultivation lay within the boundaries of subdivision 1. Rectification could be decreed only upon proof that the parties intended that a further parcel of land, precisely identified, was to be included in the sale.

---

81 *Pukallus v Cameron* (1982) 43 ALR 243, at 247; *Medical Defence Union v Transport Industries Insurance Co Ltd* (1986) 6 NSWLR 740.

82 *Westland Savings Bank v Hancock* [1987] 2 NZLR 21, at 29.

83 (1973) 128 CLR 336.

84 (1982) 43 ALR 243.

85 *Ibid*, at 251.

In contrast with these cases, the New Zealand Court of Appeal, in *Dundee Farm Ltd v Bambury Holdings Ltd*,[86] granted rectification where the evidence established that the vendor intended to sell and the purchaser intended to buy certain farmland but, by mistake, an additional piece of land comprised in another title was included in the agreement. The court considered that the written agreement did not reflect the parties' bargain. Nor was the inclusion of an additional lot the subject of further negotiation.[87]

Rectification can also be ordered for a unilateral mistake in circumstances that give rise to an inference of sharp practice[88] or unconscionable dealing.[89] In *Roberts v Leicestershire County Council*,[90] rectification of a contract for the erection of a school was permitted where the plaintiff had submitted a tender based upon a contract period of 18 months and the defendants had prepared a contract based upon a completion period of 30 months. Although, prior to the execution of the agreement one of the officers of the council had discovered the error, the council chose not to inform the plaintiff. The price of the work would have been considerably higher had the completion date been 30 months. However, in *Riverlate Properties v Paul*,[91] the Court of Appeal declined to order rescission of a lease with the option of rectification where relief was sought for a mistake which was unknown to the defendant.[92] Russell LJ observed:[93]

> It may be that the original concept of reformation of an instrument by rectification was based solely on common mistake, but certainly in these days rectification may be based on such knowledge on the part of the defendant. See, for example, *A Roberts & Co v Leicestershire County Council*. Whether there was, in any particular case, knowledge of the intention and mistake of the other party must be a question of fact to be decided on the evidence. Basically, it appears to us that it must be such as to involve the defendant in a degree of sharp practice.

---

86 [1978] 1 NZLR 647. Further, see *Whiting v Diver Plumbing Ltd* [1991] 1 NZLR 560 where there was an obvious omission.

87 *Ibid*, at 653.

88 *Riverlate Properties v Paul* [1975] Ch 133, at 141; [1974] 2 All ER 656, at 660; *Commissioner for New Towns v Cooper GB Ltd* [1995] 2 All ER 929.

89 *Thomas Bates Ltd v Wyndham's (Lingerie) Ltd* [1981] 1 WLR 505, at 515; 522. Further, see *Misiaris v Saydels Pty Ltd* (1989) NSW Conv R 55; 474; *Johnstone v Arnaboldi* (1990) 2 Qd R 138; *State Rail Authority of NSW v Ferreri* (1990) ANZ Conv R 211.

90 [1961] Ch 555; [1961] 2 All ER 545.

91 [1975] Ch 133; [1974] 2 All ER 656; adopted in *Commerce Consolidated Pty Ltd v Johnstone* [1976] VR 724, and *Leighton v Parton* [1976] 1 NZLR 165.

92 See *Paget v Marshall* (1884) 28 Ch D 255; [1881–85] All ER 290. On common mistake, see *Solle v Butcher* [1950] 1 KB 671; [1949] 2 All ER 1107.

93 [1975] Ch 133, at 140; [1974] 2 All ER 656, at 660.

Rectification has also been ordered in the Court of Appeal of Queensland in relation to a mutual mistake of law, in *Winks v WH Heck & Sons Pty Ltd*, where the parties believed that the terms of the written contract legally bound the purchaser to recognise timber rights associated with the vendor's earlier sale of those rights to another when they did not. Rectification was granted so that the contract conformed to the parties' true understanding.[94] The court differed from the view expressed in the dissenting opinion of Higgins J in the High Court of Australia in *Bacchus Marsh Concentrated Milk Co Ltd v Joseph Nathan & Co Ltd*[95] that equity did not permit rectification where the mistake related to the legal interpretation of provisions in a contract. It is submitted that the better view is that adopted in *Winks*. Rectification should be declined for a mistake of law or interpretation only if the other party does not share the misapprehension.

A court may order rectification and specific performance in an appropriate case.[96] Rectification will not be permitted when to do so will interfere with the rights of third parties or the contract, if rectified, could not be performed.[97] A right to rectification is assignable.[98] A party will not be precluded from seeking rectification because a claim has been made under an unrectified agreement;[99] however, rectification cannot be ordered if the original agreement has been wholly performed.[100] Sometimes, it may be more appropriate to seek an order for the implication of a term rather than rectification.[101]

The Contractual Mistakes Act 1977 (New Zealand)

In New Zealand, the rules of common law and equity relating to the relief which could be claimed for mistake by a party to a contract have been abrogated and the jurisdiction to grant relief in cases of contractual mistake is governed by the Contractual Mistakes Act 1977. The Act was the result of a report by the Contracts and Commercial Law Reform

---

94 *Winks v WH Heck & Sons Pty Ltd* (1986) 1 Qd R 226, following *Re Butlin's Settlement Trusts* [1976] Ch 251.

95 (1919) 26 CLR 410, at 451, followed in *Issa v Berisha* (1981) 1 NSWLR 261, at 265.

96 *United States v Motor Trucks Ltd* [1924] AC 196 (PC).

97 *Coolibah Pastoral Co v Commonwealth* (1967) 11 FLR 176; *Nobleza v Lampl* (1986) 85 FLR 147.

98 *Majestic Homes v Wise* (1978) Qd R 225; *Latec Investments Ltd v Hotel Terrigal Pty Ltd* (1965) 113 CLR 265.

99 *Market Terminal v Dominion Insurance of Australia* (1982) 1 NSWLR 105, but subsequent words or conduct consistent with a particular interpretation of a contract may preclude reliance upon an opposite interpretation. *Standard Portland Cement v Good* (1983) 57 ALJR 151 (PC).

100 *Caird v Moss* (1886) 33 Ch D 72.

101 See Mason J in *Codelfa Construction Pty Ltd v State Rail Authority of NSW* (1982) 149 CLR 337, at 346.

Committee, on the effect of mistakes on contracts.[102] The Act expressly excludes the doctrine of *non est factum*, the law relating to the rectification of contracts, the law relating to undue influence and cases involving fraud, breach of fiduciary duty, and misrepresentation whether fraudulent or innocent. Also excluded from the operation of the Act is the Illegal Contracts Act 1970, ss 94A and 94B of the Judicature Act 1908 which relate to the recovery of moneys paid under mistake of law or fact and the Frustrated Contracts Act 1944.[103] Mistake is expressly said to include both a mistake of fact and law.[104] The rights of third parties are protected if the person to whom a disposition is made acts in good faith and did not have notice at the time of the disposition that the property was the subject of, or the whole or part of the consideration for a mistaken contract.[105] In order to more fully comprehend the scheme of the legislation, ss 6 and 7 are comprehensively set out below.

Section 6 of the Act provides:

(6)(1) A court may in the course of any proceedings or on application made for the purpose grant relief under s 7 of this Act to any party to a contract:

(a) If in entering into that contract:

(i) that party was influenced in his decision to enter into the contract by a mistake that was material to him, and the existence of the mistake was known to the other party or one or more of the other parties to the contract (not being a party or parties having substantially the same interest under the contract as the party seeking relief); or

(ii) all the parties to the contract were influenced in their respective decisions to enter into the contract by the same mistake; or

(iii) that party and at least one other party (not being the party having substantially the same interest under the contract as the party seeking relief) were each influenced in their respective decisions to enter into the contract by a different mistake about the same matter of fact or of law; and

---

102 May 1976. Further, see Sutton, RJ, 'Reform of the Law of Mistake in Contract' (1976) 7 NZULR 40.

103 Section 5(1) and (2).

104 Section 2(1).

105 Section 8.

(b) The mistake or mistakes, as the case may be, resulted at the time of the contract:

(i) in a substantially unequal exchange of values; or

(ii) in the conferment of a benefit, or in the imposition or inclusion of an obligation, which was, in all the circumstances, a benefit or obligation substantially disproportionate to the consideration therefore; and

(c) Where the contract expressly or by implication makes provision for the risk of mistakes, the party seeking relief or the party through or under whom relief is sought, as the case may require, is not obliged by a term of the contract to assume the risk that his belief about the matter might be mistaken.

(6)(2) For the purposes of an application for relief under s 7 of this Act in respect of any contract:

(a) A mistake, in relation to that contract, does not include a mistake in its interpretation.

(b) The decision of a party to a contract to enter into it is not made under the influence of a mistake if before he enters into it he becomes aware of the mistake but elects to enter into the contract notwithstanding the mistake.

Section (7) provides:

(1) Where by virtue of the provisions of s 6 of this Act the court has power to grant relief to a party to a contract, it may grant relief not only to that party but also to any person claiming through or under that party.

(2) The extent to which the party seeking relief, or the party through or under whom relief is sought, as the case may require, caused the mistake shall be one of the considerations to be taken into account by the court in deciding whether to grant relief under this section.

(3) The court shall have a discretion to make such order as it thinks just and in particular, but not in limitation, it may do one or more of the following things:

(a) Declare the contract to be valid and subsisting in whole or in part or for any particular purpose;

(b) Cancel the contract;

(c) Grant relief by way of variation of the contract;

(d) Grant relief by way of compensation.

(4) An application for relief under this section may be made by:

(a) Any person to whom the court may grant that relief; or

(b) Any person where it is material for that person to know whether relief under this section will be granted.

(5) The court may by any order made under this section vest any property that was the subject of the contract, or the whole or part of the consideration for the contract, in any party to the proceedings or may direct any such party to transfer or assign any such property to any party to the proceedings.

(6) Any order made under this section, or any provision or any such order, may be made upon and subject to such terms and conditions as the court thinks fit.

(a) Judicial applications of the Act

Although the Act was described by McMullin J in the Court of Appeal in *Conlon v Ozolins*[106] as remedial, it has not led to many reported applications for relief. This would suggest that it has not had any adverse effect on the security of contract the importance of which s 4(2) of the Act expressly asserts. However, it is also likely that a conservative interpretation of what constitutes mistake under s 6(1)(a)(iii) has considerably restricted any remedial operation that might have been intended. There has been a fundamental judicial disagreement in the Court of Appeal on the jurisdiction of a court to grant relief under this subsection which has had the effect of largely preserving the common law, 'outward manifestation of consent', approach based on a case like *Smith v Hughes*.[107]

(b) Mutual mistake under s 6(1)(a)(iii) of the Act

In one of the first reported cases on the ambit of this subsection, *McCullough v McGrath's Stock & Poultry Ltd*,[108] Mahon J considered that the common law still prevailed in relation to the formation of a contract and the Act was limited purely to the relief that might be granted. This approach was subsequently held to be incorrect by the Court of Appeal

---

106 [1984] 1 NZLR 489, at 505.
107 (1871) LR 6 QB 597; [1861–73] All ER 632, and see discussion, pp 107–08 below.
108 [1981] 2 NZLR 428.

in *Conlon v Ozolins* because, in the opinion of the majority, such an approach would undermine the remedial purpose of the legislation. McMullin J, in this regard, observed further that:[109]

> ... there is nothing in the Contractual Mistakes Act nor the report of the Committee to support the view taken by Mahon J which, if adopted, would severely restrict the operation of the Act itself. In enacting the Contractual Mistakes Act, Parliament provided an entirely new code applicable to every case of mistake which fitted its framework. It replaced with its own provisions the old and unsatisfactory rules of common law and those others which equity had evolved in an endeavour to mitigate the harshness of the former. Thus, a person who is a party to a contract, to which some element of mistake attaches, must now look to the statute and no longer to the common law or equity for his remedy, if there is to be one. To hold that the *Smith v Hughes* principle still operates to defeat the application of the Act would be to deprive the statute of much of its force; it would ignore the very wording of s 5(1) which expressly says that the Act shall have effect in place of the rules of the common law and of equity governing the circumstances in which relief may be granted on the grounds of mistake. Therefore, in so far as it holds that the operation of estoppel by representation is not excluded by the Contractual Mistakes Act, *McCullough v McGrath* was wrongly decided.

In *Conlon v Ozolins*, the majority, Woodhouse P and McMullin J, considered that s 6(1)(a)(iii) of the Act applied in relation to an agreement for the sale and purchase of land. In that case, a vendor and purchaser had entered an agreement for the sale of a block of land. The vendor, who was an elderly woman, had some difficulty in explaining herself in English which was not her native language. She had only intended to sell three lots but a fourth, including the back garden of her home, had been mistakenly included in the agreement. There was evidence that, had all four lots been for sale, the purchase price would have been much higher. The plaintiff, who sought specific performance of the agreement, was found to have been ignorant of the vendor's mistake. The majority considered that both parties were labouring under different mistakes as to the area of land sold.[110] Since there was a benefit to the purchaser substantially disproportionate to the consideration paid under the contract, the vendor was entitled to relief under s 7 and the case was remitted to the trial judge for further consideration. Somers J, however, in a strong dissent was critical of this reasoning and considered that there was an absence of any mistake on the part of the purchaser. Hence, in his view, the provisions of s 6(1)(a)(iii) of the Act, which required the

---

109 *Ibid*, at 504.

110 Further, see *Engineering Plastics Ltd v J Mercer & Sons Ltd* [1985] 2 NZLR 72.

parties to have made a different mistake about the same issue of fact or law, were not satisfied. In the opinion of Somers J, if the majority approach were correct there would be few, if any, cases of mistaken intent that could not be claimed to fall within this provision of the Act.[111] The approach of Somers J was subsequently adopted by Wylie J in *Shotter v Westpac Banking Corporation*[112] and Tipping J in *Shivas v Bank of New Zealand*.[113] In *Paulger v Butland Industries*,[114] the Court of Appeal, of which Somers and Wylie JJ were members, described *Conlon v Ozolins* as:[115]

> ... a decision on its particular facts. It is not authority for invoking the Act where one party misunderstood the clearly expressed intention of the other, or where one party meant something different from the plain meaning of his own words. For then the mistake is one in the interpretation of the contract, and the party making it cannot avail himself of the Act. This distinction was made and applied in *Shotter v Westpac Banking Corporation*.

However, it may be argued that *Shotter*, *Shivas*, and *Paulger* were cases where the claimants for relief did not evidence any genuine mistake that could justifiably have invoked the provisions of s 6(1)(a)(iii). It may be argued that in each of these cases, relief was sought under the Act in a belated attempt to resile from financial obligations which the claimants had clearly freely undertaken. However, a later decision of the Court of Appeal in *Mechenex Pacific Services Ltd v TCA Air Conditioning (New Zealand) Ltd*[116] affirmed the view that the Act did not abrogate *Smith v Hughes*[117] and thus effectively preserved the objective theory of the formation of contracts. The plaintiff, TCA, was approached by Mechenex to supply air conditioning coils and the latter supplied a copy of the specification that was relevant. TCA indicated that it could supply machinery of a type and form similar to that specified and that the coils offered were 'for the duties given in the specification'. It was not, however, made clear in the evidence what 'duties' meant. Attached to the quotation were schedules giving the performance detail of the machinery and attention was further drawn to these in the body of the quotation. The schedules indicated that the particular machinery required water flow at 5.39 litres per second whereas Mechenex required, and its specification referred to, machinery that could function at four litres per second. Mechenex, when it learned that the machinery was unsuitable,

---

111 [1984] 1 NZLR 489, at 508.

112 [1988] 2 NZLR 316, at 330.

113 [1990] 2 NZLR 327, at 358 following *Paulger v Butland Industries* [1989] 3 NZLR 549.

114 [1989] 3 NZLR 549.

115 *Ibid*, at 554.

116 [1991] 2 NZLR 393.

117 (1871) LR 6 QB 597; [1861–73] All ER 632.

refused to accept delivery and argued that, in accepting the quotation it had ordered, '32 coils as per your quotation ... as per spec supplied', and as a consequence contended that consensus sufficient to constitute a binding agreement was absent. Further, it submitted that TCA had caused the mistake in that it had led Mechenex to believe that its product had met its specification and so could not enforce the contract. Alternatively, it relied on s 6(1)(a)(iii) to claim relief. The Court of Appeal held, however, following *Smith v Hughes* that there was a binding contract and that TCA had not misled Mechenex in any respect. Nor was there any mistake on the part of TCA so that s 6(1)(a)(iii) could not be invoked. The court considered any mistake on the part of Mechenex was simply caused by its failure to read the accompanying schedules before accepting the quotation.

The judgment in *Mechenex* effectively rejected the remedial approach taken by Woodhouse P and McMullin J to s 6(1)(a)(iii) in *Conlon v Ozolins* and affirmed the application of the principle in *Smith v Hughes* that if there is an outward manifestation of accord then the parties will be generally held to their contract albeit that one party may have made a genuine mistake on a material matter. The concern of the courts in eschewing the more liberal interpretation favoured by the majority in *Conlon v Ozolins* appears to be essentially that it would threaten the security of contract and disrupt commerce. Cases such as *Paulger* would suggest that the court was concerned that there may be a flood of rather unmeritorious claims. Fears that a liberal interpretation or remedial approach would undermine the security of contract or cause the floodgates to open seem exaggerated, however, since it should not be overlooked that it is only where the plaintiff can evidence a genuine mistake and a substantial disparity in consideration that the court has jurisdiction to intervene. Even assuming in *Mechanex* that there was evidenced a mutual mistake as to the type of coil, it is difficult to see that this led objectively to a substantially unequal exchange of values or a conferment of a benefit disproportionate to the consideration that Mechanex was obliged to pay. Mechanex was simply asked to pay the price that a reasonable buyer of the coils would have had to pay albeit that they were later discovered to be unsuitable for the purpose for which Mechanex wanted them. Only if the second limb, namely s 6(1)(b) is construed so as to operate subjectively could it be said that there was any disparity in benefit in that the coils could not be used by Mechanex.[118]

---

118 For example, on an objective approach to s 6(1)(b), the buyer in *Smith v Hughes* could arguably have succeeded in claiming relief because the price paid for the new oats was, it would seem, a very high price and much higher than anyone commercially would have paid for new oats. Under the Act, however, it would seem that since the buyer had ample opportunity to satisfy himself that the oats were new, having had a sample given to him, a court could legitimately decline to order relief on the ground that he had been careless in entering the contract.

Conlon v Ozolins was a very different case. There was found to be a substantial disparity in the consideration provided for the four lots over the three that the vendor thought she was selling so that the purchaser was found to have been substantially enriched by the vendor's mistake. The approach that was taken by the majority to the issue of whether there was a mistake of the kind that fell within s 6(1)(a)(iii) was, it is submitted, defensible, and a remedial approach to the legislation similarly so. The evidence clearly established that the vendor believed she was selling three lots and the purchaser believed, no doubt fortified by the agreement, that he was acquiring four lots. The parties were plainly not *ad idem* over the areas of land that the vendor intended should be sold and this would appear to be a mutual mistake concerning the same matter of fact that fell within the provisions of the subsection. The concept of common law estoppel as manifested purely by the signature of a party to an agreement can work injustice where there is no true accord and a mistake has led or will lead to a manifest inequality in the exchange of values.[119] It was not suggested in *Conlon v Ozolins* that the purchaser had, on the strength of the agreement, adversely altered his position which would have weighted the argument against relief more heavily in his favour and certainly against any setting aside of the agreement without appropriate compensation. When assessing the measure of relief, if any, that should be granted under the Act, a court is empowered to take into account the extent to which the party seeking relief caused the mistake. The court could decline relief altogether or tailor the measure or nature of relief in a case where the mistake had caused the other party to injuriously change his or her position.[120] In a case like *Mechanex*, for example, assuming the jurisdictional factors to have been satisfied, the court could legitimately have declined relief on the ground that Mechanex had been careless and should stand any loss that might arise. Thus, even where a mistake sufficient to invoke jurisdiction to grant relief is evidenced, a court has an important curial role to play under the Act and may choose not to grant relief, or grant only partial relief in an appropriate case. Indeed, this occurred in *Slater Wilmshurst v Crown Group*,[121] where, hav-

---

119 On the principle of *Freeman v Cooke* (1848) 2 Exch 654; [1848] 154 ER 652.

120 In *Ciochetto v Ward* [1987] BCL 231, the negligence of the vendor in providing an erroneous area of land in a sale and purchase agreement was one reason for declining relief under the Act. See also, *Engineering Plastics Ltd v J Mercer & Sons Ltd* [1985] 2 NZLR 72. There, adopting the majority approach in *Conlon v Ozolins* to mistake, a vendor was permitted to recover the cost of importing a product and a substantial part of its anticipated profit, where there had been a mistake as to price caused by the purchaser's lack of care in reading a quotation for the product and the contract was varied to reflect a less favourable price for the vendor than the price quoted. This case would probably be decided differently on the issue of whether there was an operative mistake under s 6(1)(a)(iii). See further on relief where a party was at fault in signing an agreement, *Denning v Tri-Star Customs and Forwarding Ltd* [1996] 3 NZLR 630.

121 [1991] 1 NZLR 344.

ing ruled that the case was one where the court had jurisdiction to grant relief under the Act, Gallon J ruled that Crown should not be granted relief because it had been seriously at fault in taking appropriate steps to ensure it had clear title to sell land to Slater, a purchaser who had sold the property on prior to completion. However, it would appear that, in the light of *Paulger and Mechenex*, the proponents of the more conservative common law approach, as evidenced in *Smith v Hughes*, have succeeded in restricting greatly the remedial value of s 6(1)(a)(iii).[122]

(c) Mistakes under s 6(1)(a)(i) and (ii) of the Act

In *Denning v Tri Star Customs and Forwarding Ltd*,[123] it was held that s 6(1)(a)(i) covered not only cases where the party knew the other was mistaken, but also included the situation where a party ought to have appreciated that the other was mistaken. In adopting this interpretation, Salmon J would appear to have opted for a wider jurisdiction to relieve against unilateral mistake than that conferred under the general law which assumed sharp practice. Salmon J considered, however, that this approach was consistent with the wide ranging relief that was available under the Act. In order, however, for a court to grant relief, a claimant must also show that the mistake resulted in a substantial disparity in the consideration or in a substantially unequal exchange of values. Actual or constructive knowledge of a mistake *per se* does not give rise to relief. Similarly, in relation to s 6(1)(a)(ii), the fact that there is a shared or common mistake will not automatically lead to relief. It is only where the mistake has led to a substantial disparity in terms of s 6(1)(b) that a court will be able to intervene.

Section 6(1)(a)(ii) has been applied to allow relief in *Ware v Johnson*[124] where the court considered that there was a common mistake as to the condition of kiwi fruit plants which had resulted in a substantial disparity in the consideration provided under the contract. In *Phillips v Phillips*,[125] the Court of Appeal held that a consent order affecting the division of property should be set aside where the parties had proceeded

---

122 Professor DW McLauchlan, in 'Mistake as to the Contractual Terms under the Contractual Terms Act 1977' (1986) 12 NZULR 123 and 'The Demise of *Conlon v Ozolins*' (1990) 14 NZULR 229, advances the view that *Conlon v Ozolins* was incorrectly decided. The submission is made above that the majority view is defensible and is consistent with a restitutionary approach to mistake. It is submitted that, in any event, to remove doubt, the Act should be amended to give a court discretion in appropriate cases to grant relief in cases where a genuine mistake is shown to exist that has lead to a substantial contractual imbalance with the proviso that the extent of relief may have to be balanced against any detriment incurred by the party who seeks to uphold the apparent bargain.

123 [1996] 3 NZLR 630.

124 [1984] 2 NZLR 519.

125 [1993] 3 NZLR 159.

under a common mistake that there was a valid and enforceable oral agreement and it was established that the *de facto* wife had received substantially less under that agreement than she was entitled to enjoy at law. In *Slater Wilmshurst v Crown Group*,[126] a common oversight wherein both parties had forgotten that there was a serious impediment to the sale and purchase of a property which led to a very significant exchange in values was held to attract the provisions of the Act although relief was declined because the vendor had been seriously remiss in taking the appropriate steps to investigate title and the purchaser had on sold.

(d) Mistaken interpretation under s 6(2)(a) of the Act

Since s 2 expressly provides that a mistake includes a mistake of law, relief under the Act will be available for a mistake of this kind unless pursuant to s 6(2)(a) the mistake involves an issue of interpretation of the contract. As an additional ground for denying relief in *Shotter*,[127] *Paulger*,[128] and *Shivas*,[129] the courts have also invoked the provisions of s 6(2)(a) so as to deny relief. In *Paulger*, the Court of Appeal observed of s 6(2)(a):[130]

> Parliament plainly intended to maintain the well-established principle that contracts are to be construed objectively, and to avoid the great uncertainty that would arise were a party to be permitted to plead as a mistake that he understood the contract to mean something different from its plain and ordinary meaning.

Care should, it is suggested, be taken not to allow s 6(2)(a) to negate a remedial application of the Act, when it is plain that the parties acted on a mutual misapprehension as to a legal incident of the contract.[131]

In certain circumstances, rectification, which is unaffected by the Act, might be available to remedy a mistake of law if it can be established for example, that both parties had entered into an agreement on the basis of a common understanding concerning a legal incident of the agreement which the written document did not as a matter of legal interpretation reflect. Otherwise one of the parties may be unjustly enriched.[132]

---

126 [1993] 3 NZLR 344.

127 [1988] 2 NZLR 316, at 331.

128 [1989] 3 NZLR 549, at 553.

129 [1990] 2 NZLR 327, at 362.

130 [1989] 3 NZLR 549, at 553. Further, see *Engineering Plastics Ltd v J Mercer & Sons Ltd* [1985] 2 NZLR 72, at 83.

131 See McLauchlan, DW, 'The Demise of *Conlon v Ozolins* (1990–91)' 14 NZULR 229, at 247–52.

132 See *Winks v WH Heck & Sons Pty Ltd* [1986] 1 QD R 226, following in *Re Butlin's Settlement Trusts* [1976] Ch 251; and discussion, p 124.

CHAPTER 6

Frustration of Contract

Frustration of a contractual transaction gives rise to important issues of unjust enrichment. Where a contract is rendered ineffective because the parties are discharged by a supervening event from further performance, benefits and losses may have accrued that without adjustment may unjustly enrich or conversely unjustly cause loss to a party. Two fundamental issues arise in relation to frustration which are considered below. First, when is a contract discharged for frustration? The second is what, if any, relief is available in order to prevent unjust enrichment when a contract is discharged for frustration?

The doctrine of frustration

Frustration has it modern origins in *Taylor v Caldwell*.[1] There, the defendants agreed to let a concert hall to the plaintiffs for a consideration of £100 a day. The hall burnt down before the first day of the concert causing the plaintiff to claim damages for breach of contract. Blackburn J observed that since the music hall had ceased to exist without fault of either party, both parties were excused from performance.[2] In later cases, judicial attention was focused on the appropriate approach to the issue of what constituted a frustrating event. There were two principal theories which had much in common.[3] The first was known as the 'implied term approach' and the second as the 'construction approach'. The implied term approach permitted a court to declare a contract frustrated if, after an examination of the contract and the circumstances in which it was made, it could be inferred that the parties must have agreed that the existence of certain facts constituted the foundation of the contract and that if this foundation disappeared the parties obligations towards one another would be dissolved. This theory depended heavily on the assumption that, as reasonable persons, the parties would have agreed upon the term had they considered the possibility

---

1   (1863) 3 B & S 826; [1861–73] All ER 24.

2   *Ibid*, at 840; 30.

3   In *National Carriers Ltd v Panalpina* [1981] AC 675, at 686–88; 1 All ER 161, at 165, Lord Hailsham identifies five different theories of frustration. Lord Wilberforce observed, however, that the various theories shade into one another. *Ibid*, at 693; 170. Further, see Brennan J in *Codelfa Construction Pty Ltd v State Railway of NSW* (1981–82) 149 CLR 337, at 409.

of the frustrating event occurring.[4] This approach, however, did not gain universal approval. In *Denny Mott & Dickson v Fraser & Co Ltd*,[5] Lord Wright considered that it was artificial. The reality, as Lord Wright perceived, was that the parties did not anticipate the supervening event and as such it was possible, if asked, that their views would differ as to what should happen as a result of the occurrence of the supervening event. In determining whether a supervening event should absolve the parties from their obligations under a contract, Lord Wright considered that the factors for consideration were, on the one hand, the terms and construction of the contract read in the light of the surrounding circumstances and on the other, the events which had intervened.[6] This approach has been described as the construction approach to frustration. It does not rest upon any presumed intention of the parties but on an assessment as to whether the supervening event so radically altered the obligations of the parties that the contract, if performed, would be fundamentally different from the contractual obligations the parties had assumed.[7]

The approach suggested by Lord Wright gained approval in the House of Lords in *Davis Contractors v Fareham UDC*.[8] Lord Reid expressed a similar reservation about the implied term approach.[9] Lord Reid considered that frustration depended in most cases not on any implied term but on the true construction of the terms in the contract read in the light of the nature of the contract and the relevant surrounding circumstances when the contract was made. When considering the nature of the obligations undertaken and the surrounding circumstances, a court was entitled to take into consideration extrinsic evidence in order to determine the nature and extent of a contractual obligation. Lord Radcliffe observed that a contract would be regarded as frustrated and automatically dissolved where, without default of either party, a contractual obligation has become incapable of being performed because the circumstances in which performance is called for would render it a thing radically different from that which was undertaken by

---

4   See *Tamplin Steamship Co Ltd v Anglo-Mexican Petroleum Products Co Ltd* [1916] 2 AC 397, at 404; [1916–17] All ER 104, at 107; *Hirji Mulji v Cheong Yue Steamship Co Ltd* [1926] AC 497, at 504; [1926] All ER 51, at 55 *per* Lord Sumner. In Australia, see the judgment of Latham CJ in *Scanlons New Neon Ltd v Tooheys Ltd* (1943) 67 CLR 169, at 195–97. In New Zealand, see *Trustees of the Fountain of Friendship Lodge v Tait* [1939] NZLR 571.

5   [1944] AC 265, at 275–76; [1944] 1 All ER 678, at 683.

6   *Idem.*

7   See Lord Simon in *National Carriers Ltd v Panalpina Ltd* [1981] AC 675, at 702; [1981] 1 All ER 161, at 176.

8   [1956] AC 696; [1956] 2 All ER 145.

9   *Ibid*, at 720–21; 153–54.

the parties.[10] The approach in *Davis Contractors* has been adapted by the High Court of Australia in *Brisbane City Council v Group Proprietary Ltd*[11] and *Codelfa Construction Proprietary Ltd v State Rail Authority of NSW*.[12] In New Zealand, this approach was also adopted by the Court of Appeal in *Roberts v Independent Publishers Ltd*.[13]

The nature of the frustrating event

Often difficult questions of assessment are involved in determining whether an event causes a contract to be so radically different from the contract contemplated by the parties that it should be regarded as frustrated. Whether a frustrating event is sufficient to completely absolve the parties from their obligations to one another will depend upon a consideration of the contract as a whole. In *Denny, Mott & Dickson v Fraser & Co Ltd*,[14] for example, the House of Lords concluded that an option to acquire a timber yard was defeated on the introduction of timber control orders which operated to frustrate the principal trading agreement between the parties. Early cases of frustration had involved situations where performance had been excused because of supervening illegality or because the subject-matter of the contract had perished or been destroyed.[15] However, in *Krell v Henry*,[16] the Court of Appeal considered that frustration also included cases where an aspect essential to a contract had failed to materialise so that the contract could not be performed as contemplated. There, the contract was construed to contemplate the occupation of certain rooms on certain dates for the purpose of viewing the coronation of King Edward VII. The coronation did not take place on those dates and the contract was held frustrated thereby absolving the defendant from having to pay for the hire of the rooms. Similarly, in *Hirji Mulji v Cheong Yue Steamship Co Ltd*,[17] a charterparty was held frustrated where a ship had been requisitioned in circumstances that rendered the contract impossible to perform and thereby deprived the charterer of any benefit under the agreement. In Australia, frustration has been successfully invoked to dissolve a

---

10 *Ibid*, at 728–29; 160.

11 (1978–79) 145 CLR 143, at 162 *per* Stephen J.

12 (1982) 149 CLR 337, at 356–57 *per* Mason J; at 380 *per* Aickin J. Applied in *Beatson v McDivitt* (1988) 13 NSWLR 134.

13 [1974] 1 NZLR 459.

14 [1944] AC 265; [1944] 1 All ER 678.

15 *Williams v Lloyd* (1628) W Jo 179; [1628] 82 ER 95; *Coggs v Bernard* (1703) 2 Ld Raym 909; [1703] 92 ER 107; *Rugg v Minet* (1809) 11 East 210; [1809] 103 ER 985; *Taylor v Caldwell* (1863) 3 B & S 826; [1861–73] All ER 24.

16 [1903] 2 KB 740; [1900–03] All ER 20.

17 [1926] AC 497; [1926] All ER 51.

contractual relationship in *Brisbane City Council v Group Projects Limited.*[18] The Crown resumed ownership of certain land which was formerly controlled by a council. Group Properties had entered into an agreement with the council for the development of the land on certain conditions being satisfied. The resumption of the fee simple by the Crown was considered to fundamentally alter the nature of the obligation which the developer had entered into with the council so that the agreement was frustrated. Further, in *Codelfa Construction Proprietary Ltd v State Rail Authority of NSW,*[19] the High Court of Australia held that an agreement to construct an underground railway was frustrated where it was contemplated by both the Railway Authority and the contractor, Codelfa, that the project could be completed within a certain time because excavation would not be threatened or time lost as a result of attempts to injunct for nuisance caused by the excavations. The Authority had mistakenly informed Codelfa that it would not encounter difficulties of this kind. However, subsequently, Codelfa encountered such difficulty and had to alter its method of work substantially so as to avoid litigation with the result that the contract was late in completion. Codelfa sought to recover loss of profits and increased costs from the Authority and in order to do so argued that the original contract had been frustrated. The High Court considered that the events that had occurred had caused the contract to be performed in a manner radically different from that which the parties had contemplated and the original agreement had been frustrated.

Whether a supervening event operates to frustrate a contract in law is a question of degree. A court will not find frustration lightly in order to dissolve a contractual relationship, as the following cases illustrate.[20] In *Tamplin Steamship Co Ltd v Anglo-Mexican Petroleum Products Ltd,*[21] a majority of the House of Lords held that the fact that a ship, which was the subject of a charter-party, was requisitioned by the British government for war service was insufficient to frustrate the charter-party where it was impossible to say that the ship would not be released to allow for the further performance of the agreement. In *Tsakiroglou & Co Ltd v Noblee Thorl,*[22] the closing of the Suez Canal did not frustrate a contract to supply Sudanese buyers with groundnuts that were to be delivered at Hambourg and shipped during a certain period. Although freight

---

18   (1978–79) 145 CLR 143.

19   (1982) 149 CLR 337.

20   *Davis Contractors Ltd v Fareham Urban District Council* [1956] AC 696, at 727; [1956] 2 All ER 145, at 158.

21   [1916] 2 AC 397; [1916–17] All ER 104. *Cf Hirji Mulji v Cheong Yue Steamship Co Ltd* [1926] AC 497; [1926] All ER 51.

22   [1962] AC 93; [1961] 2 All ER 179. Further, see *The Eugenia* [1964] 2 QB 226; *The Captain George K* [1970] 2 Lloyd's LR 21; *Kodros Shipping Corp v Empresa Cubana de Fletes 'the Evia'* [1983] 1 AC 736; [1982] 3 All ER 350.

and insurance was more expensive around the alternative route which was the Cape of Good Hope and the time of delivery a few weeks longer, this was considered insufficient to constitute a fundamental change in the contract. In *National Carriers Ltd v Panalpina Ltd*,[23] a lease for a warehouse was the subject of a claim of frustration where there was closure of a street granting access to the warehouse. Although by the time access to the warehouse was restored the lessee would have lost two out of five years remaining use of the warehouse and their business would have been seriously disrupted, the House of Lords held that the closure was not sufficiently serious to amount to a frustrating event. In Australia, in *Scanlon's New Neon Ltd v Tooheys Ltd*,[24] the High Court held that contracts for the hire of neon lights were not frustrated even though orders made under the national security legislation prohibited the illumination of the signs thereby largely depriving the hirer of much of the expected benefit of the hire. In the leading New Zealand case of *Roberts v Independent Publishers*,[25] the Court of Appeal held that an agreement containing an option for Independent Publishers to acquire the plaintiff's shares in a certain company in exchange for cash or shares in Independent Publishers had not been frustrated by the fact that Independent Publishers had become a private company with some perceived personal disadvantages for the plaintiff. The fact that a bargain has become uneconomic due to inflation will not be sufficient to constitute frustration.[26] The fact that an obligation under an agreement becomes illegal to perform in its entirety will not absolve a party from performing such part as could be achieved without illegality.[27] Thus, in *Eyre v Johnson*,[28] a tenant was not absolved from all responsibility under a covenant for repair merely because it became illegal to spend more than a limited amount each year on decoration or repair.

---

23 [1981] AC 675; [1981] All ER 161. This case held that the doctrine of frustration applied to a lease. Formerly, there was doubt as to whether frustration applied to leases, see *Cricklewood Property & Investment Trust Ltd v Leightons Investment Trust Ltd* [1945] AC 221; 1 All ER 252. In *Firth v Halloran* (1926) 38 CLR 261, at 269, Issacs J considered that frustration could apply to leases. Further, see *Maori Trustee v Prentice* [1992] 3 NZLR 344, where a substantial increase in rent did not amount to frustration. On taking up the lease it was held that the defendant had accepted the risk of such a change.

24 [1943] 67 CLR 169. Cf *Denny Mott & Dickson Ltd v Fraser & Co* [1944] AC 265. In New Zealand, in *Wellington College v Guardian Trust Ltd* [1945] NZLR 606, the temporary application of wartime fiscal regulations governing rents did not operate to frustrate the lease.

25 [1974] 1 NZLR 459.

26 *British Movietone News Ltd v District Cinemas Ltd* [1952] AC 166, at 186 per Lord Simmonds and in New Zealand, *Gore District Council v Power Co Ltd* [1996] 1 NZLR 58.

27 For illegality as a frustrating event, see *Metropolitan Water Board v Dick, Kerr & Co* [1918] AC 119; [1916–17] All ER 122; *Denny Mott & Dickson Ltd v Fraser & Co* [1944] AC 265, at 272.

28 [1946] KB 481; 1 All ER 719.

Assumption of risk and frustration

A factor which may be influential in the assessment of whether a super-vening event may be regarded in law as frustrating a venture is the question of risk. If an event should have been contemplated as a possibility, it may be successfully contended that its eventual occurrence should not be treated as frustrating an agreement. In *Codelfa Construction*,[29] the High Court allowed Codelfa's claim despite the fact that the nature of the work must have excited some concern that the completion date might be affected by exposure to litigation. However, the mistaken belief and representation to Codelfa by the Authority that the project would be immune from litigation affected Codelfa's tender.[30] To have held Codelfa to the agreement would have unjustly enriched the Authority and would have meant that Codelfa was bound to a contract that was radically different from that which either of the parties had contemplat-ed. It is instructive to compare *Codelfa* with *Davis Contractors v Fareham UDC*.[31] It will be recalled that the House of Lords declined to hold that a construction contract was frustrated for delay attributable to there being insufficient labour to complete the contract by the nominated date. The necessity for a constant and sufficient supply of labour was apparent to Davis Contractors at the time of the agreement. Although it was an essential consideration affecting the tender and the completion date, the risk of delay was foreseen and could have been the subject of special provision in the agreement protecting the contractor. Lord Reid observed that the most that could be said was that the delay that was occasioned through the default of neither party was greater in degree than was to be expected.[32] It was not caused by any new and unforeseeable factor or event. The project simply proved to be more onerous but it never became a project of a different kind from that contemplated in the con-tract. Although Lord Radcliffe expressed sympathy for the contractor, the contract in his Lordship's view could not be said to have been frustrated.

Another case that illustrates the risk factor in determining whether frustration has rendered a contract ineffective is *Amalgamated Investment Ltd v John Walker & Sons Ltd*.[33] A purchaser sought rescission of an agree-ment for the sale and purchase of a property which had been acquired for the purpose of development. After the agreement had been executed, the property was designated a protected building which meant that it could not be the subject of development. The consideration paid under the agreement reflected the value of the property assessed on the basis that it

---

29 [1982] 149 CLR 337.

30 Mason J observed that the doctrine of frustration in circumstances of this kind was closely related to the concept of mutual mistake. *Ibid*, at 360.

31 [1956] AC 696; [1956] 2 All ER 145. See discussion, p 136.

32 *Ibid*, at 724; 156.

33 [1976] 3 All ER 508.

could be re-developed. The purchaser contended that the vendor knew that the property had been acquired for development purposes and the designation, which was at the time of execution of the contract unknown to either party, was so radical a change that the agreement had been frustrated. The Court of Appeal dismissed the developer's claim on the grounds that the risk of designation was a risk which every purchaser had in contemplation. The plaintiffs had been aware that the risk existed and was one that they had to bear. The vendor had not warranted planning permission would be given for the development and the contract was not as a result of the listing so radically different that it could be said to have been frustrated. Sometimes the parties may attempt to make provision for a frustrating event in a contract. Whether the express provision accommodates the particular contingency or not is a question of construction.[34]

Fault and frustration

A further consideration in cases of frustration is fault. In order for a supervening event to constitute frustration, it must occur independently of the fault of either of the parties.[35] A party cannot rely on self-induced frustration to resile from a contract.[36] However, the rule that a party cannot rely on self-induced frustration does not require he or she to prove affirmatively that the frustrating event was not self-induced. In *Joseph Constantine SS Ltd v Imperial Smelting Corp Ltd*,[37] an explosion on a ship rendered a charter-party impossible to perform. The owners were successfully able to claim that the agreement had been frustrated even though it was possible that the owners had been negligent. However, this was one of only three possible reasons for the explosion and, in the absence of the charterer being able to establish that the owners were negligent, the agreement was dissolved by frustration. The mere fact that a party has by some act or omission prevented the performance of a contract does not necessarily preclude the other party from contending that an agreement is frustrated. In *Shepherd & Co Ltd v Jerrom*,[38] for example,

---

34 *Kodros Sipping Corp v Empresa Cubana de Fletes 'The Evia'* [1983] 1 AC 736; [1982] 3 All ER 350; *Claude Neon Ltd v Hardie* (1970) Qd R 93.

35 *Taylor v Caldwell* (1863) 3 B & S 826; [1861–73] All ER 24; *Paal Wilson & Co v Partenreederei Hannah Blumenthal* [1983] 1 AC 854, at 909; [1983] 1 All ER 34, at 44.

36 *Bank Line Ltd v Arthur Capel & Co Ltd* [1919] AC 435, at 452; [1918–19] All ER 504; *Mertens v Home Freeholds Co Ltd* [1921] All ER 372; *Maritime National Fish Ltd v Ocean Trawlers Ltd* [1935] AC 524; [1935] All ER 86.

37 [1942] AC 154.

38 [1987] 1 QB 301. Further, see *Hare v Murphy Brothers Ltd* [1974] 3 All ER 940. More generally on frustration and contracts of employment, see *Marshall v Harland & Wolff Ltd* [1972] 2 All ER 715 where a contract of employment was held not to be frustrated for illness where there was an absence of evidence of permanent incapacity. Cf *Notcutt v Universal Equipment Co Ltd* [1986] 3 All ER 582, where the nature of the illness, namely, a heart attack, had rendered the contract of employment impossible to perform. In Australia, see *Finch v Sayers* (1976) 2 NSWLR 540.

an apprentice contended that a contract of apprenticeship was not frustrated where he had been sentenced to a period in borstal for his part in an affray. The apprentice argued that frustration could not be invoked to permit his employer from terminating his contract because the supervening cause had arisen as a result of his own actions. The Court of Appeal held that a sentence of borstal training was a supervening cause that was neither foreseen nor provided for by the parties at the time of the agreement and it rendered the performance of the agreement radically different from that which the parties had contemplated. Further, the court held that the apprentice was unable to rely on his own default. His criminal conduct was unrelated to his contract and the sentence of borstal training constituted the frustrating event.

A party cannot, however, rely on frustration where an inability to perform a contract has arisen from an independent frustrating event that is collateral to a contract. Thus, in *Universal Corporation v Five Ways Properties Ltd*,[39] a purchaser of property in England was unable to claim that the agreement was discharged for frustration when he was unable to complete the purchase because of supervening foreign exchange restrictions in Nigeria which precluded his access to the necessary finance to complete the purchase.

Restitution consequent upon frustration

The effect of the doctrine of frustration is that a contract is automatically discharged upon frustration being established. Unfair consequences can flow from holding parties to a contract which is radically different from that which they contemplated and so, where these circumstances exist, the parties will be mutually discharged from performing their obligations. However, frustration could under the general law work injustice. The common law did not assist a party to a contract to receive reimbursement even though he or she had expended moneys or performed a service for the benefit of the other party prior to the frustrating event if, in the contract, the obligation to pay was conditional upon complete performance.[40] Nor, for some time, did it assist a person to recover moneys that had been paid in advance of a frustrating event in anticipation of receiving a benefit under a contract. In *Chandler v Webster*,[41] it was held that frustration only excused the parties to a contract from performance

---

39 [1979] 1 All ER 552.

40 *Cutter v Powell* (1795) 6 Term 320; [1795] 101 ER 573; *Appleby v Myers* (1867) LR 2 CP 631.

41 [1904] 1 KB 493.

of their obligations from the time of the frustrating event. Since the contract was in force until that time, a party, who had paid money in advance in the expectation of receiving a benefit under the contract, was not entitled to sue for the return of his money even though prior to the frustrating event the benefit had not been received. The loss was considered to lie where it fell. Only if a payment had been earned prior to the frustrating event in the partial performance of the contract was it recoverable.[42] *Chandler v Webster*, however, was disapproved in *Fibrosa Spolka Akcyjna v Fairbairn Lawson Combe Barbour Ltd*.[43] There, the plaintiff claimed the return of money which constituted part payment for certain machinery which was to be forwarded to Gdynia in Poland. Gdynia became enemy controlled territory and the contract was held to be frustrated since its completion was not a temporary impossibility but likely to be prolonged because of the war. The plaintiff contended that it was entitled to the repayment of the advance payment because there had been a total failure of consideration. It was held that the plaintiff was entitled to judgment and that the claim for moneys had and received survived independently of the contract where there had been a total failure of consideration. Lord Wright observed:[44]

> The claim for repayment is not based on the contract which is dissolved on the frustration, but on the fact that the defendant has received the money and has, in the events which have supervened, no right to keep it. The same event which automatically renders performance of the consideration impossible, not only terminates the contract as to the future, but terminates the right of the payee to retain the money which he has received only on the terms of the contract performance.

It was also recognised in *Fibrosa* that the common law was deficient in cases of this kind because it was unable to apportion any amount which could be set-off in consideration of expenditure by a defendant in partially performing his or her obligations under a contract.[45] This was not, however, a consequence in *Fibrosa* where the defendant acknowledged that it would not suffer loss because the machinery could be sold profitably elsewhere.

---

42 *Hirsch v Zinc Corporation Ltd* (1917) 24 CLR 34; *Westralien Farmers Ltd v Commonwealth Agricultural Service Engineers Ltd* (1936) 54 CLR 361; *cf Re Continental C & G Rubber Co Pty Ltd* (1919) 27 CLR 195.

43 [1943] AC 32; [1942] 2 All ER 122. Mason CJ in *Baltic Shipping Co v Dillon* (1993) 176 CLR 344, at 355, observed that *Fibrosa* correctly reflects the law in Australia.

44 *Ibid*, at 65; 137.

45 *Ibid*, at 72; 141 *per* Lord Wright.

Statutory relief for the consequences of frustration

(a) The English model

Shortly after *Fibrosa*, the Law Reform (Frustrated Contracts) Act 1943 was enacted to govern relief for frustration of a contract in English law.[46] This enactment was adopted in New Zealand in the Frustrated Contracts Act 1944[47] and in Victoria with the Frustrated Contracts Act 1959. It provides a statutory remedy to relieve against unjust enrichment consequent upon the frustration of a contract. Certain contracts are excluded form its operation. The Act binds the Crown. It does not apply to charter-parties other than time charter-parties or a charter-party by way of demise. Nor does it apply to contracts (other than a charter-party) for the carriage of goods by sea. Contracts of insurance are also excluded from the Act, as are certain frustrating events relating to the sale of goods.[48] The Act does not apply where a contract contains a provision which upon its true construction was intended to take effect in the event of the frustrating event occurring. Should such a contractual provision be in issue, a court is entitled to take into account the provisions of the legislation and grant relief only in so far as it is consistent with the contractual provision to do so.[49] Accrued rights to payment that can be properly severed from the remainder of the contract that is frustrated are protected under the Act.[50]

Two provisions of the Act substantially govern the jurisdiction of a court to grant compensation for the consequences of a supervening frustrating event. Under the first, a court is obliged to order the repayment of moneys paid to a contracting party in advance once a frustrating event has occurred.[51] This provision envisages that moneys will be repaid even though the consideration for the payment may not have totally failed. In this respect, the legislation affords a wider claim to relief than the common law could provide. However, this right of recovery is qualified. If the party to whom the sums were paid or payable incurs expenses before the time of discharge in or for the performance of the contract, a court may, if it considers it just to do so, having regard to all the circumstances of the case, allow the retention of the whole or any part of the moneys otherwise recoverable not being a sum that is in excess of the expenses incurred. In *Lobb v Vasey Housing Auxiliary*,[52] it was held in Victoria that the onus of establishing that an amount should be retained fell upon the party seeking to retain a part or all of the advance.

---

46 See McKendrick, E, 'Frustration, Restitution, and Loss Apportionment', in Burrows, A (ed), *Essays on the Law of Restitution*, 1991, p 147, Clarendon Press, Oxford.

47 Moran, P, 'Restitutionary Principles and the Frustrated Contracts Act 1944' (1980–83), 4 Auck Univ LR 56.

48 Section 4(5)(c) (NZ); s 3(1)(c) (Vict).

49 Section 2(3) (UK); s 4(3) (NZ); s 4(3) (Vict).

50 See s 4(4) (NZ); s 4(4) (Vict).

51 Section 1(1) (UK); s 3(2) (NZ); s 3 (2) (Vict).

52 [1963] VR 239.

The second provision enables a court to grant compensation for the performance of services by a party who has not received payment or reimbursement for any part of that service prior to the discharge of the contract.[53] Where the performance benefits the other party to the contract before the time of discharge, there shall be recoverable such sum as a court considers just. In assessing compensation, a court cannot award more than the value of the benefit that has been conferred. A court must also consider what effect the circumstances giving rise to the frustration or avoidance of the contract has had in relation to the benefit received. It is also empowered to determine the amount of expenses incurred including overheads and other work performed before the time of discharge by the benefited party in or for the performance of the contract including any sums paid or payable by him or her to any other party pursuant to the contract and retained or recoverable by that party under the Act. Where a party has assumed an obligation under a contract in exchange for which a benefit has been conferred on another person as part of the consideration for the contract (whether that person is a party or not) the benefit so conferred is required to be treated as a benefit for the person who had assumed the obligation.[54]

In assessing the value of expenses incurred by any party in relation to either provision, a court may include, without prejudice to the generality of the provisions, such sum as appears to be reasonable in respect of overhead expenses and in respect of any work or services performed personally by that person.[55] Insurance payments, however, are not to be taken into account unless an obligation to insure was imposed by an express term of the contract or by some other enactment.[56]

(b) Judicial consideration of the legislation

The legislation was considered by Robert Goff J (now Lord Goff) in *BP Exploration Co (Libya) Ltd v Hunt (No 2)*.[57] This case involved a determination of the compensation that should be paid to BP Exploration by Hunt following frustration of an agreement to exploit an oil concession consequent upon its confiscation by the Libyan government. Hunt had purchased an oil concession under a former government and had entered into an arrangement with BP Exploration which resulted in the latter spending considerable sums in prospecting and eventually realising a substantial amount of oil, some of which was allocated to Hunt under the terms of contract. Under the agreement it was provided that

---

53 Section 1(3) (UK); s 3(3) (NZ); s 3(3) (Vict).
54 See s 3(6) (NZ); s 3(6) (Vict).
55 See s 3(4) (NZ); s 3(4) (Vict).
56 See s 3(5) (NZ); s 3(5) (Vict).
57 [1982] 1 All ER 925.

Hunt's obligation to pay for his share of the plaintiff's development expenses and other costs did not require him to personally pay, but BP was to look for reimbursement solely from Hunt's share of the oil that was extracted. Robert Goff J was asked to determine the basis upon which Hunt should have to compensate BP Exploration. First, it was held that s 2(3) of the Act,[58] which Hunt argued exonerated him from personal liability, did not apply because the obligation in the agreement, whereby BP Exploration undertook not to seek reimbursement from Hunt personally, was discharged with the remainder of the contract by the supervening frustrating event.[59] In assessing the sum which Hunt should have to pay for the services rendered by BP Exploration, Robert Goff J made certain important general observations.

(a) The Act was not intended as a general power to apportion losses or expenses. Expenses could only be the subject of an award in terms of the specific provisions in the Act. Nor was it an Act that was concerned to place the parties in the position in which they would have been if the contract had been performed. The Act provided a remedy that was designed to prevent unjust enrichment.[60] This did not mean that a party could expect compensation for every kind of expenditure that might be incurred under a contract for some expenditure might confer no benefit at all on the other party.[61]

(b) In so far as the provision concerning restitution for the performance of a contractual service was concerned, as in the present case, the proper method of assessing benefit was the product of the service rendered and not the services themselves.[62] Thus, a party would not be entitled to compensation for services rendered in reliance upon the contract unless it could be demonstrated that those services benefited the other. A party could not, for example, be compensated for the construction of part of a building which had burnt down as a result of a frustrating event, thereby depriving the defendant of any benefit from the performance of the work.[63] Conversely, Robert Goff J considered that, if a benefit were established, a performing party would be entitled to restitution even though, had the frustrating event not occurred, the contract would have constituted an unprofitable bargain for the contractor.[64] Further, it was held that the fact that payment was expressed to be consequent upon completion

---

58 Section 4(3) (NZ); s 4(3) (Vict).

59 [1982] 1 All ER 925, at 943. The House of Lords upheld the approach of Robert Goff J on this point. *Ibid*, at 990–91 *per* Lord Brandon.

60 *Ibid*, at 938.

61 *Idem*.

62 *Ibid*, at 939.

63 *Ibid*, at 942.

64 *Ibid*, at 938.

in performance was insufficient to exempt the contract from the operation of the Act. Unless it was made expressly a term of the agreement, in which case s 2(3) came into play, relief was available under the Act even for an entire contract where payment was said to arise on completion.[65]

(c) Where the claim was for compensation for services rendered, the measure of recovery was limited to the amount of the defendant's benefit and was not the measure of recovery that would normally be associated with a claim in *quantum meruit* or *quantum valebat*, namely the reasonable value of the plaintiff's performance.[66]

(d) In assessing what was just compensation, a court could take into account the terms of the contract.[67] The terms might serve to indicate the scope of the work, the nature of the risk undertaken, and remuneration and so be relevant to the sum awarded in respect of such work. The contract sum would constitute some evidence of what would be a reasonable sum to award for the plaintiff's work. Robert Goff J considered that it might be unfair to award more than the contractual consideration or a rateable part of it in respect of services rendered.

Robert Goff J considered that BP Exploration had enhanced the concession and benefited Hunt enormously although the circumstances surrounding the expropriation had reduced the value of this benefit. Further, Robert Goff J acknowledged that the assessment of what constituted a just sum imposed a difficult burden on a court in a case of this kind. In assessing what was a just sum, it was considered that the contract provided valuable guidance.[68] Compensation should be assessed on the basis of expenses incurred by BP in providing the benefit for Hunt. In this regard, Hunt was required to pay the sum that he would have been required to pay to BP under the contractual provisions for what was described as oil reimbursement less the amount that had been already been paid to BP under the contract. The sum paid by way of compensation was, as Robert Goff J perceived, substantially less than the actual benefit to Hunt of BP's services.[69] Finally, in having regard to the method of assessing compensation, the court considered that the provisions of the Act did not permit a court to add in a time value representing the advantage to Hunt that had accrued as a result of his having enjoyed the benefit of BP's industry without full reimbursement over a considerable period of time.[70] The

---

65 *Ibid*, at 943–44. *Cf Cutter v Powell* (1795) 6 Term Rep 320; [1775–1802] All ER 159; *Appleby v Myers* (1867) LR 2 CP 651; [1861–73] All ER 452.

66 *Ibid*, at 942. Further, see Chapter 4, pp 73–74.

67 *Ibid*, at 943.

68 *Ibid*, at 958.

69 *Ibid*, at 960.

70 *Ibid*, at 959.

approach of Robert Goff J to assessment was upheld in the Court of Appeal. Lawton LJ made the important observation that the Act did not require a judge to perform an accountancy exercise which, in any event, might produce differing results. What was just was what the trial judge considered appropriate and an appellate court would not interfere unless the method of assessment was so plainly wrong that it could not be regarded as just.[71]

(c) The Frustrated Contracts Act 1978 (New South Wales)

In New South Wales, frustration is governed by the Frustrated Contracts Act 1978. This Act embodies a complicated statutory scheme which, unlike the English legislation, is aimed primarily at equalising losses and benefits rather than granting restitution for unjust enrichment. The Act similarly binds the Crown and does not apply to charter-parties except a time charter-party or a charter-party by way of demise. Nor does it apply to a contract (other than a charter-party) for the carriage of goods by sea, a contract of insurance or to contracts where the parties have agreed that it should be excluded.[72] Further, it does not apply to a contract embodied in another instrument or agreement constituted by the memorandum or articles of association or rules or other instrument or agreement constituting or regulating the affairs of companies, credit unions, building societies, co-operatives, trade unions or partnerships in any case where the frustrating event furnishes a case for the winding up or dissolution of any of these bodies.[73] The Act applies to obligations under a contract which are frustrated and cannot be severed from the remainder of the contract.[74]

Part II of the Act is concerned with accrual of rights of action before frustration. If rights of action have accrued before the frustrating event, s 7(1) limits the available cause of action to damages which must be assessed with regard to the fact that the contract has been frustrated.

The provisions relating to compensation for expenditure and benefits received which are set out in Part III of the Act appear rather complex. Division I of Part III relates to performance of obligations other than promises to pay money. In cases of this kind, s 11(2)(a) provides that where a contract is frustrated and part but not the whole of the performance to be given by a party under the contract has been received before the time of the frustration, the performing party shall be paid an amount equal to the attributable value of the performance except where

---

71 *Ibid*, at 980. For criticism of the approach of Robert Goff J, see Stewart, A and Carter, JW, 'Frustrated Contracts and Statutory Adjustments; the Case for Reappraisal' (1992) 51 CLJ 66, at 98–100.

72 Section 6(1)(e).

73 Section 6(3)(2).

74 Section 6(3).

the attributable cost of the performance exceeds the attributable value. Attributable value is defined as an amount equal to the value of the proportionate allowance for that performance reduced by the lost value of that performance. Attributable cost is defined in the Act to mean first, where there is no incidental gain to the performing party, an amount equal to the reasonable cost of performance. However, this may alter if there is an incidental benefit to the performing party defined as any property or improvement to property acquired or derived by the performing party which is not comprised in any performance or expended or disposed of in giving performance. An example of this is seen in a building contract where materials that the contractor has retained after the frustrating event could be used on another job. In such cases, the reasonable cost may be reduced by the amount of the incidental gain.

Where the amount of the attributable cost exceeds what is defined as the proportionate allowance (meaning such part of the agreed return for complete performance of the contract as is appropriate to be charged having consideration for the extent to which the performance has been reduced), the attributable cost will be taken to be such part of the reasonable cost of the performance as is equal in amount to that proportionate allowance. Section 11(2)(b) provides that where the attributable cost of the performance exceeds its attributable value, an amount can be paid by way of compensation that is equal to the sum of:

(i) the attributable value of the performance; and

(ii) one-half of the amount by which the attributable cost of the performance exceeds its attributable value.

An example may assist to comprehend these rather complex provisions. A contractor agrees to perform certain construction work for an owner, the total contract price to amount to $10,000 with the work to be performed in six months. If a frustrating event occurs within this period so that the contractor is absolved from completing the contract, the contractor will be permitted the attributable value of the performance which is the proportionate allowance for that performance reduced by the lost value of that performance. Assume that the contractor has completed two-thirds of the work when the frustrating event occurs. Assume also that the work is diminished in value for the owner by one-third. For example, in the case of a building, a substantial fire may have diminished the value of the partially completed work because a certain amount of redecoration and reconstruction will be required thus reducing the benefit of the contract to the owner by one-third. The general rule under s 11(2)(a) would permit compensation in the sum of $3,333.33 being the value of the proportionate allowance for performance, ie two-thirds of the price less a third for the lost value of that performance.

Assume, however, that the attributable cost was to be assessed as the proportionate allowance for the work, which being two-thirds complete was $6,666.66. There being no incidental gain for the contractor (such as there might be, for example, if the contractor acquired materials that could be used on another job). The amount to be paid to the contractor by virtue of s 11(2)(a) and (b) will be $4,999.99 calculated as follows:

Attributable value	$3,333.33
<u>Plus</u> one-half of the amount by which the attributable cost of the performance exceeds its attributable value	<u>$1,666.66</u>
	$4,999.99

The intention of s 11(2)(a) and (b) is that the parties should share losses equally that arise from frustration. Thus, in this example, the contractor has to suffer an equivalent loss in compensation for his actual service to the actual loss in real benefit that is suffered by the owner. Section 15 of the Act, however, permits a court to dispense with these provisions if the application would be manifestly inadequate or inappropriate, would cause manifest injustice or would be excessively expensive. The Act differs from the English model in that compensation for services is not dependent or limited to the upper value of the benefit actually received by the party for whom services are performed if the attributable cost exceeds the attributable value of the performance. Thus, in the example given above, the upper level of compensation payable under the English model would be limited to the sum of $3,333.33 or the attributable value being the actual benefit received. It would also seem that if the contractor has made a bad bargain, such as where his or her actual costs exceed the contract price, he or she will not be advantaged by the frustrating event. This is because the attributable cost can never be assessed at more than the proportionate allowance for the contract.[75]

Where money has been paid to another person as part of or as part of an agreed return for the performance of the contract by the other party and the contract is frustrated, s 12 makes provision for the return of the sum paid. However, where the party who has to repay the money has suffered a detriment as a result of partial performance, he or she will be able to deduct one-half of the amount that would be fair compensation for the detriment suffered. Should the performing party have received any property or improvement to property as a result of attempting to perform the contract, s 12 further provides that the other party shall be entitled to one-half of the value of the property or improvement so acquired or derived. Again, the Act seeks to apportion benefits and losses. These provisions may also be departed from under s 15 if their application would be manifestly inadequate, inappropriate, or would cause manifest injustice or be excessively expensive.

---

75   Section 11(1).

(d) The Frustrated Contracts Act 1988 (South Australia)

This Act also envisages a profit and loss sharing formula for the assess-ment of compensation after frustration. Again the formula is complicated. Section 7(1) provides that on frustration there will be an adjustment between the parties so that no party is advantaged or disadvantaged in consequence of the frustration. Section 7(2) contains a statutory formula for assessing the adjustment which may be dispensed with if, in the opin-ion of a court, there is a more equitable basis for making the adjustment. The statutory formula envisages that the value of contractual benefits received up to the date of frustration by each party to the contract will be assessed at the date of frustration and the values will be aggregated. From this will be deducted the value of the contractual performance of each party to the contract and those values are also aggregated. The remainder is to be notionally divided between the parties, with an adjustment made between them, so that there is an equalisation of the contractual return of each at the figure notionally arrived at by subtracting the aggregate perfor-mance from the aggregate benefit and halving the balance. The contractual return of a party means the figure, which may be positive, zero or nega-tive, obtained by subtracting from the value of the contractual benefits of that party the value of the contractual performance of that party.

In assessing the value of performance in cases where the performance does not consist of a monetary payment (the value of which is able to be derived or deduced from the provisions of the contract), the value of the performance will include the party's actual costs in carrying out his or her contractual obligations together with a reasonable amount for work and labour.[76] In addition, if a party would (assuming the contract to have been fully performed) have made a profit or loss, the percentage profit or loss will be estimated and the amount of the performance increased or reduced by that percentage.[77] It is immaterial that the other party to the contract may have received no benefit. Contractual performance also includes reliance costs that a party incurs preparatory to the perfor-mance of a contractual obligation.[78] If a party performs a contractual obligation after a frustrating event of which he or she is unaware, the value of the performance may be taken into account.[79]

In assessing benefits, the effect of the frustrating event is to be taken into account.[80] Where the frustrating event diminishes the value of the contractual benefit, the conduct of the party, who may be responsible for some negligent act or omission leading to an event that is extraneous

---

76 Section 3(2)(c)(i).
77 Section 3(2)(c)(ii).
78 Section 3.
79 Section 7(6).
80 Section 3(3).

to the contract, will also be of relevance. If the risk by law or custom is to be born by a particular party, who should have in accordance with good business practice been insured, the diminution in value of the benefit will be notionally regarded as a benefit received by that party.[81] A benefit may include benefits that are received otherwise than under the contract but at a cost to the party in such a way that it forms part of the value of the contractual performance of that party, or in circumstances in which the receipt of the benefit constitutes part of the contractual performance of that party.[82]

An example may serve to illustrate the application of this statutory formula. Assume that a contractor agrees to perform work for which he is to be paid $10,000. At a cost to himself in relation to materials and labour of $4,000, he constructs a building which was about two-thirds complete when a fire prevents the completion of the work and frustrates the contract. Assume that the work was uninsured and there was no obligation by law or custom that insurance should be effected. Assume also that the profit the contractor would have received, assessed on a *pro rata* basis for the work carried out, would be $500 and that he retained $1,000 worth of materials which could be used on another project. Finally, assume that the building after the fire was worth $4,000.

Aggregate benefits, under the formula in s 7(2),would include:

Value of building after fire	$4,000.00
Plus value of remaining materials	$1,000.00
	$5,000.00

Aggregated performance:

Cost of material and labour	$4,000.00
Percentage profit	$ 500.00
	$4,500.00

Aggregate benefit	$5,000.00
Less Aggregate performance	$4,500.00
Equals	$ 500.00

Notional remainder (equal division)	$ 250.00

Under s 7(2), the contractor will be entitled to payment of his contractual return being his benefits, in this case, retained materials of $1,000.00 less his costs of performance (ie materials and labour and lost profit of $4,500.00) being a sum of $3,500.00. To his contract return, the sum of

---

81 Section 3(4).
82 Section 3.

$250.00 should be added thereby entitling him to payment from the owner of compensation in the sum of $3,750.00. The owner's contractual return equates with the reduced value of the building being a sum of $4,000.00, but from this is subtracted $250.00 being his share of the notional remainder which is paid as an adjustment to the contractor. The remaining sum of $3,750.00 constitutes the owner's equalised contractual return.

Like the other statutory regimes, the Act does not apply to a charter-party that is not a charter-party by time or demise. It does not apply to carriage of goods by sea other than an appropriate charter-party. Nor does it apply to contracts of insurance, partnership agreements, or a contract under which an association is constituted or provides for rules governing the administration of, or rights of membership in an association.[83] It binds the Crown. It does not apply if a particular part of the contract to which the frustrating event applies is severable from the remainder of the contract.[84] Nor does it apply if, according to the proper construction of the contract, the obligation is to survive a certain supervening event.[85]

Accordingly, it can be seen that the statutory regimes considered above differ considerably in the extent of relief which can be granted to the parties to a frustrated contract. The New South Wales and South Australian legislation, which allow for profit and loss sharing, permit a greater measure of relief for the performance of services than the English model which does not allow compensation for services that do not result in a benefit for the recipient of the service. The ability to claim reliance costs, prior to the performance of a contractual obligation, is expressly recognised in the South Australian legislation. It may be argued that a more extensive right of recovery is preferable to one that is linked exclusively to the actual benefit conferred because both parties under a frustrated contract are innocent of wrongdoing and losses and benefits should be equalised or adjusted as equitably as possible.[86]

---

83 Section 4(2).

84 Section 6(2)(a).

85 Section 4(1)(b).

86 See the essay of McKendrick, E, 'Frustration, Restitution, and Apportionment', in Burrows, A (ed), *Essays on the Law of Restitution*, 1991, p 168, Clarendon Press, Oxford.

CHAPTER 7

Illegal Contracts

Unjust enrichment is an important consideration in the law relating to illegal contracts. Whether a court should treat a contract as illegal is often a difficult question raising issues of public policy. The consequences of a finding of illegality can, however, have important consequences where benefits have been received or losses or expenses incurred pursuant to an illegal contract. The principles upon which a court should act in deciding whether a contract is illegal and the circumstances in which restitutionary relief may be permitted are considered below.

Ex turpi causa non oritur actio

As a general rule, a court will not lend its assistance to enforce a contract which is illegal. Hence, in *Holman v Johnson*,[1] Lord Mansfield observed:[2]

> The principle of public policy is this: *Ex dolo malo non oritur actio*. No court will lend its aid to a man who founds his cause of action on an immoral or an illegal act. If from the plaintiff's own stating or otherwise, the cause of action appears to arise *ex turpi causa*, or the transgression of a positive law of this country, then the court says that he has no right to be assisted. It is on that ground the court goes; not for the sake of the defendant, but because they will not lend their aid to such a plaintiff. So if the plaintiff and the defendant were to change sides and the defendant was to bring his action against the plaintiff, the latter would then have the advantage of it; for where both are equally in fault, *potior est conditio defendentis*.

In that case, the vendor, who was resident in France, was permitted to recover the price of tea which he had delivered to the defendant in France. Although the vendor was aware that the defendant intended to smuggle the goods into England to avoid duty, the court considered that because the tea had been delivered in France, the agreement was complete and involved no violation of English law. It would have been otherwise had the contract provided for the delivery of the tea in England since that would have involved the vendor in smuggling if the duty had not been paid.[3] This principle is also illustrated in *Pearce v*

---

1   (1775) 1 Cowp 344 ; [1775] 98 ER 1120.
2   *Ibid*, at 343; 1121.
3   See *Geismar v Sun Alliance and London Insurance Ltd* [1978] QB 383; [1977] 3 All ER 570.

Brookes.[4] A coach builder failed in an action to recover the hire for a brougham which had been let out to a prostitute on the ground that the contract was for a purpose that was contrary to public morality. The principle that a court will not lend its assistance to enforce a contractual transaction that is tainted with illegality is founded upon public policy.

Agreements that are prohibited at common law or under statute

Agreements are illegal if they are prohibited under common law or by statute. Most cases of illegality today will involve the application of a statutory prohibition. If certain activity is prohibited, a contract which is directed at pursuing that activity will be illegal and void. In *Cope v Rowlands*,[5] an unlicensed broker was not permitted to recover for work carried out without the appropriate licence. Baron Parke observed:[6]

> It is perfectly settled, that where the contract which the plaintiff seeks to enforce, be it express or implied, is expressly or by implication forbidden by the common or statute law, no court will lend it assistance to give it effect. It is equally clear that a contract is void if prohibited by a statute though the statute inflicts a penalty only. And it may be safely laid down, notwithstanding some *dicta* apparently to the contrary, that if the contract be rendered illegal, it can make no difference, in point of law, whether the statute which makes it so has in view the protection of the revenue, or any other. The sole question is whether the statute means to prohibit the contract.

In that case, statutory interpretation of the applicable legislation permitted the court to infer that a purpose of the legislation was the benefit and security of the public who had to rely on brokers. Thus, the prohibition on unlicensed brokers[7] impliedly tainted brokerage contracts negotiated with unlicensed persons. The proliferation of statutes and

---

4   (1866) LR 1 Ex 213; [1861–73] All ER 102. Further, see *Cowan v Milbourn* (1867) LR 2 Ex 230 where the contract was for blasphemous purposes. Further, see Chapter 13 on Restitution and Crime, pp 343–44.

5   (1836) 2 M & W 149; [1836] 150 ER 707.

6   *Ibid*, at 157. In so far as it was suggested that there was no distinction between legislation protecting the revenue and that for the protection of the public, later cases would suggest a greater potential for a court to strike down an agreement for illegality where the statutory prohibition was for the public protection. Indeed, that was one of the factors that was telling in *Cope v Rowlands*, and further, see *Victorian Dayelsford Syndicate Ltd v Dott* [1905] 2 Ch 624, at 629–30; but it is not the only consideration, Gibbs ACJ in *Yango Pastoral Company Pty Ltd v First Chicago Australia Ltd* (1978) CLR 410, at 414 citing *St John Shipping Corporation v Joseph Rank Ltd* [1957] 1 QB 267, at 287; [1956] 3 All ER 683, at 690 and *Shaw v Groom* [1970] 2 QB 504, at 518.

7   Further, for agreements impliedly prohibited, see *Victoria Dayelsford Syndicate Ltd v Dott* [1905] 2 Ch 624; *Cornelius v Phillips* [1918] AC 199.

regulations governing all manner of commercial and social activity led Devlin J in *St John Shipping Corporation v Joseph Rank*,[8] to say:[9]

> If a contract has as its whole object the doing of the very act which the statute prohibits, it can be argued that you can hardly make sense of a statute which forbids an act and yet permits to be made a contract to do it; that is a clear implication. But unless you get a clear implication of that sort, I think that a court ought to be very slow to hold that a statute intends to interfere with the rights and remedies given by the ordinary law of contract. Caution in this respect is, I think, especially necessary in these times when so much of commercial life is governed by regulations of one sort or another which may easily be broken without wicked intent.

Devlin J went on to make the important point that in a less serious case of a breach of a statute or regulation, a failure to enforce a contract may have unfortunate consequences and result in a party being unjustly enriched. In this regard, Devlin J observed:[10]

> Persons who deliberately set out to break the law cannot expect to be aided in a court of justice, but it is a different matter when the law is unwittingly broken. To nullify a bargain in such circumstances frequently means that in a case, perhaps of such a triviality that no authority would have felt it worthwhile to prosecute, a seller, because he cannot enforce his civil rights, may forfeit a sum vastly in excess of any penalty that a criminal court would impose; and the sum forfeited will not go into the public purse but into the pockets of someone who is lucky enough to pick up the windfall or astute enough to have contrived to get it. It is questionable how far this contributes to public morality.

This sentiment was also articulated by the High Court of Australia in *Yango Pastoral Company Pty Ltd v First Chicago Australia Ltd*.[11] The High Court held that a provision in the Commonwealth Banking Act which provided for heavy fines for corporations that carried out unlicensed banking business in Australia did not preclude the bank from obtaining restitution of arrears on a mortgage and guarantees given by Yango in order to secure a debt when the bank was not possessed of the appropriate authority to carry out banking. Gibbs CJ,[12] following the observations of Devlin J in *St John Shipping Corporation v Joseph Rank Ltd*, observed that

---

8   [1957] 1 QB 267; [1956] 3 All ER 683. Applied in *Hayes v Cable* (1961) NSWR 610 to uphold a building contract performed without council approval. Further, on building agreements and local authority approval, see *Doug Rea Enterprises Pty Ltd v Hymix Australia Pty Ltd* (1987) 2 Qd R 495. Also, see *Capricornia Electricity Board v John M Kelly Pty Ltd* (1992) 2 Qd R 240; *cf Carey v Hastie* [1968] NZLR 277.

9   *Ibid*, at 288; 690.

10 *Idem*.

11 (1978) 139 CLR 410.

12 *Ibid*, at 414. To similar effect Mason J, at 425.

the fundamental issue was whether the statute meant to prohibit the contract. The statute should be construed in the ordinary way and a court should have regard to all relevant considerations. No single consideration, however important, should be regarded as conclusive.[13] The court unanimously decided that the legislation did not expressly or impliedly prohibit the making of contracts of loan albeit that the bank in doing so might render itself liable to penalty for carrying on an unlicensed business. A reason given for declining to hold the loans void for illegality was that such an interpretation would mean that investors would be prejudiced and the defendant would gain a windfall. In this regard, Mason J observed:[14]

> ... the effect of relieving the defendants from their contractual obligation to repay money to the plaintiff would not be confined to the substantial detriment resulting to the plaintiff. The ability of the plaintiff to meet its obligations to its investors and other creditors depends, in part if not entirely, on its ability to enforce the terms of repayment of its contracts of loan with persons such as the defendants. To hold the contract unenforceable at the suit of the plaintiff would be to provide a windfall gain to the defendants and other borrowers in a similar position, and, although indirectly, to impose substantial hardship on those who originally made funds available to the plaintiff.

If an agreement is expressly or impliedly prohibited by law, it will be void *ab initio*[15] unless the statute expressly or impliedly provides otherwise. Even though deceived by the other party to the agreement, an innocent party will not be able to enforce the agreement unless he or she falls within the class of persons expressly protected by a statute.[16] Thus, in *Mahmoud v Ispahani*,[17] the plaintiff was unable to sue for non-payment for delivery of linseed oil sold to the defendant who falsely misrepresented that he was licensed to receive the product. The fact that the plaintiff had been deceived was no answer to the defendant's plea of illegality on the contract. This would seem a harsh application of the *ex turpi causa* principle.

---

13 [1957] 1 QB 267, at 287; [1956] 3 All ER 683, at 690. The observations of Devlin J were considered in New Zealand, prior to the introduction of the Illegal Contracts Act 1970 in *Strong v Bava and Co Ltd* [1960] NZLR 166; *Dromorne Linen Co Ltd v Ward* [1963] NZLR 615; *Berrett v Smith* [1965] NZLR 460; *Carey v Hastie* [1968] NZLR 277.

14 (1978) 139 CLR 410, at 428.

15 *Cope v Rowlands* (1836) 2 M & W 149; [1836] 150 ER 707. Further, see *Yango Pastoral Company Pty Ltd v First Chicago Australia Ltd* (1978) 139 CLR 410, at 413, Gibbs ACJ, at 430 *per* Jacobs J; and for a case where the statute was held to provide otherwise, see *Batu Phat Ltd v Official Assignee* [1933] AC 691.

16 *Gray v Southouse* [1949] 1 All ER 1019; *Kiriri Cotton Ltd v Dewani* [1960] AC 192. Further, see *Berrett v Smith* [1965] NZLR 460.

17 [1921] 2 KB 716. The court left open the question of redress for the deceit on some other ground, see Bankes LJ at 726, Scrutton LJ at 730. *Cf Shelly v Paddock* [1980] 1 All ER 1009; *Saunders v Edwards* [1987] 2 All ER 651.

Agreements that are *prima facie* legal, but are embarked upon for an illegal purpose or are intended to be performed illegally

A contract may appear legal on its face but either or both of the parties may have entered it for a illegal purpose or intended to perform it in a way which is unlawful.[18] Where both parties intend to perform a contract which is *prima facie* legal in an unlawful manner, a court will not lend its assistance to either party seeking to enforce the contract. Similarly, if parties enter into a contract which is *prima facie* capable of being performed lawfully but, to the knowledge of both, is to be performed in an unlawful manner, the contract will be unenforceable.[19] In JM *Allan Ltd v Cloke*,[20] the English Court of Appeal declined to allow the plaintiff to recover the hire of a roulette table and gaming equipment which, to the parties' knowledge, was to be used in a manner that was unlawful even though it could have been hired and used in a manner which did not contravene the law. The fact that the parties did not know that the intended manner of performance was unlawful was no answer to the illegality. Where, however, only one of the parties intends to perform the agreement unlawfully or, subsequently, determines to perform the agreement in an unlawful manner, a court will not allow illegality to be pleaded as a defence. In *Archbold (Freightage) Ltd v S Spanglett Ltd*,[21] for example, the plaintiff was permitted to recover damages for loss of freight which, unknown to the plaintiff, was carried by the defendant in an unlicensed motor vehicle thereby rendering the performance of the contract unlawful. Pearce LJ, having concluded that the contract was not one that was expressly or impliedly prohibited by statute, said of the defendant's contravention of the statute:[22]

> No question of moral turpitude arises here. The alleged illegality is, so far as the plaintiffs were concerned, the permitting of their goods to be carried by the wrong carrier, namely a carrier, who unknown to them, was not allowed by his licence to carry that particular class of goods. The plaintiffs were never *in pari delicto* since they did not know the vital fact that would make the performance of the contract illegal.

If the agreement embodies a stipulation which will, if performed, render the contract illegal, a court will not allow the party in default to rely on the illegality if the other party was unaware that performance would be illegal. Thus, in *Fielding and Platt Ltd v Najjar*,[23] the plaintiffs, at the

---

18 See *Pearce v Brookes* (1866) LR 1 Ex 213; [1861–73] All ER 102.

19 See *Buckland v Massey* (1985) 1 Qd R 502.

20 [1963] 2 All ER 258. Further, see *Ashmore Ltd v Dawson Ltd* [1973] 2 All ER 856.

21 [1961] 1 QB 374; [1961] 1 All ER 417.

22 *Ibid*, at 388; 424.

23 [1969] 2 All ER 150.

request of the defendant, invoiced certain goods which were to be delivered in Lebanon in a way which, unknown to the plaintiffs, was intended to mislead Lebanese authorities and facilitate an illegal importation. The Court of Appeal considered that, even if the stipulation as to performance had been a term of the contract, the defendant could not plead illegality unless he could show that the plaintiffs had knowledge of it and were actively participating in the transgression.[24] Conversely, in *Alexander v Rayson*,[25] the plaintiff was unable to sue for rental on a lease because he had deliberately entered into an arrangement which was designed to conceal the true rateable value of the premises. For the same reason, in *Scott v Brown, Doering McNab & Co*,[26] the plaintiff was unable to obtain rescission of an agreement to purchase shares on the ground that he had entered into the arrangement with a dishonest intention of rigging the market.

Where the illegal purpose or performance involves a breach of statute, difficult issues may arise. In these cases, close scrutiny of the relevant legislation and its objects and a critical examination of the surrounding circumstances is required before a court declines to lend its assistance to the enforcement of a contract for illegal performance. In this regard, the approach does not differ from that adopted where the issue is whether the terms of a contract contravene a statute. As Devlin J observed in *St John Shipping Corporation v Joseph Rank Ltd*, whether it is the terms of the contract or the performance of it that is called into question, the test is just the same: is the contract, as made or as performed, a contract that is prohibited by statute?[27] In this regard, it has been judicially recognised that public policy may sometimes be better served in the case of a statutory violation by enforcing the agreement. In *Vita Food Products Inc v Unus Shipping Co Ltd*,[28] Lord Wright observed that it should not be forgotten that the rule by which contracts (forbidden by statute or declared to be void) are in proper cases nullified for disobedience to a statute is a rule of public policy only and public policy understood in a wider sense

---

24 *Ibid*, at 152–53 *per* Lord Denning MR. A court will not assist a plaintiff who knowingly participates in the breach of the law of a friendly foreign country. *Foster v Driscoll* [1929] 1 KB 470; *Ralli Bros v Compania Naviera Sota y Aznar* [1920] 2 KB 287; *Regazzoni v KC Sethia (1944) Ltd* [1957] 3 All ER 286. Query whether this applies to revenue laws, see the observations of Viscount Simonds suggesting the contrary in *Regazzoni v Sethia (1944) Ltd, ibid*, at 292. *Ralli Bros* was distinguished in *Re O'Connors Bills of Costs* (1993) 1 Qd R 423.

25 [1936] 1 KB 169. Applied in *National Mutual Life Association of Australia Ltd v G H Hallas Pty Ltd* [1992] 2 Qd R 531. Distinguished in *Gray v Pastorelli* [1987] WAR 174, where the documents could not facilitate an illegal purpose.

26 [1892] 2 QB 724.

27 [1957] 1 QB 267, at 284; [1956] 3 All ER 683, at 688, and further, see the discussion in *Carey v Hastie* [1968] NZLR 277.

28 [1939] AC 277, at 293; [1939] 1 All ER 513, at 523, cited with approval by Jacobs J in *Yango Pastoral* (1978) 139 CLR 410, at 432; and in New Zealand in *Carey v Hastie* [1968] NZLR 277, at 281.

may at times be better served by refusing to nullify a bargain except on serious and sufficient grounds. This approach was taken in Australia in *Farrow Mortgage Services Pty Ltd v Edgar*,[29] where the Federal Court permitted the enforcement of loans that had been made in contravention of legislation regulating building societies in Victoria. Although performance of the loan agreements involved violation of provisions of the legislation, the court asked the same question posed in *Yango*; did the legislation by implication require the loans to be declared unenforceable? A reason for declining to do so was that investors would suffer if the loans were not repaid and borrowers would enjoy windfall gains.[30]

Related contracts

An agreement may be affected by illegality if it is aimed at furthering a collateral illegal transaction. Thus, in *Spector v Ageda*,[31] the plaintiff was a solicitor who sought to enforce a loan which had been made in order to enable the borrowers to repay a loan from an unlicensed money-lender. The plaintiff, who had acted for the borrower in the original money lending transaction, was aware that the original loan contravened the money-lending legislation but did not advise the defendant. It was held that the plaintiff was unable to enforce the loan which she had made with the knowledge that the original advance was illegal.[32]

Severance of an illegal term

A term of an agreement which requires the performance of an illegal act may be severed from the agreement if it is not an essential part of the agreement. The High Court of Australia considered this issue in *Thomas Brown & Sons Ltd v Fazal Deen*.[33] The plaintiff deposited by way of bailment gold and gems with the defendant. The deposit of gold was illegal under exchange control regulations in force at the time. After the safe in which the items had been stored went missing in unexplained circumstances, the plaintiff sued to recover the gold and the gems. The defendant's claim that the whole transaction was tainted with illegality was rejected by the High Court which held that the contract was clearly severable and the plaintiff was entitled to recover the gems.[34] The

---

29 (1993) 114 ALR 1. Further, for Australian decisions where courts declined to hold contracts illegal for illegal acts in performance, see *Ross v Ratcliffe* (1988) 91 FLR 66; *Frank Davies Pty Ltd v Container Haulage Group Pty Ltd (No 1)* (1989) 98 FLR 289; *Re O'Connor's Bills of Costs* (1993) 1 Qd R 423.

30 *Ibid*, at 18.

31 [1973] Ch 30; [1971] 3 All ER 417.

32 *Ibid*, at 44; 427.

33 (1962) 108 CLR 391.

34 *Ibid*, at 411, following an observation of Jordan CJ, in *Mcfarlane v Daniell* (1938) 38 SR NSW 337 that 'if the elimination of the invalid promises changes the extent only but not the kind of contract, the valid promises are severable'.

approach in *Fazal Deen* was adapted by the Privy Council in *Carney v Herbert*.[35] The court rejected the defendant's argument that the creation of mortgages to finance the purchase of shares in contravention of the New South Wales companies' legislation was essential to the transaction and thereby rendered the entire agreement unenforceable. In rejecting this argument and holding the defendants bound by the agreement, the Privy Council held that the provision relating to the mortgages was severable and that public policy did not require the court to impugn the transaction. The court held that the issue of severability was one of construction and did not involve an examination of the parties' intentions at the time of formation of the contract.[36]

Restitution of moneys paid pursuant to an illegal contract

A restitutionary claim will not, in general, under English law place a party to an illegal agreement in a more advantageous position. Two decisions of the English Court of Appeal are in point. In *Berg v Sadler and Moore*,[37] it was held that a plaintiff, who had falsely pretended that he was entitled to purchase goods, was not entitled to either the goods or the return of the money paid in consideration of their supply. Lord Wright MR said of the plaintiff's claim to the return of his money:[38]

> To maintain an action for moneys had and received, he has to prove the exact circumstances in which the money was paid, and the circumstances which he says entitle him on grounds of justice to have an order of repayment. If, however, he proceeds to that proof, he can only establish his claim by proving the facts which show that he was engaged in this criminal attempt to obtain goods by false pretences. The court, on well established principles, will refuse to give its aid to any claim which can be established only by proving facts of that nature.

In *Harry Parker Ltd v Mason*,[39] the Court of Appeal again declined to assist a plaintiff to recover money from his agent which he had given to him for an illegal purpose. Du Parq LJ observed:[40]

> In my opinion, a principal seeking to recover from his agent money which he handed to him for an illegal purpose is in no better case,

---

35 [1985] AC 301; [1985] 1 All ER 438.

36 *Ibid*, at 316; 447, disagreeing with observations to the contrary in *Brew v Whitlock (No2)* [1967] VR 803, at 811–12.

37 [1937] 2 KB 158; [1937] All ER 637. Further, see *Simpson v Bloss* (1816) 7 Taunt 246; 129 ER 99, where the plaintiff was unable to recover in an action for moneys had and received moneys paid to extinguish a debt as a result of an illegal gambling transaction.

38 *Ibid*, at 163; 641.

39 [1940] 4 All ER 199.

40 *Ibid*, at 204.

when he seeks relief from a court of law or equity, than the contracting party seeking to recover back payments made by himself to another party to the contract (who is not his agent) for an illegal consideration. In neither case will the courts order the repayment of the money.

This approach was adopted by the High Court of Australia in *George v Greater Adelaide Land Development Company Limited*.[41] It was held that a purchaser was unable to reclaim instalments of the purchase price of land, which he had paid under an illegal agreement for sale, despite the agreement being expressly made subject to compliance with the relevant legislation. A restitutionary claim may, however, be permitted where an agreement is not illegal but merely unenforceable. In *Pavey & Matthews Pty Ltd v Paul*,[42] the High Court of Australia held that a construction contract that did not meet the requirements of the Builders Licensing Act in New South Wales because it failed to sufficiently describe the work that was required to be performed under the contract was unenforceable although the builder had completed the work requested by the owner. It was held, however, that the statutory prohibition did not preclude the plaintiff from successfully claiming remuneration under a *quantum meruit*. The court heavily relied on the approach taken to restitutionary claims otherwise unenforceable under the Statute of Frauds.[43] In cases of this kind, where work has been carried out but there has been an omission to record the transaction, the courts have permitted recovery on a *quantum meruit* for a reasonable sum. *Pavey & Mathews* illustrates how it is necessary to carefully consider the relevant legislation, its objects and the surrounding circumstances before taking the more drastic step of declaring an activity illegal and denying any restitutionary reimbursement for services rendered.[44] Although an important object of the legislation was the elimination of claims based on poor workmanship and excessive remuneration for unjustified or inflated claims for variations, this object was not at variance with a claim for reasonable remuneration for work that had been

---

41 (1929) 43 CLR 91. Applied in *Reid Murray Developments WA Pty Ltd v Hall* [1968] WAR 3.

42 (1986) 162 CLR 221.

43 See *Horton v Jones (No 1)* (1934) 34 SR (NSW) 359; *Turner v Bladin* (1951) 82 CLR 463; *James v Thomas H Kent & Co Ltd* [1951] 1 KB 551. Further, see *Scott v Pattison* [1923] 2 KB 723; *Merrell v Loft* [1895] 13 NZLR 738, and the discussion of *Pavey & Matthews Pty Ltd v Paul* in Chapter 4, p 69.

44 As, for example, in *Cope v Rowlands* (1836) 2 M & W 149. The distinction between an illegal contract and one merely unenforceable for non-compliance with the equivalent of the Statute of Frauds was considered in *Slobbe v Combined Taxis Co-operative Society Ltd* [1973] 2 NZLR 651, at 652–53.

performed by the plaintiff at the defendant's request.[45] To deny the plaintiff a *quantum meruit* for his work in these circumstances would have allowed the defendant to be unjustly enriched.[46]

Recently, however, in *Nelson v Nelson*,[47] the High Court of Australia has sanctioned restitution of property conveyed by the plaintiff for a fraudulent purpose in circumstances that would suggest a more liberal approach to restitution in cases of illegality than is favoured by English courts. This important decision is considered below.

Exceptions to the *ex turpi causa non oritur actio* principle

Courts have mitigated the potential for hardship that the *ex turpi causa* rule can cause by insisting on a rigorous examination of a statute to ascertain whether, expressly or impliedly, a contract is illegal in its formation or performance. At least where a contract is not illegal in its formation, an innocent party to an illegality in performance will not be affected by the *ex turpi causa* principle. Further, the courts may avoid an application of the principle by severing illegal terms in an agreement. There are, however, a number of other means by which it is possible to avoid the application of the *ex turpi causa* principle.

(a) The parties are not *in pari delicto*

Where the purpose of a statutory provision is the protection of a class of individuals to whom the plaintiff belongs, the plaintiff will be able to obtain restitution for any illegal payment or other benefit provided to another in breach of the statute. In *Kiriri Cotton Co Ltd v Dewani*,[48] a tenant sought to recover a rental premium paid to a landlord contrary to the provision of the Uganda Rent Restriction Ordinance 1949. Neither party thought they were doing anything illegal. Both parties in this regard were mistaken. Although a tenant had no express statutory power to recover, the Privy Council allowed the tenant to recover the premium on the ground that the parties were not *in pari delicto* because the prohibition on receiving premiums was imposed on the landlord for the tenant's protection. Accordingly, the responsibility for the mistake

---

45 In *Pavey & Mathews Pty Ltd v Paul* (1986) 162 CLR 221, at 263–64, Deane J considered the manner in which a *quantum meruit* claim could be approached to assess what was fair and just. Where a *quantum meruit* assessment based on reasonable value would be greater than the contract price, it would be appropriate to have regard to the latter and discussion, pp 175–76 and Chapter 14, pp 351–52.

46 *Cf* the money-lendor cases, *Kasumu v Baba-Egbe* [1956] AC 539; *Mayfair Trading Co Proprietary Ltd v Dreyer* (1958) 101 CLR 428 and discussion, pp 175–76 and Chapter 14, pp 351–52.

47 (1995) 184 CLR 538; (1996) 70 ALJR 47. See discussion, pp 171–74.

48 [1960] AC 192. Further, see *Gray v Southouse* [1949] 2 All ER 1019.

rested with the landlord.[49] However, if the plaintiff is unable to establish that the legislation is directed at protecting a particular class of persons to whom he belongs rather than the public at large, he or she will be unsuccessful in claiming restitution under this exception. Thus, in *South Australian Cold Stores Ltd v Electricity Trust of South Australia*,[50] the High Court of Australia declined to allow the plaintiff to recover excess charges paid under the Prices Act 1948. The court held that the Act was passed for the benefit of the general public to control inflation rather than for the protection of electricity consumers as a class. The court also considered that a claim to restitution was excluded because there was a provision in the Act whereby a court could order repayment of excess charges when imposing a penalty for contravention of the Act. Kitto J, however, observed that where a statute was intended to protect a certain class of person then a court should permit a plaintiff to recover even though the legislation provides penalties for breach.[51] In saying this, Kitto J criticised the contrary view expressed by Denning LJ in *Green v Portsmouth Stadium Ltd*[52] that where a statute provides certain penalties for a breach, the presumption is that no other remedy is available.[53] In a subsequent decision, *Kiriri Cotton*, Lord Denning, however, did not repeat the view he had expressed earlier in *Green*. In the light of the more liberal approach of English and Australian courts[54] to recovery of *ultra vires* taxes from the revenue, it may transpire that the *in pari delicto* exception and the limitation of the kind considered in *South Australian Stores* will have to be reconsidered.

Where the plaintiff, as in *Kiriri Cotton*, is not *in pari delicto* with the defendant because he or she comes within a protected class, a mistake as to the legal nature of a payment will allow the plaintiff to pursue a restitutionary claim for the recovery of moneys illegally paid to the defendant. Mistakes of law may also be the subject of restitutionary claims where the parties are *in pari delicto* if the defendant has fraudulently misrepresented the law.[55] However, in *Harse v Pearl Life Assurance Co Ltd*,[56] an innocent misrepresentation as to the legality of a life insurance policy on which the parties were said to be *in pari delicto* was held to be an insufficient ground

---

49   *Ibid*, at 203–06.

50   (1965) 115 CLR 247.

51   *Ibid*, at 258.

52   [1953] 2 QB 190; [1953] 2 All ER 102.

53   *Ibid*, at 195; 104.

54   *Woolwich Building Society v IRC (No 2)* [1993] AC 70; [1992] 3 All ER 737; *Commissioner of State Revenue (Vic) v Royal Insurance Australia Ltd* (1994) 182 CLR 51.

55   *British Workman's and General Assurance Co v Cunliffe* (1902) 18 TLR 425; *Hughes v Liverpool Victoria Friendly Society* [1916] 2 KB 482; *Kiriri Cotton Co Ltd v Dewani* [1960] AC 192, at 204.

56   [1904] 1 KB 559.

to permit recovery of insurance premiums. In *George v Greater Adelaide Land Development Company Ltd*,[57] the High Court of Australia approved the Harse principle when declining to permit instalments of the purchase price of a property under an intended sub-division to be recovered where the parties were *in pari delicto* concerning the illegality of the transaction and both shared a mistaken belief that the agreement for sale and purchase was legal when it was not. A mistake of fact, however, as to the legality of a contract may permit restitution, even though there is no fraud associated with the mistake. In *Oom v Bruce*,[58] a shared mistake of fact was sufficient to permit restitution of insurance premiums when a contract of insurance relating to goods destined for Russia was rendered illegal because war had broken out between England and Russia. As a consequence of the judgment of the High Court of Australia in *David Securities Pty Limited v Commonwealth Bank of Australia*,[59] the distinction between payments made under mistake of law and fact has now been abrogated. A payer will be able to recover payments made under a mistake of law subject to defences of consideration,[60] adverse change of position demonstrated by the payee,[61] estoppel or payment made pursuant to a genuine compromise of a *bona fide* claim.[62] In that case, the High Court reversed the judgment of the Federal Court which had held that the payment of withholding tax by a borrower was irrecoverable as a mistake of law.[63] Although the High Court did not determine the case on this ground, it would seem that the payments should have been recoverable in any event because the parties were not *in pari delicto*.[64] It is arguable, however, that even if the parties are *in pari delicto*, a mistake of law should *prima facie* entitle a payee to recovery and the *Harse* principle should no longer apply. To deny recovery where the payment is made under a mistake as to the legality of a transaction is to permit the unjust enrichment of the party who has acquired a benefit under the transaction. The fact that the payer is genuinely mistaken about the illegality of a transaction diminishes any moral turpitude associated with a contract being illegal.

---

57 (1929) 43 CLR 91. Further, see *Cheers v Pacific Acceptance Corporation Ltd* [1960] SR (NSW) 1.

58 (1810) 12 East 225; 104 ER 87.

59 (1992) 175 CLR 353.

60 *Ibid*, at 380–83.

61 *Ibid*, at 384–86.

62 *Ibid*, at 395.

63 Further, see *J & S Holdings Ltd v NRMA Insurance Ltd* (1982) 41 ALR 539.

64 (1992) 175 CLR 353, at 384; 400.

(b) Where the defendant has behaved unconscionably towards the plaintiff

If the defendant has acted oppressively, fraudulently, or has acted in breach of a fiduciary relationship owed to the plaintiff, the plaintiff will be allowed restitution.

(i) Oppression

In *Smith v Cuff*,[65] the plaintiff was able to recover a payment demanded by and made to a creditor in consideration of the creditor agreeing to a compromise to settle the plaintiff's debts. This constituted a fraud on the other creditors. Recovery was permitted on the grounds of oppression. In *Andrews v Parker*,[66] it was held that a plaintiff could plead undue pressure to recover property transferred under an alleged illegal agreement. However, in *Callaghan v O'Sullivan*,[67] the plaintiff was denied restitutionary relief where he submitted to a corrupt demand and intimidation by police officers in an effort to stifle a prosecution concerning himself and his daughter. The court held that submission to threats of this kind offended public policy and the payments could not be recovered. It may be argued however that, where a bribe or other illegal benefit is derived through duress or undue pressure, public policy is better served by ordering the defendant to surrender his ill-gotten gains.

(ii) Fraud

In *British Workman's and General Assurance Ltd v Cunliffe*,[68] it was held that premiums could be recovered where they were paid as a result of a fraudulent representation that a policy of insurance taken out by the plaintiff was valid. This case was approved by the Court of Appeal in *Harse v Pearl Life Assurance Company*.[69] The court, however, declined to allow restitution where a representation as to the validity of a contract was innocently made, the parties being said to be *in pari delicto*. It may be argued that this distinction is unsatisfactory. Where a party is induced into entering an agreement by the other party's misrepresentation as to its legality, recovery should be permitted to deprive that other party of the windfall.[70]

---

65 (1817) 6 M & S 160; 105 ER 1203. This exception is also recognised in *Harse v Pearl Life Assurance Co* [1904] 1 KB 559 and *George v Greater Land Development Co Ltd* (1929) 43 CLR 91.

66 (1973) Qd R 93.

67 [1925] VLR 664.

68 (1902) 18 TLR 425.

69 [1904] 1 KB 559.

70 See Dickson, B, 'Restitution and Illegal Transactions', in Burrows, A (ed), *Essays on the Law of Restitution*, 1991, p 185, Clarendon Press, Oxford, and discussion, pp 164–66.

A plaintiff may be able to avoid the consequences of illegality by suing in deceit. In *Shelley v Paddock*,[71] the plaintiff successfully claimed damages for false representations that the defendants were alleged to have made in regard to a real estate transaction. The purchase of a house in Spain involved payments made in contravention of exchange control legislation. However, the plaintiff had no knowledge that these payments were illegal. In *Saunders v Edwards*,[72] the plaintiff, who had purchased the lease of a flat, was the victim of a false representation that the flat included a roof terrace. He had, however, contrived to reduce the stamp duty payable by having the agreement include a false amount for chattels. Notwithstanding his fraudulent conduct, he was permitted to recover. The Court of Appeal considered that the defendant's moral culpability greatly outweighed the plaintiff's and the defendant should not be able to keep the fruits of his fraud. The illegal apportionment was considered to be wholly unconnected with the plaintiff's cause of action in tort. Conversely, in *Thackwell v Barclays Bank*,[73] the court declined to permit a plaintiff to recover damages from a bank for the conversion of a cheque because it formed part of a fraudulent re-financing transaction to which the plaintiff was a party. The court, however, accepted an 'affront to conscience' test which the defendant bank had submitted should be applied in cases where the plaintiff was a party to the illegal activity.[74] The conscience test gained greater credence in the Court of Appeal in *Saunders v Edwards*[75] but was eventually rejected by the House of Lords in *Tinsley v Milligan*.[76] Lord Goff observed in this case that it was by no means self-evident that the public conscience test was preferable to the present strict rules-based approach that English courts had adopted for 200 years.[77]

---

71 [1980] 1 All ER 1009.

72 [1987] 2 All ER 651. *Cf Neal v Ayres* (1940) 63 CLR 524, at 532 where knowledge by the vendor that a purchaser of a hotel would trade unlawfully did not preclude the plaintiff from suing in deceit, since it was extrinsic to the dealing which formed the foundation of the contract, and, therefore, did not corrupt it. Similarly, false and misleading claims under the Trade Practices Act 1974 were not excluded by illegal performance by the plaintiff of a long distance haulage business, *Brownbill v Kenworth Truck Sales (NSW) Pty Ltd* [1982] 59 FLR 56.

73 [1986] 1 All ER 676.

74 *Ibid*, at 687.

75 [1987] 2 All ER 651, at 660–65; *Euro Dam Ltd v Bathurst* [1990] 1 QB 1; [1988] 2 All ER 23; *Howard v Shirlstar Container Transport Ltd* [1990] 3 All ER 366.

76 [1994] 1 AC 340; [1993] 3 All ER 65.

77 *Ibid*, at 363; 80. In *Nelson v Nelson* (1995) 184 CLR 538, at 596; (1996) 70 ALJR 47, at 79–80, Toohey J adopted a more sympathetic approach to the conscience test which accords more with the approach of the High Court generally in that case to issues of restitution and illegality.

(iii) Breach of fiduciary duty

In *Re Ferguson*,[78] a company was permitted to claim restitution of loans made to a director which were unlawful and made in contravention of his fiduciary duty. Knowledge of the illegal nature of a transaction in *Sykes v Stratton*[79] precluded a plaintiff from recovering moneys paid to a solicitor for the performance of an agreement that breached exchange control regulations. However, in *Weston v Beaufils*,[80] Hill J declined to permit a solicitor to plead illegality where he had advised his client, the plaintiff, to transfer properties to him as part of a fraudulent scheme to avoid tax. The court held that by advising the plaintiff to deal with his properties in this way the solicitor had acted in breach of his fiduciary obligation. Accordingly, it would be unconscionable for the defendant to be enriched by his own breach of fiduciary duty.[81]

(c) Repentance

In *Taylor v Bowers*,[82] the plaintiff had delivered his stock-in-trade to a third party for the purpose of defeating his creditors. Without his knowledge, the goods were sold to the defendant who had knowledge of the fact that the assignment from the plaintiff to the third party was a sham. Before the illegal purpose was put into effect, the plaintiff sought to recover his goods. He was permitted to do so because he had resiled from the illegal arrangement before it had been perfected with any prejudice to creditors. Mellish LJ observed:[83]

> If money is paid or goods delivered for an illegal purpose, the person who had so paid the money or delivered the goods may recover them back before the illegal purpose is carried out but, if he waits till the illegal purpose is carried out, or if he seeks to enforce the illegal transaction, in neither case can he maintain an action; the law will not allow that to be done.

In *Kearley v Thomson*,[84] Fry LJ, whilst expressing some disquiet about the correctness of the principle expounded by Mellish LJ, considered that it had no application where the illegal purpose had been carried

---

78 (1969) 14 FLR 311.

79 (1972) 1 NSWLR 145.

80 (1994) 122 ALR 240.

81 *Ibid*, at 267.

82 (1876) 1 QBD 291; [1874–80] All ER 405; *Hastelow v Jackson* (1828) 8 B & C 221; 108 ER 1026; *Symes v Hughes* (1870) LR 9 Eq 475.

83 *Ibid*, at 300; at 407.

84 (1890) 24 QBD 742. The principle of *locus poenitentiae* is, however, now well entrenched, see *Kiriri Cotton Co Ltd v Dewani* [1960] AC 192, at 202–03; *Tinsley v Milligan* [1994] 1 AC 340, at 374; [1993] 3 All ER 65, at 89 *per* Lord Browne-Wilkinson.

into effect in a material way.[85] In *Berg and Sadler v Moore*,[86] Lord Wright MR, refused to permit restitution of moneys paid in order to illegally obtain goods by a false pretence. Lord Wright MR observed:[87]

> The defendant's position therefore, is that they are in possession of the money, which has passed to them under a contract *prima facie* lawful, but which has turned out to be a contract tainted by fraud, so far as the plaintiff is concerned. The defendants can rely on the principle *potior est conditio possidentis*, and the court will refuse to re-open the transaction, or order the money to be paid, on a total failure of consideration.

In Australia, decisions of the High Court support the approach taken in *Kearley v Thomson* that restitution should be denied if there has been a partial performance of the unlawful purpose. *Payne v McDonald*,[88] *Perpetual Executors and Trustees Association of Australia Ltd v Wright*[89] and *Martin v Martin*[90] were each concerned with plaintiffs who sought to contest ownership of land on the ground that settlement had been effected in order to defeat the plaintiffs' creditors. In each case, the court considered that proof of an intention to defraud creditors was insufficient to preclude the plaintiffs from asserting title. Evidence was also required that the plaintiffs had succeeded in whole or in part.[91] In *Martin v Martin*, the court said of sham arrangements of this kind:[92]

> When that is the case there must, under Australian case law, be further inquiry and it must be ascertained whether the unlawful purpose was in any degree carried out or, on the other hand, the intending law breaker recanted before any necessity arose of using the cover he had thus provided or else virtuously refrained from using it.

In *Weston v Beaufils*,[93] Hill J had to consider whether the plaintiff could have certain properties re-conveyed to him which he had placed in the name of his solicitor pursuant to an arrangement whereby certain properties were transferred by the plaintiff into the name of a solicitor in order to assist the plaintiff to deceive the Commissioner of Taxation in

---

85 *Ibid*, at 747.

86 [1937] 2 KB 158; All ER 637.

87 *Ibid*, at 166; 643.

88 (1908) 6 CLR 208.

89 (1917) 23 CLR 185.

90 (1963–64) 110 CLR 297.

91 *Payne v McDonald* (1908) 6 CLR 208, at 213.

92 (1963–64) 110 CLR 297, at 305. More recently, *Freedom v AHR Constructions Pty Ltd* (1987) 1 Qd R 59; English authority would appear to deny recovery on proof of fraudulent intent, see *Gascoigne v Gascoigne* [1918] 1 KB 223, *Tinker v Tinker* [1970] 1 All ER 540, *cf Tribe v Tribe* [1995] 3 WLR 913.

93 (1994) 122 ALR 241.

relation to stamp duty. His Honour doubted, however, in the absence of evidence, that the Commissioner had been deceived that the illegal purpose was effected unless the various dispositions of property were seen as the implementation of the illegal purpose.[94] Hill J also doubted whether there could be any genuine repentance in a case where the arrangement was frustrated by the defendant declining to perform thereby forcing the plaintiff to commence proceedings which would inevitably expose the fraud.[95]

More recently, however, the High Court of Australia in *Nelson v Nelson*[96] suggested that it would not regard itself as bound to deny restitutionary relief merely because a fraudulent object had been effected. The plaintiff in that case was permitted restitution of a property which had been transferred into the names of her children in order to fraudulently acquire a subsidy for financial assistance for the purchase of a second property even though in order to defeat the presumption of advancement that arose in favour of her children she had to reveal the fraudulent nature of the transaction. A majority of the court considered that as a condition of her being granted equitable relief she should, however, have to pay back the subsidy she had received. In arriving at this decision, the court was influenced by the fact that the legislation contained a statutory scheme for recovery and there were, in addition, criminal penalties for fraud.[97] There was, therefore, little reason to expose the plaintiff to serious loss with the consequence that the defendant, her daughter, would be unjustly enriched.[98] This case would suggest that Australian courts will now look more to the nature of the illegality, the policy or object of the legislation or rule of public policy governing the transaction, and whether there exist alternative methods of penalising errant conduct, rather than simply whether the fraudulent object has been achieved or there has been repentance. It is suggested that this is a better approach than an approach which draws a rigorous distinction based on repentance alone. Even where the dishonest object has not been achieved, public policy would suggest there be some limits to recovery in cases of this kind. Thus, as Lord Alvanley observed in *Tappendon v Randall*,[99] courts could not easily permit a plaintiff recovery of money or property given to hire an assassin even though the criminal purpose is not achieved. Conversely, *Clegg v Wilson*[100] is open to doubt. The plaintiff there transferred property to the defendant in considera-

---

94 *Ibid*, at 268.

95 *Idem*.

96 (1996) 184 CLR 538; (1996) 70 ALJR 47.

97 *Ibid*, at 570; 63 *per* Deane and Gummow JJ, at 616; 90–91 *per* McHugh J.

98 *Ibid*, at 597; 80 *per* Toohey J.

99 (1801) 2 B & P 467; [1801] 126 ER 1388.

100 (1932) 32 SR (NSW) 109.

tion for the latter's promise not to give evidence in relation to criminal proceedings that had been commenced against the plaintiff's son. After proceedings had been withdrawn, the plaintiff was permitted to recover the property. It is submitted that a court should not assist a plaintiff to restitution of property or money when the plaintiff had so clearly manifested an intention to suborn a witness and so seriously perverted the course of justice.

(d) Reliance on a collateral claim

Collateral actions that do not depend on any assertion of illegality by the plaintiff will succeed even though the cause of action arose out of an illegal contract or arrangement. In *Strongman Ltd v Sincock*,[101] a builder was permitted to recover damages from an architect who had failed to obtain the necessary licence in order to enable the work to be lawfully performed. The Court of Appeal upheld the plaintiff's claim on a collateral contract even though the illegality precluded the owner being sued directly for the contract price. It was considered relevant that the plaintiff was unaware that a licence had not been obtained and that he had not been negligent either. The court accepted that it was the universal practice for an architect to obtain the requisite licence.

Where a plaintiff is able to assert a proprietary right to property, the fact that it has been derived from criminal activity will not preclude the plaintiff from obtaining restitution. A court is not concerned with how the property came to be acquired. Thus, in *Gordon v Metropolitan Police Chief Commissioner*,[102] the plaintiff was permitted to recover the proceeds of illegal betting arrangements in an action for moneys had and received. There was no statutory right of forfeiture, and the court would not imply a power to confiscate money which belonged to the plaintiff. Buckley LJ posed the question:[103]

> But what is the cause of action in the present case? The plaintiff had the property and the possession. His cause of action is exhaustively stated by saying that he sues the defendant for having deprived him of his property. The defendant seeks to say: 'True, it is your property, but it ought not to have been your property; forms no part of the cause of action.' If the property is taken from the plaintiff on that ground, it is taken by confiscation. There is no ground of public policy upon which the defendant should keep that which under no circumstances is his. It may be that the plaintiff never ought to have acquired that property, but having acquired it, his cause of action to

---

101 [1955] 2 QB 525; [1955] 3 All ER 90. Further, see *Gregory v Ford* [1951] 1 All ER 121. Cf *Askey v Golden Wine Co Ltd* [1948] 2 All ER 35.

102 [1910] 2 KB 1080; [1908–10] All ER 192.

103 *Ibid*, at 1098; 201.

recover it from the person who deprives him of it arises only from the fact of deprivation.

This principle was approved in Australia in *Russell v Wilson*.[104] There, the High Court considered that it was not a defence for the police to refuse to surrender property seized on the grounds that it had been obtained illegally or that it might be used for an illegal purpose. In *Golan v Nugent*,[105] however, leave to re-plead a defence to an action for the recovery of indecent books was granted by a majority of the High Court on the ground that the seized materials were of such a nature that, on grounds of public policy, they should not be returned to the plaintiff. Central to the success of claims of this kind is the need for the plaintiff to show a proprietary interest and an immediate right to possession of land[106] or goods. In *Bowmakers Ltd v Barnett Industries Ltd*,[107] the plaintiff was able to sue successfully for damages for the failure by the defendant to deliver up machine tools which had been the subject of illegal hire purchase agreements. The defendant conceded that property was vested in the plaintiffs for the purposes of the action thereby giving the plaintiff an immediate right of possession.[108] Bowmakers was followed by the Privy Council in *Singh v Ali*,[109] where the plaintiff, who had purchased a lorry under an unlawful agreement from the defendant, was able to claim damages from the defendant who had repossessed the property and sought to deny the sale. Although the contract of sale was illegal, it was held to be sufficient to vest the property in the plaintiff. Where, however, the plaintiff has to rely on illegality in order to assert a proprietary claim, the action will fail. In *Taylor v Chester*,[110] a plaintiff sought to recover half of a £50 bank note which he had deposited with the defendant as security for a loan. The deposit was made for the purpose of prostitution and in order to establish his right of possession, the plaintiff had to reveal the unlawful purpose for which the note had been given. In *Thomas Brown & Sons Ltd v Fazal Deen*,[111] the plaintiff was unable to recover gold unlawfully bailed to the defendant under the exchange control regulations because, in order to establish his entitlement to possession and avoid a statute of limitation, he had to prove a contract of bailment and a refusal by the bailee to comply with his

---

104 (1923) 33 CLR 538.
105 (1988) 166 CLR 18.
106 *Feret v Hill* (1854) 15 CB 207; [1843–60] All ER 924.
107 [1945] KB 65; [1944] 2 All ER 579.
108 See *Penfolds Wines v Elliot* (1946) 74 CLR 204, at 227.
109 [1960] AC 167; [1960] 1 All ER 269.
110 (1869) LR 4 QB 309; [1861–73] All ER 154.
111 (1962) 108 CLR 391.

request for their return.[112] As we have seen, an illegal agreement will not prevent the transfer of a proprietary interest. The rationale for this was explained by Lord Denning in *Singh v Ali* as:[113]

> ... the transferor, having achieved his unworthy end, cannot be allowed to turn around and repudiate the means by which he did it – he cannot throw over the transfer. And the transferee, having got the property, can assert his title to it against all the world, not because he has any merit of his own, but because there is no one who can assert a better title to it. The court does not confiscate the property because of illegality – it has no power to do so ...

This principle, however, will be subject to the expression of a contrary legislative intent. If a transaction is expressly said to be illegal and of no effect, there can be no exchange of proprietary interests.[114]

In *Tinsley v Milligan*, a majority of the House of Lords applied the *Bowmaker's* approach to an equitable claim. A woman claimed a share in a property to which she had contributed to the purchase price which had been placed in the sole name of another with a view to both parties fraudulently obtaining welfare benefits. The House of Lords granted her relief because she was able to establish her interest in the property without resort to the illegal nature of the claim on the basis of a resulting trust. A majority of the House of Lords held that the same approach should apply to equitable relief as applied to common law claims. In Australia, however, there is a suggestion in the judgment of the High Court of Australia in *Nelson v Nelson*[115] that the court may depart from a rigorous application of the *Bowmaker's* approach in an appropriate case. Although *Nelson v Nelson* involved a claim for equitable relief, it may be argued that if, as in that case, the court was prepared to grant relief where the fraudulent nature of a transaction was exposed it should also adopt a similar approach in relation to common law claims where any compelling public policy reason for denying relief is absent. Indeed, McHugh J was critical of the *Bowmaker's* principle suggesting that it was of doubtful worth as a deterrent.[116] In the opinion of McHugh J, attention should be focused on the nature of the illegality, the objects of the legislation, any alternative methods of penalising the illegality, and deterrence should not be disproportionate to the harm associated with the breach.

---

112 *Ibid*, at 412.

113 [1960] AC 167, at 176–77; [1960] 1 All ER 269, at 272–73. Further, see *Scarfe v Morgan* (1883) 4 M & W 270; [1835–42] All ER 43; *Kingsley v Sterling Industrial Securities Ltd* [1966] 2 All ER 413; *Belvoir Finance Co Ltd v Stapleton* [1970] 3 All ER 664.

114 *Joe v Young* [1964] NZLR 24.

115 (1996) 184 CLR 538; (1996) 70 ALJR 47.

116 *Ibid*, at 610; 87–88.

(e) Equitable assistance to mitigate the effects of an illegal contract

In *Lodge v National Union Investment Company Ltd*,[117] Parker J declined to order delivery up of securities mortgaged to an unregistered money-lender unless the mortgagor agreed to repay the money which had been advanced to him. However, in *Kasumu v Baga-Egbe*,[118] the Privy Council doubted the correctness of this decision. Lord Radcliffe ordered the delivery up of securities given to a money-lender without requiring repayment of the loan. Lord Radcliffe considered that, in providing that a loan which failed to satisfy the provisions of the legislation could not be enforced, the statute prohibited a court from indirectly assisting the money-lender to enforce the loan. To impose terms as a condition of relief would conflict with the policy of the legislation. Subsequently, in *Mayfair Trading Co Pty Ltd v Dreyer*,[119] a majority of the High Court of Australia held that the plaintiff was not liable to repay a loan arising out of a money-lending transaction and ordered the return to him of collateral security documents. The majority[120] adopted the approach in *Kasumu v Baba-Egbe*, in preference to an earlier decision of the court in *Langman v Handover*,[121] which had followed *Lodge* and required repayment of the capital borrowed as a condition of relief.

Respect for a statutory prohibition on enforcement of a money-lender transaction was also evidenced in *Orakpo v Manson Investments Ltd*.[122] The House of Lords held, reversing an earlier ruling of the Court of Appeal in *Congresbury Motors Ltd v Anglo-Belge Finance Co Ltd*,[123] that the objects of the Money-lenders Act should not be undermined by declaring that a money-lender could be subrogated to an unpaid vendor's lien in relation to land that had been the subject of an earlier purchase with finance provided by the money-lender. To have recognised an equitable lien in these circumstances would have plainly circumvented the policy of the legislation which was intended to prohibit relief for money-lenders who did not comply with the Act. Even if, ordinarily, equity will by subrogation allow a lender a lien where finance has by arrangement between the borrower and the lender been applied directly by the lender in the purchase of a property, the imposition of a lien in *Orakpo*

---

117 [1907] 1 Ch 300.

118 [1956] AC 539. Further, see *Cohen v Chester Ltd* [1939] 1 KB 504; [1938] 4 All ER 188.

119 (1958) 101 CLR 428.

120 *Ibid*, at 452–56.

121 (1929) 43 CLR 334, at 453. *Langman v Handover* was followed in *White v Pacific Acceptance Corporation* [1962] SR (NSW) 60.

122 [1978] AC 95. *Orakpo* has, however, been criticised by Beatson, J, 'Unjust enrichment and the Moneylenders Act' (1978) 41 MLR 330; and Lord Goff and Jones, G, *The Law of Restitution*, 4th edn, 1993, p 67, Sweet & Maxwell, London.

123 [1971] Ch 81.

would have undermined the object of the statute which required security interests to be recorded. In this regard, Lord Salmon considered that it would not be proper to apply an equitable doctrine for the purpose of enabling a money-lender to escape from the consequences of his breach of the statute particularly if to do so would also enable him to recover his money much earlier than he was entitled to do under the contract of loan.[124]

If an equitable interest arises by operation of law, is not in conflict with a statutory prohibition and does not involve an assertion of illegality, as in *Tinsley v Milligan*,[125] restitution will be ordered even though property was acquired for an illegal purpose. English courts will not, however, permit recovery if the plaintiff has to reveal the illegality in order to claim equitable relief. In *Chettiar v Chettiar*,[126] for example, the Privy Council declined to assist the plaintiff to defeat a presumption of advancement and recover property settled on his son on the ground that it had been effected for an illegal purpose. This approach, however, was rejected by the High Court of Australia in *Nelson v Nelson*,[127] where relief was granted to a woman who had transferred property into the names of her children in order to effect an illegal object. Relief was ordered on the basis that she surrender her ill-gotten subsidy. *Nelson v Nelson* would suggest that the High Court has chosen not to continue to slavishly follow the proscription of Lord Mansfield in *Holman v Johnson*[128] or adopt the strict rules based approach to restitution and illegal transactions favoured by the English courts. Rather, it is likely that Australian courts will be able to effect restitution, at least in equity, where the objects of any governing legislation will not be defeated and justice can otherwise be achieved.[129] To this end, the approach is not unlike that adopted by New Zealand courts under the discretionary legislative scheme considered below.

A further means of obtaining equitable relief was suggested in *Farrow v Edgar*.[130] The Court of Appeal of New South Wales observed in this case that, where transactions were illegal in performance rather than in formation, there was greater latitude to permit equitable relief. The court, however, did not have to resort to this approach in that case because the loans in issue were held not to be illegal.

---

124 [1978] AC 95, at 111.

125 [1994] 1 AC 340; [1993] 3 All ER 65.

126 [1962] AC 294; [1962] 1 All ER 494.

127 (1994) 184 CLR 53; (1996) 70 ALJR 47. See Rose, FD, 'Gratuitous Transfers and Illegal Purposes' (1996) 112 LQR 386.

128 (1775) 1 Comp 344; [1775] 98 ER 1120.

129 Further, see *Hurst v Vestcorp* (1988) 112 NSWLR 394, at 417 *per* Kirby P, at 445–46 *per* McHugh J. Cf *Henderson v Amadio* (1996) 140 ALR, 391, at 562–65 where restitutionary relief was declined because of a serious transgression of prospectus requirements.

130 (1993) 114 ALR 1, at 18–19.

The Illegal Contracts Act 1970 (New Zealand)

When rejecting the application of a 'public conscience' test in *Tinsley v Milligan*,[131] Lord Goff referred to the discretionary approach adopted in New Zealand under the provisions of the Illegal Contracts Act 1970. Lord Goff considered that the House of Lords was unable to replace a system based on strict rules which had existed for over 200 years by judicial decision so as to introduce a discretionary system based on conscience. His Lordship conceded, however, that the present system, although principled, was indiscriminate in its effect and capable of producing injustice.[132] Lord Goff rightly identified this as a concern of law reformers in New Zealand, and the reason for the introduction of the Illegal Contracts Act. Indeed, in one of the earlier decisions on the Act, McMullin J, in *Dreadon v Fletcher Development Co*, observed:[133]

> Most cases before the courts on illegality of contract are cases in which the illegality is the result of statute or regulation. It was the need to remove the over-severe consequences which sometimes flow from a breach of the less important of the very large number of regulations which a managed welfare state seems to require ... and not so much to deal with the consequences of common law illegality that the Illegal Contracts Act was enacted.

Lord Goff considered that before a discretionary system was implemented, there should be a study of the matter by the Law Commission.[134] Such an inquiry should have to embrace not only the perceived advantages and disadvantages of the present law but also the likely advantages and disadvantages of a system of discretionary relief with particular reference to the New Zealand experience. New Zealand courts have had to consider illegality under the Act on a number of occasions and the cases would suggest that the discretionary approach has not inhibited trade or commerce or caused great difficulty.[135] Indeed, the discretionary approach may well have enhanced the settlement of disputes particularly in cases where the breach is of a technical or less serious kind. The courts have discouraged litigants who have attempted to take unconscionable advantage of illegality. It would appear that the courts have sensibly

---

131 [1994] 1 AC 340, at 363–64; [1993] 3 All ER 65, at 80.

132 *Idem.*

133 [1974] 2 NZLR 11. McMullin J cited as an example of a harsh application of the rule, *Carey v Hastie* [1968] NZLR 24. Further, to similar effect, see Cooke J in *Harding v Coburn* [1976] 2 NZLR 577, at 581.

134 [1994] 1 AC 340, at 364; [1993] 3 All ER 65, at 80.

135 Earlier concern that this would be the case seems to have been largely misplaced. See Furmston, MP, 'The Illegal Contracts Act 1970' (1970) 5 NZULR 151; and McLauchlan, DW, 'Contract and Commercial Law Reform in New Zealand' (1984–85) 11 NZULR 36, at 40–41. For a more optimistic treatment of the Act, see Beck, A, 'Illegal Contracts in Action' (1989) 13 NZULR 389.

pursued the Act's objective to ameliorate, where appropriate, the consequences of illegality.[136]

(a) The legislation

Under the Act, which binds the Crown,[137] an illegal contract is defined as any contract that is illegal in law or in equity whether the illegality arises from the creation or performance of the contract. An illegal contract includes one that contains an illegal provision whether that provision is severable or not.[138] It is further provided that a contract that has been lawfully entered into shall not become illegal or unenforceable because its performance is in breach of an Act unless the Act expressly provides or its object clearly so requires.[139] Illegal contracts are declared to have no effect. Similarly, dispositions made pursuant to an illegal contract are declared to have no effect.[140] In this regard, any rule of law or equity to the contrary is abrogated. This provision is, however, expressly made subject to the express provisions of the Act or of any other enactment.[141] A further exception protects a third party who is a *bona fide* purchaser for value of property which constitutes a disposition from a party to an illegal contract if the third party did not, at the time of the disposition, have notice that the property was the subject of, or the whole, or part of the consideration for an illegal contract. Protection is also given to a disposition made by or through a person who may become entitled to the property under a disposition of property by a party to an illegal contract.[142]

On the important issue of relief, s 7 provides that subject to the express provisions of any other enactment, a court may, in the course of any proceedings, or upon application for that purpose, grant to any party to an illegal contract any relief by way of restitution, compensation, variation of the contract, validation of the contract in whole or in part, or for any particular purpose or otherwise as the court thinks fit. Relief is similarly available to any party to a contract who is disqualified from enforcing it by reason of the commission of an illegal act in the course of its performance or any party claiming through such a party. Relief may also be sought by a party to the contract or any other person for whom it is material to know whether relief will be granted. It is expressly provided in s 7(3) that in considering whether to grant relief, the court shall have regard to:

---

136 An expression used by Richardson J to describe the correct approach to the Act, in *Re AIC Merchant Finance* [1990] 2 NZLR 385, at 389. Further, see Dickson, B, 'Restitution and Illegal Transactions', in Burrows, A (ed), *Essays on the Law of Restitution, op cit*, pp 194–96 concludes that a discretionary approach is preferable to the rules based system.

137 Section 4.

138 Section 3.

139 Section 5.

140 Section 6(1).

141 *Idem.*

142 Section 6(1)(a)(b).

(a) the conduct of the parties;

(b) in the case of the breach of an enactment, the object of the enactment and the gravity of the penalty expressly provided for any breach thereof; and

(c) such other matters as it thinks proper.

Section 7(3), however, provides that a court shall not grant relief if it considers that to do so would not be in the public interest. Under s 7(4), a court may grant relief even though the person, to whom relief was granted, entered into the contract, or committed an unlawful act, or unlawfully omitted to do an act with knowledge of the facts or law giving rise to the illegality but the court is required to take such knowledge into account in exercising its discretion.[143] A court has the power to vest property that was the subject of, or the whole, or part of the consideration for an illegal contract in any party to the proceedings. Further, it may direct any such party to transfer or assign property to any other party to the proceedings.[144] A court may make orders on such terms and conditions as it thinks fit.[145]

(b) Judicial applications of the Act

Initially, there was some doubt as to whether contracts which were proscribed by statute as void or of no effect could be the subject of relief under the Act.[146] However, to entertain such a qualification or exemption as McMullin J first emphasised in *Dreadon*,[147] would have seriously inhibited the operation of the Act. In *Harding v Coburn*,[148] the court held that in order to fall outside the provisions of the Act, a contract had to be governed by legislation expressly excluding the operation of the Act. Cooke J observed:[149]

> The limiting word 'express' is significant. It suggests that Parliament meant to rule out arguments based on implication or inference. Only when there is obvious inconsistency is the other enactment to prevail.

---

143 Section 7(4).

144 Section 7(5).

145 Section 7(6).

146 *Slobbe v Combined Taxis* [1972] NZLR 354, at 360; [1973] 2 NZLR 651.

147 [1974] 2 NZLR 11, at 19.

148 [1976] 2 NZLR 577, at 584–88. Approved in *Ross v Henderson* [1977] 2 NZLR 458, at 465.

149 [1976] 2 NZLR 577, at 584. In *AIC Merchant Finance Ltd* [1990] 2 NZLR 385, the Court of Appeal held that the relevant provisions of the Securities Act expressly precluded the court validating illegal allotments under the Illegal Contracts Act but did not preclude the court granting relief by way of compensation under the Act. The Securities Act was not a code which governed relief but, in so far as the provisions of that Act applied to render an allotment invalid and of no effect, the provisions of the Illegal Contracts Act governing relief were limited to compensation and validation of the illegal allotments was not permissible.

(c) Validation

One of the most important features of the legislation has been the power to validate a contract. The Court of Appeal upheld validation in *Harding v Coburn*[150] where, as a result of a mistake on the part of a purchaser's solicitor, a farm had been purchased without the necessary consent required under the Land Settlement Promotion and Land Acquisition Act, an object of which was to prevent the aggradation of farmland. The purchaser in that case did not own any other farmland and had made a mistake as to the form of the agreement used. Where a defendant unconscionably attempts to take advantage of an illegality, a court may assist the plaintiff by validating the contract. Thus, in *National Westminster Finance New Zealand Ltd v South Pacific Rent-a-Car Ltd*,[151] the Court of Appeal upheld a claim to validate a series of illegal hire purchase agreements relating to motor vehicles which the defendant attempted to resile from on the ground of illegality. It was found that the plaintiff had been advised at the time of entering the agreements with the defendant's predecessor that they were valid and the plaintiff had accordingly advanced finance for the acquisition of the motor vehicles. The agreement had been in force for some time before the share-holding in the company was acquired by the defendant who sought to take advantage of the illegality by declining to honour the agreements and gain a consequent windfall.[152]

In *Catley v Herbert*,[153] the plaintiff and the defendant, who had been in business together as orchardists had entered into an agreement to dissolve their association. The arrangement they entered into unwittingly violated the provisions of s 62 of the Companies Act, which prohibited a company from giving financial assistance for the purchase of its own shares. There being no prejudice to any creditors or any shareholders, the agreement was validated. However, in *Euro-National Corporation Ltd v NZI Bank Ltd*,[154] validation was declined where a complex scheme of arrangement which was conceded to be illegal had been clearly contrived with the assistance of professional advisers so as to minimise the plaintiff's financial embarrassment and advantage the defendant. Similarly, in *Equiticorp Industries Group v The Crown*,[155] validation was declined where the Crown had been found to have wrongfully profited from the sale of its shares in a large steel concern which had been illegally financed by Equiticorp. Since it was considered that the Crown had

---

150 *Ibid*. Further, see *Hurell v Townsend* [1982] 1 NZLR 536.

151 [1985] 1 NZLR 646 (HC), 655 (CA). Further, where the circumstances of the case also justified validation, see *France v Hight* [1990] 1 NZLR 345.

152 *Ibid*, at 654.

153 [1988] 1 NZLR 607.

154 [1992] 2 NZLR 739. Further, see *Lower Hutt City Council v Martin* [1987] 1 NZLR 321.

155 [1996] 3 NZLR 612, considered further, p 299.

deliberately not investigated the source of funds, it was considered contrary to the public interest to validate the purchase. To do so would in the opinion of the court have been to condone dishonest and commercially unacceptable behaviour. Validation was also refused by the Court of Appeal, in *House v Jones*,[156] where the conduct of the purchaser's solicitor involved a succession of defaults in complying with the Land Settlement Promotion Act and a period of five years had passed since the nominated settlement date. During that time, farm prices had greatly increased and the value of the dollar had diminished so that it was considered unjust to allow the purchasers to complete five years later. Where an illegal provision has not been validated because it was offensive to the policy of the legislation, a court may sever the offending provisions so that an agreement may otherwise take effect.[157]

(d) Compensation

A claim for restitution or compensation for use of a motor car as a taxi was sought in *Broadlands Rentals Ltd v Bull*.[158] A taxi had been acquired by the plaintiff under an illegal hire agreement. The taxi had been used for approximately 100,000 miles before it was repossessed by Broadlands. At first instance, the plaintiff was awarded the sum of $3,275.25 being the money he had paid by way of hire. However, the trial judge awarded Broadlands a sum of $825 for the use of the vehicle calculated at an interest rate of 10% per annum on the capital outlay for the motor vehicle for the period of hire. The Court of Appeal, whilst not allowing Broadlands to profit from the transaction, increased the sum awarded to $2,625, which reflected what was considered to be a fair amount for depreciation in the value of the vehicle between the time of its lease and the date of possession. The Court of Appeal considered that the Act was not intended to be punitive, although it was observed that *inter partes* it might well be reasonable to exercise the discretion under s 7 to ensure that the party more culpable does not profit at the expense of the other.[159] In *Re AIC Merchant Finance Ltd*,[160] the Court of Appeal also ordered that investors with AIC be compensated for invalid securities that had been issued to them reflecting their investments. The securities were held to be illegal under the relevant legislation pertaining to the issue of securities because there was no registered prospectus in place. The Securities Act expressly prohibited invalidation but it was

---

156 [1985] 2 NZLR 288.

157 *Edwards v O'Connor* [1989] 3 NZLR 448; *Supercool Refrigeration and Airconditioning (Liq) v Hoverd Industries Ltd* [1994] 3 NZLR 301.

158 [1976] 2 NZLR 595.

159 *Ibid*, at 600.

160 [1990] 2 NZLR 385.

held that this did not, as a matter of construction, extend to preventing a court from granting compensation or restitution to the investors under the Act for an amount which they would have received had their securities been valid. Emphasis was placed on the underlying legislative intent which was to protect investors. The court was also persuaded by the fact that, if these subscribers were treated simply as unsecured creditors, they would receive nothing in the company's liquidation.

(e) Residual discretion to grant relief in cases falling outside the operation of the Act

In H*owick Building Co v Howick Parklands Ltd*,[161] it was considered that, had an agreement entered into between the plaintiff and the defendant contravened the Commerce Act which expressly excluded the operation of the Illegal Contracts Act 1970, there was a residual discretion to enforce a contract where it would have been unconscionable to allow the defendant to rely on a defence of illegality. The defendant had deliberately encouraged the plaintiff to believe that the legality of the scheme would not be challenged until it later became opportune for the defendant to resile from the contract. Although both parties had entertained a doubt about the legality of the scheme, the court considered that the defendant by its actions had effectively misled the plaintiff into not proceeding with a re-arrangement or revision of the agreement earlier. Accordingly, the defendant had assumed primary responsibility in relation to any possible contravention of the Act.[162]

---

161 [1993] 1 NZLR 749.
162 *Ibid*, at 767–68.

CHAPTER 8

Breach of Contract

Restitution may be sought to prevent the unjust enrichment of a party following the rescission of a contract by an innocent party upon repudiation by a party in default. Claims to restitution are not, however, exclusively limited to the innocent party. In some circumstances, a contract-breaker may be entitled to claim restitution of moneys paid under the contract or claim reimbursement for services rendered where it would be unconscionable for the innocent party to retain the benefit of the services without payment. The circumstances in which restitutionary relief will be afforded an innocent party or the party in default will be considered below. In this regard, it is also useful to compare restitutionary relief under the general law with a statutory discretionary scheme such as that embodied in the Contractual Remedies Act 1979 in New Zealand which is discussed in the final part of this chapter.

The innocent party

If there has been a breach of a term that can be regarded as constituting an essential or fundamental obligation of a contract[1] or one that goes to the root of a contract so that the innocent party is deprived of any substantial benefit under the contract,[2] he or she may rescind the contract and sue for damages. Similarly, the innocent party may rescind the contract and claim damages if the defaulting party's acts or omissions evidence an intention to repudiate the whole contract or carry it out in a manner inconsistent with his or her obligations.[3] Rescission in this sense does not mean today, however, that the contract is discharged *ab initio* as it once did. The parties are discharged only as to their obligations that are prospective.[4] Rights that have accrued are enforceable. The innocent party may, however, elect to affirm the contract and simply sue for damages for breach.[5] Should he or she elect to rescind the contract, the innocent party may, in some circumstances, initiate a restitutionary claim for the return of moneys paid in advance or upon a *quantum meruit* or *quantum valebat* for the reasonable

---

1   *Schuler v Wickman Machine Tools Ltd* [1974] AC 235; *DTR Nominees Pty Ltd v Mona Homes Pty Ltd* (1978) 52 ALJR 360, at 364.
2   *McDonald v Dennys Lascelles Ltd* (1933) 48 CLR 457, at 477 *per* Dixon J; *Hongkong Fir Shipping Co Ltd v Kawasaki Kisen Kaisha Ltd* [1962] 2 QB 26.
3   *Shevill v Builders Licensing Board* (1982) 149 CLR 620, at 625 *per* Gibbs CJ.
4   *McDonald v Dennys Lascelles Ltd* (1933) 48 CLR 457, at 477.
5   Affirmation is considered further, Chapter 9, pp 211–13.

cost of services rendered or goods supplied.[6] The merits of a restitutionary claim in these circumstances are debatable and it has been argued that
the injured party should be limited simply to a claim for damages where a
contract has been rescinded for wrongful repudiation.[7] Although some
English cases[8] have allowed a measure of double recovery in this context,
the better view advanced by the High Court of Australia, in *Baltic
Shipping Company v Dillon*,[9] is that a plaintiff should not be able to invoke
cumulatively a remedy in damages and a claim to restitution so as to permit double recovery consequent upon breach. In that case, the High Court
of Australia held that if a passenger had been entitled to restitution of a
fare paid in advance for a cruise on a ship which sank, she would not have
been entitled to damages for breach of contract as well.

(a) Recovery of moneys paid in advance upon a total failure of consideration

Where moneys have been paid in advance for the performance of an
obligation under a contract and there is a total failure on the part of the
recipient to perform that obligation, the remedy of moneys had and
received is available to enable the innocent party to obtain restitution of
the advance payment. The action for moneys had and received upon a
total failure of consideration was one of the grounds of relief recognised
by Lord Mansfield in *Moses v Macferlan*.[10] In order for there to be recovery, the failure of consideration must deprive the party making the payment of any substantial benefit under the contract. Two Australian cases
illustrate the necessity for consideration to have failed substantially. In
the first, *Shaw v Ball*,[11] it was held that the action for moneys had and
received did not lie for the recovery of advance payments of the purchase price under a contract for the sale of a business which included

---

6   *Ettride v Vermin Board of the District of Merat Bay* [1928] SASR 124; *Brookes Robinson
    Pty Ltd v Rothfield* [1951] VLR 405; *Earthworks and Quarries Ltd v Eastman & Sons Ltd*
    [1966] VR 24. Exceptionally, a restitutionary claim may be available where a
    contract has been mutually abandoned. *DTR Nominees Pty Ltd v Mona Homes Pty
    Ltd* (1978) 138 CLR 423. A restitutionary remedy for a *quantum meruit* has been
    allowed where a contract that was unenforceable has been validly terminated by
    the plaintiff for breach. *Matthes v Carter* (1955) 55 SR (NSW) 357. *Brookes Robinson
    Pty Ltd v Rothfield* [1951] VLR 405; *Gino D'Allesandro Constructions Pty Ltd v Powis*
    (1987) 2 Qd R 40.
7   See discussion, pp 190–92.
8   *Heywood v Wellers (a Firm)* [1976] QB 446, at 458; *Millars Machinery Co Ltd v David
    Way & Son* (1935) 40 Com Cas 204.
9   (1992–93) 176 CLR 344.
10 (1760) 2 Burr 1005; [1760] 97 ER 676.
11 [1963] 63 SR (NSW) 910. *Cf Hunt v Silk* (1804) 5 East 449; [1804] 102 ER 1142, recov-
    ery of an advance payment was denied where a lessee had entered into possession
    of premises prior to the lessor defaulting in executing a lease. Lord Ellenborough
    considered that this constituted partial execution of the agreement. Also, see *Marsh
    v McKay* [1948] St R Qd 113.

goodwill, plant, stock and a lease of the premises in which the business was to be conducted. The purchaser had entered into possession of the premises and had commenced business. The court considered that the purchaser had received substantial performance of the contract although there had been no formal assignment of the lease of the premises to the purchaser. In *Baltic Shipping Company v Dillon*,[12] a passenger on a cruise ship, 'the Mikhail Lermantov' claimed the return of the total price of her ticket for a cruise after the ship had sunk off the New Zealand coast. The High Court held that the plaintiff could not recover. She had enjoyed the benefit of the cruise for eight days and thus had received partial performance of the contract. Mason CJ observed:[13]

> Where ... an innocent party seeks to recover money paid in the expectation of the entire performance by the contract-breaker of its obligations under the contract and the contract-breaker renders an incomplete performance, in general, the innocent party cannot recover unless there has been a total failure of consideration. If the incomplete performance results in the innocent party receiving and retaining any substantial part of the benefit expected under the contract, there will not be a total failure of consideration.

Restitution was allowed for total failure of consideration in *Rover International Ltd v Cannon Film Sales Ltd*.[14] Rover was permitted to recover instalments paid under an agreement in which Cannon was to provide films which could be copied and distributed by Rover in Italy. Under the agreement, Rover had expected to derive a share of the gross receipts of exhibiting the films it had processed. Cannon subsequently discovered that the agreement which Rover had entered into was invalid because Rover had not been incorporated at the time the agreement had been executed and took advantage of this to disclaim any further contractual commitment to Rover. Although some films had been delivered to it under the agreement, the Court of Appeal considered that Rover had been deprived of its bargain by the fact that the agreement was void *ab initio* and accordingly it was unable to distribute the films and earn profits. The delivery of the films was a mere incidence of the performance of the contract and did not in the view of the court constitute partial performance.[15] In New Zealand, the Court of Appeal

---

12 (1992–93) 176 CLR 345. Further, see *Marsh & McLennan Pty Ltd v Stanyers Transport Pty Ltd* [1994] 2 VR 232.

13 *Ibid*, at 350. The requirement that there be no substantial benefit may assist to explain the old case of *Giles v Edwards* (1797) 7 TR 18; 101 ER 920. Recovery of an advance payment was permitted where there had been an extremely small benefit to the plaintiff in trees measured and corded by the defendant which the trial judge appeared to consider was insufficient to constitute partial performance.

14 [1989] 1 WLR 912; [1989] 3 All ER 423.

15 *Ibid*, at 924–25; 433–34 *per* Kerr LJ.

in *Martin v Pont*,[16] held that an investor was entitled to recover moneys that had been given to his accountant for investment purposes. The moneys had been stolen by an employee with the result that the intended investment did not materialise and accordingly there had been a total failure by the defendant to perform his part of the bargain.

As *Rover* illustrates, a court will closely scrutinise an agreement to ascertain the nature of the obligation or promise that the recipient of an advance payment has undertaken to perform. The fact that the innocent party has derived a benefit collaterally from an agreement will not preclude reliance on the action for moneys had and received if the recipient of an advance payment has failed to essentially perform his or her obligations under an agreement. In *Rowland v Divall*,[17] the plaintiff purchased a motor car and used it for several months. The defendant did not have title to the vehicle and the plaintiff was compelled to surrender it to the true owner. Subsequently, the plaintiff sued the defendant to recover back the purchase money he had paid on a total failure of consideration. The Court of Appeal held that he was entitled to recover the purchase money although he had enjoyed the use of the car for some time. What he had contracted for was not the use of the car but title and the right to lawfully possess it, whereas what he had received was unlawful possession which had exposed him to the risk of action by the true owner.[18] The action for moneys had and received, upon a total failure of consideration, will fail if there has been partial performance because the common law was not able to apportion.[19] It would seem that, at least where consideration can be apportioned or benefits easily restored, restitution should be available even though there is no total failure of consideration.[20] This view has recently been affirmed by Lord Goff in *Goss v Chilcott*.[21]

---

16 [1993] 3 NZLR 25. Further, see *Hill v Smith* (1844) 12 M & W 618; [1844] 152 ER 1346; *Bostock v Jardine* (1865) 3 H & C 700; [1865] 159 ER 707.

17 [1923] 2 KB 500; [1923] All ER 270; *Warman v Southern Counties Car Finance Corp Ltd* [1949] 2 KB 576; [1949] 1 All ER 711. For a more extreme application of the rule, see *Butterworth v Kingsway Motors* [1954] 1 WLR 1286 where the purchaser was able to recover the purchase price on a total failure of consideration even though he had used the car for some months and had waited one more week before rescinding the contract, the vendor would have perfected his title.

18 *Rowland v Divall* has been criticised on the basis that the purchaser was enriched by being able to use the car for a considerable period of time. However, it is difficult to see why the vendor should recover anything when it was not his car to sell and the purchaser was exposed to a potential claim in conversion. Note, s 101(1)(g) of the Goods Act 1958 (Vict) provides statutory relief and allows a vendor to recover the 'fair value' of any use of the goods before termination of the performance of the contract where the vendor acted honestly and reasonably in selling the goods.

19 See *Whincup v Hughes* (1871) LR 6 CP 78, at 85–86.

20 *David Securities Pty Ltd v Commonwealth Bank of Australia* (1992) 175 CLR 353, at 383. Further, see Birks, P, *An Introduction to Restitution*, reprint 1993, pp 242–45, Clarendon Press, Oxford.

21 [1996] 3 NZLR 385.

Exceptionally, part of an advance payment might also be claimed successfully where a transaction involved more than one contract and some contracts remained unperformed. In *Rugg v Minett*,[22] for example, the plaintiff paid in advance for various casks of turpentine which had been auctioned by lots. The casks were left in the defendant's warehouse where they were destroyed by fire before the plaintiff had taken actual delivery. The plaintiff sued to recover the purchase price in an action for moneys had and received. The court observed that the seller had performed its obligations in relation to certain of the casks so that property in them and consequently risk had passed to the plaintiff prior to the fire. In so far, however, as the defendant had omitted to perform its obligations in relation to the remainder, the risk remained with the sellers and the action for moneys had and received was available to recover the price paid for them.

Should a party elect not to rescind a contract for a total failure of consideration when the opportunity to do so presents, restitution will be declined. In *Hunt v Silk*,[23] a lessee remained in possession of premises after it became apparent that the lessor was in default of his obligations to repair the premises and provide a lease. It was held that the plaintiff had voluntarily elected to remain in possession of the premises after being aware of the lessor's defaults thereby precluding his later reliance on rescission and the remedy of moneys had and received. Similarly, in *Yeoman Credit v Apps*,[24] a hirer of a defective motor vehicle was unable to recover an advance payment and instalments of hire because he had not rescinded the agreement on learning of the defects, which were substantial, but instead had retained the vehicle for a further three months paying further instalments of hire. The Court of Appeal considered that these actions constituted an affirmation of the agreement and deprived the hirer from relying on a claim to recover for moneys had and received upon a total failure of consideration.

(b) *Ultra vires* payments

Where advance payments have been made pursuant to a contract which is *ultra vires* one of the parties to make, the money can be recovered in an action for moneys had and received upon a failure of consideration. Recently, in *Westdeutsche Bank v Islington LBC*,[25] Lord Goff and Lord Browne-Wilkinson observed that the claim for moneys had and received was based on failure of consideration and unjust enrichment

---

22 (1809) 11 East 210; [1809] 103 ER 985.
23 (1804) 5 East 449; [1804] 102 ER 1140.
24 [1962] 2 QB 508; [1961] 2 All ER 280.
25 [1996] 2 WLR 802; [1966] 2 All ER 961.

and not on any implied promise to pay, or in equity on the basis that the payer retained a beneficial interest in the money.[26] As a result, it was held that, although the bank was entitled to recover moneys paid to the council in relation to an interest swap arrangement which was *ultra vires* the powers of the council, it was not entitled to claim compound interest which was a power considered by a majority to be exclusively within the jurisdiction of equity to award.

(c) Compensation for services rendered under a contract that has been wrongfully repudiated

(i) Damages for reliance expenditure

Where a party sustains a loss by reason of a breach of contract, he or she is entitled to be compensated in damages and placed in the same position as if the contract had been performed.[27] An innocent party will usually claim damages for breach of contract and these will generally be assessed as the net profit being the difference between the expenses, justifiably incurred by a plaintiff in the discharge of contractual obligations, and the amount of gross receipts. Where the contract suggests that no net profit would be made or there is a difficulty in demonstrating what the profit would be, the innocent party will be able to recoup as damages expenditure which has been incurred in the discharge of his or her contractual obligations. In this case, the damages claimed may be described as reliance damages or damages for wasted expenditure.[28] The contract-breaker is, however, able to plead in mitigation that such expenditure would not have been recouped even if the contract had been fully performed. The onus of proof of a losing contract rests on the contract-breaker because the law presumes that a person would not have entered into an agreement in which costs would not be recovered.

These principles are illustrated in Commonwealth of *Australia v Amann Aviation Pty Ltd.*[29] Amann sued the Commonwealth for damages arising out of the wrongful cancellation of a contract to carry out aerial coastal surveillance. Amann had spent a very significant sum in acquiring specially equipped aircraft but it had insufficient aircraft to carry out

---

26 *Ibid*, at 808 *per* Lord Goff, 833–39 *per* Lord Browne-Wilkinson; *cf South Tynside Metropolitan Borough Council v Svenska International* [1995] 1 All ER 545.

27 *Robinson v Harman* (1848) 1 Ex 850; 154 ER 363, applied by Gibbs CJ in *Wenham v Ella* (1972) 127 CLR 454, at 471, and Mason CJ in *Commonwealth of Australia v Amann Aviation Pty Ltd* (1991) 174 CLR 64, at 80.

28 See *McRae v Commonwealth Disposals Commission* (1951) 84 CLR 377.

29 (1991) 174 CLR 64; further, see *Cullinane v British Rema Manufacturing Co Ltd* [1954] 1 QB 292; [1953] 2 All ER 1257; *Anglia Television Ltd v Reed* [1971] 3 All ER 690, *Ccc Films (London) Ltd v Impact Quadrant Films Ltd* [1985] QB 16 and the discussion of *Amann* by Treital, GH, 'Damages for Breach of Contract in the High Court of Australia' (1992) 108 LQR 226.

its obligations under the contract which would have allowed the Commonwealth to lawfully terminate the agreement. Instead, the Commonwealth adopted an erroneous procedure for cancellation and consequently its termination of the contract was unlawful. The expenditure incurred by Amann was considerably more than any net profit that it was anticipated Amann would derive from performing the contract. An additional complicating factor, however, was that Amann expected to obtain a further contract after the present one expired because it would have been in a much better position than any competitors to secure such a contract. Were it to secure a further contract, substantial profit was anticipated. The High Court of Australia held that Amann was entitled to claim its reliance expenditure. The prospects of Amann securing a further contract were considered good and the court found that this was a factor that was in the contemplation of the parties when they entered into the agreement. This, and the fact that the issue of whether the Commonwealth would have lawfully terminated the contract was conjectural meant that the net profit lost by Amann was difficult to establish. The Commonwealth bore the onus of establishing that Amann's reliance expenditure would not have been recouped had the contract not been unlawfully cancelled. It was unable to do this so Amann was entitled to claim its wasted expenditure.

(ii) *Profit as a restitutionary component of damages*

A related issue on the question of damages for breach is whether a plaintiff can claim restitution of any profit that the contract-breaker has derived from a breach.[30] It was argued, in *Surrey County Council v Bredero Homes Ltd*,[31] that local authorities who owned adjoining land should be entitled to damages for the lost opportunity of earning additional revenue where, in breach of a covenant restricting it to building a certain number of houses, a developer had proceeded to construct additional houses without consulting the councils. The plaintiffs were unable, however, to show that the value of their adjoining property had been injuriously effected by the breach of covenant. Since damages in contract were compensatory and no loss to adjoining property was established, the Court of Appeal awarded the plaintiffs only nominal damages for the breaches of the covenants.[32] The argument that the plaintiffs had lost an opportunity to derive a bonus for agreeing to a

---

30 See Lord Goff and Jones, G, *The Law of Restitution*, 4th edn, 1993, p 416, Sweet & Maxwell, London, where the possibility of a restitutionary claim is considered.

31 [1993] 1 WLR 1361.

32 In particular, see *Steyn LJ*, *ibid*, at 1369.

variation was dismissed as a fiction.[33] Steyn LJ characterised a claim of this kind as one in restitution and in doing so approved Brightman J's approach in *Wrotham Park Estate Co Ltd v Parkside Homes Ltd*.[34] Substantial damages were awarded in that case for breach of a restrictive covenant in lieu of injunctive relief which Steyn LJ considered to be in the nature of a restitutionary claim.[35] When assessing damages, Brightman J had awarded the plaintiff an allowance for a proportion of the profit derived from the development that was attributable to the defendant ignoring a restrictive covenant on the number of homes that could be constructed. Although the plaintiff could not establish any actual loss to his property, Brightman J held that the plaintiff must pay a fair price for its actions in ignoring the covenant because the plaintiff would have otherwise been in a strong position to demand a premium for allowing a relaxation of the covenant. In a later case, *Jaggard v Sawyer*,[36] however, the observation of Steyn LJ that this was a restitutionary claim was doubted, awards of this kind being there described as truly compensating the plaintiff for loss.[37] It may be argued, however, that awards of damages that reflect a profit component are legitimately described as restitutionary because they are imposed to prevent the unjust enrichment of the defendant at the expense of the plaintiff.

(iii) Restitutionary claims for reliance expenditure

The fact that reliance expenditure may be claimed as damages where loss of profit is difficult to assess, as *Amann*[38] illustrates, may constitute a reason why there are few reported cases today in Australia of claims for *quantum meruit* or *quantum valebat* arising from a wrongful termination of a contract. Indeed, it has been suggested that the innocent party's redress should be confined to action on the contract and that a claim in restitution should not be available because rescission for repudiation no

---

33   *Ibid*, at 1370–71. See Sharpe, RJ and Waddams, SM, 'Damages for Lost Opportunity to Bargain' (1982) 2 OJLS 290, Waddams, 'Restitution as Part of Contract Law', in Burrows, A (ed), *Essays on the Law of Restitution*, 1991, p 211, Clarendon Press, Oxford. It may be argued that Steyn LJ was incorrect to so peremptorily dismiss this argument. By analogy with the loss of an opportunity of a renewal of a contract in *Commonwealth v Amman Aviation Ltd* (1991) 174 CLR 64, the savings attributable to the developer's default could be argued to represent a lost opportunity to earn additional revenue for the relaxation of the covenants. If this was a loss that was within the contemplation of the parties on ordinary principles relating to the assessment of damages, it should be compensatable as a head of common law damages, or at least be permitted as a restitutionary component of such a claim.

34   [1974] 1 WLR 798; [1974] 2 All ER 321.

35   [1993] 1 WLR 1361, at 1369.

36   [1995] 1 WLR 269.

37   *Ibid*, at 281 *per* Sir Thomas Bingham MR; at 291 *per* Millet J.

38   (1991) 174 CLR 64.

longer avoids a contract *ab initio* as it once did, but merely discharges the parties prospectively from performing their obligations. However, the courts have continued to allow such claims consequent upon rescission for breach. In *Renard Constructions Pty Ltd v Minister for Public Works*,[39] for example, the Court of Appeal of New South Wales held that, although rescission of a contract for wrongful repudiation did not rescind a contract *ab initio*, a restitutionary claim was available. A claim to restitution will be preferred where the plaintiff's damages for breach will be less than the value of his or her services assessed on the basis of a *quantum meruit*. It may happen, for example, that the plaintiff has entered into a contractual arrangement that would have, if performed, provide little profit or even more disastrously, constitute a loss for the plaintiff. In *Lodder v Slowey*,[40] for example, the Privy Council considered that a contractor was entitled to claim for the reasonable cost of services provided to a council under an agreement where the council had wrongfully entered and prevented the contractor from completing the work. The jury had returned an answer to a question which suggested that had the contractor been able to complete the contract it would not have earned any profit. Given that reliance damages may be reduced if the defendant can show that the plaintiff would not have been able to fully recoup them had the contract been performed, as *Amann*[41] illustrates, then the restitutionary remedy will similarly benefit a plaintiff who would have incurred a loss had the contract been performed. Some may consider this incongruous, however, in defence of the restitutionary claim it may be argued that by repudiating the contract the defendant has lost the protection of any advantageous ceiling that the contract might have afforded.

This approach was adopted by Kerr LJ in *Rover International Ltd v Cannon Films Ltd (No 3)*.[42] It was considered incorrect that a party should seek to resile from a contract by pleading that it was void for incapacity yet in other respects attempt to rely on the contract to limit the level of remuneration on a *quantum meruit*.[43] Goff and Jones consider, however, that a restitutionary claim should never exceed a rateable proportion of

---

39 (1992) 26 NSWLR 334, at 277–78 *per* Meagher JA; *Iezzi Constructions Pty Ltd v Watkins Pacific Qld Pty Ltd* (1995) 2 Qd R 350.

40 [1904] AC 442 and in the Court of Appeal (1901) 20 NZLR 321. This case was decided at a time when rescission for repudiation meant that a contract was discharged *ab initio*. Further, see *Hoenig v Issacs* [1952] 2 All ER 176, at 180. A claim to a *quantum meruit* is not available where the contract has been completed, see *Boyd & Forest v Glasgow and South Western Railway* (1915) SC (HL) 20.

41 [1991] 174 CLR 64.

42 [1989] 1 WLR 912; [1989] 3 All ER 423, and further, see *Greenmast Shipping Co SA v Jean Lion & Cie SA, The Saronios* [1986] 2 Lloyd's Rep 277.

43 *Ibid*, 924–25; 436.

the contract price.[44] They criticise the Californian case of *Boomer v Muir*[45] where a contractor was able to recover a sum considerably in excess of the contract price to which he would have been entitled had the contract not been unlawfully terminated. In defence of this result, however, it would appear that the contractor was not in fact unjustly enriched because the cost of performance had, so the jury found, been considerably increased by the defendant's repeated delays which ultimately led the plaintiff to leave the site prior to completion and lawfully rescind the contract. In cases of this kind, it is suggested that, although a court may have regard to the contact price in fixing an amount of a restitutionary award, this should not protect a person from liability to pay increased compensation by way of a *quantum meruit* where he or she has wrongfully contributed to the innocent party's increased costs.[46]

A *quantum meruit* claim may also extend to work and related expenditure that has been undertaken by the plaintiff pursuant to the contract in preparation for conferring the ultimate end-product on the defendant. Thus, in *Planche v Colburn*,[47] the plaintiff contracted with the defendant to prepare a manuscript on a topic for a periodical publication for a certain sum. The plaintiff commenced work on the manuscript but, before delivery of it, the defendant abandoned the publication due to its lack of success. The plaintiff was permitted to recover a sum assessed by the jury on a *quantum meruit* for the fruits of his labour. In *Brenner v First Artist's Management Pty Ltd*,[48] Bryne J in the Supreme Court of Victoria, considered *Planche v Colburn* without criticism and observed that a benefit may take many forms and that it should not be limited merely to an economic benefit.[49]

---

44 Goff and Jones, *op cit*, 4th edn, pp 424–28; Jones, G, in Finn, PD (ed), *Essays on Restitution*, 1990, pp 4–5, Law Book Co Ltd, Sydney. Further, see Dawson, F and McLauchlan, DW, *The Contractual Remedies Act 1979*, 1981, p 160, Sweet & Maxwell, London, where it is also suggested that the contractual ceiling should operate to limit the recoverable sum under a *quantum meruit*. In *Pavey & Matthews Pty Ltd v Paul* (1986) 162 CLR 221, at 263–64 Deane J considered that the contract price could be considered on a claim for a *quantum meruit*.

45 (1933) 24 P 2nd 570, considered by Fisher J in *Newmans Tours Ltd v Ranier Investments Ltd* [1992] 2 NZLR 68, at 93 who appeared to support the view that restitutionary claims should be limited by the contract expectation.

46 See Meagher J in *Renard Constructions Pty Ltd v Minister for Works* (1992) 26 NSWLR 234, at 276–78; also *Iezzi Constructions Pty Ltd v Watkins Pacific Qld Pty Ltd* [1995] 2 Qd R 350.

47 (1831) 8 Bing 14; [1831] 131 ER 305. Beatson, *loc cit*, at 82–83; Goff and Jones, 4th edn, *op cit*, p 426 also appear to take the view that, in cases of this kind, the plaintiff should be limited to a claim in damages although Jones appears less certain of this in *Essays on the Law of Restitution*, *op cit*, pp 4–5.

48 [1993] 2 VR 221, at 258. Further, see *Automatic Fire Sprinklers v Watson* (1946) 72 CLR 435.

49 As Beatson has argued; [1987] CLP 71.

The party in default

(a) Recovery of moneys paid in advance

A contract-breaker may recover advance payments of the purchase price unless the payment may fairly be described as a deposit paid in order to ensure that the contract is performed.[50] If the payment is no more than a deposit it will not be recoverable in an action for moneys had and received. In *Dies v British & International Mining & Finance Corporation*,[51] the purchaser had bought arms for a price of £135,000 paying £100,000 in advance. Though the purchaser declined to accept delivery of the guns, the plaintiff succeeded in recovering the payment. It was held that there was nothing in the agreement which indicated that the payment was intended or believed by either party to be in the nature of a guarantee or deposit for the due performance of the contract. It was further considered that there would be a manifest deficiency in the law if, when the buyer had paid for his goods in advance but was unable to accept delivery, the vendor could retain the goods and the money quite irrespective of whether the money so retained bore any relation to the amount of damage sustained. The seller, in such circumstances, has a remedy in damages and could set-off his or her claim against any claim for the return of the purchase price. This approach was also taken by Dixon J in the case of land in *McDonald v Dennys Lascelles Ltd*.[52] Dixon J observed:[53]

> When a contract stipulates for payment of part of the purchase money in advance, the purchaser relying only on the vendor's promise to give him a conveyance, the vendor is entitled to enforce payment before the time has arrived for conveying the land; yet his title to retain the money has been considered not to be absolute but conditional upon the subsequent completion of the contract.

In *Baltic Shipping Co v Dillon*,[54] Mason CJ preferred to view these cases as payments made conditional upon performance. Mason CJ, however, was careful to distinguish cases of advance payments for the sale of land or goods from contracts which required the payee to perform work and incur expense before completing performance of his or her obligations under the contract. In the latter situation, Mason CJ considered that it would be unreasonable to regard the payee's right to retain the money as conditional upon performance of the contractual obligation unless the

---

50   *Freedom v AHR Constructions Pty Ltd* (1987) 1 Qd R 59.

51   [1939] 1 KB 724.

52   (1933) 48 CLR 457 following *Mayson v Clouet* [1924] AC 980; note *Reid Motors Ltd v Wood* [1978] 1 NZLR 325.

53   *Ibid*, at 477.

54   (1992–93) 176 CLR 345, at 351–53.

contract manifested a contrary intention.[55] The distinction is illustrated in *Hyundai Heavy Industries Co Ltd v Papadopoulos*.[56] A purchaser defaulted in the second of five advance payments for the cost of a ship that was being constructed. Under the terms of the contract, if the purchaser defaulted in paying the instalment, the shipbuilder had, in addition to other contractual remedies, the right to retain money already paid and sell the ship at public auction. As a result of the default, the shipowners claimed the value of the second instalment from the guarantor, Papadopoulos. Papadopoulos claimed, following *Dies*,[57] that the purchaser would have been entitled to have recovered the instalment paid on cancellation had it been paid and accordingly the shipbuilders were unable to recover the value of the second instalment under the guarantee. The House of Lords held, however, that *Dies* was distinguishable because the contract in the present case was not simply for the sale and delivery of a ship but for its construction as well.

Where the contract expressly provides that on rescission advance payments are to be forfeit, equity may grant relief. In *McDonald v Denny Lascelles Ltd*,[58] Dixon J suggested that there was a limited jurisdiction to relieve against forfeiture of instalments on the default of a purchaser of land if the purchaser, as a term of equitable relief, subsequently agreed to perform the contract. In *Stockloser v Johnson*,[59] a majority of the Court of Appeal took a more robust approach. There, a purchaser agreed to buy plant and machinery. The contract provided that the purchase price should be paid by instalments and that in default the vendor was able to rescind the contract, forfeit the instalments that had already been paid and resume possession. Having defaulted, the vendor rescinded the contract and forfeited the instalments paid. The purchaser, who was financially unable or unwilling to complete the contract, contended that the vendor should make restitution of the paid instalments because the forfeiture clause was penal and unconscionable. Although declining to grant relief, a majority of the court, Somervell LJ and Denning LJ, considered that equity could relieve against forfeiture of instalment payments if it would be unconscionable to allow forfeiture. Denning LJ described this as an equity of restitution. Whether forfeiture would be unconscionable was to be assessed at the time the application for forfeiture was made. Romer

---

55 *Ibid*, at 352–53.

56 [1980] 1 WLR 1129; [1980] 2 All ER 29.

57 [1939] 1 KB 724.

58 (1933) CLR 457, at 578–79. Further, see *Legione v Hateley* (1983) 152 CLR 404 where relief against forfeiture of the purchaser's interest in land was granted even though the time of settlement was expressed to be of the essence. *Cf Ciavarella v Balmer* (1983) 153 CLR 438; *CSS Investments Pty Ltd v Lopiron Pty Ltd* (1987) 76 ALR 463; *Stern v McArthur* (1988) 81 ALR 463.

59 [1954] 1 QB 476; [1954] 1 All ER 630.

LJ, however, adopted a more conservative approach, expressing the view that there was no jurisdiction to relieve against a forfeiture clause after rescission unless the vendor had been guilty of fraud, sharp practice or some other unconscionable conduct. The mere fact that forfeiture might produce a harsh result was not sufficient to justify equity's intervention. Subsequently, in *Galbraith v Mitchenall Estates Ltd*,[60] Sachs J indicated a preference for the more conservative approach of Romer LJ and declined to grant relief against forfeiture where the hirer of a caravan was, under the terms of hire, able to retain a substantial advance payment and repossess the caravan which was subsequently re-sold. Although the forfeiture provision was described as harsh, the court declined to intervene in the absence of evidence of sharp practice by the hirer. This approach is also consistent with recent English authority which resist equitable interference with contracts unless the recipient of a benefit under the contract has been guilty of sharp practice or other unconscionable behaviour.[61] Sharp practice was present, however, in *BICC v Burndy Corporation*,[62] where the plaintiff had seemingly snapped at an opportunity to terminate a contract when it owed the defendant far more under a contract than the defendant owed it for late payment of an instalment. The court granted the defendant relief against forfeiture of its proprietary interest in certain patents that was out of all proportion to the breach. Sharp practice and an unconscionable desire to take advantage of a purchaser in possession's default in paying instalments of purchase was also sufficient for a majority of the High Court of Australia in *Stern v McArthur*[63] to grant relief and order specific performance of a contract for the sale and purchase of land. The purchaser had been in possession of the property for some years and had constructed a house on the land with the result that, had equitable relief not been ordered, the vendor would have been unjustly enriched.[64] Restitution may be ordered on condition that the party seeking relief account to the other for any benefits received.[65] In subsequent English cases, relief against forfeiture has been held to be limited to claims involv-

---

60 [1965] 2 QB 473, at 483 taking the view that the Court of Appeal in *Campbell Discount v Bridge* [1961] 1 QB 445; 2 All ER 97 did not endorse the majority view in *Stockloser v Johnson*. Further, see *Campbell Discount v Bridge* [1962] 2 AC 600, at 626, at 614 *per* Lord Simonds and 626 *per* Lord Radcliffe, where it was asserted that courts of equity never undertook to serve as a general adjuster of bad bargains.

61 See *National Westminster Bank v Morgan* [1985] AC 686, at 708; [1985] 1 All ER 821, at 830; *O'Connor v Hart* [1985] 1 AC 1000, at 1041; [1985] 1 NZLR 159, at 171.

62 [1985] 1 All ER 419.

63 (1988) 81 ALR 463. Relief was refused in relation to the forfeiture of retention moneys consequent upon a failure by the contractor to complete work under an entire contract. *Kratzman Holdings Pty Ltd v University of Queensland* (1982) 1 Qd R 682.

64 *Cf Steedman v Drinkle* [1916] 1 AC 319; [1914–15] All ER 299 where a forfeiture clause of instalments of purchase price was treated as a penalty and relief was granted in not dissimilar circumstances.

65 *Lexane Pty Ltd v Highfern Pty Ltd* (1985) 1 Qd R 446.

ing the forfeiture of proprietary or possessory rights and not contractual or commercial rights.[66]

(b) Compensation for services rendered under a contract

A party in default under a contract for the performance of a service will be entitled to sue for any payment or instalment that falls due prior to his or her abandonment or repudiation of a contract if the conditions for payment have been satisfied.[67] However, a party in default under a contract which is entire, that is payment is conditional upon performance, is not usually entitled to any payment. In *Sumpter v Hedges*,[68] a builder sought to recover on a *quantum meruit* for services rendered for a lump sum payable on his completing the erection of certain buildings. The builder abandoned the work prior to completion. The Court of Appeal held that he was unable to claim reimbursement for any part of the services rendered. The owner was entitled to have the work completed by another contractor and the mere fact that he took the benefit of the construction which was situated on his land did not give rise to any new contract or obligation to pay on a *quantum meruit* for the work that had been partially performed.[69] However, where the work under an entire contract has been substantially completed, the recipient will not be able to decline payment but will be able to claim a deduction for the cost of rectification of the defects to conform with the contract. This principle was laid down by the English Court of Appeal in *Dakin & Co Ltd v Lee*,[70] and has been subsequently adopted in Australia.[71] In *Hoenig v Issacs*,[72]

---

66 *Scandinavian Trading Tanker Co AB v Flota Petrolera Ecuatoriana, The Scaptrade* [1983] 2 AC 694; [1983] 2 All ER 763; *Sport International Bussum BV v Inter-Footwear Ltd* [1984] 2 All ER 321.

67 *Ettridge v Vermin Board of the District of Murat Bay* [1928] SASR 124; *McLachlan v Nourse* [1928] SASR 230; *McDonald v Dennys Lascelles Ltd* (1933) 48 CLR 546; *Westralian Farmers Ltd v Commonwealth Agricultural Service Engineers Ltd* (1936) 54 CLR 361; *Hyundai Shipbuilding & Heavy Industries Co Ltd v Pournaras* [1978] 2 Lloyd's Rep 502; *Hyundai Heavy Industries Co Ltd v Papadopoulos* [1979] 1 Lloyd's Rep 130; [1980] 2 All ER 28; *Bank of Boston Connecticut v European Grain and Shipping Ltd* [1989] AC 1056; *Elkhoury v Farrow Mortgage Services Pty Ltd* (1992) 114 ALR 541.

68 [1898] 1 QB 673.

69 *Ibid*, at 716. *Cf Williams v Roffey Brothers* [1990] 1 All ER 512 where a fresh agreement was entered into after the contractor indicated it could not complete the contract on the existing terms.

70 [1916] 1 KB 566, as explained by Bankes LJ in *Vigars v Cooke* [1919] 2 KB 475, at 483. In *Arcos v Ronaasen* [1933] All ER 646, the House of Lords did not apply the substantial compliance rule to a sale of goods.

71 See *Hunter v Council of West Maitland* (1923) 23 SR (NSW) 420; *Corio Guarantee Corporation Ltd v McCallum* [1956] VLR 755; *Simpson Steel Structures v Spenser* [1964] WAR 101.

72 [1952] 2 All ER 176.

the Court of Appeal allowed the plaintiff's claim for the contract price less a deduction based on the cost of making good defects where the plaintiff had substantially completed the work. In *Bolton v Mahadeva*,[73] the Court of Appeal, conversely, declined to permit the plaintiff to recover the price for the installation of central heating and other work where the defendant was able to show that the installation did not perform effectively and was so defective that it could only be rectified by the expenditure of a considerable sum.

Further exceptions to the principle, that ordinarily a claim for payment cannot be made on an entire contract unless the work has been completed, arise where the defendant has requested a variation in the contract[74] or has waived defective performance by taking advantage of the work in circumstances where there was an option to refuse to accept the work in its defective state.[75] A restitutionary claim may also be entertained where the defendant has acquiesced in a performance that differs from the contractual obligation, in circumstances that render it unconscionable not to pay a reasonable sum for the service. In *Steele v Tardiani*,[76] the High Court of Australia permitted the plaintiffs to recover on a *quantum meruit* where the service they performed did not meet the contract specification. There was evidence, however, that the defendant had sought to take advantage of the plaintiffs' incomplete performance and had accepted the benefit of the work. Unlike the owner in *Sumpter v Hedges*, the defendant in this case had been guilty of sharp practice.

It may appear harsh to allow the recipient of a benefit under an entire contract to retain that benefit without payment because the contract has not been totally performed. Should restitution be allowed in relation to that part of the benefit that has incontrovertibly benefited the recipi-

---

73 [1972] 2 All ER 1322.

74 See *Christy v Rowe* [1803–13] All ER 740 where a variation in the terms of a charter was requested by the charterer's consignees of cargo thus entitling the shipowner to claim recovery *pro rata* from the charterer for the cost of freight. Also, see *Greenmast Shipping Co SA v Jean Lion & Cie SA, The Saronios* [1986] 2 Lloyd's Rep 277. Where the shipowner deviates but discharges cargo to a consignee at the agreed port of discharge, there is a breach of the contract, however slight the deviation. *Hain Steamship Co Ltd v Tate & Lyle Ltd* (1934) 39 Com Cas 259 (CA); [1936] 2 All ER 597.

75 *Hoenig v Issacs* [1952] 2 All ER 176, at 181 *per* Denning LJ.

76 (1946) 72 CLR 386, at 405 *per* Dixon J.

ent?[77] In *Sumpter v Hedges*,[78] for example, it may be argued that the contractor should have been able to recover for the amount of work he had done on the building which could be used as a foundation for its completion by another builder. Any additional expense incurred as a result of having to have another contractor complete the work would be recoverable by the owner in damages, which could be set-off against a restitutionary claim by the contractor for the partial performance. In the case of non-performance arising out of the contractor's inability to perform because of liquidity difficulties, it may be argued that, in the event of bankruptcy, the recipient of the partially completed work should not be unjustly enriched at the expense of the general creditors of the bankrupt contractor. The problem with this argument, however, like the difficulty with relief against forfeiture of instalments, is that the contractor has contracted for and accepted the risk that work would not be paid for unless completed. The owner similarly contracted for the benefit of an assurance that the work would be completed according to the contractor's undertaking. Whilst it is difficult not to have sympathy for the view that restitution should be allowed in circumstances of this kind, in the absence of legislative intervention, it would be incorrect to allow a claim in restitution under the general law which has the effect of contradicting the express terms of the contract.

The Contractual Remedies Act 1979 (New Zealand)

The Contractual Remedies Act 1979 substantially altered the law in New Zealand in relation to the restitutionary relief that was available to the parties to a contract consequent upon breach.[79] The rules of law and equity governing discharge of a contract have been abrogated.[80] A party may

---

77 See Goff and Jones, *op cit*, 4th edn, pp 444–45 in which it is mooted that a restitutionary claim should be permitted where the benefit is incontrovertible. Further, see Birks, P, 'In Defence of Free Acceptance', in Burrows, A (ed), *Essays on the Law of Restitution*, 1991, pp 137–41, Clarendon Press, Oxford. The English Law Commission in its Draft Bill No 121, 'Pecuniary Restitution on Breach of Contract' recommended *pro rata* remuneration. Also, Restatement of Contracts 2nd para 374, comment b, provides that a party in breach may have restitution for any benefit that he has conferred, by way of part performance or reliance, in excess of the loss that he has caused by his own breach. In practice, many building contracts contain the right to progress payments which limit any hardship caused by the rule in *Sumpter v Hedges*. In England, the Apportionment Act 1870 allows apportionment subject to a contrary intention in relation to rents, annuities, dividends and other periodical payments in the nature of income. Annuities include salaries and pensions and query wages. Further, see s 144 of the Conveyancing Act 1989 (NSW); s 232 of the Property Law Act 1974 (Qld); s 64 of the Law of Property Act 1936 (S Aust); s 131 of the Property Law Act 1969 (WA); s 2 of the Apportionment Act 1871 (Tas); s 4 of the Appointment Act 1905 (ACT); Appointment Act (S Aus), Northern Territory.

78 [1898] 1 QB 673.

79 For a comprehensive treatment of this subject, see Dawson, F and McLauchlan, DW, *The Contractual Remedies Act 1979*, 1981, Sweet & Maxwell, NZ.

80 Section 7(1).

cancel an agreement where there has been a breach of a stipulation which the parties either expressly or by implication regarded as essential,[81] or where the effect of the breach of stipulation is to substantially alter the incidence of liability or benefit under the contract for the cancelling party.[82] Substantiality, in the statutory context, is a matter of fact, degree and impression. It has been said to have the same flavour as 'significantly' and 'considerably'. It has also been said to be equally incapable of arithmetical analysis.[83] Where cancellation is lawfully effected, the innocent party is entitled to damages for the breach. Section 8 requires the innocent party to communicate the fact of an intention to cancel to the defaulting party or, if that is not reasonably practicable, the intention to cancel may be evidenced by some overt means that are reasonable in the circumstances. Cancellation may be by words or conduct that evidences an intention to cancel.[84] Cancellation has the effect of discharging the obligations of the parties, so far as unperformed obligations are concerned, but it does not divest the parties of moneys paid or property transferred, so far as the contract has been performed prior to cancellation.[85] A party is not entitled to cancel the contract if, with full knowledge of the repudiation or breach, he or she has affirmed the contract and rescission have been abrogated.[86] In this regard, it would seem that affirmation will arise under the Act if a party, with full knowledge of the circumstances relating to the default, proceeds to enforce or perform the contract even though he or she is unaware of the right to cancel.[87] The Act does not affect the Sales of Goods Act 1908, in so far as discharge of a contract relating to the sale of goods is concerned,[88] but a misrepresentation relating to the goods will fall within the Act unless there is express provision in the contract to the contrary.[89]

---

81 Section 7(4)(a).

82 Section 7(4)(b).

83 See *MacIndoe v Mainzeal Group Ltd* [1991] 3 NZLR 273 at 284, *per* Richardson J.

84 See *Chatfield v Jones* [1990] 3 NZLR 287, resale of property by the vendor evidenced an intention to cancel but communication of cancellation did not take place until the service of amended proceedings for damages.

85 Section 8(3); *Prendergast v Chapman* [1988] 2 NZLR 177; *Brown v Langwood Photo Stores* [1991] 1 NZLR 173.

86 Section 7(5). As to affirmation, see *Jolly v Palmer* [1985] 1 NZLR 658; *Hughes v Huppert* [1991] 1 NZLR 474; *Westpac Finance Ltd v Winstone Industries* [1993] 2 NZLR 247; *Crump v Wala* [1994] 2 NZLR 331.

87 See the discussion in *Crump v Wala*, *ibid*, at 337–38 on the elements of affirmation, and the discussion of affirmation in relation to rescission for misrepresentation, Chapter 9, pp 211–13.

88 *Finch Motors Ltd v Quin (No 2)* [1980] 2 NZLR 519.

89 See *Crump v Wala* [1994] 2 NZLR 331.

Either party to the contract, or person claiming through a party,[90] may claim relief under s 9(2)(a) of the Act, which provides that a court may make orders relating to the vesting, transfer, assignment or delivery of possession of real or personal property that was the subject of the contract or the consideration for it. Further, s 9(2)(b) provides that a court may direct any party to pay to the other such sum as the court thinks just. In *Brown v Langwoods Photo Stores*,[91] Cooke P observed that the court has a wide jurisdiction under s 9 to make orders that ensure that cancellation does not have an ultimate inequitable effect. Section 9(2)(c) enables a court to direct any party to the proceedings to do or refrain from doing, in relation to any other party, any act or thing as the court thinks just. When considering what, if any, relief should be given, the court is directed under s 9(4)to have regard to the following factors:

(a) the terms of the contract;

(b) the extent to which any party to the contract was or would have been able to perform it in whole or in part;

(c) any expenditure incurred by a party in or for the purpose of the performance of the contract;

(d) the value, in its opinion, of any work or services performed by a party in or for the purpose of the performance of the contract; and

(e) such other matters as it thinks proper.

In so far as orders relating to property are concerned, a court is precluded from making an order if it is of the opinion that to do so would be inequitable.[92] Third parties who have acquired the possession of or interest in any property, the subject of the contract, for valuable consideration and in good faith are protected.[93] Any sum obtained under s 9 of the Act must be taken into account in assessing any damages awarded[94] or may be set-off against damages awarded for breach.[95]

Section 9 enables a court to grant relief for breach to an innocent party who has, for example, paid moneys in advance and received a partial benefit in exchange prior to repudiation. Thus, the common law rule relating to total failure of consideration, as illustrated in *Baltic Sipping Corporation v Dillon*,[96] has been abrogated. However, any sum received

---

90 Section 9(7)(a) and (b). Under s 9(7)(c), there is the unusual provision permitting any other person to make application if it is material to know whether relief under the section would be granted.

91 [1991] 1 NZLR 173, at 177.

92 Section 9(6).

93 Section 9(5).

94 Section 10(1).

95 Section 10(2).

96 (1992–93) 176 CLR 344.

would have to be taken into consideration in any award of damages. Where an innocent party seeks reimbursement for services rendered rather than damages, a court must consider the provisions of the contract so that if the party has entered into a disadvantageous or losing bargain this may affect the amount of compensation ordered. In this regard, the remedy of *quantum meruit* allowing reasonable compensation for services rendered irrespective of whether the innocent party would have received a profit as illustrated in *Lodder v Slowey*[97] is no longer applicable. Where the defaulting party by his or her actions has contributed to additional costs this will be a factor that a court will be able to consider when granting relief under s 9. Further, the Act allows the contract-breaker to claim relief. Thus, in so far as a contractor in default is able to show that he or she has conferred a benefit on the innocent party the rule in *Sumpter v Hedges* no longer applies and relief may be given. Similarly, advance payments of purchase price may be the subject of relief if a purchaser is in breach. However, it is doubtful whether s 9 governs relief where under the express terms of an agreement payments are expressly said to be forfeit. Section 5 envisages that express provisions in a contract governing a remedy for breach will take priority over the statutory remedies.[98] In these circumstances, a party in default who seeks to argue for relief from the application of forfeiture provisions in a contract would seem still to have to rely on equitable principles. In *Young v Hunt*,[99] for example, it was held that a forfeiture clause relating to liquidated damages was penal, unenforceable and s 5 had no application because an express remedy was provided for in the contract.

(a) Judicial applications of the Act

There have been comparatively few cases concerning the application of the Contractual Remedies Act involving restitutionary considerations since it was passed in 1979. In *Brown & Doherty Ltd v Whangarei County Council*,[100] it was held that the Act supplanted the common law relating to breach and a claim in *quantum meruit* was no longer available. In so far as advance payments of purchase price are concerned, the decisions have been predictable. In *Codot Developments Ltd v Potter*,[101] a purchaser who had repudiated a contract for sale and purchase of land was entitled to recover an advance payment which represented one-half of the purchase price under s 9, less a deduction for the vendor's losses. In

---

97 [1904] AC 442.

98 See *MacIndoe v Mainzeal Group Ltd* [1991] 3 NZLR 273 where the contractual provisions were not held to be inconsistent with the Act.

99 [1984] 2 NZLR 80.

100 [1990] 2 NZLR 63.

101 [1981] 1 NZLR 729.

Worsdale v Porglase,[102] it was held that an advance payment of 10% of the purchase price, expressed to be a deposit, was not recoverable by defaulting purchasers under s 9.

The courts have, however, more controversially taken an expansive view of their jurisdiction to grant relief under s 9 of the Act. In *Gallagher v Young*,[103] it was held that a purchaser who had lawfully cancelled a contract for the sale of land under s 9 of the Act was entitled to recover the purchase price together with interest. Although damages could have been assessed on the same basis, Greig J considered that s 9 gave the court a wide jurisdiction to do justice between the parties. There was no necessity under that section to apply the strict rules as to damages and a just order under s 9 might replace an inquiry as to damages altogether. A similar view was taken by Fisher J in *Newmans Tours Ltd v Ranier Investments Ltd*.[104] Fisher J considered that s 9 was not narrowly confined to restitutionary considerations but could embody reliance and expectation interests appropriate to damages considerations as well.[105] In that case, expenditure incurred pursuant to a contract for the purchase of travel companies by Newmans was recovered as reliance costs under s 9 with appropriate credit given to the vendor for incidental benefits derived under the partly performed agreement and a deduction attributable to a failure by Newmans to more expeditiously mitigate its losses. One of the more important aspects of the case was the fact that Newmans were allowed to recover a proportion of the consideration paid under s 9 even though the agreement had been partly performed because shares in one company had been transferred and Newmans desired to retain this company. This approach would not have been available under the common law which could not apportion in this way and would allow recovery of an advance payment only if there had been a total failure of consideration. It would seem, however, that following the approach of the High Court of Australia in *Commonwealth of Australia v Amann Aviation Pty Ltd*,[106] the losses claimed under s 9 could have been claimed in any event as reliance damages under the general law, assuming the plaintiff had not made a losing bargain, and therefore it was unnecessary to take an expansive approach to s 9. Had the Legislature intended there to be a more radical change by, in effect, subsuming the power to award damages under

---

102 [1981] 1 NZLR 723.

103 [1981] 1 NZLR 734.

104 [1992] 2 NZLR 69.

105 Citing the terminology of Fuller, LL and Perdue, WR, 'The Reliance Interest in Contractual damages' (1936) 46 Yale LJ 52, at 53–54. Fisher J considered that generally expectation interest should be preferred to reliance or restitutionary interests so that a losing bargain could affect the measure of relief granted for reliance or restitutionary losses at 93–94.

106 (1991) 174 CLR 64. Further, see *Ccc Films (London) Ltd v Impact Quadrant Films Ltd* [1985] QB 16, noted by Fisher J in *Newmans v Ranier* [1992] 2 NZLR 68, at 93.

s 9, then it would seem that it could have dispensed with damages as a remedy altogether. In this regard, a further concern is that both Greig J in *Gallagher v Young* and Fisher J in *Newmans Tours Ltd v Ranier Investments Ltd* asserted a general power to make monetary awards under s 9 free of the fetters which normally circumscribe damages claims.[107] Although a somewhat radical approach, it is an approach that has received judicial approval by the Court of Appeal in *Thomson v Rankin*.[108] However, the principle of consistency and certainty, upon which losses are assessed following repudiation of a contract, is a topic of considerable commercial importance. On a related topic, Hammond J observed in *Crump v Wala*,[109] that one should not lightly jettison hard-earned intellectual capital carefully evolved by judges over several centuries. Having said this, the Act does not seem to have troubled courts greatly. Perhaps this is because the powers contained in s 9 are sufficiently widely expressed to have induced the parties to compromise and effect settlement of their claims following repudiation rather than litigate.

---

107 This development has been criticised, see Coote, B, 'Remedy and Relief under the Contractual Remedies Act 1979' (1993) 6 JCL 141; McLauchlan, DW, 'The "New" Law of Contract in New Zealand' [1992] NZ Recent Law Rev 436, at 456–59; Watts, P, 'Restitution' [1993] NZ Recent Law Rev 425, at 429.

108 [1993] 1 NZLR 408, at 410 *per* Cooke P; at 413 *per* Anderson J. As to assessment of damages, see *McElroy Milne v Commercial Electronics Ltd* [1993] 1 NZLR 39.

109 [1994] 2 NZLR 331. Speaking of an analogous situation in relation to the wide remedies available under the Fair Trading Act 1986.

CHAPTER 9

Misrepresentation

There are two kinds of representation that are actionable; a fraudulent representation and one that, although innocently made, is nevertheless false. In the case of a mere misrepresentation, although the common law was limited in the relief it could grant, equity was able to invoke the important remedy of rescission to grant appropriate relief to prevent unjust enrichment.

The elements of an actionable misrepresentation

To be actionable, a misrepresentation must constitute a false representation as to a past or present assertion of fact or as to the present or existing state of mind or belief of the representor.[1] A representation as to future intention or a promise which is not carried out is not actionable unless it forms a term of an agreement that is legally binding.[2] Similarly, an honestly held opinion or belief is not actionable;[3] but one that is recklessly given with no regard to the truth is actionable as a fraudulent misrepresentation if it relates to a matter which is material and pertains to an existing belief of the representor.[4] A fraudulently held belief and misrepresentation of the law is also actionable as a misrepresentation.[5] In order to be actionable, a misrepresentation must be material.[6] Further, in order to be actionable, a representation must have in fact induced the agreement.[7] A representee is not bound to make

---

1   *Greene v R* (1949) 79 CLR 353, at 357; *Edgington v Fitzmaurice* (1885) 29 Ch D, 459 at 483; [1881–85] All ER 856. *Cf Yorkshire Insurance Co Ltd v Craine* (1922) 31 CLR 27, at 38.

2   *Maddison v Alderson* (1883) 8 App Cas 467; [1881–85] All ER 742; *Allan v Gotch* (1883) 9 VLR 371. It may, however, found an estoppel and be actionable on that basis. See the discussion in Chapter 4, pp 78–79.

3   *Bisset v Wilkinson* [1927] AC 177; [1926] All ER 343. If the representor has no knowledge of what he purports to represent, then that may constitute a misrepresentation. *Field v Shoalhaven Transport Ltd* (1970) 3 NSWLR 96, at 99–100.

4   See *Derry v Peek* (1889) 14 App Cas 337; [1886–90] All ER 1; *Balfour v Hollandia Ravensthorpe* (1978) 18 SASR 240; *Ritter v North Side Enterprises Pty Ltd* (1975) 132 CLR 301; *Newark Engineering (NZ) Ltd v Jenkin* [1980] 1 NZLR 504.

5   *Public Trustee v Taylor* [1978] VR 289.

6   *Smith v Chadwick* [1881–85] All ER 242; *Sibley v Grosvenor* (1916) 21 CLR 469; *Neal v Ayres* (1940) 63 CLR 524; *Field v Shoalhaven Transport Pty Ltd* (1970) 3 NSWLR 100; *Australian Steel & Mining Corporation Pty Ltd v Corben* (1974) 2 NSWLR 202; *Simons v Zartrom Investments Pty Ltd* (1975) 2 NSWLR 30.

7   *Smith v Chadwick* (1884) 9 App Cas 187; *Gould v Vaggelas* (1984) 157 CLR 215; *Savill v NZI Finance* [1990] 3 NZLR 135.

inquiry even though inquiry would have shown a representation to be false.[8] A false misrepresentation may be negated by inspection and awareness that it was false.[9] If, however, the victim has been induced to enter the agreement because of a misrepresentation, the mere fact that there were other matters which influenced his or her judgment will not prevent a victim from seeking redress.[10, 11] If, having made a representation, the representor subsequently discovers the information is inaccurate, he or she is under an obligation to communicate the error to the representee.[12] A half-truth or distortion will also constitute a misrepresentation.[13] Mere silence will not constitute a misrepresentation unless there exists a legal obligation of disclosure or the representor has effectively withheld information so that any representation that has been made is incomplete and inaccurate. Where there is a duty of disclosure, such as in the case of a contract *uberrimae fidei* or in the case of a fiduciary relationship, a failure to disclose may entitle the party to whom the duty is owed to rescind a contract.[14]

Fraudulent misrepresentation

If a misrepresentation is made with intent to defraud and induces a person to enter an agreement, then the innocent party can sue the fraudulent party at common law for damages for deceit. Actual damage suffered by the innocent party is an essential element of this action[15] and he or she is under an obligation to mitigate loss.[16] In addition, he or she might elect either to affirm or rescind the contract. An innocent party may rescind for a fraudulent misrepresentation without resort to legal proceedings, however, it might be considered more prudent to formally seek to have the contract rescinded if the fraudulent party will not accept termination and there is a possibility that third parties might be

---

8 *Clark v Clark* (1882) 8 VLR 303.

9 *Holmes v Jones* (1907) 4 CLR 1692; *Gipps v Gipps* (1978) 1 NSWLR 454.

10 *Edginton v Fitzmaurice* (1885) 29 Ch D 459; [1881–85] All ER 856; *Field v Shoalhaven* (1970) 3 NSWLR 100; *Wilcher v Steain* (1961) 79 WN (NSW) 141; *Leighton Properties Pty Ltd v Hurley* (1984) 2 Qd R 534.

11 *Smith v Hughes* (1871) LR 6 QB 597; [1861–73] All ER 632; *Bell v Lever Bros Ltd* [1932] AC 161, at 227; [1931] All ER 1, at 32; *Scott & Co Ltd v Lloyd* (1906) 4 CLR 572; *Fry v Daly* [1988] VR 19.

12 *Jennings v Zilah-Kiss* (1972) 2 SASR 493; *Carlton & United Breweries Ltd v Tooth & Co Ltd* (1986) 7 IPR 581.

13 *Jones v Bouffier* (1911) 12 CLR 579, at 617–18; *Lockhart v Osman* [1981] VR 57.

14 *Dalgety & Co Ltd v Australian Mutual Provident Society* [1908] VLR 481, *Magee v Penine Insurance* [1969] 2 QB 507; [1969] 2 All ER 891.

15 *Gans v Riley* (1913) 15 CLR 731, at 734.

16 *S Gormley & Co Pty Ltd v Cubit* [1964-65] NSWR 557, at 561–63; *McAllister v Richmond Brewing Co (NSW) Pty Ltd* (1942) 42 SR (NSW) 187, at 192.

affected. In *Alati v Kruger*,[17] the High Court of Australia held that if a false representation has become a term of the contract in the nature of a warranty, the representor could not sue for damages for breach of warranty and at the same time take proceedings for rescission. An innocent party could, however, commence proceedings for rescission and claim damages for deceit as well.[18]

Innocent misrepresentation

If an innocent misrepresentation is incorporated as a contractual promise, obligation or term of a contract, the representee will have an action in damages on the contract, in which case the measure of damages will be assessed generally as the loss of the victim's expectation or bargain. However, if the innocent misrepresentation is not embodied as a contractual term, then relief under the general law is limited. The common law did not allow damages for a mere misrepresentation that was not a term of the contract. It was not until 1963 that the House of Lords in *Hedley Byrne & Co Ltd v Heller & Partners Ltd*[19] mitigated this rule by recognising a claim for damages where there had been a negligent misrepresentation and the parties were in a special relationship. This cause of action is available where there is a contractual relationship and a party can show that he or she has relied on a carelessly made representation and that such reliance was reasonable.[20] Subsequently, the Misrepresentation Act 1967 was enacted in the United Kingdom. This Act empowered a court to award damages for an innocent misrepresentation unless the representor could show that he or she had reasonable grounds to believe and did in fact believe up to the time that the contract was made that the facts represented were true.[21] This reform was adopted in South Australia[22] and the Australian Capital Territory.[23] It effectively creates a statutory claim in damages for negligent misrepresentation. There is, however, a distinction in relation to the nature of the defences that are available for such a claim. In South Australia, there is greater protection for a principal against the innocent misrepresentations of agents or parties who act on behalf of the principal. It is a defence if the principal was not the person by whom the representation was made and did not know and could not reasonably

---

17 (1955) 94 CLR 216, at 222.

18 *O' Keefe v Taylor Estates Co Ltd* [1916] St R Qd 301; *Ivanof v Phillip M Levy Pty Ltd* [1971] VR 167, at 171–72.

19 [1964] AC 465; [1963] 2 All ER 575; *Mutual Life and Citizens Assurance Co Ltd v Evatt* [1971] AC 793.

20 *Esso Petroleum v Mardon* [1976] QB 801; [1976] 2 All ER 5; *Ellul and Ellul v Oakes* [1972] 3 SASR 377.

21 Section 2(1) Misrepresentation Act 1967 (UK).

22 Section 7(1) Misrepresentation Act 1971–72 (S Aust).

23 Section 4(1) Law Reform (Misrepresentation) Act 1977 (ACT).

have been expected to know that the representation had been made or that it was untrue.[24] In the Australian Capital Territory, however, it is more difficult for a principal to escape liability for the misrepresentation of an agent or a person acting on his or her behalf because, in such a case, both the principal and his or her representative must have reasonable grounds for believing that the representation was true and must in fact believe that it was so up until the time the contract was made.[25] A provision in a contract that purports to exclude or restrict liability or the remedies arising from a misrepresentation will have no effect unless fair and reasonable.[26]

Equity, however, in the 19th century, started to give limited relief to those who were the victims of innocent misrepresentation. Rescission of agreements or a refusal to specifically perform agreements that had been induced in this way were the measures that equity favoured in order to prevent unjust enrichment.[27] It was considered, however, at least in England, that the right to rescind was lost if the misrepresentation had become a term of the contract.[28] This approach does not appear to have been followed in Australia where it has been held that the right to rescind a contract for innocent misrepresentation is not lost by reason of the misrepresentation having become a term of the contract.[29] In the United Kingdom, legislation has subsequently been enacted that allowed rescission for an innocent misrepresentation even though it has become a term of a contract.[30]

Rescission

It is with the remedy of rescission that we are primarily concerned in our consideration of restitution and misrepresentation. The scope of this remedy at common law was limited. The remedy was not available unless the subject-matter of the contract could be restored to the wrong-doer by the party seeking rescission. In these circumstances, the injured

---

24 Section 7(2) of the Misrepresentation Act 1971–72 (S Aust).

25 Section 4(2)(b) of the Law Reform (Misrepresentation) Act 1977 (ACT).

26 Section 8 of the Misrepresentation Act 1971–72 (S Aust); s 6 of the Law Reform (Misrepresentation) Act 1977 (ACT).

27 *Torrance v Bolton* (1872) 8 Ch App 118; *Wauton v Coppard* [1899] 1 Ch 92.

28 *Pennsylvania Shipping Co v Campagnie Nationale de Navigatione* [1936] 2 All ER 1167, at 1171; *Leaf v International Galleries* [1950] 2 KB 86; [1950] 1 All ER 693.

29 *Leason Pty Ltd v Princes Farm Ltd* (1983) 2 NSWLR 381; *Academy of Health and Fitness Pty Ltd v Power* [1973] VR 254; *Simmons v Zartom Investments Pty Ltd* (1975) 2 NSWLR 30. Considered in *Accounting Systems 2000 (Developments) Pty Ltd v CCH Australia Ltd* (1993) 114 ALR 355. On the issue of misrepresentations that have become terms of a contract for the sale of goods, see discussion pp 214–15.

30 Section 1 of the Misrepresentation Act 1967 (UK); also s 6(1)(a) of the Misrepresentation Act 1971–72 (S Aust); s 3(a) of the Law Reform (Misrepresentation) Act 1977 (ACT).

party would be left to his or her action in damages.[31] However, equity had greater flexibility and was able to make allowances or grant compensation where the subject-matter had deteriorated significantly so that rescission might be effected wherever it was practically just to do so.[32] Where fraud was involved, equity was prepared to intervene in a more robust way to prevent ill-gotten gains being unconscientiously retained. In *Spense v Crawford*,[33] for example, the House of Lords granted rescission to a vendor who had been induced to part with his shares in a company as a result of the purchaser's fraudulent misrepresentation. The vendor was ordered to repay the price of the shares and compensate the purchaser for certain losses sustained on the sale of a parcel of the shares in exchange for a transfer of the shares to the vendor and an accounting for dividends derived by the purchaser from the transaction. Lord Wright said of the defendant that though he had been fraudulent, he must not be robbed, nor must the plaintiff be unjustly enriched as he would be if he got back what he had parted with and kept what he had received in return. The purpose of the relief was not punishment but compensation.[34]

Where the subject-matter of a contract is no longer in existence, rescission will be refused. Thus, where a partnership, in which the innocent party was induced to take shares, was converted into a limited liability company, the court declined to grant rescission since the shares were wholly different in nature and status from those that were originally transferred.[35] However, the mere fact that the subject-matter has diminished or deteriorated will not preclude a court from granting rescission in an appropriate case. In *Lagunas Nitrate Co v Lagunas Syndicate*,[36] Lindley MR observed that if this case had involved a fraudulent misrepresentation, the court would have been prepared to grant rescission of a contract relating to the sale of a mine even though it had been substantially worked out. A similar approach was taken in Australia by the

---

31 *Clarke v Dickson* (1858) EB & E 148; [1858]120 ER 463.

32 *Erlanger v New Sombrero Phosphate Co* (1878) 3 App Cas 1218; [1874–80] All ER 271, at 286 *per* Blackburn J.

33 [1939] 3 All ER 271, at 288–89 *per* Lord Wright. On the question of jurisdiction to rescind for fraud, see *Alati v Kruger* (1955) 94 CLR 216, at 223–24 *per* Dixon J; *Vadasz v Pioneer Concrete Ltd* (1995) 130 ALR 570, at 576–79.

34 *Idem.*

35 *Western Bank of Scotland v Addie* (1876) LR 1 SC & Div 145.

36 [1899] 2 Ch 392. Similarly, in *Erlanger v New Sombrero Phosphate Co* (1878) 3 App Cas 1218; [1874–80] All ER 271, rescission was ordered where a mine had been sold to the company and worked for some time because the vendor had acted in breach of fiduciary duty in the conduct of the sale. Where certain shares had dropped in value, rescission was granted to the purchaser after his broker, in breach of fiduciary duty, had sold them without disclosing that they personally belonged to him. *Armstrong v Jackson* [1917] 2 KB 822; [1916–17] All ER 117.

High Court in *Alati v Kruger*.[37] In that case, a purchaser of a business entered into possession only to discover that various false representations had been made relating to turnover. The purchaser claimed rescission which was opposed on the ground that the business had deteriorated. However, rescission was ordered because the purchaser had not contributed to the deterioration. As a condition of making the order, the purchaser had to account for the chattels which had been conveyed as part of their value as well as the stock-in-trade that had been diminished by the plaintiff's use. The vendor also argued that, in subsequently discontinuing the business, the purchaser had lost the ability to rescind. This argument was rejected on the ground that the vendor knew of the purchaser's desire not to proceed with the contract and could have taken steps to protect any goodwill. Fullager J considered, however, that a purchaser in possession could not act irresponsibly and abandon a business precipitately and without notice. Should deterioration occur in these circumstances, a claim to rescind could fail or, as a condition of rescission, a purchaser might have to pay compensation for any diminution in the value of the business. In cases of innocent misrepresentation, a court may also grant rescission where there has been a substantial reduction in the value of the subject-matter. Thus, in *Adam v Newbigging*,[38] the court ordered rescission of a transaction involving the acquisition of a share in a partnership, which had become insolvent after the agreement had been entered into, even though a misrepresentation relating to the prospects of the partnership was not fraudulent. Given that damages were unavailable for innocent misrepresentation, it is not surprising that in a deserving case equity should have granted rescission of contracts even though the subject-matter of the contract had substantially diminished.

Counter-restitution[39] or the restoration of benefits acquired by the party seeking rescission may be ordered as a condition of rescission as *Spence v Crawford*[40] illustrates. In *Brown v Smitt*,[41] the High Court of Australia held that counter-restitution should be made to a purchaser in possession who had effected permanent improvements or necessary repairs that were not merely ephemeral or matters of taste.[42] It was held

---

37 (1955) 94 CLR 216; *Vadasz v Pioneer Concrete Ltd* (1996) 184 CLR 102. For earlier Australian cases, see *Brown v Smitt* (1924) 34 CLR 160; *Ballantyne v Raphael* (1889) 15 VLR 538; *Robinson v Abbott* (1894) 20 VLR 346; *Wheeler v Atkinson* (1925) 28 WALR 12.

38 (1886) 34 Ch D 582; [1886–90] All ER 975.

39 A term used by Mason CJ in *David Securities Pty Ltd v CBA* (1992) 175 CLR 353, at 383.

40 [1939] 3 All ER 271.

41 (1924) 34 CLR 160. Further, see *Rawson v Hobbs* (1961) 107 CLR 466; *JAD International Pty Ltd v International Trucks Australia Ltd* (1994) 50 FCR 378.

42 *Evans v Benson & Co* [1961] WAR 12.

in *Koutsonicolis v Principe (No 2)*[43] that where a purchaser had the benefit of living on a property prior to rescission, it was necessary to allow a fraudulent vendor some compensation for lengthy occupation attributable to the purchasers being unable to afford another house before the litigation was finalised. The court considered that otherwise the purchasers would be unjustly enriched. However, the court declined to order the purchasers to pay the full market rental which would have meant that they could not have afforded alternative accommodation.

A court may order that an innocent party be indemnified for losses that arise directly from the contract but will not allow those that arise as an incidental consequence of the contract. Thus, in *Newbigging v Adam*,[44] in addition to an order for rescission, the innocent party was entitled to an indemnity against partnership debts and losses that arose from his acquiring a partnership share. In *Brown v Smitt*,[45] the High Court of Australia held that a party seeking rescission was not entitled to claim collateral losses such as were involved in carrying on business on land, which was purchased consequent to a fraudulent misrepresentation. To allow recovery of consequential losses would indirectly allow equity to grant damages, a concept which had been rejected in *Newbigging v Adam*. In the United Kingdom, under the Misrepresentation Act,[46] a court has a wide discretion in an appropriate case to mitigate hardship and award damages in lieu of rescission if this is considered to be more equitable. A similar statutory discretion exists in South Australia[47] and the Australian Capital Territory.[48]

Limitations on rescission

(a) Affirmation

The opportunity to rescind will be lost if a representee, instead of taking steps to avoid a contract, acts in such a way that a reasonable person would consider that he or she had elected to perform. A representee must, however, possess knowledge of the facts that give rise to the right to rescind. The law is uncertain as to whether, in addition, he or she must be aware of the right to rescind. In *Estates Pty Ltd v Melevende*,[49] a

---

43 (1987) 48 SASR 328.

44 (1886) 34 Ch D 582; [1886–90] All ER 975, at 984–85 *per* Lord Bowen. See *Redgrave v Hurd* (1882) 20 Ch D 1; *Whittington v Seale-Hayne* (1900) 82 LT 49.

45 (1924) 34 CLR 160.

46 Section 2(2). Note, a court in equity may have jurisdiction to order compensation in lieu of rescission, see *Greater Pacific Investments v Australian National Industries Ltd* (1996) 89 NSWLR 143, considered, p 309.

47 Section 7(3)(4)(5)(6) Misrepresentation Act 1971–72 (S Aust).

48 Section 5 of the Law Reform (Misrepresentation) Act 1977 (ACT).

49 [1965] VR 433.

case of fraudulent misrepresentation, the full court of Victoria considered that awareness of the right to rescind must also exist. In *Sargent v ASL Developments*,[50] Stephen J observed that a distinction might be drawn between contractually conferred rights and agreements that did not set out the options available to an innocent party. In the former situation, awareness of the facts giving rise to a right to elect to pursue one of the available contractual remedies, would be sufficient because a party could not be heard to say that he or she was unaware of the terms of a contract.[51] Mason J also appeared to support this opinion and tentatively preferred the approach that knowledge of the circumstances giving rise to the right to elect should be sufficient to constitute affirmation in cases of contract as well as in interests in property.[52] Subsequent Australian cases have taken different approaches.[53] It would seem difficult to contend that there was any true election where a party was ignorant of his or her legal rights or the options available even though aware that a misrepresentation was false. On the other hand, contracts are merely voidable for misrepresentation and if a party chooses not to investigate the remedies that might be available on ascertaining that a representation is false, but acts in such a way that any reasonable person would infer that he or she was content to proceed with the agreement and the other party does so, then the representee might be estopped from subsequently claiming a right to rescind.[54]

Affirmation requires proof of an unequivocal act evidencing an election not to avoid the contract.[55] Acts which are merely consistent with

---

50 (1974) 131 CLR 634.

51 *Ibid*, at 644–45. [1970] 2 All ER 871. Further, see *Khoury v Government Insurance Office (NSW)* (1984) 165 CLR 622, at 633–34; *Immer v Uniting Church* (1992) 112 ALR 609, at 618–19.

52 And semble, it would seem even if there was fraud, *ibid*, at 658.

53 In *Parker v Registrar-General* (1976) 1 NSWLR 343, it was held that, in respect of a contract induced by fraud, affirmation required not only knowledge of the falsity of the representation but also knowledge of the right to rescind. In *Re Hoffman* (1989) 85 ALR 145, the court held that knowledge of the facts giving right to elect was sufficient and it was unnecessary to show that the innocent party was also aware of the right to rescind even in a case of fraud. In New Zealand, see the discussion in *Crump v Wala* [1994] 2 NZLR 331, at 336–37; and the discussion in *Hughes v Huppert* [1991] 1 NZLR 474, at 477–78 where Gallen J spoke of a 'real and genuine affirmation in the circumstances of the case'.

54 See the judgment of Jordan CJ in *O'Connor v SP Bray Ltd* (1936) 36 SR (NSW) 248, at 258–61; *Ritter v North Side Enterprises Ltd* (1975) 132 CLR 301, at 304 *per* Gibbs J; *Kammins Ballrooms Co Ltd v Zenith Investments Ltd* [1971] AC 850, at 883 *per* Lord Diplock.

55 *Brown v Smit* (1924) 34 CLR 160, at 167–68; *Elders Trustee and Executor Co Ltd v Commonwealth Homes and Investment Co Ltd* (1941) 65 CLR 603, at 618; *Sargent v ASL Developments Ltd*, *ibid*, at 648, *per* Stephen J, at 657 *per* Mason J; *Miller v Barrellan (Holdings) Pty Ltd* [1982] 2 BPR 9543, at 9549; *Motor Oil Hellas Refineries SA v Shipping Corp of India The 'Kanchenjunga'* [1990] 1 Lloyd's Rep 391, at 398 *per* Lord Goff; *Neylon v Dickens* [1978] 2 NZLR 135 (PC); *Connor v Pukerau Store Ltd* [1981] 1 NZLR 384, at 386 *per* Cooke J; *Jolly v Palmer* [1983] 1 NZLR 685; *Hughes v Huppert* [1991] 1 NZLR 474; *Cycle Manufacturing Co v Williamson* [1993] 1 NZLR 454, at 465.

the continuance of a contract do not necessarily constitute affirmation.[56] Affirmation may involve a conscious act of election which is communicated to the other party. It does not have to involve a conscious or deliberate act, however, but may involve such conduct as would lead an ordinary bystander to infer that a contract had been affirmed.[57] Once an election has been made, a party cannot seek to rescind a contract unless another and separate ground arises.[58] It is immaterial that the other party to the contract is unaware of the facts upon which the electing party might have chosen to have rescinded the contract.[59]

(b) Delay

An innocent party may be prevented from rescinding a contract where he or she has been guilty of delay after gaining knowledge of the facts establishing a right to rescission. Whether delay will constitute affirmation will depend on its duration, the nature of the acts which have been occurred in the interval and their effect on the other party.[60] In some cases where rescission has been granted, there have been very lengthy delays.[61] Rescission of contracts for the sale of goods cannot, however, be delayed indefinitely. In the case of sales of specific goods under sales of goods legislation, the right to rescind may be lost on the passing of property, a condition thereby being treated as a warranty limiting relief to damages.[62] In *Leaf v International Galleries*,[63] a lapse of five years was sufficient to bar the purchaser's right to rescind a contract for the sale of a painting and obtain restitution of the purchase price, even though he had been ignorant of the invalidity of an innocent misrepresentation that the painting was a Constable. Since the purchaser only learnt the truth when he came to sell the painting, this may seem a rather harsh

---

56 *Immer v Uniting Church* (1992) 112 ALR 609, at 611 *per* Brennan J, at 620 *per* Deane J.

57 *Tropical Traders Ltd v Goonan* (1964) 111 CLR 41, at 55 *per* Kitto J; *Immer v Uniting Church* (1992) 112 ALR 609, at 620 *per* Deane J; *Kadner v Brune Holdings Ltd* (1973) 1 NSWLR 498; *Zucker v Straightlace Pty Ltd* (1978) 11 NSWLR 87, at 96; *Champtaloup v Thomas* (1976) 2 NSWLR 264, at 274–75.

58 *Elder's Trustee and Executor Co Ltd v Commonwealth Homes and Investment Co Ltd* (1941) 65 CLR 603; *Newbon v City Mutual Life Assurance Ltd* (1935) 52 CLR 723; *Sargent v ASL Developments Ltd* (1974) 131 CLR 634, at 656.

59 *Zucker v Straightlace Pty Ltd* (1987) 11 NSWLR 87, at 96.

60 See *O'Connor v SP Bray Ltd* (1936) 36 SR (NSW) 248, at 261–62 *per* Jordan CJ; *Sargent v ASL Developments Ltd* (1974) 131 CLR 634, at 646 *per* Stephen J; *Immer v Uniting Church* (1992) 112 ALR 609, at 611 *per* Brennan J.

61 See *Armstrong v Jackson* [1917] 2 KB 822; [1916–17] All ER 117 *per* McCardie J and the cases cited. Further, see the discussion of laches in *Erlanger v New Sombrero Phosphate Co* (1878) 3 App Cas 1218, at 1231 *per* Lord Penzance, at 1279 *per* Lord Blackburn.

62 For example, s 16(3) of the Sale of Goods Act 1896 (Qld); s 16(3) of the SGA 1958 (Vic); s 11(3) of the SGA 1895 (W Aust); s 14(3) of the SGA 1896 (Tas); s 16(3) of the SGA (NT).

63 [1950] 2 KB 86; [1950] 1 All ER 693.

decision. However, the case turned on a combination of rules. First, a delay in seeking rescission of five years meant that there had been acceptance under the provisions of the relevant legislation governing sales of specific goods. The Court of Appeal considered that it would be injurious for commerce if buyers were to be able to rescind sales of goods after lengthy periods of delay.[64] Since there had been delay sufficient to preclude rejection of the goods on the ground that the misdescription breached a term of the contract, the court considered that the buyer should be left to his remedy in damages for breach of warranty and should not be able to claim rescission for a prior misrepresentation. In Australia, in *Leason Pty Ltd v Princes Farm Pty Ltd*,[65] Helsham CJ, however, held that an executed contract of sale of a chattel could be rescinded and the purchase price returned on the ground of innocent misrepresentation even though the misrepresentation was incorporated as a term of the contract. If the merchandise is reasonably capable of being restored to the vendor in good condition and the defect is not one that would be immediately apparent to a prudent purchaser, it is

---

64 For a recent discussion of this kind of problem in New Zealand, see *Crump v Wala* [1994] 2 NZLR 331, at 336–37.

65 (1983) 2 NSWLR 381. This approach has now been confirmed in New South Wales by the amendment of the Sales of Goods Act 1923, by s 4(2A) of the Sales of Goods Amendment Act 1988. See also *Kramer v McMahon* (1970) 1 NSWLR 194; *Simons v Zartom Investments Pty Ltd* (1975) 2 NSWLR 30 where rescission of a contract to purchase real estate was ordered for an innocent misrepresentation that had become a term of the contract and the purchaser was not limited to a claim for compensation under the agreement. Also, to similar effect is *Academy of Health and Fitness Pty Ltd v Power* [1973] VR 254, considered by Lockhart and Gummow JJ in *Accounting Systems v CCH Australia Ltd* (1993) 114 ALR 355. There, in regard to s 52 of the Trade Practices Act 1974 (Cth), it was held that the fact that a misrepresentation was a term of a contract did not preclude a court from granting relief under the statute for false and misleading conduct. For some time there was doubt as to whether equitable relief for a mere misrepresentation could be given in Victoria in relation to sales of goods. See *Watt v Westhoven* [1933] VLR 458 where it was held that the effect of the Victorian Goods Act 1893, which preserved the rules of the common law in relation to the effect of misrepresentation would, as a matter of statutory construction, exclude rescission in equity of a contract for the sale of goods for innocent misrepresentation by the vendor in the absence of a total failure of consideration. These provisions also apply in Queensland, s 61(2) of the Sales of Goods Act 1896, Western Australia, s 59(2) of the Sale of Goods Act 1895, Tasmania, s 5(2) of the Sales of Goods Act 1896, the Northern Territory, s 4(2) of the Sales of Goods Act 1972. Further, see *Riddiford v Warren* [1901] 20 NZLR 572. Note that the law in Victoria has now been modified by s 100 of the Goods Act 1958 which provides that where a buyer enters into a sale of goods as a result of an innocent misrepresentation, the buyer is entitled to rescind if he or she would have been able to rescind had the misrepresentation been fraudulent. This provision applies to a sale of goods where the cash price does not exceed a certain price, or where the goods are of a kind ordinarily acquired for personal, domestic or household goods or consumption. *Cf Graham v Freer* (1983–84) 35 SASR 424 where it was held that the rules of common law include the rules of equity under s 59(2) of the Sale of Goods Act 1895 (S Aust) and the equitable remedy of rescission for innocent misrepresentation is applicable to a contract for the sale of goods even though the misrepresentation was a term of the contract. In New Zealand, pre-contractual misrepresentations, in relation to sales of goods, are governed by the provisions of the Contractual Remedies Act 1979, see *Crump v Wala* [1994] 2 NZLR 331.

submitted that a contract for the sale of goods should be able to be rescinded for innocent misrepresentation even though the purchaser has taken delivery of the goods and there has been delay in effecting rescission. In the United Kingdom, the Misrepresentation Act 1967[66] has conferred a right to rescission of a contract for innocent misrepresentation even though it has been incorporated as a term of the contract, thereby appearing to reverse this aspect of the reasoning in *Leaf v International Galleries*. This reform has been adopted in South Australia[67] and the Australian Capital Territory.[68]

(c) Third party interests

Since a contract is merely voidable for misrepresentation if a third party *bona fide* and for value obtains an interest in the subject-matter of the agreement, the opportunity to rescind will have been lost.[69] A good illustration of this is *McKenzie v McDonald*.[70] There, a land agent assumed the role of adviser to an elderly woman, who he knew was in financial difficulties, and made an agreement with her whereby she was to sell her farm to him and he was to sell to her a dwelling house and shop in exchange. The agent over-valued the shop and under-valued the farm. He also suppressed information concerning the market value of the farm and wrote a disparaging report about it. The purchaser claimed rescission of the agreement and the reconveyance of the properties together with an account. The court held that rescission was impossible because third parties had acquired interests in the farm; however, the agent was ordered to pay compensation for his fraudulent dealing in relation to the valuations. The court permitted the agent to take over the shop and the dwelling for a certain sum if he desired to do so. A shareholder, who has been induced to take shares in a company through fraud, will lose the right of rescission on winding-up proceedings being commenced because rescission will prejudice the rights of creditors.[71] A mere assignment, however, will not be sufficient to bring this principle into play since the assignor will take subject to the equities having priority over his or her interest. Any remedy the assignee might have in these circumstances will lie against the assignee.[72] In exceptional circumstances, a court may grant rescission in such a way that third

---

66 Section 1.

67 Section 6(1)(a) of the Misrepresentation Act 1971–72 (S Aust).

68 Section 3(a) of the Law Reform (Misrepresentation) Act 1977 (ACT) and s 62(1A) of the Sale of Goods Act 1954 (ACT).

69 See *Phillips v Brookes Ltd* [1919] 2 KB 243, and discussion in Chapter 5 on Mistake, pp 116–19.

70 [1927] VLR 134.

71 *Oakes v Turquand and Harding* (1867) LR 2 HL 325; [1861–73] All ER 738.

72 *Abram Steamship Co Ltd v Westville Shipping Co Ltd* [1923] AC 773.

party rights are protected as, for example, where one party is ordered to hold certain interests on trust for the third party.[73]

(d) Executed contracts and the loss of the right to rescind for innocent misrepresentation

Two important cases limiting rescission for innocent misrepresentation where contracts have been executed are *Seddon v North Eastern Salt Co Ltd*[74] and *Angel v Jay*.[75] In *Seddon*, a purchaser of shares in a company was unable to rescind the transaction after he had profitably traded in the shares for some time after learning of the misrepresentation as to their value. Although the case appears justifiable on the ground of affirmation, it, like its successor *Angel v Jay*, came to be regarded as authority denying rescission for innocent misrepresentation after an agreement had been executed. In *Angel v Jay*, a lessor had innocently misrepresented that drains were in good condition when they were defective. The lessee entered into possession and occupied the premises for six months. It was held that the lessor could no longer rescind because the contract had been executed.

These cases enlarged a rule of conveyancing, advanced in *Wilde v Gibson*,[76] which denied relief to a purchaser of real estate where the misrepresentation related to a defect in title. Although the rule in *Wilde's* case might be considered prudent to ensure purchasers carefully requisitioned title and thus advance an orderly system of conveyancing, it was unfortunate that it was extended more widely to incorporate cases like *Seddon* and *Angel v Jay*. In *Leaf v International Galleries*, Denning LJ was critical of the rule in so far as it applied to cases other than those involving requisitions as to title but a majority of the Court of Appeal were more cautious in their criticism of the appropriate width of the rule. In Australia, in *Svanosio v McNamara*,[77] the High Court affirmed the rule in so far as an innocent misrepresentation concerning land was concerned. It was held that there could be no rescission of an executed contract for the sale of land on the basis of mistake or misrepresentation unless fraud was present or there was a total failure of consideration. In *Leason Pty Ltd v Princes Farms Ltd*,[78] Helsham CJ considered that the limi-

---

73 *Waters Motors Pty Ltd v Cratchley* [1964] NSWR 1085.

74 (1905) 1 Ch 326; [1904–07] All ER 817.

75 (1911) 1 KB 666; [1908–10] All ER 470.

76 (1848) 1 HL Cas 605, at 632–33; *Manson v Thacker* (1878) 7 Ch D 620; *Allen v Richardson* (1879) 13 Ch D 524.

77 (1956) 96 CLR 186, at 198–99, 209–11; *Wilson v Brisbane City Council* [1931] St R Qd 360; *Kramer v Duggan* (1955) 55 SR (NSW) 385; *Cousins v Freeman* (1957) 58 WALR 79; *Dean v Gibson* [1958] VR 563. In *Grogan v 'The Astor' Ltd* (1925) 25 SR (NSW) 409, Long Innes J regarded the rule as applicable to a sale of shares but not an allotment of shares.

78 (1983) 2 NSWLR 381.

tation should play no part in relation to sales of goods. However, in *Vigmig v Contract Tooling*,[79] Wood J considered both the judicial and academic criticisms of the rule but felt constrained, as a first instance judge, to apply the rule so as to deny rescission in relation to a executed contract for the sale of a business. The rule in *Seddon's* case and *Angel v Jay* has not been followed in Canada.[80] In *Senanayake v Cheng*, the Privy Council considered that, in regard to a purchase of a partnership share, the more important issue was whether *restitutio in integrum* was substantially possible and would be timely, just and fair. It was considered that the term 'executed' was inappropriate to describe a continuing business arrangement. The rule in *Seddon* and *Angel v Jay* was eventually abolished in the United Kingdom by the Misrepresentation Act 1967.[81] The Act confers a right to rescind a contract for innocent misrepresentation even though the contract has been performed.[82] This right not only extends to contracts relating to personal property but also to contracts for the sale or disposition of land or an interest in land. Similar legislation was enacted in South Australia and the Australian Capital Territory. In New South Wales and Victoria, there has been reform abolishing the rule in relation to sales of goods.[83]

The Trade Practices Act 1974 (Cth)

A consideration of misrepresentation requires some mention of the effect of s 52(1) of the Trade Practices Act 1974 which is of considerable importance in relation to corporations.[84] This Act provides civil remedies where a corporation in trade or commerce engages in misleading or deceptive conduct. This section has been widely used against corporations that have induced persons to enter into contracts as a result of misrepresentations in the course of negotiations. It is unnecessary to establish any deliberate intention to mislead as there is with a fraudulent misrepresentation under the general law.[85] It is sufficient under the Act to show that the conduct engaged in was objectively deceptive or misleading, that is to say, it led someone into error or was capable of doing so. Focus is upon effect rather than intention. Relief is available to

---

79 (1987) 9 NSWLR 731.

80 *Northern & Central Gas Corp Ltd v Hillcrest Collieries Ltd* (1975) 59 DLR (3rd) 533, at 600.

81 Section (1).

82 Section 6(1)(b) of the Misrepresentation Act 1971–72 (S Aust); s 3(b)(c) of the Law Reform (Misrepresentation) Act 1977 (ACT).

83 Section 4(2) of the Sales of Goods Amendment Act 1988 (NSW). Also, s 100 of the Goods Act (Vict), 1958.

84 See further for statutory intervention in relation to certain consumer transactions, the Fair Trading Acts, Qld, 1989; SA, 1987; Tas, 1990; Vic, 1985; NSW, 1987; W Aust, 1987; ACT, 1992; Consumer Affairs and Fair Trading Act 1990 (NT); New Zealand, 1986.

85 *Hornsby Building Information v Sydney Building Information Centre* (1978) 140 CLR 216.

those who have been the victims of misleading and deceptive conduct even if they are not parties to a contract or privy to it.[86] It is not limited simply to conduct which is deceptive of members of the public in their capacity as consumers of goods.[87] It must, however, be deceptive or misleading conduct that is 'in trade and commerce' and not merely 'in relation' to it.[88] Cases involving false and misleading conduct have covered a wide range of commercial activity.[89] A misrepresentation as to a future intention is misleading unless there are reasonable grounds for making it at the time it is made.[90] A misrepresentation is actionable under the Act although it constitutes a term of a contract.[91] Silence may also be relied upon to show a contravention of the section where the circumstances give rise to an obligation to disclose relevant facts.[92] Attempts to disclaim liability for misstatements in negotiations afford no defence if it can be established that misleading or deceptive conduct has been engaged in and has been the cause of loss.[93]

Section 53 also provides civil remedies when representations are made in connection with the supply of good and services in trade or commerce. It prohibits the making of false representations as to certain defined qualities of those goods or services including their grade, composition, standard, age, approval, sponsorship, performance, characteristics and uses. Section 53A also prohibits a corporation from making false and misleading representations in trade or commerce that relate to certain defined qualities that are associated with the promotion, sales or grants of interests in land.

Under s 82, an aggrieved party can recover from the offending party the amount of loss and damage he or she has suffered. A court under s 87 has wide powers to make appropriate orders to compensate for loss

---

86 *Janssen Cilag Pty Ltd v Pfizer Pty Ltd* (1992) 109 ALR 638; *Accounting Systems v CCH Australia Ltd* (1993) 114 ALR 355.

87 *Bevanere Pty Ltd v Lubidineuse* (1985) 59 ALR 334; *Concrete Constructions (NSW) Pty Ltd v Nelson* (1990) 169 CLR 594, at 601; *Unilan Holdings v Kerin* (1992) 107 ALR 709.

88 *Concrete Constructions (NSW) Pty Ltd v Nelson, ibid,* at 602–03.

89 See *Byers v Dorotea Pty Ltd* (1986) 69 ALR 715 (false representations relating to units sold on the Gold Coast in Queensland); *Chiarabaglio v Westpac Banking Corp* (1989) ATPR 40–971 (misleading representations in relation to overseas currency loans); *Roymancorp Hempston Holdings Ltd* (1986) 65 ALR 302 (misrepresentations to the term of a lease of a business); *Neilson v Hempston Holdings Ltd* (1986) 65 ALR 302 (misrepresentations as to the occupancy rate of a motel in the negotiations for its sale); *Bateman v Slatyer* (1987) 71 ALR 553 (misrepresentation made in connection with a sale of a retail store franchise).

90 Section 51A (1986).

91 *Accounting Systems v CCH Australia Ltd* (1993) 114 ALR 355.

92 *Henjo Investments Pty Ltd v Collins Marrickville Pty Ltd* (1988) 79 ALR 83; *Rhone Poulenc Agrchimie SA v UIM Chemical Services* (1986) 12 FCR 477; *Demagogue Pty Ltd v Ramensky* (1992) 110 ALR 608; *Winterton Constructions Pty Ltd v Hambros Australia Ltd* (1992) 11 ALR 649; *Warner v Elders Rural Finance Ltd* (1993) 113 ALR 517.

93 *Pappas v New World Oil Developments* (1993) 117 ALR 304.

or damage. Further, a court may declare the whole of or any part of a contract to be void, may vary a contract, refuse to enforce any or all of the provisions of a contract, may direct the return of money or property, or the payment of the amount of loss suffered. In so far as there is a power to validate a contract, s 87 goes further than the general law. However, s 87 requires loss or damage to be proven, whereas in equity, relief could be given on proof of a misrepresentation without this being established. Restrictions on rescission such as affirmation, lapse of time and the impossibility of effecting *restitutio in integrum* are not fetters on the exercise of the powers under s 87 but are matters that a court may consider in its discretion.[94] The High Court of Australia has held that damages under the Act should be assessed on a tortious basis.[95] The popularity of the statutory remedy and the less exacting criteria for liability than misrepresentation under the general law has meant that s 52 is commonly invoked in cases where a corporation has been involved in false or deceptive behaviour in trade or commerce. The statutory remedy may be claimed in addition to relief under the general law.[96]

Misrepresentation and the Contractual Remedies Act 1979 (New Zealand)

(a) The legislation

Significant changes to the general law in New Zealand have been made in relation to misrepresentation under the Contractual Remedies Act 1979. Under this Act, the common law and equitable rules relating to rescission for misrepresentation have been abrogated.[97] The same rules govern relief, including an award of damages, whether the misrepresentation is innocent or fraudulent.[98] Cancellation of a contract may arise for misrepresentation where the parties have expressly or impliedly agreed that the truth of the representation is essential to the cancelling party,[99] or the effect of the misrepresentation is to substantially reduce the benefit of the contract or increase the burden of the contract, or will make the benefit or the burden substantially different from that which was represented.[100] A party is not entitled to cancel, if with full knowledge of the misrepresenta-

---

94 *Creative Landscape Design Centre Pty Ltd v Platz* [1989] ATPR 40–980.

95 *Gates v City Mutual Life Assurance Society Ltd* (1986) 160 CLR 1; *Netaf Pty Ltd v Bikane Pty Ltd* (1990) 26 FCR 305; *Poseiden Ltd v Adelaide Petroleum NL* (1991–92) 105 ALR 25; *Scanhill v Century Australia Pty Ltd* (1993) 120 ALR 173; *Cut Price Delis Pty Ltd v Jacques* (1994) 126 ALR 413.

96 See *Mister Figgins Pty Ltd v Centrepoint Freeholds Pty Ltd* (1981) 36 ALR 23, at 48; *Westwill Pty Ltd v Heath* (1989) 52 SASR 461.

97 Section 7(1).

98 Section 6; s 7(3)(a).

99 Section 7(3)(a).

100 Section 7(4).

tion, he or she affirms the contract.[101] Under the Act, affirmation, it would seem, arises where a party elects to proceed with the contract even though he or she may not appreciate that there is a right to cancel, whereas under the general law it is uncertain whether mere knowledge of the facts giving rise to a right to rescind is sufficient to constitute affirmation irrespective of whether the innocent party was aware of the right to rescind.[102] Besides the right to cancel, a party who is the victim of a misrepresentation, whether innocent or fraudulent, has the right to claim damages.[103] However, the torts of deceit and negligent misrepresentation are abolished.[104] Damages are assessed on a contractual basis as if the misrepresentation were a term of the contract.[105] Where a contract expressly provides for a remedy in respect of misrepresentation or makes express provision concerning the remedies provided for under the Act, the contractual provisions operate in place of the relief provided by the Act.[106] However, there is a restriction placed on the ability of a party to contract out of liability for representations made in connection with pre-contract negotiations. Any provision of this kind is subject to a court's scrutiny as to whether it is fair and reasonable.[107] Factors such as whether the parties have been legally represented, the subject-matter and the respective bargaining strength of the parties are relevant to this inquiry.[108]

Where a contract is cancelled for misrepresentation, a court may grant relief under s 9 of the Act. If it is just and practicable to do so, a court may make orders relating to the vesting of property, the payment of money or do such other act in relation to the other party as a court thinks just. A court may have regard to the contract terms, the extent to which any party to the contract was or would have been able to perform it, any expenditure by a party in the performance of the contract, the value of

---

101 Section 7(5) See *Jolly v Palmer* [1985] 1 NZLR 685; *Hughes v Huppert* [1991] 1 NZLR 475; *Cycle Manufacturing Co v Williamson* [1993] 1 NZLR 454.

102 See discussion, pp 211–12, but query *Hughes v Huppert, ibid,* at 477–78.

103 Section 6(1)(a).

104 Section 6(1)(b).

105 Section 6(1)(a). *Walsh v Kerr* [1989] 1 NZLR 490. Further, see the helpful discussion of damages by Barker J in *New Zealand Motor Bodies v Emslie* [1985] 2 NZLR 569 and Hammond J in *Crump v Wala* [1994] 2 NZLR 331, at 341–42. Contractual damages are assessed by reference to expectation loss together with consequential loss that is within the contemplation of the parties at the time of the formation of the contract. *Cf* the remedy under s 13(a) of the Fair Trading Act 1986 where damages for false and misleading conduct are assessed on the basis of consequential losses being recoverable. *Ibid,* at 341–42.

106 Section 5.

107 See *Herbison v Papakura Video Ltd* [1987] 2 NZLR 527 where the court upheld a disclaimer clause where *inter alia* both parties had been independently advised. *Cf Bird v Brickle* [1987] 2 NZLR 542, where the court ruled that a disclaimer clause did not oust the Act where there had been fraud.

108 Sections 4(1) and (2).

any services performed, any benefits or advantages gained by the other party to the contract, and any other relevant matters in determining what, if any, orders should be made.[109] No orders shall be made that interfere with the estates or interests in property of a *bona fide* purchaser for value who is not a party to the contract.[110] Further, a court is precluded from making any order that would deprive a party to the contract of property, if that party has so altered his or her position in relation to the property, (whether before or after cancellation) that it would be inequitable to make an order under s 9.[111]

(b) Judicial applications of the Act

There have been few cases under the Act in relation to misrepresentation. However, it is clear that, whilst enabling victims of innocent misrepresentations to sue for damages, the Act has made it more difficult for the representee to effectively rescind or resile from a contract if a misrepresentation is not considered to be one that the parties have expressly or impliedly treated as essential. In *Young v Hunt*,[112] a purchaser of a business claimed the right to cancel the sale for misrepresentation as to turnover and recover the purchase moneys and general damages. The vendor claimed that he had wrongfully repudiated the contract thereby entitling her to cancel. It was held that, although there had been a misrepresentation as to the turnover, this was not shown to be essential nor was it so significant that cancellation should be permitted. Accordingly, there had been a wrongful cancellation which entitled the vendor to terminate the agreement and claim damages. The court, however, considered that the purchaser was entitled to some relief under s 9 of the Act and granted him compensation which was set-off against the damages awarded to the vendor for wrongful cancellation. Similarly, in *Jolly v Palmer*,[113] it was held that, although, there had been a misrepresentation by a vendor's agent as to the government's value of a property which materially affected the value of the consideration the purchasers received, it was not so significant that it could entitle the purchasers to cancel. In any event, the court considered that the purchaser, with knowledge of the falsity of the information, had elected to affirm the agreement by seeking finance and taking other steps that were inconsistent with a desire to cancel. However, in *Sharplin v Henderson*,[114] the Court of Appeal held that a real estate agent's misrepresentation as to

---

109 Section 9(4).
110 Section 9(5).
111 Section 9(6).
112 [1984] 2 NZLR 81.
113 [1985] 1 NZLR 658.
114 [1990] 2 NZLR 134.

the boundaries of a property was sufficiently substantial to enable the purchaser to cancel the agreement. The area of land was estimated as 25% less than that for which the purchaser had bargained.

Although the Act does not apply to repudiation of contracts relating to sales of goods which are governed by the Sales of Goods Act 1908, it has been held in *Crump v Wala*,[115] that it does apply to misrepresentations made in relation to pre-contractual negotiations relating to sales of goods. In that case, however, the purchaser was found to have elected to have affirmed the contract by attempting to resell the merchandise, to which the misrepresentation related, over a period of weeks and was accordingly held to be limited to a claim for damages.

---

115 [1994] 2 NZLR 331.

CHAPTER 10

Benefits Acquired Through Duress, Undue Influence or Derived from an Unconscionable Bargain

In this chapter, restitution of benefits derived from duress, undue influence or unconscionable bargains will be considered. Where a person has derived benefits, whether contractual or otherwise, through improper pressure being applied, the transaction should be closely scrutinised to ensure that the victim has not been unconscionably deprived of his or her property or has entered into obligations that are oppressive with the consequences that the party exercising improper pressure has been unjustly enriched.

Duress

(a) Threats of bodily harm

The action for moneys had and received will lie to recover moneys paid over as a result of threats to do harm to the payer. In *Moses v Macferlan*,[1] Lord Mansfield said that the action lay[2] for money acquired through imposition, express or implied, or extortion, or oppression. A modern illustration of this rule is to be found in the New Zealand case of *Dandoroff v Rogozinoff*.[3] Where the plaintiff recovered money from a former business partner that had been extorted from him by threats of violence. Contractual transactions will also be set aside where a party has been threatened with physical harm. In *Barton v Armstrong*,[4] the Privy Council set aside an agreement where it was established that pre-contractual negotiations had included death threats made by Armstrong to Barton. A majority of the Court of Appeal held that Barton was not entitled to relief because he had failed to show that he would not have entered into the agreement with Armstrong had there been no threats. The Privy Council, however, upheld Barton's appeal. Once it was established that he had made the threats, Armstrong had the burden of proving that the threats and other unlawful pressure had not contributed at all to Barton's decision to contract. If, as the trial judge had found, Armstrong's threats were a reason for Barton's executing the deed, Lord Cross considered that he was entitled to relief even though Barton might well have entered into the agreement if Armstrong had not resorted to coercion.[5]

---

1   (1760) 2 Burr 1005; 97 ER 676.
2   *Ibid*, at 1013; 681.
3   [1988] 2 NZLR 589.
4   [1976] AC 104; [1975] 2 All ER 465; (1974) 3 ALR 355.
5   *Ibid*, at 119; at 475; 366.

(b) Threats to interfere with property

If money is paid to relieve a threat to property, the payment will be regarded as involuntary. An action for moneys had and received will lie to recover money paid as a result of extortion of this kind. In *Maskell v Horner*,[6] the Court of Appeal held that a plaintiff, who had paid money under protest to the owner of a market to prevent his goods being seized, could recover the money in an action for moneys had and received. Buckley LJ observed:[7]

> ... the plaintiff is entitled, I think, to recover upon the ground that the payments which he made were not made voluntarily, but were made under the pressure of the defendant's threat to seize and sell his goods in default of payment and were made not without objection but under protest.

In that case, there was evidence that the plaintiff's goods had been seized on an earlier occasion; however, an apprehended threat of seizure will suffice. In *Mason v The State of New South Wales*,[8] the High Court of Australia allowed a carrier to recover fees unlawfully levied for interstate travel. The carrier had paid under protest. Under the relevant legislation, it was an offence to carry goods without the appropriate licence or exemption. A person who did so was liable to penalty. There was also a power to seize vehicles and business records pending investigation and legal proceedings. Although there was no evidence of any actual threat of seizure, there was evidence that the legislation was policed. Dixon CJ observed:[9]

> The moneys were paid over by the plaintiffs to avoid the apprehended consequence of a refusal to submit to the authority. It is enough if there be just and reasonable grounds for apprehending that, unless payment be made, an unlawful and injurious course will be taken by the defendant in violation of the plaintiff's actual rights. The plaintiffs were not bound to wait until the illegality was committed in the exercise of a void authority.

A similar approach applies where a person enters into an contract in order to obtain the release of his or her goods that are being unlawfully withheld. In *Hawker Pacific Pty Ltd v Helicopter Charter Pty Ltd*,[10] an agreement to pay a sum of money and release the defendant from

---

6   [1915] 3 KB 106; [1914–15] All ER 595.

7   *Ibid*, at 123; at 601.

8   (1959) 102 CLR 108.

9   *Ibid*, at 117. Cf *Air India v Commonwealth* (1977) 1 NSWLR 449 where it was held that it was hardly reasonable to fear that the Commonwealth would determine the leases of seven major airlines because of a rent dispute. Considered further in *Esso Resources v Gas and Fuel Corp* [1993] 2 VR 99, at 104 *per* Gobbo J.

10   (1991) 22 NSWLR 299.

certain liability as to repair work it had performed on the plaintiff's helicopter was set aside. The defendant had led the plaintiff to believe that the helicopter, which the plaintiff required urgently, would not be released unless agreement was reached. The Court of Appeal of New South Wales considered that the principles, which applied to payments made under duress of goods, should also apply to contracts affected by duress of this kind.

(c) Economic duress

An action for moneys had and received will lie to permit a payer to recover money that has been paid to avert the consequences of a threat made by the payee to unlawfully interfere with a legal obligation owed to the payer. Contractual transactions, induced by coercive conduct of this kind, will be voidable in equity. The intimidation must constitute a violation of a legal obligation. Pressure that is illegitimate, in this sense, has been described as economic duress.[11] In *Smith v William Charlick Ltd*,[12] the High Court of Australia considered that a miller was not entitled to recover payments made to the Wheat Harvest Board which was responsible for negotiating the price for wheat sold on behalf of growers. The Board considered that the miller had unfairly obtained an advantageous price for the wheat that had been supplied to it and sought to exact a higher price after the wheat had been delivered. The Board informed the miller that it would not be able to purchase any more wheat unless it agreed to pay a higher price. The miller agreed to pay a higher price for the wheat it had already acquired because it would not have been able to procure wheat from any alternative source and this would have caused it to be unable to continue in business. The High Court held that the miller was not entitled to restitution. The miller had paid the money knowing full well that the Board could not lawfully make such a demand; however, the Board was not in breach of any legal obligation to the appellant. In the opinion of Issacs J:[13]

> ... there was on the facts ... no breach of legal duty to the wheat owners, and no legal wrong to the respondent, and no statutory provision in the respondent's favour which guarded against the Board's action as any undue advantage taken of the situation.

---

11 See Lord Scarman in *Pao On v Lau Yiu* [1980] AC 614, at 635–36; [1979] 3 All ER 65, at 79. Mere commercial pressure was insufficient to permit a court to intervene in *Magnacrete v Douglas Hill* (1987–88) 48 SASR 565.

12 (1924) 34 CLR 38.

13 *Ibid*, at 63.

Issacs J described actionable duress in these terms:[14]

'Compulsion' in relation to a payment of which refund is sought, and whether it is also variously called 'coercion', 'extortion', 'exaction', or 'force' includes every species of duress or conduct analogous to duress, actual or threatened, exerted by or on behalf of the payee and applied to the person or property or any right of the person who pays or, in some cases, of a person related to or in affinity with him.

Higgins J, in his dissenting judgment, however, considered that the threatened refusal of the Board to deal with the miller constituted a fraud on the Board's statutory power and the pressure applied was 'illegitimate', so that recovery should be allowed.[15]

Illegitimate pressure was seen in *Nixon v Furphy*[16] and in *Re Hooper & Grass' Contract*,[17] where purchasers were able to recover excess payments made under protest in order to avert threats by the vendors to unlawfully rescind contracts. The New South Wales Court of Appeal, in *T A Sundell & Sons Ltd v EMM Yannoulatos (Overseas) Pty Ltd*,[18] also held that a plaintiff could recover the excess price it had paid for a quantity of galvanised iron which the defendant had unlawfully refused to supply unless the plaintiff agreed to pay above the contractual price. The court rejected the argument that compulsion was limited to duress of goods. The Australian approach to economic duress was followed in England in *The Siboen and the Sibotre*[19] and in *The Atlantic Baron*.[20] Both judgments were subsequently referred to with approval by the Privy Council in *Pao On v Lau Yiu*[21] and the House of Lords in *Universal Tankships Inc of Monrovia v International Transport Workers Federation*.[22] In *Pao On*, Lord Scarman observed:[23]

In their Lordship's view, there is nothing contrary to principle in recognising economic duress as a factor which may render a contract voidable, provided always that the basis of such recognition is that it must amount to coercion of the will, which vitiates consent. It must be shown that the payments made or the contract entered into was not a voluntary act.

---

14 *Ibid*, at 56.
15 *Ibid*, at 66–68.
16 (1925) 25 SR (NSW) 151.
17 [1949] VLR 269.
18 (1956) 56 SR (NSW) 323.
19 [1976] 1 Lloyd's Rep 293.
20 [1979] 1 Lloyd's Rep 89; [1978] 3 All ER 1170.
21 [1980] AC 614; [1979] 3 All ER 65.
22 [1983] 1 AC 366; [1982] 2 WLR 803.
23 [1980] AC 614, at 635–36; [1979] 3 All ER 65, at 79.

In *Atlas Express Ltd v Kafco (Importers and Distributors) Ltd*,[24] a carrier unsuccessfully sued to recover freight charges which the defendant agreed to pay in excess of the original contractual price under a threat that otherwise the carrier would not perform its contract. The defendant operated a small business which imported and distributed merchandise. The defendant believed it could not afford to lose the carrier's service because it would be very difficult to obtain another contractor to carry its goods. Failure to supply would also affect the defendant's business. The court considered that the defendant had agreed to the increased price under an illegitimate threat.[25]

The fact that consideration has been paid will not prevent a court from avoiding an agreement obtained through economic duress. In *The 'Siboen' and the 'Sibotre'*,[26] Kerr J considered that it should not make any difference if there was some purely nominal but legally sufficient consideration, a view which Mocatta J shared in *The Atlantic Baron*. Mocatta J observed that if the contract was void the consideration would be recoverable in quasi-contract. If it was voidable, equity would rescind the contract and order the return of the consideration.[27]

A contract will only be rescinded if illegitimate pressure is applied to induce the other party's consent to the contract. Mere commercial pressure will not suffice.[28] Illegitimate pressure, however, may consist not only of threatened breaches of contract but tortious wrongdoing as well. In *Universal Tankships Inc of Monrovia v International Transport Workers Federation*,[29] the House of Lords upheld the recovery of a payment made to the defendant union after it had participated in unlawful industrial action. The unlawful activity consisted of the blacking of the plaintiff's ship so that it could not sail unless various demands were met. Corrupt bargains will also lead to restitution. Where a debtor pays a creditor

---

24   [1989] QB 833; [1989] 1 All ER 641.

25   Compare this case with *Alec Lobb (Garages) Ltd v Total Oil GB Ltd* [1983] 1 WLR 87; [1983] 1 All ER 944, on appeal [1985] 1 WLR 173; [1985] 1 All ER 303. *Cf CTN Cash and Carry Ltd v Gallaher Ltd* [1994] 4 All ER 714, the Court of Appeal declined to find duress where there had been a compromise of a dispute made after a lawful threat to withdraw credit facilities.

26   [1976] 1 Lloyd's Rep 293, at 335–36.

27   [1979] 1 Lloyd's Rep 89, at 98–99; *Vantage Navigation Corp v Suhail* [1989] 1 Lloyd's Rep 138.

28   See *Pao On v Lau Yiu* [1980] AC 614; *Alec Lobb (Garages) v Total Oil (Great Britain) Ltd* [1983] 1 WLR 87; [1983] 1 All ER 944; *'The Siboen and The Sibotre'* [1983] 1 WLR 87; [1983] 1 All ER 944; in Australia, *Smith v William Charlick Ltd* (1924) 34 CLR 38; *Crescendo Management Pty Ltd v Westpac Banking Corp* (1988) 19 NSWLR 40; *Equiticorp Finance Ltd v Bank of New Zealand* (1993) 32 NSWLR 50; *Magna Crete Ltd v Hill* (1987–88) 48 SASR 565; *Deemcope Pty Ltd v Cantown Pty Ltd* [1995] 2 VR 44; in New Zealand, *Moyes & Groves Ltd v Radiation New Zealand Ltd* [1982] 1 NZLR at 369; *Aotearoa International Ltd v Scan Carriers A/S* [1985] 1 NZLR 513; *Walmsley v Christchurch City Council* [1990] 1 NZLR 199, also *Shivas v Bank of New Zealand* [1990] 2 NZLR 327.

29   [1983] 1 AC 366; [1982] 2 WLR 803.

under duress and in fraud of other creditors, the debtor will be entitled to have the compromise set aside and restitution made of the payment.[30] A corrupt demand or undue pressure may also lead to a successful claim to restitution.[31]

(d) Compromise

Where unlawful pressure has induced agreement, a contract will be voidable in equity unless it can be established that the party seeking relief deliberately chose to compromise. The absence of any protest, the fact that the party threatened had legal advice, and the availability of alternative legal remedies are matters which are relevant to the issue of whether or not there was coercion of the will sufficient to vitiate consent.[32] In *Pao On*, the defendants had agreed to sell some shares in a company named Fu Chip to the plaintiffs in exchange for the plaintiffs selling certain property to Fu Chip. The value of the shares in Fu Chip was fixed at a certain price. Anxious that the plaintiffs would not sell the shares and so depress their market value, the defendants, who held a majority of the shares in Fu Chip, required the plaintiffs to enter into an arrangement whereby the shares would not be sold for a year. After agreement had been reached, the plaintiffs threatened not to perform unless agreement to a more advantageous variation was reached. This required the defendants to enter into an agreement to indemnify the plaintiffs should the shares fall in value during the period they were required to hold them. The defendants were anxious to complete the transaction otherwise public confidence in Fu Chip, which had recently become a public company, might be jeopardised and, accordingly, they sought legal advice. They were informed that the plaintiffs could be legally compelled to perform the existing agreement. However, they deliberately chose to avoid litigation and agreed to the new arrangement. Unpredictably, Fu Chip shares slumped with the result that the defendants declined to honour the agreement contending there was no consideration for the promise of indemnity and further that consent had been induced by duress. The Privy Council held that there was consideration for the indemnity agreement and also that the indemnity should not be set aside for economic duress. Even if the plaintiff's threats were unlawful, the defendants, with full knowledge of their ability to enforce the existing contractual arrangements, had deliberately chosen to avoid litigation and had entered into the indemnity for commercial reasons.

If there is a genuine dispute about the obligations of parties under a contract, a compromise resulting in one party accepting an extended

---

30 *Smith v Cuff* (1817) 6 M & S 160; [1817] 105 ER 1203.
31 *Andrews v Parker* (1973) Qd R 93.
32 [1980] AC 614; [1979] 3 All ER 65.

obligation in order to avoid a threatened rescission of the contract may be considered sufficient consideration for the new agreement and prevent any subsequent action based on duress. In *Moyes and Groves Ltd v Radiation New Zealand Ltd*,[33] the New Zealand Court of Appeal declined to grant relief for economic duress where a buyer under protest had agreed to pay more than the original contract price for items imported from an overseas manufacturer by the vendor at the request of the buyer. The vendor had informed the buyer that the goods would be returned to the manufacturer if he did not agree to an increase in the price. A very lengthy period had passed between the original contract of sale and the vendor being supplied with the goods from the manufacturer. The cost of supply to the vendor in this time had increased. There was a dispute between the parties as to whether the original agreement had been abandoned as a result of the length of time that had passed. The court referred to *Pao On v Lau Yiu* and held that there was a genuine dispute as to whether the agreement was still in force because there had been a very lengthy delay in the vendor acquiring the goods and the defendant had not complained.[34] The court further reasoned that, although made under protest, the agreement to pay an additional sum constituted a binding compromise of a genuine disagreement between the parties as to their respective rights and obligations. Such a compromise, whereby the seller gave up the course of returning the items, constituted consideration for the variation in price and the agreement was enforceable. Accordingly, the vendor was able to recover the increase which the buyer had declined to pay after delivery.

(e) The value of protest

As Windeyer J observed in *Mason v New South Wales*,[35] a protest provides some evidence that a payment is involuntary; however, there was no significance in the term 'protest' for it might mean no more than an assertion that payment was grudgingly made.[36] In *Moyes and Groves Ltd v Radiation New Zealand Ltd*,[37] a genuine compromise was found even though the increase in the purchase price was paid under protest.

---

33 [1982] 1 NZLR 369 considered in *Walmsley v Christchurch City Council* [1990] 1 NZLR 199, at 208–09. In that case, Hardie Boys J held that such pressure as had been applied to secure a second agreement was not illegitimate. Further, see *General Credits Ltd v Ensworth* (1986) 2 Qd R 162, where the court refused to set aside a consent order where there had been a settlement of a genuine claim.

34 *Ibid*, at 371–72. *Cf D & C Builders v Rees* [1966] 2 QB 617, where it was held by the Court of Appeal that intimidation negated a genuine accord or settlement.

35 (1959) 102 CLR 108, at 142.

36 *Idem.*

37 [1982] 1 NZLR 369. Further, see *Esso Australia Resources Ltd v Gas Corportation of Victoria* [1993] 2 VR 99.

(f) Payments made *ex colore officii*

Extortion by a payment made *ex colore officii* occurs when a public officer demands and is paid money he or she is not entitled to for the performance of a public duty.[38] In *Steele v Williams*,[39] a payment made to a parish clerk in excess of the statutory fee for permission to search a statutory register was held to be illegal and refundable. Excessive demands for the performance of public duties were also held to be recoverable in *Morgan v Palmer*[40] and *Hooper v Exeter Corporation*.[41] In *Morgan*, money was paid for the purpose of renewing a publican's licence. Similar fees had been paid for many years and the payee, the Mayor of Yarmouth, accepted the payment in the belief that he was entitled to them by custom. The plaintiff, in *Hooper v Exeter Corporation*, sought successfully to recover money paid for landing stone for which he was not liable because it was exempt from duty.

A payment made *ex colore officii* may be recoverable even though payment was made after the service was performed. This was the case in *Steele v Williams*.[42] Further, recovery does not depend on proof of bad faith on the part of the payee. In *Morgan v Palmer*, the Mayor of Yarmouth accepted the payment in good faith believing that custom justified his accepting it. A similar approach is seen in cases involving discrimination in the payment of charges for the performance of a duty owed by a public corporation or other organisation empowered to perform a public duty. In *Great Western Railway v Sutton*,[43] the railway company carried freight for the plaintiff at a higher rate than it did for others. The plaintiff was able to recover the excess in an action for moneys had and received. More recently, in *South of Scotland Electricity Board v British Oxygen Co Ltd (No 2)*,[44] the House of Lords held that industrial consumers of high voltage electricity should be entitled to recover excess charges because they had been unlawfully discriminated against in favour of other customers who were consumers of low voltage electricity. In *Esso Resources v Gas and Fuel Corporation of Victoria*,[45]

---

38 Windeyer J in *Mason v New South Wales* (1959) 102 CLR 108, at 140.

39 (1885) 8 Exch 625; 155 ER 1502; see also *Dew v Parsons* (1819) 2 B & Ald 562; 106 ER 471. See *Ochberg v Commissioner of Stamp Duties* (1943) 43 SR (NSW) 189 where a threat to withhold probate for non-payment of excessive death duty led to restitution.

40 (1824) 2 B & C 729; [1824] 107 ER 554.

41 (1887) 56 LJ QB 457.

42 (1885) 8 Exch 625; [1885] 155 ER 1502. A point made by Windeyer J in *Mason v New South Wales* (1959) 102 CLR 108, at 141.

43 (1869) LR HL 226. Further, see *Parker v Great Western Ry Co* (1844) 7 Man & G 253; [1844] 135 ER 107.

44 [1959] 2 All ER 225.

45 [1993] 2 VR 89, at 105–07 *per* Gobbo J.

however, it was held that tariff payments made to the corporation by Esso could not be recovered by analogy with payments made *ex colore officii*. The payments were not made in reliance of authority that the payee did not have. Nor did they constitute an unreasonable charge albeit that they were imposed on the corporation by the government illegally and consequently passed on to Esso.

(g) Wrongful demands for tax or other dues by public authorities

A payment will be recoverable *ex colore officii* where an unlawful demand has been made for the performance of a public duty. However, the *ex colore officii* ground of recovery does not apply if the demand is not associated with the performance of a duty. This limitation is illustrated in *Julian v Mayor of Auckland*.[46] There, the plaintiff had made payments to the council for rates pursuant to demands which were subsequently found in separate legal proceedings to be illegal. It was held that the plaintiff could not recover because the payments had not been made to compel the council to perform a public duty. It was held that a threat of legal proceedings did not prevent the payment from being voluntary if the claim was submitted to and payment made.[47] Similarly, in England, prior to the decision of the House of Lords in *Woolwich Building Society v Inland Revenue Commissioners (No 2)*,[48] restitution had not been available for illegal or *ultra vires* demands for the payment of taxes or other dues. In *William Whitely Ltd v R*,[49] the plaintiff had paid duties for a number of years on a basis which was eventually disputed. On some occasions, the company protested. Finally, the company declined to pay and succeeded in establishing that it was under no liability to do so. The plaintiff then sought to recover the excess duties paid. It was held that the payments were not made *ex colore officii* or under any other form of duress and were irrecoverable. The fact that a payment was made under a bare threat of legal action did not render the payments involuntary.

Mistake of law was also a hurdle for a plaintiff to surmount in cases of this kind. In *Pari-Mutuel Association Ltd v The King*,[50] taxes had been paid in the belief that they were lawfully owing. The demands were subsequently held in separate litigation to have been unlawful. The plaintiff failed in its action for recovery on the ground that the payments had

---

46 [1927] 46 NZLR 453 cited with approval by Latham CJ in *Werrin v The Commonwealth* (1939) 59 CLR 150, at 158.

47 *Ibid*, at 459.

48 [1993] AC 70; [1992] 3 All ER 737.

49 (1909) 101 LT 741; [1908–10] All ER 639. Further, see *Slater v Burnley Corporation* (1888) 59 LT 636; and *Twyford v Manchester Corp* [1946] Ch 236; [1946] 1 All ER 621.

50 (1930) 47 TLR 110.

been made under a mistake of law. In Australia, a similar approach was taken by the High Court in *Werrin v The Commonwealth.*[51] There, the plaintiff had paid sales tax and sought to recover the payments after it had been established in separate litigation that the taxes had been wrongfully claimed. The High Court unanimously dismissed the claim. Latham CJ and McTiernan J were the only members of the court to expressly consider the issue of whether the payments were voluntary and held that they were. Latham CJ followed *William Whitely v the King,*[52] *Pari-Mutual Association Ltd*[53] and referred with approval also to *Julian v Auckland Harbour Board.*[54] Latham CJ and McTiernan J considered that the claim was not one made *ex colore officii* because the plaintiff had not claimed he was owed any duty that caused him to make the payments. The payments were made under a mistaken belief that they were lawfully due and were accordingly considered to be voluntary. In this regard, Latham CJ observed:[55]

> The principle appears to me to be quite clear that if a person, instead of contesting a claim, elects to pay money in order to discharge it, he cannot thereafter, because he finds out that he might have successfully contested the claim, recover the money which he so paid merely on the ground that he made a mistake of law.

The other members of the court, Dixon, Rich and Starke JJ denied recovery on the ground that a statutory prohibition on recovery applied. It would seem that mistake of law was invoked in cases of this kind as a means of protecting the Revenue and preventing a payer from re-opening a transaction after later discovering that a tax or other impost had been wrongly claimed. Although such an approach was protective of the Revenue, it condoned the unjust enrichment of public bodies who claimed to retain moneys that had been unlawfully demanded by virtue of a mistake of law. In *Mason v New South Wales,*[56] Dixon CJ observed that he had reservations about applying principles that were relevant in the case of litigation between citizens to unlawful demands having the weight of *'de facto* governmental authority'. It was, however, unnecessary to resolve that issue in *Mason* because restitution there was permitted on the ground of duress. More recently, the High Court of Australia in *David Securities Ltd v Commonwealth of Australia,*[57]

---

51 (1938) 59 CLR 150.

52 (1909) 101 LT 741; [1908–10] All ER 639.

53 (1930) 47 TLR 110.

54 [1927] 46 NZLR 453.

55 (1938) 59 CLR 150, at 159. Further, see *South Australian Stores Ltd v Electricity Trust of South Australia* (1965–66) 115 CLR 247.

56 (1959) 102 CLR 108, at 116–17.

57 (1992) 175 CLR 353. See the discussion in relation to the recovery of money paid under mistake, Chapter 2, pp 29–31.

rejected the distinction between payments made under a mistake of fact and law, and in so doing a major obstacle to recovery of illegally claimed taxes or dues from public bodies was removed in Australia. The High Court, however, considered that in cases such as *Werrin*, the refusal by the court to permit recovery of payments made pursuant to unlawful demands could be justified on the basis that a compromise of a dispute had been effected and such a compromise should not be lightly set aside.[58] In New Zealand and in Western Australia also, the distinction between payments made under mistake of law and fact has been abrogated by statute.[59] In Australia and New Zealand, it would seem that restitution of illegal taxes or dues should no longer be defeated on the basis of mistake of law.

There was, however, a decisive change in judicial approach to restitution of illegal taxes evidenced in *Woolwich Building Society v Inland Revenue Commissioners (No 2)*.[60] A majority of the House of Lords allowed a claim to interest on tax that the taxpayer had paid pursuant to an illegal demand by the Revenue. The plaintiff had successfully obtained a declaration that the payment was illegal in review proceedings commenced after payment had been made. Although the capital was repaid, the defendant unsuccessfully argued that interest was not payable on the capital because the money was repaid not pursuant to any restitutionary claim, but as a result of an implied agreement that the capital would be repaid in the event that the plaintiff was successful in the review proceedings. The plaintiff had chosen to pay the moneys and commence review proceedings rather than defend a claim and risk potentially damaging speculation that might affect its business reputation. Although a majority of the court held that interest was payable because the taxpayer was entitled to restitution of the money, their Lordships were not in agreement on the appropriate basis for it. The concern of Dixon CJ in *Mason*, that principles appropriate to private citizens claims against one another might not be appropriate in relation to claims involving *de facto* government authority,[61] was supported by Lord Goff[62] and Lord Slynn.[63] Lord Goff considered that justice required that tax be repaid unless special circumstances or some principle of policy requires otherwise and that *prima facie* the taxpayer should be entitled to

---

58 *Ibid*, at 371–76. The majority also sought to explain *South Australian Cold Stores v Electricity Trust of South Australia* (1957) 98 CLR 65 in this light, *ibid*, at 376.

59 Section 94A, 94B Judicature Act 1908, and see *Thomas v Housten Corbett* [1969] NZLR 151; *KJ Davies Ltd v Bank of New South Wales* [1981] 1 NZLR 262. In Western Australia, ss 124 and 125 Property Law Act 1969 (W Aust) also abolishes the distinction. See *Inn Leisure v DF McCloy* (1991) 28 FCR 151.

60 [1993] AC 70; [1992] 3 All ER 737.

61 (1959) 102 CLR 108, at 116–17.

62 [1993] AC 70, at 161; [1992] 3 All ER 737, at 756.

63 *Ibid*, at 202; at 785.

restitution.[64] Lord Goff considered that Woolwich paid neither under mistake or compulsion and restitution had to be based on the broad ground that a denial would be unconscionable.[65] Further, Lord Goff was inclined to the view that restitution should be permitted where the tax or other levy had been wrongly exacted by the public authority as a result of it misconstruing a relevant statute or regulation.[66] In also favouring restitution, Lord Slynn considered that, although the facts did not fit easily into an existing category of duress or ex *colore officii* claims, they did shade in to them.[67] Lord Slynn rejected the argument that in allowing the claim the courts would be usurping the legislative function or threaten the Revenue.[68] The question of economic stability was a matter which, however, troubled Lord Keith[69] and Lord Jauncey[70] in their dissenting judgments. In this regard, Issacs J in the High Court of Australia in *Sargood Brothers v the Commonwealth*,[71] had earlier observed that to recognise a broad head of restitution in cases of this kind would throw the finances of the country into utter confusion. The third member of the majority, Lord Browne-Wilkinson considered that the *ex colore officii* ground of recovery should not be restricted to cases involving the wrongful withholding of a person's legal rights. In his Lordship's opinion, payments made as a result of illegal demands for the payment of taxes or other public dues, should be the subject of restitution because a citizen is often unable to resist the payment without risking breaking the law or exposing himself or herself to penalties or other disadvantages.[72] Lord Browne-Wilkinson considered that he was attracted in any event to the argument that recovery was based on a close analogy to the right to recover money paid under a contract, the consideration for which had wholly failed.[73]

The *Woolwich* approach is to be preferred to one that unnecessarily favours or protects the Revenue or other public authority which wrongfully claims taxes or other dues. Whether the right of recovery is

---

64 *Ibid*, at 172; at 759.

65 *Ibid*, at 171–78; at 759–64. Further, see Lord Slynn, at 201–05, and 784–87, and the dissenting judgment of Wilson J in *Air Canada v British Columbia* (1989) 59 DLR (4th) 161, at 169, in favour of a general right of recovery of payments unconstitutionally claimed.

66 *Ibid*, at 161; 764.

67 *Ibid*, at 204; 787.

68 *Ibid*, at 204; 787.

69 *Ibid*, at 161; 750.

70 *Ibid*, at 195; 779.

71 (1910) 11 CLR 258, at 303. Further, see the judgment of La Forest J in *Air Canada v British Columbia* (1989) 59 DLR (4th) 161, at 194–97 to similar effect.

72 [1993] AC 70, at 198; [1992] 3 All ER 737, at 781.

73 *Ibid*, at 197; 781.

based on failure of consideration,[74] a more liberal consideration of *ex colore officii* claims or duress,[75] or on a broad basis of unconscientious behaviour, a citizen should be able to recover illegal or *ultra vires* payments of tax or other dues claimed by a public official. It is the cloak of officialdom and the desire to avoid official sanction or penalty that is a powerful coercive force behind the payment of taxes or other dues by law abiding citizens.[76] To deny recovery of payments, which through error or oversight have been wrongfully demanded by a public official, is to permit unjust enrichment of the Revenue. Rather ironically, if the Crown pays money out of the consolidated revenue without authority, it may obtain restitution of the payment.[77] The citizen should be similarly protected when he or she pays illegal taxes or dues. If the coffers of the Revenue or other public authority sufficiently merit protection then legislation can be enacted for this purpose as Lord Goff, in *Woolwich*, observed.[78] *Woolwich* was a case of a payment being clearly involuntary because it was always intended that the validity of the payment would later be the subject of litigation. However, restitution in cases of this kind should not be depend upon whether there has been an effective protest. Litigation is expensive and, in many cases, beyond the financial means of a citizen. A citizen should not be penalised for relying on the accuracy of a claim for tax or some other levy or impost by a public authority. Although in *David Securities Pty Ltd v Commonwealth Bank of Australia*,[79] the High Court emphasised the importance of the defence of compromise of honest claims, it is submitted that this defence, which in the case of disputes between private citizens may be a valid reason for denying recovery in cases where payments are made to settle disputes, is less appropriate in cases involving taxes or other dues unlawfully demanded by a public

---

74 See Birks, P, 'Restitution from Public Authorities' (1980) CLP 191; 'Restitution from the Executive; A Tercentenary Footnote to the Bill of Rights', in Finn, PD (ed), *Essays on Restitution*, 1990, pp 164–65, Law Book Co Ltd, Sydney. The latter essay was considered by Lord Goff in *Woolwich* [1993] AC 70, at 166; [1992] 3 All ER 737, at 754.

75 See 'Public Authorities, *Ultra Vires* and Restitution', in Burrows, A (ed), *Essays on the Law of Restitution*, 1991, p 39 *et seq*, Clarendon Press, Oxford, cited by Lord Goff in *Woolwich* [1993] AC 70, at 173; [1992] 3 All ER 737, at 760.

76 See the *dictum* of Holmes J in *Atchinson, Topeka & Santa Fe Railway Co v O'Connor* 223 US (1911) 280, at 285–86; considered with approval by Lord Goff in *Woolwich*, [1993] AC 70, at 172; [1992] 3 All ER 737, at 760; Lord Browne-Wilkinson at 198; 781; Lord Slynn at 203; 786; considered by Lord Jauncey to be inconsistent with existing English authority at 191; 776.

77 *Auckland Harbour Board v The King* [1924] AC 318; *Commonwealth v Crothall Hospital Services Ltd* (1981) 54 FLR 439; *Attorney General v Gray* (1977) 1 NSWLR 406.

78 [1993] AC 70, at 174; [1992] 3 All ER 737, at 761.

79 In *David Securities Pty Ltd v Commonwealth Bank of Australia* (1992) 175 CLR 353, the High Court of Australia at 374–75 appeared to explain *Werrin v The Commonwealth* (1938) 59 CLR 150 and *South Australian Cold Stores Ltd v Electricity Trust of South Australia* (1957) 98 CLR 65 as cases involving a compromise of a disputed claim both cases involving unlawful demands by public authorities.

authority. Nor should a public authority be able to deny restitution and take advantage of its own mistake in wrongfully demanding payment.

In *Commissioner of State Revenue (Vic) v Royal Insurance Australia Ltd*,[80] the High Court of Australia recently held that an insurance company was able to obtain restitution of stamp duties invalidly paid to the Revenue as a result of a mistake of law. In *State Bank v Federal Commissioner of Taxation*,[81] interest was awarded on the basis that the taxpayer had a right to restitution where taxes had been invalidly claimed and placed in a fund pending the outcome of litigation. In *Esso Australian Resources Ltd v Gas and Fuel Corporation of Victoria*,[82] Gobbo J held, however, that the *Woolwich* principle did not extend to a commercial agreement between Esso and the corporation, in which Esso had agreed to pay a tariff levied on the corporation by the government. Although the tariffs were subsequently found to be an illegal impost on the corporation, the payments were not recoverable by Esso in a claim for moneys had and received. Gobbo J considered that to permit such a claim could lead to claims by others further down the chain and produce uncertainty. The corporation had not declined to carry the plaintiff's gas nor had it even threatened legal action. Although paid under protest, Esso had, for commercial reasons, elected to pay and consequently was held to have submitted to the defendant's demand and compromised its position. It may be argued that this case falls into the category of a purely commercial dispute of a private rather than a public kind and is distinguishable from *Woolwich* in that it constituted a claim that was not directly brought against the appropriate public body. In a case of this kind, however, it is arguable that a payment of tax collected and paid through an intermediary like Esso should allow the taxpayer to claim restitution directly from the Revenue on the basis that the intermediary is no more than an agent for collection.

Given the flexible nature of a restitutionary claim, it may be possible for the Revenue to plead a change of circumstance. In *Royal Insurance Australia Ltd*,[83] Mason J observed that change of circumstance might afford a defence to a restitutionary claim for the recovery of invalidly paid revenue. If, for example, a local body was able to show that certain invalidly levied payments had been appropriated exceptionally for some purpose, this might afford a defence based on change of circumstance. The fact that the payer may have passed the cost of the impost on to third parties will not, however, afford a defence although the moneys may, in an appropriate case where the third party has been separately

---

80 (1994) 182 CLR 51.
81 (1995) 132 ALR 653.
82 [1993] 2 VR 99, at 107–08.
83 (1994) 182 CLR 51, at 65.

billed, be the subject of a successful claim in restitution only if the payer undertakes to hold the proceeds in trust, thus eliminating a windfall gain.[84] Restitution may be subject to legislative enactment restricting claims of this kind.[85]

Undue influence

Transactions may be set aside where undue influence has been exercised. Courts of equity have, however, never set aside gifts because of folly, imprudence, or want of foresight on the part of donors.[86] Similarly, an improvident bargain will not be rescinded merely because it was an unwise bargain. Nor will equity intervene merely because of an inequality of bargaining power between the parties. In *National Westminster Bank v Morgan*,[87] Lord Scarman observed that there had already been statutory intervention to enact restrictions on freedom of contract such as hire purchase and consumer protection legislation and doubted whether the courts should assume the burden of formulating further restrictions.[88]

(a) The concept of undue influence

Where the donee of a gift has occupied a position which has enabled he or she to exercise dominion over the donor, equity may set aside the gift. Where a contract has been induced by undue pressure or influence, equity may similarly intervene to prevent advantage being taken of unconscionable dealing. Restitution of property or benefits may be ordered so as to prevent unjust enrichment. In *Louth v Diprose*,[89] Brennan J, in the High Court of Australia, described undue influence as exploitative conduct.[90] Oppressive conduct of this kind may involve fraudulent or misleading dealing, cheating or other unconscionable acts. It may be effected by unreasonable attention, blandishments, and persuasions of

---

84 Mason J in *Royal Insurance Australia. Ibid*, at 78. See *Mutual Pools & Staff Pty Ltd v Commonwealth* (1994) 179 CLR 155, at 177; 191, followed in *Kleinwort Benson Ltd v Birmingham City Council* [1996] 4 All ER 733.

85 For example, s 4 of the Limitation of Actions (Recovery of Imposts Act) 1963, as amended by the Limitation of Actions (recovery of Imposts) Amendment Act 1993 and Schedule 6 of the State Revenue, Further Amendment Act 1995 (NSW). The State Taxation Amendment Act 1992 (Vict) was passed to ensure that moneys claimed in this way were refunded to third parties. Note, s 409 of the Income Tax Act 1976 (NZ) as to relief for excess tax.

86 *Allcard v Skinner* (1887) 36 Ch D 145, at 182–83; [1886–90] All ER 90, at 99 referred to by Brennan J in *Louth v Diprose* (1992) 110 ALR 1, at 9. See also Salmond J in *Brusewitz v Brown* [1923] 42 NZLR 1106, at 1109.

87 [1985] AC 686; [1985] 1 All ER 821.

88 *Ibid*, at 708; 830.

89 (1992) 110 ALR 1.

90 *Ibid* at 7; Lord Scarman in *National Westminster Bank* [1985] AC 686, at 705; [1985] 1 All ER 821, at 828 used the expression 'victimisation'. Deane J, in *Louth v Diprose* (1992) 110 ALR 1, at 14, also used this term.

an insidious description or by coercion or threats of violence.[91] Undue influence has been defined as an instance of equitable fraud.[92] Cases involving undue influence fall into two categories. The first category involves proven actual influence or pressure. On the other hand, the relationship between the parties may be of such a kind that a court will presume that a very advantageous gift or bargain was derived through undue influence. In this category, the onus will fall upon the advantaged party to show that the gift or transaction was entered into freely.[93]

(b) Actual undue influence

A person seeking to have a gift or a transaction set aside in equity for actual undue influence bears the onus of establishing that the gift was the product of the donee's exploitative conduct. Dixon J, in the High Court of Australia, in *Johnson v Buttress*,[94] observed that, in relation to cases of actual undue influence, facts must be proved that show the transaction was the outcome of such an actual influence over the mind of the donor that it cannot be considered a free act.[95] His Honour further described conduct of this kind as one of deliberate contrivance.[96] Two Australian cases illustrate actual undue influence. In *Farmers' Co-Operative Executors & Trustees v Perks*,[97] the plaintiff, who was the executor and trustee of the estate of a wife who had been murdered by her husband, successfully sought a declaration to set aside a transfer of her share in a farm owned by herself and her husband as tenants in common. The evidence established that the wife and her family had been exposed to a long history of violence and, because of the isolated nature of their existence, the husband was able to exercise considerable influence over her. It also established that she had assisted him to farm the property for many years, but she had relinquished her interest without any financial compensation for her effort. The High Court of Australia, in *Louth v Diprose*,[98] upheld an order for the re-conveyance of a property which had been transferred by a solicitor to his girlfriend for undue influence. Re-conveyance was upheld on the finding of the trial judge that the solicitor had purchased

---

91 *Idem.* See, also Lindley LJ in *Allcard v Skinner* (1887) 36 Ch D 145, at 181; [1886–90] All ER 90, at 99.

92 *Symons v Williams* (1875) 1 VLR 199, at 216.

93 *Allcard v Skinner* (1887) 36 Ch D 145, at 181–82; [1886–90] All ER 90, at 99–100; approved by Lord Scarman in *Morgan* [1985] AC 686, at 705–06; [1985] 1 All ER 821, at 828.

94 (1936) 56 CLR 113.

95 *Ibid*, at 134.

96 *Idem.* Further, see *Allcard v Skinner* (1887) 36 Ch D 145, at 181; [1886–90] All ER 90, at 99.

97 (1989) 52 SASR 399.

98 (1992) 110 ALR 1.

and transferred the house to the appellant because he had been infatuated with her and had become emotionally dependent on her. This had given her a position of dominance over him. She had manipulated his affections in various ways. Brennan J described her conduct as exploitative,[99] whilst Deane J observed that equity would intervene in these circumstances to prevent victimisation and unconscientious manipulation of the solicitor to part with his property.[100]

(c) Presumed undue influence

Presumed undue influence cases fall into two categories. First, those cases where the law has created protected categories and secondly, those cases where the relationship between the parties is one of dependence, reliance or confidence to such an extent that equity will presume a gift or improvident bargain was derived through a dominating influence.[101]

(i) Protected relationships

Protected relationships have been recognised in cases of parent and child,[102] guardian and ward,[103] trustee and *cestui que trust*,[104] solicitor and client,[105] physician and patient[106] and in cases involving religious influence.[107] Included also within the protected category are dispositions of property between engaged couples.[108] Where a case falls within one of the protected relationships, equity will set aside the gift or bargain unless the donee or advantaged party is able to rebut the presumption of influence.

---

99   *Ibid*, at 9.

100 *Ibid*, at 14.

101 *Allcard v Skinner* (1887) 36 Ch D 145, at 181; [1886–90] All ER 90; *Spong v Spong* (1914) 18 CLR 544, at 551 *per* Issacs J; *Johnson v Buttress* (1936) 56 CLR 113, at 134 *per* Dixon J.

102 *Lancashire Loans v Black* [1934] 1 KB 380; *Phillips v Hutchinson* [1946] VLR 270; *Powell v Powell* [1900] 1 Ch 243.

103 *Hatch v Hatch* (1804) 9 Ves 292; 32 ER 615; *Taylor v Johnson* (1882) 19 Ch D 603. Further, see uncle and niece, *Bank of New South Wales v Rogers* (1941) 65 CLR 42.

104 *Turnbull v Duvall* [1902] AC 429.

105 *Bank of Montreal v Stuart* [1911] AC 121; *Lloyd v Coote and Ball* [1915] 1 KB 242; *Westmelton (Vic) Pty Ltd v Archer* [1982] VR 305; *Re S & P* (1982) 66 FLR 315.

106 *Mitchell v Homfay* (1882) 8 QBD 587; *Radcliffe v Price* (1902) 18 TLR 466; *Williams v Williams* [1937] 4 All ER 34; *Haskew v Equity Trustees, Executors & Agency Ltd* (1919) 27 CLR 231.

107 *Huguenin v Baseley* (1807) 1 Ves 273; [1803–13] All ER 1; *Allcard v Skinner* (1887) 36 ChD 145; [1886–90] All ER 90; *Quek v Beggs* (1990) 5 BPR 11,761.

108 *Lovesy v Smith* (1880) 15 Ch D 655; *Lloyd's Bank Ltd; Bomze and Lederman v Bomze* [1931] Ch 289; *Zamet v Hyman* [1961] 3 All ER 933.

(ii) Solicitor and client

In *Lloyd v Coote and Ball*,[109] a solicitor acted for the plaintiff in the administration of the estate of her late husband. The husband had dealings with the defendant for many years and had retained his services on several occasions. After his death, the defendant procured acknowledgments from the wife evidencing outstanding professional fees which were statute-barred. She did not receive independent advice. Subsequently, in defence of an action for account, the defendant sought to rely on the acknowledgments. The court held that the acknowledgments did not assist the defendant and the items were statute-barred. Horridge J, said:[110]

> A solicitor is not permitted to take a benefit from his client unless he first advises her to take independent advice, and ... the defendant by obtaining these acknowledgments did obtain a benefit within the meaning of the rule, and the acknowledgments cannot stand.

(iii) Medical practitioner and patient

A medical practitioner in *Williams v Williams*[111] was able to retain a substantial gift made to him by a patient. The deed creating the gift had been explained to the plaintiff by her solicitor but she was not fully aware of the extent of the gift. The Privy Council considered that, although there was a relationship of a professional nature sufficient to invoke the presumption, the gift should not be set aside because the transaction was made as a result of an exercise of her free and independent will.

(iv) Gifts to clergy and religious institutions

In *Huguenin v Baseley*,[112] substantial gifts were made to a clergyman who had assisted in the management of the affairs of a woman after her husband had died. Prior to the gifts being made, she had, with the knowledge of the clergyman, dismissed her solicitors. She did not have a full understanding of the transaction into which she had entered. Accordingly, gifts to both the clergyman and members of his family were set aside because of undue influence. Gifts to a religious institution were also set aside in *Allcard v Skinner*.[113] The plaintiff, as a young

---

109 [1915] 1 KB 242.

110 *Ibid*, at 248.

111 [1937] 4 All ER 34.

112 (1807) 14 Ves 273; [1803-13] All ER 1. This case could also fall within the category of actual undue influence, since the clergyman concerned manipulated the relationship between himself and the donor so as to advantage himself and his family. Further, see *Quek v Beggs* (1990) 5 BPR 11, 761 *per* McLelland J, where a conveyance of real property to a pastor and his wife from a Church member was rescinded.

113 (1887) 36 Ch D 145; [1886-90] All ER 90.

woman, had entered a Sisterhood and had taken vows of poverty, chastity and obedience. She had been introduced to the Superior, who was a founder of the Sisterhood, by another founding member who had been acting as the plaintiff's religious confidant at the time. Under the rules which had been drawn up by a founder of the institution, she was obliged to give up her property either to her relatives, to the poor, or to the Sisterhood. The rules also stated that a sister could not seek advice of any person outside the Sisterhood without the permission of the Superior. Not only did the plaintiff make out a will leaving property to the Superior but she also made substantial gifts to the Sisterhood. The Court of Appeal held that these circumstances gave rise to a presumption of undue influence. Had she not delayed in making her claim, the gifts would have been set aside. Although she had some advice from her brother prior to entering the Sisterhood, the court considered that, at the time she made the gifts, she was not able to freely exercise her own mind concerning the disposal of her property.[114]

(v) Engaged couples

The courts have also granted special protection to engaged couples. In *Zamet v Hyman*,[115] the Court of Appeal considered the claim of an elderly widow to set aside a deed she had executed prior to her marriage in which she had agreed not to make any claim on the estate of her intended husband. The evidence established that she had trusted her husband and had been anxious to marry him. By marrying, she gave up her employment and a pension. Her husband died three years later and the children of his first marriage sought a declaration enforcing the deed. The court considered that, in these circumstances, the husband should have fully explained the consequences of executing the deed to his intended wife. Since he had not done so the deed was set aside. In modern society, however, the existence of undue influence should not be lightly presumed in cases of this kind.[116] In *Zamet v Hyman*, Donovan LJ doubted the application of the presumption to engaged couples and considered that relief should only be granted on proof of actual undue influence.[117]

---

114 *Ibid*, at 173; 94 *per* Cotton LJ; at 183–85; 97 *per* Lindley LJ; at 189–91; 104 *per* Bowen LJ. The court emphasised that the time at which the court should assess whether the gifts were affected by undue influence was at the time the gift was made, and not at the time she had entered the convent.

115 [1961] 3 All ER 933. Also, see *Page v Horn* (1848) 11 Beav 227; [1848] 50 ER 804.

116 *Ibid*, at 938 *per* Lord Evershed MR; 943 *per* Danckwerts LJ.

117 *Ibid*, at 942; In Australia, see *Johnson v Buttress* (1936) 56 CLR 113 and *Yerkey v Jones* (1939) 63 CLR 649, at 675. This point was considered by Brennan J in *Louth v Diprose* (1992) 110 ALR 1, at 7. There, Brennan J considered that 'it may no longer be correct to presume that a substantial gift made by a woman to her husband has been procured by undue influence, but the cases in which such a presumption has been made demonstrate that the relationship which places a donor at a special disadvantage may have its origin in an emotional attachment of a donor to a donee'.

(vi) Matrimonial relationships

Unlike engagement, marriage is not a relationship that will attract the presumption of undue influence.[118] The distinction can be justified on the basis that it is less natural for a person engaged and in contemplation of marriage to part with large gifts than a person in the relationship of marriage.[119] However, in *Yerkey v Jones*, where a wife argued unsuccessfully that she had become a surety for her husband as a result of his undue influence over her, Dixon J observed that the relationship of marriage had never been divested completely of what was described as an equitable presumption of an invalidating tendency.[120] His Honour considered that the burden of establishing that a wife's disposition of property or assumption of an obligation on behalf of her husband had not been improperly or unfairly procured might rest with a husband if the wife was able to show that the circumstances raised a doubt or suspicion of undue influence on his part.[121] In *Barclays Bank v O'Brien*, the House of Lords rejected a special rule for married woman in cases of this kind. Lord Browne-Wilkinson, however, considered that such transactions should still be scrutinised with care because many wives do repose in their husbands trust and confidence in their financial affairs.[122]

(vii) Other relationships of reliance and confidence

In *Johnson v Buttress*,[123] Dixon J observed that a presumption of undue influence applies whenever one party occupies or assumes towards another a position involving ascendancy or influence over that other, or a dependence or trust on his or her part. A person occupying such a position assumes a role akin to a fiduciary in that he or she assumes a responsibility to act exclusively in the interests of the person over whom there is dominance.[124] The cases in which a court has set aside gifts or contractual transactions for presumed undue influence arising out of a relationship of dominance have been described as infinitely various.

---

118 *Bank of Montreal v Stuart* [1911] AC 120; *MacKenzie v Royal Bank of Canada* [1934] AC 468.

119 *Yerkey v Jones* (1939) 63 CLR 649, at 675.

120 *Idem.* Cf *Bank of Victoria v Mueller* [1925] VLR 642, where relief was granted to a wife who sought to have a guarantee set aside. *Yerkey v Jones* was applied in *Re Halsted; ex p Westpac Banking* (1991) 31 FCR 337. In *Warburton v Whitely* (unreported, NSW Sup Ct CA, 10 February 1989), Kirby P criticised any rule of special protection as sexually discriminatory. In *Akins v National Australia Bank* (1994) 34 NSWLR 155, the Court of Appeal declined to follow *Yerkey v Jones* in so far as it was suggested that wives merited special protection as sureties. Further, see discussion, pp 252–54.

121 *Idem.* Further, see Latham CJ at 659.

122 [1994] 1 AC 180, at 188; [1993] 4 All ER 417, at 428–29.

123 (1936) 56 CLR 113.

124 *Ibid*, at 134–35. For a further application of the presumption in relation to estate agents and financial advisers, see *Union Fidelity Trustee Co of Australia Ltd v Gibson* [1971] VR 573.

Whether the presumption should apply in a particular case requires a meticulous examination of the facts.[125] The presumption does not necessarily apply because the parties are in a fiduciary relationship. In *Re Comber*,[126] the English Court of Appeal declined to apply the presumption where a mother, in the belief that she was fulfilling her late husband's wishes, assigned to her son a lease of a business owned by her husband and for many years managed by her son. Although the Court of Appeal considered that, as the manager of the business, the son was in a fiduciary relationship with his mother, the circumstances did not justify the presumption being invoked and the lease being set aside for the lack of independent advice.

(d) Presumed undue influence and gifts

In *Inche Noriah v Shaik Allie Bin Omar*,[127] the Privy Council held that a gift to her nephew by a Malay woman, who was old and illiterate, should be set aside where the nephew had management and control of her affairs. Although she had received independent advice from a lawyer who had acted in good faith, he was unaware that the gift consumed nearly all her assets and did not advise her that the more prudent course was to devise it to him in her will. It was held that, in these circumstances, the presumption of undue influence had not been rebutted. In *Re Craig*,[128] Ungoed-Thomas J set aside gifts bestowed over a four year period on a secretary-companion who been employed by an elderly man to assist him. The defendant was found to be an able and competent woman with a strong personality. The evidence established that the donor was totally dependent upon her. Within a month of commencing work, he had made his first gift of a substantial kind and he continued thereafter, without any independent advice, to make further gifts which largely dissipated his estate. Conversely, in *Re Brocklehurst*,[129] the Court of Appeal held that a gift by a wealthy and eccentric country gentleman of shooting rights over his property should not be set aside. The evidence established that the donee had performed various services for the donor during the later years of his life. The donor whilst insisting that a lease be drawn up by the donee's solicitor had refused to take independent

---

125 *National Westminster Bank v Morgan* [1985] AC 686; [1985] 1 All ER 821, at 831. In *Goldsworthy v Brickell* [1987] 1 All ER 853, at 865–69, the Court of Appeal considered the dominance rationale, suggesting that the cases of presumptive undue influence were more appropriately rationalised as cases of trust and confidence.

126 [1911] 1 Ch 723. Further, see *Union Bank v Whitlaw* [1906] VLR 711; *Jenyns v Public Curator* (1953) 90 CLR 113, at 133; *Cowan v Pigott* (1989) 1 Qd R 41.

127 [1929] AC 127; [1928] All ER 189.

128 [1971] Ch 95; [1970] 2 All ER 390.

129 [1978] 1 All ER 767.

advice. It was further considered that the relationship was not one in which the donee was in a position of dominance.

In Australia, the presumption of undue influence in relation to gifts has been considered on a number of occasions by the High Court. In *Spong v Spong*,[130] an elderly plaintiff, who was found to be mentally infirm, was successful in obtaining a declaration to set aside a gift of land made to his son who had acted as his business adviser. In *Watkins v Combes*,[131] the court upheld the rescission of a transfer of land by an elderly invalid who was incompetent to transact business. She had reposed her trust in the defendants who had offered, in return for the transfer, to look after her for the rest of her life. Similarly, in *Johnson v Buttress*,[132] a son obtained an order setting aside a transfer of land by his elderly father. Illiterate and of low intelligence, he was found to be dependent on others for advice and assistance. After the death of his wife he became dependent on the defendant who had also promised to take care of him for life. He did not have any independent advice concerning the transfer which was executed in the office of the donee's solicitor and expressed to be for natural love and affection. A gift of shares was, however, upheld in *Jenyns v Public Trustee*.[133] There, a elderly woman had successfully carried on a business for many years. She had arranged for the business to be transferred to a company at a price to be satisfied in part by the allotment to her of a certain number of fully paid shares. Nearly two-thirds of the remainder of the shares were transferred to a son who had lived with her and managed the business. He was also the person to whom she looked for advice. The transfer of the shares was upheld in this case because the donor had received independent advice before making the gift. Further, although eccentric, she was found to be fully aware of matters relating to the business and the nature of the transaction in question.

(e) Presumed undue influence in commercial transactions

The presumption has also been invoked to set aside commercial transactions in a variety of commercial situations. In *Lloyd's Bank v Bundy*,[134] the Court of Appeal set aside a guarantee made in favour of the bank by Bundy. Bundy and his son were both customers of the bank. Bundy had been requested by his son, who owned and operated a business which was experiencing financial difficulties, to provide a guarantee and collateral security over his home which the bank knew was his only

---

130 (1914) 18 CLR 545.
131 (1922) 30 CLR 180.
132 (1936) 56 CLR 113.
133 (1953) 90 CLR 113.
134 [1975] QB 326; [1974] 3 All ER 757.

asset. Although Bundy had been advised by his solicitor not to charge the house further since he had on two occasions provided security for the bank's advances, his son intimated to a new bank manager that Bundy would provide additional security. Consequently, the manager visited Bundy taking with him security documentation. At this meeting, Bundy was informed that the bank would continue to support his son only if he agreed to increase the amount of the guarantee and provide a further charge over the house. The manager did not, however, fully explain the financial position of the company. Although the son informed Bundy that the company's problems had arisen as a result of bad debts, the manager did not share this opinion. However, he did not reveal his concern to Bundy. Bundy agreed to sign the documents to assist his son. On the son's default in meeting the terms of the mortgage, the bank obtained an order for possession which the Court of Appeal set aside. Although, ordinarily, a bank did not stand in a fiduciary relationship to a customer, in this case, the court considered that there existed a sufficient relationship of trust and confidence.[135] The bank, which was fully aware of Bundy's circumstances, was also aware that Bundy was relying upon it for advice and should have advised him to seek independent advice before the securities were signed.[136]

Transactions relating to intellectual property have also been set aside where they are shown to have been induced by undue influence. In *O'Sullivan v Management Agency and Music Ltd*,[137] the plaintiff, O'Sullivan, who was a young musician, was successful in having several agreements relating to copyright and his profession as a musician rescinded. O'Sullivan relied for guidance on his manager who had negotiated production contracts on his behalf with a company of which the manager was a director. The effect of the agreements was to bind O'Sullivan in a much less advantageous way than if he had obtained independent advice. After a period, in which O'Sullivan became very successful, his relationship with his manager deteriorated, and he sought to have the agreements rescinded. It was held that the parties' relationship was based upon trust and reliance. Accordingly, undue influence was presumed and the agreements were set aside.

In New Zealand, undue influence featured in *Coleman v Myers*.[138] In this case, minority shareholders in a private family company successfully sought compensation from the managing director, Myers, and his father,

---

135 *Ibid*, at 339–40; at 765–67 *per* Lord Denning MR; at 341–42; at 767–72 *per* Sir Eric Sachs. Further, see *National Westminster Bank v Morgan* [1985] AC 686; [1985] 1 All ER 821. *Cf Commonwealth Bank v Smith* (1992) 102 ALR 453, at 476.

136 *Ibid* at 339–40; at 766 *per* Lord Denning MR; at 345–46; at 770–71 *per* Sir Eric Sachs.

137 [1985] 3 All ER 351. See also, *A Scroeder Music Publishing Co Ltd v Macaulay* [1974] 3 All ER 616; *Clifford Davis Management Ltd v WEA Records Ltd* [1975] 1 All ER 237.

138 [1977] 2 NZLR 225.

who was the chairman of the company, for their unconscionable conduct in gaining control of the company. Evidence that the relatives trusted Myers and his father and had relied on them for advice in relation to the transaction was of critical importance. Although Cooke J was the only member of the Court of Appeal to expressly refer to undue influence,[139] the other members of the court emphasised, in language appropriate to a finding of undue influence, the dominant role Myers and his father had played in the family company and the trust that had been placed in them.[140] Accordingly, they owed a fiduciary duty to the shareholders and should have disclosed relevant information and not made false or misleading misrepresentations concerning the apparent advantages of the transaction.

(f) Rebuttal of the presumption of undue influence

Once the evidence establishes a relationship of confidence sufficient to invoke the presumption, the presumption may be rebutted by establishing to the satisfaction of a court that a gift or benefit in the case of a contractual transaction was a spontaneous act.[141] Examination of the evidence may establish that this was so even though independent advice was not received.[142] In *Re Brocklehurst*,[143] for example, a gift was upheld in the absence of independent advice because it was considered to be a true act of friendship. However, the most effective means of ensuring a gift or transaction is not set aside for undue influence is to ensure that the party affected is independently advised.[144] It is unclear as to the quality of advice that should be given. Legal advice is not, however, a requisite.[145] In *Re Coomber*,[146] Fletcher Moulton LJ considered that care should be taken to ensure that the person affected fully understands the nature and consequences of the act in question. In *Inche Noriah v Shaik Allie Bin Omar*,[147] Lord Hailsham observed that the advice must be given with knowledge of all relevant circumstances and must be such as a competent and honest adviser would give if he or she was

---

139 *Ibid*, at 332–33.

140 *Ibid*, at 323–25 *per* Woodhouse P; at 371, *per* Casey J.

141 *Inche Noriah v Shaik Allie Bin Omar* [1929] AC 127.

142 See *Bakhsh Singh v Ram Gobal Singh* (1913–14) 30 TLR 138; *Inche Noriah v Shaik Allie Bin Omar* [1929] AC 127; *Linderstram v Barnett* [1915] 19 CLR 528; *Haskew v Equity Trustees Executors & Agency Ltd* (1919) 27 CLR 231, at 234; *Watkins v Combes* (1922) 30 CLR 180, at 195–96.

143 [1978] 1 All ER 767. Also, see *Williams v Williams* [1937] 4 All ER 34.

144 *Inche Noriah v Shaik Allie Bin Omar* [1929] AC 127, at 135.

145 *Idem*.

146 [1911] 1 Ch 723, at 730.

147 [1929] AC 127.

acting solely in the interests of the donor.[148] The quality of advice will also depend on the circumstances of the case. In the case of an elderly, unworldly man like Herbert Bundy,[149] or a person of little commercial experience,[150] a more precise explanation of the risks involved in the transaction will be necessary. If the adviser has insufficient knowledge of the effect a transaction will have, then the advice may be considered inadequate.[151] Further, in order for the advice to be effective, it should relate to the period in which the transaction takes place.[152] A conflict will often jeopardise the effectiveness of advice. In situations of conflict, an advisor, who is personally interested in a transaction, should insist on the party affected by the transaction seeking independent advice.[153]

An argument that the person affected by undue influence would have proceeded with the transaction irrespective of independent advice to the contrary was rejected by Sir Eric Sachs in *Lloyd's Bank v Bundy*.[154] His Lordship considered that there was normally no room for debate on the issue as to what would have transpired had independent advice been given. However, in *Haskew v Equity Trustees Executors Agency Co Ltd*,[155] Issacs J considered that the absence of independent advice should not vitiate a deed of settlement if independent advice would not have made any difference to the result. However, the court considered that the transaction in question could be explained as beneficial and a natural family settlement that, in any event, should not be set aside for undue influence.

(g) Manifest disadvantage

Equity is not ordinarily concerned with impeaching gifts that are insubstantial. In the ordinary course of life, small gifts may be explained

---

148 *Ibid*, at 135–36.

149 [1975] QB 326; at 339; [1974] 3 All ER 757; 768 *per* Lord Denning MR; at 345; 770–71 *per* Sir Eric Sachs who described the duty as 'independent and informed judgment' citing Lord Evershed in *Zamet v Hyman* [1961] 3 All ER 933. Further, see *Commonwealth Bank v Smith* (1992) 102 ALR 453, at 477–78.

150 As in *Powell v Powell* [1900] 1 Ch 243, at 247.

151 See the judgment of Salmond J in *Brusewitz v Brown* [1923] 42 NZLR 1106, at 1115–19.

152 *Allcard v Skinner* (1887) 36 Ch D 145; [1986–90] All ER 90.

153 *Bank of Montreal v Stuart* [1911] AC 120, at 139; *Powell v Powell* [1900] 1 Ch 243, at 246; *Lancashire Loans v Black* [1934] 1 KB 380; [1933] All ER 201; *Lloyd's Bank v Bundy* [1975] QB 326; [1974] 3 All ER 757.

154 *Ibid*, at 345; at 771. Further, see *Commonwealth Bank v Smith* (1992) 102 ALR 453, at 478–79; and *Brickenden v London Loan and Savings Co* [1934] 3 DLR 465, at 469; *Gray v New Augarita Porcupine Mines Ltd* [1952] 3 DLR 15 (PC); *Farringdon v Rowe McBride & Partners* [1985] 1 NZLR 83, at 93 to similar effect. The *Brickenden* principle was considered in *Stewart v Layton* (1992) 111 ALR 687, at 713–15. For further discussion, see Chapter 11, p 288.

155 (1919) 27 CLR 231, at 234.

as the product of charity, love or affection.[156] Where undue influence is alleged, equity will usually be concerned with gifts that are substantial.[157] In *National Westminster Bank v Morgan*,[158] the House of Lords also considered that equity could rescind a contractual transaction for undue influence only if it could be shown to be manifestly disadvantageous.[159] In that case, a wife and her husband mortgaged their family home to secure a loan that was urgently required to avoid a forced sale of the home by another secured creditor. The husband, who was experiencing financial difficulties with his business, had been unable to meet the repayments on the home which he and his wife owned jointly. The wife had no independent advice before entering into the arrangement with the bank. The parties fell into arrears and the bank obtained an order for possession. The wife sought to have the order set aside for undue influence on the ground that there existed a relationship of reliance and confidence between herself and the bank from which a presumption of undue influence arose. As a result, she contended that she should have been advised to seek independent advice before she executed the mortgage. The bank argued that her claim should not succeed because the transaction had not been manifestly disadvantageous to her. Further, it was submitted that she had been advantaged because the transaction had averted the threatened sale of her home. This argument, which was rejected in the Court of Appeal, succeeded in the House of Lords.[160] Subsequently, in *Bank of Credit and Commerce International SA v Aboody*,[161] the Court of Appeal held that a wife, who had given security to a bank to cover her husband's debts accrued in relation to his business, could not succeed in any of her claims to have various transactions set aside despite her husband's coercive conduct because she could not show a manifest disadvantage. In *CIBC Mortgages v Pitt*,[162] the House of Lords, however, held that the approach in *Aboody* was incorrect. A contract obtained through actual undue influence was voidable even though manifest disadvantage could not be established. Lord Browne-Wilkinson observed that undue influence of this kind was a species of

---

156 Lindley LJ in *Allcard v Skinner* (1887) 36 Ch D 145, at 185; [1886] All ER 90, at 101. See Ungoed-Thomas J in *Re Craig* [1971] Ch 95, at 103; [1970] 2 All ER 390, at 395; noted also by Lord Scarman in *Morgan, ibid*, at 706; at 830; and further, in Australia, Issacs J in *Spong v Spong* (1914) 18 CLR 545, at 550.

157 *Goldworthy v Brickell* [1987] 1 All ER 853.

158 [1985] AC 686; [1985] All ER 821.

159 Lord Scarman, *ibid*, at 706 referred to *Poosathurdi v Kanappa Chettiar* (1919) LR 47 Ind App 1 (PC) on the necessity for the plaintiff to establish that a sale was for undervalue. To similar effect, Issacs J in *Watkins v Combes* (1922) 30 CLR 180, at 194.

160 *Ibid*, at 703; at 831.

161 [1990] 1 QB 923; [1993] 4 All ER 955.

162 [1994] 1 AC 200; [1994] 4 All ER 433. Cope, M, 'Undue Influence and Manifestly Disadvantageous Transactions' (1986) 60 ALJR 87.

fraud and that a person who had been the victim of conduct of this kind was entitled to have the transaction set aside. The opinion of Lord Browne-Wilkinson also casts doubt on *National Westminster Bank v Morgan* and the necessity to establish manifest disadvantage in cases involving a presumption of undue influence. In his Lordship's opinion, the manifest disadvantage principle was inconsistent with the general rule that a fiduciary, who entered into a transaction with a beneficiary, was under an obligation to prove affirmatively that the transaction was fair in order to avoid rescission.[163]

(h) The liability of third parties for the undue influence of another

The liability of third parties for the undue influence of others will depend upon whether the third party had actual or constructive knowledge of circumstances that would put a reasonable person on inquiry. In recent years, the relevant principles have been closely examined in cases involving suretyship but they are of general application.[164] Contracts of guarantee or other transactions involving suretyship, such as the giving of collateral security for a loan, are not *uberrimae fidei*. A creditor, for example, is under no obligation to disclose to an intending surety matters that affect the credit of the debtor. It is incumbent upon the surety to initiate those inquiries and, if the creditor is asked, then a fair and accurate response should be given. A creditor is entitled to assume, in the absence of any request, that the intending surety has satisfied himself or herself of the debtor's credit unless there are unusual features relating to a particular account which the surety has been asked to guarantee, or the creditor has assumed the role of adviser. Similar considerations apply to any collateral security that a surety may provide.[165]

(i) Surety obligations affected by undue influence of which the debtor has actual or constructive knowledge

A guarantee and any collateral security may be set aside, however, if a creditor has actual knowledge that a debtor has obtained a surety through undue influence. This will include not only actual knowledge but wilfully turning a blind eye to the fact that a surety might be the

---

163 *Ibid*, at 209; 439. In Australia, the approach in *Morgan* and *Aboody* was followed in *Farmer's Co-operative Executors & Trustees Ltd v Perks* (1989) 52 SASR 399.

164 See *CIBC Mortgages v Pitt* [1994] 1 AC 200; [1994] 4 All ER 433. Further, see T*reize v National Australia Bank Ltd* (1994) 122 ALR 185.

165 *Hamilton v Watson* (1845) 12 CL & F 109; [1845] 8 ER 1339; *Goodwin v National Bank of Australasia Ltd* (1968) 117 CLR 173, at 175. Further, see the discussion of the relevant authorities by McTiernan J in *Bank of New South Wales v Rogers* (1941) 65 CLR 42, at 61; *per* Gibbs CJ in *Commercial Bank of Australia Ltd v Amadio* (1982–83) 151 CLR 447, at 463.

victim of undue influence.[166] Further, if the circumstances are sufficient to place a creditor upon inquiry, and no steps are taken to attempt to protect the surety, the creditor may be deprived of the advantage of any guarantee or security.[167] In *TSB Bank v Camfield*,[168] it was held by the Court of Appeal that, where a surety has given a charge under an innocent misrepresentation as to the extent of the charge and inadequate steps have been taken by the creditor to protect the surety, the charge will be set aside *in toto* and not merely *pro tanto* as to the amount that is in excess of the misrepresentation. It might be thought, however, that, as in *Camfield*, where the surety is content to incur an obligation less than that misrepresented, that a more equitable approach is to enforce the charge to that extent rather than set it aside completely. In *Vadasz v Pioneer Concrete Ltd*,[169] the High Court of Australia took this approach and granted only partial rescission of a contract of guarantee where there had been a fraudulent misrepresentation by the debtor of the extent of the surety's obligation.

(i) Actual knowledge

A guarantee and any collateral security may be set aside where the creditor has personal knowledge of the fact that the guarantee or security has been obtained by undue influence. A creditor will be fixed with the knowledge of an employee or agent.[170] In *Bank of Credit and Commerce International SA v Aboody*,[171] for example, the Court of Appeal held that a solicitor, who was instructed by a bank, was under a duty to report any circumstance which made it unsafe for the bank to rely on a security which a wife had provided under pressure from her husband.[172] Although the bank had instructed the solicitor with the intention that the wife should have legal advice, the solicitor did not report the fact that the husband had entered the room and placed pressure on his wife to sign. As a consequence, the solicitor's knowledge was imputed to the bank, and the security was set aside.

---

166 As to wilful blindness as opposed to mere negligent or reckless disregard see the observations of Gibbs CJ in *Giorgioni v R* (1985) 156 CLR 473, at 482. Also, Deane J in *Commercial Bank of Australia v Amadio* (1982–83) CLR 491, at 467 citing observations of Lord Cranworth LC in *Owen and Gutch v Homan* (1853) 4 HLC 997, at 1035; 'in some case, wilful ignorance is not to be distinguished in its equitable consequences from knowledge'.

167 *Barclays Bank plc v O'Brien* [1994] 1 AC 180, at 195; [1993] All ER 417, at 429 *per* Lord Browne-Wilkinson.

168 [1995] 1 All ER 951.

169 (1996) 184 CLR 102; (1995) 130 ALR 570.

170 *Lancashire Loans v Black* [1934] 1 KB 380; [1933] All ER 201; *Bank of Montreal v Stuart* [1911] AC 121. See the discussion, at Chapter 11, pp 301–02 on imputed knowledge.

171 [1990] 1 QB 923; [1992] 4 All ER 955.

172 *Ibid*, at 974; 981–82.

(ii) Constructive knowledge

Constructive knowledge is notice of relevant circumstances which would suggest to a creditor that he or she ought to make inquiry to ensure that the intended surety is not the victim of undue influence. The more suspicious the circumstances, the greater will be the need to make inquiry. Where undue influence is a real possibility, a prudent creditor will advise an intended surety to seek independent legal advice.[173] In *Lancashire Loans v Black*,[174] a young woman, who was living apart from her husband, was pressured by her spendthrift mother into signing a promissory note and giving collateral security to enable her mother to gain a further loan. It also covered the mother's past indebtedness. The defendant did not understand the nature of the transaction. Nor did she receive independent advice. Further, the documentation was signed in the presence of a solicitor who acted for the creditor, a moneylender, as well as her mother. The Court of Appeal held that the transactions should be set aside observing that the solicitor knew that she was living apart from her husband and would not receive advice from him and this knowledge could be imputed to the moneylender. In these circumstances, there was a real possibility of undue influence and the moneylender ought to have advised the young woman to seek legal advice. In Australia, a similar approach was taken by the High Court in *Bank of New South Wales v Rogers*.[175] The plaintiff had resided with her uncle since the death of her father. She relied upon him for all business advice and was induced by him to charge virtually the whole of her property in favour of the bank, as security for his overdraft, at a time when he was in dire financial difficulty. Although the plaintiff was of mature age, she had no business experience. The bank manager was aware that she lived with her uncle and, while not actually aware of their actual relationship, had reason to believe that some special relationship did exist. The manager knew that the plaintiff's property was unlikely to be redeemed. The court considered that the manager by making prudent inquiry should have realised that there was a possibility of undue influence. The relationship was sufficient for the court to presume undue influence. The bank was affected by the knowledge of its manager and had the burden of proving that the security was free from any undue influence which it could not do.[176] Accordingly, the security was set aside.

---

173 *Lancashire Loans v Black* [1934] 1 KB 380, at 416–17; [1933] All ER 201, at 214; *Bank of New South Wales v Rogers* (1941) 65 CLR 42, at 61 *per* McTiernan J; *Barclays Bank plc v O'Brien* [1994] 1 AC 180, at 195; [1993] 4 All ER 417, at 430–31 *per* Lord Browne-Wilkinson.

174 [1934] 1 KB 380; [1933] All ER 201.

175 (1941) 65 CLR 42.

176 *Ibid*, at 55 *per* Starke J; at 61 *per* McTiernan J.

(iii) Constructive knowledge and special relationships

Equity has traditionally exhibited a protective attitude to wives who have been the victims of undue influence by becoming sureties at the request of their husbands. Although marriage is not a relationship attracting a presumption of undue influence,[177] the fact that a wife is providing security is a circumstance which may place a bank on inquiry. In *Bank of Victoria v Mueller*,[178] Cussens J thought this was particularly so where the security covered a heavy past indebtedness.[179] In *Yerkey v Jones*,[180] Dixon J considered that the fact that a creditor explains a transaction to a wife will not prevent equity setting aside a transaction if undue influence by her husband induced her to consent to become a surety. Equity would intervene even if the wife understood the nature and extent of her obligations. In these circumstances, nothing but independent advice or relief from the ascendancy of the husband over her judgment would suffice to avoid the intervention of equity.[181] Equity would also grant relief to a wife where it is shown that she did not understand the transaction because her husband had misled her or acted unconscionably.[182] In circumstances of this kind, the adequacy of the steps taken by the creditor to have the transaction explained, taking into consideration the amount of deception practised by her husband and the level of her intelligence and business understanding, would determine whether relief should be granted. Dixon J, however, considered that, where a creditor had arranged for independent advice to be given, the circumstances would have to be very exceptional before equity would intervene.[183] In *Barclays Bank v O'Brien*,[184] the House of Lords showed a certain amount of ambivalence on the issue of a special rule for wives but ultimately dismissed the contention that they were deserving of a special rule. It was considered, in any event, that a creditor should not have to prove that a wife understood the nature of the transaction before any obligations of suretyship were enforced.[185] To do so, it was considered, would constitute an onerous requirement for financial institutions who

---

177 See discussion, p 243.

178 [1925] VLR 641. See also, in New Zealand, *Nixon v Fetzer* [1910] 30 NZLR 229.

179 *Ibid*, at 658.

180 (1940) 63 CLR 649.

181 *Ibid*, at 684 *per* Dixon J. Undue influence was not established and the wife's claim to be released as a surety failed.

182 *Ibid*, at 680; at 685–86 *per* Dixon J citing *Bank of Victoria Ltd v Mueller* [1925] VLR 641, at 651 with approval. In Australia, a transaction involving a wife as surety may be set aside on the grounds that it constitutes an unconscionable bargain, see *Re Halsted ex p Westpac Banking* (1991) 31 FCR 337; *Atkins v National Australia Bank* (1994) 34 NSWLR 155; also, in New Zealand, *Bowkett v Action Finance Ltd* [1992] 1 NZLR 449.

183 *Ibid*, at 685–86.

184 [1994] 1 AC 180; [1993] 4 All ER 417.

185 *Ibid*, at 195; 428.

frequently lent on the security of the matrimonial home[186] and further did not reflect the modern view that wives were not subservient to their husbands in regard to family finances.[187] Having said this, however, Lord Browne-Wilkinson referred to the opinion of Dixon J in *Yerkey v Jones* and observed that transactions in which a wife was a surety had an 'invalidating tendency',[188] because many wives still do repose trust in their husbands in relation to their financial affairs.[189] His Lordship considered that the informality of business dealings between husband and wife raised a substantial risk that the husband might have misled a wife on the extent of the risk she was undertaking.[190] Where the transaction appeared financially disadvantageous to the wife, and undue influence, misrepresentation[191] or other legal wrong by her husband was a possibility,[192] Lord Browne-Wilkinson considered that a creditor was under an obligation to reasonably ensure that a wife's consent had been regularly obtained. A creditor could avoid the intervention of equity if steps were taken to adequately warn a wife of the risks she was taking and she was informed that she should seek independent advice. If there was a probability of undue influence, the creditor would have to insist on independent advice. In this regard, Lord Browne-Wilkinson observed:[193]

> In the normal case, a financial institution will be able to lend with confidence in reliance on a wife's surety obligation provided that it warns her (in the absence of her husband) of the amount of her potential liability and of the risk of standing surety and advises her to take independent advice.

---

186 *Ibid*, at 188; 422.

187 *Idem*.

188 An expression used by Dixon J in *Yerkey v Jones* (1939) 63 CLR 649, at 675.

189 A view which Scott LJ shared in the *Court of Appeal* [1992] 4 All ER 983, at 1008–09.

190 [1994] 1 AC 180, at 196; [1993] 4 All ER 417, at 429.

191 Including concealing the true nature of the transaction, as in *Bank of Credit and Commercial International SA v Aboody* [1990] 1 QB 923, at 969; [1992] 4 All ER 955, at 978. A negligent misrepresentation will suffice, see *O'Brien* [1994] 1 AC 180, at 196; [1993] 4 All ER 417, at 428.

192 *Ibid*, at 197; 430. In the *Court of Appeal* [1992] 4 All ER 983, at 1008 Scott LJ considered liability would be incurred if the creditor had knowledge of circumstances in which undue influence was likely; *per* Purchas LJ, *ibid*, at 1013, where there was 'a real risk'.

193 *Idem*. In *Massey v Midland Bank* [1995] 1 All ER 929, the Court of Appeal considered that Lord Browne-Wilkinson's test was not meant to be exhaustive. In that case, the bank was held to have satisfied its duty even though the woman had been advised in the presence of her fraudulent lover to seek independent legal advice. In *Banco Exterior International v Mann* [1995] 1 All ER 936, a majority of the Court of Appeal held that the duty of a bank had been satisfied where it had insisted in a letter to the husband that the charge be explained to a wife by her solicitor and the solicitor certify that he had done so but the husband in fact arranged for the borrower company's solicitor to advise the wife. The more prudent practice in cases of this kind is, as Lord Browne-Wilkinson suggested, to advise the surety personally in the absence of his or her partner. Further, see *Banco Exterior International v Thomas* [1997] 1 All ER 46 where a presumption of undue influence and notice of it was rebutted by the fact that the surety had received independent advice against executing a guarantee and charge for the bank.

Lord Browne-Wilkinson also considered that this approach should apply in cases where the surety and the debtor cohabited, or, as in *Avon Finance Co Ltd v Bridger*,[194] where there was evidence that a creditor was aware that a surety reposed trust and confidence in the debtor.[195]

In *Akins v National Australia Bank*,[196] the Court of Appeal of New South Wales considered *Barclays Bank v O'Brien* and *Yerkey v Jones*, and declined to follow the observations of Dixon J. In this regard, it was considered that the availability of equitable relief pertaining to unconscionable bargains, as in *Commercial Bank of Australia v Amadio*,[197] was sufficient to protect a wife and a special rule was unnecessary. Whichever approach is taken, a prudent creditor should be alert to the possibility of a wife or any other person in a known position of dependence being coerced into becoming a surety and take reasonable steps to see that the transaction is properly explained. This burden will be discharged by advising an intended surety to seek independent advice.

If a creditor does take steps to advise the surety to seek independent advice and some intervening event for which the creditor is not responsible precludes the surety from receiving that advice, a transaction involving suretyship will not be set aside for undue influence. In *Coldunell v Gallon*,[198] the plaintiff lender had agreed to make an advance to the defendants, an elderly couple, knowing that the moneys would be given to their son for the purpose of his business. The plaintiff procured a charge from the defendants upon their home and it was anticipated that the loan would be repaid by the son. The solicitors acting for the plaintiff, who had no reason to distrust the son, sent the security documents for signing either through the post or via the son and enclosed with them letters to the defendants advising them to seek independent advice. In all probability, the son concealed the letters. The documents were executed in the presence of the son at a meeting with his solicitor. Subsequently, the son defaulted on his loan repayments and the plaintiff sought to enforce the charge. The trial judge found that the son had exercised undue influence over his parents and set aside the charge because he considered that the son had acted as agent of the plaintiff lender in having his parents sign the security documents. The Court of Appeal, however, considered that the charge should not have been set

---

194 [1985] 2 All ER 281.

195 *Idem*. This approach was adopted by Santow J in *Burke v Bank of NSW* (1995) 37 NSWLR 53. The bank was held to have had knowledge of circumstances where there was a substantial risk of wrongdoing. For a case outside the surety-creditor relationship, where an attempt to implicate a third party in the alleged undue influence of another failed, see *Tresize v National Australia Bank Ltd* (1994) 122 ALR 185.

196 (1994) 34 NSWLR 155.

197 (1982–83) 151 CLR 447.

198 [1986] QB 1184; [1986] 1 All ER 429.

aside. The plaintiff had not appointed the son as its agent. Any duty that the plaintiff owed the defendants had been discharged. The duty of the lender did not extend to ensuring that the defendants were independently advised or that they were signed in front of an independent solicitor. Oliver LJ observed:[199]

> ... the fact is that no lender can ever be absolutely sure that a guarantor is not being subjected to pressure from the principal debtor, and to require him to do more than properly and fairly point out to the guarantor the desirability of obtaining independent advice, and to require the documents to be executed in the presence of a solicitor, is to put on commercial lenders a burden which would severely handicap the carrying out of which is after all an extremely common transaction of everyday occurrence for banks and commercial lenders.

(iv) The debtor as the creditor's agent

Will the fact that documents evidencing a surety transaction have been given to the debtor be sufficient to deprive the creditor of the benefit of the transaction, if it later transpires that the debtor has exercised undue influence over the surety? The answer will depend on whether the debtor has become the agent of the bank for the purpose of having the documents executed by the debtor.[200] Some of the cases in which equity has granted relief in such circumstances are cases where the creditor also had constructive notice and was put upon inquiry of the possibility of undue influence. In *Avon Finance Co v Bridger*,[201] for example, not only did the finance company leave the security documentation to the debtor son to have executed by his elderly parents but the circumstances, known to the finance company, suggested a relationship of influence. In *Bank of Credit and Commerce International SA v Aboody*,[202] Slade LJ rejected an argument that equity could only grant relief to a surety where the creditor had given the security documents to a debtor for execution by the surety, if the circumstances were sufficient to put the creditor on

---

199 *Ibid*, at 1201; 440–41. It is doubtful whether this minimum standard could be said to have been met, however, in *Banco Exterior International v Mann* [1995] 1 All ER 936, where the creditor had written to the husband and not to the wife insisting on her solicitor explaining the transaction. The husband arranged for the debtor company's solicitor, which he owned and controlled, to advise her. A majority of the Court of Appeal, however, held that the creditor had satisfied its obligation to the wife.

200 See *Kingsnorth Trust Ltd v Bell* [1986] 1 All ER 423; *Midland Bank plc v Shephard* [1988] 3 All ER 17. Further, see *Chaplin & Co v Brammall* [1908] 1 KB 233; *Turnbull v Duvall* [1902] AC 429, *Turnbull v Duvall* was considered to be incorrectly interpreted as an agency case by Lord Browne-Wilkinson in *Barclays Bank v O'Brien* [1994] 1 AC 180; at 191–94; [1993] 4 All ER 417, at 425–27.

201 [1985] 2 All ER 281; *Coldunell v Gallon* [1986] QB 1184, at 1199; [1986] 1 All ER 429, at 439; *Midland Bank v Shephard* [1988] 3 All ER 17, at 23. *Avon Finance* was distinguished in *Tessman v Costello* (1987) 1 Qd R 283 on the ground that there was no suggestion that the lender knew of any disability in the parents.

202 (1990) 1 QB 923; [1992] 4 All ER 955.

constructive notice of the possibility of undue influence being exerted upon the surety. Slade LJ considered that, in *Avon Finance Co Ltd v Bridger*, the Court of Appeal had considered that there were two distinct bases for granting equitable relief for sureties affected by undue influence. Irrespective of whether the creditor had constructive notice, it was considered that it was inconsistent with the equitable nature of relief for the bank not to be affected by the undue influence exerted by its agent when the transaction would not exist but for the wrongful acts of it agent.[203] In *Barclays Bank plc v O'Brien*, Scott LJ construed agency to mean a true agency and not a spurious finding of agency in order to enable apparent justice to be done in hard cases.[204] It will be recalled that in *Coldunell v Gallon*,[205] the Court of Appeal reversed the finding of a trial judge that a son, who had exercised undue influence over his elderly parents, had acted as the lender's agent merely because he had obtained the execution of the security documents. As a result, the lender was able to enforce a charge taken over the elderly parents' home.

A similar approach to agency was taken by the New Zealand Court of Appeal in *Contractors Bonding Ltd v Snee*.[206] Mrs Snee, an elderly woman, agreed to provide a guarantee to a finance company, Contractors Bonding, at the request of her son, named Savage. Contractors Bonding was to furnish bond finance to Mr Savage's company, Marco Polo, on the condition that Savage and other shareholders enter into guarantees supported by caveats registered upon the titles to their homes. In return for Mrs Snee agreeing to provide a guarantee and mortgage over her home, Contractors Bonding subsequently agreed to discharge the caveats. Contractors Bonding caused the deed of guarantee to be sent to Marco Polo's office in Auckland for execution under seal and by Mrs Snee. Although Marco Polo, in this case, was the debtor, Savage was clearly advantaged by the transaction. He took the documents to his mother who resided outside Auckland. It was found that he obtained execution by

---

203 *Ibid* at 972; at 980. This approach would appear consistent with the approach of the House of Lords, in *Barclays Bank Plc v O'Brien* [1994] 1 AC 180; [1993] 4 All ER 417.

204 [1992] 4 All ER 983, at 1008. Indeed, Scott LJ questioned the propriety of the agency principle, and the explanation of *Chaplin & Co v Brammall* [1908] 1 KB 233 and *Turnbull v Duvall* [1902] AC 429 (*ibid*, at 992–93). Scott LJ preferred an approach which required proof of notice that a 'surety is a person who is likely to be influenced by and to have some degree of reliance on the debtor' (*ibid*, at 1109). Purchas LJ, *ibid*, at 1021, considered the agency principle should apply where 'the creditor entrusts to the husband himself the task of obtaining the execution of the relevant document by the wife ... '. In *Barclays Bank v O'Brien* [1994] 1 AC 180, at 194; [1993] 4 All ER 417, at 427, Lord Browne-Wilkinson considered that a debtor, who procured a person to act as surety in response to a request by a bank to arrange security, in consideration of finance being provided, did not thereby become the bank's agent. This would suggest that the House of Lords considered agency should have very limited application in cases of this kind.

205 [1986] QB 1184; [1986] 1 All ER 429. See discussion, p 254.

206 [1992] 2 NZLR 157.

undue influence. The trial judge held that the transactions relating to the guarantee and the charge over her home were related and should be set aside. Even though Contractors Bonding had no actual knowledge of any wrongdoing, knowledge of undue influence could be imputed because the documents had been entrusted to Savage for the purpose of obtaining his mother's signature. The Court of Appeal, however, disagreed.[207] There was no evidential basis for the finding that Contractors Bonding had entrusted the documents to Savage for execution. The guarantee had been sent to Marco Polo and the mortgage to a firm of solicitors, who were believed to be acting for both Marco Polo and Mrs Smee. It was incorrect to impute the conduct of the son to Contractors Bonding merely because Savage had taken the documents to her for execution. Aside, however, from whether agency was established, which was a question of fact,[208] McKay J considered that the fact that a document had been entrusted to a third party who had a motive for ensuring its execution would be a relevant circumstance in considering whether a creditor had notice of undue influence.[209]

Where documents have been handed for execution to a debtor or a third party, who is directly advantaged by the transaction, it is necessary to closely scrutinise the actions of a creditor. Given that a surety may be voluntarily undertaking a substantial commitment, it is not unduly onerous to require a creditor to ensure that the documentation is executed by the surety in the creditor's presence or before some agent, independent of the debtor, and fully explained with the opportunity given to seek independent advice so that the surety has an adequate understanding of the effect of the transaction.[210] A creditor should, as McKay J observed in *Snee*, be alive to the possibility of undue influence where documents are handed or sent for execution to a person who has an obvious interest in securing the signature of a surety. If the creditor fails to do either, the transaction may be set aside.[211]

---

207 In *Burke v State Bank of NSW* (1995) 37 NSWLR 53, at 79, Santow J indicated disagreement with the view taken by the New Zealand Court of Appeal in *Snee*, on both the question of knowledge and liability, when he held a bank liable after it had entrusted the execution of documents to a son of elderly parents.

208 [1992] 2 NZLR 157, at 183. Further, see *Burke v State Bank of New South Wales Ltd* (1994) 37 NSWLR 53 on constructive notice and agency.

209 *Idem.*

210 *Per* Dixon J in *Yerkey v Jones* (1940) 63 CLR 649, at 685. For a useful practical discussion on a solicitor's obligations, when concerned with rendering independent legal advice to guarantors in respect of secured or unsecured guarantees, see (1992) A & NZ Con R 469. Also, Lord Browne-Wilkinson in *Barclays Bank v O'Brien* [1994] 1 AC 180, at 197; [1993] 4 All ER 417, at 430.

211 *Cf Banco Exterior International v Mann* [1995] 1 All ER 936 (fns 193, 199). Where a bank was said to have discharged its obligations to a surety in very doubtful circumstances.

Unconscionable bargains

Relief may be granted in equity where a party under a special disability has entered into an improvident bargain and the other party to that transaction has sought to take advantage of the situation. Equity will not allow a person to become enriched as a result of an unconscionable abuse of a position of advantage. In order, however, to successfully claim relief, it is necessary to prove that the advantaged party had knowledge of the disability. This will include constructive knowledge as well as actual knowledge. Unconscionable advantage is taken not only where there is over reaching conduct by the advantaged party but also where there is a surreptitious obtaining of a benefit.

Where a party seeking relief is able to show that the advantaged party was aware of the disability, the bargain will be set aside unless the advantaged party has been independently advised. The approach of equity in cases of unconscionable bargains is similar to the approach taken in cases of undue influence. However, as Mason J observed, in the High Court of Australia in *Commercial Bank of Australia Ltd v Amadio*,[212] there is a difference between an unconscionable bargain and undue influence:[213]

> In the latter, the will of the innocent party is not independent and voluntary because it is overborne. In the former, the will of the innocent party, even if independent and voluntary, is the result of the disadvantaged position in which he is placed and of the other party unconscientiously taking advantage of that position.

(a) Special disability

Equity will only protect those who are suffering under a special disability or are placed in some special situation of disadvantage.[214] Historically, the remedy originated in England to avoid catching bargains made with expectant heirs.[215] It was extended to sales of property made at considerable undervalue by poor and ignorant persons who had acted without independent advice.[216] In *Richardson v Harris*,[217] the New Zealand Court

---

212 (1982–83) 151 CLR 447.

213 *Ibid*, at 461; at 474 *per* Deane J.

214 *Ibid*, at 461–63 *per* Mason J.

215 See the discussion in *O'Rorke v Bolingbroke* (1877) 2 App Cas 814, at 823; *Davies v Cooper* (1840) 5 M & Cr 270; [1840] 41 ER 373.

216 *Baker v Monk* (1864) 4 DeG J & S 388; [1864] 46 ER 968; *Clark v Malpas* (1862) 4 DeG F & J 401; [1862] 45 ER 1238; *Fry v Lane* (1888) 40 Ch D 312; and the discussion by Salmond J in *Brusewitz v Brown* [1923] 42 NZLR 1106; in England, in *Cresswell v Potter* [1978] 1 WLR 255; in Australia, in *Blomley v Ryan* (1956) 99 CLR 362, at 428–29 *per* Kitto J, and Deane J in *Commercial Bank of Australia v Amadio* (1982–83) 151 CLR 447, at 474–75.

217 [1930] NZLR 890 (SC) 915 (CA).

of Appeal set aside a transaction in which a money lender had taken advantage of a farm labourer in acquiring his only asset, a life interest in a fund set aside for his benefit. There was evidence that the plaintiff was 'palpably dull' and inexperienced in matters of finance. Further, the money-lender knew of his impoverished circumstances and his pressing financial needs. The price paid by the money-lender was considered grossly inadequate. In *Blomley v Ryan*,[218] the High Court of Australia considered that a sale made by a landowner, who was in all probability under the influence of alcohol at the time of the transaction, to have been correctly set aside. There was evidence that the aged landowner indulged habitually in drinking bouts which was known to a stock agent who had been influential in concluding the sale at the behest of the plaintiff's father. The vendor's alcoholism was also known to the plaintiff's father who was keen to purchase the property on his son's behalf. Further, the evidence established that the property could have attained a considerably higher price. The vendor had not been given any independent advice and the solicitor had not discussed the price with him. The solicitor had been instructed by the stock agent to prepare the agreement which the defendant had signed at a hastily convened meeting attended by the stock agent and the defendant's father. A majority of the High Court considered that the trial judge had been correct to refuse specific performance and to have the agreement set aside. Fullager J considered that, although drunkenness in itself was no ground to justify an agreement being set aside, it would be unconscionable to allow the plaintiff to knowingly take advantage of the plaintiff's condition. On this point, Fullager J observed:[219]

> The circumstances adversely affecting a party, which may induce a court of equity either to refuse its aid or to set a transaction aside, are of great variety and can hardly be satisfactorily classified. Among them are poverty or need of any kind, sickness, age, sex, infirmity of body or mind, drunkenness, illiteracy or lack of education, lack of assistance or explanation where assistance or explanation is necessary. The common characteristic seems to be that they have the effect of placing one party at a serious disadvantage *vis-a-vis* the other.

Kitto J said of this 'well known head of equity' that it applied:[220]

> ... whenever one party to a special transaction is at a special disadvantage in dealing with the other party because illness, ignorance, inexperience, impaired faculties, financial need or other circumstances affect his ability to conserve his own interests and the other party unconscientiously takes advantage of the opportunity thus placed in his hands.

---

218 (1956) 99 CLR 362.
219 *Ibid*, at 405.
220 *Ibid*, at 415.

Unconscionable bargains were further considered by the High Court of Australia in *Commercial Bank of Australia v Amadio*.[221] A majority of the court granted relief to an elderly Italian couple, who had become sureties, so that their son, who was considerably in debt to the bank, could have his overdraft extended. Mason J considered that the defendants were placed at a special disadvantage because of their reliance and confidence in their son, who had misled them as to his financial circumstances. Further, their age, limited command of English and absence of business experience were also matters which placed them at a disadvantage. Mason J considered that the fact that the couple believed their son to be in a prosperous enterprise, whereas, to the knowledge of the bank, the business was in very serious difficulty, placed them at a further serious disadvantage.[222] Deane J considered that the absence of any independent advice in relation to the complicated legal documentation that they were asked to sign was another matter which placed Mr and Mrs Amadio at a serious disadvantage.[223]

(b) Knowledge of the special disability

In order to succeed in a claim for relief, the plaintiff must show that the defendant knew or was aware of circumstances which would put a reasonable person interested in the transaction on inquiry. In *Blomley v Ryan*,[224] the fact that the vendor laboured under the influence of alcohol was well known to the purchaser's father and the stock agent who had been influential in obtaining the contract. Further, the circumstances in which the transaction came to be signed suggested more than surreptitious involvement. In *Amadio*,[225] the bank was also aware that the parents, Mr and Mrs Amadio, laboured under a mistaken apprehension as to the prosperity of their son and the soundness of his business ventures. Entry into the transaction for the parents was potentially disastrous though very advantageous for the bank, since the bank was secured not only for future advances but for a very substantial prior indebtedness as well. In these circumstances, the bank had an obligation to ensure that the parents were informed as to the true state of their son's financial position and had been advised to seek independent advice. Although actual dishonesty

---

221 (1982–83) 151 CLR 447. The approach in *Amadio* has been also applied in *National Australia Bank Ltd v Nobile* (1991) 100 ALR 227; *Re Halsted ex p Westpac Banking* (1991) 31 FCR 337, where a bankruptcy notice against a wife, who had become surety for her husband, was set aside as an unconscionable bargain. In New Zealand, see *Bowkett v Action Finance Ltd* [1992] 1 NZLR 449.

222 *Ibid*, at 464–68. Wilson J, *ibid*, at 468 appeared to consider that the bank was in a position of conflict because of its special relationship with Vincent Amadio.

223 *Ibid*, at 478–81.

224 (1956) 99 CLR 362.

225 (1982–83) 151 CLR 447, at 466–68 *per* Mason J; at 477–81 *per* Deane J.

was not imputed to the bank, it was the majority opinion that the bank had sufficient notice of the circumstances of the parents' vulnerability to justify the mortgage being set aside. Since, Mr and Mrs Amadio did not receive independent advice, the bank was unable to rebut the presumption that the transaction was unconscionable. Deane J described the state of mind of the bank as 'wilful ignorance'.[226] Where, however, knowledge is not present and the circumstances do not evidence the necessity for inquiry, an agreement will not be set aside even though a party is labouring under a serious disability such as dementia.

(c) Unsound mind and unconscionable bargains

Unsound mind *per se* was held by the Privy Council in the New Zealand case of *O'Connor v Hart*[227] to be insufficient to set aside a contract on the ground that it constituted an unconscionable bargain. Hart had purchased land from the predecessor in title of O'Connor, who, at the time of the transaction, had been found to have senile dementia. Hart had not known about the vendor's disability prior to entering the transaction. The Court of Appeal had set aside the agreement on the basis that there was a marked contractual imbalance in the consideration paid for the property. The court considered that the purchaser's absence of knowledge was not fatal to the claim that the agreement should be set aside. The purchaser was entitled to compensation for the improvements he had made to the property on taking possession. The Privy Council held, however, that the Court of Appeal was in error. Lord Brightman, in delivering the judgment of the Board, observed that there was no equitable fraud, no victimisation, no taking advantage, no over reaching or other description of unconscionable conduct which might have justified the intervention of equity to restrain an action at law.[228]

The issue of incapacity for senile dementia had arisen in an earlier New Zealand case of *Archer v Cutler*.[229] After a consideration of English authorities, McMullin J concluded in this case that there were no reasons in law or as a matter of policy why relief could not be granted to set aside a contractual transaction for incapacity where there had been a substantial undervalue in the sale of some land. The incapacitated party was a woman who suffered from advanced senile dementia at the time of the transaction. This was unknown to the other contracting party. Further indicia of unfairness, apart from price, was the absence of any independent legal advice, and the difference in bargaining positions

---

226 *Ibid*, at 479.

227 [1985] 1 AC 1000; [1985] 1 NZLR 159; in the Court of Appeal, [1983] NZLR 280; [1984] 1 NZLR 755; considered in *Tresize v National Australia Bank* (1994) 122 ALR 185, at 195.

228 *Ibid*, at 1024; 171.

229 [1980] 1 NZLR 386.

arising from the disparity in their respective positions. This approach was subsequently adopted by the Court of Appeal in *O'Connor v Hart*. Lord Brightman, however, considered that relief could not be granted for incapacity at law or in equity, where it could not be shown that the other party had knowledge of the disability. Lord Brightman also considered that the High Court of Australia in *McLaughlin v Daily Telegraph Newspaper Ltd (No 2)*[230] had approved the more restrictive English approach to contractual transactions affected by unsound mind.[231] Subsequently, in *Scott v Wise*,[232] the New Zealand Court of Appeal applied *O'Connor v Hart* and declined to set aside a settlement of a farm property made by a farmer who was suffering from dementia at the time of the transaction. It had not been alleged that the respondents had known of the settlor's incapacity. The settlement was characterised as a contractual transaction since there was some consideration present. The court, however, considered that a purely voluntary settlement of property could be set aside in equity even though it could not be established that the donee or recipient had knowledge of the settlor's disability.[233]

O'Connor v Hart may be considered a rather arid approach to the problem of contractual transactions, unsound mind and unconscionable bargains. In cases like *Archer v Cutler*, where there is a substantial contractual imbalance established, it should not be beyond the jurisdiction of equity to grant relief. It is very arguable that parties who suffer from serious mental illness which precludes them from fully understanding a transaction should be entitled to special consideration. It is submitted that a better solution, where a person is innocent of any wrongdoing but seeks to take advantage of a substantial contractual imbalance in a case of this kind, is to give that party an opportunity to elect whether to accept rescission of the agreement or, as the price for not doing so, redress the contractual imbalance. In cases of this kind, a court is faced with two innocent parties. The approach in *O'Connor v Hart* unfairly penalises a person, who cannot, in any true sense, be said to have assented to the disadvantageous terms of the transaction. As a condition of rescission, the person of unsound mind should be required to restore any benefits that have been derived from the transaction. In *O'Connor v Hart*, for example, the Court of Appeal allowed Hart compensation for the improvements he had effected to the property prior to the agreement being rescinded.

---

230 (1904) 1 CLR 243, at 274–75 *per* Griffiths CJ. However, this case was not concerned with a contract but with the validity of transactions made pursuant to a power of attorney given by a person of unsound mind. What was said by Griffiths CJ on the issue of contracts was *obiter*. In *Gibbons v Wright* (1953–54) 91 CLR 423, at 444 the High Court expressly left open the issue of whether a contract could be avoided where it was entered into by a person of unsound mind with a person who was unaware of the disability in circumstances of unfairness.

231 Such as *Moulton v Camroux* (1849) 18 LJ Ex 68; *Imperial Loan Co v Stone* [1892] 1 QB 599; *York Glass Co v Jubb* (1926) 134 LT 36.

232 [1986] 2 NZLR 484.

233 *Ibid*, at 493.

(d) Contractual imbalance

In *Blomley v Ryan*,[234] Fullager J observed that it was not essential that there be loss or disadvantage shown to justify a transaction being set aside where a special disability was evidenced. However, it was also observed that the existence of a contractual imbalance was a matter from which disadvantage and unconscionable dealing could be inferred.[235] This point was also made by Cooke P in *Nichols v Jessup*.[236] In an effort possibly to avoid the rigour of *O'Connor v Hart* it was considered that a gross contractual imbalance might assist a court to arrive at a finding that the advantaged party ought to have made inquiry to ascertain whether the other party was acting under a disability. Imbalance is particularly relevant in cases where actual victimisation is not proven. Where there is serious imbalance, this may point to a surreptitious course of dealing or sharp practice.[237]

(e) The Contracts Review Act 1980 (New South Wales)

The purpose of this legislation is to enable persons who have entered into contracts, which contain harsh or excessively onerous terms, to apply to a court for relief. In circumstances where a contract is found to be unjust, meaning unconscionable, harsh or oppressive, relief may be granted. A court may refuse to enforce any or all of the contract, declare whole or any part of the contract void, vary the whole or any part of the contract, or order the execution of an instrument varying or terminating the operation of an instrument transferring title to land or creating an interest in land.[238] A court, in considering whether a contract is unjust, is empowered to consider the public interest and other relevant circumstances including inequality of bargaining position, whether a person was able to protect his or her interests, the relative economic circumstances of the parties including educational background, and literacy; whether the agreement was negotiated and entered into with the assistance of independent advice, and whether any undue influence, unfair pressure or unfair tactics were exerted on the party seeking relief.[239] Also relevant are the circumstances surrounding the making of the contract, including its purpose, setting and effect, and whether it is a commercial contract. A court is not, however, entitled to have regard to injustice arising out of the contract if it was not foreseeable at the time of agreement. A court may consider the conduct of the parties after the

---

234 (1956) 99 CLR 362.
235 *Ibid*, at 405.
236 [1986] 1 NZLR 226.
237 *Ibid*.
238 Section 7.
239 Section 9(2).

contract was made, when considering whether to grant relief for a contact which is unjust, and may grant relief even though a contract has been put into effect. The Act excludes persons who have entered into a contract in the course of trade, business or profession carried on, or proposed to be carried on by that person. Farming undertakings, however, fall within the Act.[240] The Act expressly provides that it is an offence to attempt to contract out of the provisions of the legislation. A genuine compromise of a claim is protected where the claim was asserted before the making of the contract.[241] Remedies under the Act are additional to any other law providing relief against an unjust contract.[242]

Predictably, cases under the Act involve similar considerations to those cases decided under the general law relating to undue influence or unconscionable bargains. Thus, in *Sharman v Kunert*,[243] a sale of land at a considerable contractual imbalance was set aside where it was shown that the vendor was illiterate and did not have adequate advice. In *Antonovic v Volker*,[244] a contract was set aside where a real estate agent had applied unacceptable pressure on a purchaser at auction. In *Baltic Shipping Co 'the Mikhail Lemantov' v Dillon*,[245] a release of a claim for personal injuries and personal effects was set aside on the grounds that the amount for which release was given was grossly disproportionate to the damages that the plaintiff was found to be entitled. The court also considered that there was a disparity in the parties' respective bargaining positions, and the plaintiff's physical and emotional condition, at the time of signing the release, affected her ability to adequately protect her own interests. The Court of Appeal, however, in *West v AGC (Advances) Ltd*,[246] declined to grant relief to a wife who had given a mortgage over her home to a finance company primarily for the purpose of assisting her husband in business. The plaintiff had received independent advice from her son, who was an accountant, and a barrister friend not to give the security. In *SH Lock (Aust) Ltd v Kennedy*,[247] the Court of Appeal gave

---

240 Section 6(2).

241 Section 17(4).

242 Section 22.

243 (1985) 1 NSWLR 225.

244 (1986) 7 NSWLR 151.

245 (1991) 22 NSWLR 1; *Cf Webb v Australian Agricultural Machinery Pty Ltd* (1991) 6 WAR 305, a settlement was upheld where the disability of the complainant was unknown to the employer and the consideration for the release of common law liability was held, in the circumstances, to be adequate. See the observations of Malcolm CJ and Wallace JJ on the desirability of independent legal advice in such circumstances. *Cf Adenan v Buise* [1984] WAR 61. Further, on the issue of settlements and unconscionable bargains under the general law, see also *Moffat v Moffat* [1984] 1 NZLR 600.

246 (1986) 5 NSWLR 610.

247 (1988) 12 NSWLR 482.

partial relief where the plaintiff had given an unlimited guarantee to assist her son-in-law in business, she having been misled into believing that the guarantee was for a limited amount only.

The Act enables a court to grant relief in respect of an improvident contract, even though the party advantaged had no knowledge of the disability. In this sense, the jurisdiction exceeds that of a court in equity to grant relief on the ground of an unconscionable bargain. In *Beneficial Finance Corporation Ltd v Karakas*,[248] the Court of Appeal dismissed an appeal which sought to challenge relief granted to a mortgagor-guarantor in circumstances where a defence based in equity on unconscionable bargain had failed. The disability, which led to relief being granted, related to the respondent's lack of knowledge of the risks involved in guaranteeing the loan in question, taking into account the uncertainty of the venture for which finance had been advanced. Meagher J considered that the Act was remedial and should be interpreted liberally, free from the fetters imposed by analogous legal and equitable doctrines,[249] a view which Kirby P also shared.[250] Meagher J, however, cautioned against an over liberal exercise of the jurisdiction, because it was unjust for an innocent person to be deprived of valuable property of which contractual rights were a species.

(f) Supplementary legislation

Consumer protection legislation has also enhanced the court's power to grant relief from unconscionable contracts for the sale of goods and services. In Australia, under s 51AB of the Trade Practices Act 1974, a corporation is prohibited from engaging in unconscionable conduct in trade or commerce, in connection with the supply of goods or services of a kind ordinarily acquired for personal, domestic or household use or consumption.[251] Each of the states, the Territories[252] and New Zealand have enacted Fair Trading Acts, which are intended to place fetters on unconscionable conduct by individuals in relation to the provision of goods and services in certain circumstances relating to consumer transactions. Further, the Credit Acts of New South Wales (1984), Victoria (1984), Western Australia (1984), Queensland (1987) and the Australian Capital Territory (1985) restrict unconscionable conduct in credit transactions

---

248 (1991) 23 NSWLR 256.

249 *Ibid*, at 277 citing *West v AGC Advances Ltd* (1986) 5 NSWLR 610.

250 *Ibid*, at 267.

251 *Zoneff v Elcom Credit Union Ltd* (1990) 94 ALR 445.

252 Section 43(1) NSW (1987); ss 13, 28 Vic (1985); s 39(1) Qld (1989); s 52(1) South Aust (1987); s 11(1) Western Aust (1987); s 15(1) Tas (1990); s 43(1) NT (1990); s 13(1) ACT 1992. Also, see ss 14 and 23 of the Fair Trading Act 1986, New Zealand.

falling within the ambit of the Acts.[253] In New Zealand, the Credit Contracts Act 1986 gives a court wide powers to grant relief from contracts involving the provision of credit that are oppressive. Oppressive includes conduct that is harsh, unjust or unconscionable.[254] A detailed consideration of these Acts is, however, beyond the scope of this book.

---

253 For unconscionable dealing and credit transactions, see *Tirant v LNS Autos Pty Ltd* (1986) ASC 55–470; *Luffrum v Australia and NZ Banking Group Ltd* (1986) ASC 55–483; *Hammon v Alliance Acceptance Co* (1989) ASC 58, 517; *Morelend Finance Corp Pty Ltd v Westendorp* [1993] 2 VR 284.

254 See *Italia Holdings (Properties) Ltd v Lonsdale Holdings (Auckland) Ltd* [1984] 2 NZLR 1; *Anderson v Burbery Finance Ltd* [1986] 2 NZLR 20; *Manion v Marac Finance Ltd* [1986] 2 NZLR 586; *Kerr v Ducey* [1994] 1 NZLR 577.

CHAPTER 11

Benefits Derived Through Breach of Fiduciary Duty

The important issue of the liability of fiduciaries and others who are under a duty to act in good faith and not compete with their principals will be considered in this chapter. Those who do so and those, who knowingly assist in a breach of trust or receive trust property in circumstances where it ought to have been appreciated that it was not legitimately obtained, will be liable to surrender their gains. Courts have wide powers to grant remedies, generally equitable, that may be tailored to prevent unjust enrichment in the circumstances of the case. In addition to personal remedies, the issue of proprietary relief for those who have suffered loss as a result of a breach of trust will be considered. Proprietary remedies are important where trust property has found its way illegitimately into the hand of a bankrupt or insolvent company and the victim wishes to obtain priority over the general creditors of the trustee or third party who is wrongfully in possession of the property. The courts insist on a high level of probity where a duty of good faith is owed and strive to prevent unjust enrichment derived from a breach of a fiduciary obligation.

The conflict principle

In *Aberdeen Railway v Blaickie Brothers*, Lord Cranworth LC described the duty of a fiduciary, who was a chairman of directors of Aberdeen Railway, as:[1]

> ... a rule of universal application that no one having such duties to discharge shall be allowed to enter into engagements in which he has or can have a personal interest conflicting or which may possibly conflict with the interests of those whom he is bound to protect.

In that case, the plaintiff firm sought to enforce a contract for the supply of merchandise to Aberdeen Railway. The chairman of directors, who was also a member of the firm, had negotiated the contract. The House of Lords held that the contract could not be enforced because it had been obtained as a result of the director's breach of fiduciary duty to his principal, the railway company. Lord Cranworth LC went on to say:[2]

> It was Mr Blaickie's duty to give to his co-directors, and through them to the company, the full benefit of all the knowledge and skill

---

1   (1853–54) 1 Macq 461, at 472; (1843–60) All ER 249, at 252.
2   *Ibid*, at 473; 253.

which he could bear on the subject. He was bound to assist them in getting the articles contracted for at the cheapest possible rate. As far as related to the advice he should give them, he put his interest in conflict with his duty, and whether he was the sole director, or only one of many, can make no difference in principle. The same observation applies to the fact that he was not the sole person trading with the company. He was one of the firm of Blaickie Brothers with whom the contract was made, and so was interested in driving as hard a bargain with the company as he could induce them to make.

The rule that a fiduciary should not place himself in a position of conflict has been strictly applied. Thus, in *Keech v Sandford*,[3] a trustee was held liable to hold in trust a lease which the trustee had obtained personally after the lessor had declined to renew the lease for the beneficiary. Despite the fact that the trustee had attempted to secure the lease for the beneficiary, but had failed to do so through no fault of his own, he was held liable to hold it in trust thereby securing an unexpected windfall for the beneficiary. The strictness of the rule that a fiduciary must not compete with his principal applies even though there is no demonstrable loss to the principal and the fiduciary has acted honestly. Thus, in *Regal Hastings v Gulliver*,[4] directors of a company, Regal, who with Regal had taken up shares in another company, Amalgamated, with a view to acquiring certain cinemas for resale, were held liable to account to Regal for the profits they made on the sale of their shares in Amalgamated after the venture had been brought to a successful conclusion. Despite the fact that Regal would have been unable to finance the venture from its own funds and could not on its own account embark on the transaction, the directors were liable to surrender the profit they had realised. This provided a windfall gain to the incoming purchasers and shareholders of Regal who had commenced action to force the previous directors of Regal to account. This outcome could have been avoided had the directors held a general meeting and used their voting powers to approve the transaction.

A similar result was arrived at in the decision of a divided House of Lords in *Boardman v Phipps*.[5] Boardman, a solicitor to a family trust, had been asked to make inquiries on behalf of the trust with a view to improving the poor performance of a company, Lister & Harris, in which the trust had a sizeable minority shareholding. Boardman had attempted to have a beneficiary of the trust appointed to the board of the company but this was met with hostility. A trustee, Fox, who was an

---

3   (1726) Sel Cas, Ch 61; [1558–1774] All ER Rep 230. *Cf Holder v Holder* [1968] Ch 353; [1968] 1 All ER 665; *Re Thompson's Settlement* [1986] Ch 99; [1985] 2 All ER 720; applied in *Chan v Zacharia* (1983–84) 154 CLR 179.

4   [1967] 2 AC 135; [1942] 1 All ER 378.

5   [1967] 2 AC 46; [1966] 3 All ER 721.

accountant, had indicated his opposition to the trust increasing its shareholding. Without the sanction of a court, the trust was unable to acquire any further shares. However, Fox agreed with Boardman and his co-adventurer, Thomas Phipps, who was a beneficiary under the trust, that they should acquire controlling shares in the company. It was seen as an obvious advantage for the trust to have these shares held in friendly hands. Boardman and Phipps, whose interests were treated as identical in an action commenced by a dissatisfied brother and beneficiary, John Phipps, were held liable to account to the trust for the substantial capital profits that were made on their rationalisation of the company after they had acquired the shares. Although they had acquired much of their knowledge as to the potential profitability of the shareholding as representatives of the trust, they had acted openly and honestly with the trustees and the plaintiff both of whom had appeared to support the transaction. They were, however, allowed a generous discount for their endeavour which had enhanced not only their own interests but the value of the trust's shareholding.

In *Guinness plc v Saunders*,[6] however, a director of a company, who had negotiated a substantial take-over transaction, was not permitted to retain commission which had not received the sanction of the Board under the articles of the company. Nor did the House of Lords consider that there was room to make an equitable allowance in these circumstances. Not only was there a conflict since the size of the commission was derived from the value of the take-over, but his conduct constituted a breach of the articles.

The harshness of a strict application of the equitable rule is also illustrated in the decision of the New Zealand Court of Appeal in *Gathergood v Blundell & Brown Ltd*.[7] A real estate agent had personally entered into an agreement to acquire property from the plaintiff. Unexpectedly before settlement, he received a substantial offer for the property from a third party. Accordingly, he entered into an agreement to resell the property at a considerable profit. The Court of Appeal found that the circumstances relating to the resale were quite unexpected and fortuitous and the agent had not acted dishonestly. The defendant contended that he should not have to surrender the profit to the plaintiff because the agreement to resell had been made after his agreement with the plaintiff became unconditional. The Court of Appeal, however, held that the fiduciary relationship was still in existence since the defendant had not complied with the terms of the agreement relating to the payment of the deposit. Cooke P observed:[8]

---

6   [1990] 2 AC 663; [1990] 1 All ER 652.

7   [1991] 1 NZLR 405.

8   *Ibid*, at 408.

It has been said by high authority that the obligation not to profit from a position of trust or not to allow a conflict to arise between duty and interest is one of strictness and, indeed, severity; see *New Zealand Netherlands Society 'Oranje' Inc v Kuys*,[9] *per* Lord Wilberforce. Sometimes, the rule may be thought to operate a little harshly. In the present case, however, the question is which party should benefit from a windfall gain. We have no hesitation in concluding on the particular facts – and no case with facts at all close was cited in argument – that the defendant was still a fiduciary owing duties to safeguard the plaintiff's interests when the opportunity with Arthur Toye Ltd presented itself. He must have given his solicitor instructions to invite the plaintiff, as was done in February, to concur in a new arrangement about the deposit. In these circumstances, equity cannot allow him to retain the profit made by dealing with a property as to which he still owed a fiduciary duty to the plaintiff.

The rule allowing recovery of benefits gained by a fiduciary arises, as Lord Cranworth LC observed in *Aberdeen Railway v Blaickie Brothers*,[10] where there is a possibility of conflict.[11] In *Boardman v Phipps*, Lord Upjohn, in his dissenting judgment, spoke of a 'real sensible possibility' of conflict.[12] A remote possibility was insufficient, in Lord Upjohn's opinion, to require a fiduciary to surrender profits. Applying this test, it is arguable that the application of the conflict rule in *Regal Hastings v Gulliver*, *Boardman v Phipps* and *Gathergood v Blundell & Brown Ltd*, was unnecessarily harsh. In both *Regal* and *Boardman*, there was no sensible prospect of the principal acquiring the shares which resulted in profit for the fiduciary and also incidental profit for the principal since the value of the latter's shareholding was also enhanced. Indeed, *Regal* did not have the funds to do so and, had the directors not acquired the supplementary shares in Amalgamated, the venture would not have proceeded. In *Boardman v Phipps*, only an application to a court for permission to increase the trust's shareholding, which was considered by the minority Law Lords, Viscount Dilhorne,[13] and Lord Upjohn[14] to be an unrealistic proposition, could have enabled the trust to acquire the shares in Lister and Harris. In neither case was there any suggestion that the directors had acted in bad faith or in any unconscionable way in acquiring the shareholding. Rather, the transactions were for the mutual benefit of both the fiduciaries and their principals. The application of the

---

9   [1973] 2 NZLR 163; [1973] 2 All ER 1222.
10 (1853–54) 1 Macq 461; [1843]All ER 249.
11 *Ibid*, at 472; 252.
12 [1967] 2 AC 46, at 124; [1966] 3 All ER 721, at 756.
13 *Ibid*, at 92; at 734–36.
14 *Ibid*, at 131; 761.

rule in *Gathergood* also seems rather harsh. No dishonesty or sharp practice was evidenced in that case. No secret was made of the fact that the agent was purchasing personally and the subsequent offer to purchase was not made during the currency of any negotiations with the principal. The fact that the deposit had not been paid in full did not appear to cause the plaintiff any disquiet prior to settlement. In any event, that was not a matter which was in any way related to the resale and the consequent profit.

One rationale for the severe approach exhibited in these cases is that it obviates the need to inquire into the motives of the fiduciary. This rationale was advanced by Lord Eldon, in *Ex parte James*:[15]

> The doctrine as to purchase by trustees, assignees, and persons having a confidential character, stands much more upon general principle than upon the circumstances of any individual case. It rests upon this; that the purchase is not permitted in any case, however honest the circumstances; the general interests of justice requiring it to be destroyed in every instance, as no court is equal to the examination and ascertainment of the truth in much the greater number of cases.

The *dictum* of Lord Eldon was approved in *Regal Hastings Ltd v Gulliver*,[16] but, in *Boardman v Phipps*, Lord Upjohn considered that the equitable rule should be confined to the particular circumstances of the case.[17] Lord Upjohn further warned that there would be no better mode of undermining the sound doctrines of equity than to make unreasonable and inequitable applications of them.[18] Whilst it is necessary to maintain a high standard of fiduciary loyalty so that fiduciaries are not tempted

---

15 *Cf Haywood v Roadnight* [1927] VLR 512; *McKenzie v McDonald* [1927] VLR 134; *Georgieff v Athans* (1981) 26 SASR 412. Further, in relation to a property developer, see *Cook v Evatt (No 2)* [1992] 1 NZLR 676.

16 [1967] 2 AC 135, at 155; [1942] 1 All ER 378, at 381 *per* Viscount Sankey; also Lord Russell at 145; 386; Lord Wright at 155; 393; Lord Porter at 159; 395. For a further harsh application of the rule, see *Parker v McKenna* (1878) 10 Ch App 96, where James LJ rather exaggerated the importance of the rule, when he said that it was 'for the safety of mankind ... that no agent shall be able to put his principal to the danger of such an inquiry' as to whether the principal suffered any 'injury, in fact, by reason of the dealing of the agent'. This statement was, however, approved by Lord Russell and Lord Wright in *Regal*, at 148; 388; at 155; 393. A more convincing rationale is found in the judgment of Lord Herschell in *Bray v Ford* [1896] AC 44; [1895–99] All ER 1009, to which reference was made by Lord Hodson (at 111; 748) and Lord Upjohn (155; 756) in *Boardman v Phipps* [1967] 2 AC 46, at 124; [1966] 3 All ER 721, at 756. In *Bray v Ford*, Lord Herschell considered that the strict rule was not 'founded upon principles of morality' but rather 'on the danger ... of the person holding a fiduciary duty being swayed by interest rather than by duty, and thus prejudicing those whom he was bound to protect'. *Ibid*, at 51; 1011. This approach was adopted by Gaudron and McHugh JJ in *Breene v Williams* (1996) 138 ALR 259, at 289.

17 Citing Lord Selborne LC in *Barnes v Addy* (1874) 9 Ch App 244, at 251.

18 [1967] 2 AC 46, at 133; [1966] 3 All ER 721, at 782.

to shirk their responsibilities, courts should closely scrutinise transactions to ascertain whether they violate the fiduciary rule in any sensible way. As Lord Scarman said in *National Westminster Bank v Morgan*,[19] rather than apply the rule inexorably so as to provide windfall profits to principals who have not in any true sense been victims of equitable fraud, relief should only be ordered after a meticulous examination of the facts reveals a true conflict.[20]

Disclosure to and concurrence of the principal

Whether there is any sensible prospect of a conflict will very often depend upon the extent of disclosure by the fiduciary of any potential conflict. In *BLB Corporation of Australia Establishment v Jacobsen*,[21] for example, the High Court of Australia held that an Australian agent of an overseas corporation had sufficiently disclosed to his principal his involvement as a director and principal shareholder of a customer with which the corporation had unhappy commercial dealings. Further, the court held that he had sufficiently revealed matters of importance pertaining to the relationship. Similarly, after a critical examination of the evidence, the Privy Council in *Queensland Mines Ltd v Hudson*[22] upheld an appeal by Hudson who, it was claimed, had acted in breach of his fiduciary duty because he had engaged in certain mining operations by acquiring interests in them when he was the managing director of Queensland Mines. The evidence revealed however, that Hudson had done so with the full knowledge of the Board after it had become apparent that the company was not able to pursue the venture for financial reasons. Lord Scarman, when delivering the judgment of the Privy Council, considered that there was:[23]

> No real sensible possibility of a conflict of interest between Mr Hudson and Queensland Mines, and that Queensland Mines were fully informed as to the facts and assented to Mr Hudson's exploitation of the mining exploration licence in its own name, for his own gain, and at his own risk and expense.

The Privy Council in *NZ Netherlands Society 'Oranje' Inc v Kuys*,[24] similarly, upheld an appeal by Kuys restraining the society from publishing a

---

19 [1985] AC 686; [1985] 1 All ER 821.

20 *Ibid*, at 709; 831, citing Sir Eric Sachs in *Lloyd's Bank v Bundy* [1975] QB 326, at 347; [1974] 3 All ER 757, at 772.

21 [1974] 48 ALJR 372.

22 (1978) 18 ALR 1; *cf Pedashenko v Blacktown City Council* (1996) 39 NSWLR 189 where a local council did not reveal a conflict when advising and acquiring land from two ratepayers in breach of its fiduciary duty.

23 *Ibid*, at 5.

24 [1973] 2 NZLR 163; [1973] 2 All ER 1222.

rival newspaper under the name, the 'Windmill Post'. Kuys, had been a secretary and member of the society when he had acquired a paper of the same name. The society argued that Kuys was in a fiduciary relationship with it and could not profit from his position. Accordingly, the society claimed that the paper Kuys had acquired was held in trust for it. The Privy Council held, however, that the burden of financing the newspaper would be assumed by Kuys and that he should own it. In these circumstances, because there had been sufficient disclosure, he could not be held to be in breach of any fiduciary duty he might otherwise have had to hold the paper on trust.

The existence of a fiduciary obligation

A fiduciary will be under a duty of good faith to act diligently and in the best interests of his principal in certain well recognised relationships; trustee and beneficiary,[25] a promoter or director of a company[26] or partners,[27] co-adventurers,[28] master and servant,[29] solicitor and client,[30] bailor and bailee,[31] and agents.[32] The categories of fiduciary are not closed.[33] It is

25   *Keech v Sandford* (1726) Sel Cas T King 61; 25 ER 223; *Re Hallett* (1880) 13 Ch D 696.

26   *Emma Silver Mining Co v Lewis & Son* (1879) 4 CPD 396; *Bagnall v Carlton* (1877) 6 Ch D 371; *Erlanger v New Sombrero Phosphate Co* (1878) 3 App Cas 1218; [1874–80] All ER 271; *Catt v Marac Australia Ltd* (1987) 9 NSWLR 639; *Elders Trustee and Executor Co Ltd v Reeves Pty Ltd* (1987) 78 ALR 193.

27   *Parker v McKenna* (1878) 10 Ch App 96; *Birtchnell v Equity Trustees and Agency Company Ltd* (1929) 42 CLR 384; *Chan v Zacharia* (1983–84) 154 CLR 178.

28   *United Dominions Corporation Ltd v Brian Pty Ltd* (1984–85) 157 CLR 1; *Noranda Australia v Lachlan Resources* (1988) 14 NSWLR 1; *Ravinda Rohini Pty Ltd v Krizaic* (1991–92) 105 ALR 593; *Vroon BV v Foster's Brewing Group Ltd* (1994) 2 VR 32; *Dickie v Torbay Pharmacy* [1995] 3 NZLR 429. *Cf News Media Ltd v Australian Football League Ltd* [1996] 139 ALR 193.

29   *Reading v Attorney General* [1951] AC 507; *Attorney General for Hong Kong v Reid* [1994] 1 AC 324; *Timber Engineering Co Pty Ltd v Anderson* (1980) 2 NSWLR 488; *Green & Clara Pty Ltd v Bestobell* [1982] WAR 1; *Consul Development Pty Ltd v DPP Estates* (1975) 132 CLR 373; *Surveys and Mining Ltd v Morrison* (1969) Qd R 470.

30   *Nocton v Lord Ashburton* [1914] AC 932; [1914–15] All ER 45; *Clark Boyce v Mouat* [1994] 1 AC 429; *Farrington v Rowe McBride & Partners* [1985] 1 NZLR 83; *Wan v McDonald* (1992) 33 FCR 491; *Stewart v Layton* (1992) 111 ALR 687.

31   *Hospital Products Ltd v United States Surgical Corp* (1984) 156 CLR 41, at 101 *per* Mason J. Further, see *Re Hallet's Estate* (1880) 13 Ch D 696; [1874–80] All ER 793.

32   *Armstrong v Jackson* [1917] 2 KB 822; [1916–17] All ER 117; *Boardman v Phipps* [1967] 2 AC 46, at 125; [1966] 3 All ER 721, at 757; *English v Dedham Vale Properties Ltd* [1978] 1 All ER 382; *Walden Properties Ltd v Beaver Properties Pty Ltd* (1973) 2 NSWLR 815; *Lintrose Nominees Pty Ltd v King* [1995] 1 VR 524. Similarly, a vendor who knows that an agent is also employed by the purchaser as an adviser assumes a fiduciary position. *Pacifica Shipping Co v Anderson* [1986] 2 NZLR 329.

33   *Hospital Products Limited v United Surgical Corporation* (1984–85) 156 CLR 41, at 68 *per* Gibbs CJ, at 96 *per* Mason J; at 141 *per* Dawson J; in New Zealand, *see* Somers J in *Elders Pastoral Ltd v Bank of New Zealand* [1989] 2 NZLR 180, at 192–93; *Liggett v Kensington* [1993] 1 NZLR 257, at 267–68 *per* Cooke P; at 281–83; *per* Gault J; *Watson v Dolmark Industries* [1992] 3 NZLR 311, at 317 *per* Gault J.

not, however, always easy to define when a fiduciary duty arises. As Gibb CJ said in *Hospital Products Limited v United States Surgical Corporation*,[34] the fiduciary relationship is one wherein the difficulty is to suggest a test by which it may be determined whether a relationship, not within one of the accepted categories, is a fiduciary one. Indicia of a fiduciary relationship may vary from case to case. One indicia of a fiduciary obligation is that a party undertakes to act on behalf of another and not for his or her own benefit. This may include an undertaking which is voluntarily assumed without the knowledge of the principal. In *English v Dedham Vale Properties*,[35] for example, Slade J held that a purchaser, who had made a development application as the self appointed agent of the vendors prior to an exchange of contracts, was under a fiduciary obligation to inform the vendors that permission to develop had been obtained before the completion of the sale. Failure to disclose rendered the purchaser liable to account to the vendor for the profits that resulted from the successful application.

A relationship of confidence may exist in which one party undertakes or assumes the role of adviser.[36] Thus, investment consultants,[37] bankers[38] and confidants who have taken upon themselves the role of advising others have been held to be fiduciaries.[39] In *Coleman v Myers*,[40] the New Zealand Court of Appeal held that a managing director of a family company who had assumed the role of adviser to minority shareholders was a fiduciary. However, where reliance or confidence is alleged as the basis of a fiduciary obligation, care must be taken to examine closely the scope or extent of the alleged obligation. A case which illustrates this is *Clark Boyce v Mouat*,[41] a successful appeal to the

---

34 (1984–85) 156 CLR 41. This issue has received considerable academic consideration, see Finn, PD, *Fiduciary Obligations*, 1977, p 201, Law Book Co Ltd, Sydney; and also 'The Fiduciary principle', in Youdan, T (ed), *Equity, Fiduciaries and Trusts*, 1989, Carswell, Toronto; Austin, RP, 'Commerce and Equity-Fiduciary Duty and Constructive Trust' (1986) Oxford J Legal Stud 444, at 446; Flannigan, R, 'The Fiduciary Obligation' (1989) 9 Oxford J Legal Stud 285; Loughlan, P, 'Fiduciary Liability and Constructive Trust' (1989) 7 Otago LR 179.

35 [1978] 1 All ER 383.

36 See Gibbs CJ, in *Hospital Products* (1984–85) 56 CLR 41, at 68–71; Mason J at 96–100; *Day v Mead* [1987] 2 NZLR 443, at 467 *per* Casey J; *Farrington v Rowe, McBride & Partners* [1985] 1 NZLR 83, at 94 *per* McMullin J; and further, see *Liggett v Kensington* [1993] NZLR 257, at 267 *per* Cooke P, at 281–82 *per* Gault J, in dissent at 298–300 *per* McKay J; *Pedashenko v Blacktown City Council* (1996) 39 NSWLR 189.

37 *Armstrong v Jackson* [1917] 2 KB 822; *Daly v Sydney Stock Exchange* [1986] 160 CLR 371; *Estate Realties v Wignall* [1991] 3 NZLR 482; [1992] 2 NZLR 615; *Cook v Evatt (No 2)* [1992] 1 NZLR 677.

38 *Lloyd's Bank v Bundy* [1975] QB 326; [1974] 3 All ER 757; *Commonwealth Bank v Smith* (1992) 102 ALR 453.

39 *Tweedvale Investments Pty Ltd v Thiran Pty Ltd* (1996) 14 WAR 109; *Pedashenko v Blacktown City Council* (1996) 39 NSWLR 189.

40 [1977] 2 NZLR 225.

41 [1994] 1 AC 429.

Privy Council from New Zealand. In that case, a solicitor, Clark Boyce, had acted for the respondent, Mrs Mouat, on a conveyancing transaction. He also acted for her son. Mrs Mouat had agreed to mortgage her house to enable an advance to be made to her son to assist him in effecting improvements to his home. She had been told that she ought to obtain independent legal advice, and was also informed of the nature and extent of the liability to which she was exposing herself. She did not, however, proceed to obtain independent legal advice. On her son's default, she commenced a claim alleging that Clark Boyce was in breach of fiduciary duty to her in various respects including an obligation to advise her on the wisdom of the transaction. The Privy Council reversed a finding of the majority of the Court of Appeal in Mrs Mouat's favour. Lord Jauncey held that the solicitor's retainer did not, in the circumstances, extend to advising her of the prudence of the transaction and a fiduciary duty could not be relied upon to enlarge the scope of his contractual duties. In the opinion of Lord Jauncey, there being no contractual duty on Mr Boyce to advise Mrs Mouat on the wisdom of entering into the transaction, she could not claim that he nevertheless owed her a fiduciary duty to give that advice.[42]

Another indicia is vulnerability. In this regard, Mason J, in his dissenting judgment in *Hospital Products*, observed:[43]

> It is partly because the fiduciary's exercise of the power or discretion can adversely affect the interests of the person to whom the duty is owed and because the latter is at the mercy of the former, that the fiduciary comes under the duty to exercise his power or discretion in the interests of the person to whom it is owed ...

Vulnerability was an important factor in *Watson v Dolmark Industries Ltd*.[44] There, the New Zealand Court of Appeal held that a local distributor of an Australian product was under a fiduciary duty to an Australian owner of dies which had been entrusted to it for the purpose of manufacturing the product and distributing it in New Zealand. Cooke P observed that vulnerability was an important, indeed, 'cardinal' feature of a fiduciary relationship and existed in that case because the foreign owner was dependent or reliant on the local distributor for the knowledge of the extent of manufacturing and marketing in New Zealand. The mere fact that a party is vulnerable, however, is not

---

42 *Ibid*, at 437. Further, see Dawson J in *Hospital Products* (1984–85) 156 CLR 41, at 147; also at 142 citing Megarry VC in *Tito v Waddell (No 2)* (1977) Ch 106, at 230; to similar effect. For a similar approach, see *Breene v Williams* (1996) 138 ALR 259 where the High Court of Australia declined to extend the duty of fidelity between doctor and patient to incorporate a duty on the doctor's part to disclose the notes he had taken relating to consultations which were his own property.

43 *Ibid*, at 97.

44 [1992] 3 NZLR 311, at 315 *per* Cooke P. Cf *Artifakts Design Group Ltd v NP Rigg Ltd* [1993] 1 NZLR 196, at 230–31.

necessarily conclusive of a fiduciary relationship. Matters which may tell against the imposition of a fiduciary relationship are the commercial nature of a transaction and the fact that the parties have competing interests for which they have bargained at arm's length. In *Hospital Products*, the High Court of Australia held that a foreign distributor of a foreign company's products, although under a contractual duty to use its 'best efforts' to promote the sale of the company's products in Australia, was not under any fiduciary duty to do so. The majority considered that the 'best efforts' requirement obliged the distributor only to act reasonably and this was incompatible with a fiduciary duty not to compete with the interests of the principal. The parties under the distributorship had their own interests to protect and advance and this was not ordinarily conducive to a fiduciary relationship. Gibbs CJ, following an earlier decision of the High Court of Australia, in *Keith Henry & Co Pty Ltd v Stuart Walker & Co Pty Ltd*,[45] observed:[46]

> The fact that the arrangement between the parties was of a purely commercial kind and that they had dealt at arm's length and on an equal footing has consistently been regarded by this court as important, if not decisive, in indicating that no fiduciary duty arose.

Mason J, in dissent, however, considered that although a distributor of products was not within the recognised category of fiduciary, the 'best efforts' clause was not incompatible with such a relationship. Mason J considered that the distributor had a limited fiduciary obligation to protect the manufacturer's product goodwill in Australia and would have granted an account of profits derived from the sale of the distributor's competing products during the period of the agreement. In the opinion of Mason J, the distributor enjoyed a special relationship with the foreign manufacturer which rendered the latter vulnerable.

A further reminder that fiduciary obligations should not be lightly read into commercial transactions is found in the recent decision of the Privy Council in *Re Goldcorp Exchange Ltd*.[47] The Privy Council reversed a majority judgment of the New Zealand Court of Appeal in favour of investors in gold bullion who had purchased bullion from a company, Exchange, in consideration of certificates providing that Exchange would store and insure the gold, and customers could demand physical delivery on seven days' notice. Exchange also collaterally represented that the gold would be stored in a larger bulk and audited monthly. In fact, only sufficient gold was purchased to meet likely demand and on

---

45   (1958) 100 CLR 342.

46   (1984–85) 156 CLR 41, at 70. Further, see *Paul Dainty Corporation Pty Ltd v National Tennis Centre Trust* (1990) 94 ALR 225. Also, see *Moorgate Tobacco Co Ltd v Phillip Morris Ltd* (1983–84) 156 CLR 414.

47   [1994] 3 NZLR 385.

receivership there was insufficient assets to meet the bank's debenture. The investors claimed that they were entitled to a claim in priority to the bank in relation to the remaining gold that represented their investment, on the ground that Exchange owed them a fiduciary duty. Although a majority of the Court of Appeal accepted this argument, the Privy Council considered that the relationship between Exchange and the investors was not one that gave rise to fiduciary obligations. Lord Mustill considered that the essence of a fiduciary relationship was that it created obligations of a different character from those deriving from the contract itself.[48] A mere assertion that a company was obliged honestly and conscientiously to do what it had promised to do, did not constitute a fiduciary relationship. Lord Mustill observed:[49]

> It is possible without misuse of language to say that the customers put faith in the company, and that their trust has not been repaid. But the vocabulary is misleading; high expectations do not necessarily lead to equitable remedies.

A fiduciary relationship may, however, arise prior to the formation of a formal agreement regulating the parties' relationship. In *United Dominions Corporation Limited v Brian Proprietary Limited*,[50] the High Court of Australia held that a fiduciary relationship existed between prospective partners to a joint venture before formal agreement had been reached where the arrangement was one for mutual profit and property was to be held on trust. As such, an undisclosed financial arrangement securing an advance was unenforceable against the interests of a partner who did not know of its existence and did not give his consent to it. In *Ravinder Rohini Pty Ltd v Krizaic*,[51] Krizaic had agreed with one Sharma to investigate the redevelopment of a hotel site. The site was owned by Ravinder which was controlled by Sharma. Krizaic and Sharma each took action pursuant to those arrangements and development approval for the hotel site was obtained. Sharma then withdrew from the proposed redevelopment and sold the site for a substantial profit. On the issue of whether there was a fiduciary relationship existing between the parties, the court held that, irrespective of any formal agreement, there existed a fiduciary relationship between them. Davies J considered that the duty to account for one-half of the profit which was realised arose from the fiduciary duty which existed between Mr Sharma and Mr Kriziac. Such a duty existed notwithstanding that the work of the joint venture had come to an end. The joint venture had produced a valuable benefit in respect of which Mr Sharma

---

48 *Ibid*, at 400.
49 *Idem.*
50 (1984–85) 157 CLR 1.
51 (1991–92) 105 ALR 593.

was liable to account if he took advantage of it.[52] In *Hospital Products*,[53] Mason J observed that where an agreement constitutes the foundation for the fiduciary obligation, the fiduciary relationship, if it is to exist at all, must accommodate itself to the terms of the contract so that it is consistent with and conforms to them. Mason J further observed that the fiduciary relationship could not be superimposed upon the contract in such a way as to alter the operation which the contract was intended to have according to its true construction.[54] In *News Limited v Australian Football League Ltd*,[55] it was held that fiduciary duties did not exist between the League and participating clubs because the relationship between the parties could not be described as one of mutual trust and confidence. The interests of the League and the clubs were different and they had conflicting commercial interests to pursue. The clubs could, by not renewing their annual membership, terminate their relationship with the League and this was seen as also militating against any fiduciary relationship with the result that News could not be said to have induced any breach of fiduciary duty by the clubs when it influenced them to join a rival organisation sponsored by News Limited.[56]

A fiduciary obligation may, however, exist in relation to part only of the activities of parties to a transaction or series of transactions. In *New Zealand Netherlands Society 'Oranje' Incorporated v Kuys*,[57] Lord Wilberforce, in a passage adopted by Gibbs CJ in *Hospital Products*,[58] considered that a person may be in a fiduciary position *quoad* a part of his activities and not *quoad* other parts.[59] In *Breene v Williams*,[60] the High Court of Australia held that, although the relationship between a doctor and his patient may involve fiduciary obligations to the extent that the doctor could not profit at the expense of his patient or reveal private and confidential information to others, it did not override the general contractual duty to act reasonably and with due skill. There was no wider duty of a fiduciary kind that required him to disclose to his patient medical records which were his property and not the patient's.

---

52 *Ibid*, at 596. Further, see *Fraser Edmiston Pty Ltd v AGT (Qld) Pty Ltd* (1988) 2 Qd R 1; *Cf Kelly v C A & L Bell Commodities Corporation Pty Ltd* (1989) 18 NSWLR 248.

53 (1984–85) 156 CLR 41, at 97.

54 *Idem*.

55 (1996) 139 ALR 193.

56 *Cf Cummings v Lewis* (1993) 113 ALR 285 where similar considerations of competing interests led to a rejection of an argument for contribution for losses against an alleged co-adventurer. Discussed, p 62.

57 [1973] 2 NZLR 163; [1973] 2 All ER 1222.

58 (1984–85) 156 CLR 41, at 73.

59 [1973] 2 NZLR 163, at 166; [1973] 2 All ER 1222, at 1225–26; *Moorgate Tobacco Co Ltd v Phillip Morris Ltd (No 2)* (1984) 156 CLR 414, at 446 *per* Deane J; *Elders Pastoral Ltd v Bank of New Zealand* [1989] 2 NZLR 180, at 192–93 *per* Somers J.

60 (1996) 138 ALR 259.

The scope of the fiduciary duty

In *Birtchnell v Equity Trustees Executors and Agency Co Ltd*,[61] Dixon J observed:[62]

> The subject-matter over which the fiduciary obligations extend is determined by the character of the venture or undertaking for which the partnership exists, and this is to be ascertained, not merely from the express agreement of the parties, whether embodied in written instruments or not, but also from the course of dealing actually pursued by the firm. Once the subject-matter of the mutual confidence is so determined, it ought not to be difficult to apply the clear and inflexible doctrines which determine the accountability of fiduciaries for gains obtained in dealings with third parties.

Four broad categories of case may be identified where fiduciary obligations and conflict may arise giving the principal a right to restitution of profits illicitly gained in order to prevent unjust enrichment. The first relates to the expropriation of opportunities or advantages contrary to the interests of the principal. The second category involves the extent to which a fiduciary may take advantage of information gained during the relationship. The third relates to non-disclosure of matters relevant to the scope of the obligation. The final category relates to the acceptance of secret commissions or inducements.

(a) The expropriation of opportunities or advantages

Birtchnell v Equity Trustees Executors and Agency Co Ltd[63] is a classic case of expropriation of opportunity. A partner in a real estate firm, which also invested and speculated in specific transactions with clients for profit-sharing, secretly entered into a relationship with a client of the firm whereby land purchased through the firm was subdivided and resold for profit. It was argued for the partnership that the undisclosed profits made by the deceased partner were accountable to it. A majority of the High Court of Australia agreed. Rich J observed:[64]

> In these circumstances, I think it is clear that the fiduciary obligations of the partners extended to all profit-sharing arrangements with clients. It follows that the late John Porter was not at liberty to conceal from his partners information that a client was ready to or likely to share profits with the firm or secretly turn to his own account any opportunity of such profit-sharing or, whilst ostensibly performing as a partner the work of subdividing and selling land for a client, to share with that client the profits derived from the transaction.

---

61 (1929) 42 CLR 384.

62 *Ibid*, at 408.

63 (1929) 42 CLR 384.

64 *Ibid*, at 401.

Another example of expropriating an opportunity or advantage contrary to the fiduciary's interest can be seen in *Furs Limited v Tomkies*.[65] A managing director of a company, who was empowered to sell part of the company's business, negotiated a new contract of employment with a prospective employer and purchaser which included a reward for passing on valuable information belonging to the company. The purchase price of the business sold off had been reduced and in lieu the value of the information and formulae reflected in the reward was given to the fiduciary. The fiduciary was held liable to account for his profit. In *Chan v Zacharia*,[66] the High Court of Australia similarly held that a doctor, who had obtained a lease of business premises on his own account having opposed his partnership obtaining a renewal of a lease of the same premises, was held liable to hold the lease as a constructive trustee for the partnership. By his actions in opposing the renewal, he had acted in breach of his fiduciary duty. In *Green and Clara Pty Ltd v Bestobell*,[67] and *Avtex Air Services Pty Ltd v Bartsch*,[68] managers, who had competed secretly with their principals whilst in their employment, were also held liable to account for the profits that had been made.

(b) The extent to which advantage may be taken of information derived from a fiduciary relationship or as a result of a confidential disclosure

An employee, who gains knowledge of a prospective opportunity or advantage, cannot proceed to capture that advantage in competition with the principal. The strictness of this rule's application was seen in *Boardman v Phipps*[69] where a majority of the Law Lords held that the information gained was trust property and Boardman's use of it to acquire the share-holding in Lister and Harris Ltd attracted the full rigour of the equitable rule. However, as Viscount Dilhorne observed in that case,[70] unless imparted in confidence, it is only where the information gained is used in competition with the principal's interests that a fiduciary will be liable to equitable redress. For example, in *Aas v*

---

65 (1936) 54 CLR 583.

66 (1983–84) 154 CLR 178. Further, see *British Syphon Co Ltd v Homewood* [1956] 2 All ER 897; *Canadian Aero Service v O'Malley* (1973) 40 DLR (3rd) 371 *Industrial Development Consultants v Cooley*; [1972] 2 All ER 163; *Pacifica Shipping Co Ltd v Anderson* [1986] 2 NZLR 328.

67 [1982] WAR 1. Further, see *Timber Engineering Co Pty Ltd* (1980) 2 NSWLR 488.

68 (1990) 107 ALR 539.

69 [1967] 2 AC 46; [1966] 3 All ER 721, and further, see *British Syphon Co Ltd v Homewood* [1956] 2 All ER 897; *Industrial Development Consultants v Cooley* [1977] 2 All ER 163; *Queensland Mines v Hudson* (1978) 18 ALR 1.

70 *Ibid*, at 90–91; 735.

Benham,[71] a partner was not liable to account for the use of information acquired by him in the partnership which had been used for a purpose which was foreign to the partnership. Lindley LJ observed:[72]

> It is not the source of the information, but the use to which it is applied, which is important in such matters. To hold that a partner can never derive any personal benefit from information which he obtains from a partner would be manifestly absurd.

If, however, information is communicated in confidence, then equity may protect the abuse of confidence. In the case of confidential information imparted to a fiduciary, difficult issues may arise where the fiduciary seeks to put to private use the information gained during the period of a confidential relationship after that relationship has terminated. In *Cranleigh Precision Engineering Ltd v Bryant,*[73] the defendant, who had been the managing director of the plaintiff company, was injuncted after he had left the plaintiff's employment from revealing confidential information of such importance to the plaintiff as to be equivalent to trade secrets. A person may also be ordered to account for profits if the information has resulted in the manufacture of a competing product.[74] Where, however, an application has been made for a patent,[75] or a product has been placed on the market[76] and the information is in the public domain,[77] injunctive relief may be denied.[78] A person to whom the information has been imparted in confidence may be ordered to pay damages or compensation for the information used as a springboard to compete with the business of the person who had communicated the information in confidence.[79] However, the springboard period does not last indefinitely. In *British Franco Electric Pty Ltd v Dowling Plastics Pty Ltd,*[80] the court considered that sufficient time had elapsed since the

---

71 [1891] 2 Ch 244; see *Pacifica Shipping Co Ltd v Anderson* [1986] 2 NZLR 329; but *cf CBA Finance Holdings Ltd v Hawkins* (1984) 1 BCR 599, where it was held not objectionable to compete globally.

72 *Ibid*, at 255–56.

73 [1964] 3 All ER 290.

74 *Peter Pan Manufacturing Corporation v Corsets Silhouette Ltd* [1963] 3 All ER 402.

75 *O Mustad & Son v S Allcock & Co Ltd* [1963] 3 All ER 416; distinguished in *Cranleigh Precision Engineering Ltd v Bryant* [1964] 3 All ER 290.

76 *British Franco Electric Pty Ltd v Dowling Plastics Pty Ltd* [1981] 51 FLR 411.

77 *O'Brien v Komesaroff* (1982) 150 CLR 310.

78 But see where interim relief was granted, *Speed Seal Products v Paddington* [1986] 1 All ER 91.

79 *Seager v Copydex (No 1)* [1967] 2 All ER 415; and further, on the measure of damages assessed on the basis of reasonable compensation for the use of confidential information, see *Seager v Copydex (No 2)* [1969] 2 All ER 718. Further, on assessment of damages, see *Dowson & Mason Ltd v Potter* [1986] 2 All ER 419; *Saltman Engineering Co Ltd v Campbell Engineering Co Ltd* [1963] 3 All ER 413; *Peter Pan Manufacturing Corporation v Corsets Silhouette Ltd* [1963] 3 All ER 402.

80 (1981) 51 FLR 411.

invention's entry was in the public domain for the conclusion to be drawn that the defendant would no longer have any advantage over its competitors and declined to grant the plaintiff relief.

Confidential information, which is acquired in the course of employment and becomes part of the employee's skill and knowledge in the course of his employer's business, can be used competitively for private gain after the period of employment has ended unless there exists an agreement to the contrary.[81] Thus, in *Faccenda Chicken Ltd v Fowler*,[82] a sales manager was held to be entitled to canvass the customers of his former employer. It was held, however, in *Robb v Green*,[83] that injunctive relief could be granted to prevent an employee, once he has left that employment, from taking advantage of a list of his employer's customers that had been drawn up in the course of his employment. An employee, in the same case, was said to be permitted to canvass customers of his former employer whom he had committed to memory. This distinction was criticised in the New Zealand case of *SSC Lintas New Zealand v Murphy*[84] on the ground that there was no valid reason why a servant, endowed with a good memory, should be accorded more extensive rights of canvassing his master's customers than one who was not so blessed. It was the exploitation of possible confidential information regarding on-going transactions between the former employer and his customers that give rise to actionable complaint.[85] An important feature of *Lintas* was the fact that, prior to leaving his employment with Lintas, Murphy had extensively solicited custom in breach of his duty of fidelity. He had taken advantage of special information concerning Lintas and its clients in later persuading clients to transfer business to him after he had ceased employment. Undermining the plaintiff's business in this way resulted in a claim for damages being upheld for the impairment of the opportunity to retain and regain clients.

A duty of fidelity in relation to information applies whenever it is communicated in confidence.[86] There does not have to be a pre-existing

---

81 See *Printers and Finishers Ltd v Holloway* [1964] 3 All ER 731; *Baker v Gibbons* [1972] 2 All ER 759; *Stenhouse Australia Ltd v Phillips* [1974] AC 391; 1 All ER 117; *cf Wessex Dairies Ltd v Smith* [1935] 2 KB 80; *O'Brien v Komesaroff* (1981–82) 150 CLR 310; *Pioneer Concrete Services Ltd v Galli* [1985] VR 675.

82 [1985] 1 All ER 724.

83 [1895] 2 QB 315; [1895–99] All ER 1053.

84 [1986] 2 NZLR 436, at 456–58 *per* Prichard J; considered in *Peninsular Real Estate v Harris* [1992] 2 NZLR 217.

85 *Ibid*, at 456.

86 See *Albert (Prince) v Strange* (1849) 1 Mac & G 25; 41 ER 1171; *Fraser v Evans* [1969] 1 QB 349; [1969] 1 All ER 8; *Attorney General v Jonathan Cape Ltd* [1976] QB 752; [1975] 3 All ER 484; *Deta Nominees Pty Ltd v Viscount Plastics Products Pty Ltd* [1979] VR 167; *Commonwealth of Australia v John Fairfax & Sons Ltd* (1980) 147 CLR 39; *Talbot v General Television Corp Pty Ltd* [1980] VR 224; *Fraser v Thames Television* [1984] QB 44; [1983] 2 All ER 101; *Wilson v Broadcasting Corporation of New Zealand* [1990] 2 NZLR 565.

relationship in order to have confidence protected in equity. In *Saltman Engineering Co Ltd v Campbell*,[87] the Court of Appeal upheld a claim for equitable relief made by the plaintiff who had given confidential drawings to the defendant for the purpose of the defendant manufacturing a product for him. The defendant instead manufactured the product for its own purposes. The court held that the plaintiff was entitled to damages in lieu of an injunction to cover the defendant's past and present actions. Further, the defendant was liable for using confidential information that had been obtained from the plaintiff without his consent irrespective of whether there was any contractual relationship. In *Seager v Copydex Ltd*,[88] the Court of Appeal held that when information is partly in the public domain, the recipient of such information must be careful to use only that which is in the public domain. In *British Franco Electric Pty Ltd v Dowling Plastic Pty Ltd*,[89] Wootten J in the Federal Court referred to the observations of *Megarry J in Coco v A N Clark (Engineers) Ltd*:[90]

> ... where confidential information is communicated in circumstances of confidence, the obligation thus created endures, perhaps in a modified form, even after all the information has been published or is ascertainable by the public; for the recipient must not use the communication as a springboard.

As *Seager v Copydex Ltd (No 1)*[91] illustrates, liability will attach to an abuse of confidence, even though the abuse may not be deliberate or consist of a conscious plagiarism. Further, a *bona fide* purchaser for value will be amenable to injunctive relief once he or she is informed that the information has been derived from a breach of confidence.[92] Confidentiality may, however, be lost if disclosure is considered to be in the public interest. In *Lion Laboratories Ltd v Evans*,[93] the Court of Appeal considered that an injunction should not be granted to prevent the publication of confidential information concerning the absence of

---

87 [1963] 3 All ER 413. Further, see *Seager v Copydex (No 1)* [1967] 2 All ER 415; *Delta Nominees Pty Ltd v Viscount Plastic Products Pty Ltd* [1979] VR 167; *Talbott v General Television Corporation Pty Ltd* [1980] VR 224. Cf *Concept Television Productions Pty Ltd v Australian Broadcasting Corporation* (1988) 12 IPR 129; *Fraser v Thames Television* [1984] QB 44; *Wilson v Broadcasting Corporation of New Zealand* [1990] 2 NZLR 565.

88 *Ibid*, at 417.

89 [1981] 51 FLR 411, at 416.

90 [1969] RPC 41, at 47.

91 [1967] 2 All ER 415, at 417.

92 *Wheatley v Bell* (1982) 2 NSWLR 544.

93 [1985] QB 526; [1984] 2 All ER 426. Further, see *British Steel Corp v Granada Television Ltd* [1981] AC 1096; [1981] 1 All ER 417; *Schering Chemicals Ltd v Falkman Ltd* [1982] QB 1; [1981] 2 All ER 321; *Francome v Mirror Group Newspapers* [1984] 2 All ER 408; *X v Y* [1988] 2 All ER 648; *Castrol Australia Pty Ltd v Emtech Associates Pty Ltd* (1980) 51 FLR 184; *Coulthard v South Australia* (1995) 63 SASR 531.

reliability and accuracy of alcohol measuring devices, which had been manufactured and sold extensively in the United Kingdom and used by the police in the detection of alcohol related driving offences. The Court of Appeal emphasised the need to balance the private interest in maintaining confidentiality, against the public interest in gaining information concerning the reliability of an instrument used in the detection of offences which could have severe consequences. Since the device had the potential to cause a miscarriage of justice, the defence of public interest was upheld. The court also considered that the defence did not have to prove that the plaintiff had acted iniquitously. It was the view of Stephenson LJ that the media might have a duty to publish in some circumstances even if the information has been obtained unlawfully and in flagrant breach of confidence or irrespective of the motive of the informer.[94] It was also recognised that a court is entitled to consider alternative means of satisfying the public interest other than by media publication. Communication of information to the police or some other responsible body might be a preferable alternative in some circumstances.[95]

In *Commonwealth of Australia v James Fairfax*,[96] the High Court of Australia held that disclosure of confidential information at the instance of the government would be restrained only if it appeared inimical to the public interest because national security, relations with foreign countries or the ordinary business of government would be prejudiced. A similar approach was adopted in England in *Attorney General v Jonathan Cape Ltd*.[97] In that case, Lord Widgery when declining an application to restrain the publication of extracts from a book by a former cabinet minister, said:[98]

> The Attorney General must show (a) that such publication would be a breach of confidence; (b) that the public interest requires that the publication be restrained, and (c) that there are no other facts of the public interest contradictory of and more compelling than that relied upon. Moreover, the court, when asked to restrain such a publication, must closely examine the extent to which relief is necessary to ensure that restrictions are not imposed beyond the strict requirement of public need.

The public interest defence has also been invoked in relation to an attempt by the British government to prohibit disclosures by an ex-employee of the British Security Service, in a book, *Spycatcher*. The

---

94 *Ibid*, at 536; 423.

95 See *Initial Services Ltd v Putterill* [1968] 1 QB 396; [1967] 3 All ER 145; *Francome v Mirror Group Newspapers* [1984] 2 All ER 408.

96 (1980) 147 CLR 39.

97 *Attorney General v Jonathan Cape Ltd* [1976] QB 752.

98 *Ibid*, at 770–71.

book adversely exposed various facets of the service and made damaging accusations that a senior officer had been a traitor. Various newspapers were the subject of litigation. An interim injunction was granted in England[99] to prevent publication pending trial notwithstanding the book's publication in the United States. A similar claim for relief was declined in Australia.[100] The action ultimately failed in the High Court of Australia[101] because it was considered to be an attempt to vindicate the governmental interests of a foreign state which was a claim unenforceable under international law. Brennan J further considered that a court should not enforce an obligation of confidence in an action brought to protect the intelligence, secrets and confidential political information of a foreign government.[102] However, in New Zealand, a different approach was taken. In *Attorney General for the United Kingdom v Wellington Newspapers Ltd*, a claim for an injunction failed on the ground that there had been sufficient publication of *Spycatcher* to destroy confidentiality.[103] Aspects of the book contained information which it was considered should be published in the public interest, since the New Zealand Security Service had been partly recruited from the British organisation. The Court of Appeal, however, considered that, in an appropriate case, a New Zealand court could protect the security of a foreign friendly state and would in such matters ascertain the attitude of the government.

(c) Non-disclosure of matters relevant to the scope of the fiduciary obligation

In order to properly perform a fiduciary obligation, a fiduciary must disclose all relevant information that may affect the interests of the principal. Just how far a duty of disclosure extends in any case will depend upon the scope or extent of the fiduciary duty. In *Birtchnell v Equity Trustees Executors and Agency Co Ltd*,[104] a partner was obliged to account for profits made from a venture with which he became involved, contrary to the interests of the partnership. The case could also have been decided on the basis that there was an obligation to inform the partnership of any opportunities falling within the scope of the partnership business. Similarly, in *Furs Limited v Tomkies*,[105] relief was granted where there had been a failure to disclose material information relating to a

---

99 *Attorney General v Guardian Newspapers Ltd* [1987] 3 All ER 316.

100 *Attorney General (UK) v Heineman Publishers Australia Pty Ltd* (1987) 75 ALR 461. Further, see (1988) 165 CLR 30.

101 *Attorney General (UK) v Heineman Publishers Australia Pty Ltd* (1988) 165 CLR 30.

102 *Ibid*, at 51.

103 [1988] 1 NZLR 129.

104 (1929) 42 CLR 384.

105 (1936) 54 CLR 583.

business which had led to a former senior officer in a company securing a financially advantageous contract with the purchaser.

A duty to disclose may be of particular importance in cases where a fiduciary has a duty to advise. In *Nocton v Lord Ashburton*,[106] a solicitor was held liable to compensate a client for failing to advise him properly concerning the discharge of a mortgage which had the effect of benefiting the solicitor to the detriment of his client with whom he was in business. Several New Zealand cases are illustrative of this important area of fiduciary obligation. In *Sims v Craig Bell & Bond*,[107] the Court of Appeal held that a staff solicitor in a firm, who had a business relationship with clients of the firm, had a fiduciary duty to fully disclose to the clients the implications of their entering into a mortgage. There had been no attempt to do so and the solicitor had used the moneys obtained from the advance to pay a private debt. The solicitor contended that he was entitled to do so pursuant to an agreement he had with the plaintiff. The court, however, held that, even assuming such an arrangement, the solicitor and consequently the firm were under an obligation to ensure the plaintiff was fully advised and given an opportunity to seek independent legal advice. This course had not been pursued and, accordingly, the firm was held liable to make good losses sustained by the plaintiff. As to the obligations of a solicitor in a position of conflict, Hardie Boys J observed:[108]

> While the relationship of solicitor and client *ipso facto* gives rise to fiduciary duty, the particular obligations the duty imposes depend on the circumstances. Speaking generally, the obligation is one of utmost good faith. To particularise it for the purposes of the present case, it is an obligation to avoid a conflict of interest between himself and his client. It may be very difficult indeed for the solicitor to avoid such a conflict without requiring the client to take independent advice. For the client is entitled to disinterested advice, including full disclosure of what is involved and what the consequences may be. A solicitor who is himself to benefit financially from the transaction may be hard put to show that he himself has been able to give advice of that kind ...

A personal interest may include an indirect financial interest. Thus, in *Day v Mead*,[109] a solicitor, who was a director and shareholder in a company to whom the solicitor's firm had lent money, was held liable to partly compensate a client for losses incurred after he had invested in the company on the solicitor's advice. The Court of Appeal held that the

---

106 [1914] AC 932; [1914–15] All ER 45; see *Moss v Moss (No 2)* (1900) 21 LR (NSW) Eq 253.

107 [1991] 3 NZLR 535; *Haira v Burberry Mortgage Finance & Savings* [1995] 3 NZLR 396.

108 *Ibid*, at 546.

109 [1987] 2 NZLR 443. Further, see *Official Assignee of Collier v Creigton* [1993] 2 NZLR 534; *Witten-Hannah v Davis* [1995] 2 NZLR 141; *Everist v McCready* [1996] 3 NZLR 349.

solicitor had been in breach of his fiduciary duty by not advising the client to seek independent advice and in not fully disclosing the management and financial difficulties facing the company. The personal interest required to create a fiduciary duty of disclosure in cases of this kind must be one that creates a real possibility of conflict.[110] For example, in *Farrington v Rowe McBride and Partners*,[111] the Court of Appeal held that the mere association of a solicitor with a client company to whom another client had been advised to lend money was insufficient in itself to constitute personal interest. Professional remuneration from the disputed loans was not considered sufficient to constitute a pecuniary interest. The fact that no directors' fees were paid to the partner directors, the existence of only a small shareholding and the fact that there was no evidence that the defendant solicitors had deliberately diverted funds to the company to advance their own interests by virtue of their relationship with the company meant that liability could not be founded on conflict based on pecuniary interest. However, the firm was found liable to compensate its client for certain failed investments because it had not disclosed that the firm also acted for the company with whom the investments were made. Since the interests of the prospective lender would not necessarily coincide with those of the borrower, there was, in the view of the Court of Appeal, a potential for conflict. The information concerning the firm's relationship with the company should have been disclosed and the lender should have been advised to seek independent advice. In *Sims v Craig Bell & Bond*, Thorp J considered the distinction between a solicitor having a personal conflict with a client, and a conflict arising from the fact that he represented two parties to a transaction. Thorp J observed that:[112]

> ... in the case of solicitor and client conflict, the solicitor's onus extends not only to establishing that he has made full disclosure of all information relevant to the business in hand, but also to establishing that no industry he could have exerted would have obtained a better bargain for his client. Where the only conflict is a client and client conflict and the solicitor' financial interest is limited to the receipt of reasonable fees, the onus appears to go only so far as to require him to establish full disclosure of all relevant information.

The mere fact that a solicitor represents more than one party in a transaction is not necessarily objectionable,[113] although such an undertaking

---

110 *Boulting v Association of Cinematograph, Television, and Allied Technicians* [1963] 2 QB 606, at 638.

111 [1985] 1 NZLR 83; *Koya v Haira* [1995] 3 NZLR 396.

112 [1991] 3 NZLR 535, citing *Moody v Cox* [1917] 2 Ch 71; *Spector v Ageda* [1973] Ch 30; [1971] 3 All ER 417.

113 See the discussion in *Farrington v Rowe, McBride, & Partners* [1985] 1 NZLR 83; *Clark Boyce v Mouat* [1994] 1 AC 429.

can prove hazardous as the case of *Stewart v Layton*[114] illustrates. A solicitor acted for both parties in a sale and purchase of land. A conflict arose as a result of the purchaser having difficulty in settling the transaction. The solicitor declined to act further for the purchaser, but did not advise the vendor about the difficulties the purchaser was having and continued to act until the purchaser obtained another solicitor. He was held liable to compensate the vendor for losses attributable to his failure to disclose the financial difficulties of the purchaser after the conflict had arisen. If there is a potential for conflict, only full disclosure will release a fiduciary from liability. In some circumstances, however, as Richardson J in *Farrington*[115] observed, it may be impossible, notwithstanding such disclosure, for a solicitor to act for both parties.[116]

Where there has been a breach of a duty of disclosure, it is irrelevant that the fiduciary has acted honestly. Once a breach of an obligation to disclose material information has been found to exist, it is incorrect to speculate as to what course the aggrieved party might have taken had disclosure been made.[117] This absolves a court from embarking upon considerations relating to causation. It is, however, arguable that where a fiduciary has acted honestly that the full rigour of the rule should be mitigated if the fiduciary can prove that disclosure would not have affected his principal's determination to embark on a certain course of action.[118] A duty to disclose does not extend to information that is immaterial to a transaction as the Privy Council recently observed in Clark *Boyce v Mouat*.[119]

A duty to disclose exists in other relationships of confidant or adviser. In *Lloyd's Bank v Bundy*,[120] a bank was restrained from taking action to enforce security over the plaintiff's home for a loan made to him for his son's benefit. The bank had assumed the role of an adviser to the plaintiff who was an elderly man and a customer of the bank. The manager, in obtaining the security, did not disclose the parlous financial circumstances of the son who was also a customer of the bank; nor did he advise the plaintiff to seek independent advice. Similarly, in *Commonwealth Bank*

---

114 (1992) 111 ALR 687. Further, see *Lintrose Nominees Pty Ltd v King* [1995] 1 VR 574.

115 [1985] 1 NZLR 83, at 90.

116 *Idem.*

117 *Brickenden v London Loan & Savings Co* [1934] 3 DLR 465; *Farrington v Rowe, McBride & Partners* [1985] 1 NZLR 83; *Witten-Hannah v Davis* [1995] 2 NZLR 141, at 149 *per* Richardson J, at 156 *per* Mckay J; *Stewart v Leyton* (1992) 111 ALR 687, at 713.

118 See McGechan J in *Mouat v Clark Boyce* [1991] Aust & NZ Conveyancing Reports 118, at 590, considered in *Stewart v Leyton* (1992) 111 ALR 687, at 713. In *Walden Properties Ltd v Beaver Properties Pty Ltd* (1973) 2 NSWLR 815, at 847, Hutley JA considered that a fiduciary could avoid liability for non-disclosure by proving that the principal would not have acted differently if disclosure had been made. Further, see *Koya v Haira* [1995] 3 NZLR 396, at 408; *Everist v McCready* [1996] 3 NZLR 348, at 353–54 where a strict application of *Brickenden* is rejected.

119 [1994] 1 AC 429, at 438.

120 [1975] QB 326; [1974] 3 All ER 757.

of Australia v Smith,[121] a bank manager had advised the plaintiff, who was a customer of the bank, that a business proposition which involved the plaintiff purchasing a hotel from a customer was a sound proposition when it was not. The manager disclosed that the vendor was a customer of the bank but, instead of advising the plaintiff to seek independent advice, he persuaded him not to do so. The bank was held liable to compensate the plaintiff for losses that resulted from his decision to purchase the hotel. The New Zealand Court of Appeal, in *Coleman v Myers*,[122] also held that the defendant, as managing director of a company, was under a fiduciary obligation to fully inform minority shareholders of the merits and disadvantages associated with a take-over transaction. The take-over financially advantaged the defendant and he was held liable to compensate the minority shareholders for losses they incurred in giving their consent to the transaction. Similarly, in *Cook v Evatt (No 2)*,[123] an investment company failed to disclose to an investor that it had purchased real estate only a few days prior to its on-sale to the investor for a substantial profit. The company and those associated with it were held liable to account as fiduciaries for the profits they derived from the transaction.

(d) Secret commissions

A fiduciary is not able to retain a secret profit, commission, or other inducement, and will be accountable for benefits obtained in this way to his or her principal. Either an action for moneys had and received at law, or an account in equity will lie to recover profits gained as a result of a conflict of this kind. In *Reading v Attorney General*,[124] the House of Lords dismissed an appeal brought by Reading, an army sergeant, to recover moneys from the Crown which had seized a large sum of money given to Reading as bribes. He had used his position to assist others involved in selling illicit liquor in Cairo from being detected by the police. The House of Lords held that he was not entitled to recover the moneys. The Crown had a right to retain the moneys for the abuse by Reading of his duty of fidelity. A majority of the Law Lords[125] considered that the action for moneys had and received would have been available to allow the Crown to have claimed the profits and were unanimous that there could be an account based on breach of fiduciary duty.

---

121 (1992) 102 ALR 453; *Pedashenko v Blacktown City Council* (1996) 39 NSWLR 189; *Tweedvale Investments Pty Ltd v Thiran Pty Ltd* (1994–96) 14 WAR 109.

122 [1977] 2 NZLR 225.

123 [1992] 1 NZLR 676.

124 [1951] AC 507; [1951] 1 All ER 617.

125 *Ibid*, *per* Viscount Jowitt LC; Lord Porter; Lord Oaksey and Lord Radcliffe; Lord Normand expressing reservation.

Lord Porter cited *dictum* from Bowen LJ in an earlier case on restitution of secret commissions, *Boston Deep Sea Fishing v Ansell*:[126]

> ... the law implies a use, that is to say, there is an implied contract, if you put it as a legal proposition – there is an equitable right, if you treat it as a matter of equity – as between the principal and agent that the agent should pay it over, which renders the agent liable to be sued for money had and received, and there is an equitable right in the master to receive it, and to take it out of the hands of the agent which gives the principal a right to relief in equity.

We have seen how, in *Furs Limited v Tomkies*,[127] and *Birtchnell v Equity Trustees Executors and Agency Co Ltd*,[128] the High Court of Australia ordered fiduciaries to account for secret profits derived at the expense of the principal's business. As *Reading* illustrates, the principal may claim profits even though no monetary loss has been suffered. It is the abuse of the fiduciary relationship that enables the principal to recover bribes or secret commissions.

In the case of bribes, not only will the agent or bribee be liable in an action for moneys had and received, but the action will also be available against the briber for the amount of the bribe. Lord Diplock, in *Mahesan v Malaysia Government Housing*,[129] said of the remedy of moneys had and received against a briber that whatever conceptual difficulties it might raise, it was now too well established in English law to be questioned.[130] Aside from restitutionary claims against the briber and bribee, the principal may bring an action for rescission of a contract against the briber if the bribe has induced a contract,[131] or an action for deceit against both the briber and the bribee.[132] In the case of an action for deceit, the principal may recover the actual loss attributable to the corrupt dealing, whereas with moneys had and received, compensation will be limited to the amount of the bribe.[133] Where the principal elects to rescind a contract entered into with the briber, he or she may proceed to recover the bribe from the bribee. Should, however, the bribe have been recovered prior to rescission, there is no liability to account to the briber for it as a condition of rescission.[134] In *Mahesan*, the Privy Council observed, that deceit and moneys had and received were alternative and not cumulative remedies

---

126 (1888) 39 Ch D 339, at 367.

127 (1936) 54 CLR 583.

128 (1929) 42 CLR 384.

129 (1979) AC 374; [1978] 2 All ER 405.

130 *Ibid*, at 383; 411.

131 *Bagnall v Carlton* (1877) 6 Ch D 371.

132 *Salford Corporation v Lever* [1891] 1 QB 168.

133 *Mahesan v Malaysia Government Housing* [1979] AC 374, at 383; [1978] 2 All ER 405, at 411, explaining *Hovenden & Sons v Milhoff* (1900) 83 LT 41; [1900–03] All ER 848.

134 *Logicrose v Southend Football Club Ltd* [1988] 1 WLR 1256.

against both briber and bribee. Lord Diplock considered that a fraudu-lent agent was liable either for the losses incurred as a result of his fraudulent conduct or the amount of the bribe that he had been paid, but he was not liable for both. Since the losses incurred by the defrauded principal in that case were greater than the amount of the bribe, the Privy Council allowed the claim for damages and dismissed the action for the bribe.[135]

In *Attorney General for Hong Kong v Reid*,[136] the Privy Council further held that a fraudulent fiduciary was a constructive trustee of bribes and any property derived from this source. Were the investments or property to increase in value, then the principal was entitled to the benefit of the increase. Should the property fall in value, then the fiduciary remained personally liable for the outstanding amount of the bribe. Reid was a fraudulent Crown officer with the Office of the Director of Public Prosecutions in Hong Kong and had accepted large sums of money by way of bribes investing some of the proceeds in real estate in New Zealand. The Attorney General lodged caveats against the title to the properties but was held by the Court of Appeal to have an insufficient equitable interest in the properties to justify a renewal of the caveats. In upholding the Attorney's appeal, the Privy Council reversed *Lister v Stubbs*,[137] an authority that had stood for over a century. In *Lister v Stubbs*, the Court of Appeal had declined to grant an injunction to prevent a fraudulent agent disposing of property and investments acquired with the proceeds of a bribe on the ground that the relationship between the agent and his principal was one of debtor and creditor. Lord Templeman, in *Reid*, did not agree with the argument derived from *Lister v Stubbs* that to impose a constructive trust over the assets acquired with the bribe would disadvantage general creditors of the fiduciary should the latter become insolvent. To allow the general creditors to prosper from the fidu-ciary's fraud would be to allow them to be unjustly enriched at the expense of the principal to whom a duty of fidelity was owed.

Third parties and their liability for breaches of fiduciary duty

The liability of third parties in cases of breaches of fiduciary duty fall into two categories. The first occurs where the third party is involved in a transaction which constitutes a breach of a fiduciary relationship but does not receive trust property for his or her own benefit. The second occurs where the third party is involved in a transaction which

---

135 [1979] AC 374, at 383; [1978] 2 All ER 405, at 410–11. Further, see *United Australia Ltd v Barclays Bank Ltd* [1941] AC 1; [1940] 4 All ER 20, where the House of Lords held that where two remedies are available, one for moneys and had and received, and the other for tortious damages, the plaintiff was required to elect between remedies.

136 [1994] 1 AC 325.

137 (1890) 45 Ch D 1.

constitutes a breach of a fiduciary relationship and receives trust property for his or her own benefit. In both categories, the liability of the third party as a constructive trustee will depend upon the degree of knowledge that he or she has of the circumstances giving rise to the breach.

In the first category, a third party will be absolved from liability unless it is established that he or she had actual knowledge of the breach of fiduciary relationship. Actual knowledge includes wilfully turning a blind eye to a breach and may include a wilful or reckless disregard of an obligation to inquire. In the second category of liability encompassing a receipt of some benefit, a lower standard of knowledge will suffice. A third party in this category will be liable as a constructive trustee if he or she had knowledge of circumstances which would impose on a reasonable person in the shoes of the third party an obligation to inquire about the propriety of the transaction and the consequent receipt of the trust property. There has been considerable judicial debate concerning the approach which courts ought to take in cases of this kind. This has caused some uncertainty. It is important in resolving issues of this kind that the distinction between the two categories of liability be maintained.

(a) The liability of a third party who does not acquire property derived from a breach of fiduciary obligation beneficially

A third party, who takes part or assists in a breach of a trust without actual knowledge of it, will not be liable to account to a defrauded principal unless he or she receives trust property beneficially. To impose a more onerous obligation would unduly inhibit persons who have to deal with trust property as agents. Unless an agent has actual knowledge of a fraud, he or she should not be required to question his or her principal's instructions. In *Barnes v Addy*,[138] Lord Selborne LC said:[139]

> Those who create a trust clothe the trustee with a legal power and control over the trust property, imposing on him a corresponding responsibility. That responsibility may no doubt be extended in equity to others who are not properly trustees, if they are found either making themselves trustees *de son tort*, or actually participating in any fraudulent conduct of the trustee to the injury of the *cestui que trust*. But, on the other hand, strangers are not to be made constructive trustees merely because they act as the agents of trustees in transactions within their legal powers, transactions, perhaps of which a court of equity may disapprove, unless those agents receive and become chargeable with some part of the trust property, or unless they assist with knowledge in a dishonest and fraudulent design on the part of the trustees.

---

138 (1874) LR 9 Ch App 244. Applied in *Brunei Airlines v Tan* [1995] 3 WLR 64; *Wickstead v Browne* (1992) 30 NSWLR 1; *ASC v AS Nominees* (1995) 133 ALR 1.

139 *Ibid*, at 251.

In that case, Addy, who was the original trustee of a fund, appointed Barnes a trustee as he was entitled to do under the provisions of the testator's will. Addy was unaware that Barnes would act fraudulently and misappropriate the trust fund. The plaintiffs were the children and grandchildren of the testator whose inheritance had been squandered by Barnes' actions. The plaintiffs contended that the solicitors who had approved the deeds of appointment and indemnity for Addy should be held liable to account for the missing fund as constructive trustees. In the absence of evidence of actual knowledge of the fraud, the Court of Appeal rejected this contention. Similarly, in *Williams v Williams*,[140] a solicitor, named Cheese, had previously acted for a husband who had incorrectly informed Cheese that there was no marriage settlement with his wife. Later, Cheese acted for the wife. She informed a clerk in Cheese's employ that there was a marriage settlement but Cheese ignored this information. Certain property was sold by the wife in her capacity as the executor of her husband's estate. Cheese applied half of the proceeds to pay the husband's debts and appropriated a small amount in fees. Subsequently, the marriage settlement was discovered. The couple's children sued Cheese claiming that he should account for the proceeds of sale which they contended they should have had under the settlement. Whilst observing that it would not have exonerated Cheese of gross negligence,[141] the court did not consider that the circumstances justified relief in equity. It had been conceded that Cheese had acted in good faith. On the issue of the requisite knowledge necessary to render Cheese liable to account, Kay J said:[142]

> The case ... would have been different if I had been satisfied that Mr Cheese had wilfully shut his eyes – if there had been any motive whatever fairly suggested for supposing that Mr Cheese was desirous of thinking that there was no settlement. If it were proved to me upon the evidence that he had wilfully shut his eyes, and was determined not to inquire, then the case would have been very different ...

Buckley LJ in *Belmont Finance Corporation Ltd v Williams Furniture Ltd (No 2)*,[143] and Peter Gibson J in *Baden v Societe Generale*,[144] considered that the notion of wilful or 'Nelsonian' blindness included not only wilfully shutting one's eyes to the obvious, but also 'wilfully and recklessly failing to make such inquiries as a reasonable and honest man would make'. Peter Gibson J accepted this partly objective test as plainly correct[145] and

---

140 (1881) 17 Ch D 437.

141 *Ibid*, at 445–46.

142 *Idem*.

143 [1979] Ch 250, at 267; [1979] 1 All ER 118, at 130.

144 [1992] 4 All ER 161.

145 *Ibid*, at 242–43.

cited in support the views of Ungoed-Thomas J in *Selangor United Rubber Estates Ltd v Craddock No 3*[146] and Brightman J in *Karak Rubber Co Ltd v Burden*.[147] In those cases, the courts adopted an objective test in cases where the complaint was said to be one of giving knowing assistance to a breach of trust. However, a totally objective test is inappropriate in this category. In both *Selangor* and *Karak*, it may be argued that the banks, which had unwittingly taken part in the illegal use of the plaintiff companies' capital to finance take-over transactions, fell into the knowing receipt category[148] rather than the knowing assistance category. In both cases, the banks were involved in 'round-robin' advances and receipts of cheques used to pay for and facilitate the acquisitions. These transactions constituted a fraud on the plaintiff companies because their capital was illegally used to purchase their own shares. The banks had received company cheques beneficially so as to extinguish debts accrued by virtue of their advancing funds to enable the purchase of the shares to be settled. The adoption of an objective standard in these cases was defensible because the banks received the cheques beneficially in discharge of the borrower's debts and as such the cases fell within the knowing receipt category where constructive knowledge is appropriate because the recipient stands to personally gain from the transaction. In this regard, in *Eagle Trust v SBC Securities Ltd*,[149] Vinelott J more recently rejected the concept of a totally objective standard in the knowing assistance category. Although Vinelott J observed that in *Selangor* and *Karak*, a more stringent test had been suggested in cases of assistance, he did not accept that a totally objective test was appropriate in this category.[150] However, Vinelott J considered that 'Nelsonian' blindness[151] was sufficiently wide to include the more limited objective criteria of wilful and reckless disregard postulated by Buckley LJ in *Belmont Finance* and Peter Gibson J in *Baden*. In this regard, Vinelott J also indicated his support[152] for the approach of Millet J in *Agip (Africa) Ltd v Jackson*.[153] Millet J explained the distinction between the states of mind in *Baden* as:[154]

---

146 [1968] 2 All ER 1073.

147 [1972] 1 All ER 1210.

148 See the discussion of Smith J in *Ninety Five Pty Ltd (In liquidation) v Banque Nationale de Paris* [1988] WAR 132, at 173–74; Cato CB, 'Selangor Revisited; The Liability of Third Parties as Constructive Trustees' (1985) Univ of Canterbury (NZ) L Rev 363; Harpum, C, 'The Stranger As A Constructive Trustee' (1986) 102 LQR 114, at 116; Gardiner, S, 'Knowing Assistance and Receipt' (1996) 112 LQR 56.

149 [1992] 4 All ER 488, at 499–500.

150 *Idem*.

151 *Ibid*, at 497.

152 [1992] 4 All ER 488, at 497.

153 [1990] Ch 265; [1992] 4 All ER 385.

154 [1990] Ch 265 at 293; [1992] 4 All ER 385, at 405, and see also *Cowan de Groot Properties Ltd v Eagle Trust plc* [1992] 4 All ER 700, at 761.

The true distinction is between honesty and dishonesty. It is essentially a jury question. If a man does not draw the obvious inferences or make the obvious inquiries, the question is: why not? If it is because, however foolishly, he did not suspect wrongdoing, or having suspected it, had his suspicions allayed, however unreasonably, that is one thing. But if he did suspect wrongdoing yet failed to make inquiries because 'he did not want to know' (category (i)) or because he regarded it as 'none of his business' (category (iii)), that is quite another. Such conduct is dishonest and those who are guilty of it cannot complain if, for the purpose of civil liability, they are treated as if they had actual knowledge.

As the case of *Williams v Williams*[155] illustrates, however, even gross negligence will not be sufficient to render a third party liable to account for trust property that he does not beneficially receive. In order to render a third party liable as a constructive trustee, there must be some want of 'probity'[156] manifested in some deliberate wrongdoing or a wilful determination to ignore a dishonest dealing with trust property. The approach of Lord Selborne LC in *Barnes v Addy* was considered in Australia by the High Court in *Consul Development Pty Ltd v DPC Estates Pty Ltd*.[157] Stephen J[158] considered that the state of the authorities prior to *Selangor* did not support the concept of constructive knowledge in this category of case. McTiernan J,[159] in his dissenting judgment, however, considered that had it been necessary he would have adopted the *Selangor* approach. Gibbs J appeared to support an approach more consistent with that subsequently advanced by Peter Gibson J in *Baden*. Gibbs J observed:[160]

It may be that it is going too far to say that a stranger will be liable if the circumstances would put an honest and reasonable man on

---

155 (1881) 17 Ch D 437.

156 See Edmund-Davies LJ in *Carls-Zeiss Stiftung v Herbert Smith & Co* [1969] 2 Ch 276, at 302; 2 All ER 367, at 384; also Vinelott J in *Eagle Trust plc v SBC Securities Ltd* [1992] 4 All ER 488, at 499.

157 (1974–75) 132 CLR 373.

158 *Ibid*, at 408–11.

159 *Ibid*, at 378–79.

160 *Ibid*, at 398. Further, to similar effect, see Fox LJ in *Agip (Africa) Ltd v Jackson* [1992] 4 All ER 451, at 467, and Cooke P in *Gathergood v Blundell & Browne* [1992] 3 NZLR 643, at 646. In *Nimmo v Westpac Banking Corporation* [1993] 3 NZLR 218, at 228, Blanchard J interpreted Cooke P in *Gathergood* to mean that 'an assister was only liable if he had actual or "Nelsonian" knowledge, in which case the assistance rendered would have to be inherently dishonest'. In *Equiticorp Industries Group Ltd v Hawkins* [1991] 3 NZLR 700, at 725, Wylie J, and in *Marshall Futures v Marshall* [1992] 1 NZLR 316, at 325–26, Tipping J disagreed with the view expressed by Thomas J in *Powell v Thompson* [1991] 1 NZLR 597, that knowing assistance included constructive as well as actual knowledge. *Cf* Henry J in *Springfield Acres Ltd v Abacus (HK) Ltd* [1994] 3 NZLR 502 who considered that the issue in New Zealand could not be regarded as settled.

inquiry, when the stranger's failure to inquire has been innocent and he has not wilfully shut his eyes to the obvious. On the other hand, it does not seem to me to be necessary to prove that a stranger who participated in a breach of trust or fiduciary duty with knowledge of all the circumstances did so actually knowing that what he was doing was improper. It would not be just that a person who has full knowledge of the facts could escape liability because his own moral obtuseness prevented him from recognising an impropriety that would have been apparent to an ordinary man.

A similar approach was taken more recently by the Privy Council in *Royal Brunei Airline v Tan*.[161] In that case, Lord Nicholls emphasised that, in order to fix liability on a person who had not received trust property, it had to be shown that he or she had acted dishonestly. This did not, however, import a totally subjective test. Thus, if a party, taking into account his or her personal attributes and experience, so participates in a breach of trust, he or she will not be able to rely on moral obtuseness if a natural inference is that there has been a departure from the standard that would be expected of an honest person in those circumstances. In that case, a company director was found liable to account for losses attributable to the company's insolvency where funds, that should have been set aside in a separate account for the Royal Brunei Airline, had been diverted into the company's trading account. Although it was not suggested that Tan had deliberately intended to defraud the Royal Brunei Airline, he was held liable because he was aware of the fact that the diversion of the money constituted a breach of trust.

In New Zealand, in *Westpac Banking Corporation v Slevin*,[162] Sir Clifford Richmond observed that constructive knowledge would only apply to an agent who receives trust property from a trustee, if he is setting up a title of his own to funds which he has received and is not acting as a mere depository or merely as a channel through which money is passed to other persons.[163]

Liability for knowing participation in a breach of trust was found in Australia, in *Green and Clara Pty Ltd v Bestobell Industries Pty Ltd*,[164] and *Avtex Air Services Pty Ltd v Bartsch*.[165] In both cases, third parties had participated with actual knowledge in the fraudulent activities of a fiduciary and were ordered to account for the profits they derived from the transactions.

---

161 [1995] 3 WLR 64.

162 [1985] 2 NZLR 41.

163 *Ibid*, at 69. Further on this point, see *Nimmo v Westpac Banking Corporation* [1993] 3 NZLR 218. In the latter case, the *Baden* test was described by Blanchard J as 'unhelpful', and 'over-refined' (at 228).

164 [1982] WAR 1. Further, see *Timber Engineering Co Pty Ltd* (1980) 2 NSWLR 488; *Wickstead v Browne* (1992) 30 NSWLR 1; *ASC v AS Nominees* (1995) 133 ALR 1.

165 (1990) 107 ALR 539.

(b) The liability of a third party who receives trust property beneficially

Equity will order restitution of benefits derived from the receipt of trust property by third parties where the third party had constructive knowledge or notice of the fraud. In *Bodenham v Hoskins*,[166] for example, a bank had knowledge that an account had been opened by a customer named Parkes. The bank also knew that the account had been opened by Parkes for the purpose of receiving the rents of an estate that he was managing. The bank was held liable to account to the owner of the estate for the proceeds of cheques that had been drawn on the account by Parkes and paid into his private account in order to reduce his indebtedness to the bank. Kindersley VC observed that:[167]

> I am constrained to arrive at the conclusion that the bankers, although I must exonerate them from any deliberate intention to commit a fraud, were not only parties to the simple fact of the transfer, but were parties to the fraud in question – that they were aware of the circumstances which made it a fraud in Parkes to make the transfer to his private account, and, being cognisant of that throughout, they concurred in a transaction the effect of which was that for their own pecuniary benefit an act was done by Parkes which is a fraud upon the plaintiff. According to the plain principles of a court of equity such an act never can be sustained; a person cannot retain the benefit which he has derived from being a party to such an act, with such knowledge of the nature of the act.

This approach is also illustrated in *Reckitt v Barnett, Pembroke and Slater Ltd*.[168] There, a fraudulent agent named Terrington signed a cheque in such a way as to represent clearly that it was not his personal cheque and that he was signing in a representative capacity as attorney. Terrington used the cheque to pay an instalment on a motor vehicle which he had purchased from the defendant. The plaintiff, whose cheque had been misappropriated, was able to recover the proceeds from the defendant. The circumstances surrounding the signing of the cheque together with the fact that it was given for the purpose of Terrington extinguishing a private debt meant that the defendant had constructive knowledge of the fraud. Similarly, in *Nelson v Laholt*,[169] a fraudulent executor and trustee drew cheques signed 'G A Potts,

---

166 [1843-60] All ER 602.

167 *Ibid*, at 697.

168 [1929] AC 176; [1928] All ER 1.

169 [1948] 1 KB 339; [1947] 2 All ER 751. See further, *Stephens Travel Service v Quantas* (1988) 13 NSWLR 331, at 360 where a bank had notice of an arrangement between Quantas and Stephens Travel that moneys paid to the latter by customers were earmarked for Quantas and as a result it had to account for the proceeds that it had wrongly applied to reduce the agency's overdraft.

Executor of William Burns, dec' and cashed them with the defendant bookmaker for value. It was contended that, in the absence of bad faith, the estate should not be able to recover the balance of the cheque. It was held, however, that the defendant had constructive knowledge that the cheques had been misappropriated and was placed on inquiry. It was considered that the answers the bookmaker received from Potts would not have satisfied a reasonable man that the cheques were presented honestly. On the issue of knowledge, Denning J observed that:[170]

> ... if the defendant knew or ought to have known of the want of authority, as, for instance, if the circumstances were such as to put a reasonable man on inquiry and he made none, or if he was put off by an answer that would not have satisfied a reasonable man, or, in other words, if he was negligent in not perceiving the want of authority, then he is taken to have notice of it.

This approach was subsequently adopted by the Court of Appeal in *Belmont Finance Corporation v Williams Furniture Ltd (No 2)*.[171] It was held in that case that a company, City, which was paid a large sum of money from the sale of shares in a company which it owned named Belmont, was liable to account for the proceeds of the sale to Belmont which had subsequently gone into receivership with a substantial amount of debt. The proceeds of the sale of Belmont's share capital were found to have been derived through a dishonest and illegal scheme of acquisition in which Belmont's assets had been used to finance indirectly the purchase of its own share capital. Although the directors of City were absolved from dishonestly giving assistance to this scheme, City was held liable to account to Belmont as a constructive trustee of the proceeds of the sale of its share capital because the circumstances surrounding the transaction were such that City's directors ought to have known that the proceeds of sale were derived by illegally manipulating the assets of Belmont. In *Westpac Banking Corporation v Savin*,[172] the New Zealand Court of Appeal followed *Belmont* and held that Westpac was liable to account to the owner, Savin, for the proceeds of the sale of boats. An agent for the sale of the boats, Aqua Marine, had wrongfully paid the proceeds of the sale into its private trading account with the bank in order to improve its financial position. The court considered that the bank was a constructive trustee of the proceeds of sale because it was aware that Aqua Marine was an agent for sale and did not usually trade out of private stock. Similarly, the Supreme Court of Western Australia in *Ninety Five Pty Ltd (In Liquidation) v Banque Nationale De Paris*,[173]

---

170 *Ibid*, at 343–44; at 752–53.

171 [1980] 1 All ER 393.

172 [1985] 2 NZLR 41. Further, see *Lankshear v ANZ Banking Group (NZ) Ltd* [1993] 1 NZLR 481.

173 [1988] WAR 133.

followed *Belmont* and ordered a bank to account for funds which it had received beneficially as part of an illegal scheme to finance a take-over transaction. The funds represented the repayment of a loan made by the bank to enable the purchaser to settle the transaction. Although the manager did not appreciate that the transaction was illegal, he was found to have knowledge of all the relevant circumstances which would put him on notice that it was illegal. The fact that he did not appreciate that the transaction was illegal was immaterial.[174] In *Equiticorp Industries Group v Crown*,[175] Smellie J had reservations about applying constructive knowledge in the receiving category, but was able to avoid the issue because it was found that the Crown through its agents had either wilfully closed its eyes to the illegal funding arrangements by which Equiticorp had purchased Crown shares in New Zealand Steel, or had acted with reckless disregard. However, constructive knowledge is, it is submitted, an appropriate standard by which to impute liability in the receiving category because a person should not be able to take advantage of his or her own obtuseness in failing to recognise impropriety.

Where trust funds have been beneficially received by a third party with notice of a fraud, the third party should remain under a duty to account to the principal for any loss derived even though he or she has subsequently parted with the property. Although Vinelott J, in *Eagle Securities Trust plc v SBC Securities*, accepted that this would be so where actual knowledge was established, he had reservations about whether constructive knowledge would be sufficient.[176] It is submitted, however, that the fact that the property has been transferred or dissipated should not absolve a third party from a liability to account, if the property was beneficially received with constructive knowledge of a fraud. Only if the third party has received the property as a mere conduit should liability to make restitution be denied.[177]

(c) Constructive knowledge and the duty to inquire

This has been an issue that has troubled English Judges. In *Baden v S G Developpement du Commerce*,[178] Peter Gibson J considered that constructive knowledge included two states of mind. First, it involved knowledge of circumstances that would suggest dishonesty to an honest and reasonable man. Secondly, it involved knowledge that would put an honest and reasonable man on inquiry. The distinction was one of degree. Scott LJ in

---

174 *Ibid*, at 177 following Jacobs J in *International Vending Machines Pty Ltd and Companies Act* [1962] NSWR 1408, at 1420–21, approved in *Steen v Law* [1964] AC 287, at 300.

175 [1996] 3 All ER 586, at 604–05.

176 [1992] 4 All ER 488, at 507.

177 *National Commercial Banking Corporation of Australia v Batty* (1986) 160 CLR 251.

178 [1992] 4 All ER 161, at 242–43.

Polly Peck International v Nadir (No 2),[179] however, observed that the states of mind identified by Peter Gibson J were not rigid categories with clear and precise boundaries. One category might merge imperceptibly into another.[180] If the evidence established circumstances which would lead a reasonable person to recognise a payment or disposition of property had been fraudulently obtained, then the failure of a third party, who beneficially received trust property, to recognise fraud would not prevent his or her being held to be a constructive trustee however honest he or she might have been.[181] The second state of mind, however, could cause greater difficulty. The evidence might not unequivocally suggest fraud but the circumstances might be sufficiently suspicious to place a reasonable person on inquiry. The more suspicious the circumstances, the more obvious was the need to make inquiry. Where a failure to make inquiry is alleged, Brightman J in *Karak* observed that the onus was on the plaintiff to prove the causal connection between the breach of a duty to inquire and the loss.[182] This approach was also adopted by Peter Gibson J in *Baden.*[183] It was held in that case that the bank had made appropriate inquiry since it had either received answers which would have satisfied a reasonable banker that fraud was not involved, or the evidence established that further inquiry would not have revealed fraud.[184] However, the mere fact that there is a possibility of a false explanation is no defence to a party who when faced with facts which would put a reasonable person on inquiry, makes none.[185] Indicative also of the care that must be taken to closely scrutinise the facts before imputing constructive knowledge on the basis of a failure to make inquiry is the judgment of Scott LJ in *Polly Peck International plc v Nadir (No 2).*[186] Scott LJ emphasised that, before a bank could be found to have received trust funds dishonestly, there must exist grounds for such suspicion:

> The question whether the bank did or did not have an honest belief only arises after the bank has become, or ought to have become, suspicious of possible impropriety. Unless ground had been given for suspicion, no one in the Central bank would have any relevant belief at all. They would not address their minds to the impropriety or to the legitimacy of the purpose for which the funds were being moved.

---

179 [1992] 4 All ER 769.

180 *Ibid*, at 777.

181 See discussion in *Ninety Five Pty Ltd (In Liquidation) v Banque Nationale De Paris* [1988] WAR 132. *Stephens Travel Service v Quantas* (1988) 13 NSWLR 331, at 359–60.

182 [1972] 1 All ER 1210, at 1233.

183 [1992] 4 All ER 161, at 247–48.

184 *Ibid*, at 267–70.

185 *Agip (Africa) Ltd v Jackson* [1990] Ch 265, at 295; *Equiticorp Industries Group v The Crown* (1996) 3 NZLR 586, at 603.

186 [1992] 4 All ER 769.

In Australia, in *Consul Development Pty Ltd v DPC Estates Pty Ltd*,[187] the High Court held that Consul was not liable as a constructive trustee to hold properties it had acquired as a result of information received by its managing director from a dishonest employee of the plaintiff. The employee had incorrectly represented to the purchaser that his principal was not in a financial position to acquire the properties. Although the circumstances of acquisition were suspicious, the finding by the trial judge that the managing director of Consul honestly believed that the plaintiff was not interested in the properties was sufficient to absolve Consul from any further duty to inquire.

(d) Imputed liability through agents

Liability may be imputed to a principal where a person having the requisite knowledge of a transaction is the alter ego of the principle, or where the principle employs an agent to investigate a transaction in which the principle is involved and the agent does not detect misconduct in a situation where an honest and reasonable agent would have done so. In the alter ego category, liability will be imputed if the person having the requisite knowledge had management and control over the activities relating to the transaction in issue so that he or she might be said to be the directing mind of the principal for that purpose. This may mean that the person is in general control of affairs of the principal, or it may, as in *El Anjou v Dollar Holdings Ltd*,[188] mean that the person, although not holding such a substantial position, nevertheless has control over a certain transaction in a material and effective way. Where this is the case, acts that are within the authority of the agent or employee but performed for an improper purpose or otherwise in breach of fiduciary duty, will be binding on the principal although equitable remedies and rights may arise between the principal and the agent.[189] In the second category, that of the agent hired to investigate, liability will be imputed if a duty to make inquiry has arisen and the agent has failed to detect misconduct which an honest and reasonable agent would have detected, or has failed to pass on information which would have revealed misconduct. If there is no duty to inquire, however, the mere fact that an agent has acquired adverse knowledge in a capacity other than as agent for his or her principal does not mean that liability will be imputed to the latter if the information is not passed on.[190] Nor, even if there is a duty to

---

187 (1974–75) 132 CLR 373.

188 [1994] 2 All ER 685.

189 *Richard Brady Franks v Price* (1937) 58 CLR 112; *Winthrop Investments Ltd v Winns Ltd* (1975) 2 NSWLR 666; *Greater Pacific Investments v Australian National Industries* (1996) 39 NSWLR 143.

190 See *El Anjou v Dollar Holdings Ltd* [1994] 2 All ER 685, at 698; *Halifax Mortgage Services v Stepsky* [1996] 2 WLR 230.

inquire, will the principal be liable if the agent has acted in fraud of his or her principal and chosen not to pass on the information because in that case the agent will have exceeded his or her authority.[191] In *Equiticorp Industries Group v The Crown*,[192] for example, certain agents of the Crown had been employed to make inquiry into the legality of funding arrangements concerning the acquisition by Equiticorp of the Crown shares in New Zealand Steel. It was held that, in the absence of fraud by the agents, a failure to pass on relevant information concerning the illegal means of funding the purchase meant that Crown was liable to compensate Equiticorp for losses derived from the dishonest activities of certain of its directors in acquiring the shares. Where knowledge is derived from various sources, liability may be imputed to a principal based on the aggregation of knowledge of which it has possession.[193]

(e) The liability of a volunteer for the receipt of trust property

Where misappropriated trust property has been received innocently, the recipient may be required to account unless it can be established that adequate consideration was given for the property. If there has been little or no value given for the property, then he or she may be liable to surrender up any property or repay any money that he or she has been given. In *Banque Belge Pour l'Etranger v Hambrouk*,[194] a defrauded victim was able to reclaim moneys given by the thief to his mistress. The fact that the moneys had been paid into an account of the mistress did not deter the Court of Appeal from ordering repayment. Although paid into a bank account, the moneys were unmixed and identifiable as the product of the fraud. The contention that the defendant had good title to the moneys because she had acquired it as a gift and did not have notice that it had been stolen was unsuccessful. Bankes LJ observed:[195]

> To accept either of these two contentions with which I have been so far dealing would be to assent to the proposition that a thief, who has stolen money, and who from fear of detection hands that money to a beggar who happens to pass, gives a title to the money to the beggar as against the true owner – a proposition which is obviously impossible of acceptance.

---

191 *Belmont Finance v Williams Furniture* (1979) 1 Ch 250, at 262; *El Anjou v Dollar Holdings Ltd* [1994] 2 All ER 685, at 704; *Re David Payne & Co Ltd* [1904] 2 Ch 608; *Waldy v Gray* (1885) LR Eq 238.

192 [1996] 3 NZLR 586, at 602–03.

193 *National Australia Bank v Morris* [1892] AC 287; *Brambles Holdings v Carey* (1976) 15 SASR 270; *Krakowski v Eurolynx Properties Ltd* (1995) 130 ALR 1; *Equiticorp Industries Group v Crown* [1996] 3 NZLR 586, at 604.

194 [1921] 1 KB 321.

195 *Ibid*, at 327.

Of importance also is the decision of the House of Lords in *Lipkin Gorman v Karpnale Ltd*[196] where a solicitor misappropriated partnership funds which were paid to a gaming club. It was held that an action for moneys had and received would lie to allow the partnership to recover the money. Since a gaming contract was declared void under statute and the exchange of chips was only a means to enable wagers to take place, the club was unable to show that it had given value for the payments.[197] Although the club received the moneys in good faith, it was held that restitution of the proceeds of the fraud should be permitted. To deny recovery would, in the opinion of their Lordships, permit the club to be unjustly enriched at the expense of the firm.[198] In this regard, Lord Templeman considered that moneys had and received would lie to the extent that a third party was unable to show adequate consideration.[199] However, the club was permitted to set-off the amounts paid to the thief for his successful wagers. To this extent a defence of change of circumstances was recognised.[200]

The firm in *Lipkin Gorman* relied on the common law action for moneys had and received rather than an equitable tracing claim.[201] It was unnecessary to have regard to equity because the club had admitted that, if the partnership could show that the moneys received by the fraudulent partner belonged to it, the fact that it may have been mixed in the hands of the thief with moneys of his own did not matter. However, independently of a common law claim, an equitable tracing claim would have been available to the firm as both Lord Goff[202] and Lord Templeman[203] recognised. In this regard, Lord Templeman referred to *Black v Freeman & Co*, where the High Court of Australia held that money which had been stolen by a husband and given to his wife could be recovered by the victim. O'Connor J observed:[204]

> Where money has been stolen, it is trust money in the hands of the thief and he cannot divest it of that character. If he pays it over to another person, then it may be followed into that other person's hands. If, of course, that other person shows that it has come to him

---

196 [1991] 2 AC 548; [1992] 4 All ER 513.

197 *Ibid*, at 562; 520 *per* Lord Templeman citing *Clarke v Shee* (1774) 1 Cowp 197; 98 ER 1041; *Hudson v Robinson* (1816) 4 M & S 475; [1816] 105 ER 910; *Bainbrigge v Browne* (1881) 18 Ch D 188; *Shoolbred v Roberts* [1892] 2 QB 560; *Banque Belge Pour l'Etranger v Hambrouk* (1921) 1 KB 321; *Black v Freeman* (1910) 12 CLR 105; Lord Goff at 544–47; at 529–32.

198 See the reasoning of Lord Templeman, *ibid*, at 560; 517–18.

199 *Ibid*, at 560; 517.

200 See Lord Goff, *ibid*, at 577–83; 532–36. The defence of adverse change of position has been recognised in Australia in *David Securities Pty Ltd v Commonwealth Bank of Australia* (1992) 175 CLR 353, at 385–87. See discussion, pp 34–37.

201 The equitable tracing claim is considered further, pp 317–21.

202 *Ibid*, at 572; 528.

203 *Ibid*, at 566; 522.

204 (1910) 12 CLR 105, at 110. Applied in *Lord v Spinelly* [1991] 4 WAR 158.

bona fide for valuable consideration and without notice, it then may lose its character as trust money and cannot be recovered. But, if it is handed over merely as a gift, it does not matter whether there is notice or not.

Where, however, the third party is entirely innocent of wrongdoing and acts merely as a conduit, he or she will be under no liability to account. Thus, in *National Commercial Banking Corporation of Australia v Batty*,[205] a firm was not liable for the proceeds of cheques that had been dishonestly obtained by a fraudulent clerk, applied to the firms' bank account, and subsequently misappropriated by the clerk. It would follow that if the third party had knowledge that the moneys were fraudulently obtained or whilst in control of the money obtained such knowledge, liability should attach for any misappropriation.

(f) The liability of agents to account for fees derived from a tainted source

Where an agent is shown to have actual knowledge that fees are the product of a fraud, then he or she should be liable to account for those fees to the victim. The law should not protect an agent who acts without probity.[206] An agent should not, however, be liable to account for fees derived from the proceeds of a breach of trust, unless he or she has actual knowledge that the fees are the product of a dishonest misappropriation of trust property. Actual knowledge is more commercially appropriate than an approach which requires an agent to make extensive enquiries into his or her principal's honesty and the source of fees paid for professional services. This was recognised in *Re Blundell, Blundell v Blundell*,[207] where it was held that a solicitor was entitled to accept instructions from his principal on the basis that the latter was acting honestly. It was also held that the mere fact that a solicitor knew of a breach of trust was not itself sufficient to deprive him of fees earned professionally. Stirling J observed:[208]

> In order that the solicitor may be debarred from accepting payment out of the trust estate, he must be fixed with notice that at the time when he accepted payment the trustee had been guilty of a breach of trust such as would preclude him altogether from resorting to the trust estate for payment of costs, so that, in fact, the application of the trust estate in payment of costs would be a breach of trust.

---

205 (1986) 160 CLR 25.

206 See *Carls-Zeiss Stiftung v Herbert Smith & Co* [1969] 2 Ch 276, at 302; [1969] 2 All ER 367, at 384.

207 (1888) 40 Ch D 370; [1886–90] All ER 837.

208 *Ibid*, at 383; 843.

In *Carl-Zeiss Stiftung v Herbert Smith & Co*,[209] the Court of Appeal approved *Blundell*. The court rejected a claim that solicitors, who had acted for the West German 'Carl-Zeiss' Foundation, should have to account to the East German Foundation for fees derived from litigation with the East German Foundation. The firm was held to be entitled to the fees. The knowledge that a claim had been made by the East German Foundation to the assets of the West German Foundation was insufficient to require the West German Foundation to account for its fees.[210] Although the question of the extent of knowledge that would suffice to attract liability was not determined, Edmund Davies LJ gave some guidance observing that liability should depend upon an absence of 'probity'.[211] In *Eagle Trust v SBC Securities Ltd*,[212] Vinelott J also referred to the opinion of Stirling J in *Re Blundell*. However, following the approach taken by Peter Gibson J in *Baden*, it was considered that actual knowledge could include a reckless failure to make inquiry.[213] Vinelott J also observed that in a case where an agent did not give evidence or a satisfactory explanation it might be inferred that he had knowledge, if the circumstances were such that an honest and reasonable man would have inferred that the moneys were probably trust moneys and were being misapplied, and would have either not have accepted them or would have kept them separate until he had satisfied himself that the payer was entitled to use them in discharge of the liability.[214]

Remedies for breach of fiduciary duties

There are a wide variety of remedies available to a principal, who has been the victim of a breach of fiduciary relationship or confidence, in order to prevent the unjust enrichment of a fiduciary.

(a) Injunction

An injunction will lie to prevent a threatened or continuing breach of fiduciary duty or to prohibit the unauthorised use of confidential

---

209 [1969] 2 Ch 276, at 292, 298, 302; [1969] 2 All ER 367, at 374, 379, 382.

210 Further, on this point, see *La Roche v Armstrong* [1922] 1 KB 485; at 491; [1922] All ER 311, at 313; *Competitive Insurance Ltd v Davies Investments* [1975] 3 All ER 254.

211 [1969] 2 Ch 276, at 302; 2 All ER 367, at 384; and further, see the comments of Sachs LJ at 298, 379, on *Re Blundell* (1889) 40 Ch D 370; [1886–90] All ER Rep 837 and *Williams v Williams* (1881) 17 Ch D 435. Sachs LJ considered that 'these cases tend quite strongly to the conclusion that negligent, if innocent, failure to make enquiry is not sufficient to attract constructive trusteeship'.

212 [1992] 4 All ER 488, at 509.

213 See discussion, pp 293–94.

214 [1992] 4 All ER 488, at 509.

information. An injunction may be granted as interim relief,[215] or as a permanent remedy to prevent a continuing breach.[216] In addition to an injunction, an account of profits may be ordered.[217] Common law damages may also be ordered in addition to an injunction where loss results from a breach of a tortious or contractual obligation.[218] Where, as in *Saltman Engineering Co Ltd v Campbell Engineering Co Ltd*,[219] it was considered inappropriate to grant an injunction, damages may be awarded under the equivalent statutory jurisdiction of Lord Cairns' Act[220] to reflect the appropriate value of the information gained from the abuse of confidence. In a case where information used to manufacture a product is partly confidential and partly in the public domain, the user of the confidential information may be required to compensate for the misuse of information which is confidential.[221] In addition, an order for delivery up or cancellation of documentation derived from a breach of fiduciary duty or confidence may be ordered.[222]

---

215 *Speed Seal Products v Paddington* [1986] 1 All ER 91. In an appropriate case, interim relief may be sought to preserve trust assets, see *Mareva Compagnia Naviera (the Mareva) SA v International Bulk carriers SA* [1975] 2 Lloyd's Rep 509; *TDK Tape Distributor (UK) Ltd v Videochoice Ltd* [1985] 3 All ER 345; *Australian Iron & Steel Pty Ltd v Buck* (1982) 2 NSWLR 889; or to trace the proceeds of misappropriated bank accounts, or other confidential information, see *Anton Piller KG v Manufacturing Processes Ltd* [1976] 1 Ch 55; 1 All ER 779; *EMI (Australia) Ltd v Bay Imports Pty Ltd* [1980] FSR 328; *Chrysalis Records Ltd v Vere* (1982) 65 FLR 422; *Bankers Trust Co v Shapira* [1980] 3 All ER 353; *Bekhor v Bilton* [1981] QB 923; [1981] 2 All ER 565.

216 *Peter Pan Manufacturing Corporation v Corsets Silhouette Ltd* [1963] 3 All ER 402. Injunction granted for a limited period to prevent unfair competition, see *Pacifica Shipping Co Ltd v Anderson* [1986] 2 NZLR 328.

217 *Peter Pan Manufacturing Corporation v Corsets Silhouette Ltd* [1963] 3 All ER 402; *AB Consolidated v Europe Strength Food* [1978] 2 NZLR 515, at 526–27.

218 *A G Spalding Brothers v A W Gamage Ltd* [1914–15] All ER 147.

219 [1963] 3 All ER 413; Lord Goff in *AG v Observer Ltd* [1990] 1 AC 109, at 286; *Colbeam Palmer Ltd v Stock Affiliates Pty Ltd* (1986–87) 122 CLR 25, at 33; *Talbott v General Television Corp Pty Ltd* [1980] VR 224.

220 1858 (UK) 21 & 22 Vict c 27 (Chancery Amendment), considered in *Wentworth v Woollahra Municipal Council* (1982) 149 CLR 672, at 676; in New Zealand, in *Souster v Epsom Plumbing Contractors Ltd* [1974] 2 NZLR 515; *Grocott v Ayson* [1975] 2 NZLR 586. For example, s 68 of the Supreme Court Act 1970 (NSW); s 30 of the SCA 1939 (S Aust); s 38 of the SCA 1986 (Vict); s 25(10) of the SCA 1935 (Western Aust); s 11(3) of the Supreme Court Civil Procedure Act 1932 (Tas).

221 See *Seager v Copydex* [1967] 2 All ER 415, at 417. On the issue of the measure of damages, see *Seager v Copydex Ltd (No 2)* [1969] 2 All ER 710, where the Court of Appeal suggested that, in the case of information, which has no special quality, damages could be assessed on the basis of the cost of paying a consultant a fee to acquire the information. Where, however, the information was special, such as an invention, damages could be reflected in a capitalised royalty value assessed as being the market price a purchaser would be prepared to pay for the item. Further, see *Dowson & Mason Ltd v Potter* [1986] 2 All ER 418, where the Court of Appeal considered that damages could include a loss of profit, where a plaintiff intended to manufacture a product for sale.

222 See *Peter Pan Manufacturing Corporation v Corsets Silhouette Ltd* [1963] 3 All ER 402; *Franklin v Giddins* (1978) Qd R 72.

(b) Account

An account of profits will be the most usual form of personal remedy sought in cases of breach of fiduciary duty. Thus, an agent or third party, who has knowingly participated in a breach of fiduciary duty or who has used confidential information to his own advantage and has derived profits thereon, will be held liable to account for the net profits to the defrauded principal.[223] A principal, who has been the victim of a breach of fiduciary obligation, need not have suffered any loss as a condition of receiving an account of profits.[224] Further, where there has been wilful default, a fiduciary may be ordered to account for receipts or payments which ought to have been received.[225] The assessment of profits may be difficult. At least, where the breach of fiduciary duty is unintentional, *Phipps v Boardman* supports a liberal allowance to compensate the fiduciary for time and effort in gaining the profit.[226] In *O'Sullivan v Management Agency Ltd*,[227] a manager of a musician was entitled to an allowance for his time and effort including a profit component notwithstanding a finding of undue influence in procuring of contacts of management. An allowance for profit will be less predictable in cases where there has been a flagrant breach of fiduciary duty.[228] Where the fiduciary can establish that he or she has expended his or her own capital and time and effort in acquiring a profit, some compensation should be permitted.[229] An equitable lien may be granted to secure a fiduciary's claim to expenses.[230] If the defendant can show that the profit or a greater part of it was attributable to his or her industry or the intrinsic qualities and value of the goods rather than any infringement of trade mark or breach of confidence, a court may attempt to apportion the profits.[231] In *Colbeam Palmer Ltd v Stock Affiliates Pty Ltd*,[232] Windeyer J observed that, in cases

---

223 *Timber Engineering Co Ltd v Anderson* (1980) 2 NSWLR 488; *Colbeam Palmer Ltd v Stock Affiliates Pty Ltd* (1968) 122 CLR 25; *Decor Corporation Pty Ltd v Dart Industries Inc* (1991) 33 FCR 397.

224 See *Reading v Attorney General* [1951] AC 507; [1951] 1 All ER 617.

225 *White v City of London Brewery Co* (1889) 42 Ch D 237.

226 [1967] 2 AC 46; [1966] 3 All ER 721.

227 [1985] 3 All ER 351; *Estate Realties v Wignall* [1992] 2 NZLR 615.

228 See *Timber Engineering Co Pty Ltd v Anderson* (1980) 2 NSWLR 488. Cf *Cook v Evatt (No 2)* [1992] 1 NZLR 676; *Estate Realties v Wignall* [1992] 2 NZLR 615.

229 *Paul A Davies (Australia) Pty Ltd v Davies* (1983) 1 NSWLR 440; *Warman International Ltd v Dwyer* (1995) 182 CLR 544.

230 *Shirlaw v Taylor* (1991) 31 FCR 222; *Lac Minerals Ltd v International Resources Ltd* (1989) 61 DLR (4th) 14.

231 See *My Kinda Town Ltd v Son* (1982) 8 FSR 147; *Zupanovich Pty Ltd v Beale Nominees Pty Ltd* (1996) 138 ALR 107.

232 *Colbeam Palmer Ltd v Stock Affiliates Pty Ltd* (1968) 122 CLR 25. Cf *Peter Pan Manufacturing Corporation v Corsets Silhouette Ltd* [1963] 3 All ER 402, where an account of profits was ordered, which included the profit on manufacture and sales of items, and was not limited to the profit that was attributable to the use of the plaintiff's patterns and information.

of this kind, mathematical precision was impossible. All that can be expected is a reasonable approximation.[233] In *Warman International Ltd v Dwyer*,[234] the High Court of Australia considered that a distinction should be drawn between cases in which a specific asset is acquired and cases in which a business has been acquired and operated. In the case of a business, it may be inappropriate to compel a fiduciary to account for the whole of his or her profit from the conduct of a business, or his or her exploitation of a principal's goodwill over an indefinite period of time. Where a significant proportion of the profits have been generated through the energy and skill of the errant fiduciary, it may be appropriate to allow a share of the profits. However, the court held that, in general, profits should not be apportioned in the absence of an antecedent arrangement for profit-sharing but an allowance should be made for the fiduciary's skill, expertise and other expenses. The court also considered that the appropriate measure of relief was an allowance for expenses, skill, expertise, effort and resources, and net profits should be surrendered. The approach least favourable to the errant fiduciaries was adopted since the profits had been substantially derived from the exploitation of Warman's business.

Where a fiduciary has acted in breach of his or her contractual obligations and has derived profits from his or her efforts as well, the principal may be entitled to an inquiry as to damages for breach and an account of profits. In *Timber Engineering Co Pty Ltd v Anderson*,[235] the defendant employees, who were in breach of their contractual duty of good faith, were held liable to an inquiry as to damages as well as an account of profits. The argument that this would amount to double recovery was unsuccessful. However, in *Tang Man Sit v Capacieus Investments Ltd*,[236] the Privy Council held that such remedies were alternative, and not cumulative and a court could make orders requiring the defendant to give such information so that an informed election could be made prior to judgment.

---

233 *Ibid*, at 43–46.

234 (1995) 182 ALR 544.

235 *Ibid*, note double recovery doubted in *United States Surgical Corp v Hospital Products International Pty Ltd* (1982) 2 NSWLR 766, considered also by Mason J in *Hospital Products Ltd v United States Surgical Corporation* (1984) 156 CLR 41, at 115–16; *House of Spring Gardens Ltd v Point Blank Ltd* [1983] FSR 489. Further, see *United Australia Ltd v Barclays Bank Ltd* [1941] AC 1; [1940] 4 All ER 20; and *Mahesan v Malaysia Government Housing* [1979] AC 374; [1978] 2 All ER 405.

236 [1996] 1 All ER 193.

Delay in bringing an action may debar a plaintiff who has deliberately withheld commencing action from claiming profits; and, in other cases, delay may restrict the period in which profits should be assessed.[237]

(c) Rescission

Rescission of a contract may be available to a person who has entered into a contract with a fiduciary. A contract entered into between a trustee and a beneficiary may be rescinded for inadequate consideration[238] or on proof of a material breach of fiduciary duty.[239] Similarly, a contract which is the product of corrupt dealing between briber and an agent may be set aside at the request of the principal.[240] Where there exists a breach of fiduciary duty, a court will attempt to achieve practical justice[241] even though *restitutio in integrum* of the property is impossible. In equity, a court will endeavour to achieve a just result by either ordering compensation for any deterioration in the subject-matter of the contract or an account of profits against the wrongdoer, whilst requiring the innocent party to give credit for benefits received under the contract.[242] Where rescission is impossible because the innocent party is unable to restore benefits received, the appropriate remedy to obviate losses derived from a breach of fiduciary duty is the equitable remedy of compensation.[243]

Delay after a plaintiff has ascertained his or her right to rescind, which causes prejudice to the defendant, may lead a court to decline rescission.[244]

---

237 *Colbeam Palmer Ltd v Stock Affiliates Pty Ltd* (1968) 122 CLR 25; *Kalamazoo (Aust) Pty Ltd v Compact Business Systems Pty Ltd* (1984) 84 FLR 101. In intellectual property cases, profits may in the case at least of an unwitting infringement of intellectual property rights be limited to the date of the claim. See *Colbeam Palmer Ltd v Stock Affiliates Pty Ltd, ibid*, at 33–36. There has been further statutory intervention, in certain areas of intellectual property, see in Australia, s 123 of the Patents Act 1990 (Cth), s 32B(2) of the Designs Act 1906 (Cth). *Cf* s 115(3) of the Copyright Act 1968 (Cth).

238 *Tufton v Sperni* [1952] 2 TLR 516, at 522; *Tate v Williamson* (1866) 2 Ch App 55, at 60–61.

239 *Adam v Newbigging* (1888) 13 App Cas 308; *Armstrong v Jackson* [1917] 2 KB 822, at 828–29; [1916–17] All ER 1117, at 1120–22; *Daly v Sydney Stock Exchange* (1986) 160 CLR 371, at 387.

240 *Mahesan v Malaysia Government Housing* [1979] AC 374; [1978] 2 All ER 405.

241 *Erlanger v New Sombrero Phosphate Co* (1878) 3 App Cas 1218, at 1279; [1874–80] All ER 271, at 283–86; *Adam v Newbigging* (1888) 13 App Cas 308; *Armstrong v Jackson* [1917] 2 KB 822; [1916–17] All ER 117; *Alati v Kruger* (1955) 94 CLR 216, at 223–24 *per* Dixon J; *O'Sullivan v Management Agency* [1985] 3 All ER 351; *Estate Realties v Wignall* [1992] 2 NZLR 615. See discussion under misrepresentation, Chapter 9, pp 205–08.

242 See *Lord Wright in Spense v Crawford* [1939] 3 All ER 271, at 288–89; *O'Sullivan v Management Agency* [1985] 3 All ER 351, at 363. *Bendigo Central Freezing & Fertiliser Co Ltd v Cunningham* [1919] VLR 387; *Brown v Smitt* (1924) 34 CLR 160. In *O'Connor v Hart* [1984] 1 NZLR 754 (reversed in the Privy Council on other grounds) [1985] 1 AC 1000; [1985] 1 NZLR 159, the Court of Appeal, as a condition of rescinding a sale of land, ordered the purchaser in possession, Hart, to be compensated for improvements made to the property.

243 *Greater Pacific Investments v Australian National Industries Ltd* (1996) 39 NSWLR 143.

244 *Armstrong v Jackson* [1917] 2 KB 822, at 828–29; [1916–17] All ER 1117, at 1120–22; *Fysh v Page* (1956) 96 CLR 233.

(d) Compensation

If a principal can show loss, the preferred remedy may be compensation for breach of fiduciary duty rather than account. Compensation was ordered to redress a breach of fiduciary obligation by the House of Lords in *Nocton v Lord Ashburton*,[245] and has since been ordered by courts in Australia[246] and New Zealand.[247] Compensation in equity for a breach of fiduciary duty is not fettered by limitations such as forseeability or remoteness that restrict common law damages.[248] Compensation is assessed in such a way as to ensure that losses made good are only those which according to hindsight and a commonsense view of causation were attributable to the breach.[249] Compensation for a breach of a fiduciary obligation will be favoured where profits are inconsequential or difficult to compute. Loss of an opportunity to profit from a transaction may be the subject of a claim for compensation against an errant fiduciary.[250] The conduct of the plaintiff may affect the quantum of compensation awarded for breach of a fiduciary obligation. In *Day v Mead*,[251] the New Zealand Court of Appeal reduced the amount of compensation claimed for loss arising from a breach of fiduciary duty after taking into account the actions of the plaintiff and his contribution to the loss. Where a trustee has been honest but negligent, the Court of Appeal of Western Australia in *Permanent Building Society v Wheller*,[252] observed that he or she should not have to compensate a beneficiary for losses without proof that but for the breach of duty the losses would not have been incurred. In this regard, it was considered that there was a distinction in the approach that should be taken to compensation where it was based on a true breach of fiduciary duty involving dishonesty. The value of assets that have been misappropriated may be assessed as at the date of the proceedings rather than at the date of the misappropriation, if there is an adverse movement in value.[253]

---

245 [1914] AC 932; [1914–15] All ER 45.

246 *McKenzie v McDonald* [1927] VLR 134, at 146; *Re Dawson (dec'd)* (1966) 2 NSWLR 211, at 216; *Talbott v General Television Corporation Pty Ltd* [1980] VR 224; *Markwell Bros Pty Ltd v CPN Diesals Queensland Pty Ltd* (1983) 2 Qd R 508, at 523; *Catt v Marac Australia Ltd* (1987) 9 NSWLR 639, at 660; *Fraser Edmiston Pty Ltd v AGT Qld Pty Ltd* (1988) 2 Qd R 1; *Commonwealth Bank v Smith* (1992) 102 ALR 453, at 478–79; *Stewart v Layton* (1992) 11 ALR 688, at 713–15; *Chittick v Maxwell* (1993) 118 ALR 728; *Greater Pacific Investments v Australian National Industries* (1996) 39 NSWLR 143.

247 *Coleman v Myers* [1977] 2 NZLR 225; *Farrington v Rowe, McBride & Partners* [1985] 1 NZLR 83.

248 *Re Dawson (dec'd) Union Fidelity Trustee Co Ltd* (1966) 2 NSWLR 211, at 214–16; *Hill v Rose* [1990] VR 129; *Permanent Building Society v Wheeler* (1993–94) 11 WAR 187.

249 *Target Holdings Ltd v Redferns* [1996] 1 AC 421; [1995] 3 WLR 352; *Equiticorp Industries Group v The Crown* [1996] 3 NZLR 586.

250 *Biala v Mallina Holdings Pty Ltd* (1994–95) 13 WAR 11.

251 [1987] 2 NZLR 443.

252 (1993–94) 11 WAR 187.

253 *Re Dawson Deceased* (1966) 2 NSWLR 211.

(e) Constructive trust

A fiduciary who has stolen the property of his principal or has obtained property in breach of trust may be held liable to hold the property as a constructive trustee. Thus, in *Keech v Sandford*[254] and *Chan v Zacharia*,[255] property obtained in breach of fiduciary duty and in competition with the principal was the subject of a constructive trust. A constructive trust of this kind has been described as an institutional constructive trust akin to an express trust.[256] There has, however, been increasing recognition that a constructive trust may be imposed as a remedial device to prevent unjust enrichment.[257] A constructive trust of this kind does not depend on there being evidence of an unconscientious interference with a proprietary interest. For example, in *Attorney General for Hong Kong v Reid*,[258] the Privy Council imposed a constructive trust on land purchased from the proceeds of bribes. Their Lordships held that if the properties were to increase in value, then the principal was entitled to the benefit of the increase. If the properties were to fall in value, then the fiduciary remained personally liable for the outstanding amount of the bribes. Lord Templeman was not receptive to the argument, which had appealed to the English Court of Appeal a century before in *Lister v Stubbs*,[259] that to impose a constructive trust over the assets acquired with the proceeds of bribery would be disadvantageous for the general creditors of the fiduciary should the fiduciary become insolvent. Lord Templeman considered that if a trustee commits a crime by accepting a bribe which he ought to pay over to his *cestui que trust*, the bribe and any profit made

---

254 (1726) Sel Cas, Ch 61; [1558–1774] All ER 230.

255 (1983–84) 154 CLR 178. Further for the imposition of a constructive trust over the goodwill and business of a company, see *Timber Engineering v Anderson* (1980) 2 NSWLR 488, but compare the approach of Mason J in *Hospital Products v United States Surgical Corp* (1984) 156 CLR 41, at 115, where an account rather than a constructive trust was considered the appropriate remedy where there had been a dishonest interference with and undermining of the plaintiff's product and capacity to sell its product in Australia.

256 See *Westdeutshe Landesbank v Islington LBC* [1996] 2 WLR 802, at 837 *et seq*; [1996] 2 All ER 961, at 996 *et seq per* Lord Browne-Wilkinson, and see institution or remedy, *Re Jonton Pty Ltd* (1992) 2 Qd R 105.

257 Scott, AW (1955) 71 LQR 39, at 41, citing Pound, R, 'The Progress of Law' (1920) 33 Harv LR 420–21. See the discussion by Deane J of the distinction between a remedy and an institution in *Muschinski v Dodds* (1986) 160 CLR 583, at 613–17 and further, see *Re Jonton Pty Ltd* (1992) 2 Qd R 105, at 107.

258 [1994] 1 AC 321, applied in *Zobory v Federal Commissioner of Taxation* (1995) 129 ALR 484, where Burchett J held that that a constructive trust was imposed over money that was stolen as soon as it was misappropriated so that the thief was not liable for income derived from interest received even though it was mixed with a small amount of the thief's own money. The interest was treated as an accretion to the trust. See further, *FC Jones and Sons v Jones* [1996] 4 All ER 72, discussed, p 316.

259 (1890) 45 Ch D 1. Professor R Goode, strongly defended *Lister v Stubbs* in his essay, 'Property and Unjust Enrichment', in Burrows, A (ed), *Essays on the Law of Restitution*, 1991, pp 240–46, Clarendon Press, Oxford. Further, see Watts, P, 'Restitution' (1993) NZ Recent Law Rev 424, at 425.

there from should be withdrawn from the unsecured creditors as soon as the crime is discovered.[260] It is submitted that creditors should not be able to take the benefit of moneys or investments derived from a bankrupt's fraudulent dealings for which there would ordinarily be an obligation to account if insolvency had not occurred. To permit creditors to fortuitously profit in these circumstances is to allow their unjust enrichment. The imposition of a constructive trust in these circumstances is remedial and corresponds with the approach that courts in the United States have taken to the constructive trust.[261] The decision of the High Court of Australia in *Daly v Sydney Stock Exchange Ltd*[262] may merit reconsideration in the light of *Reid* and its rejection of the debtor-creditor analysis in *Lister v Stubbs*. In that case, a firm of stock-brokers, in breach of a fiduciary duty to the plaintiff, solicited moneys for investment from the plaintiff who had sought to invest in shares. The firm was in serious financial difficulties at the time. This was a matter which was not disclosed to the plaintiff by the firm before the investment was made. The firm subsequently went bankrupt before the investment could be realised. The plaintiff, for the purpose of establishing a claim under the governing fidelity fund, had to establish that the moneys had been received in trust. It was contended by the plaintiff that the firm held the moneys as constructive trustees because of their breach of duty. This argument was rejected by the High Court which held that the investment constituted a contract of loan and a debtor-creditor relationship. Gibbs CJ[263] considered that the imposition of a constructive trust would have serious ramifications in an insolvency and followed *Lister v Stubbs*. Brennan J considered that the loan was voidable but, until action was taken to avoid the investment, the borrower could not be regarded as a trustee. In the opinion of Brennan J, there was no analogy between the present case and one where a constructive trust is imposed on money or

---

260 [1994] 1 AC 324, at 336.

261 See *Beatty v Gugenheim Corporation* (1919) 225 NY 380, where Cardozo J stated, 'A constructive trust is the formula through which the conscience of equity finds expression. When property has been acquired in such circumstances that the holder of the legal title may not in good conscience retain the beneficial interest, equity converts him into a trustee'. Referred to by Goulding J in *Chase Manhatten Bank NA v Israel-British Bank (London) Ltd* [1979] 3 All ER 1025, at 1038; referred to also by Mason J in *Hospital Products Ltd v United States Surgical Corporation* (1984) 156 CLR 41, at 108, and in New Zealand, in *Elders Pastoral v BNZ* [1989] 2 NZLR 180, at 185, *per* Cooke P.

262 (1986) 160 CLR 371. Further, see *Westpac Banking Corporation v Markovic* (1985) 82 FLR 7; *Austinel Investments Australia Pty Ltd v Lam* (1990) 19 NSWLR 637; considered by Gummow J in *Stephenson Nominees Pty Ltd v Official Receiver* (1987) 76 ALR 485; *ASC v Melbourne Asset* (1994) 121 ALR 626. *Cf Neste Oy v Lloyd's Bank plc* [1983] 2 Lloyd's Rep 658; *Elders Pastoral v BNZ* [1989] 2 NZLR 180; *Liggett v Kensington* [1993] NZLR 257, reversed in the Privy Council [1994] 3 NZLR 385.

263 *Ibid*, at 379–80.

other property which is acquired by a non-fiduciary otherwise than by contract as in *Chase Manhatten Bank NA v Israel-British Bank (London) Ltd*.[264]

Chase Manhatten[265] involved a substantial payment mistakenly made by a bank and credited to the defendant bank which subsequently went into liquidation. Goulding J adopted the American approach that a constructive trust was a remedy through which the conscience of equity finds expression.[266] In the opinion of Goulding J, the payer should have a priority claim over the general creditors of the payee because the payer by paying under mistake had retained an equitable proprietary interest in the money sufficient to impose an obligation in good faith upon the payee to account.[267] In these circumstances, a constructive trust was imposed to prevent the unjust enrichment of the payee bank's creditors. There is an obvious point of distinction between *Daly* and cases like *Reid* and *Chase Manhatten*, in that the payment in the former case was advanced for the purpose of securing an investment thereby creating an immediate relationship of debtor and creditor. However, because the investment was derived in breach of fiduciary duty and was one that would have been unlikely to have been made had the investor known of the true position, it can be persuasively argued that the investment, representing the proceeds of the moneys advanced, was immediately impressed with a trust.[268] In the event of the firm's insolvency, the imposition of a remedial constructive trust based on the acquisition of the money in breach of fiduciary duty would be necessary and appropriate in order to prevent unjust enrichment of the firm's general creditors. The development of the remedial constructive trust and its relationship with the orthodox equitable tracing remedy is considered later in this chapter.[269]

Ancillary problems may arise. Should a remedial constructive trust be imposed where the agent has contributed to an investment purchased partly with the proceeds of the bribe and with his own funds? Restitutionary relief should be limited to that portion of the investment which is derived from the proceeds of the bribe or other breach of

---

264 *Ibid*, at 390–91.

265 [1981] 1 Ch 105; [1979] 3 All ER 1025.

266 *Ibid*, at 126; 1036–39, a phrase used by Cardozo J in *Beatty v Gugenheim Corporation* (1919) 225 NY 380.

267 *Ibid*, at 128; 1032. The approach of Goulding J has been rejected by Lord Browne-Wilkinson in *Westdeutsche Landesbank Girozentrale v Islington LBC* [1996] 2 WLR 802; 2 All ER 961 and see discussion, p 324.

268 Following the approach of Lord Templeman in *Attorney General for Hong Kong v Reid* [1994] 1 AC 321, at 336. See also *Re Kountze Bros* (1935) 79 F (2nd) 98, at 102, noted by Gummow J in *Stephenson Nominees Pty Ltd v Official Receiver* (1987) 76 ALR 485, at 505–06.

269 At pp 323–28.

fiduciary dealing.[270] It should not attach to the fiduciary's own property.[271] However, should the investment increase in value then a remedial constructive trust should proportionally reflect this increase. Another problem arises where assets have been acquired totally with the proceeds of the bribe but the fiduciary has improved the asset with his or her own labour and capital. If the fiduciary can establish that the value of the property has been enhanced in this way, allowance should be made for this. Where the breach has not been wilful, allowances made for maintenance and improvement of property may be more generous than in the case of a wilful default.[272] Further, where a fiduciary has acquired property in competition with his or her principal and is ordered to hold it in trust, the constructive trustee is entitled to an indemnity from his or her principal for the purchase price of the property and the cost of other outgoings and improvements.[273]

(f) Common law actions for the recovery of property

At law, an action for detinue or conversion will lie to require a fiduciary who has converted trust property to restore it to his principal. In order for an action of this kind to succeed, the plaintiff must be able to show an immediate right to possession of the property. Damages will follow from the remedy of conversion or detinue.[274] Where the plaintiff decides to waive the tort and instead claim the proceeds of the wrongful act rather than damages, an alternative action for moneys had and received may lie.[275] In *Lipkin Gorman v Karpnale Ltd*,[276] the House of Lords held that the plaintiff, a firm of solicitors, had an immediate right to possession of a banker's draft which had been fraudulently obtained by a partner because a draft had been made out to the firm. Accordingly, the firm was able to sue the defendant, a gaming club, to whom the draft had been fraudulently endorsed in conversion. Lord Goff distinguished

---

270 See *Scott v Scott* (1963) 109 CLR 649; *Paul A Davies (Australia) Pty Ltd v Davies* (1983) 1 NSWLR 440; in the *Marriage of Wagstaff* (1990) 99 FLR 390.

271 See Lord Wright in *Spense v Crawford* [1939] 3 All ER 271, at 288–89.

272 *Marriage of Wagstaff* (1990) 99 FLR 390, at 398–99. In *Dickie v Torbay Pharmacy Ltd* [1995] 3 NZLR 429, allowances were awarded to errant fiduciaries and repayment of deposit moneys as a condition of the imposition of a constructive trust.

273 *Re Sherman* [1954] Ch 653, applied in *Mansard Developments Ltd v Tilley Consultants Ltd* [1982] WAR 161.

274 In conversion, damages will be assessed as at the date of the breach; in detinue, damages will be assessed at the date of judgment, see *Sachs v Miklos* [1948] 2 KB 23; *Munro v Willmott* [1949] 1 KB 295; *Greenwood v Bennett* [1973] 1 QB 195; [1992] 3 All ER 586. An equitable claim for delivery up or specific restitution of a chattel may lie, if the chattel has some intrinsic or special value to the plaintiff. *Peruvian Guano Co v Dreyfus Brothers & Co* [1892] AC 166; *Greenwood v Bennett*, ibid, *McKeown v Cavalier Yachts* (1988) 13 NSWLR 33; *Gadsen v Strider 1 Ltd* (1990) 20 NSWLR 57.

275 See *United Australia v Barclays Bank* [1941] AC 1; [1940] 4 All ER 20; *Grace Brothers Limited v Lawson* (1922) 31 CLR 130. For waiver of tort, see Chapter 12.

276 [1991] 2 AC 548; [1992] 4 All ER 512.

Commercial Banking Corporation v Mann,[277] a decision of the Privy Council, on the ground that in that case the drafts that had been fraudulently obtained had not been made out in the name of the defrauded principal, Mann, but in the name of fraudulent third party and this meant that Mann had no right to immediate possession of them. As a consequence, Mann was unable to maintain an action for conversion of the draft or moneys had and received against the bank which had cashed the drafts and paid the fraudulent party.

A restitutionary claim for moneys had and received based on a more liberal concept of unjust enrichment was also recognised in *Lipkin Gorman.* In that case, the firm's principal claim for moneys had and received was against the club for the proceeds of cheques that had been fraudulently drawn on its account and used by a fraudulent partner for the purpose of gambling. The firm sued the club to recover the moneys that had been paid to it as wagers. Lord Goff considered that the club could not in conscience retain the money.[278] In his Lordship's view, the claim was not founded in conversion or waiver of tort but was based on a broad notion of unjust enrichment. Lord Templeman[279] also considered that the moneys could be recovered if to retain the moneys would mean that the club was unjustly enriched. The club was unable to plead that it had given consideration for the payments because the wagers were null and void under the Gaming Act. However, in so far as it had paid out on successful wagers, it was able to reduce its obligation to make restitution on the ground of a defence of adverse change of position.[280]

The action for moneys had and received is not limited to circumstances where a defrauded principal can assert a proprietary claim to money that has found its way into the hands of another that is as a result of any subtraction of the wealth of the principal.[281] Moneys had and received may lie also to recover moneys, for example, that are the result of a bribe.[282] The availability of the remedy of moneys had and received in these circumstances may be rationalised as being moneys that could

---

277 [1961] AC 1; [1960] 3 All ER 482, following *Union Bank of Australia v McClintock* [1922] 1 AC 240 (PC).

278 [1991] 2 AC 548; at 572; [1992] 4 All ER 512, at 527, citing Lord Mansfield in *Moses v Macferlan* (1760) 2 Burr 1005; [1760] 99 All ER 676, and further, see *Clarke v Shee and Johnson* (1774) 1 Cowp 197; [1774] 98 ER 1041.

279 *Ibid*, at 559–60; 517, citing Lord Wright in *Fibrosa Spolka Akcyjina v Fairbairne Lawson Combe Barbour Ltd* [1943] AC 32, at 61; [1994] 2 All ER 122, at 135.

280 [1991] 2 AC 548, at 558 *per* Lord Bridge, at 568 *per* Lord Achner, at 578–80 *per* Lord Goff.

281 An expression favoured by Birks, P, *An Introduction to the Law of Restitution*, reprint 1993, pp 135–39, Clarendon Press, Oxford.

282 *Mahesan v Malaysia Government Housing* [1979] AC 374; [1978] 2 All ER 404.

not be retained in conscience[283] or, perhaps, as a waiver of the tort of deceit.[284]

(g) The common law tracing claim

Tracing at common law may enable a plaintiff to recover property or money in a personal action for conversion or moneys had and received, where the property or money can be identified as the product of trust property that has been misappropriated. Property for the purpose of a tracing remedy of this kind may include a chose in action such as a bank debt. In *Lipkin Gorman*,[285] Lord Goff considered that the firm was able to assert a right to a chose in action, namely a debt owed to it by its bank, because its account was in credit. The money derived from this account was identified as the product of this debt. This was sufficient in the opinion of the Lord Goff to allow the firm to assert property in the money that had been paid to the club. This approach was followed in *FC Jones and Sons v Jones*,[286] where a trustee in bankruptcy of a firm was able to recover the proceeds of cheques belonging to the firm that had been given to the wife of an insolvent partner who had used them to invest profitably in commodities. The account which was in the wife's name at the commodity brokers was in substantial profit. The court held that the moneys in the account belonged to the trustee and denied the wife any allowance by way of profit because she had exclusively used the firm's money to trade.

The common tracing remedy can assist a defrauded principal to claim a priority over general creditors as *Taylor v Plummer*[287] illustrates. There, a defrauded principal was able to resist a claim brought by the assignee in bankruptcy of a fraudulent agent who had misappropriated a bank draft and converted it into doubloons which the principal had

---

283 *Moses v Macferlan* (1760) 2 Burr 1005; [1558–74] All ER 581.

284 See Viscount Simon LC in *United Australia Bank v Barclays Bank Ltd* [1941] AC 1, at 12–13; [1940] 4 All ER 20, at 29. For a critical analysis of waiver of tort, and its application to deceit, see Hedley, S, 'The Myth of Waiver of Tort' (1984) 100 LQR 653. In *Refugee Assurance Co Ltd v Kettlewell* [1909] AC 243, the action for moneys had and received was invoked to obtain premiums obtained through a dishonest representation relating to an insurance policy.

285 [1991] 2 AC 548, at 573–74; [1992] 4 All ER 512, at 528–29. It has been suggested that the common law remedy may fail if there is a transmission of funds electronically, see *Agip (Africa) v Jackson* [1990] Ch 265, at 286, and further, see *Nimmo v Westpac Banking* [1993] 3 NZLR 218, at 238–39.

286 [1996] 4 All ER 721. *Lipkin Gorman* was also applied in New Zealand in *Equiticorp Industries Group v The Crown* [1996] 3 NZLR 586, at 602.

287 (1815) 3 M & S 562; [1814–23] All ER 167, and further, Sir Peter Millet, 'Tracing the Proceeds of Fraud' (1991) 107 LQR 71. It may be argued that the common law tracing remedy is of tenuous origin involving essentially only the application of equitable principles by a common law judge in a bankruptcy matter. See Khurshid, S and Mathews, P, 'Tracing Confusion' (1979) 95 LQR 78, and Watts, P, 'Restitution' [1993] NZ Recent Law Rev 424, at 433.

subsequently acquired. The property was identifiable as the product of the draft. The principal was able to assert title to the product and thereby secure a priority over the fiduciary's general creditors. However, where money passes into general currency, the means of identification at common law will fail. Money, being a fungible, will lose its identity unless it remains unmixed with other moneys either of a fraudulent party or a third party to whom it has been paid. A common law action for moneys had and received will not be available to enable a victim to recover misappropriated money where the money has lost its means of identification and passed into general currency.[288] In *Banque Belge v Hambouck*,[289] a bank was able to recover money that had been fraudulently acquired by a thief and paid into the account of his mistress. The moneys paid into the account were unmixed and were paid into court prior to trial. In *Lipkin Gorman*, the club elected not to take the point that money derived from the fraud may have been mixed by the thief with his own money. Nor was any point taken that the moneys paid to the club was mixed with its own funds.[290] If the club had not made either of these concessions, the firm would have had to have resort to a tracing claim in equity as Lord Goff observed.[291]

(h) The equitable tracing claim

A proprietary claim based on the concept of equitable tracing was recognised by the Court of Appeal in *Re Hallet's Estate*.[292] Hallet, who was a solicitor, had misappropriated trust property. He mixed the proceeds of this property together with money of his own and other victims in his own bank account. It was held that the plaintiff, from whom he had misappropriated trust property, was able to claim a charge over funds representing her property that remained mixed in Hallet's bank account. Jessell MR also observed that, where trust funds have been misappropriated and converted into money which is used to acquire an investment, the principal can adopt the transaction and take the investment or hold it as security for the amount of the trust money expended in the purchase. Where, however, there has been a mixing of trust funds with funds belonging to the fiduciary 'and the proceeds have been invested, it was said that the principal is limited to a charge or equitable

---

288 *Orton v Butler* (1822) 5 B & Ald 65; 106 ER 1329; *Foster v Green* (1862) 7 H & N 81; 158 ER 726, but see *Miller v Race* (1758) 1 Burr 452; [1758] 97 ER 398.

289 [1921] 1 KB 321.

290 See Lord Goff [1991] 2 AC 548, at 572–73; [1992] 4 All ER 512, at 528.

291 *Idem.*

292 (1880) 13 Ch D 696; [1874–80] All ER 793, at 796, applied in *Re Clifton* (1923) 26 WAR 41; *Brady v Stapleton* (1952) 88 CLR 322; and further, see *Black v S Freedman & Co* (1910) 12 CLR 105; *Stephens Travel Service International Pty Ltd v Quantas Airways* (1988) 13 NSWLR 331.

lien over the investment.[293] Further, the High Court of Australia in *Scott v Scott*,[294] held that the estate of a defrauded testator was entitled to a proportionate share in the increase in value of a property which a trustee had acquired partly with trust moneys and partly with his own. The fact that the trustee had repaid the moneys prior to his death did not absolve his estate from liability. Conversely, in *Re Tilleys' Wills Trusts*,[295] the estate of a trustee who had mixed trust funds and private funds in a bank account did not have to account for profits derived from investments made by the trustee with the assistance of an overdraft facility. Although the trust funds had reduced the overdraft, there was no deliberate use of those funds to facilitate the investments. In the opinion of Ungoed-Thomas J, the trustee's breach halted at the mixing of the funds in her bank account.[296] Where, however, land is acquired in breach of fiduciary duty with trust money and moneys derived from a loan secured against the land, the fiduciary has been held liable to hold the land as constructive trustee for the principal. In *Paul A Davies Pty Ltd v Davies*,[297] the Court of Appeal of New South Wales held that *Scott v Scott* did not apply where the fiduciaries, who were directors of a company, had not used their own money in the purchase of a property but had, in addition to the unauthorised use of trust funds, provided the balance of the purchase price by way of a mortgage secured over the purchased property. The fact that the directors had a personal commitment on the mortgage did not, in the court's view, justify an application of *Scott v Scott*. A liberal allowance was, however, made to the fiduciaries for their time and effort spent in securing the profit.[298] In *Hagan v Waterhouse*,[299] where trust property in which the trustees held a two-thirds interest had been mortgaged and the proceeds consequently used to derive profits, a proportionate amount of the profits was awarded to the trust of one-third.

---

293 *Ibid*, at 709; 796. Further, *Re Diplock* [1948] Ch 465, at 521. However, the Australian approach is more robust in this aspect. Where it is possible to sever mixed property, the principal may elect to take his or her appropriate share; *Brady v Stapleton* (1952) 88 CLR 322, and this may include also money that has been mixed with money of the fiduciaries. *Stephens Travel Service v Quantas* (1988) 13 NSWLR 331. It was considered there that a charge would be more appropriate where the principal did not want to take property that had diminished in value (at 347).

294 (1963) 109 CLR 649, at 664. A proportionate share of profits in a bookmaking business was allowed in *Hagan v Waterhouse* (1991) 34 NSWLR 308.

295 [1967] Ch 1179.

296 *Ibid*, at 1193.

297 (1983) 1 NSWLR 440; in *Marriage of Wagstaff* (1990) 99 FLR 390.

298 Further, see in *Marriage of Wagstaff, ibid*, at 399.

299 (1994) 34 NSWLR 308. *Cf* the more rigorous approach in *FC Jones & Sons v Jones* [1996] 4 All ER 721 where profits were not allowed where trust moneys were used to profitably speculate.

The Court of Appeal, in *Re Diplock's Estate*,[300] held that the tracing remedy was available to preserve trust property which had been misapplied by executors of Caleb Diplock's estate and given to various charities. Where a charity had mixed trust money with its own and had used the mixed fund to purchase land, the claimant next of kin were permitted a charge over the land.[301] However, where the money from the executors had been used in the alteration or improvement of assets which the institution already owned, the court considered that it would be inequitable and impractical to grant a charge.[302] The court also declined to grant relief where the money had been used to discharge an encumbrance over land[303] or in relation to the repayment of an unsecured loan.[304] As to investments, the court considered that it was permissible to allow the next of kin to trace into stocks that had been purchased with the funds.[305] Where there had been an accretion of the Diplock acquired stock with stock purchased by a charity with its own reserves, a charge proportionate to the Diplock contribution over the stock was recognised.[306]

If trust property has been misappropriated and the proceeds wrongfully paid into a bank account, a defrauded principal will be able to trace into the mass of assets that have been acquired as investments out of the proceeds of the account. In *Space Investments v Canadian Imperial Bank*,[307] the Privy Council considered that if a bank misappropriated trust funds and paid them into a general account, a tracing claim would be available generally against the assets of the bank. Lord Templeman observed:[308]

> A bank in fact uses all deposit moneys for the general purposes of the bank. Whether a bank trustee lawfully receives deposits or

---

300 [1948] Ch 465; 2 All ER 318; affirmed *sub nom Ministry of Health v Simpson* [1951] AC 251; [1950] 2 All ER 1137.

301 *Ibid*, at 546; 360.

302 *Ibid*, at 547–48; 360–61.

303 *Ibid*, at 548–50; 361–62. This aspect was doubted in *Boscawen v Bajwa* [1996] 1 WLR 328.

304 *Idem*.

305 *Ibid*, at 554; 363.

306 *Ibid*, at 555–56; 364–65.

307 [1986] 3 All ER 75; criticised by Goode, R, 'Ownership and Obligation in Commercial Transactions' (1987) 103 LQR 443, at 445–47. *Cf*, in support, Jones, G, 'Tracing Claims in the Modern World' (1987) King's Counsel 15; considered by Cooke P in *Liggett v Kensington* [1993] 1 NZLR 257, at 274; also Birks, P, *An Introduction to the Law of Restitution*, 1985, p 377 *et seq*, Clarendon Press, Oxford. In *Stephenson Nominees Pty Ltd v Official Receiver* (1987) 76 ALR 485, at 505–06, Gummow J considered that the approach in *Space Investments* was helpful in a case where a beneficiary under a constructive trust dealt with the constructive trustee as a fiduciary and general creditors did not do so. In his Honour's view, in these circumstances, the case for preferring the beneficiaries to the general creditors was more apparent. This approach was adopted in *ASC v Melbourne Asset* (1994) 121 ALR 626, at 649.

308 *Ibid*, at 76–77.

wrongfully treats trust money as on deposit from trusts, all the moneys are in fact dealt with and expended by the bank for the general purposes of the bank. In these circumstances, it is impossible for the beneficiaries interested in trust money misappropriated from their trust, to trace their money to any particular asset belonging to the trustee bank. But equity allows the beneficiaries, or a new trustee appointed in place of an insolvent bank trustee, to protect the interests of the beneficiaries, to trace the trust money to all the assets of the bank, and to recover the trust money by the exercise of an equitable charge over all the assets of the bank.

Space Investments was followed in New Zealand in *Liggett v Kensington*.[309] A majority of the Court of Appeal held in that case that investors in bullion purchased from a bullion company, Exchange, were owed a fiduciary duty because Exchange had represented prior to sale that the bullion would be held by the company and stored on behalf of a purchaser. This did not occur. The purchase moneys were applied from time to time in the acquisition of bullion to meet certain of the commitments. On the insolvency of the company, contractual commitments to the investors far exceeded bullion stocks held by the company at the date of the receivership. By a majority, the court held that the investors were entitled to trace and assert a charge over the remaining bullion in priority to the bank which had a floating charge over the assets of the company. The Privy Council, however, upheld Exchange's appeal and rejected the contention that the contractual provisions relating to the investments imposed a fiduciary obligation on Exchange.[310] In any event, even if a fiduciary relationship existed, the court considered that the circumstances surrounding the transactions would not have justified a proprietary claim to the remaining bullion because a separate and sufficient stock of bullion never existed. In the opinion of Lord Mustill, what the non-allocated claimants were really attempting to achieve was to attach the proprietary interest, which they maintained should have been created over the non-existent stock, to wholly different assets.[311] A further reason for not recognising a proprietary claim was that the investors' money had been paid into an overdrawn account and had ceased to exist. Lord Mustill observed:[312]

> Their Lordships should, however, say that they find it difficult to understand how the judgment of the Board in *Space Investments LT v Canadian Imperial Bank of Commerce Trust Co (Bahamas) Ltd*, on which the claimants leaned heavily in argument, would enable them to overcome the difficulty that the moneys said to be impressed with a

---

309 [1993] 1 NZLR 257.
310 [1994] 3 NZLR 385.
311 *Ibid*, at 400.
312 *Ibid*, at 405.

trust were paid into an overdrawn account and thereupon ceased to exist: see, for example, *Re Diplock*. The observations of the Board in *Space Investments* were concerned with a mixed, not a non-existent, fund.

As *Liggett's* case illustrates, an equitable tracing claim will fail where trust property has been dissipated. It will also be lost where the trust property has been acquired by a *bona fide* purchaser for value.[313] In the case of a volunteer, who has acquired trust property, the extent of restitution will, as *Diplock* illustrates, depend on what is considered fair and practicable in the circumstances. The recognition of a change of circumstances defence by the House of Lords in *Lipkin Gorman*,[314] in the case of a common law claim, may also assist a volunteer who has expended moneys innocently on other than usual items to resist an equitable tracing claim.

(i) The rule in *Clayton's* case

Difficulties may arise where there is insufficient money in a fund to satisfy the competing demands where there has been a mixing of funds provided by more than one victim of fiduciary fraud. In *Clayton's* case,[315] it was held that, in the case of a current account between debtor and creditor, drawings are to be attributed to earlier payments into an account in the absence of agreement to the contrary. *Clayton's* case did not involve a claim against a fiduciary but the principle has been recognised and applied somewhat guardedly in relation to misappropriated trust property. It is a rule, however, that is liable to displacement if the circumstances do not lend themselves by agreement or to the practicalities of the case. In *Hallet*,[316] whilst affirming the relevance of *Clayton's* case to cases involving misappropriated trust funds, Jessell MR held that the rule was displaced where a trustee had withdrawn funds leaving a balance in his account sufficient to satisfy the misappropriation of the trust fund. The funds withdrawn were deemed to be the trustee's own money. In *Re Oatway*,[317] it was similarly held that where an investment was purchased out of a bank account in which the trustee had mixed trust moneys and his own and had subsequently applied the balance of the fund for his own purposes, the rule in *Clayton's* case did not apply. Where various trust funds have been blended in one account, *Clayton's*

---

313 *Black v Freeman* (1910) 12 CLR 105, at 109; *Jacobsen v Ross* [1995] 1 VR 337. In *Lord v Spinelly* [1991] 4 WAR 158, a recipient of property was held liable to account for the diminution of the value of assets he enjoyed as a volunteer.

314 See discussion, p 303.

315 (1816) 1 Mer 572; [1814–23] All ER 1. Applied in *ANZ Banking Group Ltd v Westpac Banking Corporation* (1987–88) 164 CLR 662, at 676.

316 (1880) 13 Ch D 696; [1874–80] All ER 793, at 805–06.

317 [1903] 2 Ch 356. Applied in *Hagan v Whitehouse* (1994) 34 NSWLR 309.

case will govern the priority of payments out of the account.[318] Thus, in *Re Stenning*,[319] where a solicitor had blended moneys of various clients into one account, it was held that the money of the first client must be considered to have been misappropriated by the solicitor with the result that it had disappeared and the tracing remedy was lost for that client. *Clayton's* case was also considered in *Re Diplock*.[320] The Court of Appeal in this case, declined to extend the rule beyond bank accounts to stocks which had been purchased out of Diplock moneys and accounted for as part of a mass of stock, the greater amount of which the charity had acquired independently of the Diplock gift. Some of the stock had been sold by the charity and it was contended that the charity should be deemed to have sold off its stock first leaving the Diplock stock intact. It was held that such an approach was inappropriate and, to the extent that the mass was reduced, the loss should be born rateably in proportion to the respective amounts invested.[321] In other cases, *parri passu* sharing may be the most equitable resolution. In *Sinclair v Brougham*,[322] the House of Lords considered that the most equitable and practical resolution of the issue of priority between depositors who had made *ultra vires* loans to a Society, and shareholders of the Society should consist of a *parri passu* sharing in the assets of the Society that remained after the general creditors had been paid. In *Barlow Clowes International Ltd v Vaughan*,[323] the Court of Appeal considered, in the circumstances of that case, that it was contrary to either the express or presumed intention of investors to apply the rule in *Clayton's* case. *Parri passu* rateable sharing in the balance available for distribution was ordered. In New Zealand in *Re Registered Securities*,[324] it was also held that *Clayton's* case should not apply in regard to the interests of competing *cestuis que trust* where the circumstances did not merit the application of the rule. The investor claimants there were ordered to share proportionately to the extent of their contribution to the available assets.

---

318 See *Re Hallet* (1880) 13 Ch D 696; [1874–80] All ER 793. Applied in *Hodges v Kovac Estate Agency Pty Ltd* [1961] WAR 19.

319 [1895] 2 Ch 433, at 435–36.

320 [1948] Ch 465; 2 All ER 318.

321 *Ibid*, at 553–56; 364–65.

322 [1914] AC 398; [1914–15] All ER 622. Further, see *Re Securitibank Ltd* [1978] 1 NZLR 97. Note that *Sinclair v Brougham* was expressly disapproved by a majority of the House of Lords in *Westdeutsche Landesbank Girozentrale v Islington LBC* [1996] 2 WLR 802; [1996] 2 All ER 961.

323 [1992] 4 All ER 22.

324 [1991] 1 NZLR 545. Also, see *Re Ararimu Holdings* [1989] 3 NZLR 487.

(j) The lowest intermediate balance principle

In *Roscoe v Wynder*,[325] it was held that a claimant to a tracing remedy may only trace funds in a general trading account which represents the lowest intermediate balance of the account. In that case, the general trading account, into which trust and personal funds had been blended, had been dissipated by the trustee well below the amount of the trust funds. The trustee subsequently paid additional sums into the account and drew on it for his own purposes with the result that there was a larger credit balance at the time of his death but it was insufficient to fully cover the amount of trust moneys that had been misapplied. The court considered that the tracing claim was limited to the sum which represented the lowest intermediate balance of the account.

The relationship of the equitable tracing claim to the remedial constructive trust

The orthodox approach in relation to the imposition of a constructive trust after *Diplock*[326] required a claimant to establish a breach of a fiduciary duty with regard to the misapplication of trust property. Recently, a constructive trust has been imposed to prevent the unjust enrichment of a fiduciary where profits from bribes were derived from a breach of a duty of fidelity rather than the misapplication of trust funds. Thus, in *Attorney General for Hong Kong v Reid*,[327] the Privy Council allowed the Crown's claim to an equitable interest by reason of the imposition of a remedial constructive trust in properties in New Zealand which had been acquired through the proceeds of bribes paid to Reid during his employment with the Crown in Hong Kong. The argument that a debtor-creditor relationship existed between the victim and the dishonest employee so that a trust could not be imposed failed to impress Lord Templeman who rejected earlier English authority in point.[328] Constructive trusts have been imposed independently of a fiduciary relationship. In *Chase Manhatten Bank NA v Israel-British Bank (London) Ltd*,[329] for example, Goulding J considered that there did not have to be a fiduciary relationship in the trust sense in order to permit the plaintiff to

---

325 [1915] 1 Ch 62. This approach was seemingly approved by the Privy Council in *Re Goldcorp Exchange Ltd* [1994] 3 NZLR 385 (PC), at 404. Considered without disapproval in *ANZ Banking Group Ltd v Westpac Banking Corporation* (1987–88) 164 CLR 662, at 678.

326 [1948] Ch 465; 2 All ER 318. See Megarry VC in *Tito v Waddell (No 2)* [1977] Ch 106, at 230; and further, see Dawson J in *Hospital Products Ltd v United States Surgical Corporation* (1984) 156 CLR 41, at 142, on the necessity for a prior fiduciary relationship.

327 [1994] 1 AC 324.

328 See *Lister v Stubbs* (1890) 45 Ch D 1.

329 [1981] 1 Ch 105; [1979] 3 All ER 1025.

claim a constructive trust to prevent unjust enrichment. A fiduciary obligation to account could arise where the payee received money that it could not conscientiously retain. This had occurred because the plaintiff bank had mistakenly paid a substantial sum of money to the payee bank which subsequently became insolvent. It was held that an equity arose because the mistaken payer retained an equitable interest in the money and the conscience of the payee was subject to a fiduciary duty to respect that interest.[330] Mistake negatived the intention on the part of the payer to benefit the payee. Retention of the funds as a windfall for the general creditors was considered unjust in these circumstances and a constructive trust was imposed to secure the proceeds of the mistaken payment for the plaintiff. Although the judgment of Lord Browne-Wilkinson in the House of Lords in *Westdeutsche Landesbank Girozentrale v Islington LBC*[331] would suggest that Goulding J was incorrect to regard the payer as retaining an equitable interest in the money, nevertheless, the imposition of a remedial constructive trust, it is submitted, was justified to prevent what would otherwise have been a gross case of unjust enrichment. In *Westdeutsche*, it was argued that a bank which had engaged in an interest swap agreement that was *ultra vires* the local authority could not claim, in addition to a personal remedy to restitution, a proprietary right to the property based on a resulting trust since it had intended to part with its money. Lord Browne-Wilkinson's observations were, accordingly, *obiter*[332] and, of the other members of the House of Lords, only Lord Goff mentioned *Chase* and expressly declined to review the decision. If the criticism of Lord Browne-Wilkinson in *Westdeutsche* does result in the rejection of the concept of the remedial constructive trust, should a case like *Chase* come before the House of Lords, it is submitted this would be an unfortunate result. The imposition of a constructive trust should not, as Lord Browne-Wilkinson appears to suggest, depend on whether the payee was fixed with knowledge before its insolvency of the mistaken payment or whether it was not discovered until afterwards. It is submitted that even if the payee did not realise the mistake before it became insolvent, it was a glaring injustice for the liquidator to attempt to treat the money subsequently as the payees for the benefit of the general creditors, and equity should be sufficiently flexible to recognise a remedial constructive trust to prevent unjust enrichment in these rather exceptional circumstances.[333]

---

330 *Ibid*, at 118–19, 128; 1032. Further, see *Sinclair v Brougham* [1914] AC 398, at 419–20; [1914–15] All ER 622, at 632 *per* Lord Haldane.

331 [1996] 2 WLR 802; 2 All ER 961.

332 *Ibid*, at 837; 996. Note that in *Re Goldcorp Exchange Ltd* [1994] 3 NZLR 385, at 404, Lord Mustill reserved his opinion also on the reasoning in *Chase*.

333 Analogous reasoning is to be found in Lord Goff's defence of *Sinclair v Brougham* in *Westdeutsche v Landesbank v Islington LBC* [1996] 2 WLR 802, at 813; [1996] 2 All ER 961, at 973.

An even more radical departure from the orthodox requirement of the presence of a fiduciary relationship was seen in *Neste Oy v Lloyd's Bank*.[334] There, a constructive trust was imposed where a payment was received by directors of a company in circumstances where it was inevitable there would be a total failure of consideration for the payment, because the moneys had been received as consideration for the performance of a contract on the very day the company ceased trading. It was considered that the money could not in good conscience be retained for the good of the general creditors. The concept of a remedial constructive trust also received consideration by the Court of Appeal of New Zealand in *Elders Pastoral v BNZ*.[335] Elders, who acted as a stock agent and had sold livestock belonging to a farmer, knew the bank had security over the stock. Cooke P adopted the approach in *Neste Oy v Lloyd's Bank*[336] and held that it was unconscionable for Elders to retain the proceeds in discharge of the farmer's debts to it. Somers J adopted a more orthodox approach and, having examined the security, concluded that the farmer owed a fiduciary duty to the bank to apply the proceeds to the bank in discharge of its obligations. As the farmer's agent, Elders could be in no better position than the farmer to claim the proceeds of sale. However, Somers J also appeared to acknowledge the existence of a remedial constructive trust. His Honour said of this remedy:[337]

> It has come to be used as a device for imposing a liability to account on persons who cannot in good conscience retain a benefit in breach of their legal or equitable obligations. Its evolution or extension as a remedy may not yet have come to an end.

Subsequently, in *Liggett v Kensington*,[338] the New Zealand Court of Appeal had to consider whether investors in gold bullion should have priority to the remaining assets of a company in liquidation, Exchange, over a bank as debenture holder. It had been represented to investors by Exchange that the bullion would be stored in its vaults sufficient to meet

---

334 [1983] 2 Lloyd's Rep 658. This case was considered without criticism by the Privy Council in *Re Goldcorp Exchange* [1994] 3 NZLR 385, at 404.

335 [1989] 2 NZLR 180. This case has been the subject of some criticism by Meagher Gummow Lehane, *Equity: Doctrines and Remedies* (1992), 3rd edn, Butterworths, pp 66–67; however, it is submitted that whether on the remedial constructive trust approach adopted by Cooke P or the more orthodox approach taken by Somers J, to have allowed Elders to have retained the proceeds of the loan, when they had sold the stock, as an agent, knowing that there was a chattel security over the loan in favour of the Bank would have been a plainly unconscionable result.

336 [1983] 2 Lloyd's Rep 658.

337 [1989] 2 NZLR 180, at 193. Both Cooke P and Somers J (*ibid*, at 185;193) adopted the view advanced by Lord Goff and Jones, G, *The Law of Restitution*, 3rd edn, 1986, p 77, Sweet & Maxwell, London that it was unnecessary to found a tracing claim in equity upon the existence of a fiduciary relationship.

338 [1993] NZLR 257. Cf *Stephens Travel Service International Pty Ltd v Quantas Airways* (1988) 13 NSWLR 331.

demand and insured on behalf of investors. This did not, however, occur. The actual method of operation was to hold only sufficient stocks to meet requests for delivery. As a consequence, contractual commitments far exceeded bullion stocks and the other assets of the company. A majority of the Court of Appeal held that the investors were entitled to priority to the debenture holder. Cooke P considered that the investors had relied on Exchange and this had created a fiduciary relationship which entitled the investors to trace into the bullion assets of Exchange. Since the investors were able to claim an equitable charge on the assets of Exchange, this charge ranked in priority to the bank's floating charge which crystallised later.[339] Cooke P described the trust as orthodox and disclaimed reliance on the concept of a remedial constructive trust.[340] Gault J also considered that Exchange was in breach of a fiduciary obligation[341] and observed that, had he not been able to find that Exchange was a fiduciary, he would have been prepared to impose a remedial constructive trust over the bullion stocks.[342] However, in that event, he would have remitted the matter for further consideration on the issue of whether the bank as debenture holder had knowledge of circumstances giving rise to the investors' interests. Gault J indicated that he would be reluctant to give priority by way of a remedial constructive trust if the bank had taken security without notice of the circumstances giving rise to the misapplication of investors' funds.[343] The Privy Council,[344] however, declined to uphold the investors' claim either on an orthodox fiduciary approach or an approach based on a remedial constructive trust. Although the Privy Council did not dismiss the concept of a remedial constructive trust, Lord Mustill, in delivering judgement, considered there was no reason to deprive the bank of the advantage of its security. The investors were not labouring under any mistake as in *Chase Manhatten v Barclays Bank*. Nor could it be contended that there was any total failure of consideration as there had been in *Neste Oy v Lloyd's Bank* because the investors had what they bargained for, a contract for the sale of unascertained goods. Lord Mustill observed that the fact that the claimants were private citizens, whereas their opponent

---

339 *Ibid*, at 274, citing *Space Investments v Canadian Imperial Bank* [1986] 3 All ER 75, at 76–77, where Lord Templeman considered that a bank which wrongfully appropriated trust moneys was under an obligation to repay the money out of the assets of the bank in priority to customers and general creditors. Lord Templeman considered that the fact that there could not be any specific tracing into a general asset of the bank did not preclude a tracing claim from succeeding because a bank uses all deposit moneys for its general purposes.

340 *Ibid*, at 272.

341 *Ibid*, at 281.

342 *Idem*.

343 *Ibid*, at 283–84.

344 *Re Goldcorp Exchange* [1994] 3 NZLR 385.

was a commercial bank, could not justify the court in simply rejecting the bank's valid security. To do so would stretch the nascent doctrine of the remedial constructive trust past breaking point.[345]

Professor Goode has warned of the need to consider the interests of the general creditors before a remedial constructive trust is imposed.[346] The further the case is from the trust model and the traditional or orthodox proprietary claim based on a fiduciary's misuse of trust property, the greater the claims of general creditors will generally be to share *parri passu* in the bankrupt's available assets. Where property has been derived through a breach of fiduciary duty, however, the general creditors should not be able to gain a windfall derived through dishonesty. Thus, it has been argued earlier that in a case like *Daly v Sydney Stock Exchange*,[347] a remedial constructive trust could legitimately be imposed where a principal can establish that money has been transferred to a fiduciary in breach of the latter's duty of good faith even though that may mean overriding a debtor-creditor relationship. Nor, it is submitted, should the general creditors of an insolvent payee be able to benefit from a mistaken payment as Goulding J recognised in *Chase Manhatten*. Although in *Westdeutsche Landesbank Girozentrale v Islington LBC*,[348] Lord Browne-Wilkinson alone rejected the concept of a remedial constructive trust as imposed in *Chase*, it is arguable that the wider approach is justified where there would otherwise be a clear case of unjust enrichment and it is unconscientious for the recipient, in that case the liquidator of the payee, to retain the moneys. It is not a disservice to equitable notions of trust and conscience to compel an otherwise recalcitrant liquidator to acknowledge the priority of the mistaken payer in such circumstances. The imposition of a remedial constructive trust in *Chase* is an indubitably fairer and better result than the obviously unjust enrichment of the creditors. However, in other cases it will be more difficult to justify defeating the interests of general creditors by the imposition of a remedial constructive trust. In so far as it suggests a remedial constructive trust may be imposed where there has been a total failure of consideration, *Neste Oy v Lloyd's Bank*[349] illustrates a very liberal and rather exceptional application of the remedial constructive trust as a foundation for relief in a commer-

---

345 See discussion [1994] 3 NZLR 385, at 401–04.

346 Goode, R, 'Property and Unjust Enrichment' in Burrows, A (ed), *Essays on the Law of Restitution*, 1991, pp 241–44, Clarendon Press, Oxford.

347 (1986) 160 CLR 371. See discussion, p 313.

348 [1996] 2 WLR 802; [1996] 2 All ER 961.

349 [1983] 2 Lloyd's Rep 658. *Cf Mac-Jordan Construction Ltd v Brookmount Erostin Ltd* [1992] BCLC 350, a breach of an obligation to hold certain retention moneys under a building contract as a trustee was held not to entitle the appellant to a proprietary interest in the moneys in the hands of the receiver appointed by a debenture holder and for a discussion of this case and the various approaches, see Scott, SR, 'Recovery of Advance Payments' (1990–91) 14 NZULR 375.

cial transaction. Indeed, it is arguable that where money is paid pursuant to a commercial transaction, even if the transaction be *ultra vires* one of the parties, the payer should not be preferred to other disappointed creditors on the insolvency of the payee.[350] Just as the High Court of Australia in *Hospital Products*[351] exhibited restraint when declining to find that a commercial transaction between two parties who had negotiated at arm's length gave rise to a fiduciary relationship, so should the courts exhibit similar restraint in relation to the imposition of a remedial constructive trust in commercial transactions. Indeed, the judgment of the Privy Council in *Goldcorp Exchange Ltd* constitutes a reminder that commercial transactions should be closely scrutinised before a fiduciary obligation or a remedial constructive trust is found to exist.

Exemplary damages and interest

A power to award exemplary damages in cases involving breaches of fiduciary duty has been recognised in New Zealand.[352] The legitimacy of a jurisdiction to award exemplary damages in cases involving a breach of fiduciary duty is, however, doubtful.[353] A plaintiff can usually be adequately compensated without resort to punitive awards. In addition to a claim for account or compensation, awards of costs and interest should provide adequate redress. In cases where simple interest is awarded, the general rule is that it is for the purpose of compensating the plaintiff for the detriment that he or she has suffered for being out of his or her money and it is not intended as a punishment for the defendant for being dilatory in settling a claim.[354] A factor that may be taken into account, however, is whether the defendant has derived any benefit from having the use of the money until judgment.[355] In *State Bank of NSW v Swiss Bank Corporation*,[356] the Court of Appeal declined to hold that an award of interest under s 94 of the Supreme Court Act 1970 entitled Swiss bank to a restitutionary allowance where there was no evidence that the State Bank had derived a benefit from moneys which it had

---

350 Such an opinion was expressed by Lord Goff in *Westdeutske Landesbank v Islington LBC* (1996) 2 WLR 802, at 809, 815; (1996) 2 All ER 961, at 968; 974.

351 (1984–85) 156 CLR 41.

352 *Acquaculture Corporation v New Zealand Mussell Co Ltd* [1990] 3 NZLR 299, at 301 *per* Cooke P; *Cook v Evatt (No 2)* [1992] 1 NZLR 676; *Watson v Dolmark Industries* [1992] 3 NZLR 311; Aitken, L, 'Developments in Equitable Compensation: Opportunity or Danger' (1993) 67 ALJ 596.

353 This approach is criticised by Meagher Gummow Lehane, *Equity: Doctrines and Remedies*, 1992, 3rd edn, Butterworths, p 888.

354 *Batchelor v Burke* (1981) 148 CLR 448; *Swiss Bank v State Bank of New South Wales* (1993) 33 NSWLR 63.

355 *Woolwich Equitable Building Society v Inland Revenue Commissioners* [1993] AC 70.

356 (1995) 39 NSWLR 350, at 360–61.

received by mistake and paid over to a third party. Where a fiduciary, however, uses trust property for investment or in the course of business or trade and it can be shown or assumed that a profit equal to or greater than compound interest has been made, compound interest may be ordered.[357] An attempt to extend an award of compound interest to an action for moneys had and received failed in *Westdeutsche Landesbank Girozentrale v Islington LBC,* although two members of the House of Lords were in favour of such an award on a claim in restitution.[358] In New Zealand, in *Equiticorp Industries v The Crown,*[359] it was held that compound interest should not be ordered against the Crown since it was engaged in the task of running the country for the public good, rather than being engaged in trade and commerce.

---

357 *Burdick v Garrick* (1870) 5 Ch App 233; *Wallersteiner v Moir (No 2)* [1975] 1 All ER 849; *O'Sullivan v Management Agency* [1985] 3 All ER 351; *Southern Cross Commodities v Newing* (1987) 5 A CLR 1110; *Hagan v Waterhouse* (1994) 34 NSWLR 308; *Biala v Mallina Holdings Ltd* (1994–95) 13 WAR 11; *National Bank of New Zealand Ltd v Development Finance Corporation of New Zealand* [1990] 3 NZLR 257; *General Communications Ltd v Development Finance Corporation of New Zealand Ltd* [1990] 3 NZLR 406.

358 [1996] 2 WLR 802; 2 All ER 961, at 819–21, 979–81 *per* Lord Goff; at 856–58, 1015–16 *per* Lord Woolf.

359 [1996] 3 NZLR 586.

CHAPTER 12

Tort

Two aspects involving restitution for unjust enrichment derived from tortious wrongdoing will be considered in this chapter. The first concerns waiver of tort which has declined in significance today and plays little part in a modern law of restitution. The second concerns the availability of a restitutionary component in damages awards reflecting a defendant's profit rather than the plaintiff's loss which is of greater importance today.

Waiver of tort

Historically, the concept of waiver of tort arose as a result of the increasing availability of *assumpsit* and the remedy of moneys had and received to enable the recovery of the proceeds of torts. In *Lamine v Dorell*,[1] the administrator of an estate sued in an action for moneys had and received to recover the proceeds of the sale of debentures that had been gathered in by an administrator whose appointment was subsequently revoked. The action was defended on the basis that it was misconceived and the plaintiff should have brought an action in detinue or trover. However, although the court acknowledged the plaintiff could have sued in conversion or detinue, the action for moneys had and received was also considered an available alternative means of recovery. In this regard, Holt CJ considered that the claim was similar to those where actions for moneys had and received had been allowed to enable an official to recover moneys that had been wrongfully received by a person who did not lawfully hold office, an action which was said to have crept in by degrees.[2] In an earlier case of *Howard v Wood*,[3] the Court of King's Bench had permitted the plaintiff to claim fees in an action for moneys had and received that had been paid to the defendant under an invalid grant. It had been contended that the plaintiff should have commenced an action in trover for the money or an action on the case for disturbing him in his office. However, the

---

1 (1701) 2 Ld Raym 1217; [1701] 92 ER 303. For other early cases of moneys had and received to recover the proceeds of tortious wrongdoing, see *Lightly v Clouston* (1808) 1 Taunt 112; [1808] 56 ER 128 where the plaintiff was able to recover the proceeds of the defendant's wrongful seduction of the plaintiff's apprentice. Further, see *Hunter v Prinsep* (1808) 10 East 378; [1808] 103 ER 818 where owners of goods wrongfully sold by a shipper were able to claim the proceeds of sale in an action for moneys had and received.

2 *Ibid*, at 1217.

3 (1679) 2 Lev 245; [1679] 83 ER 540.

court held that there was sufficient precedent to permit the plaintiff to recover in an action for moneys had and received.

Prior to the Common Law and Procedure Act 1852, a claim in tort could not be joined in the same proceedings with a claim for moneys had and received.[4] The action for moneys had and received was treated as analogous to a contractual claim because of the fictitious implied contract theory. Since tort and contract claims prior to the Common Law Procedure Act 1852 could not be joined in the same proceedings, the action for moneys had and received based on implied contract could not co-exist as an alternative remedy to a claim in tort in common proceedings. Where the plaintiff prior to the Common Procedure Act 1852 elected to commence proceedings alleging moneys had and received so as to recover the proceeds of a defendant's tort, he or she was said to have waived the tort. The term waiver of tort was, however, a misnomer.[5] In reality, a plaintiff who sued in *assumpsit* was not waiving the tort or electing between two inconsistent rights[6] but was simply electing between two alternative remedies. This point was forcefully made by Lord Atkin in *United Australia v Barclays Bank Ltd*.[7] Lord Atkin observed that in the ordinary case the plaintiff never had the slightest intention of waiving, excusing or palliating the tort.[8] The notion of waiver had also been developed by some judges who had rationalised the action for moneys had and received as based upon a fictitious agency.[9] Such an approach was also condemned by Lord Atkin who observed:[10]

> I protest that a man cannot waive a wrong unless he either had a real intention to waive it, or can fairly have imputed to him such an intention, and in the cases which we have been considering there can be no such intention either actual or imputed. Fantastic resemblances of contracts, invented in order to meet requirements of the law as to the forms of action which have now disappeared, should not in these days be allowed to affect actual rights. When these ghosts of the past stand in the path of justice clanking their medieval chains, the proper course for the judge is to pass through them undeterred.

---

4   See *United Australia Ltd v Barclays Bank Ltd* [1941] AC 1, at 53; [1940] 4 All ER 20, at 46 *per* Lord Porter.

5   See Hedley, S, 'The Myth of Waiver of Tort' (1984) 100 LQR 653.

6   See *Sergent v ASL Developments Ltd* (1974) 131 CLR 634; *Ciavarella v Balmer* (1983) 153 CLR 438, at 449; *Dombikin Holdings v Grail* (1991) 5 WAR 563.

7   [1941] AC 1; [1940] 4 All ER 20.

8   *Ibid*, at 28–29; 36.

9   *Ibid*, at 26–27; 37. For a true illustration of ratification of an agent's acts, see *Vershures Creameries Ltd v Hull and Netherlands Steamship Co Ltd* [1921] 2 KB 608, considered by Lord Atkin in *United Australia Ltd v Barclays Bank Ltd*, *ibid*, at 31; 38–39.

10 *Ibid*, at 29.

There were certain advantages for a plaintiff in suing in *assumpsit* rather than in tort. A tort claim could not survive the death of the tortfeasor whereas a claim in *assumpsit* did.[11] Waiver of tort was available for conversion, trespass to land or goods, deceit, and extortion, however, it was not available in all cases of tort, most notably cases of defamation or assault.[12] Waiver of tort was also advantageous where the plaintiff could assert that wrongdoing had enabled the defendant to receive a profit which a plaintiff desired to recover without proving actual loss.[13] Thus, in a case involving a bribe, the principal could claim the proceeds even though he or she could not establish an actual loss. Conversely, as in *Mahesan v Malaysia Government Officer's Co-operative Housing Society Ltd*,[14] where the plaintiff was able to prove an actual loss greater than the proceeds of the bribe, the plaintiff could claim in tort rather in restitution. Double recovery, in these circumstances, however, was not permitted.[15]

Modern applications of waiver of tort

There are very few modern cases where waiver of tort has been considered. In *Grace Brothers Limited v Lawson*,[16] the High Court of Australia declined to allow Grace Brothers to maintain an action against an auctioneer for conversion of goods or moneys had and received, where it had declined any interest in the goods and had by its actions in delivering the goods to the auctioneer represented that he should account to the owner for the proceeds of sale. The auctioneer had sold the goods on the direction of a fraudulent third party whom he believed to be the owner and had paid over the proceeds to him. The true owner subsequently successfully claimed against Grace Brothers for the losses arising from the fraud although, as Issacs J recognised, he also would have had a claim against the auctioneer for conversion or moneys had and received were he to have elected to proceed in that way.[17] In *Commercial Banking Company of Sydney Ltd v Mann*,[18] the Privy Council declined to

---

11   *Hambly v Trott* (1776) 1 Cowp 371; 98 ER 1136. Further, see *Phillips v Homfray* (1883) 24 Ch D 439 where a failure to complete inquiries relating to compensation for trespass prior to the defendant's death meant that the earlier decree lapsed. The tort rule on the effect of death in the United Kingdom was abrogated by s 1 of the Law Reform (Miscellaneous Provisions) Act 1934 (UK), and was further modified by s 1 of the Proceedings Against Estates Act (UK).

12   *United Australia Ltd v Barclays Bank Ltd* [1941] AC 1, at 12–13; [1940] 4 All ER 20, at 26 *per* Viscount Simon LC.

13   *Reading v Attorney General* [1951] AC 507; [1951] 1 All ER 617; *Mahesan v Malaysia Government* [1979] AC 374; [1978] 2 All ER 405.

14   [1979] AC 374; [1978] 2 All ER 405.

15   *Idem.*

16   (1922) 31 CLR 130.

17   *Ibid*, at 134.

18   [1961] AC 1; [1960] 3 All ER 482.

permit a solicitor, Mann, to entertain claims for conversion or moneys had and received in relation to the proceeds of various bank cheques that had been fraudulently obtained by a partner and made out in the name of a third party who had cashed them and received the proceeds from the bank. It was held that the plaintiff could not establish ownership to the cheques which had been obtained by the unauthorised acts of his partner. It was assumed (and their Lordships considered rightly so) that if the tortious claim failed so must the action for moneys had and received.[19]

In this regard, however, it is useful to compare *Lipkin Gorman v Karpnale*[20] where the House of Lords had to consider whether a firm of solicitors could recover money that had been fraudulently misappropriated by a partner of the firm and paid to a gaming club for the purpose of gambling. In that case, a fraudulent partner had inveigled a cashier of the firm into making out cheques to cash which he signed and from which he subsequently received cash exchanging it for gaming chips at the club. The firm claimed to recover the moneys paid to the club as moneys had and received on the ground that the club had given no consideration for the payments. In so far as the action for moneys had and received was concerned, the House of Lords held that the action was available to recover the money which had been stolen from the firm. It was also held that the club, in providing gaming chips and the opportunity to wager, had not given lawful consideration for the payments. Both Lord Templeman and Lord Goff considered that such an action would lie to prevent the club being unjustly enriched.[21] Lord Templeman and Lord Goff, however, considered that the action for moneys had and received could lie to prevent unjust enrichment independently of any tortious claim. Indeed, there could not be any claim to conversion since the money had been paid to the club and had passed into currency.[22] Lord Goff observed:[23]

> The cases in which such a claim has succeeded are, I believe, very rare ... This is probably because at common law, property in money like other fungibles is lost as such when it is mixed with other money. Furthermore, it appears that in these cases the action for moneys had and received is not usually founded upon any wrong by the third party, such as conversion; nor is it said to be a case of waiver of tort. It is founded simply on the fact that, as Lord Mansfield CJ said, the third party cannot in conscience retain the

---

19 *Ibid*, at 8; 484.

20 [1991] 2 AC 548; [1992] 4 All ER 512.

21 *Ibid*, at 559–60; 517 *per* Lord Templeman; at 572; 527–28 *per* Lord Goff.

22 *Miller v Race* (1758) 1 Burr 452; [1758] 97 ER 398.

23 [1991] 2 AC 548, at 572; [1992] 4 All ER 512, at 527. Further, see *Clarke v Shee and Johnson* (1774) 1 Cowp 197; 98 ER 1041.

money – or as we say nowadays, for the third party to retain the money would result in his unjust enrichment at the expense of the owner of the property.

Indeed, it is doubtful whether the concept of waiver of tort holds anything of significance for the modern law of Restitution.[24] Waiver of tort was important for lawyers faced with the development of the action for moneys had and received and the need to comply with technical requirements of pleading and joinder prior to the Common Law Procedure Act 1852. Its principal use today is likely to be in cases where it is easier for a plaintiff to claim the proceeds of the tort than have to establish loss or damage. Further, the action for moneys had and received may be advantageous in those jurisdictions which permit a longer limitation period in contract than in tort. In *Chesworth v Farrer*,[25] for example, it was held that the action for moneys had and received was analogous to a contractual remedy and survived a limitation period which precluded the plaintiff commencing a tortious action to recover goods that had been bailed. In *Beaman v ARTS Ltd*,[26] Denning J considered, however, that a plaintiff should not be able to avoid a limitation period that precluded a tort claim by suing in assumpsit. The latter it is submitted is the more appropriate approach when the foundation for the claim in moneys had and received lies in tort.

Election and waiver of tort

A person will have elected to pursue one of two inconsistent remedies as opposed to inconsistent rights when, with knowledge of the circumstances giving rise to relief, he or she determines to pursue one of the two options and obtains judgment or satisfaction. Having obtained judgment or satisfaction, the alternative remedy cannot be pursued.[27] In *United Australia v Barclays Bank*,[28] the House of Lords had to consider the issue of election in relation to a claim in conversion to recover the

---

24 See the discussion advanced by Hedley, S, 'The Myth of Waiver of Tort' (1984) 100 LQR 653, at 674–79.

25 [1967] 1 QB 407.

26 [1948] 2 All ER 89, at 92–93. For a similar approach, see Corbin, AL, 'Waiver of Tort and Assumpsit' (1910) 19 Yale LJ 221, at 235–36.

27 *United Australia v Barclays Bank* [1941] AC 1, at 29–31; [1940] 4 All ER 20, at 37–38 *per* Lord Atkin.

28 [1941] AC 1; [1940] 4 All ER 20. Further, see *Re Simms* [1934] 1 Ch 1 where the election to pursue a tortious claim deprived the trustee in bankruptcy of any opportunity of seeking profits derived from the conversion of the bankrupt's assets by a receiver. *United Australia Bank v Barclays Bank Ltd* has been applied in Australia, in *Suttons Motors Pty Ltd v Campbell* (1956) 56 SR (NSW) 304; *Ciavarella v Balmer* (1983) 2 NSWLR 439; *Chomley v Union Bank Australia Ltd* [1951] SASR 152 and was distinguished in *Registrar General v Behn* (1980) 1 NSWLR 589. In New Zealand, *Thornton Hall Manufacturing v Shenton Apparel Ltd* [1989] 3 NZLR 304; *LC Fowler & Sons Ltd v St Stephens Board of Governors* [1991] 3 NZLR 304.

proceeds of a cheque that had been stolen and cashed by the bank with the proceeds being paid to a third party. The plaintiff had earlier commenced an action against the third party for the amount of the cheque as moneys lent or had and received but discontinued this action prior to judgment. The Court of Appeal in the present proceedings held that, in bringing the earlier action for moneys had and received against the third party, the plaintiff had elected to waive the tort and could not subsequently commence proceedings for conversion against the bank. The House of Lords held, however, that election did not arise until judgment had been entered or satisfaction given. In any event, the bank was liable for conversion of the cheque independently of the third party's liability. However, had the plaintiff successfully obtained relief against the third party, further recovery against the bank would not have been permitted.

Restitutionary awards as a component of damages in tort

Generally, damages in tort will be assessed on the basis of compensating the plaintiff for loss or damage caused by the tortfeasor.[29] However, on some occasions, the plaintiff will have suffered little or no loss or damage but the tortfeasor will have gained a benefit as a result of his or her wrongful conduct. In these circumstances, issues arise as to whether damages should include a restitutionary component reflecting the profit to the defendant of his or her wrongdoing and further, if a restitutionary award is appropriate, the means by which it should be assessed.[30]

(a) The way-leave cases

A trespasser who has wrongfully deprived a person of land is liable to pay a reasonable sum for the dispossession by way of mesne profits.[31] Way-leave was also allowed as a component of damages in cases where the defendant had trespassed on the plaintiff's land and had used it surreptitiously for his own advantage.[32] In *Phillips v Homfray*,[33] the owners of a colliery entered into an agreement to purchase the adjoining land of a landowner without disclosing the fact that they had taken a considerable

---

29 In Australia, see *Butler v Egg & Pulp Marketing Board* (1966) 114 CLR 185, at 191.

30 For further consideration of this topic in Australia, see Tilbury, 'Restitutionary Damages' a paper published for the NSW Bar Association CLE Seminar, 5 June 1995. In England, Birks, P, *An Introduction to the Law of Restitution*, reprint 1993, Chapter 10, Clarendon Press, Oxford.

31 *Swordheath Properties v Tabet* [1979] 1 WLR 285; [1979] 1 All ER 240 and see discussion in *Strand Electric and Engineering Co Ltd v Brisford Entertainments Ltd* [1952] 2 QB 246, at 252–53; [1952] 1 All ER 796, at 799–800.

32 *Martin v Porter* (1839) 5 M & W 351; [1839] 151 ER 149; *Jegon v Vivian* (1871) LR 6 Ch App 742.

33 (1871) 6 Ch 770. The decrees were subsequently rescinded after the defendant's death on the basis that the inquiries had not been completed prior to their death. *Phillips v Homfray* (1883) 25 Ch D 439. For an interesting discussion of these cases, see Mason, K and Carter, JW, *Restitution Law in Australia*, 1995, pp 642–43, Butterworths, Sydney.

quantity of coal from his adjoining land without authority and had also carried coal from their own mines under his land. Lord Hatherley, in addition to setting aside the agreement, allowed the landowner compensation for the value of the coal taken from his land and ordered an inquiry as to the amount of compensation that should be paid to the plaintiff for the use that had been made of his land.[34] This approach was adopted in *Whitwham v Westminster Brymbo Coal and Coke Company*,[35] where, in addition to damages being ordered for the diminution in the value of land caused by the unauthorised tipping of spoil on the plaintiff's land, the defendant was ordered to pay compensation for the use that had been made of the plaintiff's land in crossing over it to dump the spoil. The principle of way-leave was extended to a case of unauthorised use of the plaintiff's land. Rigby LJ considered that damages for the use of another's land could be assessed by inquiry as to any customary rate for way-leave in the locality but, in the absence of a local rate, the court could fix an appropriate sum to compensate the plaintiff for the unauthorised use of his land.[36] Since the parties had agreed on a certain sum that would be appropriate, the court in that case was absolved from making further inquiry.

(b) Restitutionary aspects of damages awards

The issue of how far profits may be claimed as a restitutionary component of tortious damages, where the plaintiff's property has been used by the defendant to acquire a profit, is uncertain. The colliery cases illustrate that damages could be ordered for the unauthorised extraction of coal from the plaintiff's land even though the plaintiff was not in business of that kind. If the plaintiff could prove that the extraction of the coal was carried on dishonestly, the plaintiff was entitled to be compensated at a higher rate than if the extraction was carried out with no dishonest intent. If dishonesty was proven, the owner was entitled to be compensated at the rate appropriate to coal cut and hewn without deduction for the expenses associated with mining the coal.[37] However, if the coal had not been acquired dishonestly, the owner was compensated at a lower net rate with the expenses associated with mining the coal being credited to the defendant. The value of the coal would usually be the market rate at the

---

34 *Ibid*, at 780–81. The jurisdiction to grant compensation arose in the opinion of Lord Hatherley because a court in equity had the power to grant compensation in respect of a continuously accruing damage *de die in diem* arising from a continuous trespass underground, which could only be stopped by injunction restraining any further conveyance of coal through the plaintiffs property (*ibid*, at 780–81).

35 [1896] 2 Ch 538.

36 *Ibid*, at 543–44.

37 *Martin v Porter* (1839) 5 M & W 351; [1839] 151 ER 149; *Phillips v Homfray* (1871) 6 Ch 770, at 780. *Cf Wood v Morewood* (1842) 3 QB 440; *Jegon v Vivian* (1871) LR 6 Ch App 742.

time of extraction unless the circumstances suggested that some other rate would be more appropriate. In *Livingstone v Rawyards Coal Company*,[38] the House of Lords considered that an appropriate award of compensation for coal taken illicitly from the plaintiff by an adjoining colliery should be assessed on a royalty basis calculated at the rate the colliery owner would have been prepared to pay. The circumstances were exceptional because the landowner was unable to dispose of it to anyone other than the adjoining collieries because of the location of the land. The trespass was also found to be unintentional.

Where a person has unlawfully remained a trespasser on residential property, the owner is entitled to damages for the trespass without adducing evidence that he or she would or could have let the property to someone else. The measure of damages will be the value to the trespasser of the use of the property for the period of the trespass. In *Swordheath Properties Ltd v Tabet*,[39] it was held that the normal measure would be the ordinary letting value of the property. The principle that a person may be compensated for the use or wrongful use of his or her land even though loss is not shown to exist, has been followed in Australia. In *Yakamia Dairy Pty Ltd v Wood*,[40] it was held that where the defendant had wrongfully depastured cattle on the plaintiff's land, the plaintiff was entitled to an agistment fee which was payable even though he was unable to show any actual loss. In *Bilambil-Terranora Pty Ltd v Tweed Shire Council*,[41] the Court of Appeal of New South Wales awarded damages to a landowner who had gravel taken illegally from his property by the council. Even though it was almost certain that the company could not have obtained planning approval to operate the gravel pit commercially, it was held that that the landowner was entitled to damages assessed at the market value of the gravel extracted less the cost of severance. Mahoney JA considered that to deny the plaintiff an award, even though it could not have commercially exploited the gravel, would have allowed the council to profit from its wrongdoing.[42] A royalty method of assessment, however, was rejected[43] and the defendant was credited with an allowance for the cost of extracting the gravel. In *LJP Investments Ltd v Chia Investments Ltd*,[44] it was held that a restitutionary

---

38   (1880) 5 App Cas 25. Considered in Australia, in *Bilambil Terranora Pty Ltd v Tweed Shire Council* (1980) 1 NSWLR 465.

39   [1979] 1 WLR 285; [1979] 1 All ER 240.

40   [1976] WAR 57; *cf Gilchrist, Watt, & Cunningham v Logan* [1927] St R Qd 185 where the plaintiff was able to establish a greater loss than agistment value.

41   (1980) 1 NSWLR 465.

42   *Ibid*, at 494.

43   The trial Judge and Samuels JA had favoured an award based on a royalty assessment.

44   (1989) 24 NSWLR 499.

component for damages for trespass to land could reflect the peculiar value of the use to the trespasser rather than the market value of the land use. Chia had deliberately placed scaffolding on the plaintiff's land in such a way as to encroach on the plaintiff's air space for the purpose of completing a development. It had sought permission to do so but the plaintiff had declined permission unless a substantial sum was paid. Chia ignored the plaintiff's refusal to grant permission and proceeded to erect and use the scaffolding. A mandatory injunction was ordered but subsequently leave was granted to the plaintiff to claim damages for trespass. Chia had in this case acquired a very substantial profit in terms of the enhanced value of its development by the trespass and this was reflected in the amount of the restitutionary damages awarded, namely, $37,380, even though the valuation of the air space was only $800. The higher award reflected the price that the plaintiff had asked as consideration for permitting the trespass; a price which the court considered that Chia would have been prepared to pay to complete the development had it not chosen to trespass. This reflected the actual value of the saving to Chia for its trespass.

A similar approach is seen in English cases involving breaches of restrictive covenants and other unlawful interferences. Thus, in *Wrotham Park Estate Co v Parkside Homes Ltd*,[45] Brightman J, in assessing damages in lieu of an injunction, awarded the plaintiff an allowance for a proportion of the enhanced value of a development attributable to the defendant choosing to ignore a restrictive covenant on the number of houses that could be built in the development. The plaintiff could not establish any actual injurious loss to its property, however, Brightman J considered that the defendant should pay a fair price for choosing to breach the covenant in lieu of an injunction because the plaintiff would have been in a strong bargaining position had the defendant negotiated a price for waiver of the covenant. In *Stoke City Council v W & J Wass Ltd*,[46] the Court of Appeal, however, declined to extend this principle to a plaintiff who claimed to recover damages for nuisance arising from an unlawful rival market. The plaintiff, who was licensed to hold a market, was unable to show that he had derived any actual loss from the defendant's market. The court considered that the plaintiff, in order to recover in a case of this kind, had to prove actual loss. Whilst a remedy of injunction might have been available to prevent the operation of an unlawful same-day market, it was held that the award of damages on the user principle would lead to the owner of the market obtaining a

---

45 [1974] 2 All ER 321. This approach was followed in *Bracewell v Appleby* [1975] Ch 408; [1975] 1 All ER 993 in relation to the encroachment on a right of way; *Carr-Saunders v Dick McNeil Associates Ltd* [1986] 1 WLR 922; [1986] 2 All ER 888 in relation to interference with the right of light.

46 [1988] 1 WLR 1406; [1988] 3 All ER 394.

greater measure of relief than would be justified by the nature of his right.[47] The court observed that in patent cases, an infringement would lead to the infringer having to pay a reasonable fee by way of damages,[48] however, this analogy was not considered appropriate in *Wass*. Nourse LJ considered that a rival market did not involve a use of the plaintiff's property in a way which would deprive him of the opportunity to hold his own market and, if there were losses incurred as a result of the unlawful competition, that could be compensated on proof of damage in the usual way.[49] Whilst indicating a reluctance to extend the user concept of restitutionary damages to a case of this kind, the court did not question the propriety of the award of damages in *Wrothham Park*. In *Jaggard v Sawyer*,[50] the Court of Appeal also upheld the approach of Brightman J in *Wrothham Park*, declining, however, there to permit the plaintiff a ransom price as damages in lieu of an injunction for the unauthorised use of a cul-de-sac where it was shown that the proposed use would cause only a small injury to the plaintiff. The court, however, considered that damages in cases of this kind were not restitutionary but were truly compensatory, although the enhanced profit was a factor which a court was entitled to take into account in its assessment of the amount of compensation that should be paid to the plaintiff. In this regard, it would appear that the Court of Appeal differed from the view earlier expressed by Steyn LJ in *Surrey County Council v Bredero Homes Ltd*[51] that the approach of Brightman J in *Wrotham Park* constituted an award of damages on a restitutionary basis.[52] It is arguable, however, that damages assessed on the basis of the defendant's gain or saving may legitimately be described as restitutionary damages albeit that they are intended to compensate the plaintiff for a breach of covenant or some unlawful interference. In a case of this kind, the extent of compensation will very much depend on the attitude of the defendant and the value of the benefit derived from his or her wrongful conduct rather than necessarily any measured or quantifiable actual loss to the plaintiff.

Recognition of a restitutionary award has also been applied in cases involving damages for interference with goods and other assets of a plaintiff. Thus, in *Strand Electric and Engineering Co Ltd v Brisford*

---

47 *Ibid*, at 1409; at 404–05 *per* Nicholls LJ.

48 *Meters Ltd v Metropolitan Gas Meters Ltd* (1911) 28 RPC 157; *Watson Laidlaw & Co Ltd v Pott Casels and Williamson* (1914) 31 RPC 104; *General Tire and Rubber Co v Firestone Tyre and Rubber Co Ltd* [1975] 2 All ER 173.

49 [1988] 1 WLR 1406, at 1414; [1988] 3 All ER 394, at 401.

50 [1995] 1 WLR 269.

51 [1993] 1 WLR 1361, at 1369.

52 [1995] 1 WLR 269, at 281 *per* Sir Thomas Bingham MR; at 291 *per* Millet J.

Entertainments Ltd,[53] the defendant detained some switchboards which had been installed in a theatre because they could not otherwise effectively market the theatre for sale. The plaintiffs ordinarily hired the switchboards. It was held that the defendant was liable to pay damages, in addition to the value of the switchboards, assessed as the market value for the use of the goods that amounted to a saving for the defendant during the period of their detention. Denning LJ described the plaintiffs' damages as resembling an action in restitution:[54]

> The claim for a hiring charge is ... not based on the loss to the plaintiff but on the fact that the defendant has used the goods for his own purposes. It is an action against him because he has had the benefit of the goods. It resembles an action for restitution rather than an action for tort. But it is unnecessary to place it in any formal category. The plaintiffs are entitled to a hiring charge for the period of detention and that is all that matters.

The fact that the plaintiffs might have been unable to find a hirer was considered irrelevant. Romer LJ strongly refuted this argument:[55]

> In my judgment ... a defendant who has wrongfully detained and profited from the property of someone else cannot avail himself of an hypothesis such as this. It does not lie in the mouth of such a defendant to suggest that the owner might not have found a hirer, for, in assuming the property, he showed that he wanted it and he cannot complain if it is assumed against him that he himself would have preferred to become the hirer rather than not have had the use of it at all.

Strand Electric has been followed in Australia in *Gaba Formwork Contractors Pty Ltd v Turner Corporation Ltd.*[56] Giles J in the Supreme Court of New South Wales, awarded damages in this case based on a hiring fee, in addition to the value of the goods detained, on the basis that the plaintiff might have hired out the goods. It was considered irrelevant that the plaintiff had not evidenced an available market for its materials.

In commercial cases, particularly, it may be anticipated that higher awards reflecting a profit component will be recognised where the defendant has acted in contumelious disregard of the plaintiff so as to achieve greater savings and profit from the use of a plaintiff's assets.

---

53   [1952] 2 QB 246; [1952] 1 All ER 796. Applied in *Penarth Dock Engineering Co Ltd v Pounds* [1963] 1 Lloyd's Rep 359; *McAlpine and Sons Ltd v Minimax Ltd* [1970] 1 Lloyd's Rep 397; *Hillesden Securities Ltd v Ryiack Ltd* [1983] 2 All ER 184.

54   *Ibid,* at 247; 801.

55   *Ibid,* at 256-57; 801.

56   (1993) 32 NSWLR 175. It was distinguished in *McKenna and Armistead Pty Ltd v Excavations Ltd* (1957) SR (NSW) 515; *Egan v State Transport Authority* (1982) 31 SASR 481; referred to with apparent approval in *Yakamia Dairy Pty Ltd v Wood* [1976] WAR 57.

Care should, however, be taken in cases of this kind not to award a sum which unfairly penalises the wrongdoer. Some recognition should be had for the profit attributable to the defendant's industry and investment of capital in an enterprise. Generally, it is submitted that an appropriate upper level would be the measure of profit that the savings for the wrong-doer derived from the unlawful interference represents, as *Chia* would suggest. Where the interference has been unintentional, it may be appropriate to decline any restitutionary award based on profits. Thus, in *Re Sims*,[57] a bankrupt's estate was not permitted to claim profits derived by a receiver who, in good faith but wrongfully, had taken over certain of the bankrupt's contracts. The court considered that since the bankrupt could not have performed the contract, his estate should not enjoy the profit that had been derived in good faith through the bankrupt's industry.

---

57 [1934] Ch 1.

CHAPTER 13

Crime

Profits from crime

Where a person commits a crime, he or she will not usually be permitted to profit from it. Thus, in *Cleaver v Mutual Reserve Fund Life Association*,[1] Florence Maybrick was found guilty of the murder of her husband. It was held against public policy for her administrators, who had been appointed under the provisions of the Forfeiture Act 1870 to claim the proceeds of an insurance policy that her husband had taken out on his life for her benefit. There was a resulting trust of the proceeds of his insurance for the children of the deceased. A similar approach was taken in the *Estate of Crippen*.[2] After Crippen had been found guilty of the murder of his wife and executed, his mistress claimed a grant of the administration of Crippen's wife's estate. Sir Samuel Evans P in refusing a grant observed that the human mind revolts at the idea that a person could derive an advantage in such circumstances.[3] Plainly, to allow claims such as these to succeed would be unconscionable and would constitute unjust enrichment of an extreme kind.

Courts in the United Kingdom are, however, able to modify forfeiture under s 2(2) of the Forfeiture Act 1982 if the justice of the case requires. In *Re K (Deceased)*,[4] a wife had been exposed to gratuitous violence for some years from her husband. The court applied the provisions of the exemption where she had accidentally shot and killed her husband during the course of frightening him with a loaded gun. In Australia, the strict public policy approach adopted in the United Kingdom has not been so rigorously applied. In *Public Trustee v Fraser*,[5] the Supreme Court of New South Wales declined to apply a rigid rule in relation to murder or manslaughter but preferred a discretionary approach relevant to the moral culpability of the offender. In *Public Trustee v Evans*[6] and *Re Keitley*,[7] courts in New South Wales and Victoria have declined

---

1   [1892] 1 QB 147; [1891–94] All ER 335.
2   [1911] P 108; [1911–13] All ER 207. Further, see *Re Giles (deceased)* [1972] Ch 544; *Gray v Barr* [1971] 2 QB 554.
3   *Ibid*, at 209.
4   [1985] Ch 85.
5   (1987) 9 NSWLR 433.
6   (1985) 2 NSWLR 188. *Cf Public Trustee v Fraser* (1987) 9 NSWLR 433.
7   [1992] 1 VLR 583.

to order forfeiture in cases of domestic violence. In both cases, the courts considered that the lower level of the applicants' moral culpability permitted them to accede to interests in their deceased husband's estates. More recently in *Troja v Troja*,[8] when dismissing an appeal against forfeiture by a woman, who had been acquitted of the murder of her husband on the ground of diminished responsibility, the New South Wales Court of Appeal were divided on the merits of a discretionary approach in manslaughter cases. In the lower court, Waddell CJ in equity, had suggested that it would be appropriate to adopt legislation along the lines of that adopted in the United Kingdom.[9]

Accrued proprietary rights

The policy of the law against declining a person to profit from crime did not extend to dispossessing people of property which had been derived from criminal activity if the person was able to assert an accrued proprietary right in the property prior to its seizure or confiscation by police. In *Gordon v Metropolitan Police Chief Commissioner*,[10] the plaintiff was permitted to recover the proceeds of illegal betting arrangements in an action for moneys had and received. The money had been given to the plaintiff albeit for an illegal purpose and seized by the police during a raid. The plaintiff was able to assert a right of ownership in the money. There was no statutory power of confiscation and nor was the Court of Appeal prepared to imply one. It was held that there was no public policy reason to dispossess a person of property which was his and to recognise such a power would amount to confiscation.[11] This approach was adopted in Australia by the High Court in *Russell v Wilson*,[12] where it was held that, in the absence of an order for the forfeiture of money or valuable securities seized by the police being made by the court upon the respondent's conviction for illegal gambling, the respondent was entitled to their return even though they constituted the product of an illegal horse-racing sweep.

Statutory confiscation of the proceeds of crime

Although there was no common law power of confiscation, legislatures have recognised the importance of confiscation or forfeiture provisions in order to deter criminals by attaching the fruits of their crimes. Thus, in *Russell v Wilson*, the relevant gaming legislation contained a power to

---

8   (1994) 33 NSWLR 269.
9   See the Australian Capital Territory Forfeiture Act 1991.
10   [1910] 2 KB 1080; [1908–10] All ER 192.
11   *Ibid*, at 1098; 201 *per* Buckley LJ.
12   (1923) 33 CLR 538. Further, see *Golan v Nugent* (1988) 166 CLR 18.

confiscate the product of an illegal sweep although no order was made in that case by the trial judge. In more recent years, legislatures, motivated by the significant profits that may be made by organised crime and in particular by drug dealing, have enacted provisions which are intended to impose significant penalties by confiscating property that has been used to facilitate serious crime. Further, in most modern statutes, there is a power to impose pecuniary penalties aimed at confiscating any benefits that have been acquired or derived as a result of a serious crime. Legislation of this kind has been described as draconian in the sense that courts have jurisdiction to impose orders which do not necessarily reflect the actual benefit realised from the criminal activity in addition to other penalties that are imposed upon conviction.[13] However, in practice, courts appear to consider an element of proportionality in the orders that are imposed.

(a) Pecuniary penalty orders

Legislation in certain of the Australian states and Territories,[14] the Commonwealth[15] and New Zealand,[16] make provision for the imposition of pecuniary penalties upon conviction for serious criminal offending.[17] The prevention of unjust enrichment under confiscation legislation is aimed at deterring offenders from committing crime. The legislation is directed at the proceeds derived by an offender from criminal activity and is not confined to the actual profit derived by a particular individual from his or her offending. Legislation that provides for pecuniary penalty orders in confiscation statutes,[18] empowers a court to assess the value of any benefit derived by a person convicted of a serious offence as defined

---

13 *R v Smith* [1989] 2 All ER 948; *R v Simons* (1993) 98 Cr App R 100; *R v Pedersen* [1995] NZLR 386, at 390 *per* Cooke P.

14 For example, Crimes (Confiscation of Profits) Act 1989 (Qld); Confiscation of Proceeds of Crime Act 1989 (NSW); Crimes Confiscation of Profits Act 1986 (Vict) as amended by the Crimes (Confiscation of Profits) (Amendment) Act 1991; Crimes Confiscation of Profits Act 1988 (Western Aust) as amended by Crimes (Confiscation of Profits) Amendment Act 1990 and Acts Amendment (Confiscation of Criminal Profits) Act 1992; Crimes (Confiscation of Profits) Act 1993 (Tas); Crimes (Forfeiture of Proceeds) Act 1992 (NT).

15 Proceeds of Crimes Act 1987 (Cth).

16 Proceeds of Crime Act 1991 (NZ).

17 See Freiberg, A, 'Criminal Confiscation, Profit, and Liberty' (1992) 25 ANZJ Crim 44.

18 For example, ss 13–14 of the Crimes (Confiscation of Profits) Act 1989 (Qld); ss 24–25 of the Confiscation of Proceeds of Crime Act 1989 (NSW). In NSW, the Act contains specific provisions in s 28 dealing with pecuniary penalty orders in relation to drug offending; ss 12–13 of the Crimes Confiscation of Profits Act 1986 (Vict) as amended by the Crimes (Confiscation of Profits) (Amendment) Act 1991; ss 15–16 of the Crimes Confiscation of Profits Act 1988 (Western Aust) as amended by Crimes (Confiscation of Profits) Amendment Act 1990 and the Acts Amendment (Confiscation of Criminal Profits) Act 1992; ss 21–22 of the Crimes (Confiscation of Profits) Act 1993 (Tas); ss 10–11 of the Crimes (Forfeiture of Proceeds) Act 1992 (NT); ss 26–27 of the Proceeds of Crimes Act 1987 (Cth); ss 26–27 of the Proceeds of Crime Act 1991 (NZ).

in the legislation, and a court may order a person to pay to the state a pecuniary penalty equal to the value so assessed. When assessing the value of the benefit, a court is required to consider the money or the value of property that came into the possession or control of the defendant, the value of any other benefit derived from the defendant having committed the offence, the market value associated with doing a particular criminal act, the value of the defendant's property and the defendant's income and expenditure.[19] When assessing a pecuniary penalty, the expenses and outgoings of the defendant in connection with the commission of the offence cannot be deducted so that the benefit involves the gross and not the net or actual benefit realised after expenses have been deducted.[20]

The courts have not been in universal agreement on the appropriate approach to take to the question of pecuniary penalties. There has been a difference of approach on the question of whether a benefit means an actual benefit or whether a benefit that is only temporarily received is sufficient to justify a pecuniary penalty order. Thus, the question posed is whether a drug courier, who has received money or property that has been handed over subsequently to a third party, is liable to a pecuniary penalty order even though no actual or permanent benefit has been derived? In *R v Fagher*,[21] the Court of Criminal Appeal of New South Wales considered that benefit meant the defendant's share of gross proceeds and not the total money handed to him before the proceeds were divided. Although temporary possession of property could not be considered a benefit, the Federal Court in *Cornwell*[22] was of the view that an appellant was liable to a pecuniary penalty for the value of the marijuana he received even though he had agreed to pay certain sums to third parties. These payments were regarded by the court as expenses or outgoings rather than as division between co-offenders of the gross proceeds of the transaction and were consequently not deductible from the gross benefit. The appellant was, accordingly, held liable to a penalty assessed in relation to the total gross value of the benefit without deduction for the value of the payments made to third parties. In *Nieves*,[23] the Court of Criminal Appeal of Victoria considered that a court should not concern itself with sharing arrangements made between convicted persons or with others when considering the issue of jurisdiction, but actual value was a matter which could ultimately be considered in relation to the

---

19 Victoria and Western Australia have different provisions in relation to assessment, see s 13 (Vict); s 16 (Western Aust).

20 See *Re Tillotson* (1995) 1 Qd R 86. This provision is not contained within the provisions governing assessment of a pecuniary penalty in Victoria or Western Australia.

21 (1989) 16 NSWLR 67.

22 (1990) 49 A Crim R 122.

23 (1991) 51 A Crim R 350.

actual pecuniary penalty imposed. This approach was subsequently endorsed by same court in *R v Peterson*.[24] It was observed in this case, that in a disputed case a court should embark on an inquiry designed to ascertain the value of a benefit actually derived by a person as a result of committing an offence when assessing the value of a pecuniary penalty. In *R v Pederson*,[25] the Court of Appeal of New Zealand considered similarly that a court should not take into account whether a defendant had an obligation to pay part of the proceeds derived from a crime to somebody else when determining whether a defendant was liable to a penalty order, although this was a factor that might, in a court's discretion, constitute justification for imposing on the defendant a lesser amount by way of pecuniary penalty. Cooke P observed, however, that the Act was not a fiscal or taxing statute but its purpose was to deter serious crime:[26]

> Being a measure designed to deter serious crime by demonstrating emphatically that it does not pay, the Proceeds of Crimes Act should be judicially administered in that spirit. In simple cases of serious drug selling, the courts should be slow to award less than the maximum penalties against sellers. This is a move in a necessary direction involving recognition that imprisonment is not an adequate remedy for crime.

The pecuniary penalty order is accordingly wider in scope than a benefit assessed in purely restitutionary terms on the basis of unjust enrichment in that it is not limited to the actual benefit received by the criminal. There is power under some statutes relating to pecuniary benefits for a court to lift the corporate veil and treat as individual property, property that is under the effective control of that person.[27]

(b) Forfeiture orders

There is provision for the forfeiture of property that is tainted under confiscation legislation enacted in Australia and New Zealand in relation to serious criminal offending.[28] Tainted property means property that is used in or in connection with property, or derived or realised

---

24 [1992] 1 VR 297. Further, see *Ex parte McGee* (1995) 1 Qd R 623.

25 [1995] 2 NZLR 386.

26 *Ibid*, at 391.

27 For example, s 27 of the Confiscation of Proceeds of Crime Act 1989 (NSW).

28 Section 8 of the Crimes (Confiscation of Profits) Act 1989 (Qld); s 18 of the Confiscation of Proceeds of Crime Act 1989 (NSW); s 7 of the Crimes (Confiscation of Profits) Act 1986 (Vict) as amended by the Crimes (Confiscation of Profits) (Amendment) Act 1991; s 4 of the Crimes (Confiscation of Profits) Act 1986 (S Aust); s 10 of the Crimes (Confiscation of Profits) Act 1988 (Western Aust) as amended by Crimes (Confiscation of Profits) Amendment Act 1990 and Acts Amendment (Confiscation of Criminal Profits) Act 1992; s 16 of the Crimes (Confiscation of Profits) Act 1993 (Tas); s 5 of the Crimes (Forfeiture of Proceeds) Act 1992 (NT); s 19 of the Proceeds of Crimes Act 1987 (Cth); ss 15–16 of the Proceeds of Crime Act 1991 (NZ).

directly or indirectly by a person, or as a result of the commission of a serious offence. As with pecuniary penalty orders, these are deterrent provisions aimed a prohibiting criminal offending. In deciding whether or not to order forfeiture, a court is required to take into account the use that is ordinarily and has been intended to be made of the property and any hardship that may reasonably be likely to arise if the property is forfeit. There is jurisdiction under the various confiscation acts for the Crown to make application for restraining orders and other information gathering orders prior to trial, and of a person charged with a serious offence.[29]

Clearly, where property has been derived from a crime it may be forfeit.[30] Similarly, property that can be identified as the exchange product of a crime should be liable to forfeiture. Thus, if a car purchased with drug money is sold and the proceeds can be identified or have been used in the purchase of some other property found in the possession of a defendant, then, upon conviction, the money or exchange product should be liable to forfeiture.[31] However, more difficult questions arise where the basis of the forfeiture application is the mere use of property to facilitate a crime. There have been differences in judicial approach to this question. One approach asserts that there is no jurisdiction to consider forfeiture unless there has been a substantial use of the property,[32] however, the other approach does not require evidence of substantial use. Rather, the degree of use is a factor to consider in determining whether an order should ultimately be made.[33] A court under confiscation legislation of the kind that is being considered here does not have the power to make orders forfeiting part of the offender's interest in any fractional amount.[34]

Proportionality is an issue for consideration in cases relating to confiscation. A Western Australian case of *Rintel*[35] illustrates proportionality and the operation of the legislation. There, the Crown sought forfeiture of land and a motor vehicle that had been used for drug purposes. Drugs had been stored in a house and conveyed in a motor vehicle for sale. The trial judge had declined to make forfeiture orders in relation to either

---

29 For example, s 36 (search warrants), s 43 (restraining orders). See *NSW Crime Commission v Younan* (1993) 31 NSWLR 44 on the approach of a court to a relaxation of a restraining order to enable a defendant to meet legal expenses; s 58 (production orders), s 65 (search powers), s 68 (monitoring orders), Confiscation of Proceeds of Crime Act 1989 (NSW).

30 In *R v Hood* (1988) 54 NTR 1, land acquired out of the proceeds of drug dealing was forfeited under the Poisons and Dangerous Drugs Act 1983, now repealed.

31 See *R v Grant* (1979) 2 NSWLR 478.

32 *R v Ward, Marles and Graham* (1987) 33 A Crim R 60, at 65.

33 *R v Hadad* (1989) 16 NSWLR 476, at 482 *per* McInerney J; *R v Rintel* (1991) 3 WAR 527, at 530–31 *per* Malcolm CJ.

34 *R v Bolger* (1989) 16 NSWLR 115; *R v Dunsmuir* [1996] 2 NZLR 1.

35 *Idem.*

item of property. The Court of Appeal upheld the Crown appeal in part. It was held that there was insufficient use of the premises to justify a forfeiture order for the land[36] but, in relation to the motor vehicle, a majority of the court considered that, in the light of the respondent's previous convictions and the seriousness of the crimes for which he was convicted, an additional penalty was justified. Accordingly, the motor vehicle was the subject of a forfeiture order.[37] The Crown also failed to secure forfeiture of land and a motor vehicle in *R v Ottens*.[38] There, the Crown applied for the forfeiture of a pastoral lease in the Northern Territory held by a company of which Ottens, who had been convicted of cultivating a large crop of cannabis, and his wife were the principal shareholders. Forfeiture was rejected on the grounds that the drug cultivation occupied only an infinitesimal proportion of the land and also because it would adversely affect the interests of Ottens' family who were not involved in his offending. A motor vehicle which was the subject of a related application for forfeiture was found only to have been associated in a minor way with the offending. Forfeiture of it was declined because it was considered that this would constitute hardship since it was also required for family purposes.[39] In analysing the objects of the forfeiture provisions, Martin CJ observed that they included depriving an offender of the physical and financial ability and the power of opportunity to continue to engage in proscribed conduct, deterring the offender from crime by undermining the ultimate profitability of a venture and the protection of the community by curtailing the cumulation of prohibited items as well as preventing the unjust enrichment of the offender.

(c) Restitution or compensation orders

The power to order restitution or compensation may be contained in statutes proscribing criminal activity and dealing with penalties. Whether restitution is ordered will often depend on the financial ability of a defendant to pay. In sentencing, it is not uncommon for an offender to make restitution or enter into an arrangement to effect restitution in order to mitigate sentence. This is a matter that may be legitimately considered by a sentencing judge when deciding the appropriate penalty to impose upon conviction for an offence.[40]

---

36 Orders for forfeiture of land was also refused in *R v Anderson* (1992) 61 A Crim R 382 on the grounds of hardship. It was refused in *R v Galek* (1993) 70 A Crim R 252 on similar grounds but it was permitted in *R v George* (1992) Qd R 351 because the land was used almost exclusively for an unlawful purpose.

37 Forfeiture of a motor vehicle used for transporting drugs was ordered in *R v Mackie* (1982) 18 NTR 42.

38 Supreme Court, Darwin, 18 April 1994. An application was declined in *R v George* (1992) 2 Qd R 351 on the ground that the use of the vehicle for an unlawful purpose was an isolated occurrence.

39 The adverse effect that forfeiture would have on third parties was considered in *R v Hadad* (1989) 16 NSWLR 476.

40 *O'Keefe* [1992] 60 A Crim R 201, at 204.

CHAPTER 14

Defences to Claims in Restitution

In this chapter, consideration will be given to the principal defences that are relevant in relation to claims in restitution. Most have been discussed in earlier pages of this book and will be summarised here.

Contrary legislative intention or rule of public policy

The availability of restitution is subject to a contrary intention incorporated in legislation or a rule of public policy governing a particular transaction. This requires a court to consider closely the objects or purpose of legislation. This principle is illustrated in *Orakpo v Manson Investments Ltd*.[1] In relation to an application to set aside a money-lending transaction, the House of Lords held that it would defeat the policy of the legislation to permit the money-lender subrogation to an unpaid vendor's lien. The House overruled earlier English authority to the contrary.[2] *Orakpo* illustrates how transactions entered into by lenders, that seriously transgress the objects of legislation governing lending transactions, will not be indirectly enforced by the courts by resort to equitable doctrine even though a denial of restitution may mean that a party is enriched. In contrast, in *Pavey & Matthews Pty Ltd v Paul*,[3] a majority of the High Court of Australia held that recognition of a restitutionary claim for building work that had been performed did not impugn the policy of legislation that rendered oral contracts unenforceable by the contractor.[4] Although the builder was unable to enforce an oral contract, this did not preclude restitution for a *quantum meruit* for the reasonable value of work that the owner had requested. The legislation was not intended to deprive a contractor of all reimbursement for work carried out at the request of an owner but was intended to protect an owner against excessive charges that were not substantiated in writing.

In relation to the application of company law principles, a similar approach is seen in *Sinclair v Brougham*[5] and *Re Cleadon Trust Ltd*.[6] In

---

1   [1978] AC 95; [1977] 3 WLR 229. See Chapter 4, pp 175–76. Further, for similar applications, see *Kasumu v Baga-Egbe* [1956] AC 539 and *Mayfair Trading Co v Dreyer* (1958) 101 CLR 428; *Leho Holdings Pty Ltd v Deutsche Bank (Asia) AG* (1988) 2 Qd R 30.

2   *Congresbury Motors Ltd v Anglo-Belge Finance Co Ltd* [1971] Ch 81.

3   (1986) 162 CLR 221.

4   Distinguishing money-lender cases, *ibid*, at 229–30 *per* Mason CJ and Wilson J, at 261–64 *per* Deane J, at 269–70 *per* Dawson J.

5   [1914] AC 398; [1914–15] All ER 622.

6   [1939] 1 Ch 286.

Sinclair v Brougham, the House of Lords held that depositors who had made payments to a society that were *ultra vires* the borrowing powers of the society were unable to recover the money in a action for moneys had and received.[7] Although the reasoning was in part based on the out-moded implied agreement theory of restitution rather than the more liberal approach taken in later cases based on a court imposed obligation, it is unlikely that the House would have been prepared to favour restitution at the expense of the *ultra vires* doctrine, even though the society received an undoubted benefit because its assets were greatly increased by the *ultra vires* deposits.[8] Similarly, in *Re Cleadon Trust Ltd*, one of the majority members of the Court of Appeal, Scott LJ, considered that to permit the lender, Creighton, restitution of the payments made by him to reduce the indebtedness of the Cleadon subsidiaries when the resolution purporting to confirm the loan was invalid in that it did not comply with the Articles, would mean that the court would be seen to condone a flagrant abuse of the Articles of Association.[9] Although the company received an undoubted benefit as a result of the debts being discharged, in that it was released from its liability under a guarantee of the debts of the subsidiaries, it was the opinion of Scott LJ that the court could not have assisted Creighton to recoup his payments even assuming that a restitution was otherwise available on a more liberal basis than implied contract.[10]

Similarly, public policy may be against restitution. We have seen this demonstrated in cases involving illegal transactions[11] or criminal offending.[12] However, care must be taken to ensure that greater injustice is not achieved by declining restitution. Thus, in *Nelson v Nelson*,[13] the High Court of Australia ordered restitution of a woman's home that had been placed in the names of her two children in order to allow her to fraudulently acquire a second home by obtaining a subsidy under the Defence Service Homes Act 1918, on condition that she repay the subsidy. It was held that since the Act contained penalties for fraud, there was no

---

7 [1914] AC 398; [1914–15] All ER Rep 622, at 414–18, 630 *per* Viscount Haldane LC, at 433–34, 638 *per* Lord Dunedin, at 440, 642 *per* Lord Parker, at 452, 648 *per* Lord Sumner.

8 The *ultra vires* doctrine was considered in *Ashbury Railway Carriage and Iron Co v Riche* (1875) LR 7 HL 653. In *Sinclair v Brougham, ibid*, Lord Dunedin expressed some disquiet concerning the application of the *ultra vires* doctrine in these circumstances, as did Lord Goff more recently in *Westdeutsche Landesbank v Islington LBC* [1996] 2 WLR 802, at 813; [1996] 2 All ER 96, at 972–73.

9 *Ibid*, at 311. Considered by Young J in *Cadorange v Tanga Holdings* [1990] 20 NSWLR 26, at 39.

10 *Idem. Cf Craven Ellis v Canons Ltd* [1936] 2 KB 403; [1936] 2 All ER 1066.

11 *Berg v Sadler & Moore* [1937] 2 KB 158; [1937] All ER 637.

12 See *Re Crippen* [1911] P 108; [1911–13] All ER 207 and the cases cited in Chapter 13 on Restitution and Crime, pp 343–44.

13 (1995) 184 CLR 538; (1995) ALJR 47.

further reason to penalise her by denying her restitution of the home. In other circumstances, fraudulent conduct will not be so benevolently considered. In *Re Gasbourne Pty Ltd*,[14] for example, it was held that assuming a restitutionary remedy was otherwise available for share-holders, who had discharged a tax liability of their company, restitution from the company should be denied because the inability of the company to discharge its own liability had been directly attributable to their own improper conduct with regard to the company.

Bona fide purchaser for value

The defence of *bona fide* purchaser for value is available to an action for moneys had and received. In *Aiken v Short*,[15] the valid discharge of a debt was one reason for denying the payer restitution of money paid under mistake. In *Porter v Latec Finance Pty Ltd*,[16] it was the opinion of a majority of the High Court of Australia that a debt existed, had been validly discharged and consideration provided even though the debtor had fraudulently misrepresented his identity to both the payer and the payee. Accordingly, a claim to recovery of a payment on the grounds of mistaken identity failed. A claim that consideration had been provided for payments of withholding tax made by a customer in the mistaken belief that they were lawfully owing was rejected by the High Court of Australia in *David Securities Pty Ltd v Commonwealth Bank of Australia* because the obligation of the bank to pay withholding tax was not one that could be lawfully imposed on its customer and the responsibility for ensuring that the legislation was complied with fell upon the bank. Consequently, it could not rely on its own ignorance of the law so as to claim that it had provided a reduced interest rate in consideration of the customer agreeing to pay withholding tax. In *Lipkin Gorman v Karpnale Ltd*,[17] the House of Lords held that a gaming club had not given consideration for stolen money that it received from a thief in exchange for gaming chips because the wagers were null and void under gaming legislation. *Bona fide* purchaser will also defeat equitable claims such as tracing claims[18] and also will prevent rescission of a contract for wrong-doing where third party interests are involved.[19]

---

14 [1984] VR 801. Further, see *Henderson v Amadio* (1996) 190 ALR 391 where restitution was denied because a prospectus failed to comply with legal requirements.

15 (1856) 1 H & N 210; [1843–60] All ER 425.

16 (1964) 111 CLR 177, at 185 *per* Barwick CJ, at 198–99 *per* Taylor J, at 208–09 *per* Owen J. More recently, for the discharge of a debt as consideration for a mistaken payment, see *Griffiths v Commonwealth Bank of Australia* (1994) 123 ALR 111.

17 [1991] 2 AC 548; [1992] 4 All ER 513. In New Zealand, see *Martin v Pont* [1993] 3 NZLR 25.

18 *Black v Freeman* (1910) 12 CLR 105, at 109.

19 See p 362.

Compromise of an honest claim

Compromise of an honestly made claim is an important defence to a restitutionary claim as Mason CJ observed in *David Securities Pty Ltd v Commonwealth Bank of Australia*.[20] It is in the public interest that disputes be resolved without resort to litigation and settlements should not be lightly set aside. Even in cases involving illegitimate threats to break contracts, courts have consistently refused to set aside settlements when it appears that the parties have deliberately chosen the lesser option of compromise rather than litigation. Thus, in *Pao On v Lau Yiu*,[21] the Privy Council considered that the plaintiff had received legal advice and had entered a new and less advantageous agreement deliberately and for commercial reasons. In *David Securities*,[22] Mason CJ considered that the refusal of the High Court to order restitution of wrongfully paid taxes and charges in the earlier cases of *Werrin v Commonwealth*[23] and *South Australian Cold Stores v Electricity Trust of South Australia*[24] could be justified, not on the ground that the mistaken payments involved questions of law rather than fact, but because, in both cases, the plaintiffs had elected to pay rather than litigate and had accordingly chosen to compromise. However, whilst avoidance of litigation and the settlement of claims is to be encouraged in litigation between private citizens, the defence of compromise is less appealing in cases involving illegal demands by public authorities, as Dixon J observed in *Mason v New South Wales*.[25] It has been suggested earlier that a defence of compromise is inappropriate in cases involving taxes or other dues unlawfully demanded by a public body.[26] In *Woolwich Building Society v Inland Revenue Commissioners (No 2)*,[27] a majority of the House of Lords ordered restitution of interest earned on payments that had been wrongfully demanded by the revenue and paid by the taxpayer in order to avoid potentially damaging speculation that might affect its business reputation. Lord Goff[28] and Lord Slynn[29] considered that principles that might be appropriate in relation to citizens' claims against one another were not appropriate in relation to claims involving *de facto* government

---

20 (1992) 175 CLR 353, at 374–76.
21 [1980] AC 614; [1979] 3 All ER 65; *Moyes and Groves Ltd v Radiation New Zealand Ltd* [1982] 1 NZLR 368.
22 (1992) 175 CLR 353, at 376 *per* Mason CJ.
23 (1938) 59 CLR 150.
24 (1957) 98 CLR 65.
25 (1959) 102 CLR 108, at 116-117.
26 See Chapter 10, pp 231–37.
27 [1993] AC 70; [1992] 3 All ER 737.
28 *Ibid*, at 167; 756.
29 *Ibid*, at 201; 785.

authority. *Woolwich* suggests a less tolerant approach to the retention of illegally demanded taxes or dues by public authorities than had formerly been the case. In the light of *Commissioner of State Revenue v Royal Insurance Ltd*,[30] where the Revenue was ordered to repay *ultra vires* stamp duties it had collected from Royal, it is likely that Australian courts will also be unsympathetic to claims by taxing authorities to withhold *ultra vires* payments on the ground that in making payment the taxpayer had chosen to avoid litigation and accordingly compromised his or her claim.

Change of position

One of the most important developments in restitution has been the recognition of a defence of change of position. This is a particularly important defence in relation to the recovery of moneys paid by mistake although it has wider application to other cases of moneys had and received. Change of position is important because it allows a court to more fully consider the competing equities of a claimant payer and a defendant payee in order to evaluate whether restitution should be ordered in cases where the payer is able to show a *prima facie* case of unjust enrichment. If a payee is able to show an adverse change of position as a result of the receipt of money, a court may refuse restitution.[31] This defence is considered more fully in Chapter 2.[32]

Estoppel

Estoppel may operate to deny a claimant restitution if, as a result of a misrepresentation or some other reprehensible conduct such as a breach of obligation owed by the plaintiff to the defendant, the defendant is able to assert that he or she has suffered a change of position or detriment.[33] There must exist a causal connection between the representation or conduct complained of and any detriment suffered by the party claiming estoppel. In *Jones v Waring and Gillow Ltd*,[34] Lord Sumner considered that the detriment the defendants complained of, being the release of their goods as a result of their being handed the plaintiff's cheques made out in their name by a rogue, was not attributable to the plaintiff's conduct but rather was an act done in response to the rogue's fraudulent reasons for being given the cheques. Where, however, the

---

30 (1993–94) 182 CLR 51.

31 *David Securities Pty Ltd v Commercial Bank of Australia* (1991–92) 175 CLR 353, at 385 *per* Mason CJ.

32 See pp 34–37.

33 See *R E Jones Ltd v Waring and Gillow Ltd* [1926] AC 670, at 693; [1926] All ER 36, at 46 *per* Lord Sumner, at 701; 50 *per* Lord Carson.

34 [1926] AC 670, at 692–93; [1926] All ER 36, at 46.

party claiming estoppel is at fault, estoppel will not be able to be relied upon in defence of a restitutionary claim.[35] The operation of estoppel as a defence to restitution of money paid under mistake has been considered earlier.[36]

Estoppel, however, is not limited in application to money claims but is a doctrine of general application. If, for example, the plaintiff unacceptably delays in taking appropriate action to invoke equitable relief so as to set aside a transaction that is voidable and as a result the defendant suffers detriment or an adverse change of position, the plaintiff may be estopped from having the transaction rescinded.[37] In these circumstances, estoppel is closely related to the defences of laches, acquiescence, and affirmation or election which are considered below.[38]

Restrictions on equitable relief

(a) 'Clean hands'

If a person seeks the assistance of equity to effect restitution, misconduct on his or her part that bears an immediate and necessary relationship to the equity sought may result in relief being denied.[39] Associated with this maxim is the principle that he who seeks equity should be prepared to do equity. This has been described as a broad principle of equity and one that has been said not to depend upon any refined or technical requirement. Thus, in *Nelson v Nelson*,[40] the High Court of Australia allowed a woman to recover a house that she had transferred into the names of her children for a fraudulent purpose on condition that she repay a subsidy that she had fraudulently received to the appropriate authority. To deny the plaintiff restitution would have meant that her daughter, who alone had opposed restitution, would acquire a substantial windfall. In *Moffat v Moffat*,[41] the Court of Appeal of New Zealand, as a condition of setting aside an unconscionable matrimonial property agreement, ordered the applicant not to oppose her husband making the appropriate application

---

35 *Larner v London County Council* [1949] 2 KB 683; [1949] 1 All ER 964.

36 See discussion in Chapter 2, pp 32–43.

37 See the discussion of *Hawker Pty Ltd v Helicopter Charter Pty Ltd* (1991) NSWLR 299, at 304.

38 In *Allcard v Skinner* (1887) 36 Ch D 145, at 189; [1886] All ER 90, at 102, Lindley LJ said that he would not distinguish between the expressions, acquiescence, laches, election not to avoid a voidable transaction, ratification or confirmation. McMullin J in *O'Connor v Hart* [1983] 1 NZLR 280, at 296, observed that 'the precise lines of demarcation between estoppel, acquiescence, and election are not easy to draw'.

39 *Meyers v Casey* (1913) 17 CLR 91; *AG (UK) v Heinemann Publishers Aust Pty Ltd* (1987) 8 NSWLR 341; *Fai Insurances Ltd v Pioneer Concrete Services Ltd* (1989) 15 NSWLR 552.

40 (1996) 184 CLR 538; (1995) 70 ALJR 47.

41 [1984] 1 NZLR 600.

to the court for the division of property under the relevant legislation governing matrimonial property. This principle may have to give way to a contrary legislative intent.[42]

(b) Acquiescence

Relief may be refused where the party seeking relief has delayed to such an extent in seeking to have a transaction set aside that it can be inferred that the party has acquiesced in what has occurred. Mere delay will not suffice to constitute acquiescence. Whether delay will be sufficient to constitute acquiescence will depend on its length and the nature of the acts which have been done in the interval and any detriment that has been occasioned by the other party as a result.[43] In some cases, where rescission has been granted, there have delays of some years.[44] However, knowledge of the facts giving rise to a possible or potential claim and a consequent unexplained delay may lead to an inference that a claimant had deliberately chosen not to pursue a remedy and subsequently, in making a claim, has had a change of heart. In *Allcard v Skinner*,[45] for example, a majority of the Court of Appeal held that, although the plaintiff would have been successful had she acted promptly in having the gifts set aside after she had left the Sisterhood, her delay in bringing a claim for five years meant that she should fail. The majority considered that, after leaving the Sisterhood, she had the means to assert her rights and knowledge of the facts from which a claim of right might arise.[46] She was free from the influence of the Sisterhood and had access to legal advice had she desired to pursue the matter. Her delay justified an inference that she had elected not to disturb the gifts.[47]

---

42 In relation to money-lender transactions, see *Kasumu v Baga-Egbe* [1956] AC 539.

43 See *O'Connor v SP Bray Ltd* (1936) 36 SR (NSW) 248, at 261–62 *per* Jordan CJ; *Sargent v ASL Developments Ltd* (1974) 131 CLR 634, at 646; *Immer v Uniting Church* (1992) 112 ALR 609, at 611 *per* Brennan J.

44 See *Armstrong v Jackson* [1917] 2 KB 822, at 830–31; [1916–17] All ER 117, at 1123 *per* McCardie J and the cases cited. Further, see the discussion of laches in *Erlanger v New Sombrero Phosphate Co* (1878) 3 App Cas 1218, at 1231–34 *per* Lord Penzance, at 1279–81 *per* Lord Blackburn.

45 (1887) 36 Ch D 145; [1886–90] All ER 90.

46 *Ibid*, at 192; at 104 *per* Bowen LJ. Further, see *Bullock v Lloyd's Bank Ltd* (1955) Ch 317; [1954] 3 All ER 726. In *Avtex Airservices v Bartsch* (1990) 107 ALR 539, at 569, Hill J doubted whether 'knowledge alone of the facts which give rise to the claim said to have been waived was sufficient'. His Honour considered there needed 'to be knowledge as well of what rights emerge from those facts'.

47 *Ibid*, at 186–89; at 102 *per* Lindley LJ; at 191–93; at 104 *per* Bowen LJ; in partial dissent on this point, Cotton LJ at 173–75; at 94. *Cf Kerr v West Australian Trustee* (1937) 39 WALR 34 where a son had no opportunity for independent advice and the gift to his father was successfully impeached for undue influence after the father died.

(c) Laches

A relevant limitation period[48] will defeat a claim to restitution; however, aside from this, prejudice to the defendant and change of circumstances attributable to laches or delay may also mean relief is denied. In *Allcard v Skinner*, there was no evidence that the Sisterhood had incurred any particular expense as a result of delay although Lindley LJ appeared rather sympathetic to the view that it had.[49] Laches was accordingly not made out as a ground for declining relief. In *Fysche v Page*,[50] the High Court of Australia observed that, in cases where rescission of a transaction was sought, relief might be denied if delay had placed the party, whose title was impeachable, in an unreasonable situation or if, because of a change of circumstance, it would give the party claiming relief an unjust advantage or would impose an unfair prejudice on the other party to a transaction. In *Baburin v Baburin (No 2)*,[51] the Queensland Court of Appeal upheld a decision not to grant equitable relief to a plaintiff who had delayed making a claim relating to a transfer of shares in a private company for 19 years. The court considered a number of factors militated against the granting of relief. These included a finding that the increased value of the shares was largely the result of personal services provided by the defendants for the company in the intervening period. Further, the plaintiff had stood by and accepted benefits at the defendant's instigation consisting of unearned wages and dividends. There had been a change in the nature of the rights attached to the shares and a transfer of an interest in the shares to an innocent third party. A relevant witness, who might have assisted the defence, had died and other documents had been destroyed. No satisfactory explanation for the delay was given. In *Orr v Ford*,[52] however, a majority of the High Court of Australia declined to accept a defence of laches on the ground that, whilst prejudice arising from a loss of evidence that might have been available earlier is a proper consideration in relation to laches, in that case, the loss was speculative and accordingly laches was not made out.

---

48 Limitation periods in the case of restitutionary claims require close attention to the relevant statutes and will vary depending on the nature of the claim. This subject is comprehensively dealt with in Mason, K and Carter, JW, *Restitution Law in Australia*, 1995, pp 912–42, Butterworths, London.

49 *Ibid* at 188–89; 102.

50 (1956–57) 96 CLR 233, at 243. Also, see *Hourigan v Trustees Executors and Agency Co Ltd* (1934) 51 CLR 619, at 629–30; *Lamshed v Lamshed* (1963) 109 CLR 440, at 453.

51 (1991) 2 Qd R 240. Further, see *Bester v Perpetual Trustee Co Ltd* (1970) 3 NSWLR 30 where a 20 year delay did not bar relief.

52 (1988–89) 167 CLR 316. Applied in *Websdale v S & JD Investments Pty Ltd* (1991) 24 NSWR 573.

(d) Affirmation

Affirmation constitutes an unequivocal act involving an election not to avoid the contract.[53] Acts which are merely consistent with the continuance of a contract do not necessarily constitute affirmation.[54] Affirmation may be exercised by a conscious act of election which is communicated to the other party. It need not, however, involve a conscious or deliberate act but may arise as a result of the party's conduct in doing an act from which a court or an ordinary bystander would infer that he or she was affirming the contract or had acquiesced in the defendant's conduct.[55] For example, in *The Atlantic Baron*,[56] Mocatta J considered that the absence of protest, the fact that a final payment for a ship being without qualification, and the delay in advancing a claim were sufficient indicators of an intention to affirm an agreement that was voidable for economic duress. Mocatta J held that the fact that the plaintiff did not actually intend to affirm was irrelevant. Considered objectively, the plaintiff's conduct was consistent only with affirmation. Once an election has been made, a party cannot seek to avoid a contract unless another and separate ground arises.[57] It is immaterial that the party is unaware of the facts upon which the electing party might have chosen to have rescinded the contract.[58]

To affirm, a person seeking relief must be aware of the facts or circumstances which give rise to a right to seek relief. It is uncertain whether he or she must be aware of his or her legal rights.[59] If, however, a party chooses not to investigate the remedies that might be available on learning of circumstances that would give rise to a right to rescind and acts in such a way that any reasonable person would infer that he or she was content to proceed with the contract, estoppel may operate to preclude rescission or other equitable relief on proof of detriment or adverse

---

53 *Brown v Smit* (1924) 34 CLR 160, at 167–68; *Elders Trustee and Executor Co Ltd v Commonwealth Homes and Investment Co Ltd* (1941) 65 CLR 603, at 618; *Sargent v ASL Developments Ltd, ibid,* at 648 *per* Stephen J, at 657 *per* Mason J; *Alleyn v Thurecht* [1983] 2 Qd R 706; *Miller v Barrellan (Holdings) Pty Ltd* [1982] 2 BPR 9543, at 9549; *Motor Oil Hellas Refineries SA v Shipping Corp of India. The 'Kanchenjunga'* [1990] 1 Lloyd's Rep 391, at 398 *per* Lord Goff; *Neylon v Dickens* [1978] 2 NZLR 135 (PC); *Connor v Pukerau Store Ltd* [1981] 1 NZLR 384, at 386 *per* Cooke J; *Cycle Manufacturing Co v Williamson* [1993] 1 NZLR 454, at 465.

54 *Immer v Uniting Church* (1992) 112 ALR 609, at 611 *per* Brennan J, at 620 *per* Deane J.

55 *Tropical Traders Ltd v Goonan* (1964) 111 CLR 41, at 55 *per* Kitto J; *Immer v Uniting Church* (1992) 112 ALR 609, at 620 *per* Deane J; *Kadner v Brune Holdings Ltd* (1973) 1 NSWLR 498; *Zucker v Straightlace Pty Ltd* (1987) 11 NSWLR 87, at 96; *Champtaloup v Thomas* [1976] 2 NSWLR 264, at 274–75.

56 [1979] 1 Lloyd's Rep 89; [1978] 3 All ER 1170.

57 *Elder's Trustee and Executor Co Ltd v Commonwealth Homes and Investment Co Ltd* (1941) 65 CLR 603; *Newbon v City Mutual Life Assurance Ltd* (1935) 52 CLR 723; *Sargent v ASL Developments Ltd* (1974) 131 CLR 634, at 656.

58 *Zucker v Straightlace Pty Ltd* (1987) 11 NSWLR 87, at 96.

59 See discussion, pp 211–12.

change of position by the other party to a transaction.[60] In New South
Wales, the Court of Appeal considered affirmation in *Hawker Pacific Pty
Ltd v Helicopter Charter Pty Ltd*[61] in relation to a claim to rescind a contract for duress. An owner claimed duress had influenced him to enter
into an agreement with a repairer relating to the terms of payment for
repairs to a helicopter. The repairer argued that the plaintiff had
affirmed the agreement in falsely asserting that it would pay, according
to the terms of the agreement, for some time before seeking to have the
agreement rescinded. The Court of Appeal, however, declined to accept
that the respondent had done so. Having referred to the *Atlantic Baron*,
Priestley JA observed that affirmation was not an intelligible legal category in its own right. In order to prove affirmation, the appellant had to
show either that the respondent elected not to avoid the contract or was
estopped from asserting a right to avoid it.[62] An election did not have to
be made immediately on becoming aware of a legal right to rescind. A
party might keep the question open so long as the other party to the
transaction did not suffer detriment.[63] Further, Priestley JA considered
that election must be unequivocal in the sense that it was only consistent
with one of two sets of rights and inconsistent with the exercise of the
other.[64] In this case, the actions of the owner did not cause the other prejudice and nor did they lead to an inference that the owner had elected to
affirm the agreement. Priestley JA considered that estoppel applied only
where, in ignorance of a legal right to elect, the conduct of the party seeking to avoid the agreement had been such as to amount to a representation to the other that the agreement had been affirmed thereby causing
the latter to suffer prejudice. The evidence did not establish conduct
amounting to a representation. Nor was the repairer able to show prejudice.[65] As to prejudice, Handley JA observed that there must be material
or significant disadvantage or detriment in order to found an estoppel
which was not evidenced in that case.[66]

---

60 See the judgment of Jordan CJ in *O'Connor v SP Bray Ltd* (1936) 36 SR (NSW) 248, at
    258–61; *Ritter v North Side Enterprises Ltd* (1975) 132 CLR 301, at 304 *per* Gibbs J;
    Kammins Ballrooms Co Ltd v Zenith Investments Ltd [1971] AC 850, at 883 *per* Lord
    Diplock.

61 (1991) 22 NSWLR 298.

62 *Ibid*, at 304.

63 *Idem*, citing Mason J in *Sargent v ASL Developments Ltd* (1974) 131 CLR 634, at 656.

64 *Idem*, citing Stephen J, in *Sargent v ASL Developments Ltd*, *ibid*, at 646.

65 *Ibid*, at 305. See *Goldsworthy v Brickell* [1987] 1 All ER 853, at 872–73.

66 *Ibid*, at 306–07. Further, see Dixon J in *Thompson v Palmer* (1933) 49 CLR 507, at 547;
    and in *Grundt v Great Boulder Pty Ltd* (1937) 59 CLR 641, at 679; *Newbon v City
    Mutual Life Assurance Society Ltd* (1935) 52 CLR 723, at 734 *per* Rich, Dixon and Evatt
    JJ; *Territory Insurance Office v Addlington* (1992) 84 NTR 7.

(e) The impossibility of effecting *restitutio in integrum*

In cases where a contractual transaction is voidable and liable to rescission, relief may be denied because the contract has been wholly or partly performed and it is impossible to restore the parties fully to their respective positions; that is, restitution in integrum is impossible. A court in equity, however, will not be dissuaded from setting aside a contact, that it considers should not in conscience stand, on the ground that precise restoration to the parties' pre-contractual position is impossible. A court will look to all the circumstances of the case and attempt to restore the parties as completely as possible to their pre-contractual positions.[67] This requires a court to consider practical justice in the particular circumstances of the case. For example, in *O'Sullivan v Management Agency Ltd*,[68] it was contended that the agreements which O'Sullivan had entered into with his manager and his manager's group of companies should not be set aside because they had been partly performed. The Court of Appeal held, however, that this was not a bar to the agreements being set aside and the companies were ordered to disgorge their profits made at O'Sullivan's expense and account to him for these. The manager and his companies were entitled to reasonable remuneration including a profit element for work carried out gratuitously or under the agreements because they had assisted the plaintiff to prosper.[69] Practical justice also extends to losses where the defendant is not guilty of misconduct in a morally reprehensible sense. Having referred with approval to *O'Sullivan's* case, in *Cheese v Thomas*,[70] the Court of Appeal upheld an order dividing the net proceeds of a house sale in accordance with the parties' proportionate contributions to the purchase. The plaintiff was the aged great-uncle of the defendant and the house had been purchased in the expectation that the plaintiff would reside in it until he died and thereafter it would belong to the defendant. The court held that the realised loss on the sale of the property should not fall exclusively on the defendant who, although presumptively in a relationship of undue influence to the plaintiff in relation to the purchase, had not acted in a manner which was morally reprehensible. The court observed that it would not be equitable for the defendant to bear the entire loss.[71] Even where *restitutio in integrum* is impossible and a contract cannot be set aside, equity can remedy the wrongdoing by ordering an account of

---

67 The principle of *restitutio in integrum* and its application is considered further, pp 208–211, and defences to rescission, pp 211–17.

68 [1985] 3 All ER 351.

69 *Ibid*, at 367.

70 [1994] 1 All ER 35.

71 *Ibid*, at 43.

profits or equitable compensation.[72] This occurred in *Greater Pacific Investments v Australian National Industries Ltd*.[73] There, a transaction that had been entered into by ANI in breach of fiduciary duty could not be rescinded because the vendor GPI was unable to restore benefits that it had received; however, GPI successfully obtained compensation for its losses.

(f) Third party interests

Restitution will usually be denied if third parties have *bona fide* and for value acquired an interest in the subject-matter.[74] *Bona fide* purchasers for value will also be protected against tracing claims in equity.[75] Exceptionally, a court may grant rescission in such a way that third party rights are protected as where one party is ordered to hold certain interests on trust for the third party.[76] Third parties may similarly be protected under statutory provisions such as those present in the Contractual Mistakes Act 1977,[77] the Illegal Contracts Act 1970,[78] and the Contractual Remedies Act 1979,[79] relating to relief for mistake, illegality, and breach of contract in New Zealand.

---

72 See *Coleman v Myers* [1977] 2 NZLR 225. Further, see *Catt v Marac Australia Ltd* (1987) 9 NSWLR 639. Rogers J considered that equitable compensation was not limited to circumstances where there had been rescission of a contract. On compensation generally, see Street J in *Re Dawson (dec'd) Union Fidelity Trustee Co Ltd* [1966] 2 NSWLR 211, at 216; *Farrington v Rowe McBride & Partners* [1985] 1 NZLR 83; *Commonwealth Bank v Smith* (1992) 102 ALR 453, at 477–80; *Stewart v Layton* (1992) 111 ALR 688, at 713–71. Also, see Davidson, IE, 'The Equitable Remedy of Compensation' 13 Melb U LR 349.

73 (1996) 39 NSWLR 143, further see *Equiticorp Industries Group v Crown* [1996] 3 NZLR 586, and discussion, Chapter 11, pp 310–11.

74 See *McKenzie v McDonald* [1927] VR 134, discussed p 215; *Coolibah Pastoral Co v Commonwealth* (1967) 11 FLR 176 (rectification denied); *Lewis v Avery* [1972] 1 QB 198, at 207; [1971] 3 All ER 907, at 910–12, where Lord Denning MR voiced his concern for the protection of third party *bona fide* purchasers in the case of voidable transactions. Discussed pp 118–19.

75 See *Black v Freeman* (1910) 12 CLR 105, at 109.

76 *Waters Motors Pty Ltd v Cratchley* (1964) NSWLR 1085.

77 Section 8.

78 Section 6(1)(a)(b).

79 Section 9(5).

INDEX